CRIMINALS AND CROCODILES
Policing in Rhodesia

Arnold Woolley

TSL Publications

First published in Great Britain in 2023
By TSL Publications, Rickmansworth

Copyright © 2023 Arnold Woolley

ISBN: 978-1-915660-32-9

The right of Arnold Woolley to be identified as the author of this work has been asserted by the author in accordance with the UK Copyright, Designs and Patents Act 1988.

All rights reserved. No part of this publication may be reproduced, stored in a retrieval system or transmitted, in any form or by any means without the prior written permission of the publisher, nor be otherwise circulated in any form of binding or cover other than that in which it is published and without a similar condition being imposed on the subsequent buyer.

Photos copyright Arnold Woolley

Cover by : White Magic Studios

The Way In

Hooray for the UK tax man; because without him, or perhaps her, I never would have joined the British South Africa Police, or to be more geographically precise, the Rhodesian police force. In 1964, after a tour of duty in Nyasaland, now Malawi, as a probationary member of the UK's Colonial Police Force, I was back in England, aged 25, wondering what next to do with the rest of my life. Prime Minister Macmillan's "Winds of Change" were blowing strongly through Africa and Great Britain was busy "Getting Out of Empire." Because of that, permanent and pensionable status within the Colonial Police Service was no longer available, although further tours "On Contract/Gratuity" were on offer. On my way from Nyasaland to Cape Town, to embark on a mail ship to the UK for a six-month long period of accrued leave, I had stopped off in Rhodesia and taken a brief look at the country and at the BSA Police. I was impressed by both, but, with some seven years of police work behind me, holding the rank of inspector and earning £720 per annum, I felt that the recruiting officer's offer of a full seven months of basic training in Tomlinson Depot, with a starting rank of Constable, on a wage of £540 per annum, was a bit of an insult, so I had politely walked away from it. I had an offer from the East Sussex Constabulary to join them; to go on a full year of training at Bramshill and come out of that with a Station Sergeant's rank. That was an attractive offer, but I had enjoyed my time in Africa and the call of sunshine, blue skies and wide open and wild country was a strong one. Besides which, I also had a verbal offer from the Rhodesian Post Office, to join them at a middle management level to help develop their security department.

It was into the middle of my puzzling about the future that the tax man stepped, by way of a formal tax demand, for some £1,000.00, which was quite a significant sum, representing as it did, a year and a half of my Colonial Police Salary. That was not to say that I had failed to pay tax on my salary for three and a half years and on my accrued leave and gratuity. That I had done. However, that payment had been made to the Nyasaland

Government. The letter advised that if I was resuming permanent residence within the UK, I was required to make payment to the UK tax man and then recover my money from the Nyasaland authorities. That raised a small problem, because in April 1964, Nyasaland, as a British Protectorate, had achieved independent status as Malawi. I was vividly aware of some of the problems that others had already had in attempting to obtain refunds from the Malawi Tax Department and of battles that were still going on. After a couple of weeks of fruitless correspondence between me and the Inland Revenue, I received a blunt letter advising me that it was not their task to recover my tax payments from the Malawi Government and transfer it to my UK account, but mine and mine alone. If I was intending to remain in the UK, I was required to pay up on the demand presented or be on the receiving end of a court action for the debt. The tone of the letter was officious, curt and bordered on the belligerent. My response to that letter was to book passage on the Southern Cross steamship, leaving Southampton for Cape Town and places further on, on 4th November. That two-week sea voyage was routine and uneventful until the deck cricket competition was held. Individual players signed on the lists on the noticeboards, according to their country of origin. As might be expected, after a day or so of the lists being up on the boards, there were a couple of countries with sufficient names to be able to form a couple of teams, while others mustered just one. In particular, the South African team was clearly somewhat short-handed. My offer to join them, to make up their number was welcomed. After a day or two of practice activity, the competition got under way for real. It was a case of team names drawn from a hat, on a straight knock-out basis. The South African team and the team from Great Britain ended up contesting the final on a day when the sky was blue, the sea was calm and the number of spectators was large.

The GB team won the toss but decided to put South Africa in to bat first. Worryingly for the team I was part of, wickets tumbled all too quickly. When it was my turn to bat, in middle order, I managed to survive long enough to reach the individual retirement marker of 25 runs, which made our final total a respectable one. In my permitted couple of overs of bowling I managed to take three wickets, which also helped towards our eventual victory over the GB team. It was all very enjoyable, pleasant and light-hearted, but as I was about to leave the games-deck I was confronted by a fellow passenger. She was an elderly lady, diminutive in stature. She was something of a character. She had appeared every day in entirely black clothing from her gleaming leather shoes to the top of her hat of the straw boater style. Her hat was decorated simply with a black band and a generous cluster of imitation black cherries. No matter what the weather was, she carried with her a rolled umbrella which was as black in colour as the rest of her chosen garb. I had played a few hands of Bridge in her company and judged her to be of lively mind, feisty nature and very British. "Young man," she stated, in a voice loud enough to be heard for yards, "You are British through and through. What on earth did you think you were doing, playing for those foreigners and helping them win? I shall never speak to you again!" She punctuated her words with the delivery of several sharp raps on my shoulders with her rolled umbrella. Having delivered her admonishment, she whirled about smartly and walked away. As she went, one of the other passengers who had seen and heard her commented to me with a smile on his face, "That's put you in your place my friend and I'll bet she keeps her word!" She did!

That was how and why, towards the end of November 1964, I returned to Rhodesia, intending to take up employment with the Rhodesian Post Office. While waiting for the processing of my formal application to join the post office, I had accommodation at the Salisbury YMCA. In those first few days in the country, I wandered unhurriedly around Salisbury. I took in the central park, the main streets with modern shops and of course, walked to the top of the Salisbury Kopje, from where, like many before me, I stood for quite a while, studying the industrial site close below and the rest of Salisbury spread out beyond. October's high heat was gone and the rains had started, but walking was very pleasurable. The YMCA itself was located on Salisbury Street, which I rapidly discovered was generally regarded as being "on the wrong side of the tracks," in that it was in the city's acknowledged red-light area. After evening meal on the first day, I was invited by residents already there to join them in a "sundowner" as early evening drinks were usually described, imbibed at leisure on the first-floor veranda. From that lofty vantage point, they indulged in some truly wild gambling – strictly for cigarettes! The game consisted of looking down at the cars circulating around the blocks within view and estimating how long it would be before a particular driver made a choice from the strolling "Mahouries" plying their age-old trade and disappeared with her in his car. I had no problem understanding the word "Mahourie" as it was used sometimes in Nyasaland, although the more common appellation was "Mkazi wa ganyu" meaning, quite literally, "Little while wife." I had been at the YMCA about a week – and lost cigarettes every evening – when Bob Smith, my contact within the post office, advised me that the security manager's training course that I was supposed to be joining on 1st December 1964, had been put back indefinitely, but that there was a counter hand's course starting that date, which they wished me to join, with a transfer to security to be available sometime in the future, after a year or so doing counter duties to equip me with some clear understanding of post office routines and procedures from the bottom up.

I was still mulling over that somewhat unwelcome re-arrangement when a liveried police "bee-car" pulled up one morning outside of the YMCA. On entering the building, the co-driver inquired if there was anyone named Woolley staying there. On hearing that conversation, I stepped forward and identified myself to the European constable. "OC Depot wants to see you," he advised, somewhat curtly, eyeing me up and down. "Any idea why?" I asked. The reply was a shake of his head, followed by, "We've been told to find you and take you to see him. That's it. You ready?"

All I could do under the circumstances was to nod an acceptance of the situation and follow him out of the building and into the waiting police car, an Austin Cambridge saloon. The drive to Morris Depot was not a long one. Once there I was escorted to the depot office, a simple turn of the century red brick built square building, large enough to hold what appeared to be four smallish offices. The building had a red painted corrugated iron roof and a broad veranda, on which I was asked to wait, while my escort went inside one of the offices.

A couple of minutes later he re-appeared. "OC will see you now," he said, motioning me towards the door. As I stepped in through the door, the uniformed police officer behind the broad desk stood up. He gestured to a chair in front of it. "Sit down, Mr Woolley. Perhaps you remember me? Assistant Commissioner Wright? I nodded as I moved forward and we both sat. "Yes Sir. You and I spoke last April."

"We did indeed," he confirmed. "I saw your name in the immigration lists a few days ago and remembered our conversation at that time and your decision to turn us down." I shrugged. "The offer was a bit too basic, Sir."

Ascom Wright gave an understanding nod. "May I ask what brings you back to Rhodesia, Mr Woolley?" "Of course, Sir. Apart from the climate and the country, I have an offer to join the postal service, in their security department. It was a bit more attractive than what you offered me."

He nodded slowly and thoughtfully then leaned forward. "I can offer you a more attractive arrangement now, Mr Woolley. That is, if you might still be interested." He paused and looked inquiringly at me.

"I've signed nothing yet, Sir. My application is still being processed." "Good, because I can now offer you a shortened course through depot and a starting pay rate at the top of the constable's scale. That's £720.00 per annum, Mr Woolley." He leaned back, raised his eyebrows and waited. "How long would that shortened course be, Sir and how long before a promotional step up in pay might be possible?"

Ascom Wright's eyebrows sank to normal position. "Six weeks in depot, provided you pass the exams at that stage of the course. As for pay, that would depend on you. You could sit sergeant's exam after three years. With your background and experience I would judge that you would stand a good chance of making it at that time." He reached into a tray on the desk and handed me a large manila envelope. "If you decide to accept our latest offer, all the papers you need are in there."

I took the envelope from him and flicked quickly through the papers inside it. They all looked very standard to me, which caused me to ask, "Is that shortened course in depot and the top pay rate actually written in these papers, Sir? If they're not, how do I know they are contractually valid?"

Ascom Wright could have taken exception to that, but he did not. Instead, he stood up with just a trace of a smile creeping on to his face. "That is a very good point, Mr Woolley. If you are feeling like accepting our fresh offer, you can have my hand on it right now and a letter confirming our conversation with you by tomorrow." He offered his hand across the desk and looked very directly straight into my eyes, without a blink or waver. I decided then and there that he was a man of his word. I rose from my chair and shook his hand. "Welcome to the BSAP, Mr Woolley, I'm sure you won't regret it." His serious, suntanned face creased into a full, broad smile that included his eyes. "Just remember that when we meet again it will be salutes, not handshakes. Meanwhile, let me get that bee car to return you to your lodgings."

On Tuesday, 8th December 1964, I duly reported to Morris Depot, where I was formally attested and enlisted into the British South Africa Police as 007207H Constable Woolley, Arnold. On that same day, six of us formed the nucleus of Recruit Squad 9 of 1964. In numerical order we were:

7202 Pieterse, Jacob Cloete
7203 George, Clive Richard
7204 Grant, Anthony Young
7205 Gunston, Colin
7206 Phillips, Christopher Robin
7207 Woolley, Arnold

From the conversations which took place as we introduced ourselves to each other, I discovered that my fellow recruits were either born and bred in Rhodesia or in South Africa. They all appeared to be some years younger than I was. Once we had attested, we were introduced to Inspector Gerry Winchcombe, who was to be our squad instructor for the duration of our training course in Morris Depot. We were allocated a wooden barrack block with twenty-four single iron framed beds in it, three windows on each side wall and doors at either end. On each of the beds was a kapok filled mattress, along with two pillows, two sheets and a single, thin, blanket. Gerry Winchcombe advised us that our training activities would formally commence the following week, when a further number of recruits from the UK were expected to join us. One of the first things he did was to demonstrate just how we were to make our beds and how they were to be left in the morning once we went on parade. He also advised us that until the squad was complete in numbers, we could expect to be engaged upon "assorted activities" as he put it. He also pointed out that for official purposes we were already 9 Squad of 1964. Meanwhile, he required that a squad leader be elected from among us. On that issue he gave us until the next day to sort out who it was going to be. He also introduced us to the essentials of the depot, those being the location of the ablutions block that we were to use, the tarmac parade ground which was positioned between the sacrosanct green square, upon which nobody trod and the mess hall in which all recruits ate their three meals per day and the back serving hatch of the mess hall, where mugs of tea were available at tea-breaks throughout the day. His final admonishment, as he left us to our own devices at the end of that afternoon was, "You are all confined to camp until further notice, so don't go sneaking out for a night on the town!"

That evening, after an unexciting but ample meal in the mess hall, where we were the butt of much ribald commentary from more senior recruits, we nucleus members of Recruit Squad 9 of 64 sat around our sparse quarters and began to get to know each other a little better than our brief introductions earlier in the day. During the course of that first evening and well before the duty bugler signalled lights out, it became crystal clear that I was some five to seven years older than the others and the only one with previous police experience. The result was that I was nominated to be the leader of the squad. That squad decision was formally agreed and confirmed by Inspector Winchcombe the next day, most of which was spent doubling here, there and everywhere around the entire acreage of Morris Depot, from the stables area at one end to the Police Sports Club and grounds at the other. Even in the lightweight civilian clothes that we were wearing and with all of us in shorts, it was sweaty going in the sticky heat of that December day. In that initial tour around, we stopped at, and received input about, the lecture rooms, the camp hospital, the armoury, the saddlers' shop, the police reserve offices and parade ground, the swimming pool, the athletics track, the assault course, the administration block, the NCO's quarters, mess and bar, the officers' mess and of course, the Guardroom, which contained defaulters' cells; rapid entry into which we were threatened with, should we misbehave in any way during our stay in Morris Depot. We were also shown the outdoor riding school, the stables and the watering troughs for the horses. For me, one of the most welcome and interesting locations was the Forensic Team's Building, to the right and downhill from the main entrance. I had, very successfully, taken advantage of the admirable skills of Dr Thompson and his excellent team in my years of policing in Nyasaland and looked forward to being able to do so in future.

That day, also in the morning, two more locally recruited members joined us. They were:

   7208 Addison, Keith Roland
   7209 Bolas, Stanley

In the afternoon, we were marched off, at the double of course, to the Ordnance Stores and the Tailors' Shop, where our basic kit and uniforms were issued to us. The method of issue was simple and direct. In a clear area in the stores there were blankets on the floor. Piled up on the blankets were all of the items of kit that required no personal fitting. Everything from sailor style canvas kitbags to leather notebook covers, to handcuffs, water bottles and whistles on lanyards. The PT kit stood out clearly and ominously. For the items that needed sizing for personal fit, we were carefully measured, one by one. Those of us who fitted, reasonably well, into the standard proportions of small, medium or large sizes received and signed for the articles then and there. Others of us who required some adjustments before any reasonable fit might appear were detailed off to return in a couple of days to collect outstanding items, which of course we duly did. With very good cause, as some were to learn to their cost a while later, we were warned to mark every article of our uniforms and kit with our force numbers and names just as soon as we got them. Thursday, 10th December 1964 gave me no grief, because I had grown quite used to the definitely military "short back and sides" that went with the wearing of police uniforms at that time. For some of the others, it was bit more traumatic as their treasured civilian mode hair locks tumbled under the scissors and clippers of the camp barber. There was no asking about what we might want. It was simply a case of standing loosely at ease in a group outside until called and then sitting down and still in the barber's chair until the job was done. Eventually, all equally well shorn, we returned to our barrack block where mirrors appeared, checks were made and gasps of, "My mother'll kill me," and, "I've been scalped!" were among the more printable of the agonized comments. In the middle of our agonizing and commiserating Gerry Winchcombe strode in. "Right, you lot. It's time to get you all sorted out with a batman. Follow me." Gerry Winchcombe led us to a spot near the horse lines where there were a score or so of African civilians sitting around. At a word from our instructor, the Africans, all male and adult, rose to their feet and stood in a loose group, facing us.

"These are all approved and experienced camp batmen," Gerry Winchcombe explained. "You pick one to do your laundry, polishing and ironing for the rest of your time in depot. Treat them fairly. Make sure you pay them the going rate and pay them on time. If you look after them, they'll look after you. That's the way it works. Remember this. Most of these guys have been working here for years. They know the ropes better than you ever will. If you're wise, you'll let them do what's needed and not try to tell them what you think is needed, day by day. Take a look. Each one of you will choose one of them. Whichever one it is, you then let them start working on your kit. In another day or so, you'll be in uniform and on parade. Bad turnout on any parade will get you in trouble, quick as a flash and on extra parades behind the guard. Working well with your batman is essential. Because of that, it has to be a two-way arrangement. If the one you choose agrees, that's that. However, they have the right to say no and they sometimes do, even though they all want the work and the pay." Gerry Winchcombe wagged his Malacca cane at us and said, "Right then. Starting with you, Pieterse, make your choice."

The first four pairings were made in rapid succession. Names were exchanged and notes were duly made by Gerry Winchcombe. However, when Clive George's turn came, the individual he chose shook his head, then, without hesitation he pointed directly at me and said, in clear English, "I'll work for that one!"

Gerry Winchcombe spotted the angry scowl on Clive George's face. "Pick another one," he snapped, which Clive duly did.

The next two pairings were made smoothly and then it was my turn. "Excuse me, Sir," I said to our instructor, "But I'm only due to be in depot for six weeks or so. Whoever I choose will be out of work again when I leave. I think these guys need to know that before I ask one of them to work for me. They might prefer to wait until the rest of the squad arrives next week and get a job with somebody who will be here for the whole six months."

"That's a fair point, Woolley," Gerry Winchcombe acknowledged. He turned to the remaining would-be batmen. Gesturing at me he repeated what I had said, advising the remaining work seekers that there would be others arriving in a few days who would be in depot for a full course and that if they wanted to, they could leave now and come back when the further recruits were present. A few of them heard what was said and quietly moved away. Among those who remained was the fellow who had turned down Clive George.

"Which one do you want, Woolley? They all know the score now."

I pointed at the fellow who had turned down Clive George. "Do you still want to work for me? The answer was a slow, deliberate nod. "Then he'll do for me Sir," I stated. That was how Romeo and I teamed up. I never regretted my choice. A couple of days passed before I felt comfortable enough to ask him why he had turned down Clive George to work for me. Romeo, who was more than middle-aged and whose hair was beginning to go grey at the edges replied simply and without hesitation. "That one is trouble, Sir." In that, his judgement proved sound.

There were no such luxuries as electric irons available to our batmen. To smooth and smarten our washed and starched uniforms they all wielded irons that weighed a ton and were heated by charcoal lumps on the inside. The activity of ironing was accompanied by much swinging of the irons and much puffing and blowing too. However, despite the primitive tool, the batmen did a remarkably good job in keeping us smartly turned out and fully up to the demandingly high parade ground standard that was needed to see us safely through the morning and afternoon parades that shortly became a standard part of each day at depot.

I shall pass lightly over the many hours spent polishing webbing and leather belts and shining boots and shoes and every bit of brass, from anklet buckles to BSAP shoulder flashes. Suffice to say that it took some of the others a while before they learned just how to wrap a polishing cloth around the first and second fingers of their right, or left, hand as the case was and tuck it neatly into itself so that it would stay in position for long enough to allow the time-honoured method of bulling our shoes, boots, leggings, belts and cap straps to transform the surface of raw stained brown leather into something acceptably bright and shiny. It also took a while before some members of the squad finally learned how to put on properly the yards of cloth and tape that made up a pair of short puttees, let alone a pair of long puttees. I use the word properly because if they were wound too tight around ankle and calf, cramps often occurred. However, if they were not tight enough, they started to come undone and unwind. That was how the first member of the squad to end up behind the guard got there. Clive George's loosely fitted puttees started straggling behind him, so he received a verbal warning and some instruction. When he managed to repeat the same default, a day or so later, that was it. Clive was fortunate in that we had no saddles or number one kit at that time, let alone an allocated horse, so his default merely cost him a bit of time and some extra effort from his batman. "The Guard" that defaulters such as Clive had to parade behind was the daily evening parade of senior squad recruits and Depot Staff who were to form the overnight patrols. It was their task to make regular checks on the security of all buildings within Morris Depot. Being told off and put behind the guard did not sit well with Clive, whose mutters about it drew very little sympathy from the rest of the squad. On that matter of the preparation and identification of our kit, I also made sure that every item I had carried my newly acquired force number and, if space allowed, my name too.

As one might expect, depot was not a quiet place during daylight hours. From the traditional bugle call of reveille through to the last one of lights out, the bustle and noise was continual. Bawled orders rang out almost continually and from all directions and the rhythmic beat of boots on tarmac hardly ever ceased, or so it seemed. The roadways were a source of much movement, of individuals, squads and transport of all kinds, from cycles through to the heavy vehicles used as personnel carriers. Besides those, there was the steady clip-clop and neighing of horses and the braying of the mules hauling the service carts around. Altogether it was a steady cacophony. For the first day or two each new, unfamiliar noise had us sticking our heads outside of our allotted quarters to discover what might be causing it. Once each was mentally rationalised and catalogued it simply became background hum.

On the 14th December 1964, we were joined by just one more recruit, 7210 THORNTON, Malcolm Ian. In the middle of that afternoon, Insp. Winchcombe called me from our hut to tell me that there was a group of new recruits due at Salisbury Airport next day, on a routine BOAC flight from London. He instructed me to be available outside the Guardroom by 09:00hrs on the 15th, to travel with him to meet the newcomers once they had landed and cleared immigration. "I want you in boots, leggings, tunic, shorts and cap; all bright, shiny and smart. Got it?" His Malacca cane tapped my chest for emphasis.

"Yes, Sir!" I responded, although I felt a bit puzzled because we had barely started to get used to our standard depot dress of short sleeved grey shirts, blue long trousers and service cap, with webbing anklets and belt.

"Good. I want a pass-out parade turnout from you Woolley," he admonished. "I want them to get a clear understanding of what to expect, so get yourself off to the barber right now for starters!"

I knew enough not to point out that it was only four days since my last visit to the camp's barber. Instead, I replied, "Right away, Sir," turned smartly on my heels and marched off towards the barber's shop where I explained my re-appearance after just so short a while.

On hearing my story, the barber's face cracked into a positively evil grin that I sensed boded no good for what little hair I had left after the previous visit. "Sit you down then," he invited with a sweeping gesture of his arm towards a vacant chair. "Let's make Inspector Winchcombe a happy instructor, shall we…?"

When I eventually returned to our squad hut the several occupants promptly took one look at my damned near quarter inch crew-cut style hair and promptly commenced asking questions and offering opinions about it, none of which were complimentary. When I explained my conversation with Gerry Winchcombe and tomorrow's task, they began to understand why I had scarcely any hair left on my head.

Chris Phillips turned to Clive George and said, "You still reckon you want to be squad leader? You've done nothing but moan about your haircut as it is. I reckon you'd have gone barmy if the barber had done that to you."

Clive just scowled, spat on the polishing cloth wrapped round his right hand and got on with bulling his issue leather belt.

I set off to find Romeo, who, fortunately, was not far away, busy ironing. When I explained what was required for the next morning, he just nodded and said in a quite matter of fact way and without breaking the steady rhythm of his ironing, "It will be alright, Ishe. You will be number one for shine, starch and creases. I will see to it."

With that almost casual reassurance ringing in my ears, I returned to our hut and doubled my own efforts to create a shine on dull brown leather. With a full evening of spit and polishing, broken only by evening meal and a cup of tea, I was quite glad when the bugle-call for lights out sounded from the darkness outside.

The following morning was a dry and bright one, horizon to horizon blue sky, with the glaring yellow ball of the tropical sun doing its best to convince the unknowing that the rainy season never existed as it rapidly pushed the temperature into the eighties.

After a PT parade, a shower and breakfast, Romeo appeared with my uniform for the day. A quick look at it told me he had indeed been as good as his word. A few minutes before 9:00 a.m., I reported, as instructed, to the Depot Guardroom, where I found Insp. Winchcombe waiting. He was dressed as I was, with the addition of a cane under his arm and a clipboard in his left hand. Decked out in cap, tunic and shorts, with boots and leggings, and belt and brace, I duly thudded to a formal halt in front of him and barked out, "7207 Constable Woolley, reporting for duty as instructed, Sir." Gerry Winchcombe just nodded and let his eyes begin a detailed audit of my front, from cap to toe-cap. Wordlessly he walked around behind me, where he paused long enough to complete his examination of my turnout. "Take off your cap," he instructed, which order I promptly complied with. There was a brief silence before Insp. Winchcombe said, "Cap back on and stand at ease." He walked around to face me again as I complied with the given instructions.

"In a couple of minutes, Woolley, there will be a Land Rover and a Bedford flatback arriving here. Then we shall go to the airport to collect the rest of your squad. I don't want that uniform of yours creased up on the journey, so you will travel standing upright, in the back of the Bedford. There's enough metalwork there to hold on to. You can put your cap in the cab so that doesn't get lost on the way. Until the transport arrives, just stay put."

The importance of getting me to the airport in good order was underlined after the transport arrived. The two African drivers, in blues and soft caps, reported to Insp. Winchcombe. "Get the tailboard down and get this recruit up there without mucking up his uniform. I don't want him climbing up over the side. Got it?"

"Yes, Sir," they replied smartly.

That was how it was that I travelled standing upright directly behind the driving cab on the back of the Bedford lorry from Morris Depot to Salisbury Airport, taking in the sounds and sights of Salisbury and its suburbs along the way. Once at the airport I was carefully unloaded under the watchful eye of Insp. Winchcombe and re-united with my cap before he and I proceeded into the main terminal.

As we approached the building a BOAC 707 sank noisily but gracefully from the sky, settled gently onto the runway and completed its landing. Insp. Winchcombe looked at his wristwatch, "That's the one with your lot on it, Woolley. Let's give them a proper BSAP welcome, eh?" Without waiting for any answer from me, he headed off until we were standing inside the main building, which, although clearly busy, was not crowded. Insp. Winchcombe carefully selected a spot a few paces from and directly in front of the archway from which the arriving passengers, having cleared customs and emigration, would come.

"You just stay here, at ease, Woolley," Insp. Winchcombe instructed, "While I go through to find them." He took a couple of steps, then paused for a moment and looked back at me as if having an afterthought. "Oh. You can take off your cap, Woolley. Under your left armpit will do. Leave it there until I tell you to put it back on." As I obeyed that instruction he walked on and vanished from sight.

Standing as I was, almost smack in the middle of the bustling but not crowded concourse, I sensed a few curious glances directed my way by others standing around to greet incoming passengers. Perhaps because I had already had better than seven years in police uniform, being the subject of a bit of eyeballing was no worry at all, so I just stood there, at ease and waited as instructed as at first a trickle, then a rush, of incoming passengers poured out from the archway, into the arms and greetings of the waiting people, to be shepherded away, along with their assorted baggage.

The rush dwindled to a trickle. The concourse had almost emptied, yet there was still no sign of Insp. Winchcombe or the incoming recruits. I began to wonder what was causing the delay. Then it was that the cluster of nine young men appeared, gazing curiously around them. With them they had a small mountain of suitcases, trunks, haversacks and overnight bags, some being carried, the rest on trolleys. At their head was Insp. Winchcombe, who carefully steered them to where I was, by then somewhat conspicuously, standing.

A few feet distant he called the group to a halt and pointed at me with his cane. "Take note you lot," he instructed. "This is Recruit Constable Woolley. He has been elected Squad Leader of 9 Squad of 1964, which is the training squad you will be assigned to once you are formally attested later today. If you have any questions or concerns while you are undergoing training in depot, start by asking him. If he can't sort it out, it is his job to find somebody who can do so, which is usually me. Any questions?"

There was a pause and a bit of head shaking, before one of the new arrivals who I later discovered was Taffy Lovell, who had dark hair at almost shoulder-length, stuck up his hand. With a clear grimace of concern and in a voice full or horror, he asked, "Do we all have to have that kind of haircut, Sir?"

"You'll get used to it," Insp. Winchcombe replied, glancing unsympathetically at him. "Now let's get you lot to the transport and get you into depot and attested." Turning his face towards me once again, he raised his cane until the end briefly touched his cap brim. The unspoken instruction was clear enough. I set my cap on my head and snapped into a full attention stance, with head up, chin in, chest out but shoulders down and stomach in. "Lead off, Woolley. You know the way."

As I executed a parade-ground about-turn and marched away towards the glass entry and exit doors I clearly heard one of the new arrivals mutter in a stage whisper, "Bloody Nora, I thought we were here to join a police force, not the bleedin' army!"

That was how the following individuals added themselves to the growing number of members of Squad 9 of 1964:-

7211 Biddulph, Peter William
7212 Brown, Dennis Antony
7213 Bruce, James Hogg
7214 Gent, Henry Watson
7215 Inman, Howard James
7216 Lovell, Maldwyn Leslie
7217 Tedford, John Dill
7218 Whittaker, Richard
7219 Wood, Paul

Later that day, after the new recruits had all been allocated beds, had had their first meal in the canteen and returned from their visit to Police HQ to be attested, we began to introduce ourselves, exchange backgrounds and learn something of the various motivations that caused the new arrivals to sign on.

Over the next few days, as Christmas loomed, the squad began to come together as a unit. When it came their turn to attend the barber's shop, the trepidation on the faces of the newcomers was clear to see. Their collective relief on being generally left with more hair on their heads than I had, was quite marked. So much so that Harry Gent, who was about my own age, with police force experience from the UK, asked me about it. When I explained that it had been by special instruction of our Squad Instructor, he scratched his chin thoughtfully for a moment, then offered, "Something of a psychologist then; or just a nasty sadistic bastard?"

"Something of each would be my guess, Harry," I replied. "The problem is that we don't presently know the proportions of the mix and that could be important." There that particular conversation ended.

With the squad at full strength the festive season came and went rapidly and somewhat liquidly for some. The guard room cells got to be busier than usual and assorted members of several squads ended up parading, with full kit, at evening time behind the guard outside the Depot Guardroom, after having been found unsteady on their feet at early morning parades. For us, the highlight of it was wrapping Insp. Winchcombe's car in pink toilet paper, complete with a massive pink bow on top, while he was having lunch on Christmas Day.

One day early in the New Year, after a few loosening-up exercises, we were introduced to the quarter mile long circuit of the running track. "I want you to do just two laps this morning," Insp. Winchcombe advised us. "That's half a mile. For today you can take your own time but remember that we need a sub-five-minute mile out of each you in a fortnight or so, if you are to pass the fitness standard."

Running has never been one of my strengths. My lungs never seem to have been shaped for top cardio-vascular performance. In fact, during my apprenticeship years in Brighton, the annual TB scan usually resulted in me being called back for further examination and I was quite used to the technicians' comments of "Don't like the look of your chest, young man!" as they peered at the x-rays. With that history behind me, I viewed the running track with jaundiced eyes and set off at a steady jogtrot. Gradually the squad sorted itself into a sort of running ability order. Johnny Tedford simply took off and finished his two laps before several of us, including me, had done one. Howard Inman, Colin Gunston and Chris Phillips, too, were obviously quite at home on the track. At the back of the group, Harry Gent, Taffy Lovell and I all sort of jogged along until we were across the line for the second time, way over the indicative time.

As the final half-dozen or so of us finished and tried, hands on hips and doubled over, to get our breath back, a uniformed rider appeared, atop one of the depot horses. Drawing his mount to a halt at the top of the bank to the track he called to Insp. Winchcombe, "Don't bother to call them to attention, Mr Winchcombe. Half of them look as though they wouldn't make it. How far have they done?" I recognised the voice. It was Ascom Wright.

"Just half a mile, Sir, but it's their first time on the track this morning." Insp. Winchcombe replied, drawing himself to attention.

"Very well, Inspector. Keep them at it. We don't want any failures and drop-outs, do we? Especially Squad Leaders." With that, he turned the horse and rode off at a rising trot that looked effortless, leaving the rest of us to get our breath back.

As he rode out of sight, Insp. Winchcombe strode over to where I was slowly getting my breathing back to normal. "I don't know why, but Mr Wright has clearly got his eye on you, Woolley," he said warily. "Whether that is a good thing or a bad thing only time will tell, but if you fail any of the fitness standards, I don't think you should expect any favours. Got it?"

In the rarefied air of the highveld, it was all I could do at that moment, to gasp a, "Yes, Sir," in reply and continue to wonder just how the more recently arrived Johnny Tedford and others could manage to do as well as they had.

Strangely, it was not any failure of physical fitness that led to one of our number dropping out. It was more of a physiological abnormality that the standard medical examination was never designed to detect. As we changed from walking, doubling, or trotting around the camp area, fitted into our uniforms and shaped up into an orderly and well-drilled group, recruit constable 7202 Jacob Cloete Pieterse, far better known by then as "Yarpie," encountered a growing problem. He simply could not march!

Try as hard as he could, and he did try, with encouragement from everyone and several visits to the camp hospital, Yarpie simply could not sustain a steady marching rhythm. After perhaps fifty or a hundred yards of "Left, right, left, right, swing your arms," and so on, the unfortunate fellow would break step, with a hop, skip and jump and drop out, complaining of intense cramp. Those of us on the squad who had previous police experience felt sorrier for him than others, for we knew how little real "marching" he would be called upon to do once through Depot and out to a station. We all felt that he would manage perfectly well, once through pass-out parade. Eventually, towards the end of January 1965, he was given an honourable discharge, on medical grounds. It was a gloomy day for the squad when Yarpie handed in his issued kit, packed his civilian bags, shook hands all round and left.

In those early days we also came face to face with the assault course. It was another of our instructors, Insp. "Tackie" MacIntosh, who led us to it one rainy morning. "There you are," he declared, waving his hand in the general direction of the dozen or so assorted obstacles. "Three minutes is the pass time you will need in about a month from now. Fail that and you're in trouble. Today we'll go and have a look at the obstacles one by one first and then you can spend the rest of this PT period sorting out your own best individual way around it. You'll get enough practice at it to give you all a fair chance on the day. Any questions?"

"What's the record, Sir?" asked Howard Inman. Insp. MacIntosh looked him up and down before answering. "Two minutes, twenty seconds," he stated flatly. "Fancy your chances of bettering it?"

Inman shook his head, an expression of pure innocence all over his rain wet face. "No, Sir. Particularly not on a soaking wet day like today. Those blue gum poles are slippery as hell and we're wearing rubber soled PT shoes."

The next half-hour was a careful exercise in overcoming the treacherous combination of log ramps, rope swings, vertical walls and climbing frames, monkey swings, concrete culvert pipes, rope walks and balancing bars that comprised the assault course. Most of us, careful though we were, managed to slip, slide or fall off from one or other of the obstacles. My timing and grip let me down on the monkey swing bars, but I did manage to stay upright when I landed in the water-filled pit below. Not that only being soaked from the knees down was any victory, because with the way the rain was coming down, we were all quickly soaked from head to toe anyway.

Clive George was less fortunate when he attempted the rope swing over another water-filled trench. His grip failed when his body was out of vertical, so his landing in the water was almost horizontal. He refused an offered hand out and scrambled on to relatively dry land cursing and swearing, which our instructor promptly told him off for. When we were done, Insp. MacIntosh had us form up into squad order in threes, ready to quick march or run back to the main part of depot and take a hot shower before breakfast. "Right," he said, before ordering us on our way, "Next time, when it's dry you can race each other over that little lot. Anyone who breaks his neck gets an honourable discharge and the slowest one gets to end up behind the guard in full dress order. Got it?"

Soggy nods from all let him know that he had got his message across.

Having set the cheerful thought of more assault-course work into our minds, he ordered me to double the squad away to quarters for a shower and breakfast while he promptly turned away into the rain for a run on his own.

The moment Insp. MacIntosh was out of sight Clive George broke ranks and began to sprint away in the direction of our quarters and the ablution blocks. My bellow of, "Where the hell do you think you're going to Clive?" brought the reply of, "F… you, Woolley, I want a hot shower." He just kept sprinting away. I let him go, ordered the rest of the squad into a quick march and then double time over the half mile or so back to the road outside our quarters, where I halted and dismissed them.

A few minutes later, as I made my way to the shower block, Harry Gent caught up with me. "You're going to have to slap him down sooner or later," he advised me conversationally. I nodded my agreement and then added, "It's all a matter of timing, Harry."

"Don't leave it too long," Harry advised. "He's busy muttering behind your back and the more that goes on the worse it will get. For the present, most of the squad are quite happy with you as leader. He's the only one who seems to have a bit of a thing about a Brit being squad leader."

I smiled at Harry. "I suspect he'll have a bit of a thing about anyone being squad leader. Unless it's him of course!"

Harry laughed. "You could be right," he agreed.

Inside the shower block there was no sign of the subject of our conversation. If he had indeed got in and out of the showers before us, to ensure that his shower water was hot, he had moved very fast indeed. Mind you, in the steamy heat of a Rhodesian summer, a cold shower was often more enjoyable than a hot one.

At breakfast time I worked it so that I had a seat directly across the table from Clive George. With others of our squad sitting around us I quietly told him that whether he liked me or not, or whether he wanted somebody other than me, perhaps himself, as squad leader was immaterial. Decisions had been made and that was that. Now the important issue was that the squad should work as a team and all support each other because there would come a time for everyone to show their strength and particular talents and other times when our own individual weaknesses would need a little help from squad-mates if we were to all see the course through successfully.

My quiet words were met with a tart, "Easy for you. You've got just six weeks. The rest of us are here for seven months. Squad leader you may be. Just don't try pushing me around. That's all." He pushed back from the table, gathered his plate and utensils and turned away.

Sitting around the large refectory type table were most of our squad. I looked around at each of them and said, "If anyone other than Clive wants to throw his hat into the ring, I'm quite happy to have another ballot for leader." Heads shook all around and that was the end of it, for then.

Before Christmas we encountered our first pay parade. No such delicacies as payment into bank accounts and carefully confidential pay slips. Every recruit in depot paraded on the hard square in front of a table, behind which sat the paymaster flanked by a couple of assistants. Squad by squad, names and numbers were called out in order of seniority. So too were the pay rates and the amount of cash due to be handed over. When my £720.00 per annum pay rate was loudly declared there were a few exclamations and one or two questions muttered in the assembled squads. Chief Inspector Trangmar silenced them with a stentorian bellow. I, just as those already paid had done, duly marched out, slammed to a halt before the paymaster, took one step forward, saluted, received my pay, in my left hand, in notes and coin, saluted once again, took a step back, performed a right about turn and marched back to my position in the ranks.

With Christmas and New Year gone, the squad shaped up rapidly into the standard routine of depot. At 06:00hrs it was PT, come rain or shine, although mostly when it was wet, we were steered towards the gymnasium, within which were all the usual bars, ropes and other bits of exercise equipment. At 07:30hrs the canteen opened for breakfast. At 09:00hrs. it was morning inspection parade, followed by lessons of all kinds, from typewriting to arms drill, right through to 12:30 when we were dismissed, ready for lunch at 13:00hrs. At 14:00hrs it was afternoon parade, followed by more lessons and instruction periods. In the tea-breaks, mealtimes and off duty hours we talked, talked some more and even more after that, right through until "Lights Out" sounded and the need for a good night's sleep became the priority.

It was during the chattering of the evening times that I discovered I was not the only one who, because of previous police experience, had been promised a short course through depot. Harry Gent, Johnny Tedford and Peter Biddulph had each been offered no more than three months. They had all been assured, back in the UK that provided they passed the mid-course exams, they would be released from depot at the three-month point. They were just a bit envious of the fact that I had been offered an exit from depot at six weeks, once our first exams and the fitness tests were over.

As January 1965 passed, it was clear to me that, for our Instructors it was developing the physical fitness of the squad which was, for the moment, the priority aim of our training.

In those weeks our visits to the running track grew more frequent. The distance we ran increased too. Once everyone could cover the half-mile in reasonable time, we moved up to a third circuit of the quarter mile track. In later weeks we covered the fourth circuit as well. John Tedford, Howard Inman, Chris Phillips, Colin Gunston and Dick Whittaker were always the fastest, well inside what was required, right from the start. I was always the tail-end Charlie, steadily and reliably a handful of seconds over the standard needed, which was something of a worry.

Classroom lectures were at a minimum while the physical activities took precedence. We were introduced to the swimming pool, part of the police recreation club facilities, where a jump, or a dive from the high board was mandatory, whether you could swim or not. Possessing just about as much swimming skill as my running skills, I jumped. One or two others who could not swim at all, were required to take a leap of faith, landing in the water where the very good swimmers like 7220 Rob Elliot were waiting to save them from drowning. Taffy Lovell enjoyed the pool so much that he promptly spent most of the next weekend there. However, being just a bit unwary of the strength of the tropical sun and a wee bit relaxed from a toot or two, he promptly dozed off to sleep on a poolside lounger after one Saturday drinking session. The result was a painfully lobster red back and legs and a lesson hard learned.

If one or two of us were short on running and swimming skills, most of the whole squad was short on the ability to type. In that direction, we met with one of the notable attractions of Morris Depot. That attraction was Miss Anne Lovell, whose purpose was to teach us typing and administration. Miss Lovell was tall, shapely, slim, trim and attractive. She was also fully aware of the effect that she had on male recruits and more than capable of keeping them in place without creating offence or warfare. After our first encounter with her it became clear that being seated in front or behind her, when she bent over our typewriters to assist any of us recruits, was totally distracting. She also made it clear that she did not date recruits and that pinching or patting her bottom was a "Behind the Guard" offence.

There came a day when one of our number succumbed to temptation. As Annie Lovell, dressed in a tight-fitting pencil skirt, bent over to offer instruction to Johnny Tedford, a paper pellet, fired from a hand-held stretched rubber band, a few desks away, thwacked sharply into her right buttock. Miss Lovell yelped, swung round and firmly slapped Harry Gent's face, he being the nearest one to her. The class promptly fell about, laughing. "Not me Miss!" Harry protested, left hand to his reddening cheek, "Look." He bent down, picked up the offending paper pellet and offered it to her. Fast realising what had happened, Miss Lovell gasped, "Oh, I'm so sorry," and retreated, with as much dignity as she could, to the front of the classroom, from where she declared, "This lesson is ended!" and hurried out.

Near the end of January 1965, our insignia and our ranks changed. Until then, there were both African Constables and European Constables in the Force. Somewhat suddenly, those of us in the European Training Camp, the Morris Depot, all became Patrol Officers, with one single golden coloured bar upon each of our epaulettes.

Those European Constables who had completed three years of service put up two golden bars on each shoulder and European Sergeants suddenly became Section Officers with three bars on each shoulder. The much-respected Sergeant's stripes disappeared as far as European personnel were concerned. It took many days before everyone became used to the new system and titles. For a long while, assorted wisecracks about the changes abounded.

Once our instructors got the impression that most of the squad had mastered basic foot drill, it was time for us to get familiar with the weaponry that was a necessary part of policing in Africa. Not that it was ever used lightly against people, for the Force's record was that no civilian had been killed by a member right from the end of the Matabele Rebellion of 1896, through to modern times. The Force Motto of "Pro Rege, Pro Lege, Pro Patria," was one that was taken very seriously by all members.

The Depot Armoury instructors were headed by Insp. Dave Perkins, assisted by Sgt Eric Kennelly. When Insp. Perkins asked of us who had handled firearms before, most of us raised our hands. Even the younger element who were mostly local had handled hunting rifles and shotguns of one kind or another, as they shot for the pot or undertook hunting for the assorted vermin that troubled farmlands throughout the country. On that first occasion, Insp. Perkins asked the question, "Anyone know what the most dangerous kind of firearm is?" There was a bit of a silence, so I raised my hand. "An empty one, Sir," I stated firmly. There was a loud snigger from Clive George.

Insp. Perkins looked sharply at him. "You think that's funny?"

"It's a stupid answer, Sir. Empty weapons can't kill."

Insp. Perkins gave Clive George a long hard look. Then he reached round behind him and lifted a picture-framed service style web belt from the table. The top half of the belt, between the brass buckles at the back, was clearly missing. The edges to the hole showed up as shredded and roughened. "Pass that around," he said. "Take a damned good look at it and remember it well, because the recruit who was wearing it was killed a year or two ago when his spine was blown in half right here in this armoury by another recruit holding a Greener shotgun that he thought was empty."

The sombre trophy was passed from hand to hand and back to Insp. Perkins who put it down on the table before turning back to us once again. "Golden rule of handling firearms is that no weapon is empty until you have proved that it is. Got it?"

There were nods from all around. Even from Clive George.

For the purposes of weapons training and arms drill there was no such thing as a personal firearm at that stage. When needed we all drew Mark IV .303 Lee Enfield rifles from the armoury and handed them in at the end of the drill period. At other times we began to get familiar with assorted handguns and sub-machine guns: .38 and .45 Revolvers, 9mm Automatics of assorted makes and both 9mm Sterling and Uzi sub-machine guns. We were also shown and had explained to us the full workings of the latest 7.62mm FN semi-automatic rifle. I say, "the latest", because there was just one of the original models of the FN in the armoury. Section Officer Eric Kennelly brought the older item and one of the latest ones out to show us. He quickly demonstrated the assembling and dis-assembling of the latest item, extolling its 20-round magazine and many benefits over the .303 SMLE and even the newer SLR. He was a little less enthusiastic about the older FN, confessing that the weapon had arrived some years before, but without any instruction manual or toolkit, so apart from being able to "break" it at the hinge point forward of the butt, they had not been able to remove the magazine or fully dis-assemble it. One by one we were all able to familiarise ourselves with the new style FN and told to look forward to the day when that weapon would be fully available to all members of the police force.

While others were handling the assorted weapons that day, I took a long hard look at the older style FN. In doing so, something struck me. Whereas the new FN had a toolkit built into the hand grip behind the magazine, the older version did not. When I looked to see if there was a butt-trap that might house such a toolkit, again there was not. That had me puzzled because I could not see the purpose of requiring a fully separate toolkit. Then something clicked in my mind. I reached for a 7.62 bullet. A couple of moments later I called Sgt Kennelly over and showed him the fully dis-assembled rifle. He stared at it for a moment and then demanded to know how I had done it. I duly demonstrated how it was done, using just a live cartridge. Sgt Kennelly bellowed for Insp. Perkins, showed him my handiwork and explained how I had done it. Insp. Perkins promptly had me re-assemble and dis-assemble the rifle in front of him. When I had done that successfully he grinned hugely and said, "Well done lad," before turning to Sgt Kennelly and saying, "Don't let him near a 20mm cannon shell or he'll have the whole damned depot in pieces!"

No training depot would be complete without kit inspections, so we had our fair share of those. For the first while it was each Saturday morning. Every item of issued kit, with uniforms, had to be laid out on our beds in immaculate order, with each of us standing to attention at the foot of the bed as Inspectors Winchcombe, MacIntosh or one of the other instructors peered, poked, prodded and examined until they were satisfied, or had found sufficient fault to merit a "Behind the Guard!" instruction. This was a time when the batmen really came into their own. Each had a copy of the layout photograph and each, I am very sure, had a private collection of oddments, such as buttons, badges and articles of uniform, so that anything missing could be produced and laid out. Romeo was a marvel of good order and precision. It was his efforts that kept me from any default in this particular requirement and I was very grateful for it. Others were less fortunate. Mind you, there was one such inspection when we could all have been in dire trouble. We had prepared our beds for the 09:00hrs inspection, seen off our batmen and were all standing at ease in the barrack block when a smart figure, unfamiliar to us, but properly dressed in full uniform, with Section Officer's bars up and swagger cane under his left armpit, strode boldly into the room. "Right, you lot. Inspection has been delayed. I want you outside. Now. Fall in on the parade ground and wait until I join you. Get to it. At the double! Move!"

We had been there long enough to have become accustomed to obeying orders promptly and without question, so out we went, rapidly. In a short while the entire squad was drawn up in parade order on the tarmac a hundred yards away from and out of sight of our quarters, standing easy and awaiting the appearance of the Section Officer who had given us the order to parade. We had been standing there for about five minutes without any instructor coming near us when Insp. Winchcombe approached us. I promptly drew the squad up to attention. "What the devil is the squad doing here Woolley?" He demanded. I explained the reason. Insp. Winchcombe's face tightened. "Get the squad back to their quarters Woolley. You've been had!" He turned about and marched off towards the Depot Office.

There was no orderly march back to quarters. It was a mad dash as daylight dawned that we had been hoaxed. What we found was wreckage. Beds had been overturned and bedding had been pulled off from beds. Uniforms and equipment were everywhere, from ceiling beams to locker tops and elsewhere, much inside, but quite a lot outside. As we grimly surveyed the shambles we noticed that we had an audience. Most all of the recruits in depot, apart from our squad, were within view, staring at our barrack block with broad grins and much laughing at our discomfort. One wag bellowed, "Come on you lot. It's two minutes to inspection. Get your fingers out!"

The jeers, cheers and laughter at our situation were cut short by the bugle call for parade for those not on kit and barracks inspection. As the audience hastened away, we began to set beds upright and gather our scattered kit and equipment. It was then that those of us who had marked our kit and equipment benefited from the time spent doing it. Several of the squad who had not bothered to do so struggled to sort out their own gear from the pile of un-marked stuff.

Insp. Winchcombe's arrival in the block went almost un-noticed until he bellowed, "Belt up and quieten down!" As silence established itself, he gazed around tight-lipped. Once his roving gaze had encompassed the totality of the shambles, he turned to me. "Today's inspection parade for this squad is cancelled, Woolley. So is the rest of this morning's routine. You'll spend the time between now and midday getting this mess sorted out. I want a list of any damaged or missing kit with me before sixteen hundred hours today." He gave a curt nod, turned about and headed for the door, where he paused and looked back. "Do any of you have any idea who did this?" There were assorted mutters in the negative and much shaking of heads, including mine. "Okay," Insp. Winchcombe said flatly. "Let's just call it a part of your training." He paused and then added warningly, "Just make sure that it doesn't happen again." With that admonishment he went, leaving us to put right our beds, bedding and belongings and discuss angrily just who might and might not have been responsible. That we never did find out.

Our PT activities were mostly routine affairs. On rainy mornings using the pommel horses, spring-boards, vaulting boxes, and beams, along with the ropes, we were put through our paces in the gymnasium. When it was dry, we did our exercises out in the open, on the Police Reserve Hard Square. On such occasions, one of the more interesting episodes was log-drill. The "logs" were Caber length chunks of blue gum trees, perhaps better known as Australian eucalyptus trees. In weight these logs were about 400lbs. In teams of six we threw the logs horizontally up in the air and caught them on the way down. We lifted them over our heads one handed and two handed. We tucked them under our armpits, one side and the other and did bending exercises with them. On occasions, three of us at each end carried the logs on our shoulders while each of us in turn hung by arms and legs from the centre of the log and tried to pull, push or lever from his position under another log carried by one of the other members of the squad.

We also discovered that the seating tiers around the sports field were easy to deal with when we were asked to run up and down the gangways as fast as we could on our own, but not quite so easy to cover when hopping on one leg or the other and far less easy when ordered to undertake the same up and down exercise with another squad member as a piggy-backed burden. Mostly that was done in paired-off fashion, weight for weight, but when Insp. Winchcombe, with straight face and perhaps just a hint of a gleam in his eye, set the light-weight Chris Phillips to carry the much heavier weight of Ox Grant, it was mission impossible, resulting in total collapse of the pair and much ribald laughter from the rest of us.

Our schedule of running around the track gradually stepped up as our fitness grew. We also commenced a series of longer runs one afternoon of each week. Very rapidly it became clear that we had some fine athletes among our number, such as John Tedford, Chris Phillips, Howard Inman, Rob Elliot and, to give him his fair due, Clive George. Their natural abilities in the gym, the swimming pool, on the track or over longer distances, were clear for all to see. Others performed adequately, while a few of us, me included, had to work just as hard as our variously limited abilities permitted, as we strove towards the levels that would see us safely through the Preliminary Examination stage of our training.

In the classroom, those of us who had previous police experience found little difficulty in assimilating the input relating to Common and Statutory Laws and Force Standing Orders, basically because Rhodesian Law followed the Roman-Dutch Legal System which had much in common with UK Law in general.

As January progressed, it became clear to those of us who had been promised short spells of training, that the date of our Preliminary Examination and the physical tests that went with them, was ill-defined and uncertain. Peter Biddulph, Harry Gent, John Tedford and I had a few conversations over the subject. I conceded that the squad had to be treated as a whole and that the time I had been in depot before the British contingent had arrived on 15th December could hardly be counted as training. Nevertheless, we four were all keen to escape just as soon as we could, from the confining and regimented rules of depot and get out to station postings wherever they might be. In that, we were allowed some choice, between Town and District. With my background service in Nyasaland, I had no hesitation in indicating a preference for a District posting.

January 1965 finished without any examination date appearing. That milestone caused some more discussion between us. As Squad Leader I did have a better opportunity than anyone else to talk over squad problems with our instructor. When I did just that over the subject of shortened courses for some of us and exam dates, Insp. Winchcombe advised me that the examination dates varied squad by squad, depending upon the progress each squad was making. He pointed out that not much real training had occurred before the New Year, so perhaps I and the others involved had best reckon from the start of the year rather than from when we had enrolled. "You and the others need to concentrate more on the importance of passing those exams and rather less on the importance of the date they may take place," he admonished. That was the message that I had to take back to the others. None of us liked it, but at that time, nobody felt like making a scene over it.

In early February, the most senior squad in Morris Depot completed their 6 months of training. After a very impressive Pass-Out Parade they moved out, heading for Driver Training School at Cranbourne. That created the chance for us in 9 Squad of 1964 to move into the quarters they had vacated. That was Bodle Block, which provided rooms which two of us could share, which was a considerable improvement in our previous situation. I promptly took a photograph of the entire squad on the day we moved in. Lots of happy, smiling faces. It was a couple of days after that move that our usual training routine was briefly disturbed, at very short notice. As policemen we were not greatly interested in the politics of the land, but we were all well-aware of the rapidity with which previous British colonies were being granted independence and somewhat wary of majority rule and the ills it had already brought about elsewhere. Certainly, with my background in Nyasaland and with several interesting conversations with Dr Hastings Banda behind me, I was well-aware of the impending break-up of the Federation of the Rhodesias and Nyasaland and wondering just how independence for Southern Rhodesia, as it then was, would turn out. Clearly in connection with that subject, a gathering of tribal chiefs from all over Rhodesia had been arranged by the government. To facilitate that Ndaba, to use the Chishona word for it, the chiefs from all over the country were summoned to Salisbury. Those from the most distant parts were to be transported by train to and from the capital. The trains needed to be guarded on their journeys to and from, so the entire body of depot recruits was called into action.

Following a succinct but adequate briefing, we drew .303 rifles, real live ammunition, torches and batteries, all of which we might be called upon to use. After that, our overnight gear and our raincoats were packed into our sailor-style canvas kitbags and away we were carted, aboard a Bedford 5 tonne flat-back lorry, for the short journey to Railway Avenue and Salisbury Station. There Squad 9 of 64 boarded the scheduled morning train destined for Beira, with Umtali as a routine stop on the way. Our task was to travel to

Umtali, spend a few hours at Umtali Police Camp and then escort a few score of tribal chiefs on the overnight train back to Salisbury. After that, we were to remain in Morris Depot, at instant readiness in case of any unforeseen eventualities while the Ndaba was going on. Once the gathering in Salisbury was over, we were to escort the same group of chiefs safely back to Umtali on the night train to Beira and get ourselves back to Salisbury on the following morning train. To all of us it appeared like two and a half days of mission and probably not a lot of sleep in that time. I remember well the different attitudes within the squad over the job ahead of us. The born and bred Rhodesians regarded it as a bit of a drag, while those of us from further afield welcomed the chance to see something of the country that we had chosen to be policemen in. The only down-side of it, for those of us on the supposed promise of a shortened course in depot, was that it pushed our Preliminary Examinations three days further away.

What struck me on that journey to Umtali was the agricultural order that had clearly been established by the European farmers over the years. Neat and tidy fields of maize, tobacco, cotton and sorghum were everywhere. Farm homesteads, mostly of red-painted corrugated iron roofed bungalows with broad verandas sheltered below stands of tall blue gum trees, with jacaranda, acacia and mopani in abundance. Iron roofed or thatched quarters for the farming labour force, were located not far from many of the farmhouses. Small dams were more plentiful than I had ever envisaged and cattle too. The change to Tribal Reserve land was startling, because the abundance of grass and trees suddenly vanished at the boundary fences. Traditional thatched huts crowded together in clusters, village by village, interspersed with grazing lands and well-tended fields of maize and sorghum. One clear memory I have of that first journey is of seeing in the tribal areas as many goats as cattle and noting for the first time the "contour ridging" on the hillsides, both greater and lesser, designed to prevent the heavy rainstorms carrying away downhill the thin layer of arable soil. It was also clear that in the tribal lands, trees were few and far between.

As I was to learn, the issues of compulsory contour ridging and cattle dipping were aggravations that the local politicians ruthlessly exploited in their drive to create and grow trouble between local people and the government.

The weather was good for viewing the countryside and the Garrett engine up front chuffed and puffed steadily as it covered the miles at an unhurried pace. The train carriages were hardly modern, but were sturdy and comfortable, with upper and lower bunks for overnight travel. For this daytime run the upper bunks were pulled up and tied out of the way while the lower ones were used as seating. A corridor at the side led to an open veranda at the end of each coach so that progress from one swaying coach to the next was something to be undertaken carefully. Inspector Winchcombe and I both patrolled up and down the first-class and second-class carriages, although we left our weaponry with the others in our own compartments. Overall, our wanderings drew little attention from the other passengers, because white, and for that matter, black, police officers travelling by train was, as we subsequently learned, a very routine happening.

After disembarking at Umtali, we were transported to the police camp on the edge of town, directed to the Single Quarters and told to make ourselves comfortable and await further instructions. That evening we were transported back to the railway station where a number of carriages were drawn up alongside a platform. Without fuss or palaver we were allocated in teams of eight to one or other of the coaches, with instructions to be visible and vigilant on the verandas between coaches and in the corridors. One compartment was allocated to us for our kitbags and for rest and relaxation as we rotated on and off watch for the journey to Salisbury. Shortly after we joined the coaches, several buses and other vehicles began to arrive. From them disgorged the several score or so of Tribal Chiefs and a number of Village Headmen from the region who had been summoned for the meeting in Salisbury. Accompanying them were an assortment of District Commissioners, their civilian assistants and uniformed messengers. Altogether, it was a cheerful, bustling hubbub of colour and noise.

It was interesting, at least for me, to note the extreme variety of dress chosen by the individual delegates. Many were in traditional tribal dress, which I suppose is best described as robed and blanketed, while others wore totally westernised shirts, trousers and jackets, or even suits. Their footwear varied from nothing, through the very common tyre-tread sandals, to shiny leather shoes. Several of them were displaying their brass insignia pendants, curved or square according to status. The assortment of flywhisks and even feathered head-dresses was considerable. Here and there I noticed a ceremonial axe or zi-stick, some in the hands of those dressed in suits, clearly a sign that despite the many changes brought about following the arrival of the Europeans in the land, some old traditions still clung on strongly. The other first impression was of considerable age, maturity and dignity among them all. Once the assorted passengers were all aboard and settled, the few coaches were pulled away from the platform and shunted off into a siding area to await the night train from Beira to Salisbury, which our coaches were due to be attached to. In that marshalling yard there were overhead lights aplenty and little need for us on guard duty to use our torches.

Our own efforts to safeguard our human cargo were augmented by foot patrols, one with a police dog, supplied from Umtali Urban Police Station. As ever on any inactive duty in company, we talked over the cause of the gathering and the background tensions between Great Britain and Southern Rhodesia, over the break-up of the Federation of the Rhodesias and Nyasaland and the demands from local nationalists for immediate black majority rule. One common viewpoint prevailed among the born and bred Rhodesians. That was that between the tribal divisions, the political differences and the inherent corruption among many of the Africans placed into positions of power and influence, any precipitate move towards black majority rule would inevitably lead to lawlessness, inter-tribal fighting inefficiency and an exodus of the white population that was the stabilising and progressive force in the land. It was pointed out for the benefit of us outsiders that the country had been a Self-Governing Colony since 1928, that there were already 20 out of the 100 seats in parliament which were guaranteed for black representatives, with plans to grow that number gradually towards parity and then a majority in 25 to 30 years' time, so as to provide a slow and steadily incremental move towards majority rule, rather than the sudden handing over that had caused so much trouble elsewhere in Africa and indeed all around the world since Great Britain commenced its exodus from empire, following the Second World War.

Late in the evening our carriages were shunted out of their holding position and attached to the rear of the Beira to Salisbury train and off we went. As we moved away from the lit area it became a case of "Torches on!" and "Keep your eyes open!" Nobody actually told us what we were to keep our eyes open for, although our briefing had contained the instruction that if the train were fired upon, we were to return fire without waiting for any order to do so.

Fortunately for everyone concerned, the journey was uneventful. The hours and the miles rolled by and watches changed routinely, without incident, until we pulled into Salisbury Railway Station, where a fleet of local busses was waiting to carry the chiefs and headmen away to the conference venue. Once they were all gone, under escort from Salisbury Town Police, we were driven back to depot. After returning our weaponry to the armoury and getting a late breakfast inside us, we were ordered to rest and recover through the remainder of the day, but to be ready for the return journey that evening.

Whatever the substance of the Ndaba had been in detail, none of us recruits were made aware of, but one thing was clear as we prepared to escort the train back to Umtali that evening. The mood of the chiefs had changed. The conversations were more subdued and the periods of silence more evident. Clearly a great deal more personal and collective reflective thinking was going on, before they settled down to sleep, while we recruits reprised our original routine for the escorted journey to Umtali. If the mood of the chiefs was sombre, the mood of the weather had changed also. Rain teemed down the whole way. Where torch beams had cut bright tunnels of light through the previous night and a whole host of stars had fought a twinkling competition in the moonless sky above, this night was different, very different! Heavy clouds poured down a welter of raindrops that created a shimmer on every surface they encountered. The light beams from our torches were pierced through and through by myriads of shiny droplets and the penetrative power of each beam was markedly diminished. When I experimentally raised my .303 and sighted along the barrel as I stood on the drenched veranda between coaches, the teeming power of the rainfall defied any accurate alignment. It was the kind of atmosphere where hitting the proverbial barn door from the inside could have been difficult. All we could do was to shelter as much as we could, wipe the spraying water from our eyes frequently and hope that on a night such as that, any bad guys with evil intent might just want to stay at home.

Eventually, before dawn and after a wet, uncomfortable, but uneventful trip, we arrived at Umtali, where we saw the assorted chiefs safely on to their home-going transports, before heading off to the District Police Camp for some breakfast and a few hours of rest. Later in the day, we boarded the next passenger train back to Salisbury and the continuation of our basic training course.

It was a couple of days after that escort activity that the squad was introduced to the routine of watering the riding horses. On this occasion we were marched down to the horse lines and handed over to Sgt John Pearce, one of the equitation instructors. As days went by, it was a bit difficult to know whether it was he, or one or two of the horses tied to the lines that gave us the hardest time. Sgt Pearce certainly made it clear that first time that we were of far less value and importance than his four-legged charges. "These," he stated forcefully, waving his riding crop at the line of equines waiting to be watered, "are well-trained, intelligent and useful members of the Force, which is far more than you lot presently are. Just like you, some of them don't get on with each other. Some of them won't get on with you and you won't get on with some of them. However, they still need to be fed, watered, groomed, mucked out, cared for and, for some of you, actually ridden. That riding bit is some weeks away yet. For today, all that I want of each of you is that you take one of these horses, untie it, walk it to the watering troughs and let it drink until it decides it has had enough. Once it has had enough, you're to lead the horse back into its own stall in the stables." The flow of his speech halted momentarily as he used his riding crop to point to one of the stable buildings. "Each horse has its name and number on the stall door and you can find the number of whichever horse you've got hold of engraved on its front near-side hoof." The riding crop became a pointer once more. "When you've returned your horse to its stall you are to remove its head-collar. You will then leave the stall, with the head-collar and lead rope, carefully closing and bolting the door behind you. Hang the head-collar and lead rope on the tack board inside the stables and fall in out here again." Sgt Pearce's eyes wandered penetratingly over the squad. "How many of you have ever ridden or handled horses?" he inquired. A few hands went up, all but one from the Rhodesian members of the squad. The only member of the British element whose hand went up was Tony Brown. When Sgt Pearce asked what his experience with horses was, Tony replied simply, "I was in the Household Cavalry, Sgt." That sent Sgt Pearce's eyebrows momentarily skywards. "Were you, indeed?" he mused. "Then you can show us all how it's done. The others can follow your good example." He gestured towards the tied horses. "One last piece of advice for you all. When you untie your horse, keep a firm grip on its lead-rope and head-collar, because some of them won't want to go where you want them to go." He gestured to Tony Brown. "Fall out and show us how it's done then."

Under the eagle eye of Sgt Pearce, Tony Brown marched the few paces to the nearest of the tied horses. Without fuss or bother he patted a hand on its back and patted, stroked and talked his way forward until he was able to get a firm grip on the head-collar with his right hand and give the tied lead rope a sharp tug that untied the knot holding it to the line. Without any trouble at all, Tony turned the horse around and began to lead it towards the watering troughs.

Leaving Tony to his own well-controlled devices, Sgt Pearce turned to the rest of us and said, "That's how it should be done. Now let's see how the rest of you get on. Fall out one by one, get a horse from the line and get it watered. You first, Woolley! "

I headed for the horse to the right of the one Tony Brown had chosen. For no other reason than it gave me a bit more room to turn the horse round me once I had it untied. Having never handled a horse before, I followed Tony's example, made manual and voice contact with the animal and attempted to act and speak as if this was something which I had done a thousand times. On either side of me the other members of the squad were closing in on their chosen horses, some boldly and others timidly, that was for sure.

After that, it took less than a minute before Sgt Pearce' prophesy about the horses having minds of their own was proved right, because some of those horses definitely had ideas other than that of going to the watering troughs. One or two kicked at one end or struck out at the other as they were untied. A couple of others decided to try to bite as they were being untied while one or two of them promptly reared up, pulled lead-ropes free from their handlers' grips and took off at a gallop along the horse lines, urged on by Sgt Pearce's voice yelling, "Get hold of those horses or you're behind the guard tonight, for a week!" The lightweight Chris Phillips did as Sgt Pearce had instructed and hung on gamely to head-collar and lead rope, only to be lifted off his feet and carted away, accompanied by Sgt Pearce's bellow of, "Hang on tight and send us a postcard when you get there!"

The horse I had hold of made a half-hearted attempt to pull free, but other than that it was reasonably well-behaved, for which I was very grateful. Along with a few of the other members of the squad who had also managed to keep hold of their horse, I started to follow Tony Brown and his horse towards the watering troughs.

As the mayhem gradually subsided, loose horses were caught and the fractious ones were calmed down. Amid the confusion of both horse and human noise and activity, Sgt Pearce was here, there and everywhere, fast with a word of advice, a quick helping hand or a cussing for one or two of the squad who he felt were being idle or stupid. When Clive George got bitten and promptly kicked out at his horse's leg, it was Clive who got a verbal roasting, not the horse. Slowly, after some several minutes, every one of our squad had his horse at the watering troughs, where we ignorant ones quickly learned that horses are likely to splash, among other things, when they drink. Eventually, somewhat damp and having learned just a little bit about the depot horses, we had them all returned to their appropriate stalls and were released to go about the rest of the day, after a quick shower.

After a few days the matter of watering the horses became a routine one. We learned that most of the horses were okay once they realised who was in charge. Certain of the horses, like *Quince* and *Winch* had particularly evil temperaments. Whether in or out of their stalls, given half a chance, they bit, kicked, stamped, bucked, barged and reared with little or no provocation. Even Tony Brown, who quickly stood out as the most capable horse-handler among us, treated those two animals warily.

7204 Tony Grant was never known to any of us as anything other than "Ox" because that was how he introduced himself. It was easy to see why he had earned that nickname. He was damned near as broad as he was tall and every way round, it was all solid muscle. That he was well nick-named was demonstrated one day on the horse watering duties when he ended up with a three-year-old colt called *Kim*. On that particular day, *Kim* was clearly feeling lively. While being led towards the troughs, he kicked, barged, pulled and bit as best he could. It got him nowhere with Ox, who was from a farming background, could ride well and knew a thing or two about most animals. At the troughs, once he had had his fill, *Kim* thrashed his head from side to side in the water and liberally splashed all within range. Then he tried to climb up on the trough with both front hooves. Fortunately, Ox had firm hands, a steady nerve and enough weight to keep the pesky colt under control, pull him around and away from the troughs and head off towards the stables. However, when they reached a point a few yards short of their stable block door, *Kim* decided to stage a protest. He just stopped moving and stood still. Ox pulled on the head-rope. *Kim* pulled back. Stalemate! Without a word, Ox simply stepped back alongside the stubborn colt and ducked under him. He wrapped an arm around each front leg and, before the puzzled colt could do anything more, straightened up and started walking forward. *Kim*, with both forelegs firmly gripped and off the ground, had no option but to walk forward on rear legs alone, all the while with the most astounded look I have ever seen on a horse's face.

Eventually, our squad graduated to the stage where we were to start grooming the horses occasionally, as well as watering them. As fortune would have it, it was raining, so our first attempt at grooming activity was undertaken with the horses in their stalls, wearing their head-collars and tied to rings in the walls. Clive George and Colin Gunston had both irritated Sgt Pearce recently, so they were allocated the two awkward horses. The rest of us, as we walked along the length of the stable building, simply turned into the stall of the first horse we came to that was not being groomed and got on with the job in hand, watched over by both Sgt Pearce and Insp. Matchett.

Purely by chance I ended up at the door to the stall occupied by RH *Yeovil* and promptly pulled up short. That was because I was looking over the door at the saddest, sorriest horse I had seen in a long time. The poor animal was a chequerboard of gashes, cuts, scrapes and bruises, from nose to tail, none of which showed any signs of having received any medical attention. Most were dirty, muddy and had straw sticking to congealed or still fresh blood. *Yeovil* was also, quite reasonably, not wearing a head-collar and not tied up, but standing dejectedly facing the stall door, in a welter of droppings that suggested his stall was overdue for mucking out. Not far from the door, on the inside, was a very battered and upside-down bucket that appeared once to have held the stall's water provision.

"You, horse, are one sorry-looking specimen," I offered conversationally as I slid back the bolt, "You are cuts and scrapes all over, so how the dickens I'm supposed to groom you I know not." I put down my grooming kit on the wall and slipped carefully into the stall. *Yeovil* began to turn, somewhat slowly and clearly painfully, in order to bring his back end around. I sensed a kick was coming, so stepped in close as fast as I could, grabbed a handful of his mane and an ear and snapped at him, "Stop it! You are in no condition to pick a fight with anyone or anything. If you want some water and your injuries cleaned up, stand still and behave!"

I let go of *Yeovil*'s ear and mane, put my hands on my hips and glared at him, ready for anything he might try. For a moment we remained eyeball to eyeball as it were, then *Yeovil* slowly stretched out his neck, opened his mouth, clamped his teeth very gently over my left forearm, more carefully than viciously and looked up at me as if to say, "See, I can still bite if I want to!" before just letting go and then standing quietly, with his nose gently nudging the battered bucket I took what was clearly an equine hint, picked up the battered container and shortly returned with it duly filled. I was barely inside the door for the second time before *Yeovil* stuck his head into the bucket and damned near drained it dry.

After that interesting introduction, I just set about trying to carefully clean the unfortunate animal's assorted wounds, picking out pieces of straw, twigs and tarmac gravel here and there and gently wiping the poor horse down with handfuls of straw, because it looked as though he had not been groomed in days. Whenever I touched a very sore spot, *Yeovil* jerked away and whickered, but made no attempt to kick or stamp. As I worked on him, I kept up a running commentary for the horse, telling him what I was going to do next. Frequently I moved up to his head to give him a gentle pat and a scratch between his ears before going back to clean around the next injury. After about a half hour of careful work I straightened up from my monologue and labours to see Insp. Matchett leaning on the stall's gate, quietly watching what I was doing. The expression on his face made me ask, "Anything wrong, Sir?" Insp. Matchett shook his head. "Nothing at all, lad. You just keep on doing what you're doing but have a word with me when you've finished." With that he turned away and marched off. A few minutes later Sgt Pearce wandered by, being so casual about his meanderings that it was almost comical in the way that he pretended not to be interested in what I was doing. By that time, I felt I had done what I could with the horse's multiple injuries, so I had started to clear up the droppings and separate the dry straw from the wet, moving *Yeovil* about as I needed to. On seeing what I was up to, Sgt Pearce stepped away a few paces, yelled for one of the African stable hands and sent him off to fetch a wheelbarrow. To me he said, "Shove that soiled stuff out of the stall and leave it to the labourers. It's time to fall in."

I did as I was instructed, quickly spread some fresh straw for *Yeovil* to bed down on if he wanted to and then took myself off to join the squad standing easy outside.

When the squad was all together Insp. Matchett told Tony Brown to march them away. He waited until they were moving off and then asked me. "Who told you to try to groom *Yeovil*, Woolley?" I shrugged. "Nobody Sir. His was the first unattended stall I came to so I just got on and did what I could for him, given the state he's in."

Insp. Matchett pursed his lips, "As I understand it, Woolley, you've never ridden or handled horses before?" It was a statement as much as a question. "Never, Sir, but I usually get on well with animals and that seemed to help. Can I ask what happened to *Yeovil*, Sir? He is in a bit of a state."

"He got hit by a car on a morning ride through town yesterday. He was knocked over hard enough to cause him to roll and slide a couple of yards on a freshly gravelled bit of road. It's lucky he only suffered the superficial damage he did. Just for your information, he's put two of the labourers in hospital and kicked a half-dozen more since then. What I want to know is how come he didn't do the same to you the moment you went into his stall?"

I shrugged. "I've no idea, Sir. I just talked to him and then got on and did what I did and he let me do it. That's it, Sir."

Insp. Matchett nodded thoughtfully. "Now you know the full story and the damage *Yeovil* has done in the past couple of days, would it bother you to go back and tend to him again?"

"No, Sir," I said. "I think he and I can get along."

Insp. Matchett turned to Sgt Pearce who had by then joined us. "Have a word with Winchcombe. I want Woolley down here morning and evening for the next week or so. He can work on *Yeovil* until the horse has recovered."

Sgt Pearce just nodded. That was how it was that I found myself acting as nurse to a battered horse for the next many days and not working to precisely the same schedule as the other members of the squad. In that time *Yeovil* behaved like a gentleman. I was able to clean and disinfect his wounds, change his water bucket and muck out his stall without any trouble at all. There came a day when I was finally able to walk him out to the watering troughs, under the eagle eyes of Sgt Pearce and Insp. Matchett and return him to his stall. That first time was a slow and steady journey, but there was improvement each day thereafter until eventually it was decided by the instructors that *Yeovil* no longer needed my personal brand of care and attention and I returned to the regular schedule of training along with the rest of the squad.

As for *Yeovil*, he, so I was informed, promptly bit the next recruit who went into his box and broke his thumb!

A couple of days after I finished as *Yeovil*'s temporary groom, the simmering antagonism, between Clive George and me came to a head. One of the tasks handed down to the squad leader was to delegate one member of the squad, every morning, to collect mail during the lunch break, from the depot office. On that particular day, it was Clive's turn. He had nodded when I gave him the task in the morning, but after lunch I discovered that the job had not yet been done.

Seeking to find out why not, I located Clive in the room he now shared with Chris Phillips. He was sitting on the side of his bed, polishing his boots before the afternoon parade at 2:00 p.m. When I asked him about the mail collection he just shrugged and went on talking to Chris. When I repeated my question, he carefully put down his boot and cloth, looked up at me and said, very deliberately, "I don't have to take orders from a c---- like you!"

Hitting someone while they are seated is hardly fair, so I invited him to stand up and repeat what he had just said.

Instead of accepting my invitation he just said, "F--- off!"

At that, I compromised and hit him on his left cheekbone as hard as I could with an open-handed slap from my right arm.

I have to admit that Clive came up swinging a whole lot faster than I thought he would. I got my head away from his attempted right uppercut but collected a solid left hook to my right temple. If Clive was faster than me, his arms were shorter so a couple of straight lefts from me brought a smear of blood from his nose. Our brief scrap was brought up short by Chris Phillips shoving himself in between us at the same time as the first bugle call for afternoon parade sounded.

"If you two are late for parade you'll both be behind the guard!" he stated flatly. "If you want to finish this later that's fine, but not right now!!"

Clive and I glared at each other, but both realised the sense of what Chris had just said. Wordlessly we both obeyed the early warning call, so that we arrived on parade on time as required. It was routine that our squad instructor inspected us as we paraded, both morning and afternoon, before sending us off to the appropriate location for that time. On this occasion,

Insp. Winchcombe started as usual with our right marker, Pete Biddulph and worked on from there. When he reached me a few places along in the front rank, he eyed me up and down and then said, "What happened to your face, Woolley?"

"Walked into a door, Sir," was my prompt reply.

Our squad instructor nodded wordlessly and passed on along the three ranks until he arrived in front of Clive George. After looking him up and down he commented, "I suppose you're the door that Woolley walked into."

"Yes, Sir," Clive agreed.

Insp. Winchcombe nodded again and passed on. That was all that he ever said about it. At the end of the afternoon, when I was required to march the squad back to our allotted quarters, I asked Clive if he wanted to finish the scrap or shake hands and forget it.

"I didn't think you'd have the guts to hit me," was his response. To that I replied, "And I didn't think you'd be as fast as you were, so maybe we're quits?"

Clive nodded. We shook hands and that was that. There were comments of approval from the squad members around us. Relations between Clive George and myself were never totally friendly after that, but a degree of mutual respect existed, which prevented any more trouble.

As we headed for our shared rooms, Harry Gent stepped up alongside me and muttered, "I think that's cleared the air a bit. It was needed, you know. He's been telling too many people that you're yellow and he could take you any day he wanted to. Now he knows he was wrong. That's why he chose not to finish it later."

"For which decision, Harry, I for one am very glad," I remarked and walked contentedly on.

Some few days later there occurred a most peculiar incident. It was one that I was never ever able to quite get to the bottom of. Evening meal had been completed and the sun had set, so that the depot area was lit only by artificial light. I was inside our allocated quarters when I realised that there was a growing crescendo of voices some short way away outside. The tone of the voices carried both excitement and anger, so I went out to see what was causing it. In a small clear area among the buildings which formed our quarters were perhaps forty or more recruits, all ringed around and enclosing one single recruit who was being pushed, shoved, spun and punched around the circle of recruits around him. When he fell to the floor he was picked up and thumped and spun around some more. Most of the shouting was of the nature of "Come on you yellow bastard. Fight! Put your fists up and fight! You're a coward! We're gonna cream you, you runt," and so forth. Their victim's hands were hanging limply at his sides and his only response was a somewhat feeble, muffled, "I'm not fighting! I'm not fighting!"

Coming in unexpectedly as I did, from behind them, I was able to push my way through to the front of the circle. What I saw going on was ugly, cowardly, pack-rat behaviour. What I quickly realised was that the victim was Colin Gunston, who was one of the youngest members of our squad, 9 of 1964.

His visibly bloodied face and dishevelled clothing told me he had already taken a pounding. I sensed a need to stop it. Fast! I let out a parade-ground roar of "Belay that you pack-rats, he's had enough!" That unexpected bellow created a moment of surprise which I used to grab hold of Colin and barge my way out of the angry, belligerent circle, pushing their unresisting erstwhile victim ahead of me.

Before the pack could organise themselves to prevent it, I had Colin safely into the shelter of a portico styled entrance way to one of the barrack blocks close by. With him leaning against the door behind me I placed myself between the two front pillars of the portico and turned to face the decidedly angry and noisy mob, whose members were by then voicing their opinions of me for interfering.

One of them came at me, head down and fists swinging wildly. At times like that, Queensbury Rules go out of the window and vivid memories of childhood days and self-survival skills hard-learned amid the bomb-dumps of the East End of London, after WWII, come rapidly flooding back.

"That's dirty!" yelled one of the angry mob as my forehead, knees and feet worked harder than my fists to drop my first adversary. "So is a mob of forty to one," I snapped back. "If you buggers want a scrap, I'll give you one, as long as it's one at a time." My raised fists and the individual groaning at my feet seemed to give them a moment of reflection. "We don't want you, you stupid bastard. It's him behind you we want!" came from somebody else.

"Why?" I demanded. "What's he done?"

"That's our business," one of them shouted.

About then I heard the door behind me open. A quick glance over my shoulder told me that somebody was pulling Colin Gunston inside the building. Later I discovered it was Brian Gunston, Colin's older brother who was also in depot at that time, but in a squad ahead of us.

"This business is going to get you all behind the guard for a week if you keep it up." I reminded them sharply over the hubbub. At that point, over the heads of the mob facing me, I caught a brief glimpse of a tall figure in instructor's uniform peering around the corner of a building a score of yards away.

From somewhere in the crowd there was a cry of "Rush him. He can't fight all of us at once!" There was another cry of "Let's trough him!" That brought roars of approval and the throng surged forward. As lots of them came at me in a rush the individual I had flattened wrapped his arms round my calves. Very rapidly I was swept off my feet and carted away towards the horse lines and the watering trough, with the whooping, cheering and jeering crowd tagging along behind. With a couple of people holding each arm and leg and the other dozens whooping encouragement I had no chance of escape. A dunking in a horse trough by fellow recruits was a recognised punishment for anyone who upset fellow recruits by being smelly for lack of a shower or was caught pinching another recruit's gear or such. Wearing just a light shirt, shorts and sandals, I was not going to suffer much, so I just let them carry me along. However, I do not like bullies, so I said, "You have your fun now, but when I come out of the trough, I'm coming after you, one by one. Just rely on that." I also made sure I had a good look at the faces of those carting me along.

To chants of "Dunk him! Dunk him!" I was duly dumped into the nearest concrete watering trough. Those holding my legs and my right arm promptly let go, but one of those holding my left arm kept a firm grip on my wrist and levered down so that my left elbow grated along the top of the trough wall. It was painful, damaging and quite deliberately done. I gritted my teeth and said nothing but marked well the individual who had done it. He eventually let go and stood back with his fellow members of the dunking crew, all laughing as I heaved myself out of the trough and stood there for a moment, dripping water and facing the cheers and jeers of the on-looking dozens.

Without haste or a single word, I wiped the water from my eyes, face and head and shook myself like a dog to rid myself of the worst of the water. Then I carefully bent over and wiped excess water from my thighs, knees and lower legs. That unobtrusively put me where I wanted to be, which was in an almost sprinting start position, from which I suddenly launched myself, flat out, at the clustered dunking group, my eyes and intentions set on the individual who had levered down on my left arm.

It may have been one against eight, discounting the on-lookers, but it was the eight who fled and the one who pursued. The eight rapidly started to split up. That I did not mind, because I had eyes and intention on just one, for starters. As I have already set out, I am no runner. Despite the white-hot anger that was driving me I sensed that my quarry was leaving me behind as we pelted up the slight slope towards the barrack blocks. For the second time that evening, up ahead, I briefly sensed the presence of a tall figure in instructor's uniform. My quarry turned around the corner of the first block with me a few paces behind. When I turned that same corner, I had to pull up sharply. My quarry was on the ground, still rolling and Sgt Pearce was standing on one leg, rubbing his lifted right shin and swearing.

Grateful for whatever collision had occurred, which, in hindsight, I suspected was not accidental, I ignored our riding instructor and closed in on my target, who was trying to get to his feet. I let him straighten up and then, admittedly perhaps before he was fully ready for or expecting it, I hit him hard enough to put him down again.

"That's for my elbow!" I snarled at him and turned away, intending to set off after any of the others that I could find.

"Where do you think you're going Woolley?" Sgt Pearce demanded as I moved to pass by him.

"I'm going hunting, Sir." I offered. "I've seven more pack rats to sort out." Sgt Pearce, now firmly upright on both feet, shook his head. "Not tonight!" he stated flatly. He pointed his swagger cane at the recruit I had flattened. "That's enough for now. Get into some dry clothes and then take yourself off to Camp Hospital and get that arm looked at. You're bleeding worse than a stuck pig."

I looked down at my left arm. It was red from elbow to fingertips. By then quite a few recruits, including some of those who had attended my troughing had caught up and were looking on. Seeing some of my own squad among them, Sgt Pearce called out for them to step forward. He picked out Tony Brown and Harry Gent. "You two see that Woolley gets into dry clothing, gets that arm attended to and stays out of trouble until tomorrow morning. We can sort out whatever caused this rumpus then."

He turned to the onlookers and snapped, "The circus is over. Get back to your normal routines for now, but I think some of you had better be prepared to answer a few questions come tomorrow. Move yourselves!"

I was duly escorted by Tony and Harry for the rest of that evening until lights out sounded, first back to quarters for a change into dry clothing and then on the brief walk to Camp Hospital, where my left elbow scrapes were fortunately found to be more messy than serious. A dressing, some bandaging, orders to rest it for 24 hours and a sling sorted it out. As we walked and talked it became clear that none of us knew what had started the nonsense with Colin Gunston. When I asked where Colin was and about his injuries my two escorts were only able to tell me that as far as they knew he was okay, but a bit bruised and battered. When I eventually caught up with Colin, in our quarters that was just about how he was. A bit puffy of face and eyes and somewhat tender about the body, but not seriously hurt.

When I asked what had started the trouble, he just shrugged and said he did not feel like talking about it, so that was that. Clive George, who had apparently missed all the noise and nonsense, listened to the general chatter about what had gone on. Then he turned to me and asked, "Did you really have a go at all eight of them?"

I nodded. "They buggered off and I only caught up with one of them. That was when Sgt Pearce put in an appearance."

Clive looked hard at me. "You're mad!" he stated. I think it was a compliment.

The following morning, with my left arm in a sling, I was excused PT and lined up with the Sick Parade when the 09:00 Morning Parade was called. Tony Brown took control of the squad for that parade. Later in the morning as I was standing watching the rest of the squad doing arms drill, Insp. Winchcombe came along to inquire what I knew of the disturbance of the last evening. I related what had gone on and how it had ended. At the conclusion of my story I asked, "Are there likely to be any repercussions, Sir? I did let fly a bit here and there." Insp. Winchcombe looked at my sling. "We get worse injuries than that on the assault course. As for whoever you clouted, it seems there's no broken bones and nobody is complaining. Provided that the OC Depot accepts it as just a harmless bit of horseplay that will be the end of it. If I were you, I'd get that sling off just as fast as I could and put last evening's events firmly out of my mind."

It was advice I gladly complied with.

It was a day or so after that event that I received a reminder about standards. It was a hot, bright, Saturday afternoon and I had decided to walk into town to buy a few personal items. I was dressed in a white long-sleeved shirt, open at the neck, slacks and polished leather shoes. I duly booked out of depot at the Guardroom and set off. Just outside the gates, I saw Ascom Wright. He was riding towards me, at a walk, on one of the depot's horses. As he neared me, I bade him a polite, "Good afternoon, Sir,"

He reigned in his horse and said, "Good afternoon to you, Mr Woolley. Where are you going?"

"Into town, Sir. I've a few personal bits and pieces I need."

Mr Wright gestured towards me with his riding crop. "Not dressed like that, if you don't mind, Mr Woolley."

I glanced down at myself. I thought I was quite neat and tidy. "I'm sorry you disapprove of my attire, Sir. This was about standard for out of uniform shopping activities up in Nyasaland. What do I need for here, Sir?"

"Jacket and tie, Mr Woolley, that's what!" He leaned somewhat towards me and offered, almost conspiratorially, "In Nyasaland they have hot weather. Down here we have standards. Let's maintain them, shall we?"

His question was clearly an order. "Very good, Sir. I'll go back and get into something more suitable." I did an about turn and started back towards the gates of depot.

Mr Wright kneed his horse forward and walked it briefly alongside me. "You'll be doing your first PT tests and written exams next week, Mr Woolley. Good luck with them. And don't worry yourself about that incident the other evening. I've closed the file on it and you can take it from me that it has done you no harm." With that, he urged his mount into a trot and moved on towards the stables, while I headed for my room to add a jacket and tie to my clothing. I was grateful for Ascom Wright's assurance over the recent fracas, but just a bit bothered about four circuits of the running track in a time I had never yet been able to achieve.

The following week was one of changed pattern. Classroom and evening revision sessions on Common and Statute Law took priority over other activities. As the days passed, members of the squad spent much time sat on chairs or beds, reading and silently memorising, or wandered thither and yon, reciting chunks of Force Standing Orders and The Police Act. Those of us less than fully familiar with horses had to try to remember the assorted bits and pieces of horse anatomy and equine stable and feeding needs. On that score, our expert was Tony Brown, whose horse skills rapidly proved that he had not wasted his years in the Household Cavalry in the UK. There was also much sorting through the many books and documents that might be needed to see our way through the necessary Administration and Finance exam.

The Monday morning PT session was dedicated to indoor tests. Press-ups, Pull-ups, Rope Climbs and the like were crammed into that one morning in the gym. We all sweated and strained, but nobody failed. The written exams were scattered through the week.

One by one we worked out way through what was required. Inevitably we carted the papers away, compared answers and worried about the bits and pieces that we had forgotten to set down within the allotted time.

A few raindrops delayed our test on the assault course, so it was not until the Wednesday that we turned out to face that particular brute. By then we had all been over the course on several occasions. After the first time, it was a case of cheerfully competing against each other following a massed start. On this occasion, we each set off at half-minute intervals, so that our efforts could be individually timed, as was needed. It was also very useful to have somebody ahead of you to attempt to catch up with and somebody behind you, to try to stay ahead of. My previous efforts on the assault course had always resulted in a sort of mid-squad position each time we had undertaken it. My slim build and long arms and legs allowed me to climb well and crawl through culverts a bit faster than the stockier members of the squad. Also, going over the top of the high wall and the net climb gave me no problem as I also had no particular fear of heights. One or two others had that problem, so moved more slowly than I did. The result was that I made it comfortably within the allotted two and a half minutes, but nowhere near as fast as Howard Inman, who simply flew at it as if he had wings. He completed the course in record time and in front of the recruit who had started immediately ahead of him.

In the cool of the Thursday morning, we turned out in our PT kit to tackle the mile run. Nothing had been said to me by any of the squad, but as we lined up across the track to all start at the same time, Colin Gunston and

Chris Phillips positioned themselves on either side of me. "We're your pacemakers, Arn. Squad decision. We'll pace-make for you for the first three laps, then go for it ourselves." As a final piece of advice, he added. "Just stay close behind us and remember to breathe deeply and swing your arms as you run."

There was no time for me to ask questions because Insp. MacIntosh's cry of "Ready. Get Set. Go!" was followed by a sharp blast on his whistle and that was that. The usual speed merchants were soon out in front with the rest of us following along, becoming more and more stretched out as each lap was completed. I stuck close to Colin and Chris, who were running side by side, at a pace decidedly slower than I knew they both could do. We quickly became the tail-enders. We were encouraged along at the end of each lap by Insp. MacIntosh's time calls and urges to, "Speed it up a bit." At the end of the half-mile we three were just about on time. For me, that third lap was the hard one. Chris sensed that I was struggling. He dropped back alongside me and urged, "Swing your arms more. It will help lengthen your stride. And remember to breathe deeper." It was sound coaching advice, which I did my best to follow. It certainly helped.

Way up ahead, the natural runners were finishing, in times of 4 minutes 15 seconds or so, while I tried to concentrate on swinging my arms more, to lengthen my stride and deepen my breathing. As arranged, when we started the final lap, Colin and Chris took off and sprinted round to ensure they completed the mile run in good time. For the last couple of hundred yards, I was urged along by those who had already finished. Shouts of, "Keep your head up," "Swing your arms more," and "You can do it," all definitely helped me to make that special effort as our instructor loudly counted down the last few seconds against the last few dozen yards. On his "Three" I crossed the finish line. As I folded over and tried to gasp back some of my vanished breath, Tacky MacIntosh made a note on his clipboard and declared loudly, "Four Fifty-Seven, Woolley!" Those were the second-best words I ever heard during my time in Morris Depot. Once I had regained some of my missing breath, I had a quick word with my two pacemakers. "When we next get to the bar," I gasped, "the drinks are definitely on me. Several of them!"

It was a good dozen or more years later that I was finally diagnosed as having a hiatus hernia, which eventually explained why I was no great runner.

At least with the physical tests it was a quick and clean decision, clear to all at the end of each particular test. The problem with any written exam is that no matter how well you feel you have answered the questions there is always that nagging doubt. Have you properly understood the question? Have you answered the question correctly? If you have been "on target" have you covered most, if not all, of the points that would earn you marks? Fortunately, with any exam that carries a pass mark you do not have to be at the top of the scoresheet. It is getting to or above that necessary numerical line that is the important bit and knowing that much has to be a matter of waiting until somebody has marked the papers, which takes time.

As that week of examinations moved along and each test or exam became history, the post-mortems grew in number and intensity. Did a particular question mean this, or did it mean that? How many facts equalled a point in the answer? How much did spelling and grammar count in the scheme of things. Everything was chewed over, worried about and compared. The Friday afternoon's announcement of results was a concern for everyone, for different reasons. I did not wish to do any longer in depot than I needed to, which, all being well, was that Friday. It was the same for the other experienced policemen in the squad who had, like me been offered short courses. As for the others, they were all well aware of the threat of being back-squaded should any failure occur. Anxiety and stress made that week a difficult one, in which tensions and probably blood-pressures too, rose. Small upsets grew into arguments, harsh words and squabbles that quickly became physical. I was grateful for the assistance of the calmer members like Harry Gent, Peter Biddulph and Tony Brown in maintaining a strong sense of unity and purpose within the squad.

Eventually, with all of us seated in the administration lecture room, Insp. Winchcombe, arrived, carrying a sheaf of papers on a clipboard in his hand. Whatever he was, Gerry Winchcombe was not of a sadistic nature. He got on with the task of delivering the results without delay. His rapid glance around the rows of desks told him nobody was absent. He waved the papers and clipboard briefly and said, evenly, "Except for Woolley, the entire squad will move on to begin riding school training and the next phase of your time in depot, on Monday, because you've all passed in all subjects." He looked directly at me and said, "Stop looking so worried Woolley, because you too have passed. You are to report to Driving School at Cranbourne at 09:00hrs on Monday morning to start your Driver Training Course." He paused briefly to let the relieved sighs and comments of "Thank heavens" subside before continuing. "Don't get too cocky, you lot. As I've said, you've all passed each of your exams. That's the good news. The bad news is that one or two of you have only just made it and will need to do a bit better next time round because it gets harder from here on in, which includes the riding school part. Now you can all take yourselves off for a tea-break while I put the results up on the noticeboard for you to read in detail."

Not needing any further bidding, with happy expressions, joyful words and congratulatory handshakes all round we took ourselves out into the bright sunlight and streamed off to the tea bar. As luck would have it, Romeo was in our quarters, attending to my uniforms. When I somewhat apologetically informed him that I was leaving Morris Depot and heading for Driving School at Cranbourne on Monday morning, he politely cut through my apologies. "Ishe, I can work for you while you are at Driving School. It is no problem." Those helpful words made me feel a whole lot better and that was the way it worked out. Later that day, after some detailed study of the list of results, most of us found our way to the Police Sports Club at the playing fields, where we celebrated with something just a little stronger than tea.

As I drifted off to sleep that night the few words "…Report to Driving School at Cranbourn," kept echoing in my mind. Those were the best few words I had heard in all my weeks at Morris Depot. That night I slept soundly on them.

Cranbourne had been the first airstrip for Salisbury, originally for civilian aircraft and then, before and after WWII, as an RAF training base. In the years since the war the suburbs of Salisbury had grown up and surrounded it and a brand-new airport had been developed elsewhere. After that, the old airport location had been handed over and developed as the BSAP's Driving School. The school's member i/c at that time was Inspector John Dolby. His attitude towards disciplinary requirements was simple. If he spoke, recruits obeyed. Any contravention of that resulted in an invitation to face up to him behind the canteen after five o'clock. The habit, so I was told, was for bare fists, if that was agreeable, or with gloves on for the softies, as he put it more than once in the weeks that I was there.

Much of the main runway still existed and foot drill on and along that was a regular activity, in between lectures and practical sessions in Land Rovers and on Motorcycles, as those of us on the basic driver training course worked towards gaining what was a Grade IV police force qualification, before finally being posted out to an operational Police District and Station, or heading for a Town posting, or, if chosen, to the Administration Branch or a Technician's position. Authority to drive the "Bee Cars" for Traffic Section, the Highway Patrol Cars, or Heavy Vehicles required further driver training courses.

The accommodation at Cranbourne was typically RAF from WWII, with long barrack blocks divided into rooms that were shared by two recruits. The lecture rooms were basic, simple desks, with blackboards and a screen for training film projection. Back then, the reader might need to be reminded, such things as whiteboards existed. Computers and power-point presentations had yet to be invented. In fact, it was rare to have even a flip-chart facility. Arriving on my own as it were, rather than as part of an arranged group, I was required to fit in with the members of the last squad that had recently passed out from depot and to pick up on the driver training in mid-course. When I reported to him in the main office, Insp. John Dolby scanned through my papers and scowled. "You have licences for both cars and motorcycles I see." He did not even look up to see my confirmatory nod. "All that means is you're full of bad habits that we are going to have to knock out of you. Crawford's on his own. You can share with him."

That was my welcome to the Driving School. I am not too sure that 7154 Thomas Andrew Crawford really appreciated my sudden and unexpected arrival, because he had rather spread himself around the room which we were now to share for the remainder of the time his squad were under training. For the moment I merely stacked my metal trunk and kitbag in a vacant corner and set off to find the lecture room in which he and the others of his squad were receiving instructions. That first lecture that I joined was a film on driving and driving techniques and what happened when driving went wrong, for one reason or another. It was definitely not a film to be lightly put before the squeamish, but with my experiences gained in the UK and having served as provincial fatal accident investigation officer for a year in Nyasaland, there was little in it that I had not experienced in real life. It clearly did get through to one or two of the younger and less experienced recruits who found themselves without much appetite at lunchtime.

When the film and analysis of it were over and lunchbreak was declared, I made myself known to Tom Crawford and explained the sudden, unannounced invasion of his quarters. Tom did ask me who had decided I was to share a room with him. My answer of "Insp. Dolby," brought a terse, "Well, that's that then," and an assurance that he would clear space for my gear that evening. Those few short weeks during which he and I shared quarters at Cranbourne later proved to be a fortunate interlude that was to save my own life and some others some three years later and far away from Cranbourne Barracks.

The quality of the driver training was second to none. We cleaned and polished more two and four wheeled items of transport than we liked, many of them at disgustingly early hours of the morning. That was followed by breakfast and then into the daily routine, which started off with a period of foot-drill, clearly designed to wake us up again after our meal. The remainder of the day was occupied with a very effective method of training which I recognised from my Army Cadet years. It consisted of a theory lecture, followed by periods of discussion, practice and then practical application. It did work well.

We studied the Highway Code and Driver Training Manual until we could recite almost the whole of both off by heart and pored for hours over stripped down and cut away samples of vehicles of various sorts so that each of us had a pretty good working knowledge of the mechanics and systems of the vehicles. As it was pointed out to us on numerous occasions, there are not many garages out in Districts, so knowing how to cure a few of the basic causes of breakdowns was time well spent.

Of the time at Cranbourne, two incidents stick firmly in my mind. The first was the day when we routinely paraded for the usual morning session of foot-drill, which, on that occasion, Insp. Dolby decided to take himself, which was not unusual. When we proved to be a bit messy and untidy in executing his foot-drill orders, he decided we were still half asleep and needed waking up, so we should do some drill "at the double." That was no real problem because we were all fairly fit, but, when it started to pour with rain and Insp. Dolby called to the office for a raincoat for himself, but left us to get soaked, some muttering arose. Insp. Dolby certainly seemed to think of himself as a bit of a drill-pig. Basically, he knew his stuff and had a capable voice which he enjoyed using, letting us march away some distance before ordering an about turn or other action that would eventually bring us back towards him.

On this occasion, he had us marching away from him and back past him and then back towards and past him again, along the runway, at the double. All the while we were getting wetter and wetter. Finally, as we were doubling away from him once more, somebody up front said, "Ignore the next order. We didn't hear it because of the noise of our boots, the rain and the distance." Somebody warned, "He'll have you with the gloves off behind the canteen." "Not if we all stick together," came the terse reply. There was a quiet chorus of "Okays" and "Rights" at that. The result was that when Insp. Dolby's distant "At the double, about turn," reached us, we just kept on going. When he repeated the order, we ignored that too. When we reached the perimeter fence some quarter mile away, we simply marked time at the double, still in neat ranks as a squad and waited.

Insp. Dolby caught up with us a few minutes later. He made no attempt to order us to a halt but kept us marking time at the double. In a voice that clearly carried his vexation he snapped, "What the f--- do you lot think you're doing?" He didn't wait for an answer before going on, "I ordered you to about turn. Why didn't you?" A dozen or more voices quickly assured him we had not heard any such order, probably because of the distance we had been from him and the pouring rain and noise of our drill boots at the double on the tarmac.

Insp. Dolby's highly coloured and thin-lipped expression clearly told us that he did not believe a word of our explanation. If any single one of us had, at that moment, burst out laughing I have no doubt we would all have been in deep trouble. Perhaps fortunately, our exertions and the discomfort of marking time at the double in pouring rain subdued any inclination towards mirth. Straight faces and straight backs were all that he got from us. After a couple more minutes of just glaring at us as we continued to mark time at the double, Insp. Dolby nodded grimly, then bellowed, "About turn. For...wards," and set us off towards the offices and quarters where he eventually dismissed us without further comment.

When it came to the motorcycle training, I was allocated a 250cc Matchless, not the largest of machines by far. Standing a bit above six foot in height I did rather tower over it, so much so that even Insp. Dolby noticed it. "You look like a drum on a pea!" was his observation as he passed by one morning. Apart from what I might have looked like, I had no problem with that allocation, because it was one of the lighter machines available, so that much easier to handle over gravel, sand and rock. Nyasaland may have given me a good deal of experience of driving Land Rovers and Bedford Crew-cars, which definitely gave me an advantage in the Land Rover driver training, however, in Nyasaland we never did use motorcycles and my motorcycling in the UK had been on standard tarmac roads. That kind of experience certainly did little to assist with staying upright aboard a motorcycle on the purely earth/gravel dirt roads and sandy tracks all around Salisbury.

One would never have accused any of our instructors of having a sadistic streak, but there were times when some of them managed to find ways of making our training very interesting, very interesting indeed! One of those was when Insp. Dolby himself decided to lead us in and around the Borradaile Quarries. It was rough riding in the extreme, with precarious tracks, little more than small animal game trails, that zig-zagged up and down the disused quarry walls and jumbled moonscape of rock and gravel in heaps, piles, mounds and ridges, with pools of water to drop into if a rider got it wrong, which several did. To give him his due, Insp. Dolby led from the front and asked us to do nothing that he had not demonstrated first. However, he seemed to expect and indeed demanded, equal expertise from a bunch of recruits whose skills varied from not too bad, right down to only started riding a motorcycle a week or two ago. He certainly gave us the impression that his humour factor rose according to the number of us who finally tumbled off from our machines during any particular motorcycling training excursion.

It may have been memories of a certain drill period in the rain on the airfield runway that caused him to lead us on another day on a training ride along the banks of the Makabusi River. Insp. Dolby's advice of, "Just follow along and see if you can keep up with me," was all the instruction we received. The trees and bushes were in full foliage and visibility was a bit limited. Each twist, turn, drop or climb appeared without a lot of time for study, calculation and planning. Purely by luck, I was Tail End Charlie on that run, for which position I ended up being very grateful. That was because Insp. Dolby chose a footpath which, after a mile or so, led across a broad gulley which was five or six feet deep running down towards the river on our left. The interesting bit was that the footpath, without warning, led out across the gulley horizontally, atop the concrete box sections carrying a mains water pipe. The pipe was about a foot in diameter, so the top of the concrete encasement was no more than eighteen inches across. As I approached the gully that was still out of sight to me, I was close up on the back wheel of the motorcycle in front of me. There were a series of yells, curses and sounds of crashing motorcycles ahead of us. The recruit ahead of me braked safely to a halt and I drew up close behind. We found ourselves looking at a scene of mechanical carnage. A score of yards or so ahead of us, where the far side of the gulley was and the concrete box disappeared into the ground once more, Insp. Dolby was seated on his machine, looking back. Between us there were a dozen or more machines and riders in all sorts of upset positions on the ground six or eight feet below the top of the concrete covered pipe.

We last two riders were able to stand our machines and go to the aid of our less fortunate fellows, who had all tumbled from the top of the concreted-in pipe and landed in and on the bushes and rocks in the gulley bed. When we had it all straightened out, two of the motorcycles were un-serviceable and two of our number had sustained injuries that, while fortunately not serious, meant that they would not be riding a motorcycle for a few days.

The story that appeared later that day was that Insp. Dolby, knowing the tracks well, had led our unsuspecting ride out on to the very narrow pipe-way and, as was quite possible, had ridden straight across without trouble. The problem began, because, when he was at the far bank, Insp. Dolby chose not to continue on, but to stop, put his feet down and look back. Each of the riders behind him in turn found themselves not "out on the proverbial limb" as it were, but very definitely "out on a narrow concrete slab and having to come to a halt." Bikes rapidly dropped off on either side as speed fell off and balance failed.

The rider directly behind Insp. Dolby who had come off relatively lightly, challenged our instructor with, "What the Devil did you stop there for, Sir?" only to be told in sweet and innocent tones, "I did tell you all to come across one by one, you know. Perhaps you didn't hear me?"

Trainee Squad 1. Instructor 1. Honours even!

Eventually, the days and weeks of driver training led to formal test drives and rides that did not include quarries or assorted riverbanks, for which we were all grateful. It was with a sense of great relief and satisfaction that I achieved my Grade IV police driving authority. Just a little later that same day, I received the advice that I had been posted to Fort Victoria Province along with instructions to report to Provincial HQ there as soon as transport could be arranged.

When I said my farewell to Romeo, I paid him up to date and handed him a little something extra, along with a few words of thanks for his efforts on my behalf over the past few months. In response he thanked me for my generosity, took two paces backwards, came to a very passable stance of attention, threw up a smart salute, said, "Pitane bwino, Bwana," which is Chinyanja for "Go well, Sir," before marching smartly away.

The Guardroom, 1965

Below
Blatherwick Memorial Morris Depot January 1965

New Boys

From left to right: Standing, 7204 Antony "Ox" Grant, 7223 Dave Reacord, 7206 Chris Phillips, 7203 Clive George. Squatting, the middle three: 7220 Rob Elliot, 7205 Colin Gunston, 7207 Arnold Woolley (The Author) and squatting in front, 7202 Jacob "Yarpie" Pieterse

59

Part way through training in depot

From left to right:- Back Row:- 7207 Arnold Woolley (The Author), 7218 Richard Whittaker, 7205 Colin Gunston, 7215 Howard Inman, 7213 James Bruce, 7219 Paul Wood. Middle Row:- 7155 Ernie Mason, 7195 Matthew Webster, 7203 Clive George, 7204 Anthony "Ox" Grant, 7216 Taffy Lovell, 7212 Tony Brown, 7214 Harry Gent, 7220 Robert Elliot, 7211 Peter Biddulph, 7217 John Tedford. Front Row:- 7183 Brian Gunston, 7206 Chris Phillips, 7223 Dave Reacord, 7202 Jacob "Yarpie" Pieterse

Fort Victoria Province & Mashaba Police Station

Fort Victoria was a small Province in police terms. So much so that it had only one District, which, of course, had the same boundaries as the Province. The town area contained four police establishments. A large building on the main road to the north housed both Provincial and District administrative offices. The police camp housed the European Single Quarters, Police Reserve Headquarters, Fort Victoria Rural Police Station, Provincial Radio Branch Headquarters, the armoury and the Police Club building, which was of relatively modern construction compared to the remainder of the buildings, which were all pre-war in date, with typically red painted corrugated iron roofs. In the middle of the urban area there was, not unreasonably, Fort Victoria Urban Police Station. That stood not far from the bell tower and one wall, which were the last standing remains of the original fort, built at the time of the Pioneer Column's passage through the area in 1890. To match the police station positioned in what I shall loosely name as the European part of the town, Mucheke Police Station and camp were situated in Mucheke Township, the town's residential area for the African population.

In the main police camp in the town area the club was called "The Phoenix." The club was aptly named, having been recently built out of the ashes of a far older building which had, just a little mysteriously, caught fire and totally burned to the ground a couple of years back. Assistant Commissioner Peter Sherren, later to be Commissioner, had, reputedly, stopped any attempt to save the old buildings and contents, commenting as he stood and watched it burn, "It's insured and it's about time we had a new building anyway," As I found out in future days, Peter Sherren was no fool.

Arriving from Salisbury by Land Rover somewhat late in the day, I was provided temporary accommodation in the European members' Single Quarters. The following morning, a dry warm and bright day towards the end of March, I made sure that I was up and about early. I carefully dressed myself in boots, leggings, cap, tunic and shorts, as befitted a district uniformed policeman and set off to walk the short distance from the mess at Rural, through the European residential area to report to Provincial HQ. There I handed my route instructions document to Staff Inspector Jack Bacon, the provincial clerk. He carefully read through the document, ordered me to sit down and wait and then vanished through one of the three doors to the office. He returned a few minutes later, paused long enough to scribble a note on the route instructions and shoved the paper towards me.

"You've been posted to Mashaba," he advised cheerfully as I picked up the travel document. "Member-in-Charge is Inspector Bernard Cavey. You'll find he's a good man to work for. It's only a half-hour drive from here, out along the road to Shabani. I've asked them to send a vehicle in to collect you from the mess at Rural Camp. Take yourself back there now and just wait until your transport arrives. Good luck!"

It did not take me long to walk the mile or so back to the mess, pondering all the way over just what sort of police station I was headed for and just who I would be working with. Back at the mess, I gathered my trunk, hold-all and kitbag and settled down in the lounge, impatient to be on the way to my allotted posting. Fortunately for my impatient frame of mind, that wait was not a long one. Quite soon a uniformed police Land Rover appeared. The patrol officer driving it came into the mess lounge, spotted me and my gear and walked across with his hand out. Barry Lane (6520) and I exchanged handshakes and names and together we stowed my gear in the back of the vehicle without wasting any time. As Barry drove us along, he gave me an outline of the station, upon which he had been serving already for several months.

My clearest recollection of that journey is Barry's enthusiasm for his posting at Mashaba, as it was then commonly called. He was clearly happy to be there and was certain that I would be too. As he explained for me while he drove, Mashaba existed mainly because of the Asbestos Mines. The names of the larger ones he rattled off with cheerful familiarity as Gaths, King and Temeraire. As I was to find out in coming weeks, there were other, somewhat smaller mines, such as DSO, Boss and Rex. Gaths, which produced the then more commercially attractive long fibred asbestos, as against the short fibred stuff, was the principle one, being large enough to merit having its own hospital.

"It's not a big place," Barry cautioned, "but it's got a lot of friendly people on the mines and it's not far from Fort Vic." I soon discovered that hardly any of the Europeans in the area used Fort Victoria Town's full name. It was simply "Fort Vic," or, for the African population, "Masvingo." That, in the local Shona/Kalanga dialect means "Walls" which was a bit of borrowed glory as it were because the name really derived from its proximity to the Zimbabwe Ruins a dozen miles to the south-west of the town.

The road that Barry was driving along was at least a decent one as far as my experience of travel in Africa was concerned. It was a full nine feet width of well-made tarmac with a few feet of decently maintained earth/gravel to either side. As each oncoming vehicle approached, Barry carefully steered to the left, without losing speed. The vehicle gave a very notable lurch as the nearside tyres dropped off from the tarmac and onto the gravel. Each oncoming vehicle did the same. As the vehicles, of whatever size, disappeared behind us, Barry carefully edged the Land Rover back to the right and on to the full width of the tarmac surface, until the next oncoming vehicle appeared, when the whole process was repeated.

"Got to look out for the washaways and soft spots," Barry warned at one passing as our vehicle's nearside wheels left the tarmac surface and dropped quite a bit. "If you hit a bad one it can catch you out unless you've got a decent grip on the steering wheel." It was a piece of sound advice that I welcomed and benefitted from in future days.

Our journey of about twenty-five miles took us from the relatively flat European farming and ranching lands around Fort Victoria to the distinctly hilly country that surrounded Mashaba. Part way along we passed a signposted turn-off leftwards to Mushandike Dam. In answer to my obvious question, Barry explained that the dam provided water for the European farming area downstream of the dam wall and acted as a nature reserve and recreation area for fishing and sailing. "Got to be a bit careful there," Barry warned, "Because along with the bass, bream and catfish, there's crocs as well."

In answer to my question about the population of the police station's area, Barry shrugged. "Not too sure. Fifteen to twenty thousand Afs I suppose and a couple of hundred of us whiteys."

Nearing Mashaba the colour of the soil changed. Whereas Fort Victoria was surrounded by soil that was mostly brownish in colour, that around Mashaba was much more red. As I was later to learn, it was that redness that caused the Africans to call the area Mashava for short, or in full, Magomo Mashava, meaning red mountain.

Eventually, a signpost indicated another junction off to the right and the presence of the police station complex, a couple of hundred yards away, up a slight incline.

The layout of the place was a simple one. Station offices existed in between the mess and the Member-in-Charge's house, with the African Staff quarters not far away. For me, the most pleasant surprise was the well-kept and colourful set of flower beds fronting the veranda to the main office. For recreational purposes there was a laterite surfaced tennis court adjacent to the mess building.

Barry wasted no time in helping me get my gear unloaded and into the single quarters room that had been allocated to me. After that, he steered me to the main office building. On the way, we passed a 44 gallon drum. Nothing very strange about that, but it was what was perched on the top of it that really caught my eye. It was the bleached white skull bones of a hippopotamus. Barry caught my interested look. "We have problems with them up and down the Tokwe River and around Mushandike Dam. We have to shoot the occasional one, here and there, when they do too much damage to local crops. The Boss shot that one in February. We stuck it in an anthill until all the flesh had been eaten away. Now it's just waiting to be sorted out as a souvenir for when the Boss goes on retirement in a year or so."

A day or two later, in a quiet moment, I took a couple of photographs of that drying set of bones.

When we reached the Member-in-Charge's office, Barry introduced me to Inspector Bernard Cavey, Section Officer Peter Nicholls (5921) and Patrol Officer Ian Harries. I got the impression that they had all gathered together in order to meet the new man on the station and generally check him out so to speak. Some word of my past experience must have preceded me, because once he had received my route instructions and the usual pleasantries had been dispensed with, Bernard Cavey said, "I believe you've done some prosecuting in the past." It was more a statement than a question.

"Just a bit, Sir," I confirmed. "I often assisted the police prosecutors in Hove and earned a Class 2 prosecutor's authority in Nyasaland."

"Good," was Bernard Cavey's cheerful reply. "You can help Peter with the court work tomorrow. It'll give you an idea of the variety of the workload here. We all take turns in being duty officer for the week, starting at 16:00 hours on a Friday. That earns you the following weekend off. And when I say "Off" I mean just that. You do whatever you want to, but you do it off station. I also like you single men to get away for at least one evening a week whenever you are not the duty officer. That way you won't get bush-happy and start talking to the walls of your room or go picking fights with each other. Meanwhile, there's a desk in the main office for you to work at, so off you go."

The rest of that day I spent exchanging small talk with Pete, Barry and Ian, learning the layout of the offices and being taken for a brief introductory ride around the main mining company complexes. That evening, after a fairly basic but filling meal and another hour or two of small-talk in the mess lounge over an ale or two, I headed off to bed at a reasonable hour, content to be where I was and content also to let the morrow bring whatever it might.

The first thing that the morrow brought was an early rising for a cup of tea before attending Stable Parade at 06:15hrs. Not that there were any horses to attend to, but the Land Rovers and station motorcycle had to be regularly checked upon, ticked off as okay or marked up as needing repair or service on the daily maintenance log and generally made as bright and shiny as their age and usage allowed.

When Stable Parade ended at 07:00hrs, it was a quick scramble for a wash and shave, then breakfast before putting on the dress order for the day and setting off for the offices for 08:30. I mention dress order for the day, because that depended upon what each of us had as planned duties for each day. Routinely it was boots, leggings, shorts, grey shirt and cap, with our non-officer pattern Sam Browne belt. Court duties saw us in shoes, stockings, shorts and tunic, topped off by a cap. Nominally, when wearing the grey short-sleeved uniform shirt, we were supposed to wear a blue tie with it. However, it was common habit for that item to be dispensed with outside of the main towns. Mashaba was certainly not one of the main towns and Insp. Cavey was not one to stand on too much ceremony, so we enjoyed the open neck rule so long as the weather was decent and provided that we were operating within our own station area.

For me, assisting SO Nicholls, the dress order for that first full day was shoes, stockings, shorts, tunic and cap. By the time that I joined him in his office, Pete had the court roll all prepared. Minor cases, mostly involving pleas of guilty and the likelihood of a modest fine, were dealt with by having only a few sheets of essential information behind a Docket Record Form. More awkward and serious cases were compiled within a stiff cardboard folder with investigation diary forms, statements, documentary exhibits and formal charge sheets. As assistant to Pete, my task was to ensure that every set of the investigation papers was ready for each case as it was called. That meant checking that the paperwork for the case, greater or lesser, was all there and that every accused person, witness and all exhibit items, physical or documentary, were ready to hand as required.

Mashaba was nowhere near big enough to merit a resident magistrate, so the periodic court was presided over by one of the magistrates from Fort Victoria. On this particular day, it was Mr Stainer. His full name was Charles John Henry Boyce Stainer.

He was, as Pete warned me, a bit of a stickler for proper court procedures and attention to detail. He did not suffer fools lightly. He had a short-fused temper and a dry wit that he was just as likely to exercise equally on police prosecutors, their assistants, accused persons or witness for either side.

Once the court room had been called to stand by the Clerk and Mr Stainer had seated himself comfortably in the traditionally styled chair, behind the equally traditionally styled dark mahogany bench, he gazed intently all around until his eyes settled upon me. After a moment or so of piercing gaze he turned his attention to Pete. "Good morning, Mr Prosecutor," he said drily. "I see you have a new assistant. Perhaps you might care to identify him for me. I do so like to know who I am telling off as the day proceeds."

Totally unflustered by that opening, Pete, who, like us all, was still on his feet waiting for the instruction to sit and proceed with the cases on the role, stated simply, "Patrol Officer Woolley, Sir. He was posted to Mashaba yesterday and is assisting me today. He has some prosecuting experience from service in the UK and Nyasaland."

Mr Stainer's eyebrows rose noticeably. "Has he indeed?" he said, with a heavy emphasis on the indeed. "I hope somebody has told him that a little knowledge is often a dangerous thing. Especially in my court?"

"I am sure that he will take the utmost care to look, listen and learn as the day goes on," Pete responded evenly.

"Very well. You may all sit." He waited as we all sank to our respective seats and the rustling noises ceased. "Kindly get on with the first case if you will, Mr Prosecutor."

To give him his due, Mr Stainer was a very proficient magistrate. He had a good team with him too. His Clerk and his Interpreter were both very much on the ball. The prison staff and our police details also all seemed to be on best performance. Accused persons came, were dealt with promptly and departed.

Part way down the list of cases one African Male Adult was brought in to face a charge of stocktheft from a local European Ranch bordering on the Tribal Trust Land to the north of the station. One head of cattle had been taken. Investigations had led to the accused, whose home huts had been found to contain a great deal of beef from a recently slaughtered animal. Such a weight of evidence had been discovered that the accused had admitted the theft under a warned and cautioned statement and had indicated his intention to plead guilty, which he duly did.

With the statement of agreed facts submitted, Mr Stainer turned to the accused and, through the interpreter, asked him if he had anything to say in mitigation before he was sentenced. Via the interpreter, the accused pleaded that it was not he, himself, who had committed the offence, but the bad spirits that dwelt within him and over which he had no control because, like all bad spirits, they were very powerful.

Mr Stainer listened attentively as the interpreter translated, most carefully, from Chishona to English, just what the accused had said. He let a moment of silence hang in the air, before saying, "Mr Interpreter, please advise the accused that although I am a European, I have lived in Africa long enough to understand how powerful those evil spirits are. Therefore I sentence his evil spirits to six months imprisonment with hard labour for this offence. However, I do believe he had better go along too, to keep them company."

As the accused was led away, Mr Stainer, with just the trace of a smile on his face, called, "Next case please, Mr Prosecutor," and the court session proceeded to an uneventful conclusion, for which, I, for one, was very grateful. In later days, when I assisted and, on some occasions, stood in for Pete and became "Mr Prosecutor" for the day, the court sessions did not turn out so satisfactorily. I left those court sessions considerably and deservedly chastened but always better informed for the next one.

Later in the day, back at the station offices, Pete and I sorted out the paperwork arising from the court activities. We cleared and endorsed fingerprint records for cases that had been finalised, ready for their despatch to HQ records, made notes on front covers of the files, closed those dockets which had been finalised, whether Statutory Records (SR), or Criminal Records (CR), closed the respective entries in the Crime Register, sent cases involving prisoners who had been remanded in custody back to their respective investigating officers for further work and completion and closed down, one way or another, every entry on the Court Roll for the day. Only then were we able to sit back, relax and say to each other, "Job done!"

That afternoon I met up with Mujere Mapuvire, usually known as "Shorty," for which there were perhaps two reasons. He really was knee-high to the proverbial grasshopper. The second item was that he was missing most of the finger joints of his left hand. He had been a miner at Gaths Mine for a few years, but then encountered a miss-hap and the hand injury that deprived him of that job. There were then of course no requirements for injured workers to be compensated or pensioned off. They were simply discharged. However, Shorty had, so I was advised by the station sergeant, been one of the good workers on his shift. His supervisor spoke up for him and he was provided with training to become a cook/houseboy for one of the white miners. That job he had held down satisfactorily for a few years, until his employer had, a couple of months before my arrival at Mashaba, decided to return to South Africa. When I arrived on station, Barry had kindly agreed to let me use his personal batman for a few days and had tasked the station sergeant with finding me a batman of my own, as quickly as was possible. Shorty was approved of by one and all and came with a very glowing letter of recommendation from his previous employer. I agreed to take him on, on a month's trial basis.

The police team at Mashaba, was a busy and friendly one, from top to bottom. It was also a happy one. Insp. Cavey was a very fair and thoughtful boss to work under and Pete, Barry and Ian were easy to get along with. However, barely a week or two after I arrived, the night-time quiet of the mess quarters was broken by the sound of swearing and shattering glass. The disturbance was clearly coming from the lounge. Barry and I arrived on the veranda, from our bedrooms, as if in synchronised motion and headed for the source of the noise. In the lounge, where the lights were on, was Ian Harries, dressed in civvies. He was wandering, rather unsteadily, around the lounge, which had windows on two opposite sides. In his circulating, he was punching, lefts and rights, at a couple of pictures on the walls without windows and at the windows where they existed. Fortunately for him, the windows had mosquito gauze on the insides, which his fists had not gone through, although the panes of glass outside had broken. He had not been quite so lucky in punching the glass covered pictures, as his generously bleeding knuckles clearly showed. We did not really need to ask what the cause of his evil mood was, because as he struck out with his lefts and rights, he was shouting, repeatedly, amid some cruder expletives, "The bitch said 'No!' The bitch said 'No!'"

It took the combined efforts of both of us to get Ian to stop his rampage and sit down. A quick glance at the knuckles of both of his hands suggested that a stitch or two would be in order. We took turns to get back to our bedrooms to get adequately dressed to go out, then marched the somewhat protesting Ian out to the station Land Rover and then up to the Gaths Mine Hospital. An hour or more later we returned to the police station with Ian sporting two well bandaged hands. A decidedly sheepish expression crept on to his face as we showed him exactly how his injuries had been earned; something he appeared to have little memory of. Although certain events of the evening might not have imprinted themselves too well in his mind, others clearly had, because as we left his bedroom, he was still muttering viciously, "The bitch said, 'No!'"

The following morning there was just a little bit of explaining that Ian had to do in front of the boss before normal daily routine swung into gear. Not a lot was ever said about the incident, or the damage. The damage was put right quietly, fresh pictures appeared in the mess lounge and Ian had a bill to pay. Whether that incident had anything to do with it, or whether it was because, technically, Ian was the senior PO on station, a week or so later there came unexpected news of a transfer for him. The lowveld at Triangle and Hippo Valley, had been developing as an irrigated estate area, fed by the waters of Lake Kyle. More and more jobs were being created and the population was rising, fast. Along with that rising population, criminal activity was rising also, so the area needed additional staffing to support those already at Triangle Police Station. The story went that as Hippo Valley Estates began to grow so rapidly, a Patrol Officer and a Constable from Triangle were sent to set up, under canvas, a new Police Post, until some more permanent arrangement might be made. A couple of weeks earlier, so we heard, the uniformed pair had arisen at dawn to find over four hundred would-be complainants clustered politely but impatiently around their tents. The outnumbered pair called for back-up, temporary reinforcements were sent and one of the force's pioneer detachments appeared in double-quick time, to erect more substantial, if still impermanent, offices. The population of the area was still increasing. Ian was to be an additional pair of hands to deal with the growing workload.

That transfer for Ian came at the end of April. Pay day had come and gone and I had cash to get to my bank account. As Ian was travelling to Hippo Valley via Fort Victoria and had said that he intended to stop off there to do some shopping, I asked him if he would mind making a payment into my Barclays Bank account there. That he agreed to do, so, armed with all of his kit and an envelope from me, containing the bank's half of a paying-in slip and £50.00 in cash, Ian shook hands all round and departed.

A month or so later, I received a routine periodic statement of my current account with Barclay's Bank. There was no trace of any payment into it of the £50.00 I had handed to Ian. On discovering that, I had a quiet word with my boss. As there had been no witnesses to my handover of the envelope to Ian, I accepted that there was little that I could do about it, although, at the then pay-rate of £720.00 per annum, before tax etc., £50 was a lot of money. Upon hearing what I had to say, Bernard Cavey's face tightened. He reached for the phone and dialled. While I listened, he made arrangements for me to have an interview with Propol, Senior Assistant Commissioner Peter Sherren, later that same day.

In Mr Sherren's office at Provincial HQ, I repeated what I had told Inspector Cavey and presented my bank account records, showing a certain regular pattern that had been broken. Mr Sherren studied the stub in my paying-in book, then reached for the phone on his desk and arranged for me to make a telephone call to Hippo Valley. When Ian Harries came on the line, I inquired of him if he remembered the envelope containing the bank slip and £50.00 cash I had handed him the day he left Mashaba. Ian denied any knowledge of it. I reminded him of the exact time and place of the handover and reminded him of the notes on the paying-in book's stub. Ian still firmly denied any such event. Mr Sherren, who had been listening in, motioned to me to end the conversation, which I did. When both handsets were down on their cradles, Mr Sherren said, somewhat apologetically, "You know you won't get your money back, don't you?"

"Yes, Sir," I replied, "but staying quiet about what Patrol Officer Harries has done would be a second wrong. He needed to know that he has not got away with it without being found out and the Force needed to know that he cannot be trusted."

Mr Sherren nodded as he rose from behind his desk and escorted me to the closed door of his office, which he opened. "I'm sorry I can do no more than take note of this event, Mr Woolley, apart from saying that you've done the right thing in coming forward." With that note of approval to send me on my way, I returned to Mashaba, where I duly related what had gone on to Insp. Cavey. After that, it was just a matter of a lesson hard learned and getting on with being a policeman. That last bit was helped by the arrival of PO Pete Wilson as replacement for Ian Harries. Pete was a born and bred Rhodesian. His attitude towards the African population was interesting. He had an intense dislike of what he called the Kaffir Mentality. That had little or nothing to do with colour. It was all about equality. "If the bugger speaks my language, looks me in the eye and can hold a sensible conversation I'll ignore his colour, but if he is one of those who wants to chase you and me and every other white person out of the country, just because we're white, then he's likely to feel the knuckles of my fist!"

Not long after his arrival at Mashaba there was a wee bit of a riot at the Gaths Mine Beerhall. It started over allegations of watered-down Chibuku Beer. Pete and I and half a dozen constables attended the scene. The instigator of the trouble was still performing and attempting to whip up anger among others. Pete, with me close by his shoulder, pushed, shoved and thrust his way through the throng until he was facing the noisy one. Unnoticed by almost everyone, except perhaps me, Pete's right boot raked down the noisy one's left shin bone and descended on to his instep. The noisy one yelled in pain, clutched his left shin and hopped on his right foot. Pete promptly hooked the man's right foot from under him and down he went. Pete pointed down at the fallen drinker, called loudly to the African Police behind us, "Arrest this man for being drunk and incapable in a public place." Then he stood there, glaring at the scores of others in front of him.

"Securu ndiyani?" he roared. (Who's the senior person here?) A grizzled and diminutive fellow was eventually pushed forward. Pete pulled a couple of coins from a pocket. Turning to one of the barmen behind the long counter, he slapped the coins on the hard surface and called for a gallon of their standard Heinrich Chibuku brew. When the startled barman finally did as requested Pete grabbed the large container, handed it straight to the oldster and demanded that he taste it and tell everyone if it was good or bad.

It was admirable psychology. There was no way that that oldster was going to refuse, or complain about, a full gallon of Chibuku Beer handed to him for free. As the would-be agitator was being hustled away by our constables, the oldster lifted the great pot and took a good long draught. Umpteen score of drinkers suddenly went quiet. After a long moment, the oldster stopped swallowing. He held up the noticeably diminished gallon pot and declared firmly, "Ari Bwino!" (It is good!) Despite the fact that he spoke in Chinyanja, for there were many Nyasas among the miners, his approval of the quality of the beer was clear. There were roars of agreement from the crowd. Within minutes, the normal drinking pattern and level of noisy chatter settled in and the threatened rioting was forgotten.

Pete's somewhat individualistic way of resolving problems was not always strictly according to the book. Motorcycle patrols of the surrounding area were routine matters. We had a regular pattern of visits to make, to ranches, schools, irrigation schemes, townships and senior tribal figures. The patrol reports we put in went on record and were subject to inspection at monthly and annual visits of senior officers. I well recall the day when Pete asked me if I had time to drive him out to a particular farm in the purchase area right on our border with Chilimanzi as he had court summonses to deliver there. I did not have any great workload on at the time, so quite readily agreed, although wondering just a little why Pete did not wish to drive himself.

After a drive of something less than an hour we arrived at our destination. Pete, assisted by the constable who was with us, duly served the court papers and we began the return journey to Mashaba. As I started to drive off, Pete suggested that I go via a bit of a detour because he wanted to see if a certain businessman based at a nearby township, was back from Harare and available for a statement about a recent store robbery. I had no problem with that, so off we went, with me driving, Pete sitting in the front passenger seat and our constable behind us on the bench seat. I was quite used to the village dogs running beside the vehicles that passed their individual patch of territory. They ran alongside, snarling, yapping and occasionally biting at tyres, often to their cost. Eventually they stopped chasing and went back home, there to wait until the next chaseable vehicle passed by.

On this trip with Pete, many dogs chased us over short distances. I ignored them and Pete appeared to do the same. That is, until we approached one quite large kraal, when Pete suggested that I should slow down a bit. That I duly did. As expected, a few local dogs came out to confront and challenge our passage past their home. One was a big brute. Whatever its ancestry, its attitude matched its size. Pete had to pull his left elbow well within the cab window to prevent the beast taking a chunk out of his forearm. It was then that Pete pulled out the .38 revolver that he had secreted inside his shirt tucked behind his belt. As I kept driving, Pete opened the passenger door with his left hand, waited until the huge dog tried to get between the door and the side of the vehicle and then shot it through the head with his handgun.

There was a jolt as the rear near-side wheel went over the downed dog. When I looked back in the mirror, it was laying in the roadway, unmoving. Villagers were running towards it.

"What the heck was that all about?" I asked as my foot pressed a little harder on the accelerator.

"That damned thing bit me when I was up here on motorcycle patrol a week or so back." Pete explained. "If I had not been wearing boots and leggings it would have had a chunk out of my calf. It damned near had me off the motorcycle on that occasion. It was past time that somebody put it down."

In May and for once on time, the rainy season faded away. Dry weather activities revived. Along with other routine duties, I began to meet with members of the European Field Reserve, most of whom were ex-servicemen. Over most weekends there were afternoon shoots on the local rifle range, which the station staff had responsibility for keeping in good usable order, with the assistance of the reservists, many of whom were very proud of their abilities with assorted weaponry. Range controls were tightly enforced, whether the Range Officer for the event was one of the senior reservists, or Insp. Cavey himself. As I rapidly learned, every single one but the smallest of police stations had an associated rifle range and a police reserve contingent. Teams competed against each other locally and in open competitions at the many rifle ranges all around the Province and elsewhere.

The competitors' abilities over distances from 100 to 1000 yards were adequately tested by a variety of shooting disciplines. Skills in grouping, rapid fire, snap shooting, falling plates and hanging gongs were aggregated into team and individual totals and trophies awarded at the end of the day or afternoon.

My ability to achieve decent scores using the Mark IV Short Metford Lee Enfield .303 rifle was duly noted in the practice sessions. Because of that, I became a member of the Police Station Shooting Team during my all too short stay at Mashaba.

Unlike many other Members-in-Charge, Bernard Cavey did not indulge in the common practice of immediately sticking the new man on as Duty Officer for the next week. Upon my arrival he had carefully re-arranged the roster so that he, Pete, Ian and Barry each took a turn ahead of me before listing me in that role. The result of that was that I had a relatively easy familiarisation period in those first few weeks.

The roadway between Mashaba and Fort Victoria was much used. It carried a great number of heavy lorries burdened with asbestos, travelling to the railhead at Fort Victoria, as well as native buses and much other traffic of assorted size and weight. The Traffic Accident Report Book (TARB) that had to be completed by police details for each incident became a familiar set of pages for all of us, from constables through to the Member-in-Charge. Often it could be closed by M i/c Station as requiring no further police action. If the accident required some further action, the TARB became part of whatever greater docket was being created. It might be something as simple as a Deposit Fine of perhaps $10.00 for a bald tyre, or something as serious as a charge of Causing Death by Dangerous Driving. It was a wise policeman who filled out his TARBs diligently, because the pages, or the entire book, often became documentary exhibits in court cases or even inquests. On those occasions, inaccurate, sloppy and untidy TARBs could, and did, cause significant embarrassment to their compilers and to the Police Force as a whole. Solicitors and barristers gave no quarter when any opportunity arose to denigrate a police witness and score points for their clients, the accused person.

Early on in my Nyasaland police work I managed to muddle a vehicle registration number when investigating a death caused through negligent driving. Since that particular case depended upon questions of technical precision, relating to speed, distance and visibility, my inability to be precise over that one detail brought ridicule down on my personal skills and on the skills of my superiors who had also missed spotting my error. The result was that a guilty driver escaped punishment and I determined to never again make a slip-up like that. I am not too sure that I achieved that aim on every occasion in future years, but I did give it my best shot.

The other lesson I learned from harsh experience in the UK and Nyasaland was to carefully **read** every document, at least the evening before, in every case that I was required to present in court. It was perhaps that collection of experiences that led me to be able to save Barry Lane's blushes when he, having done an excellent job in dealing with a tricky case where driver negligence had caused many thousands of dollars of damage and injured several people, made a simple slip-up. Barry had done all of the difficult work well, but when preparing the documentary exhibits which were the plans of the scene, he had managed to wrongly transcribe the original measurements in yards into the same figures but marked them off as feet. Because it was a defended case, the necessary evidential documents had been provided already to the defence lawyers. It was very likely that that team would spot the error and play hard upon it. It was necessary to draw that potential sting. so, once court was in session, I made clear what had gone on, apologised for it and offered a corrected plan.

With Mr Stainer presiding, I did wonder what dry witticism my corrective efforts might draw, but, as it turned out, after the defending solicitor had let loose with a scathing attack on the faulty plan and sought to cast doubt about the ability of the Police Force and PO Lane in particular, to rightly investigate whether it was daytime or night-time, it was Mr Stainer who hit back on our behalf.

"To err is human," he intoned. "To forgive is reputedly divine. The error here has been noted, apologised for and offered up for correction at the first available opportunity. Perhaps a little divinity in your response might have been appropriate?"

The defence solicitor had sufficient acumen to take it that although the magistrate's last sentence had been phrased as a question, it was actually far from that. He bowed his head in submission and sat down, muttering, "Very well, Sir," as he did so.

Eventually, the accused was convicted and fined. However, it was not just a victory for the police force, but, more importantly, a victory for those innocent parties who had suffered loss and injury in that traffic accident, because the conviction opened up, for them, the route to compensatory payments from the guilty driver's insurance company.

Sadly, over my service years, I encountered many cases where the guilty driver was convicted but had no valid insurance policy to provide reparation for the innocent victims.

Every police station I served upon had a store of anecdotes, handed down through the years, about the dedication or the daftness of those who had served there before, both black and white. One such item was explained later to me when I commenced my first week as Duty Patrol Officer. It was a simple enough report, in the middle of one afternoon, of a relatively minor road traffic accident in the low density European residential area of Gaths Mine. A motorist had hit and injured a dog. Keen to get swiftly to the scene, I grabbed my clipboard and paperwork, made a quick raid on the station armoury to draw a revolver in case I had to put down the injured dog, called for one of the constables on standby to come with me, instructed the charge office orderly to book us out and scooted along the veranda to inform Pete Nicholls what I was off to do.

"Okay," he said. "Get to it then, but don't do a Fox!" The comment puzzled me, but then was not the time to start asking for explanations. Duty called!

The scene of the accident was not far away. The dog, a Labrador type, was very dead, the private car involved was barely dented and the male adult European driver was having a perfectly reasonable and sympathetic conversation with the dog's owner, another European from a bungalow nearby, when we arrived on the scene. The owner of the dead dog assured me that he was able to see to the disposal of his pet himself, the documentation for the car involved and its driver was all in order and the vehicle had no actionable defects. That made it a very simple and straightforward TARB, which I duly completed in short order. I delivered a few words of sympathy to both parties, exchanged two handshakes and that was that. Back at the station I asked Pete Nicholls about that "Don't do a Fox!" comment.

The story was simple. A year back, European Constable Fox, a fairly new policeman, had gone out to attend a similar accident in the low-density residential area of Gaths Mine. That one had involved a badly injured cat, which Const. Fox had decided needed putting out of its misery. Equipped as I had been more recently, with a .38 revolver, Const. Fox carefully lifted the unfortunate moggy's head with his left hand, put the muzzle of the revolver against the suffering animal's forehead and pulled the trigger. He did succeed, so Pete related, in putting the cat out of its misery, but he also blew a bullet hole through the palm of his own left hand.

"That's why I cautioned you not to do a Fox," he ended with a grin.

It was a couple of days later that I discovered the second reason why European Const. Fox's name was indelible in the memories of the station staff. It was related to me that the accident-prone policeman had driven back to station in one of the Land Rovers on one occasion, parked the vehicle outside and left it to be ready whenever next required. I have mentioned that the police station at Mashaba was up a slope a couple of hundred yards from the Fort Victoria to Shabani main road. Hold that thought. Now imagine that you are a local rancher, innocently and routinely driving back from Fort Victoria, through Mashaba, on your way home, when suddenly you have to slam on the brakes to avoid a grey painted series II Land Rover, with "Police" plates and painting all over it, but with nobody in it, that you see to be slowly but steadily crossing the road from right to left just ahead of you.

Imagine then watching the Land Rover run down the embankment slope of the roadside, lurch resolutely into the ditch at the bottom and come to a stop, delicately but precariously balanced vertically on its nose, all of which activity was apparently caused by Const. Fox forgetting the essential act of putting on the handbrake before leaving the vehicle. The photographs of the Land Rover in that somewhat unique pose appeared in the force's magazine, *The Outpost* shortly after the event. I suppose it was little wonder that European Const. Fox was no longer at Mashaba when I arrived there.

It was during my first week as Duty Patrol Officer that I encountered my first murder case as a member of the BSAP. One evening toward midnight I was awakened by the night office orderly. A report had come in that an

African woman had been killed in the high-density residential quarters on Gaths Mine. Without wasting time, I gathered all the bits and pieces that might be needed, including my personal camera, collected a duty constable from the charge office, loaded a body-box into the Land Rover, booked out in the Occurrence Book and set off. My constable companion knew his way around and very efficiently guided me to the mine's main office, from where the incident had been phoned in and where the initial informant was waiting for us to arrive.

As I discovered, the Mine's General Manager was also waiting in the office, along with a couple of the mine's African employees. There did not appear to be anyone present who I could immediately identify as an accused person.

The story was simple, but tragic. The killer was one of the African shift workers, occupying quarters No. 60 in the Single Men's section of the compound. That evening, being off shift, he had gone to the beerhall on the mine property. There he had had a few pints of Chibuku, the national brand of native local brew, chatted up one of the local Mahuris and returned with her to his modest accommodation. Some while later, an argument had occurred. Neighbours had heard angry shouting and then some screaming, which had suddenly been silenced. A concerned employee had gone to see what was going on. He found the Mahouri laying naked, on her back on the pieces of cardboard put down on the concrete floor of the room to act as a mattress. She appeared to have been stabbed more than once, around the chest and neck. He had noticed blood on the floor and walls. The man in the room with her was sitting on a small stool, holding his stomach with one hand and a blood-stained home-made knife in the other. The concerned employee had called for help from neighbours. Together they carried the stabbed Mahouri the fortunately short distance from the scene to the mine hospital, where she was pronounced dead. The suspected killer, although apparently injured, had been able to walk to the hospital with them. He was in a bed in the hospital, with other employees guarding him.

With assistance from the constable with me, I made a few notes, recorded a list of names of potential witnesses and then followed the miners as they guided me to the hospital's African ward, where they identified the suspect, who was laying in one of the beds, but who was clearly not asleep.

The first item to sort out was the matter of whether or not the suspect could speak English to any degree. He could not, so the constable with me carefully translated my words for him. I started to formally Warn and Caution him as a suspect in the murder of a presently un-named female adult African. Before I could even finish writing the formal words of the caution, the accused took a deep breath and began to relate how the Mahouri and he had agreed a price for her services in the beerhall, but, when she had delivered her services for him and was preparing to leave, she had demanded a greater sum. That had caused an argument, she had pulled a knife from her clothes and stabbed him in the belly with it. That made him lose his temper, so he had taken the knife from her and stabbed her once with it, to stop her stabbing him again. When he had finished his tale and after he had had it read back to him, he signed it and the constable and I did the same.

Leaving the suspect under the constable's guard, I went to take a look at the dead woman's body laid out on a slab in the hospital's small mortuary. There were several puncture wounds evident at her chest and her throat had been seriously cut. The mine doctor who had been called out to attend the incident advised me that the stomach wound the suspect had suffered was relatively superficial and that the suspect could be released to police custody later that day. I made arrangements to collect the dead woman's body later that day and the suspect also. With the mine manager's assistance, I arranged for the scene to be guarded and protected until daylight and then returned to the police station for a short while of sleep and a hasty breakfast, before returning to Gaths Mine to relieve the constable I had left guarding the suspect and to examine the scene and collect the remains of the victim.

To state that the mine single men's accommodation was basic would be an understatement. The bedroom to number 60 was barely eight-foot square, with a small window and just one internal door leading to and from the combined kitchen/dining-room. The dead woman's clothing was still laying scattered around on the few pieces of cardboard on the floor. What blankets there might have been had been used to wrap the Mahouri's body in on the way to hospital.

I recorded what was necessary, made sketches and took photographs of the scene, with its copious blood stains, particularly one massive spray of blood rising two feet up from the floor on one wall. That was clearly arterial blood-flow. The only injury that would have created that was the slashed neck, where the later full post-mortem confirmed that the carotid artery had been severed. That meant the woman had been laying, head back and shoulders to the floor, close to the wall, when her throat had been slit. There was also the interesting question as to how a naked woman might have pulled a knife from clothing she was clearly not wearing. There was one further telling piece of evidence. In the clothing of the accused at the hospital and within the rooms at the scene, no trace of any money could be found. Neither was there any money in the dead woman's clothing at the scene.

The knife itself was clearly a home-made affair, with a handle carved from a bovine's horn. Nothing in the suspect's living quarters linked him to the knife. Nobody who knew him had ever seen him with it. Similarly, when we investigated where the Mahouri lived, those she had associated with claimed they had never seen her with such an item either. Even a full search around the suspect's home kraal in the Mtilikwe Reserve a couple of dozen miles away turned up nothing to firmly link him with the knife. In due course the case went to High Court in Fort Victoria. My photographs of the bloodstains at the scene became a focal point in the argument over what had and had not happened. The detailed picture of the blood sprayed up the wall confirmed the full post-mortem result and the expert opinion of the doctor as to the likely position of the dead woman when her throat had been cut. The accused was convicted of murder and sentenced to several years in prison.

While that murder case was progressing, on the 13th May 1965, there occurred another kind of tragedy that also etched indelible memories into the software of one's brain. The rainy season was really over, but the climate chose to throw up one last weather front, with rain, thick cloud and thunderstorms.

It was mid-morning when the telephone call came in, from one of the area's ranchers, to say that he believed, from information given to him by one of his African ranch-hands that a light aircraft had crashed in a wooded area on his ranch. As befitted the nature of that phone call, it was put through by the constable telephonist on duty to the Member-in-Charge. Inspector Cavey promptly called Pete, Barry and me into his office and warned us to be ready to move out once some confirmation of the crash was obtained. He made an urgent phone call to air traffic control at Salisbury Airport. It took only a few minutes for that location to confirm that it had indeed lost radio and radar contact with a light aircraft flying into Salisbury from Johannesburg. With all of us standing listening, Inspector Cavey relayed the news of the suspected light aircraft crash as recently reported to him. After a few minutes of conversation, he put the phone down and turned to us.

"They want us to get out there asap," he stated flatly. "There were two on board the plane. They want a search for any survivors or bodies and for us to secure the crash site and the wreckage for later collection and investigation by their air accident investigators who will head for here once we can confirm the report of the crash. I'll stay here as comms link. I want one of you Patrol Officers here with me. You're the junior man Arnold, so it had better be you. The rest of you grab some constables and get moving."

As the others began to stir, I said, "With respect, Sir, I may be the junior detail on station, but unless anyone else has dealt with an aircraft crash before, I may be a bit more use out at the scene, because I have."

Bernard Cavey's, "Hold it!" stopped the movement of the others towards the door. To me he said, "Go on, but no long stories. There isn't time."

"A French Air Force Dakota flew into the side of a mountain called Chiradzulu in Nyasaland. That crash killed 38 paratroopers and the whole aircrew. I was involved in the aftermath of that. This one is going to need a lot of photography for the record. The quicker they're taken, the better. I've my camera in my room and a lot of unused film in it."

Inspector Cavey made up his mind instantly. "You grab your camera Arnold and get out to the scene with the others. Barry, you stay here with me." As we left his office, Insp. Cavey's bellow of, "Don't forget to book out!" reminded us all that hurry or no hurry, station routines had to be properly observed. In this case, our departure had to be written into the Occurrence Book on the charge office counter. That logged all personnel movements, hour by hour and day by day. Who was involved in whatever occurrence it was, the time of a report, or time out and in and the reasons why, along with which vehicle was being put to use.

By the time I had grabbed my camera along with the station's traffic accident first aid kit, complete with splints, just in case, Pete and Barry had rounded up our station sergeant and a few of our constables and shepherded them into a Land Rover. With Pete at the wheel, we took off in a wheel-spinning hurry down the slope towards the tarmac road and turned towards Shabani and the alleged crash site.

A half hour later, Pete was able to confirm, via our police vehicle's VHF radio, that the report was all too genuine. With guidance from the rancher and his employee, there was no delay in us getting to the scene. The wreckage of the light aircraft was clearly visible among the thin grass and scrub trees of the area. Two things were obvious from the start. The first was that the aircraft had come down hard and fast and probably almost vertically, because the area of scattered debris was no more than a hundred yards in diameter. The second was that it was not a survivable crash. The battered but relatively intact body of the pilot was still strapped into his seat, which had been torn loose from its proper position and lay some yards from the wrecked engine and clear of the battered remnants of the main portion of the fuselage. The passenger's body was no longer in a seat. It lay chest down, some few yards from the pilot and nearer to the remains of the plane's tail. At first, I could see no head to the body, but on getting closer, I discovered that the passenger's head, although dis-articulated from the spine, was actually present, tucked in a macabre tidiness under the right armpit.

I took a whole lot of film shots of the two bodies amid the wreckage, making sure that I had every angle covered before anyone else set foot anywhere near them. Once I had that much on film and had carefully established the extent of the wreckage field I set about taking more photographs until I felt I had coverage of the entire scene. Once that was done, we set about combing the area for any personal effects belonging to the two dead men. Pete made a radio call to the station, requesting body-boxes, a supply of torches and permission to remove the bodies of the crash victims before darkness.

Within the hour and without disturbing anything else, we completed the grim task of searching through the pockets of the two dead men, for any items of identification and other personal possessions. Those we bagged and labelled. The bodies themselves we recovered into the coffin-shaped metal body-boxes that were part of every station's routine equipment. That necessary handling of the dead men suggested there was barely an unbroken bone in either body. In that handling, we were able to return the passenger's head to a more conventional position. In a respectful and sombre silence we loaded the body-boxes into the back of the Land Rover. Pete instructed two constables to stay there on first shift guarding the scene. Then we set off, as dusk was falling, to return to Mashaba Police Station, from where we arranged for the onward transportation of the bodies of the two victims to refrigerated storage in the mortuary at Fort Victoria General Hospital, there to await formal post-mortem examination.

Inspector Cavey listened intently to our detailed de-briefing on what we had encountered at the scene. A series of phone calls arranged for government air crash investigators, prisons staff, with a gang of prisoners and a few of us police details to gather at the crash site early next day. The issue of lifting the engine, the heaviest part of the wreckage, was dealt with by arranging for some sheerlegs and pulleys, capable of being powered by a winch on the front of one of our station's Land Rovers.

With all of the necessary arrangements made, we took ourselves off to our various home quarters, to get cleaned up, eat, sleep and be refreshed for the demands of the following day. All of us that was, except for Barry Lane, who was that week's Duty Patrol Officer. He drew the short straw of having to make before and after midnight visits to the crash site in order to change over the pairs of constables guarding it.

The following morning, at the crash site and once us police details had carefully explained our procedures of the previous day, the department of civil aviation's investigators took over. Once they had photographed and measured as they needed and peered at the settings of the various control surfaces at the time of impact, they instructed us, aided by the prison officers and prisoners, to recover every scrap of the aircraft that we could find, load it on to a Bedford 5-ton flat-back lorry that we had guided as close to the scene as the terrain allowed and re-assemble the shattered remains, as best we could, on land at the side of Mashaba Police Station.

Particularly poignant was the reverence with which the African prisoners treated the pilot's seat and the area where the passenger's body had lain. On their realisation that there were bloodstains present, they carefully scraped together handfuls of the dry, dusty soil and used them to cover over every visible trace of dried blood. Only when that was done did they feel happy to start shifting the debris. I added a few more photographs to those already on my camera as the recovery process went on, piece by piece, greater and lesser, until we were sure we had everything except the engine block loaded onto the lorry.

The exercise of recovering the engine was made a great deal easier because of the score or so of cheerful "Bandits" as we generally called them. They gathered, lifted, pulled and worked with a will once it had been explained to them just what was needed. Aided by the sheerlegs and a Land Rover winch, the engine was finally safely stowed on the lorry. We made a couple of shoulder-to-shoulder sweeps across the debris field, just to make sure we had overlooked nothing, or at least nothing significant, before we drove away with a final thought or two for the two lives lost and the bereaved families many miles away.

Before lunchtime, we were back at Mashaba Police Station where we made a break for a quick bite to eat. After that, Barry and I booked out of the station, heading for Fort Victoria General Hospital and the mortuary facility there, where I met, for the first time, but by no means the last, Dr Ascough, the senior Government Medical Officer, or GMO as they were usually referred to. To him I handed over the Post-Mortem Request Forms relating to the two dead men. Dr Ascough read carefully through the paperwork, then looked at Barry and me and asked the question that often cropped up where Post-Mortem Examinations were needed. "How much detail do you want?"

That was a very kindly, indeed human, question for many reasons. In cases where the cause of death was obvious it was a case of not only wasting valuable medical time if an investigating officer insisted on a fully detailed post-mortem, but it was also necessary to give a thought to the relatives. It was the families and relatives, whether, black, white, religious or irreligious, whose body was either relatively undisturbed, or had been seriously opened at skull, face, neck, thorax and abdomen, had had organs and specimens removed for examination and analysis and then been rather crudely and obviously sewn back together, or were able to receive a body for disposal that was in relatively undisturbed and therefore less distressing, condition.

"A cause of death compatible with them being involved in an aircraft crash would do it, Doc," Barry replied without hesitation. It was the answer I too would have given.

The white-coated African Medical Assistant pulled open in turn the refrigerated drawers containing the blanket-wrapped bodies of the pilot and passenger and unwrapped each sufficient for us police officers to provide formal identification by name and confirm that we had helped recover them from the site of the crash, which we described. That was a very necessary closing of the chain of evidence in such cases.

Doctor Ascough declined to have the bodies lifted on to the post-mortem examination table and declined also the offer of necessary instruments for sawing and cutting.

Instead, he simply carried out a visual and manual external examination of each of the dead men. As he rocked the passenger's disjoined head to and fro, he slowly shook his own, his expression sombre. When he was finished, he motioned for his assistant to slide shut the two refrigerated trays on which the dead men lay.

Turning to Barry and me, Doctor Ascough asked quietly, "Do you know what caused the crash?"

"Pilot error, we believe," Barry stated. "The civil aviation boys told us the pilot was not instrument rated. He ran into a heavy weather front somewhere between Belingwe and Mashaba. He should have turned back into clear skies but chose to fly on, probably became dis-orientated and that was that."

Doctor Ascough nodded wordlessly and reached for the paperwork.

"The tragic irony of it is, Doctor," I put in, "that they were flying to Salisbury to attend the funeral of a relative. Not wanting to miss paying their last respects was probably why the pilot flew on instead of turning back. Now the families have two more funerals on their hands."

Only when he had finished writing did Doctor Ascough reply. "Let's hope," he offered as he handed the necessary documents to Barry, "that nobody else suffers a similar fate travelling to the funerals of these two unfortunate individuals."

On our walk back to the Land Rover, Barry perused the paperwork. "Cause of Death," he stated, reading from the papers relating to the pilot. "Death due to multiple internal and external injuries consistent with having been involved in an aircraft crash." He switched papers, looked at the second sheet for a moment and continued, "This one's the same. With a bit of luck, the family will never know the poor bugger's head was tucked neatly underneath his arm, will they?"

"Not if the undertakers are up to their job," I replied. "A bit of stitching and a shirt with a high collar will do it."

When we arrived back at Mashaba, Barry handed over the necessary documents to Pete Nicholls before I got my camera and we both went to take a look at the wreckage, now laid out in proper position, one piece to another. With permission from the government investigators, I took a few more photographs to complete the set relating to the crash and agreed to have copies made of all of my photographic work, to be sent on to the investigators, which is what I did. The original set of slides is still with me. From our conversation with the investigators, it appeared that the most likely cause of the accident was that the inexperienced pilot had hit heavy turbulence, at relatively low level and become inverted without realising it. When Barry and I both looked incredulous at that remark, the two men, both experienced pilots themselves, assured us it could and did happen. The nose of the aircraft would have dropped towards the ground, creating pressure underneath the pilot's feet, making him feel that the aircraft was stalling. His natural response would have been to push the control stick forward and increase engine power, instead of pulling the stick back towards him so as to complete a full loop, if he had the height, or realising he was inverted and correcting that situation. Failing either of those corrective moves, the aircraft had hit the ground under full power and very nearly vertical, from the control surface settings and the visual evidence.

In due course the two Sudden Death Dockets were closed after a paperwork inquest finding of "Death due to multiple injuries arising from involvement in an aircraft crash." The Civil Aviation Authority's file was eventually closed after a finding of "Pilot error, caused by inexperience."

When I completed my first spell as Duty Officer, Insp. Cavey asked me where I was going for the weekend. I had to point out to him that I had no transport of my own yet and apart from the police station staff, really had not had time to form the kind of personal friendships that might take me off station for a weekend. At that he agreed I could stay on station, but he clearly was not happy about it.

Towards the end of my second spell as Duty Officer, Insp. Cavey called me in to his office. "I've got a job for you for the weekend. Right up your street. There's a very large croc been sighted in Mushandike Dam. It's taken one of their breeding herd of eland and it needs shooting before it takes any more. I've arranged a rondavel to be made available for you from Friday evening and some fishing tackle too. Draw a rifle from the armoury, report to the senior ranger at reception there before dark. Barry can drive you out there on a road patrol and collect you on Sunday at dusk to bring you back. You can spend your time fishing, game viewing and croc hunting all in one go. The rondavels are fully equipped, so all you need to do is take enough food for those couple of days."

That was how it happened that I spent a very enjoyable two days occupying one of the thatched roofed and low walled visitor rondavels at Mushandike Nature Reserve, which had the dam at its centre. I was made more than welcome by the ranger in charge and his African staff, who provided me with all the fishing tackle I needed and kept me provided with live bait of every kind, from grasshoppers to grubs and worms. The staff showed me the spot, a favourite watering point for animals within the reserve, where the eland had been taken and warned me that the croc, which had been seen to take the animal, was "Makuru!" meaning very big, perhaps twenty foot or so. They cautioned me to be careful when fishing and to stay well back from the edge if I chose to fish from the rocks where the water was deep. It was advice that I fully intended to follow, for my experiences in Nyasaland had included having to deal with the sudden death of a local man who had been fishing from low rocks on the shores of Lake Nyasa. In his excitement of trying to land what was probably a large fish on the end of his line, he made the mistake of standing too close to the water's edge. Onlookers saw the tail of a large croc suddenly rise out of the water. It swept the unfortunate fisherman off the rocks and into the water. As he struggled to clamber back on to the rocks, the croc grabbed him in its jaws and dragged him under water. Nothing was ever seen of him again. I had no intention of making the same fatal mistake.

For two thoroughly enjoyable days, with good weather to help, I relaxed and enjoyed the amenities of the tourist facilities and walked, watched game and fished as the fancy took me. One of the African rangers, a tall, lanky individual named Josepa, accompanied me much of the time as I walked the shoreline and much of the whole of the game fence that demarcated the reserved area. He had been one of the staff there for many years and knew the area well. It was good to encounter, once again, the noisy quiet of the African bush; to listen to the warning grunts of a troop of baboon and the higher call of francolin in the long grass. In the evening I was able to sit and watch the stars in all their glory, undimmed by the glare of electric lights. There was nothing in the way of big game there, but ample in the way of antelope, from tiny duiker up to the eland which were as large as a horse, or damned near so. Josepa also showed me the sizeable deposit of Beryl not far from the dam wall and two sets of ancient cave paintings.

For those two days I was able to walk and fish in glorious weather, under a wide blue sky. My African guide introduced me to the delicacy of "macimbe" which is the local name for the large caterpillars commonly found all over the country, anywhere there are musasa trees. At that time of the year, with the weather beginning to warm up, the caterpillars start falling out of their chosen trees. The caterpillars are fearsome looking black fellows, up to five centimetres long, covered with long grey hairs. When they start falling out of the musasa trees, they do so in considerable quantity. Each one hits the ground with a clearly audible plop. As I had already learned from my Nyasaland encounters, hairy caterpillars of most kinds are things to be very wary of and stay well away from. However, "macimbe" are not like most hairy caterpillars, the grey hairs on these caterpillars don't shoot, sting or itch, they are soft and harmless. The caterpillars feed on the leaves of the musasa trees. Once they begin to drop to the ground, they become a sought-after delicacy for the locals and for the occasional European brave enough to try them. Around Harare, the African name for Salisbury, so my companion told me, they are called "madoro" but that is only due to the difference between the Kalanga and Chishona dialects.

On discovering that I had actually eaten flying ants, in Nyasaland, Josepa insisted that I should gather a couple of good handfuls of the wriggly macimbe fellows, for eating when they were cooked and dried. Back at the rondavel he cheerfully showed me how to squeeze the innards out, give them a quick rinse and then a few minutes of boiling in salted water. When they were cooked, he set them out to dry. I had to carry them back to the mess in Mashaba to finish drying out properly, but, when I did eat them, a few days later and much to the disgust of Barry and Pete, who both turned their noses up at the offer of the local delicacy, I found it easy to do so. Like the flying ants, they have a firm and crunchy texture, with a mild peppery flavour.

Although I never saw a single trace of the croc, which was shot a couple of weeks later, by the senior ranger, I did manage to catch a good haul of bream and catfish, one or two of which I ate myself, but most of which I was able to give to Josepa and the other rangers, black and white, who had made me so welcome.

With a thoughtful boss like Bernard Cavey, who I thanked profusely for arranging that very interesting weekend away and friendly and helpful advice from Pete Nicholls, Mashaba was one of the happiest stations that I ever worked on. Locally, Balmain's store provided a wide range of general store goods that meant little need to travel far for most of the daily routine necessities of life. To add to that convenience, there always seemed to be some reason or another, every few days, for a police vehicle, or one of the motorcycles, to be sent through to Fort Victoria. Routine repairs and servicing of our vehicles, the need to deliver or collect papers and personnel, High Court Sessions and training days, all gave us opportunities to get a few hours away from the usual routine of the police station and to take a few minutes to purchase bits and pieces not available in Mashaba.

Mind you, I suspect I should be careful in using that word routine. Yes, there was a set pattern to the running of the station, day by day. That much of the routine was regular, reliable, orderly and predictable. However, what was far from regular, reliable and orderly, as the last few pages may have suggested to you already, was the nature and burden of the workload.

For everyone there were quiet weeks, busy weeks and some that fast became frantic ones, particularly for the Duty PO. You may take it that Bernard and Pete did try to ensure that everyone had a fair share of work on hand at any one time. Incidents of whatever kind, those that were reported during ordinary office hours, were allocated out fairly, turn by turn. It was the out of ordinary working hours reports that produced, without fail, the "Feast or Famine" effect. Whoever was Duty PO for the week was not automatically excluded from a fair share of the workload that arrived during ordinary working hours. However, once the Duty PO was called out to attend whatever it was, after hours, that incident, whatever its simplicity or magnitude, became the responsibility of that duty officer.

At the beginning of June, I collected one of those "interesting" weeks as Duty PO. The weekend passed routinely. I dealt with the one daytime and one night-time road patrol that were regularly carried out at weekends by the Duty PO, carefully staying in constant radio contact with the station, in case any more pressing report might be received in my absence. No such urgent summons arrived.

Even the daylight hours of the Monday passed routinely. Just, I am sure, to lull me into the thought that the remaining four days were going to be a doddle. It was after dinner on the Monday evening that the fun and games started. I was lounging around in the mess, reading a newspaper, when I heard a car travelling fast up the incline from the main road. It slid to a noisy halt outside the charge office. A minute or so later the phone rang. It was the duty constable. The report was that a vehicle had hit a cyclist and injured him, a couple of miles out of town on the Fort Victoria Road. There was a need for police and an ambulance at the scene. I left the charge office orderly to record the details of the helpful African motorist and allow him to proceed on his way to Shabani which was his destination.

I grabbed everything I might need, linked up with the duty constable and set off for the scene in respectably fast time.

What I found was not a simple traffic accident. Readers unfamiliar with Africa will need to reflect that long before the European arrived there in 1890 or so, the local people had footpaths they had used for scores, if not hundreds, of years. When us Europeans constructed roads from here to there and everywhere, those roads cut across umpteen of those traditional footpaths. As the African learned to use the wheel, which he had not yet invented himself, or copied from outside, before 1890, carts and bicycles began to appear. Put a local beer-drink together with a local man riding on his unlit bicycle, intent on going from the beer-drink to his home on the other side of the main road, together with a heavy goods vehicle, a tipper truck loaded with asbestos, travelling fast towards Fort Victoria and you have all the ingredients for a cake-full of calamity.

The accident was on a tight bend of the unlit road. The lorry had come to a halt half on and half off the tarmac, facing Fort Victoria. At first, I could see no sign of the cyclist. The lorry itself was unlit. Not unnaturally, the crash had by then drawn a horde of locals, crowding everywhere all over the road. There was urgent work to be done to get them all clear of the road and get some warning signs out on either side of the crash site, before any other vehicle came round the corner fast and hit the lorry or turned itself over in trying to swerve around it. I pulled the police Land Rover to a halt a safe distance from the rear of the lorry and climbed out, leaving all the lights on. Clutching my powerful box-battery torch I walked up to and then along the side of the lorry. The torchlight revealed tyre marks, scrapes and bloodstains. Only when I flashed my torch along the length of the lorry did I notice the buckled bicycle wheel wedged under the upright vehicle, just to the rear of the right front wheel. I also realised that the onlookers were all standing without speaking. The silence was eerie. As I reached the front of the lorry, an African man climbed down from the driving cab.

"Are you the driver?" I asked. He nodded. "Where's the cyclist?" I continued. The lorry driver pointed in the general direction of the buckled bicycle. "Upo," (There). "Yafa!" he concluded (He's dead!). At that moment the constable with me joined us, carrying two reflective "Police Ahead" signs. "Ask the driver to put on the lorry's lights," I instructed him, which he did. At that request the lorry driver shook his head. "Ha pana," he intoned. (There are none!) That was all I needed; a reportedly injured cyclist who was in fact dead and a heavy lorry being driven on a main road, after dark, without any lights working.

In something of a hurry, I instructed the constable to get the warning signs set up on either side of the crash scene, at least one hundred full strides away and then got down on the gravel of the roadside in order to see just what the condition of the cyclist underneath the lorry really was. It was not a pretty sight. Cyclist and cycle had been caught by the suspension and other metalwork on the underside of the heavy vehicle and dragged some several yards before the vehicle came to a halt. Buckled cycle and buckled rider were intertwined in one bloodstained tangle. There was no doubt at all that the unfortunate cyclist's life was extinct.

A careful examination of the gruesome tangle beneath the lorry made me think it could be extracted if the lorry could be jacked up perhaps three or four inches. It was a rare lorry in Africa that travelled far without a jack. Fortunately, this one was well equipped to change tyres if needed. The toolbox held a very usable heavy-duty jack.

With the lorry driver's assistance, I made sure the vehicle was firmly in gear, with handbrake hard on, before he and I set about placing the jack, prior to attempting to lift the offside front corner. All the while, the several dozen onlookers maintained their eerie silence. The constable with me returned about then, assuring me that the warning signs were well-placed, better than a hundred full paces away on each side.

With the lorry driver working the jack and some assistance from my constable, we were able to extract the twisted bicycle and mangled rider from beneath the lorry. Handling the dead man as respectfully as we could, we separated human remains from metal ones and laid the body out, face upwards alongside the tarmac surface in front of the heavy vehicle. When I put the beam of my torch on to the dead man's surprisingly undamaged face, the eerie silence broke. Several of the bystanders rushed forward, shouting, screaming and wailing. Some began to shout and shake their fists at the lorry driver who promptly tried to climb back into the lorry's cab, even though it was still jacked up.

"They know him, Ishe," my constable shouted above the din, gesturing at the dead man. "He is their relative."

"Okay but get them off of the road and well back. If anything comes round that corner too fast while they're all over the road, we'll have some more fatalities on our hands." I pulled the lorry driver away from the angry onlookers, stowed him safely in the police Land Rover and returned to the front of the lorry. I was barely in time. Above the wailings I heard the noise of a vehicle approaching fast, from the Fort Victoria direction.

On seeing the flashing of my torch and belatedly realising there were people all over the road, as well as the lorry, the driver, who had either not seen, or seen and chosen to ignore, the police ahead warning signs, slammed hard down on the brakes. Inevitably, with his front wheels turned for the bend, the back end of the car slid away from his control and the vehicle began to fishtail. To give the driver his due, he controlled the fishtailing vehicle well. As it slid to a tyre-squealing halt, broadside across the road, barely a couple of feet from my toes, I noted it was a shiny black Mercedes-Benz sports car. The driver was a middle-aged European male adult.

"What the hell do you think you're doing flashing me down like that, with people all over the road," he snarled angrily.

"Did you not see the "Police Ahead" warning sign that's on the gravel verge a hundred yards or more back there?" I asked evenly, gesturing in the direction he had just driven from.

"No, I was in a hurry," he answered, just a trifle defensively.

"So was he," I informed him, shining my torch beam on to the mangled and blood-stained body of the cyclist barely six feet from him. He took one look and was violently sick, vomiting food and, from the smell, a fair load of liquor, all over the door, dashboard and driver's compartment of his car.

When he was finished retching, he dragged a handkerchief from his coat pocket and wiped his face, before looking at me once more and hissing, "Damn you! You've ruined my car and my evening!"

"And maybe saved your life too. Who knows?" I replied. "You may drive on round the lorry whenever you're ready." With that I turned away from him and got on with what was needed to properly investigate and process the fatal traffic accident on hand.

With a final yell of, "You'll hear more of this!" which I never did, the driver of the sports car drove round the lorry and away, not quite as fast as he had approached.

A radio call for a body-box and a couple more constables helped bring the crash scene under proper control and protect it until daylight hours when I was able to make a full examination of what the road surface evidence was and to take some photographs to add to the sketches and measurements. The circumstances of the crash and the absence of any lights in working order on the lorry meant that the accident had to be treated as a case of causing death by negligent driving. The vehicle, one of the Temeraire Mine fleet, had to be impounded and properly examined by vehicle inspectors. The bicycle had to be properly examined too. That examination revealed that the bicycle had no effective brakes. There was a post-mortem to arrange and inquiries to be made at the beer-drink the dead man had come from directly before the accident. It amounted to quite a lot of work to be done over the next few days and even weeks.

Back at Mashaba Police Station after breakfast time, all of us involved in the case overnight headed for our respective quarters to try to grab a few hours of sleep before a meal at lunchtime and then resuming duty for the afternoon.

Dawn on the Wednesday brought a report of a suicide by hanging of an African woman from one of the Purchase Area farms. The purchase areas were hectares of land that usually bordered European farming areas. The land was divided into smallholdings that could be bought only by Africans, male or female. I make that point because it is not usually known by Europeans that in the tribal areas it is only women who can be allocated land. That land allocation is usually provided only when there is a marriage. That is because it is recognised that after the marriage, the female will have a husband and children to feed. As her family might grow, so the woman can apply to the kraalhead for the allocation of a greater area of land for her family. The purchase area lands were stepping-stones to enable the progressive African farmers, male or female, to get onto the commercial food production ladder.

Responding to the report of the suicide, I collected my clipboard and camera, arranged for a body-box to be placed in one of the station's Land Rovers, called for one of the duty constables, one who knew the way to the scene and set off. Stable Parade, breakfast and the pile of docket work in the in-tray on my desk would just have to wait.

The dead woman turned out to be one of two wives of a farmer who owned one of the purchase area farms. She had two young children by and lived contentedly with her husband and his first wife who was some years older. The problem was that her husband had failed to pay the full bride price, or "lobola" that had been agreed with the dead woman's father at the time of the marriage a half-dozen or so years before. The dead woman's father had ordered her back home, along with her children, to be married off to a businessman from a township not far away. That was because the businessman was someone who was able to pay an agreed lobola sum, cash in hand, on the wedding day.

Not wishing to be parted from her happy family, hating the man she was being sold to and feeling unable to go against her father and the strength of tribal custom, she had cooked a meal for her family, seen everyone off to sleep the previous evening and gone quietly out into the nearby wooded area, with a length of twisted leather rope in her hands. She had climbed a mopani tree, tied the rope to a limb and around her neck and dropped from the branch.

When my constable and I reached the farmhouse, we found the dead woman's husband tied hand and foot, leaning back against the wall of the house and weeping copiously. Having found his second wife missing at dawn he had searched for her, found her dead and returned to the farmhouse to get a rope with which to go out and hang himself alongside his dead wife. His first wife had called on neighbours and friends to tie him up in order to stop him taking his own life and deepening the family tragedy. All that I could do was to listen sympathetically to the tragic story, treat the dead woman's remains with dignity and properly document the suicidal event. As we prepared to leave the farm, with a Sudden Death Book fully filled out, I asked, via my constable, what the farmer intended to do once I had left and he was released.

"I will hang myself," was the firm declaration duly translated into English for me. "His mind is twisted from grief." His first wife warned me. "He will do it."

I raised a silent eyebrow at my constable, who nodded firmly in response to my unspoken question. There was only one answer to that threatened second tragedy. I carted him off and detained him at the police station for the week that it took to arrange a post-mortem, complete the paperwork and release the body for burial. In such cases, some Members-in-Charge permitted investigating officers to return bodies to their home locations, others refused to do so in order to save mileage. Bernard Cavey was one of the humane ones. He fully supported my preventive detention of the farmer and the return of that man's dead wife's body to the farm. By then, one of his adult sons, from his first marriage, had arrived on the farm. That man worked on the mines near Johannesburg. He also spoke good English so that he and I were able to converse directly. After a conversation with his father, he advised me that his father's mind was no longer twisted. He would bury his second wife with love and with sorrow, but he would not harm himself afterwards. That was because he could now see that it was his duty to raise their two children safely to adulthood, so that he would now do.

When I prepared to drive away in the police vehicle and shook hands all round, the farmer handed me a dozen hen's eggs in thanks for having prevented him from hanging himself in the immediate aftermath of his second wife's suicide. Police rules dictated that I should decline them. In tribal custom it would have been an insult to do so. I have always believed that rules are for the guidance of wise people and the blind obedience of fools, so tribal custom won and the constable working with me went off to his quarters later in the day with the eggs in his hands and a smile on his face.

Having had a somewhat lively week as duty patrol officer, I was looking forward to my weekend off, but I was caught completely on the hop when my boss called me in and said, "With the kind of week you have just collected, I want you off station for the next couple of days. Got it?"

"I've still not got a car yet, Sir," I protested, "and I really don't have anywhere to go to."

My boss gave an almost evil grin. "Oh yes you do," he declared. "There's an inter-services shoot at Gwelo this weekend. One of the annual biggies. The range officer could do with an assistant and you're it. Since that will be an official duty, you can take the station motorcycle to get there. Report to Gwelo Central. They have a spare room in the mess that you can doss down in. You can leave there when the competition is finished on Sunday afternoon."

"You never know," he added as an afterthought, "if one of the police teams is short of a member, you might even get to join it."

I never did discover what strings my crafty boss had pulled to get me off station and into a bit of competitive socializing, but I was not too surprised to discover, when I reached Gwelo, that there was indeed a vacancy for me to step into. Despite using a borrowed .303 that I had little time to zero and get used to, I was not the lowest scorer in the Gwelo Rural Team that I became part of for that enjoyable and relaxing weekend away.

The ranchers in the area around Mashaba were careful to protect and encourage the wildlife on their property, or wild animals passing through on the hunt for best pastures to graze upon. The wildlife faced continual depredation from both African and European poachers. I had no time for the poachers of any colour who set snares and left cattle and wildlife to die slowly and painfully. Not much less either for the Europeans, from towns and mines, who could have obtained licences and permits legitimately, but who chose to hunt illegally and often by torchlight at night. They were indiscriminate in what they killed, both in type and quantity, often returning in a short while to where they had had success.

One such episode began with the inevitable telephone call to the station, made by a local rancher. "Mac" McLeod was getting on somewhat in years but was still fit and active. He was often referred to as "Mad Mac" by other Europeans in the area. However, as I discovered, all of his mental marbles were still rolling in the right direction. Mac, so I learned, had been a District Commissioner in the days between the wars. He had two families. The first by his European wife, who had died a few years earlier and the second by a Matabele woman, who, as Mac told me, quite proudly, was of "Esanzi Ndebele" stock, meaning "Of the Royal House of the Matabele Tribe." Both families existed quite amicably on the same ranch, which Mac maintained very well, compared to one or two of his neighbours whose ranches I visited for one reason or another during my time at Mashaba.

Mac's second family had heard a gunshot in the middle of the night. A look around early after dawn had located traces of footprints and indications of a steinbok, a small antelope, having been killed. The report arrived during one of my duty weeks, so off I went, on the station's motorcycle, with a constable on the pillion seat, to investigate the case.

Mac McLeod and one of his African employees guided us to the scene.

"Not a lot you can do, perhaps, but I felt I had to report it because this is the third time this month," Mac advised. "The first time it was a warthog, the second a duiker. That size of animal suggests it's somebody shooting for the family pot, not for biltong or to sell on. The rains this past year have not been too good and the crops have suffered. There's a lot of hunger about."

That was all too true. The trees were limp leafed, the grass was sparse and browning and the soil itself was dry and dusty. I made a few basic notes, took a photo of the bloodstain and took a good look at the spoor left by the poachers.

Constable Mzvondiwa, who was with me that day, took one look at the tracks. "Two of them, Ishe. Both wearing tyre-tread sandals," he observed.

And that's where they rested the firearm," I suggested, pointing to the impression of a firearm butt-plate at the base of a small scrubby tree. "A firearm and tyre-tread sandals suggests a couple of individuals from the Purchase Area, surely?"

Const. Mzvondiwa and Mac both nodded their agreement. "Can I leave you to it?" Mac asked. "I've got quite a lot to do around the ranch. I'll leave my two lads to help you."

As Mac drove off, the four of us began to scour the area around the scene.

I probably had just a little more tracking skill than the average BSAP member who was straight out of a town or UK lifestyle. I had been well tutored by both black and white game rangers in Nyasaland and my eyesight was sharp. I noticed a blemish on the sole of one of the two sets of sandals. It was easy to pick it up in the dry dusty surface. When I pointed it out to my three companions they all agreed. Between the four of us we located the direction of movement of the two poachers and set off to follow their spoor. It was less than a half mile to the boundary of the ranch. There we located the point at which the poachers had entered Mr McLeod's land. On the other side of the barbed wire fence there was a well-used dirt track, wide enough for a Land Rover or a scotch-cart, the animal drawn two-wheeled cart commonly used by Africans. There the ground evidence told us that the poachers had left two cycles, which they had boarded and ridden away on, in the general direction of Chilimanzi African Purchase Area, a dozen or more miles away to the north.

It was still early in the morning. The dirt track through the ranching area did not seem to have been disturbed or used much yet that day. "Let's see how far we can get," I suggested. The others agreed, although it was more in hope than expectation that we set out to follow the tyre marks of the two cycles. Perhaps, as a reward for hard work and determination, luck was with us that day, or maybe it was that luck had deserted the poachers.

A half-mile or so along the track, the tyre mark of one of the cycles grew broader than it had been. "It is puncturing," Mzvondiwa remarked. Shortly after that we traced where the pair had stopped and got off from their cycles. The scarred sandal showed up well. Immediately thereafter the broad tyre mark narrowed again. The tyre had obviously been pumped up hard again. That mishap for the poachers gave us a chance, so we pushed on, finding more places where the two had had to dismount and re-inflate the defective tyre.

Eventually, some three hours later, we reached the homestead area of one of the Purchase Area farms. The farm itself was neat and tidy, with a set of traditionally built round huts set back not far from the track that we had been following. A dozen assorted fruit trees, orange, lemon and mango formed a small orchard. Close to the huts the skin of a small buck was pegged out to dry and cure in the sunlight. The members of the farming family were seated in a circle around an open fire. Resting on the traditional three stones of the fireplace was a three-legged iron pot containing the cooked meat from the poached steinbok. Until our unexpected appearance interrupted them, the family had been enjoying a meal of sadza, cooked maize meal, with the cut up and stewed meat from the steinbok as the relish to go with it.

The two poachers, who turned out to be the farm owner and his brother, both sitting barefoot by the fire, were highly surprised by our appearance, especially the appearance of a "murungu" a white man, on foot. They wanted to know how we had been able to follow them, so we explained the defective tyre and the distinctive mark in the sole of the one pair of tyre-tread sandals.

There was no ill-will during the investigation there. We collected the pegged out raw skin of the buck, located the two pairs of sandals, the bicycles, the lawfully held single-barrelled twelve bore shotgun that had been used and removed the cooking pot, which was still half full of meat, from the fire. Warned and cautioned statements and a photograph that linked skin, fireplace and huts in one shot, were all that we needed. If ever poachers had been caught red-handed, they had been. In answer to the question why they had gone poaching, the reply was a simple phrase, "Nyara, Ishe!" meaning hunger. Not so much a lack of maize meal, for the farm store was full, but a lack of fish, meat or even beans, to act as relish to go with the bulk of the sadza.

The shotgun became an exhibit, also the cooking pot and meat. To carry that item, we slung it on a pole so that two people at a time could share the load. Since I had no radio with me, it was just a matter of gathering the evidence, formally arresting the accused persons and setting off to walk back the way we had come. It was late in the afternoon before we reached Mac McLeod's ranch, from where we were able to telephone for a vehicle to collect the accused persons and the exhibits. Mac McLeod's surprise at our success was as evident as had been that of the accused persons themselves.

Back at the station I eventually got to catch up on replacing the quantity of liquid that I had sweated out over about eighteen miles of walking to catch the poachers. It was quite a lot.

When the case came to court, the two accused persons pleaded guilty. When asked by Mr Stainer if they had anything to say in mitigation of sentence, their only complaint was that Const. Mzvondiwa and the two farm workers had eaten almost all of the cooked meat in the pot, on the way back to the ranch, yet none had been offered to them.

"I should think not," was the magistrate's straight-faced reply, "such an action could have been construed by this court as an improper inducement to you to plead guilty."

He promptly sentenced them both to three months' imprisonment with hard labour.

If luck had been the reason for success in that particular case of poaching, it was a detailed tip-off that led to the arrest and imprisonment of one of the Gaths Mine European employees, who, so it turned out, had also been poaching. The informant, a European shift-worker on Gaths Mine, was put through to Member-in-Charge. On completion of his conversation with the miner, Insp. Cavey briefed Pete Nicholls, Pete Wilson and myself on what he had been told. Basically, it was that the informant lived next door to the house of one of the European shift bosses, who was, apart from reputedly being thoroughly disliked by those he was in charge of, both black and white, a known and regular night-time poacher. The story went that the shift boss drove out quite frequently, accompanied by one or other of his household servants, to do some poaching. On the clarity of the information provided by the informant, who had willingly identified himself, we were able to obtain a search warrant. Backed by the authority of that document, Pete Wilson and I carried out a search of the home of the suspect. Our search turned up over two hundredweight of biltong, dried venison, in sacks in the garage. In the fridge and deep freeze inside the house we found the hearts of fourteen antelope, from duiker to eland.

Despite our finding of that quantity of meat, the accused miner refused to give any accounting for it being in his possession. "Given by friends. Some of it a long time ago," was the only thing he was willing to say. His wife was equally obdurate. The case was going nowhere other than a technical offence or two under the Wildlife Act, until we spoke at length with the two household servants employed by our suspect and his family. Oh boy, did they spill the beans. It was a lesson in human relationships. If you bully your shift staff, pay your domestic employees peanuts, knock them around, shout at them and call them "Kaffirs" all the time, you must expect that some resentment will set in. It also suggested that if you are going to take your servants out on illicit activities, you need to make sure they are so well rewarded that they will not wish to see that munificence come to a halt.

With the detailed evidence provided by his domestic employees and the material evidence we two police officers had found, convictions of poaching were achieved. That hunger for cheap game meat cost the fellow his job, two family heirloom rifles, his Land Rover and a year in jail, because it turned out that he had a previous conviction, for poaching.

A few days after that, there came an early morning call from Gaths Mine. A murder had occurred overnight in the African Quarters for single men. As murder cases went, it was simple to sort out, being almost a replica of the murder case I had dealt with previously. The African Male Adult who was the accused, had been in the mine beer hall the previous evening. There he had arranged with one of the local Mahouris that, for the going rate, she would spend the night with him at his quarters. After a lengthy bout of vigorous sexual activity, she had demanded more than the agreed payment because of the length and vigour of their encounter. Arguments led to a screaming session from the Mahouri, shouting that she had been raped. When she would not stop her shouting and screaming, the accused pulled a knife from under his sleeping mat on the floor of the room and, with just one stroke, slit her throat. That act had turned the sleeping mat and the floor into a literal bloodbath. Having silenced her, the accused went to sleep beside the dead woman and then reported what had occurred to the mine police the next morning.

I duly recorded a somewhat lengthy Warned and Cautioned Statement, in which the accused freely explained the entire series of events, took photographs, backed by measurements of the room and eventually saw the case through to High Court.

While that case was being progressed and just a few days after the poaching case against the mine shift boss cropped up, I encountered another side of police activity. Insp. Cavey called me into his office one afternoon. Unusually, he instructed me to close the door behind me before motioning me to a chair. Without beating about the bush, my boss proceeded to deliver an operational briefing. "Special Branch details will be arriving on station after dark. There's an active ZANU recruitment cell at Gaths Mine that needs sorting out. The ringleader is known. He's got to be arrested, quietly if possible, so it's got to be a night-time job. Mac McGuiness and his companion will need a guide. That has to be someone who can handle a handgun safely and keep a cool head if anything develops. The quarters of the wanted man just happen to be right next door to the scene of that murder case you recently dealt with. Mac will confirm the location when he briefs you. You can guide them there and provide support if any ruckus starts, which we hope it won't. We need that organiser and every shred of paperwork in his quarters. Questions?"

"I thought membership of the Zimbabwe African National Union (ZANU) was lawful, so why is he wanted for recruiting members?"

Insp. Cavey smiled without a trace of humour. "This one is recruiting for external terrorist training. Tanzania and beyond. They've been at it for a couple of years or more now. Just how many have gone and just when they are likely to start coming back are pieces of information we're still trying to find out. That's what this evening's effort is all about. There's also some evidence of Two-Book activity. He reached into a drawer in his desk and handed me a holstered handgun. "Shoulder holster and a P39, not a 38 revolver. It's on safe and the chamber is empty. There are two magazines with it and they're both fully loaded. Get familiar with it if you need to but keep it out of sight. Mac and one of his African details will meet you outside the charge office at 01:00hrs. Full uniform for you, but you'll use their transport, not ours; Meanwhile, not a word to anyone about this conversation, that handgun, or what you are going to be doing tonight. Got it?"

"Yes Sir," I replied dutifully. I tucked the weapon and holster into my belt, pulled the grey jersey I was wearing well down to cover it and left the office. Feeling like a cross between Dick Barton and Sherlock Holmes I made my way as nonchalantly as I could to my bedroom. Once there I checked out the P39 automatic handgun. As my boss had said, it was on safe and empty. Both magazine clips were fully loaded with 9mm cartridges. I buried the handgun out of sight in my bedclothes and returned to the working offices.

The mess was quiet and in darkness when I left it and walked, box-torch in hand, across to the charge office, feeling the unfamiliar burden of the P39 under my armpit as I did so. For the record, I booked out "On road patrol round the village." Right on time a Ford Zephyr saloon car drew to a halt in front of the police station. Inspector McGuiness as he then was, in civilian attire, climbed out of the car as I walked towards it. After we exchanged handshakes and names, Mac asked one question. "Are you armed?" At my affirmative nod and a tap with my right hand under my left armpit, Mac said, "Good." He ushered me into the back of the car. Sitting in the front passenger seat was an African also in civvies. "Patrol Officer Woolley, meet Manufu." Mac paused long enough for Manufu and I to shake hands, then continued, "It's not his real name, but it will do for tonight. He knows that man we're after. There may be others with him in the quarters he occupies and there may be weapons there too. On that point we're not sure, so we go in weapons in hand and ready for any eventuality, but we do it quietly. That okay with you?" At my nod of assent, he went on, quite conversationally, "Ever shot anyone yet?"

"In riots in Nyasaland, Sir, yes."

"Okay, because being hesitant or squeamish in this kind of operation can get us all killed when we are faced with people with weapons in their hands and a willingness to use them, which these people all have, in spades. If you're ready, let's get on with it."

The drive to the edge of Gaths Mine high density residential area, or African quarters as they were usually known, took us just a few minutes. We parked the car well short of the start of the buildings and walked in on foot. In any tribal area village setting, or in the European quarters, a quiet approach would have been impossible, because of the presence of dogs. In the high-density area, dogs were not allowed to be kept, so no barking warned anyone of our presence. Between shift-changes, in the middle of the night, long after even the beer hall had shut, very few mine employees were expected to be about. Without difficulty, or even being noticed, I was able to guide my two companions to the house number that was of interest. I had wondered just how we were going to deal, quietly, with a door that would probably be locked from the inside. I need not have worried. When we reached the door we wanted, Manufu delved inside his bomber jacket and produced what was obviously a professional's set of picklocks. The house was in darkness and the street empty in the chill of the cold season night as Manufu set to work. As he worked, Mac produced a snub-nosed revolver and a shaded torch from his jacket pockets. With practised ease he screwed a silencer on to the revolver. The quiet click as he drew back the hammer of his handgun sounded loud to my nervous ears. I reached inside my issue raincoat and uniform tunic and hauled out my P39. I had already loaded it, set a round in the chamber and placed the safety catch on, before leaving my room. All I needed to do was ease off the safety catch, making that preparatory action clear to Mac.

In seconds that seemed like minutes, Manufu's work on the lock was done. I heard no clicks or rotating of tumblers but when he turned the handle and gently pushed, the door moved silently open an inch or so. At that point Manufu stepped back to allow Mac to ease the door open wide enough for he and I to step cautiously into the darkness within.

The single curtainless window allowed in some illumination from a nearby streetlight. That enabled us to avoid falling over the table, chairs and assorted boxes within the room, without any need for Mac's dimmed torch to be used. It was also quite clear that, fortunately, nobody was sleeping in that room. On tip-toes Mac and I sidled across the room to the bedroom door. As we moved that far, Manufu entered the room behind us and pushed the door into an almost-closed position. It was then that I noticed that he had a scarf pulled up to cover all but his eyes. Helpfully, the second door was half-open. From within we could hear rhythmic breathing that told of a sleeping person. Silently, weapon at the ready, Mac turned on his dimmed torch and sidled into the bedroom, with me close behind. Conveniently, the man in the simple iron-framed bed was alone and sleeping on his back under a few blankets, his head on a couple of pillows. "Hold my torch," Mac whispered, handing the dimmed light over to me. With a speed and precision that spoke wordlessly of much practice, Mac flowed silently over the few feet across the room. His left hand clamped tightly down over his target's mouth while his right hand drove the tip of the silencer on the barrel of his pistol into the man's neck under his left ear. As the man's eyes opened wide, he tried to sit up. But Mac's weight and strength were sufficient to force him back down, "Police. Make a noise or move a hand and you're dead!" he hissed, "Understand?" Without any instruction, Manufu hissed a few words in Chishona, appearing to repeat what Mac had said. To reinforce what the others had said I carefully let my P39, aimed straight between his eyes, be seen by the man on the bed.

After a moment or so of tension, the African male adult on the bed appeared to relax. "Sit up," Mac ordered, "but keep your hands where I can see them." Mac's hand still remained firmly over the man's mouth and the gun-barrel firmly under his ear, until his order was obeyed. Despite the dim light, I clearly saw Mac raise an eyebrow at Manufu and jerk his head in the direction of the man on the bed. Manufu nodded twice. We had the man we wanted.

"Check what's under the pillows," Mac instructed Manufu, who promptly did as he had been told by pulling both pillows from the bed. The thud as something heavy that had been between them hit the floor was followed by his exclamation of, "Ah!" as he bent and came up with a handgun in his grasp.

"Make sure that thing's safe," Mac instructed me. I handed both torches to Manufu, holstered my P39 and inspected the weapon that had been between the pillows. Interestingly, it was a Colt .45 Automatic. My quick check of it showed it to have a cartridge in the chamber, a full clip of ammunition in place, the hammer back and, somewhat alarmingly a safety catch that was set in the ready to fire position. I carefully let down the hammer, cleared the breach, removed the clip, made it safe and put it into my raincoat pocket. With that done, I pulled out my P39 once more and directed it again at the man on the bed.

At that point Mac removed his hand from the man's mouth, but not the gun from under his ear. "Swing your legs out and get your feet on the floor," he commanded. "Do it slowly and carefully." In obeying that instruction the man revealed that he had been sleeping wearing a pair of trousers but nothing more.

As the rudely wakened man set his feet on the floor, Mac pulled his gun back from the man's neck and stepped back. "While you get dressed, my friend," he said quietly, "our uniformed officer here will read you your rights in relation to your possession of the illegal firearm that was under your pillow."

Within a couple of minutes, the alleged recruiter of terrorists was formally under arrest and in handcuffs on a charge of being in possession of an unlicensed firearm.

When I invited him to make a reply to the formal Warn and Caution words, he just spat on the floor at my feet.

Under Mac's instructions I returned to the car and drove it, quietly and using sidelights only, as close as I could get it to the target house. Quickly and silently, Manufu and Mac bundled the arrested man into the back seat of the Zephyr. While I kept an eye – and a gun – on the arrested man, my two companions began to load books and boxes of paper gathered from the house into the boot of the Zephyr. When that task was completed, I slid across the bench seat to the passenger side to let Mac get back behind the wheel. Manufu joined the arrested man in the back of the car and we drove off.

On the way back to Mashaba Police station I extracted the .45 automatic from my raincoat and, under Mac's instruction, put it into the car's glove compartment. Outside the police station Mac stopped the car briefly to let me out. "Thanks for your company," he said as we shook hands. "I may see you again sometime." In that, he proved prophetic.

Officially, my road patrol around the village finished at 01:57hrs. Later in the morning I discreetly returned the P39 and shoulder holster to Insp. Cavey and briefed him on the road patrol. At the end of the story my boss tucked the handgun away in the drawer it had come from and looked directly at me. "For the record, your road patrol was uneventful, if anyone asks." Nobody ever did and I never did learn who he was or what became of the African with the automatic pistol under his pillow.

One of the problems for the mine managements was the habit of their employees to crowd unauthorised guests into their rather small living accommodation. With the blessing of the assorted mine managers, the police station's staff, usually supported by European police reservists and Mine Compound Police, carried out occasional raids. My first involvement in one such activity occurred on the 16th of June 1965. After a briefing by i/c station, I found myself in charge of Ian Marks and Gerry Jerome, two reservists, along with the station's entire muster of African police. Thus it was that at 9:00 p.m. that evening the score of us crammed ourselves into three Land Rovers and set off to carry out what were supposed to be surprise raids for trespassers lodging within the African staff compounds at both Kilmarnock and Temeraire mines. We started at Kilmarnock mine, driving in and parking on sidelights only and as quietly as we could. Somewhat worryingly, what we encountered suggested that we had been expected. The whole compound of over two hundred buildings was eerily quiet and lacking any pedestrian movement. Our sweep through the compound took us just under an hour to complete. At the end of the hour we had found not one single trespasser, which fitted in with a piece of information quietly whispered to one of our African constables by a family relative within one of the huts that word of our impending raid has been circulating earlier in the day, resulting in any trespassers moving out for the night, or at least as long as we might be there.

It was hard to see how word of our intended visit might have leaked out to the mine workers from our side, as our earlier warnings to staff and reservists had been that we intended to carry out night-time traffic checks, which we did, on occasions actually do. It was of course possible that the leak had come from the mine management side, as we were required to liaise with mine management in arranging the raids.

Somewhat deflated, we moved on to Temeraire Mine compound, where we fared only slightly better, by locating just two trespassers asleep in accommodation in the compound. Back at Mashaba Police Station, the two trespassers were booked into the cells for rest of the night and the entire team stood down, recorded as off duty at 11:33 p.m.

Four days later, at 07:50hrs, Ian Hulley, manager of DSO mine, telephoned in a report that an infant child of one of their married African employees had just died at the mine clinic. Given that this was an unexplained death, it caused me to record the opening of Sudden Death Docket 12 of 1965. Armed with one of our Sudden Death Record booklets, with its several pages for recording the essentials of such occurrences and in company of

Const. Musekwa, I drove the few miles to the DSO mine clinic in order to formally record the circumstances of the death, the formal identification to me of the deceased child and to convey the small body to the Gaths Mine Hospital, where the mine's very able and helpful Dr Bradley would carry out a post-mortem examination as soon as convenient. The grief of both the mother and father was real and deep. They took just a little persuading before they were willing to let me place the small lifeless figure into the body-box on the floor at the rear of the police Land Rover. Their story was simple. The child, their first and only one, had taken ill two days before. Thinking it was nothing but a cold, they had not really treated it, until this morning, when they realised its condition was serious, so brought it to the clinic, where it had died in the presence of the medical orderly there. There were no suspicious circumstances, but a formal cause of death had to be ascertained before the body could be released for burial.

At midday on the 20th June a VHF radio message arrived from Shabani Police Station, which was located about 30 miles west of Mashaba. The message was that they had received a complaint of rape, had investigated it, located the accused and witnesses and then realised that the offence had occurred a mile or so inside Mashaba Police Station's area of responsibility, so would Mashaba Police Station staff kindly deal with it. A quick word with Insp. Cavey resulted in me then briefing the very reliable Const. Musekwa to be ready to travel the following day by bus to Shabani and then escort prisoner, complainant and witnesses back to Mashaba for full investigation and documentation.

At 09:00hrs on the 21st June, shortly after I had seen Const. Musekwa safely on to a Matambanadzo Bus to Shabani, Dr Bradley phoned to advise that he had carried out the necessary post-mortem examination on the dead infant and was able to certify the cause of death as Bronchial Pneumonia.

At 10:00hrs that day, two detective constables from Fort Victoria arrived in Mashaba to investigate their station's Crime Reports 1 and 14/6/65, which were allegations of peddling political party membership cards, under the illegal "Two Book" system. That system, a particular offence under the Law & Order Maintenance Act, worked by recording the names of those who paid-up and joined, within the pages of the "Good Book", while those who initially declined were then threatened with having their names written down in the "Bad Book" and told that they "would be remembered when independence came." The two plain clothes details arrived in their own transport and once they had made their presence and purpose known to member-in-charge, they simply went about their own business. By noon, the two detectives were back on station, having arrested a Gaths Mine employee by the name of Francis Makombe. They had apparently searched his quarters at the mine compound but found nothing incriminating. However, they wanted him detained temporarily to enable further inquiries to be carried out. A routine search of Francis Makombe's clothing, prior to his detention in the cells, disclosed nothing untoward, but, somewhat curiously, his possession of three unexpected coins. Two were current Belgian coins of 20 Franc value, but it was the third one that really drew my attention. It was a British half-sovereign, gold of course and in almost mint condition. When questioned about it Makombe simply shrugged and said that he had won the coins when gambling in Fort Victoria a few days before. When I explained the origins of the gold coin to him and offered him its face value of ten shillings in exchange for it, he firmly declined the offer.

The rest of that day passed routinely as did the following morning, however, during lunch in the mess the next day, Shorty whispered to me that there was a man who wished to talk to me. He was waiting at the bottom of the mess' garden. With that intriguing message in my mind I did my best not to rush my meal. When it was right to do so, I left the table and made my deliberately unhurried way to the far end of the mess garden.

There I found a male adult African, busy weeding and tidying the garden as if he were a mess employee. Without breaking from the weeding work which he was doing, he greeted me in Chinyanja, to which I responded appropriately and then asked why he wished to speak with me. In good English he explained. "My brother is Thousand Kabinda, Bwana. He says you are a good Majoni and can be trusted."

The mention of a name from some two years back, during my time as second-in-charge of Dedza Police Station in the Angoni Highlands of Nyasaland was a bit of a surprise. It had to do with an appalling injustice and false imprisonment handed out by the Malawi Congress Party officials in the area. When the District Commissioner declined to attempt to put matters right, for fear of repercussions from the MCP, I carried out a Lone Ranger style armed raid on the MCP offices, released Thousand Kabinda, who had been kept locked up in a storeroom for more than three weeks and sent him safely on his way out of the area. My action thoroughly displeased the MCP, which resulted in a very rapid transfer.

My unexpected informant went on to tell me that Makombe, a heavy vehicle driver for Shannon Transport Company and one of the teachers on the Gaths Mine School, were all involved in the selling, under threats if refused, of Zimbabwe African National Union membership cards. According to him, the sellers were allowed to keep a cut of the take for their rewards. He also alleged that Makombe and others had been trying to recruit mine workers to go abroad for training as Freedom Fighters. The three did not keep the political party literature, membership cards or the cash in their mine quarters but hidden safely in the bush outside of the mine, or in a house in Mashaba village, which he identified for me. He further advised me that while waiting for me, he had seen a known local witch doctor surreptitiously breaking an egg on the front garden wall of the police station as part of a spell to guarantee Makombe's swift release from custody.

My unexpected informant advised me that he would try to keep me informed of happenings on the mine. I quietly thanked the fellow and walked casually away to the garden in front of the police station office block. Just where my informant had indicated, there was a freshly broken hen's eggshell sitting amid the flowers.

That afternoon, after a conversation with i/c station, I provided a full account of what had come to me from my informant to the two detectives. The information resulted in a search of the house in Mashaba village, where they discovered precisely what my informant had indicated. As a result, Francis Makombe was transferred to Fort Victoria for further interrogation. Somewhat to my surprise, a few days later he was released and returned to Mashaba.

Late on the afternoon of that day Const. Musekwa arrived back on station with the villagers he had escorted from Shabani. Fortunately for me, that case ended up with Barry Lane. That allowed me to call on Const. Musekwa to join me for the short journey to collect the dead child's body and the Death Certificate from the hospital at Gaths Mine and drive the few miles to DSO mine. There we handed the dead child's mortal remains over to its grieving parents before returning to the police station, where I was able to complete SDD 12 of 1965 and submit it for closure.

The next couple of days were quiet ones, during which I had several about what was going to be done with the score or more of trespassers now in the cells. The standard fine for those caught lodging without permission in the mine compounds was a £2 deposit fine. One or two of those in the cells had that much money with them. Others did not.

It took Insp. Cavey a few telephone calls here and there and a lengthy conversation or two, but in the end, it was decided that as every single one of our collection of trespassers was either a hawker of one thing or another, or else a genuine relative of a mine employee and all of them were there with the knowledge of the compound police who had been paid either by the hawkers or others to turn a blind eye, it would be a bit draconian to charge them with criminal trespass. In the end, after 48 hours in our cells, we carted all of them back to Gaths Mine and handed them over to the mine management, who were far more interested in finding out which of their compound police had been taking back-handers than in criminalizing the basically harmless trespassers. With that somewhat unusual decision made, we explained to them that they would not be going before the magistrate and eventually handed them over to the mine staff for whatever processing was appropriate within the mine rules. Barry Lane and I were climbing into our vehicle when the English-speaking herbalist walked over to us. "Thank you Majonis for being our friends. We Africans do not forget our friends." As he walked away, Barry turned to me and remarked, "That will put a smile on the boss's face when we tell him." Indeed, it did!

On the 25th of June a report came in of three sudden deaths. Villagers had found a mother and infant battered to death and the husband hanging by his neck from a nearby tree. With Sudden Death Booklets numbered 13 and 14 of 1965 on my clipboard and Const. Chilowa as my interpreter, I set off to the scene, not too many miles distant. The dead woman and her infant child were laying on a simple iron bed in a sleeping hut. The heads of both were battered out of recognition which explained the huge pool of congealed blood, swarming with flies, which was on the floor under the bed. That the murder weapon appeared to have been a small three-legged cast-iron cooking pot laying against the wall of the hut was evidenced by the fact that one of the three iron legs of the pot had broken off during the killing and was there to be seen, embedded deep in the woman's skull. Mercifully, both the mother and her infant appeared to have been asleep when they were killed.

Relatives of the deceased woman and infant helped me remove the entire roof of the hut so that there was enough light within for me to take photos for the record. Barely thirty yards distant, at the edge of the cluster of huts there was a mature tree. Clearly visible from the doorway of the sleeping hut with the two bodies within, I could see the body of an adult male African hanging by the neck from a branch some twenty or so feet above ground level. A trail of blood-stained footprints led from the sleeping hut to the base of the tree. Once more I used my camera to record the body hanging in the tree. It did not take long to learn the story behind the triple tragedy I was investigating and recording. The dead man had failed to make good on the lobola payments he had promised his wife's father when he asked for her to become his wife. Very recently, the father had called his daughter back as he had another man for her to be married to. One who had the ability to pay a respectable sum in lobola, right then and there.

Rather than face the loss of his wife and child, the husband had clearly killed them both and then hanged himself. It was a story I had sadly encountered before and would hear all too many times again in years to come. Once I had recorded all that was necessary, noted down the formal identifications of the three deceased persons and taken sufficient photographs to back up the written record, I positioned the Land Rover directly below the hanging figure and climbed up to the branch from which the dead man was hanging. Once I had secured a loop of rawhide rope under the armpits of the dead man and taken a hitch around the branch I was sitting on, I was able to first cut the rope which had asphyxiated the dead man and then lower his body to the roof of the Land Rover. After that, it was a matter of lowering the body into the hands of his relatives, who placed it with great care into one of the two body-boxes within the Land Rover. A few minutes later, the villagers placed the bodies of the dead woman and her infant into the second body-box. Next to them in the body-box I placed the bloodstained cooking pot, for the visual benefit of whichever doctor might end up carrying out the post-mortem examinations.

Before I left the scene, through Const. Chilowa, I recorded brief but adequate statements to cover what would have to be the opening of a murder case to cover the deaths of the mother and child. I thanked the villagers for their assistance and expressed my sorrow at the deaths of their three relatives. At that, the village headman sought an assurance that the bodies would be returned for local burial, together in a single grave which they would prepare. It was an assurance which I was happy to provide for him.

Back at Mashaba Police Station I explained to SO Nicholls and Insp. Cavey what I and Const. Chilowa had discovered at the scene of the deaths. In view of the murder aspect, the following morning I drove the dead bodies to Fort Victoria Hospital, where Dr Ascough listened carefully to the outline I provided and agreed that visual post-mortem examinations would be sufficient. The visual aspect extended just a little to the extraction and handing to me of the broken-off leg of the cooking pot from the woman's battered and miss-shaped head. With all of the essential paperwork attended to, I was able to drive straight from the hospital to the village where the triple tragedy had occurred. There I was able to return the three dead bodies to the care of their relatives, to be prepared for burial, just as they had briefly lived, together.

Like a number of other district police stations, Mashaba had a small prison nearby. It was kept supplied, from the far larger prison in Fort Victoria, with short-term prisoners, or those within a few weeks of discharge from longer sentences. Mostly "the Bandits" as they were usually referred to, were male adult Africans who had been convicted of Statutory Offences such as failing to dig contour ridges or failing to carry their identification documents. They were well fed and cared for and their work was usually lightweight, but publicly useful for the common good of the community, as directed by the District Commissioner. The working parties were always escorted by uniformed prison warders, armed with a single-barrelled Greener 12 Bore Shotgun. It was a common sight at the end of their working day to see the bandits climb aboard their Bedford flat-back and then for one or other of them to helpfully hold their warder's shotgun while that individual climbed aboard. It was not unknown for some of those prisoners, the ones who worked well, to find themselves taken on into the District Commissioners' paid workforce as uniformed messengers or such. On the 28th June 1965, it fell to me to drive to Fort Victoria Prison in order to collect several Bandits because the number at Mashaba Prison had fallen. Among them was one I had met previously. It turned out, he had been seeking work as a batman at Morris Deport some months before. Having failed in that effort, he returned to this home village in the Fort Victoria area, where he was hauled into court for failing to properly contour-ridge his field and sentenced to one month in prison.

The next few days passed routinely, but then the station received a request to carry out trespasser raids on the compounds at Gaths, Balmain and Temeraire Mines, at a time and date of our choosing and without assistance from the compound police at any of those locations. SO Nicholls had taken a spot of local leave to spend time with an Australian nurse who was working at the Gaths Mine Hospital, so I was handed the task of organising and supervising the raids. With Insp. Cavey's agreement, on the night of 3rd/4th July, at midnight, I called out for duty the entire station staff, except for a skeleton few who would man the station for the next day. Supported by a Field Reservist from each of the mines, but without the presence of any compound police, our team carried out checks at all three mine compounds, between 00:30hrs and 05:00hrs that night.

Our total tally was 44 individuals, but we also had another half-dozen flee from us once we started knocking on doors. That was something we had expected would occur, because of our limited number and the absence of a full cordon around any of the compounds. Oddly, contrary to what our first surprise raid had turned up, many of this collection had no legitimate reason for having been where we found them. Of the 44, by 09:00hrs that day 17 had paid Deposit Fines and 13 had been released after proving they did have some reasonable grounds for being there. Once again there were stories of mine compound police accepting cash in return for turning a blind eye. It took another 24 hours to get to the truth of the presence of the remaining 14 within the compound accommodations. Relatives or friends paid Deposit Fines for 12 of them. Two were found to be carrying fraudulent identification papers. Both proved to be wanted on neighbouring stations. At Insp. Cavey's behest it fell to me to brief the mine managers on the results of our raids, starting with the fact that their compound police employees were simply not doing their allotted job, which was something they were all by now well aware of.

Shortly after I was posted to Mashaba, the senior African detail on station, Sgt Madzima, retired. Out on a routine road patrol with me a few days later, one of the senior constables confided to me that he and others were happy to see the back of him because the Sgt did not treat people fairly. Apparently, he had his favourites, who were given all of the easy and pleasant work on the station, while others had a hard time of it. As a result of that conversation, I did some sifting through past duty rosters and did indeed find that there appeared to have been a decidedly uneven distribution of day shifts, night shifts and rural patrol work. I also had some conversations with Barry Lane and Ian Harries, who both agreed that Sgt Madzima had not been one of their favourite African details. With the Sgt gone on retirement, all I did was to mentally note that the constable had been telling the truth, feel relieved that Sgt Madzima was no longer a serving detail and leave it at that.

A couple of weeks after his first approach to me, Thousand Kabinda's brother had some more information for me. It was to the effect that Ex-Sgt Madzima, whose origins were local, had become a member of a closed group of adult male Africans who met, once or twice a month at various houses in Mashaba Township, to talk politics. There was a membership fee of £5 to join the group. My informant related that the group consisted of several school-teachers, a few clerks from the nearby mines and Francis Makombe.

I passed that information up the usual channels and expected that to be the last I heard of it. However, a couple of weeks later it was passed down to me, via Insp. Cavey, that CID Ft Victoria had attempted to have one of their informants join the group but that his application had been refused. Their request to me was to try to find someone who might be able to penetrate this apparently close-knit and secretive group. As a result, I used the agreed signal that I needed to speak with Thousand Kabinda's brother, which resulted in another conversation between us. At the suggestion that he might try to penetrate the group, he laughed and said simply, "I am Nyanja. They are all Chishona or Kalanga. They have refused to let even Ndebele people join them. That I know, but I will watch them for you!"

That promise from my informant produced results far quicker and far more spectacular than I expected. On the 8th July, at his request, he and I met again. The previous evening, he had followed Francis Makombe from one of the meetings, because he went into the meeting empty-handed but came out carrying a small wooden box which he hid behind some bushes alongside the main road into the Gaths Mine compound. His detailed description of the location enabled me to gather up that box under cover of an after-midnight road patrol, without an accompanying constable, at the end of the day. The box was large enough to hold an A4 paper in flat form and about six inches deep. It proved to contain a whole lot of ZANU PF propaganda literature in both English and Chishona, a supply of party membership cards and two notebooks with a list of names in them. Although not marked in any way, it was clear to me that one was the "Good Book" and the other was the very-much feared "Bad Book" used when canvassing for membership of ZANU PF. What was quite clear to me was that there were different handwritings in the notebooks, suggesting that it was not just one person who had been out and about "Two-Booking".

After catching up on a bit of sleep I once again reported my night-time escapade to Insp. Cavey, who promptly arranged for me to deliver the box and contents later that day to CID/SB in Fort Victoria, where I met for the first time with Det. Section Officer Ron Gardner, who agreed with me that my informant was a useful one and agreed that a £20 reward for his efforts so far would be appropriate. When I was able to hand that over a few days later, it certainly put a smile on my informant's face. DSO Gardner and I also agreed that we would love to be there, to see the expression on his face when Francis Makombe found the box had vanished.

It was about then, after I had been at Mashaba for some three months, that we received warning of the date of our formal Annual Inspection, to be carried out on 27th July, by our Officer Commanding Police District. That piece of information promptly sent the entire station into overdrive.

I was fully conversant with that particular annual event, from my Colonial Police days. Officer Commanding Victoria Police District was C/Supt Roy Briault, who was a good and fair officer according to everyone at Mashaba. That did not lessen the frantic dashing around throughout the couple of weeks before the inspection date. If it was immobile, it was whitewashed, painted or red polished. If it moved, it was drilled and paraded, us Europeans with our standard weaponry, the No. 4 Lee Enfield .303 rifle. Vehicles, both four and two-wheeled, were serviced, tarted-up and made as presentable as age and mileage allowed. In between, every station book, record and piece of paper was checked over and made proper.

While that added burden of spit and polish was being undertaken, routine policing went on as usual, resulting in me getting to investigate the stock-theft of a prize-winning Afrikander bull from Mr Rabe's "Rabevale" Ranch just north of Mashaba Village.

With Const. Masekwa, I set out on 8th July, to investigate that case. When I looked carefully around the last known location of the animal, which had been out in a field with other cattle overnight, I noticed an oddity in the hoof-prints of one. Mr Rabe confirmed that the missing bull had suffered a modest split in its front near-side hoof, for which it had been receiving treatment. I was certainly not a skilled tracker compared with the Bushmen and Game Rangers I had worked with in Nyasaland, but, as I have recorded in previous pages, they had taught me quite a bit about that activity, which had resulted in getting a positive result some weeks back, when investigating the poaching case on Mac Macleod's ranch. Given that success and what I was looking at on this occasion, I was prepared to give it a try, with complete support from Const. Musekwa who agreed that the damaged hoof was trackable. It took us a couple of hours of careful circling of the paddocks and boundary fences of the ranch, until we, accompanied by Mr Rabe's ranch foreman, were able to locate the tracks of the bull, along with the tracks of two individuals wearing the commonly worn tyre-tread sandals. An hour more of further careful tracking brought us within sight of a long-abandoned mine dug into the side of one of the hills some few miles from Rabevale Ranch. Mr Rabe's ranch foreman pointed to it and said, "Ma Texas!" At my puzzled look, he explained that the tunnel mouth we could see had once been the entrance to the Texas Mine, which had been an operating gold mine until a dozen years or so before when it shut due to a couple of episodes of rockfalls caused by the unstable geology of that particular area.

Closing quietly in on the mouth of the tunnel, it was clear that the beast's spoor and that of the two thieves, disappeared into it, but there was nothing to indicate that either the bull, or the thieves had come out. That posed a bit of a dilemma, since neither I, nor Const. Masekwa, or the ranch foreman was carrying any weaponry or even any method of defence if attacked. We also lacked any form of torchlight. There was also the possibility that there might be other exits to this abandoned tunnel. Armed only with two handfuls of tunnel dust, to throw into the face of any would-be assailant, I stepped warily into the tunnel, allowing my eyes to become accustomed to the dwindling light. My movements were clearly not silent enough, because from deeper within the tunnel there came a cry of "Ndiyani?" meaning "Who is it?" to which I replied loudly "Mapolisa!" At that there were sounds of movements fading into the distance, then silence. Reassured by that, I led on for a few more yards. There we found the still-warm carcass of the stolen bull, already skinned and partly butchered. Beside it were two axes and a large skinning knife which we promptly took possession of, grateful that they had not been wielded against us.

Const. Masekwa's calls for the thieves to give themselves up met with silence. With Masekwa and I each carrying an axe and the ranch foreman wielding the skinning knife we pushed further into the darkening tunnel. Some twenty or twenty-five yards further in we found the two stock thieves, who, fortunately gave themselves up without any resistance.

Back at Rabevale, Mr Rabe greeted us with a mixture of concern, surprise and pleasure. He swiftly arranged for the carcass and meat to be recovered so that the meat could be distributed as rations among his workforce and the skin handed to me as an exhibit for court purposes. Sensibly, the two accused eventually pleaded guilty to a charge of stocktheft, for which they were later, on 3rd August, jailed for the usual six months, which brought a satisfactory closure to Mashaba CR33/7/65. For clarity of understanding for readers who may not have a police background, a police station's monthly tally of offences dealt with via a fully investigated file of papers, which we called a Docket, was divided into two lists, depending upon whether the offence was a common law crime or an offence against one or other piece of Statutory Legislation. Common Law offences merited a CR entry, while Statutory Offences merited an SR entry. Minor matters, whether a Common Law Crime or a Statutory offence were often dealt with via Deposit Fines.

Seeing that I was a little bit busy with docket work of one kind or another, it was Barry Lane who went off to deal with a report on 17th July that a Mr Bower, an employee of Gaths Mine, had been apprehended by Mushandike Game Park Rangers, just after he had shot two kudu and one steinbok within the boundaries of the park. Along with Mr Bower they had detained a black man, Nelson Kassem, who had a house and small plot of land a mile or so outside Mashaba Village. That evening in the mess, Barry talked over his difficulty with that case. The two arrested men had been released pending further inquiries, because they both vehemently denied they had been poaching. Their story was that they had permission to hunt on land, owned by Suleman Kassem, brother to Nelson Kassem which land adjoined that of the National Park. While on that land, they had heard shots from within the National Park. Concerned that it might be poachers, they had driven in the direction of the gunfire and come across a half-dozen Africans, with some dogs. Allegedly, two of the group had been carrying shotguns and appeared to have just killed the two kudu and one steinbok. Bower claimed that he had put a warning round from his shotgun over the heads of the African poachers, who had then fled and taken themselves out of sight by the time two of the team of African game rangers at the park had arrived on the scene, come to all of the wrong conclusions and detained Bower and Kassem as poachers. Barry informed me that Suleman Kassem, who owned Shona Valley Farm and ran a store there had confirmed that he had allowed his brother and friend, Mr Bower, to hunt on his land, although he had warned them that there was a lack of fencing to demarcate the boundary between his land and that of the National Park and admonished them not to hunt over that ill-defined boundary.

Barry related that the two game rangers had been on foot patrol, had heard shots, gone to investigate and found Bower and Kassem close by the three dead animals and within sight of their Land Rover. All three animals had been killed by shotgun rounds and Bower had been holding a shotgun when first seen by the game rangers. They agreed that Bower and Kassem had told them the same story they related to Barry under Warn and Caution, but had not checked around to see if there was any spoor of people and dogs to corroborate what Kassem and Bower had claimed.

Barry's gut instinct was that Bower and Kassem were lying, but with insufficient evidence to rebut their story, they were going to get away with it. The following day, Barry and I and the two game rangers met up at the scene of that poaching case, intent on seeing if we could find any trace of the alleged group of African poachers and their dogs. An hour or more of scouting around turned up nothing, but with thick grass and bush rather than soil and the few game trails well-decorated with overnight movement of game large and small, that proved nothing. When we got back to Mashaba Police Station and discussed our findings with SO Nicholls and Insp. Cavey, the decision was made that there was insufficient evidence to take the two men before a magistrate, so the case was closed.

On the 22nd July I set out in the company of Const. Matsvira for a day patrol of the European Farming and Ranching Area. Visits to Grimstone Farm, Lochinvar Farm, Sans Souci Farm and Rabe Valley and Spring Spruit Ranches produced one common theme. Continual intrusions, mostly by night, of poachers who seemed to be European employees of the various mines in the area. Peter Crief, the owner of Lochinvar Farm, who was a keen conservationist, related that the previous Saturday night a stretch of his south-west boundary fence had been taken down and a Land Rover had been driven in. Whoever the occupants were, they had killed and carted away two kudu. One of his farmhands had heard the noise of an engine and had got there in time to see what he described as an old type grey Land Rover, with a box-body back and no cab being driven away with the carcass of two kudu in the back. That raised an interesting thought in my mind, as I had seen such a Land Rover parked at Temeraire Mine's main office block.

Another thought that struck me concerned the abandoned headgear to an experimental mine shaft which stood within Mr Rabe's ranch land, but close to the boundary with Lochinvar Farm. Rising better than a hundred feet to the winding wheel and top platform, I reckoned it would be a marvellous advantage-point from which to keep watch for any hunting lamp being used at night-time in that area. I put my thinking to Mr Rabe who gave me permission to use the headgear as a look-out point any time I wished to do so.

On the 24th July, I was visited once again by my regular informant. On this occasion he was not alone. With him was a very well-dressed male adult African who spoke excellent English. He explained that he was one of the clerks at Gaths Mine. He was known to, and friendly with, both Francis Makombe and ex-Sgt Madzima and was prepared to make an application to join the rather secretive group to which both belonged. From what the two related to me, the disappearance of the hidden box of political papers and canvassing books had been put down to pure misfortune. Requests had been made up-stream to ZANU PF connections in Fort Victoria for further supplies and another pair of canvassing books had been created. They also advised me that Solomon Pedzisayi, a well-known Nationalist who had recently been released from detention at Wha-Wha was back in Mashaba, where he was in contact with Francis Makombe. I thanked both, handed over the £5 membership fee for the secretive group and gave each another £5 for working with me.

My subsequent phone conversation with Ron Gardner in Fort Victoria, made from Insp. Cavey's office, brought forth the kindly caution from my boss that if I kept on coming up with all of this intelligence material, I could find myself seconded to Special Branch. Thankfully, that never happened.

For whatever reason, on the day, it was OC Province, Peter Sherren, who carried out the annual inspection, not OC District. Typical of the gentleman that he was, Mr Sherren arrived before time, but stopped his staff car well within sight at the bottom of the slope leading to the offices, until the clock told him it was right to arrive.

Fortunately, from start to finish, the day went well. He, being the renowned tennis player that he was, had caused us to carefully re-paint the white lines on the tennis court and make sure there were no unwanted holes in the net. What we could not hide was the fact that nobody ever used the tennis court. Shortly after I arrived on the police station I had made it clear that I did enjoy playing tennis. Nobody else did, so my tennis playing in spare moments was done at the Gaths Mine Recreation Club, where I was made very welcome. In his look around the station area Mr Sherren observed and commented unfavourably on the uneven and unplayable state of the tennis court. On discovering that I was a tennis player he suggested that I should get into Fort Victoria for the weekend, because the elimination process for attendance at the Police Annual Championships in Salisbury were due to take place then.

I duly attended and got involved in the selection process. Playing singles, I was soon eliminated from the contest, but, by pure chance, Det. Section Officer Gardner from Fort Victoria Central CID and I teamed up together in the doubles contest and did rather better. The final elimination match put Mr Sherren and his long-standing partner, which pair had represented the Province for the past three years and won the Salisbury tournament twice, up against us two. When Ron Gardner and I duly won the match, which was a hard-fought one, we fully expected to be asked to represent the Province at the main competition. That did not happen. We later discovered through discreet inquiries that OC Province had advised Salisbury that there would be no doubles representatives from the Province that year due to there being no pair available who were up to the required standard.

With Annual Inspection safely behind us, I decided it was time to try out Mr Rabe's night-time vantage point. With Insp. Cavey's approval and backing, I scrounged the use of two TR28 SSB radio backpacks from radio branch in Fort Victoria. Pete Wilson and I spun a coin to see who would act as the spotter on the mine headgear and who would drive the police vehicle ready to be directed on to any poachers whose night-lamps showed up. I lost, so, Const. Mzvondiwa and I set ourselves up at 22:00hrs on the Friday after the Annual Inspection, atop the old mine tower to see what might appear. After making sure that we had good radio communication between us on the mine headgear and Pete in the police Land Rover, we settled down to wait and to watch. After three hours of just watching the stars rotate slowly around the heavens, it was Mzvondiwa's sharp eyes that picked up a distant but distinct glow in the dark countryside in the area of Lochinvar Farm. My quick call to Pete brought an instant response. A half-hour or so later, Pete radio'd a brief message. All it said was, "You can come down Arn. We've got the buggers!"

As a result of that little exercise two of Temeraire Mine's European employees went to jail for poaching and a certain grey box-bodied Land Rover without a cab, along with a rifle and a shotgun, were confiscated and forfeited to the court.

On stations such as Mashaba, the European police officers acted as Driving Test Examiners. One full day per month was set aside for the purpose. African and European learner drivers booked their individual appointments and arrived in an assortment of saloon cars and light vehicles of all shapes, makes, ages and conditions of roadworthiness.

Each of us Patrol Officers and even SO Nicholls took turn and turn about to clear the appointments list for the day. We all ended up with anecdotes to relate later. The tests were of course well-regulated. There were score sheets and a set points count. A minor error or two would not necessarily be a cause for failure, but woe betide the driver who really got it wrong. My first customer was a miner's daughter whose qualified driver accompanying her was her father, an employee of Kings Mine. The lass was in her late teens, pretty as a picture and decidedly "Ooh-la-la!" When we prepared to set off, her father climbed into the back seat, clearly intent to be a passenger on the test run. That was not the normal arrangement. When I suggested that he should be waiting at the Charge Office and not travelling with us, his reply was short and blunt. "Not after the last time!" he asserted as he made himself comfortable. His daughter looked demurely ahead and said nothing, but her complexion turned bright pink. To avoid what could easily have become an altercation, I simply warned him to remain silent and motionless while the test drive was under way and cautioned him that if he made any comment or assisted his daughter in any way during the test drive that would be cause for a failure at that point.

The young lady went properly through the pre-movement requirements and set the car in motion very neatly. When I eventually had her stop once more at the police station some half hour later and failed her, she simply bit her lip while a tear coursed its way down her cheek. Before I could explain in any detail, her father threw a tantrum. The gist of it was that his daughter had driven perfectly, as he had seen from where he had been sitting and I had no grounds at all for failing her.

When he had vented his wrath on me to the point that he was breathless and finally shut up, I tapped the papers on my clipboard with its recorded list of failure points and asked, "Did you teach your daughter to drive, or did you get somebody else to do it?"

"I've taught her myself," he snapped. "I've been driving for years. Never had an accident in my life and you're suggesting neither she nor I can drive properly. You're the second idiot on this police station. The next time we'll go to Fort Victoria or Shabani."

"The young lady will still fail," I asserted firmly, because I think her bad habits are likely to have come from you. Do you want to swap places with your daughter and do a little driving for me? You can show me how good you are."

As I suspected, his pride demanded that, like it or not, he had to accept my challenge. When he was comfortably set in the driver's seat and his daughter had moved into a back seat, I motioned him forward. I deliberately directed him to drive the same route I had had his daughter drive over, even to the three-point turn, hill-start and emergency stop. When I had directed him back to the police station and got him to stop, he turned to me and somewhat belligerently demanded, "Well?" In as calm and matter-of-fact voice as I could muster, I listed his several failing defects. They included not using his rear view mirrors at all, exceeding the local speed limit, cutting corners, driving for distances with his left hand on the gear lever and only his right hand on the steering wheel and, most dreadful of all, since many cars of that time had no electronic indicators, but relied upon manual signals from the driver, whenever directed to make a right or left turn, he stuck his right arm out of the window, to make the appropriate signal, which was fine, but he also took his left hand off the steering wheel in order to change gear downwards as he approached the corner. Then, just as his daughter had done, he grabbed the wheel in both hands as the car reached each corner and turned it, one way or the other.

As the clearly angry driver opened his mouth to argue, his daughter said, rather quietly but clearly from the rear seat, "He's right Daddy. I could see it from back here." Then she burst into tears.

Just occasionally, there were moments of hilarity on the test drives, such as when a quite competent African driver driving a Ford Zephyr in basically sound order responded very smartly to my indication for an emergency stop, the last requirement of the test run. He hit the brakes hard, held the car in a straight line very well and stopped in a short distance. However, every door flew open and the boot-lid flew up, synchronised better than in any Walt Disney cartoon, proving what many Ford car owners of that time had already discovered, that the door-locks were sub-standard and unreliable. That driver I had no hesitation in passing, although I suggested to him that he needed to get the locks looked at without delay.

I had been at Mashaba for nearly six months when Insp. Cavey called me into his office. It was a Monday morning in late September. He did not beat about the bush. "How fast can you pack your gear and get over to Chibi?" Without waiting for my reply, he went on, "Section Officer Phil Mead, the Member-in-Charge over there was injured playing rugby for the police team last Saturday afternoon. He broke a bone in his back or some such. He'll be unfit for duty for some months. Propol wants you to take charge of the station temporarily, until a permanent replacement can be found for Phil Mead."

As I digested the sudden and somewhat unwelcome news, my boss continued. "We'll all be sorry to see you go, because you've settled in well here. Take it that somebody at Province feels you are capable of running a small district station. That's a pat on the back which will do you no harm in the future. If you find yourself struggling with anything, you can always phone me for advice. Got it?"

All I could say that to was, "Yes, Sir and thank you."

In something of a daze, I headed for the mess, where my batman, Shorty, was busy ironing my uniform for the next day. I explained the sudden transfer I had been given and asked him if he wished to stay in Mashaba or move across to Chibi with me. I had his reply even before he uttered a word, because at the mention of Chibi, his face lit up. When I finished speaking, he grabbed my right hand with both of his and shook it. "I will come with you, Ishe. Chibi is my home!"

The next morning, along with all my personal possessions packed into my large tin trunk and my issue kitbag, and after shaking hands with those I was leaving, I organised for Shorty to move to Chibi the next day by bus and then just sat around until the vehicle from Chibi arrived to collect me, as arranged.

Chibi – First Time Around

It was 6893 Patrol Officer Brian Oberholzer who arrived at Mashaba Police Station to transport me to Chibi. He was wearing grey shirt and tie, khaki shorts, with boots and leggings. He took one look at me, wearing my shoes, stockings, shorts and tunic and had a hearty laugh.

"Didn't anyone tell you that at Chibi we wear grey shirts all year round?" he asked as we shook hands. "Chibi has a sort of micro-climate, particularly down at the southern end where it is almost at lowveld level. Never mind, we'll get you sorted out once we get there." With that enlightening introduction done, farewells made and my tin trunk and service kitbag loaded, I climbed, somewhat regretfully and reluctantly into the front passenger seat of the Chibi Police Station Land Rover. Once I was settled, Brian keyed the vehicle's engine into life and drove out of Mashaba, along the road towards Shabani. About twenty miles or more along that road stands Mandamabwe Township. Like many other "townships" it is basically a cluster of half a dozen brick under corrugated iron buildings. Those buildings housed two general stores, a bottle store, a tailor's, a grinding mill and a motor repair garage which actually did have a petrol pump. There was no electricity supply at the township, so the petrol pump was worked by hand. The tall stand had two glass containers, side by side, each of a gallon measure. Once one of the measures was visibly full, the mechanism automatically transferred the fuel, pumped up from its underground tank to the second glass measure, while the fuel in the first glass measure was then allowed to go from the pump into the vehicle fuel tank or jerry-can or whatever container was being filled.

Brian stopped at the township to buy some fresh bread from the store that had a bakery attached to it. While Brian purchased whatever it was that he needed, I stood by the Land Rover, watching a local car being fuelled from the hand-operated pumps, the like of which I had of course seen on many occasions in Nyasaland. Once the fuelling of the vehicle was done, my eyes wandered more to the distant western horizon, A dozen or more miles away, on the far ridge, across the valley of the Lunde River, there appeared to be a steam train travelling. Not that I could hear any engine or see one. What had caught my eye was what appeared to be a greyish white smoke trail, some three to five miles long, trailing along the far horizon. When I turned to look southwards, I could see the beginnings of the granite hills that covered much of Chibi Police District.

When Brian returned to the Land Rover, clutching a cardboard box full of delightfully aromatic fresh bread and rolls, I asked him what that distant smoke trail was.

"That's dust blowing from the mine tips at Shabani." He informed me. "It's the largest asbestos mine in the world. There's a big European population there too. That place is a whole lot bigger than Mashaba. It comes under Midland Province, so we don't have anything to do with it. I've been at Chibi for a year and a half and this is the closest I've ever been. Mind you, with all of that asbestos dust blowing around, it's not a place I would want to spend much time in anyway." With that we both clambered into our transport and Brian once again drove off southwards, on the gravel road that eventually led us to Chibi Township, the police station and camp and the district commissioner's administrative and residential area. Little did I know then that some dozen years later, I would end up posted to Shabani as Station Officer, the title given to the second-in-command of larger police stations, usually commanded by a Chief Inspector.

The driver of any vehicle travelling over dirt roads at that time, way before seat belts appeared, had one advantage over his or her passengers. That being their hold on the steering wheel. It allowed the driver to be far less bounced around as corrugations, ruts, washaways and potholes threw vehicles of all shapes and sizes in all directions, often at one and the same time. I was sufficiently well experienced by then to heed well Brian's admonishment of, "Hold on tight, Arn. This road is well used and not too well maintained!"

The variety of vehicles we passed was interesting, from ox-carts to buses. Each was crammed to overflowing, with goods, with passengers and sometimes both. Being deep into the dry season, all vehicles except for the slow-moving ox-carts raised plumes of dust which they left trailing behind them to settle all too slowly. Each passing vehicle delivered to us a dust cloud in its wake that we had to battle through. Our vehicle of course delivered tit for tat. On those "pass-by" occasions, which were many, passengers could at least shut their eyes until the worst of the dust cloud had cleared. The driver of each vehicle could not indulge in that small luxury. Brian did quite a lot of blinking and wiping of his eyes with the back of a hand.

When I write of "pass-by" occasions, those readers who have never enjoyed, or suffered typical African dirt road, should discard all thoughts of two-lane roads, with a nice, tidy, lane for one way and a second, quite distinct, for the opposite direction. The road we were travelling on was wide enough for two vehicles to safely pass by each other when travelling in opposite directions. However, because the habit of drivers, of all vehicles of sizes greater and lesser, to stick to the middle of the road until some oncoming vehicle came into view, there was just one set of wheel ruts. They were deep, because they were established by the impact of many busses and lorries with all their weight and large wheel size. It took considerable skill for drivers of smaller vehicles to maintain a straight and level course at even moderate speed.

During that journey over the sometimes rutted and sometimes badly corrugated gravel road, Brian did his best to wise me up on the situation at Chibi. His first bit of information was that despite having attested only in March 1963, he had been accepted for transfer from uniform branch to CID. That transfer at such an early stage of his career, so he believed, had much to do with the growing insurgency threat and the creation of Ground Coverage Sections. Those were, I was already aware, formed of duty uniformed African police who had been selected to work in plain clothes, controlled by CID, but working from, and part of the establishment of, duty uniformed stations. All that he was waiting for was advice of the exact date that his transfer was to become effective. It was expected that it would be soon. Having informed me of that, he went on cheerfully that not only was he shortly moving on, but that the second patrol officer, Kevin Kilfoil, who was senior to him, had already submitted his resignation, effective in a few weeks, with the intention to return to the career he had come from in the UK, that of a customs officer.

Brian also added, equally cheerfully, that Sheila Mead's absence from the station for the last ten days or more meant that the daily filing and routine administrative work that was undertaken via the "Wife of Member" part-time post allocated to the station, was a bit behind.

Brian was interested to know how come somebody with barely six months in the force and with just one bar up, had been chosen to stand in for a

Section Officer in charge of a station like Chibi. I gave him a brief outline of my three years and more in Nyasaland and told him what little I knew of the how and why I had been chosen to take on the temporary role of Member-in-Charge. When I asked him if he knew exactly what had happened to Section Officer Phil Mead, Brian related that all he knew was that Phil Mead, who was a notable rugby player, had gone off to represent the BSAP in Salisbury, some two weeks earlier. During that game he had received a back injury that had needed hospital treatment and as a result he would be off duty for some months. Sheila Mead, Phil's wife had been up in Salisbury with him and was staying there for a while. Officer Commanding Victoria District had sent a radio message, yesterday, advising of my temporary transfer to Chibi as acting Member-in-Charge and that was it.

Chibi Police Station covered what was almost entirely a Tribal Trust area, with a total population of some 120,000 persons. It was roughly rugby-ball shaped, canted somewhat left of vertical on the Mercator Map Grid, bordered to the west by the Lunde River and to the east by the Tokwe River. Down much of its length ran a portion of the main road from Fort Victoria to Beit Bridge and the border with South Africa. That same road was also the main route to the fast-developing Triangle and Hippo Valley areas of the lowveld, where sizeable irrigation schemes were turning the dense bush land into viable irrigation schemes fed by the water from Kyle Dam a few miles outside Fort Victoria, not very far from the Zimbabwe Ruins.

The land that we drove through towards Chibi Township and the Government buildings was mostly typical Tribal Trust Land. It was full of wattle, daub and thatched huts, in family clusters between arable fields and patches of grazing land. The trees, mostly mopani and acacia thorn, with an occasional stand of blue gums, were few and far between and what little grass there was, appeared dry, brittle and brown rather than green. That the cattle in sight were surviving rather than flourishing could be detected from one glance at them. They were thin, ribby and underweight, without exception. Their battle for nourishment was not assisted by the existence of hordes of goats, whose grazing habits caused a great deal of harm. I lost count of the number of village dogs that ran at us and chased after us, snarling or barking furiously and snapping at our vehicle's tyres. Thoughts of my journey with Pete Wilson and his handgun ran through my head. The soil was light brown and dusty. Its nature was clearly vulnerable to the heavy rain showers of the wet season and easily whipped up by the swirling winds into short-lived dust devils. Those are miniature tornadoes that precede the rains. There was ample evidence of the impact of the agriculture development officers at the DC's Office, because every slope in the arable areas had plenty of contour ridges, designed to prevent the rainfall creating any natural wash-away effect.

Chibi Police Station itself is located close to the base of a granite kopje that stands at the eastern edge of a whole range of granite domes, for which stony hills Chibi is, as I later found out, internationally famous. Apart from the building that housed the police station offices, there was a separate radio office. A few yards from that building stood a small corrugated-iron shed. That housed the diesel generator, which was a sturdy Lister engine that provided power for the radios and electric light for the offices. Close by that was another building that housed cells and witness quarters for African civilians. The two buildings closest to the base of the kopje were the Member-in-Charge's house and the European mess and living quarters. There was also a one-time stable building which had become a garage when horses were replaced by vehicles some years ago. Close by but distinct from those there was the African Police Camp, with housing for the married and single African members. A huge baobab tree dominated a roundabout close by the main office and between that and the African Police Camp.

Brian drove straight on past the offices to the European single quarters where he helped me move my gear into the one spare bedroom and waited while I did a hasty change of uniform into the same style gear he was wearing. I was glad that I had packed my shirts and shorts carefully, so the lack of immediately recent ironing did not show up much. What I did immediately notice was the metal framework above the bed, which carried a mosquito net. At Mashaba there had been so few mosquitoes that nobody bothered with nets at night-time in the dry season, although everyone made sure they took on board their daily anti-malaria pill.

The mess building itself was just an oblong of brickwork, doors and windows under a corrugated iron roof. As one faced it, there was a kitchen to the left end, then a small dining room, then a lounge. A door from the lounge led onto a broad mosquito-netted veranda that ran the length of the rest of the building. Half-way along the length of the veranda there was a telephone extension. Off of that veranda led the three bedrooms and then at the far right-hand end, there were the toilets and a bathroom. Brian pointed out that the water supply could be a bit "iffy" because the local source was a concrete tank on top of the kopje. That tank was supplied by a nine-mile-long pipeline that started in the Tokwe River. Breakdowns of the pumping system were not unknown. The first warning, quite often, was when the water just ceased to run from the taps. To get around such events, two or three jerry-cans of water were kept in the kitchen. In the absence of any electricity supply, there were hooks and stands for Tilley or Petromax lamps and a few candle holders. When the water supplies were okay, hot water was provided by a wood-burning external boiler system.

Brian was also kind enough to warn me that there was a light aircraft landing strip a couple of hundred yards to the north of the camp, so any sudden appearances of light aircraft at low altitude and loud engine noise was nothing to worry about as the landing and take-off paths, depending on wind, were directly over the mess and Member-in-Charge's house. I was grateful for that particular piece of advice barely a couple of days later, when a Cessna light aircraft arrived quite early one morning, to collect the District Commissioner, as I found out later. It roared in over the rooftops of the police camp, without prior warning, as I was shaving. I recall thinking at that time that it was fortunate I was using a safety razor.

After Mashaba, with that location's luxury of a twenty-four hours per day electricity supply, Chibi's facilities were inevitably simple and basic. However, they were adequate, especially for anyone like me, who had survived well enough on similarly remote and primitive stations in Nyasaland.

By the time my change of uniform was achieved and my gear was stowed in my allocated bedroom, it was time for lunch, so it was in the mess lounge that I met 6291 Patrol Officer Kevin Kilfoil. Kevin, who, having attested in January 1961, had decided to stay on when he had completed his basic three years. More recently, with the Winds of Change rustling the angry leaves of independence movements all over Africa and within Rhodesia too, he had decided that there was no long-term future for Europeans in the BSA Police. His aim, and who could blame him, was for a reliable career in a civil service or police environment, with advancement on merit and an adequate pension at the end of service. To achieve that, he felt a need to return to the civilized stability of the UK.

I recall my first meal in the Chibi Police Station Single Quarters quite vividly. Not for the beefsteak, chips and peas that were put before us on the table, but more for the fact that, fortunately just as we had all finished eating and were about to retire from the dining-room to the lounge, there came the unmistakable raucous call of a dog-baboon, from way up on the kopje behind the building. That was followed by other answering calls as the troop spoke up for where they individually were. Kevin, upon hearing the first call, promptly got up, said "Excuse me, please," and dashed off in the direction of his bedroom. Brian answered my raised eyebrows with, "Kevin has a bit of a thing about baboon. He keeps a personal rifle in his bedroom and takes pot-shots at them if they show their noses. They raid the African staff's gardens if they get half a chance." Brian's words of explanation were suddenly punctuated by the crack of a .303 rifle, followed by a chorus of barking from all over the kopje. "I'll bet he's missed again," Brian commented. "Let's go see."

Accompanied by a dwindling chorus of baboon barking as the troop headed away from the threat of more gunfire, we left the dining room, crossed the lounge and headed for Kevin's bedroom, where we found him crouched at the open window, rifle at his shoulder, peering intently up at the clustered rocks. "Any luck?" Brian inquired. Kevin shook his head. "He started moving the moment I opened the window, but I think he's got some granite chips in his butt, because I didn't miss by much." He lowered the rifle, made it safe and stood. "You any good with one of these things?" he asked, holding the weapon out towards me.

"Not too bad," I replied as I took hold of the rifle and hefted it, "Besides which, I don't much like baboons either. Up in Nyasaland my first murder case, if you can call it that, was when a two-month-old baby disappeared from where the mother had left it sleeping on a mat outside a hut. It turned out that the infant had been snatched by a baboon, carted away and mostly eaten. We found the remains."

The .303 rifle I was holding was no ordinary Short Metford Lee Enfield. The fore-piece woodwork was shorter and the barrel much longer than the standard SMLE Mk IV that I had been handling for years. The magazine had a six-round capacity, instead of the usual ten and there was also a single shot loading platform that could be set across the top of the magazine. The rear sight was also of a notched "v" style, rather than an aperture.

Kevin obviously saw my puzzled frown as I examined the rifle. "That's been around since 1896," he offered. "It's a Lee-Speed by make; the predecessor of the Lee-Enfield that's now our standard issue in the Force."

It certainly was a stylish weapon and a very light and comfortable one as I discovered, when I lifted it to my shoulder and sighted along it with the barrel out of the window.

"I was going to sell it to Brian when I leave, but he won't need it now that he's off to the bright lights and big city life in CID. You can have it for a fiver if you're interested."

I lowered the .303 and stuck out my right hand. Kevin grabbed it and pumped it up and down. "Thanks," he said, "that's another item ticked off. There's some Firearm Licence Application Forms in the office. We'll get a set filled in this afternoon." He paused for just a moment, before adding, "You don't happen to want a car as well, do you?"

It turned out that Kevin owned a 1948 Studebaker sedan, for which he only wanted twenty-five pounds. After a look at it a while later and a short drive, I bought that too.

Once Kevin had safely stowed away the Lee Speed rifle, all three of us set off to walk the short distance to the police station's main building and, in particular, the Member-in-Charge's office. Brian held the door open, delivered an exaggerated bow and gestured me within. "We are both," he declared with conviction, "quite delighted to say, 'It's all yours'!"

"Thanks," I replied rather dryly, noting the presence of two generously sized desks. Each had a blotter, pen and pencil holders and a set of wooden paperwork dividers marked In, Pending, Court, File and Out. Each of those desks had a black Bakelite party line telephone on them. Both desks were tidy, but well stacked with paperwork, mostly piled up in the "In" divisions. "Which is which?"

Kevin pointed to the desk nearest to a large safe with a red telephone set on it, standing against one wall. That phone carried no party line dialling facility. "That's yours. The other one," he offered, with a broad grin, "is for your wife. Next door is the armoury and on the other side of that is the Charge Office where our African staff lurk when they are not out doing all the hard work on foot or on bicycle. Brian and I have our desks in the small office block we walked past on the way here. That's where the radio room is."

For a moment there was silence as I stood looking round the office, with its red polished floor, rush mats and one wall completely dedicated to the shelves and lever arch files numbered from 1 to 99 that held all sorts of subject papers that were in common usage, as well as copies of the Police Act and Regulation, Force Standing Orders and numerous other tomes on Statute and Common Law. A small side table carried an Olympia typewriter that gave the appearance of long service on a hard station and the station's Crime Register. Memories of similar offices in Nyasaland crowded reassuringly into the forefront of my mind.

"Well, gentlemen," I said, breaking the silence, "all you can do is to leave me to it while I go through what's here, sort it out, prioritise it and find out what needs attending to first. That should keep me busy for an hour or two. Meanwhile, whatever systems you've arranged regarding duty officer and station keys, I'll leave you to stick to until I've got a better idea of how the station functions. Once I've had a glance through the paperwork on hand, I'll take a walk around the rest of the camp. We can have another conversation after dinner this evening, if that is okay with you?" A pair of nodding heads told me that that arrangement was okay with them.

Once the two Patrol Officers had left, I moved round, sat down in the chair behind the Member-in-Charge's desk, reached for one of the two ball-point pens in my left side shirt pocket and for the first item of paperwork piled up in the "IN" tray.

An hour and a half later a tray of tea appeared. It was carried in and set down on the spare desk by the mess cook. One look at it told me that someone had set out to create the right impression. The tray, which was itself covered in a very well-ironed tea cloth, did not carry just a mug of tea, ready for drinking; it carried a white metal teapot, complete with a tea-cosy of many colours, matching jugs containing milk, made up from powder and hot water. There was also a bowl of sugar, a china cup and saucer and a small plate with a few digestive biscuits on it. I declined the cook's offer to pour tea for me, thanked him for the refreshment and sent him off. The welcome ritual of a tea-break enabled me to reflect on the picture that was building in my mind of a police station that was vastly different from Mashaba, but far more akin to one or two of the rural police stations that I had worked on in Nyasaland. Many of Mashaba's complainants had been Europeans. "The Masters & Servants Act" featured frequently there, with all sorts of complaints about the misbehaviour of houseboys, garden-boys, cooks and nannies, along with the continual poaching cases. In the Chibi paperwork I had been through since lunchtime, I had not seen a single set of case papers that had a European complainant. The cases of Murder, Housebreakings, Store-breakings, Assaults of all kinds, Thefts, Cattle Thefts and Rapes all had one thing in common. That was African complainants. Even the few cases of "Fail to Dip Cattle" and "Fail to Contour-ridge land," which originated from the District Commissioner's Office as a result of the work of the Agriculture Development Officers, carried African names as complainants on behalf of the State.

Two issues did concern me. The first being that the next court session was due on the coming Thursday, but not a lot of the casework was ready for it. The second was that the many volumes of secondary legislation neatly stowed on the shelves had not been updated by annotation for some time. Lists of annotations to existing legislation and fresh Ministerial Regulations were regular arrivals on any Member-in-Charge's desk. At Mashaba, SO Nicholls had had a firm grip on that particular work, keeping it for himself, even when he discovered that I too knew the often-intricate routines necessary to keep the records straight. The danger of not doing that particular piece of unpopular work was that a power that had been removed might be used, or a fresh regulation, needing to be implemented promptly, was never enforced. That could, and did, lead to problems on some stations. Promotion chances had been wrecked on that lurking reef in Colonial Police; that I was aware of. There was a file of papers containing outstanding Annotation Lists going back some months. It represented a lot of hours of work, but was not, of itself as much of a priority issue as was the court roll and dockets which needed to be listed on it.

In order to stretch my legs, I left my cup of tea to cool and walked out on to the top of the entrance steps and took the few paces past the triple-bolted and padlocked armoury door and entered the charge office. There was a short counter, with a small wooden gate at the end. Civilians, unless being dealt with as accused persons, or witnesses, did not proceed beyond that barrier. Behind the counter one of the constables was seated on a high stool, close by a small telephone switchboard that was the landline communication centre for the station. All calls on the party line rang in that office, whether the call was for the station or not. The station's ring call was two short and one long. Other ring calls, such as three shorts, or one short and two long, were listened to by the orderly, without response, because they were for other locations on the shared line, such as the DC's Office, the Clinic a dozen miles away, or one or two of the stores in the nearby township. When our orderly recognised a call to the station, it was his task to answer it, find out whether it was for the Member-in-Charge, or someone else and then put the call through as needed. One of the reasons why the Orderly did not stray far from the phone switchboard was the rule that incoming calls would be answered within three rings. The Orderly was also custodian of the Occurrence Book, which, theoretically, was the record of all movements to and from the station and all other incidents which, by their nature, needed to be recorded.

Not far from the Occurrence Book was a Minor Report Form Book. That essential item was supposed to be used to record just what its title stated, Minor Reports.

That meant things such as attendances at domestic disputes, raptors of all kinds taking a chicken, or goats straying into a garden and creating damage. As I was to discover in later years, certain individuals would attempt to keep their official crime figures down by not entering thefts, housebreakings, stocktheft cases or whatever, in the Crime Register, but just giving them a page number reference from the current Minor Report Form book. That kind of behaviour was a nonsense, because, where crime was genuinely rising, perhaps through development as at Triangle and Hippo Valley, or by weight of Demographic Change, the only way to attract more staff was to demonstrate that the establishment of the station was inadequate for the amount and type of crime occurring and therefore needed increasing. That was not achieved by hiding the real picture from inspecting officers.

Looking beyond the counter and the constable, I noted with approval that the charge office was neat and tidy. There was a desk for the station's sergeant and a number of tables, chairs and benches for constables and witnesses. One wall was given over to a large noticeboard with a variety of paperwork pinned up.

After exchanging a few polite words with the charge office orderly, I returned to the Member-in-Charge's office to continue plodding through the assorted paperwork. I had not been there very long when the phone rang. It was the Orderly with word that Dispol, short for Officer Commanding Police District, was on the line, wishing to speak with me.

Chief Supt Roy Briault's greeting was at least a friendly one. "Good afternoon, Woolley," he began, "How well do you swim?" My rather perplexed, "Beg pardon, Sir?" brought a little more explanation. "Well, we have rather chucked you in at the deep end, haven't we?" Despite the last two words, it was not a question.

Over the next ten minutes or so, Dispol inquired what my first impressions of Chibi were and assured me that the station would not be left without replacements when the other two Patrol Officers shortly left. To my question of just when Section Officer Mead would be returning, Dispol advised me that he would not be returning to Chibi at all. His injury was serious enough to keep him in hospital for a while, after which time he would need to be on a town station somewhere, one with physiotherapy treatment available. He went on to tell me that once the year's promotion activities were all done and dusted, probably in a couple of months, a new M i/c, a married Section Officer, would be posted to the station. Until then the position was all mine, including the Acting up Allowance. He concluded by reminding me that he was there to help if I found myself struggling and that he would be coming out for an informal visit sometime the following week, "To help sort out the matter of a handing-over certificate." His parting comment, "Keep your water-wings well inflated, Woolley. It can be tricky in the deep end," did nothing to ease my thoughts.

The rest of that afternoon rather flew by as I tried to cram in as much information as I could as fast as I could. One of the record books was titled, "Visits to Pioneer and Isolated Graves." A quick glance reminded me of the Pioneer Column's 1890 route from Belingwe, across the Lunde, through Chibi via the Munaka Pass in the line of hills of that name and then on over the Tokwe and up to Fort Victoria via Providential Pass. I realised that Chibi was likely to be rich in history and archaeology. It was a cheering prospect for my off-duty hours. It also reminded me that, as Acting M i/c, I needed to pay my respects fairly quickly to the District Commissioner at his office and to Chief Chibi, at his home not far beyond Chibi Township, a bare mile away. When I mentioned that intention later, Brian advised me that Chief Chibi was a difficult person to get to see, partly because he was old and almost totally blind and partly because he was totally traditional in his behaviour. If the spirits said "No!" then Chief Chibi said "No!" That gave me food for thought.

My afternoon musings along those lines were interrupted by Brian

Oberholzer who asked if I wanted the station generator to be kept on, to provide power for the electric light in the office if I intended to keep working on into the evening. A quick glance at the clock indicated that it was 17:00hrs, or 5:00 p.m. Another glance, outside, reminded me that the evening was not yet drawing in, which was normal at that time of year. I decided that enough was enough for day one and followed Brian out of the office and up to the mess. There, turn and turn about all three of us bathed and changed into civilian wear and settled into the lounge for a sundowner and some friendly conversation, before evening meal.

When the eating was done, we relaxed in the lounge again. Apart from the usual furnishings, a couple of Petromax oil lamps, that provided light and a generously sized fireplace, the most notable item in the lounge was the skin of a huge python. It extended at picture-rail height, all along one wall and part of the next. Brian advised me that it had been there some years, having been killed just after the Second World War, back in the granite hills, where it had taken a goat. Time had of course moved on since then. So many python had been killed that they were now rare throughout the whole country, to the extent that they were classified as Royal Game, not to be hunted or killed without a special permit.

That conversation led on to what game was and what was not still surviving in the area. On that point I learned that there were still some small antelope, duiker and steinbok, just a few kudu and not much else. Somehow, there were still a few leopard but not many, while the baboon in the area, no longer predated sufficiently by their natural enemy, the leopards, were prolific.

Kevin and Brian also informed me that the crocodile in both rivers were doing well and that the District Commissioner had a permit to shoot 52 hippo each year because that marauding animal was also not in short supply and tended to impact on villagers' crops.

We were settled comfortably in our respective "Chairs Morris" which seat is a wooden framed armchair with an adjustable back; a type of chair that was only made comfortable by thick cushions, when a visitor arrived. Bill Kennedy was an Assistant District Commissioner stationed at Chibi. As the only single European on the DC's staff, he quite often walked the short distance to the police camp for a chatter with Brian and Kevin who were much the same age as he was.

After the usual introductions, Bill joined us and picked up the threads of our conversation. It was he who related that the present DC was a bit awkward to get on with at times. His name was Cornelius Gerhardus Jacobus O'Connor. "One of the Transvaal Irish" as Bill Kennedy put it. He apparently insisted on speaking Afrikaans most of the time, although he was also perfectly fluent in English and in Kalanga, the local Chishona dialect. Bill also warned me that the DC firmly believed that he was a great white hunter. He insisted on shooting the annual allocation of hippo himself and organised numerous baboon shoots, allegedly for the benefit of the villagers, but mostly because of his liking for shooting. "The problem is," Bill explained, "he's a lousy shot. Partly because he insists on using a family heirloom, a worn out old Manlicher 8mm rifle that his father used against the British in the Boer War. It's got little penetrating or stopping power. That and his lousy eyesight!" he ended up. He waggled a warning finger at me. "If you go out hunting with him, just stay close to him and directly behind him. Anywhere else is dangerous."

That conversation also revealed that Saturday afternoons were a sort of compulsory attendance event at the DC's Office, where there were a couple of tennis courts and a small pavilion in which refreshments, from tea and coffee to a cold beer could be enjoyed. Everyone was welcome there during those afternoons, whether they played tennis or not. Our exchanges of information also brought to light that almost all our foodstuffs and basic supplies were purchased in Fort Victoria as the local township stores carried very little indeed that was of interest to Europeans. However, I was assured, the meat supplies were sourced very close by, because there was a butcher's shop, run by one of the local African traders, a half mile down the road, just beyond a narrow gorge that provided access for the road and bus route to the south-west and western parts of Chibi Tribal Trust Land.

The keeping of fresh produce at Chibi was limited by the capacity of the refrigeration equipment. The mess kitchen did have a paraffin powered refrigerator. That had limited space, much of which was usually taken up by bottles of beer. There was no freezer capacity at all. The kitchen range was gas-powered, supplied from two large cylinders positioned on the outside of the building, housed in a plywood shelter. When one cylinder ran out, demand was switched to the full one and the empty one went on the first available police transport, to Fort Victoria, for refill.

That very useful, four-way, conversation continued for a couple of hours or more before Bill departed and all three of us police officers decided that it was time for bed.

"If there's a call out," Brian advised, "that phone on the veranda will ring. It'll keep ringing until the duty PO answers it. Tonight, that's me. If there is a call, it usually wakes both of us anyway."

"Or all three of us tonight." Kevin chipped in, with feeling.

Brian ignored the comment from Kevin and went on, "We usually surface at about 5:30, for a quick cup of tea before Stable Parade at 06:00. Breakfast is at 07:30 and down to the offices by 8. After that, it's just whatever the day brings in. Lunch is at 13:00."

With that last bit of operational briefing taken on board, I decided that then was not the time to begin telling my companions what I thought of the state of the paperwork I had waded through that afternoon. I bade both others a good night, made my way to my bedroom, undressed and scrambled into bed, lifting one side of the mosquito net and ducking under it. Before getting fully settled, I made sure that the fine white netting was tucked in all around and that my arms were not laying up against it. Once I was sure that I would not be an easy target for any of the flights and squadrons of apprentice Draculas that would inevitably be about in the darkness, I relaxed and let sleep claim me.

The next morning ran smoothly along on the timetable Brian had set out. Our ever-cheerful cook set a mug of tea down beside my bed with a call of "Wake up, Ishe. It is half past five."

After a quick comfort break, a washing of hands and face and the hasty swallowing of the helpfully refreshing mug of tea, I joined Brian and Kevin on the walk down to the stables and store-room area of the camp. Although nominally a "parade," the maintenance of vehicles was carried out, for very good reasons, in civilian clothes and very definitely not the best ones either. The station's two Land Rovers and the motorcycle that made up the transport fleet were waiting for the daily mechanical check-over and wash and brush-up routine that was delivered during the daily Stable Parade. Daily check sheets were filled in and the roadworthiness, or otherwise, of each piece of transport was placed on record; a record that would be inspected by the next visiting officer, whoever that might be and whenever it might occur.

As well as the mechanical and cleanliness aspects, Stable Parade also made sure that the logbook for each vehicle was filled in up to date, with journeys matching the Occurrence Book entries and mileage all accounted for. On that point of mileage, careful note was made of when services of greater or lesser type were due. Woe be-tide the station i/c who permitted a vehicle to be overdue for a service. The Central Mechanical Engineering Department at the Government Depot in Fort Victoria carried out all the province's BSAP vehicle maintenance. Bookings for services had to be arranged to fit in with CMED's workload from all the other government departments, so it was wise to keep an eye on mileages and get bookings for service made well ahead.

That first Stable Parade told me that between the three European and the couple of African drivers on the station, a keen eye had been kept on the vehicles, for they were all in good sound order and well up to date on services. That was good to know, because well-maintained vehicles were less prone to breakdowns, and breakdowns in remote locations, often out of radio contact, were very uncomfortable occurrences, as my police work in Nyasaland had taught me.

I also took the opportunity to explain to the station sergeant and constables just who I was, my background and how come I was posted to the station as temporary and acting Member-in-Charge. When I finished my explanation, I asked if there were any questions.

"Ah, no, Ishe," Sergeant Wurayayi replied, apparently for everyone, "but we are happy to know that your one bar is telling lies."

I took that as an acceptance of my position and welcomed the comment.

Later that day I sent a constable to speak with Chief Chibi to ask permission for me to visit him. Having had the warning about the chief's traditional inclinations, I handed the constable a six-foot square black cloth, of good quality and two half-crown coins, with the request that the chief should offer them to his ancestral spirits. I instructed that constable to tell Chief Chibi that he would stay within call until the chief had received an answer from his ancestors. I warned him to take his bedroll with him. Via a direct phone call, using the direct-line phone atop the safe, I arranged to go down to the DC's office in the afternoon, to call in on Mr O'Connor.

That visit to the DC was an interesting one. If Chief Chibi was allegedly traditional and probably tribal, the area was well balanced, because so was the DC. That gentleman's manners were impeccable. He was also nobody's fool.

He was clearly well educated and well informed. His English was, despite his very heavy Afrikaans accent, straight out of the Victorian or Edwardian eras. He was somewhat above average height, slim, thin-faced and greying on top. He was dressed in a khaki safari-suit, with brown leather shoes that would have looked good on any formal military parade. He had been at Chibi for a couple of years or more and had got to know the district well. He confided that, since he was due for retirement in little over a year or so, he hoped that he would be able to finish that time at Chibi, where he and his wife were very happy. He urged me to get out and about in order to become familiar with the area and its people and reminded me that police staff were welcome to use any of the several brick-built DC's Rest Camps that were scattered around the area. As he put it to me, it was not in keeping with the status of a District Commissioner, or Member-in Charge of a police station to have to camp out under canvas or set up a camp bed on the veranda of a store in the rainy season, when out and about on duty. I somehow gained the impression that importance of status did not extend down to mere POs or junior staff of his own department.

Our conversation roamed over matters of political interest nationally and locally.

On the matters of talks between the British and Rhodesian Governments, he made it clear that he had little hope the British would see sense and grant independence before majority rule. He quizzed me at some length on my experiences in Nyasaland as that country had moved towards and gained independence. I told him a little of the outrages I had witnessed of the One-Party State situation and the beginnings of the descent towards corruption in government positions that I had seen for myself. I related to him a conversation I had had one day with Dr Banda, when I asked him why he was so keen to break up the Federation of Rhodesias and Nyasaland and Dr Banda's reply of, "Has it never occurred to you, Inspector, that it is far better to be a big frog in a small puddle than a small frog in a large one?" To that, Mr O'Connor nodded a couple of times, slowly and deeply. "Power young man; Power! That's all the African is interested in and all that he respects. Never show him any weakness. He admires strength and respects it. I learned that early on in my career and the learning has served me well. It's not that I dislike the average African. Some of them are smart and a lot of them are decent people. The problem is they hadn't yet even invented the wheel when we arrived here. There will have to be majority rule one day, but, if it comes before they are ready for it, it will all end in disaster, tears and suffering, for everyone."

We talked through the local administrative problems of getting cattle herds fully registered and making sure they were dipped regularly, in order to prevent over-grazing, keep diseases down and the value of the cattle up at sales times. He also expressed his concern over the need for good relations between all of the wings of government working in the area and the pooling of information in the face of the activities of local nationalists who were recruiting local young men and women for the purposes of external training as terrorists.

Our first encounter was a very friendly and pleasant one, which boded well for the future. It ended with him inviting me to the next Saturday tennis party, which I duly promised to attend.

On my arrival back at the police camp, I was greeted by the sight of the constable I had sent to see Chief Chibi, deep in conversation with the station sergeant.

I had certainly not expected an answer that quickly. Sgt Wurayayi advised me, with a broad grin, "Ishe, Chief Chibi had agreed to feel you. That is good."

"Feel me? What the heck does that mean?"

The sergeant's grin widened some more. "He is blind now Sir. He will take your hands and feel them. If he is happy with them, he will feel your face and head. Then he will decide if he is willing to speak with you."

"Does he do that with everyone?" I inquired, somewhat amazed by what I was hearing.

Sergeant nodded emphatically. "Everyone except his own family; or the tribal elders he has known all of his life."

"Has he said when?"

Sergeant shook his head. "He will send one of his messengers, Ishe. That is his way."

I raised my eyebrows, shook my head in wonderment and thanked both the sergeant and the constable for their part in getting me an audience with the chief. It might have been simpler, I reflected in the quiet of the office, to have just rolled up, in a vehicle, in uniform and asked to speak with Chief Chibi, as most people did. However, my encounters with tribal elders in

Nyasaland had taught me that by following their customs, far better relationships were established. As it turned out, it was worth doing it the hard way.

Between Kevin, Brian and me, we got stuck into the docket work that was on hand and particularly those cases for which an accused person was on remand. When Thursday morning arrived, the court roll was well prepared and most of the cases were at least presentable, with witnesses, both police and civilian, on hand. The courtroom was a part of the DC's complex, dating back to when those officials were the magistrates too. It was not large, but it was well appointed, with a teak desk and high-backed chair for His Worship and a proper dock for the accused persons on one side and a witness stand on the other.

A large, but simple mukwa table served to hold the papers that the prosecutor had to work through. Towards the back of the courtroom there were chairs for the public and witnesses who had finished giving evidence. Those witnesses who had yet to give their evidence were, of course, kept outside and out of hearing of the proceedings, until it was their turn to give evidence.

When Mr Stainer was ready to enter the court, sharp on 9.00 a.m., the court clerk called for everyone to rise and be silent. Once the magistrate was seated, he gestured for all present to sit and looked directly at me. "You do get around, Mr Prosecutor. I trust you have learned sufficient in past weeks elsewhere to be able to manage competently on your own?" I thought I detected just a trace of sarcasm in his tone.

"I believe so, Your Worship," I replied evenly. "After all, I have had the advantage of a most worthy tutor."

Mr Stainer uttered a gruff "Harumph" and bade me call the first case. As luck would have it, all went well. The prisons staff had those remanded in custody all ready when called for and those who had been in the police cells also arrived on call. Witnesses came and went on cue. Remands and judgements were handed down at a steady rate, until I was able to declare, just before lunchtime and mainly for the few onlookers behind me who did not have copies of the court roll in front of them, "That case completes the court roll for today Your Worship."

Mr Stainer gave the court interpreter time to translate my words into Kalanga and then call, "All rise, please." That allowed His Worship to stand

and walk, somewhat stiffly upright, through his allocated door and out of the courtroom, which promptly became a babble of voices as witnesses sought to claim travel warrants or expenses, family and friends of jailed and fined offenders argued over the results of their cases and even hurled insults and the occasional threat at those who had been complainants. Eventually, the combined efforts of police officers, prison staff and DC's messengers cleared them all from the courtroom. In the relative silence the abundance of necessary paperwork was gathered up by the three sets of officials, representing Police, Prisons and Justice, after which we all went off upon our own separate ways.

For any police station where a uniformed police officer was the prosecutor, the burden of work relating to court days did not cease when the court clerk called, "All rise and be silent, please" at the end of the last item on the roll. Back at the police station the cases had to be sorted out into those that had been completed, one way or the other and those in which the accused had been remanded, in or out of custody, to enable further investigations to be made. The former required the certification and sending off to the Criminal Records Bureau of the fingerprints of the accused person or persons, the endorsement of outcome on the case record, the provision of a "Completed" serial number for the year, the closing of the Criminal Record Book entry for that individual case and the eventual putting away of that set of paperwork in its proper place in the growing pile of records for the current year.

There was always a mental, if not physical sigh of relief uttered by investigating officers of all ranks when an accused person admitted guilt in relation to whatever they were being charged with. That might be when they were arrested and responded to a first Warn and Cautioned admonishment put by the investigating officer, or later, in answering a formal Charge Sheet. Whichever way, that allowed cases to be brought down to a documental minimum, usually no more than a half-dozen sheets, behind a Docket Record face sheet.

Just occasionally, an accused person would, upon arrest, behave quite amenably and admit whatever offence it was. They might then repeat that admission on a formal Charge Sheet, but then, if a prosecutor was so foolish as to send them off on remand, pending return of fingerprints, they would come back to court and promptly plead "Not Guilty." Sometimes that was because they had been "tutored" by hard-cases or political troublemakers already in jail. Sometimes, that was because those same jailed people threatened violence towards them, if they pleaded guilty. Whenever that change of heart happened, there had to be further remands, the taking of full statements and the creation of a greater quantity of paperwork, before any return to court, with all witnesses in attendance. Such cases then became lengthy, as they often entailed a "Trial-Within-A-Trial," during which the now denied admissions were argued over and accepted or rejected by the Magistrate, or occasionally, the Judge.

Quite often, accused persons were known and arrested very early in cases, particularly those of the nature of assaults and robberies. In those cases, the first appearance in court was a simple request for remand, to allow the case to be fully investigated and prepared for a full court hearing. That set of paperwork would be endorsed with the remand details and sent back to the investigating officer, with a request for the case to be further investigated and made ready for hearing at the next court date, usually a couple of weeks ahead.

More complicated cases, such as murders, of which there were many, might see an accused person remanded several times before they eventually appeared in court at a higher level, either a District or High Court.

It was always advisable for that closing off and further instructing of case work, arising from the court session to be done by the prosecutor him, or her, self, because that person was the only police officer who really knew what had gone on. Delegating that essential task to others who had not been present within the court was a risky thing to do, so I always made sure that if I were Mr Prosecutor for the day, then I did the aftermath work myself.

I had always felt myself to have been extremely privileged and very lucky, to have gained experience at the prosecutor's table early on in my police career. That fortunate opportunity, one which the great majority of police officers never have, enabled me to be a far more careful, inquisitive and effective investigator and documenter of cases, both complex and simple.

That first court day at Chibi also gave me a picture of the abilities of both Kevin and Brian, in investigation and documentation terms. Both were capable and industrious. The point I admired most was common to both. Despite having had a "junior detail" foisted on them and knowing full well that they had only weeks, if not days, to do before moving on, both of them pulled their weight and more, giving me every bit of support they could, for the short time that we three were together at Chibi.

On my first Saturday afternoon at Chibi, I duly took myself off, along with Kevin and Brian, all suitably dressed, to the DC's office and residential complex and the tennis courts. All told, there were ten of us. That was enough to keep both courts busy, playing doubles. Somehow nobody even suggested any singles games.

Mrs O'Connor greeted me warmly, introduced me to those I had not yet met, to Marie and Piet Visser and Brian Tullett and ran the afternoon with a gracious but firm hand. She made sure that everyone played with and against everyone else, that cold drinks were available all afternoon and, without appearing to have glanced at any timepiece, declared that tea-break was due about thirty seconds before a couple of servants appeared, bearing trays of tea, soft drinks and biscuits.

The tea, biscuits and cold soft drinks and a great deal of conversation were very much the order of the afternoon. Tennis skills were variable and the competition keen but friendly. The DC, as befitted his lightweight frame, did not hit the ball particularly hard, however, what he lacked in muscle power he more than made up for in guile. He was clearly a master of the soft touch and awkward spin techniques. He certainly gave me and most of the others, a right old run-around. During the tea-break, Mr O'Connor chattered away in Afrikaans, until his wife reminded him, gently but firmly, that several of those present did not speak that language. It soon became clear to me that there was a decidedly well established, if unspoken, social pecking-order. Mr O'Connor kept almost everyone else in order and Mrs O'Connor kept him in order. It worked well.

All in all, it was a very pleasant and enjoyable afternoon.

The following morning, just after breakfast, the telephone on the mess veranda rang. Kevin, who was duty officer for the week, identified himself in that position and began to listen, with me within earshot. He found himself talking with a European male car driver, who was demanding the presence of a police officer to sort out what he described as a serious traffic accident which had badly damaged his new Mercedes saloon car. That driver, who was speaking from a phone at the Hippo Pools Hotel, just across the Lunde River and some dozen mile south of Ngundu Halt junction, had, apparently, been driving his car from Triangle Sugar Estates to Fort Victoria.

At the junction with the main north-south road from Beit Bridge to Fort Victoria, he had turned north. Shortly afterwards, a Rhodesia Railways heavy lorry, coming downhill towards him, had shed a wheel. The wheel, freed from its mounting, had shot ahead of the lorry, crossed the centre of the road and collided with the front of his car, causing serious damage. He was demanding that a Patrol Officer should attend the scene.

Kevin listened patiently. When the clearly angry fellow stopped just long enough to draw breath, Kevin asked if anyone was hurt and whether or not both vehicles were safely drivable. The man on the other end of the line admitted that nobody was hurt and that both vehicles were still roadworthy. However, he claimed that he had the keys for the lorry and was going to hold onto them and that if somebody from Chibi was not going to attend, he would get on to Fort Victoria Police Station and demand to speak to somebody more senior there.

Normally, under this kind of circumstance, where there was no question of any Road Traffic Act offence, the drivers would have been told to exchange vehicle numbers, names, addresses and insurance details and if they wished to go beyond that, to call in to have more full details taken by their local police station when they returned home, or to any police station they happened to pass by.

However, one of the things that was troubling me was just how I was going to be able to get around and about in the area in fairly short order, before Kevin and Brian left, at a time of very limited mileage and strict petrol rationing. I detected a chance to kill two birds with one stone. I gestured to Kevin to hand me the phone, which he did, with some relief. I deliberately identified myself as "Member-in-Charge," conveniently forgetting the "Acting" bit. That title was clearly what the angry motorist wished to hear. Somebody, "in authority" was now listening to his ranting. I let him repeat his story. When he demanded a police presence to sort out the accident and the damage, as he put it, I was able to say that I and the Duty Patrol Officer would be with him just as soon as safe driving speeds permitted, which was likely be over an hour or so.

A few minutes later, Kevin and I, with a constable in the back, were in the station's Land Rover, heading for the main north-south road. On the front seat, between Kevin and I there was a clipboard with a Traffic Accident Report Book, a TARB as it was usually known, all ready to be filled in. The first fifteen miles were through the Tribal Trust Lands on a very badly corrugated dirt road; a well-used and busy one at that from the assortment of vehicles we passed, including busses. Nearing the main road, Kevin pointed out the cluster of buildings that comprised Chibi Clinic. That location had a Senior Medical Orderly in charge. The complex had male and female wards for the local villagers who needed them, an out-patient section and a busy accident and emergency room too. Most importantly, treatment was affordable at a half-crown cost, no matter what.

Once on to the main road, with its good, broad two lanes of tarmac surface, Kevin drove on as fast as the legal limit and safe driving techniques permitted. The road itself was well-maintained, the surface smooth and even. Quite a change from the rattling, banging and vibrating that was the norm for progress on the dirt roads.

A few miles south of the clinic a cluster of buildings to the left caught my attention. "Another hospital?" I asked.

Kevin nodded. "That's Ngomahuru Isolation Hospital. One part of it handles Tuberculosis cases. The other part is a Lepresaurium. Victoria Province has more than its fair share of both of those diseases."

Overall, it took us nearly an hour and a half to reach the Ngundu Halt area, deep in the hills, a few miles north of the Lunde River. On a hill, a mile or so north of the turn-off eastward to Triangle and Hippo Valley, we observed a Rhodesia Railways heavy goods vehicle, parked neatly to the left of the road, facing downhill. A little lower down the slope, on the other side, facing towards Fort Victoria, was a very shiny dark blue Mercedes saloon car with a European driver sitting in it, behind the steering-wheel. Lounging about on the bank near the lorry were a dozen or so locals. Kevin drew our vehicle to a halt behind the heavy vehicle and we three occupants climbed out. I walked down the nearside to the front of the lorry, noted that the driver's cab was empty and then glanced back along the offside. There was no sign of any wheel being missing.

I handed the clipboard and TARB to Kevin and left him and the constable to identify the driver from among those sitting on the roadside bank. I then walked across to the Mercedes. It was a very late model, with a shiny steel front bumper, chrome radiator grill and a naked lady white metal mascot atop the radiator cap. At first glance, the car appeared to be unmarked. The driver climbed out and met me by the front of his car. "It took you long enough," he snapped, before I had even had time to identify myself. "I've been here hours." His eyes settled on my shoulders. "Are you sure you're the Member-in-Charge?"

I ignored his anger and abruptness and asked if he would kindly show me the serious damage to his car that he had reported over the phone. Standing in front of his car he pointed downwards at the metal bumper. "There," he stated emphatically, his finger a few inches from a very slight dent. "And there," he declared angrily. "Car's ruined. Cost me a packet a week ago. Now it's worthless. Who's going to pay for it? That's what I want to know?"

That second blemish was harder to see than the first. It was a minute scratch on the top edge of the chrome radiator grill.

To help me keep my face expressionless, I bent forward and carefully traced a forefinger across both of the indicated blemishes. Straightening up, I asked him, "Are you sure that it was a wheel that came off and hit your car, Sir? I ask that because I can't see any wheel missing from that lorry over there?"

"It was a damned wheel I tell you. It came bowling down the hill ahead of the lorry, clouted my bumper and radiator and then bounced up and over me. I never saw where it ended up."

I left the angry driver by his car and walked over to Kevin and the constable who were deep in conversation with the driver of the lorry. His story was simple. He had seen the Mercedes approaching; then seen one of the tyre-locking rims, which were one part of his rear wheel assemblies, spinning past him on his off-side, like a fast-rolling hoop. It hit the front of the Mercedes, bounced up over it and went into the bushes at the side of the road. He stopped his lorry and climbed out of his cab to check the rear tyres. The European driver stopped, reversed back, climbed out and snatched the keys which were then still in the lorry's dashboard. They had an argument and the European drove off southwards and returned a while later saying the police were coming.

Leaving Kevin to get on with completing the TARB, I walked back to the driver of the Mercedes. "I understand that you have recorded the registration number of the lorry and the name of the driver, Sir?"

"Too damned true," was his sharp reply.

"In that case, Sir, I suggest that you provide your insurance and driver's licence details to Patrol Officer Kilfoil over there, give him the keys to the lorry and then drive on about your business. You can put in an insurance claim against the railways company, once you have an estimate of the cost of repairs. Rhodesia Railways are a fully insured company and big enough to be able to cover the cost of those repairs, even if the car is a write off."

The Mercedes driver looked hard at me. "I want him arrested. I could have been killed."

"His vehicle will be examined to find out why the part came off," I assured him. "If any negligence is involved or if the vehicle was not roadworthy when it was sent out, summonses will be served, but, right now, there are no justifiable grounds for an arrest."

Visibly unhappy, the driver of the Mercedes provided the necessary details to Kevin, handed over the keys to the lorry, climbed into his car and drove off north. Once he was out of the way, with the help of the lorry driver and the onlookers, we found the missing hoop of metal. A close examination of it showed that a locking bolt had sheared. An inspection of the rest of the vehicle disclosed that it was in perfectly good order and quite capable of being safely driven at a modest speed, to the nearest depot part-way towards Triangle. Admonishing the driver to keep his speed down, I sent him on his way.

Kevin drove us back from that highly educational accident by a different route, on wholly dirt roads, that took us through the hills, past Razi Dam, the largest one of the many in Chibi, up through the Munaka Pass and on, past our local butchery, to the police camp. By the time we got back, we were all ready for lunch.

Chief Superintendent Roy Briault was as good as his telephone word when he appeared the next week. He kept the visit very informal and very helpful. To put right the absence of the formal hand-over certificate which was always required when the top spot at any station changed hands, as they often did following routine promotions, retirements and transfers, he intended to send out the provincial quartermaster, to go through the station inventory with me. Provided no serious deficiencies turned up, I would be required to sign acceptance for the inventory and would relinquish responsibility for it whenever the next properly ranking member-in-charge appeared. On that point, at that time, he was unable to tell me who that might be, or when. What he was firm about was that I would be remaining at Chibi to support that person. I pointed out that Kevin Kilfoil was due to leave the police force at the end of the month, while Brian Oberholzer might vanish at any time now. Unless something was done about that situation, I could well find myself as the only European policeman at the station. OC District assured me that he did not intend to let that happen.

For the next few hours, with a tray of tea and sandwiches from the mess at lunchtime, we worked our way through the long list of items that were regularly checked upon by visiting officers. Aside from the cash holdings, such as the imprest account, deposit fine receipts book and intelligence reward fund, Mr Briault also went through the Occurrence Book, Minor Reports Books, Crime Register, Warrants of Further Detention, Patrol Records Book, individual Patrol Diaries, Personal Notebooks and the Ration Roll. When that lot was done, he turned his attention to the Vehicle Maintenance Records, the Incomplete Dockets and eventually, those cases which were currently under investigation.

Late in the afternoon, when the office work was done, Mr Briault decided he needed a stroll around the camp. That stroll covered the police camp, witness quarters, stores and stables and of course, the European single men's quarters and mess, before the pair of us returned to the charge office building.

Not everything was exactly as he, or I, would have liked it and my list of "Things to Keep on Top Of" was longer than I might have hoped for, but I took some heart from his parting remark, as he climbed into his car. "Well, Mr Woolley, you're still afloat. Keep it up."

As the dust from the receding car settled, Brian and Kevin appeared, wanting to know how the visit had gone. I displayed my written list of "Things to Keep on Top Of" and repeated OC District's parting remark. With that, we all agreed it was time for a beer and headed off to the mess.

A few days later, our provincial quartermaster appeared, clutching a sheaf of papers that were his copy of the formal inventory for Chibi Police Station. Despite good warning and careful preparation, it took several hours to go through every item listed, from firearms to furniture and typewriters to vehicle tools. Fortunately, all was well, even down to the tyre pressure-gauge for the Land Rover. Q-rep was pleasantly surprised. I was simply relieved. He and I put our signatures to the necessary handover certification, after which he duly departed in good time to get back to Fort Victoria before dark.

His parting remark of, "Well, Mr Woolley, now it really is all yours. Good luck with it," was a sobering one.

Not long after Q-rep's visit, Chief Chibi sent word for me to call on him. I took Const. Bude, who had been my original messenger, with me. Chibi's home kraal was a cluster of traditionally built huts. There were kitchen huts and sleeping huts and grain huts, all intermingled. At one end of the complex was a round hut that, like many in Africa, would have sat well in Iron Age Britain. It was fully twenty feet in diameter. The wattle and daub wall measured little more than five feet high. It was overlapped by the bottom end of the thatched roof that rose to perhaps fifteen feet at its peak, where there was a hole that allowed the smoke generated by the fire that sat in the centre of the hut to escape and dissipate.

The interior of the hut was dark, the thick thatch heavily smoke-stained to a shiny dark brown. Only the flickering flames of the fire, within a circle of stones, provided some light. Around the inside of the walls, there were lengths of mud benches for seating purpose and here and there on the floor were mats, some of split bamboo and others of pure woven and plaited rushes. On those mats, mostly sitting cross-legged, were half-a-dozen seriously senior grey and white-haired local men who were clearly the chief's Dare or council of elders. There was one rush mat that was unoccupied.

Chief Chibi himself was certainly of considerable age. Bearded and white haired, he was blanket-wrapped from shoulders to ankles. He was seated on a European style kitchen chair, closer to the fire than anyone else. At his chest hung the half-moon brass plate that was his formal badge of office. Const. Bude, carefully briefed, identified me to Chief Chibi and explained that, if the chief agreed to talk with me, my wish was to learn about the area, its people and their history.

When Const. Bude fell silent, Chibi made a brief reply in Kalanga and held out his hands, palms uppermost. "He wishes to feel your hands, Ishe," Bude informed me softly.

I handed my cap, which I had removed when entering the hut, to Bude and moved forward so that I could place my hands on those of the chief. For a minute or so the old man's hands roamed over my own, from fingertips to wrists. Finally, he uttered a short phrase. At that, Bude informed me that the chief wished to feel my face and head. Knowing that an awful lot might hinge on the next moments, I carefully knelt down and lifted the chief's right hand to my chin. Once more there was silence as the chief's hands passed lightly to and fro, from chin to neck, face, nose, ears, eyes and scalp.

Eventually, Chibi lowered his hands and spoke, quite briefly. There was a burst of laughter and some nodding of heads from the elders. Somewhat puzzled, I looked questioningly at Bude. "The chief says that your hair is older than your face, Ishe." On that I had to admit he was right. At 26 years of age, I was notably thin on top already.

"Is that all he says?" I asked, just a little concerned.

"No, Ishe. He has agreed to speak with you."

In the next couple of hours, seated beside my constable interpreter on the spare rush mat, I shared a meal of roasted goat, sadza and sweet beer with Chibi and his council of elders. As Chibi talked, I learned a great deal about his tribal area, which was properly called "Chivi Chako" or "Your Sin" and its people and history. I learned of how, many years back, the Chibi people had split and fought each other; of how a marriage arranged to heal the rift had ended in treachery and death, resulting in one faction being driven out across the Lunde River into Mberengwe (Belingwe) area and, when derided by the victors for being poor warriors, that defeated element had shouted back "Chivi Chako" because the victorious faction had indulged in treachery and how the name had stuck.

I learned of the hills named Nyaningwe and Nyaningwe Nema and their importance to the local people and their survival after the first raids by the Ndebele Impis.

I listened with interest to tales of hunting, of tribal skirmishes and both victories and defeats.

Chibi, or perhaps Const. Bude, drew vivid word pictures of celebrations and rituals held at Kubemberera, "the dancing place" high up on Nyaningwe Nema hill.

When Chibi's memory occasionally let him down over a detail in his stories, one or other of the elders would chip in, reminding their chief of this or that.

Eventually, Chief Chibi decided that his voice was becoming weary and that he needed to rest it. Through Const. Bude, I thanked him and the elders for sharing their history with me and asked if I might speak with them all some more on another occasion, when it would be my turn to provide the beer and the meal. Whether it was the thought of that offer, or because, as I felt, the chief was proud of his heritage and happy to talk about it, my offer was accepted. We two policemen shook hands all round and departed.

On the short drive to the police station, Const. Bude informed me that even he had heard things he had never known before and hoped that whenever I went to see the chief again, I would take him with me to interpret once again. I assured him I would be happy to do so. Fortunately, it was a promise I was able to keep.

The next Saturday afternoon's tennis party brought an invitation from the DC to join him on a hippo shoot on the Tokwe River on the following Monday. His uniformed messengers had apparently received several complaints from one village area where the hippos were numerous and doing a great deal of damage. He did make it clear that I would be going along purely as an observer, because he would be doing the shooting. That was, he was at pains to assure me, simply because the licence to cull the animals was issued to the DC's staff and not to the police force. Despite that, I felt it would be useful for me to see a bit more of the local area and gain some idea of the damage that hippo do in cultivated crops.

On the Sunday, Kevin decided that before he finally departed from Chibi, he needed to take some photographs of the police camp and area from the top of the kopje behind the station. He also confirmed what previous conversations had rather suggested. Neither he, nor Brian had ever ventured onto the kopje before. They had only ever taken pot-shots at baboon when they appeared on it. I promptly offered to make the climb with him. I too wanted to take a similar set of photographs and had been eager to have a closer look in the caves and crannies formed by the clusters of granite boulders on the hill. However, the kopje was heavily vegetated, except for the narrow maintenance pathway alongside the water supply pipelines to and from the large concrete tank. This tank was set in the small flat area that formed the lowest point of the crest on the somewhat saddle-shaped hill and could be seen from the police station. Clambering on, up and around such a thickly bushed and very broken kopje on one's own was a most unwise activity, for several reasons, which was why, despite my immediate interest in the hill, I had not yet tried to venture near it. Kevin's need for some photographs gave me an opportunity to scratch that particular itch.

In the middle of that Sunday morning, Kevin and I set off, both carrying cameras, slung over our shoulders and both carrying firearms. Kevin had his

Lee-Speed rifle and I had one of the police station's 12 Bore Greener Shotguns. At the beginning of the pipeline pathway, which rose at an angle of something around fifty or sixty degrees, I levered open the Martini-Henry action of the Greener shotgun, slid a cartridge into the breach, closed the mechanism and set the safety catch on. Kevin followed suit with his .303.

When I picked up a few pieces of rock and hurled them well up ahead of us, Kevin asked what that was for. I pointed out that we were both wearing veldtschoens, a very comfortable and common style of footwear in the bushlands. It was also a type of footwear that allowed the wearer to walk and even climb, very quietly. Most snakebite victims whom I had encountered in my travels were ones who had been climbing kopjes when bitten. Many of them had been bitten in the hand, forearm or face as they reached up and over rocks and ledges, the top surfaces of which had been blind to them as they climbed. Snakes and even scorpions, out warming up to operational temperature by basking in the morning sun, reacted instantly and aggressively when an unsuspecting hand, forearm or face suddenly loomed up close to them. My pitching of rocks well ahead of us was to ensure that whatever was up ahead of us had ample warning of our approach and plenty of time to clear from our path.

Very quickly, both Kevin and I realised that despite climbing alongside the concrete pipeline, we needed both hands to scramble up the steep slope. By mutual agreement, we slung our weapons across our backs and clambered on, stopping every dozen strides or so to pitch more rocks ahead of us until we reached the water tank itself. If it looked big from down below, close-up it appeared larger. It was fully twenty feet across, set on a concrete base that was a foot wider all around. The concrete wall was about seven feet deep. A white-painted sloping sheet-metal roof covered it. As we stood looking at it, we could hear the steady splash-splash of water pouring into it to the rhythm of the pumping machinery some miles away to the east. The structure looked good and sound, but, as we walked around it, I noticed a slight leak where the outflow pipe was. That leak had clearly been there some while, because the water had run over the edge of the concrete base and formed a small muddy area about a yard across. In the mud were footprints of birds and paw-prints of animals; one of which was that of a leopard. It was not a fresh pugmark, but that was when we both decided to unsling our respective weapons and carry them just a little more readily to hand.

Kevin decided to take a photograph of the tank and then we moved on, attempting to stick to the crest of the kopje as its spine rose up towards the northern end. The ground was covered in a tangle of dead brushwood, acacia thorn bushes, cacti and sisal. There were stacks of colourful red-hot poker plants, or canna, to name them properly, with all sorts of grasses growing between them. There were small game trails in the grasses between the rocks and the tops of several of the boulders were shiny smooth, from the feet of countless generations of rock rabbits, locally called dassies and properly named as hyrax, which clearly thrived on the hill. Those furry little fellows were much sought after by the local people for their skins, which made wonderful blankets, or karosses. For those locals, their flesh was also good eating too. On that score, no self-respecting leopard would turn his or her nose up at a meal of dassie either. As I had learned already, although only about the size of a British hare, their closest relative was the elephant. I often thought that particular relationship was one of nature's instances of going from the sublime to the ridiculous.

Given that the main purpose of our expedition that day was to get to the highest point on the kopje and take photographs, I made no effort to penetrate into any of the crevices or caves that we pushed and hacked our way past. I say "hacked" because my belt carried a water-bottle and a sheathed hunting knife, which I used to good effect where I could, all the time wishing it was the size of a panga, or machete. What I did watch out warily for were hornet or bee's nests. Upsetting either of those two types of flying fiends guaranteed an instant episode of pain, sickness and even death.

Here and there, between the bigger boulders there were suggestions of rough stone walls of undressed rocks. The areas they enclosed were far too small to be living quarters, but as defensive positions in time of trouble, they would have been very hard to assault.

Eventually, after nearly an hour and a half of hard work, we reached the north-eastern edge of the kopje. We were still about twenty or thirty feet below the actual peak, but the sheer bare granite rock rising above us was too comprehensive an obstacle for us to surmount. However, what was there pleased us both no end, because we found ourselves standing on a small terrace, behind a very old dressed stone wall that was chest high. The view was phenomenal. The flatlands of the north and east portions of Chibi Tribal Trust Land were spread out before us. The Mashaba hills and the

Mines at Shabani could all be made out clearly, despite their distance away. Closer to us were Chibi Township and the DC's office and residential area, while right at our feet, the police camp, building by building, seemed so close that we could have, had we wished to, thrown stones onto the roofs of most of them.

For a while, we were both very content to just stand there, staring and pointing out to each other bits and pieces of the landscape that were identifiable. Even in the haze that was beginning to build as the dry season progressed; the far distant twin hills of Revuri and Inyuni, close by the Zimbabwe Ruins, were easy to distinguish. As the dry season advanced and the haze over the distance thickened, those and the other hills on the horizon would gradually become uncertain outlines. They would stay that way until the first rains laid the floating atmospheric dust particles and washed the air squeaky clean. Then those hills would suddenly leap back into sharp focus, as if they had all been moved twenty miles closer.

From our position on that highest walled platform, we were better able to look down on the eastern flank of the kopje, directly behind the police mess and member-in-charge's house. From above, it was clear that there were several small flat areas within rough stone walling that appeared to have largely collapsed and a few caves and crevices too. There was one huge granite rock-face about a third of the way down which looked as though it had broken apart. What appeared to be the broken-off portion, weighing dozens of tons, was situated face-down on the largest of the terraced areas. I decided that there was a great deal more exploring to be done on the hill at another time. For the moment, we satisfied ourselves with taking all the photographs we wanted to. When that was done, we did, for a minute or two, consider taking the more direct route downwards. However, the steepness of the slope, the jumbled geological mayhem of the granite boulders and the thickness of the vegetation, were all hazards that steered us to opt for a return via the way we had come up, longer though that might be.

Our return journey was uneventful until we got to within a few yards of the water-tank. Kevin, who was in front of me, suddenly stopped and brought his rifle up to the aim position at his right shoulder, clicking off the safety catch as he did so. Following the line of the long barrel I realised that the flat ledge, where the tank sat on its concrete base appeared to have what at first looked like a thick rope decorating it. Then I realised that I was looking at the middle and tail end of one very large, dark greenish brown snake, the head of which was out of sight around the curve of the tank, near where the small leak was. I moved a couple of paces, as quietly as I could to my right, to be clear of Kevin, pushed off the safety catch of my shotgun and studied the situation. To get to the downward path we needed, we would have to pass within six feet of the wall of the tank where the pipes joined it. The snake we were looking at was at least double that length.

"Python?" Kevin queried softly.

"Wrong markings," I whispered back. "More likely a cobra, so watch it."

At that moment, the head of the snake appeared. The brute was fourteen-foot long if an inch. The broad yellow band behind its head identified it immediately. On seeing us, its head lifted, its hood flared and it kept coming. Kevin's shot passed over the top of the head of the banded cobra and scarred the concrete wall of the tank. Perhaps ducking from the passage of that near miss, the snake's head went down, nearer to ground level. My own shot hit the ground almost smack under the chin of that moving head. Earth, leaves and twigs blasted upwards. Stung, but otherwise unhurt, the cobra recoiled from the blast and fled directly away from us. Kevin got in one more shot, but that too merely scarred the tank. By the time I had another shotgun round loaded the reptile had gone from sight.

"A .303 rifle and a single shot greener-gun are not the ideal weapons for taking on an aggressive banded cobra," I said as conversationally as I could, over the pounding of my heart. "That's what comes of forgetting to throw rocks ahead of us."

Kevin grinned. "That stroppy bugger would most likely have thrown a rock straight back at us and then come after it."

I nodded agreement. "Now it's out of the way, let's get moving; before it decides to come back with some friends."

We clambered downwards to ground level without further incident and headed for the mess, where we settled down to explain the shots to Brian, to clean our weapons and enjoy a beer or two before lunch.

The following day, two matters of note occurred. The first was that my firearms licence arrived in the post. I duly handed over five pounds in cash to Kevin and completed the paperwork that legalised the transfer of his long-barrelled 1896 Lee-Speed .303 rifle to me. The second occurrence was that I accompanied the DC, as arranged, on his hippo hunt.

At that stage of the year, the Tokwe River had ceased to flow. It was, in effect, simply a dry riverbed with pools of water of greater or lesser length, volume and depth, at varying distances apart over its whole length. The hippos, which were plentiful, foraged at night and returned to submerge themselves in the cool waters of the pools during daylight hours. The culling of any species, from cane rat to elephant should be a scientifically based activity. Anything injured, lame or diseased, needed to be the first target; After that, the young bulls. Only if that targeting failed to achieve what was desired, did the guns point towards the females, the breeding stock for the future.

That scientific approach was, however, not how Mr O'Connor carried out his mission to keep down the number of marauding hippo in his area of responsibility. The journey to the Tokwe itself, a couple of miles or so upstream from the point where the Chibi Township and administrative settlement's water was drawn from, was a short one. To save mileage, I travelled in one of the Internal Affairs Department's Land Rovers, with Brian Tullet. Ahead of us in a similar vehicle were the DC himself, driven by Bill Kennedy, along with a small number of uniformed messengers.

As we neared our target area, Brian Tullet pointed out to me some areas of flattened maize, millet and rapoko. There was not much left for the villagers to reap. All caused by the night-time activities of the great lumbering animals as they each sought their fill of nightly nutrition within convenient foraging distance from the river. It was easy to see why the villagers wanted some culling done.

Having left Chibi immediately after lunch, it was still early afternoon when we reached the river. Word had been sent on ahead of what the DC intended to do. Quite naturally, there were a couple of hundred locals standing around and sitting about, all chattering like school children on an outing. The DC himself climbed out of his vehicle carrying his personal 8mm Manlicher bolt-action rifle. To back him up, Bill Kennedy was carrying an Internal Affairs Dept .303 SMLE rifle. Neither Brian nor I carried any weapon at all. Brian Tullet set the foreseeable tone of the afternoon, by whispering to me, as we alighted from our vehicle, "I'll bet you a lemonade to a crate of beer that Bill does not get to fire a single shot all afternoon." Remembering what Bill Kennedy has said about the DC believing himself to be a great white hunter, I did not take up that whispered bet.

With us nonentities standing in the background, the DC first met with the local headman and kraalheads under him. With those niceties completed, instructions were issued for all but a couple of the seniors present to remain where they were, while the rest of us walked on to where the shooting was to be done. Obediently, we followed Mr O'Connor and the local guides to the nearest of several large pools in which probably a dozen hippo were idling away the daylight hours. The water was no more than five feet deep, because the hippos were having to kneel in order to be fully submerged. Two of them were wholly out of the water, resting on the sand.

At a distance of some hundred yards or so, the DC bade us all stay put, while he walked on alone on the well-used footpath on top of the riverbank. As he neared them, the two hippos on the sandbank twitched their ears and grunted, but neither moved. After all, they were totally used to the constant movement of villagers along that pathway, so had no real cause for alarm.

When the DC was level with the two hippos, at a range of no more than thirty paces, he stopped, knelt and carefully aimed his rifle, angled downwards, at one of the two animals and fired. Despite watching carefully, I failed to see where his bullet actually struck. Both hippos were broadside on to him, both showing fully their right sides. His only precise killing spot was between the right eye and right ear of whichever beast he chose to sight on.

For some reason, Mr O'Connor decided to try to shoot for the heart. With a heavier weapon, such as a .357, a .375 or a 40-40 calibre, he might have got away with it, but not with the 8mm antique that he was wielding. All he did was to wound the animal. It squealed with pain and rage, lumbered to its feet and headed, along with its alarmed companion, straight into the water close by. As the two shapes were moving, the DC fired again, this time slapping a bullet into the rump of the second hippo before that poor beast could get into the water.

While the two wounded victims milled around, turning the pool red with their blood and thoroughly alarming the few other animals in that stretch of water, the DC waved for us to join him.

When we reached him, his eyes were shiny bright and his face was beaming. He was obviously enjoying himself. For the next ten minutes, he took pot-shots at everything that moved in the pool. Hippopotami that were young, old, male, female, all took bullets from the DC's antiquated weapon, until one of them made a bid to find a safer place. It started a stampede to get out of danger by leading those that could follow up and out of the water at the end of the pool furthest from us. Two of the group, perhaps those he had first hit, struggled to get out of the water. Both fell, thus becoming targets for more shots from Mr O'Connor's antiquated rifle.

When the slaughter was over, four dead hippos were accounted for. Others certainly had been hit, as blood spoor heading away downriver testified. Mr O'Connor seemed quite sanguine about that. When I suggested that we might need to follow and despatch the wounded ones, the DC shook his head. "They'll live, or they'll die. If they die, we'll hear about it."

That was not the way I had been taught to hunt by skilled game rangers in Nyasaland. There the rule was that you followed up on wounded animals of any kind, until you either lost spoor, or accounted for them. I had some experience of what a wounded big-game animal could do if left suffering. I had helped bury some of the victims and dealt with the sudden death dockets.

We left the villagers and a few uniformed messengers to see to the skinning and butchering of the dead hippos. The skins, to be collected the next day, would no doubt end up as sjamboks, the tough hippo-hide whips so beloved of the Afrikaner and so detested by the African. The meat would at least provide some good eating for the nearby villagers, perhaps a little compensation for their eaten and trampled crops.

In the vehicle travelling back to Chibi, Brian Tullet remarked, "Not a pretty sight, eh?"

"That," I said grimly, "is an understatement. As a great white hunter, the man's a menace."

Brian nodded. "I suggest you don't try to tell him that. He's very touchy at any challenge to his shooting and hunting skills and the excellence of that antique rifle of his. Apart from that, he really is a decent bloke to work for."

Since I was hardly in a position to comment on that final opinion, I just stayed silent.

A week or so later, the DC phoned me to say that he was going out on another hippo shoot and would, once again, welcome my company, along with a constable or two. Because the DC had asked me personally, I felt I was duty bound to go along, distasteful though the first hunt had proved.

It was with a feeling of relief that I discovered that on this occasion, Mr

O'Connor was after just one particularly big bull hippo that local people had identified as being troublesome and allegedly dangerous. The story went that it had a favourite pool which it and it alone occupied during the day, so there would be no problem identifying it milling around amid others. To me, that story sounded a bit weird, because hippos usually congregated together. However, I was proved wrong and the locals were proved right.

We found the pool. We found the hippo. When we first saw it, it had only the top of its head, its ears and eyes, out of the water. As the DC approached, rifle at the ready, the hippo simply sank fully out of sight, becoming a vague outline with its shoulders probably a foot and a half below the surface. Any skilled hunter would have waited until the poor brute put its head up again and likely despatched it with one well-aimed shot. That was not the DC's way. Clearly convinced of the power of his 8mm bullets to cut through a foot or more of water without losing clout or penetrative power, Mr O'Connor aimed and fired. Whether he hit it or not with that shot, I never knew. What I saw, was one big bull hippo as it emerged from the water and headed off downriver as fast as it could go, pursued by several 8mm bullets, fired by Mr O'Connor, just as fast as he could work the bolt action and pull the trigger of his rifle. A couple of spurts of sand told me that not every shot hit home, but, clearly, one did, because the hippo suddenly lost the use of its back legs. After shoving more cartridges into the magazine of his rifle and pushing one home into the breach, he waved us up from where we had been watching and set off ahead of us towards the roaring, wounded and semi-paralyzed hippo. From within twenty feet of the poor brute, he fired six more shots, before the animal's forelegs buckled and it pitched fully to the ground and, thankfully, breathed its last breath.

As protocol required, we all congratulated the DC on his completion of a job well done as whooping and chanting villagers descended on the carcass, knives and axes at the ready. Once again, we left the uniformed messengers to supervise the skinning and butchering of the unfortunate hippo and headed back to Chibi Village.

Fortunately, as circumstances worked out, that was the last time that I was required to accompany Mr O'Connor on a hippo shooting expedition. It was not, however, the last time I went hunting with him.

Over the next couple of weeks, Kevin and Brian both left. Kevin's departure date had long been known, but, for Brian, his advice of transfer was barely less sudden than was mine from Mashaba. A radio message arrived, giving him forty-eight hours' warning and that was that. All the while, OC District was at pains to assure me that I would certainly not be left, single-handed, to cover the work of one Section Officer and two Patrol Officers.

On that issue, the day after Brian left, 7157 Patrol Officer Reginald David Graham, who had been in depot at the same time I had been, but two squads ahead of me, arrived at Chibi.

Reg arrived along with word from Dispol that in a fortnight or so, he would be followed by Section Officer Ian Lewis, who would take charge of the station. As I soon discovered, Reg simply did everything hard. He worked hard, played hard, drove motor vehicles hard and motorcycles even harder. As time went on more than one of our trusty constables was to return, shaking, from a pillion passenger ride with Reg and describe it as "too terrible!" Reg's likings were several! Cars, motorcycles and most things mechanical. He also liked a few ales, here and there. However, I always felt that what he enjoyed most was bedding the ladies. Socially, he worked on a simple belief that a gentleman should never discriminate between single and married ladies. They were to be treated the same; which meant asking, just as soon as possible, "Do you feel like some bed exercise with me?"

Reg told me, in one of our early conversations in the quiet of the mess, that he had worked out that one in ten of the ladies, married or single, would say "yes" in answer to his direct question. That being so; the quicker he asked, "The wrong nine," as he put it, the quicker he would get to that "Number ten" woman. On occasions over the next several months, when Ian Lewis was Duty Officer for the week and Reg and I attended social events in Fort Victoria or one or other of the hotels in the Zimbabwe Ruins area, Reg's dancing partner of the moment would deliver a firm slap to his face and leave the dance floor alone. On such occasions Reg would return to our table rubbing his cheek and mutter, "Number 7" or such. That he was viewed as attractive and often charming company by married and single women was evidenced by the number of occasions upon which Reg would sidle quietly up to me and murmur, "I'll see you later, she's a ten!" before vanishing with some female in tow.

As a hard-case, Reg was actually a fraud. His hard-case exterior shattered in the presence of animals and children. I recall tears streaming down his face when we attended a fatal road traffic accident in which an African toddler was the victim. Tears also flowed when he was unable to save a newborn calf despite bottle-feeding it every few hours over a couple of days or more.

Reg did quickly cotton on to the fact that his method of riding the station motorcycle scared stiff the African staff riding pillion. Not wishing to be slowed down to a pace that made them feel comfortable, Reg avoided taking them with him, if he could. There were many occasions when he could do that. Traffic accidents on the main road, delivery of court summonses, attendance in Fort Victoria for court or vehicle servicing and so on.

It was following on from one of those occasions that I received a telephone call from OC Province. The telephone call was made for the purpose of informing Patrol Officer Graham that OC Province had seen him riding a police motorcycle on the main road to Fort Victoria, laying chest and belly down on the tank and seat with his feet stretched out straight behind him and that if he ever was seen doing that again, he would be on a disciplinary charge. Reg, when advised of the verbal warning, was genuinely nonplussed. "I was only trying to get there a bit faster," he complained.

Mentioning Section Officer Ian Lewis needs me to explain that Reg and I were only left to hold the fort between us as it were, for a couple of weeks before our new boss arrived. In those two weeks, Sheila Meade arrived to supervise the packing up of all of her and Phil Meade's household effects and their transfer, by a large removals van, to Salisbury, where Phil was fortunately recovering well from his sport-inflicted injury.

5543 Section Officer Ian David Lewis, his wife Julie and their infant daughter moved into the newly emptied and freshly spring-cleaned married quarters towards the end of September. The spring-cleaning was carried out by a gang of "Bandits" from the local prison, under supervision of a guard. Rhodesia still had "Imprisonment with Hard Labour" on the statutes, although the "hard" had virtually vanished. Prisoners still helped to keep government offices and buildings tidy and in good order and they were a common sight working to cut grass, trim flower beds and do simple road repair work wherever such was needed. Prison guards, at the end of the day, when shepherding their charges onto some flat-back lorry, ready to be returned to prison, quite routinely, in Chibi, just as I had seen in Mashaba, passed up their Greener shotgun to one or other of the Bandits, before climbing aboard themselves and recovering the weapon. Trust is, after all, a precious and wonderful thing!

Ian Lewis and I carried out a careful and thorough hand-over routine a day or so after his arrival on station. Fortunately, that procedure went smoothly. All that was needed to be accounted for was there and in its rightful place. That allowed us both to put the necessary signatures on the appropriate certificate. With that ritual behind us, I was able to hand over the station keys and take up my proper position in the Patrol Officers' Office, alongside Reg, leaving the M i/c's desk to Ian and the unoccupied "Wife of Member" desk to his wife, Julie.

To enable Ian to settle in and familiarise himself with the station, Reg and I shared the Duty Officer slot for the next couple of weeks. That was probably just as well, because, having taken over from Reg on the Friday afternoon, at 16:00hrs, as was our habit, the following morning brought word of a murder case to be investigated.

The story as reported by the local kraalhead's messenger, who had walked through most of the night, a distance of around twenty miles, in order to be at the police station early, was that there had been a beer-drink, attended by many people. Late in the evening a man and a woman, not related, had left the beer-drink together. At about midnight, a local man who had not been at the beer-drink had been walking home when he spotted a heap laying in the middle of a recently ploughed field that his family worked. Thinking that to be something strange, he had gone closer, to see what it was. He found it to be a dead woman. He left the body there and went to report to the senior kraalhead for the area, which happened to be where the beer-drink was, which was still going on. The kraalhead sent his messenger to report the death to the police.

In this instance, nobody reached for the Minor Report Form Book. The appearance of the messenger and the basic facts of his report went into the Occurrence Book, with a cross-reference to an entry in the Crime Register. Such matters were so routine in the life of any District Police Officer in that part of Africa that there was no sudden rush of activity. Nobody called for the CID. Nobody set off hurriedly in one of a fleet of police vehicles, with sirens blaring and lights flashing, accompanied by at least one ambulance. Having arrived and reported his story during Stable Parade, the messenger was provided with food and water until that Stable Parade was done, breakfasts had been had and the day's work proper could be commenced.

So, it was with a good breakfast inside me that I booked myself out in the Occurrence Book, made the appropriate entry in the vehicle logbook, gathered my clipboard, complete with investigation diary sheets and sheets of blank paper from my office and grabbed a measuring tape and my camera and shoved those into the Land Rover. I then told my new boss where I was off to, drove the Land Rover to the stables store where Const. Bude and the messenger helped me load a metal body-box, saw those two individuals into the Land Rover and drove off, to commence investigating Chibi Police Station's latest murder case, under the reference of CR48/9/65.

After an hour or more of driving, guided by our messenger informant, I was able to stop our vehicle within a hundred yards of the body. The field was as we had been told, one which had been cleared of reaped crops and already ploughed, waiting for the first rains, when it would be sown, most probably with maize seeds to produce next year's crop. At one edge of the field were a group of local men and women, sitting quietly.

Before going anywhere near the woman's dead body, I needed to speak with the man who had found it. While Const. Bude and our informant went off to find him, I photographed the scene at a distance and from a couple of different angles. By the time I had done that, the man I wanted had been found from among the onlookers and brought forward. He was barefooted and confirmed that that was how he had been when he found the body. I then had him show me exactly how he had approached the body and identify for me his own footprints in the freshly tilled soil. With that to assist I took some more photographs of the scene before commencing my own approach to the body, setting my feet into the footprints of the villager who had first discovered the dead woman's body in the field.

The woman's body was fully clothed, although she was barefooted. She was positioned face down, hands up level with her head and palms down. The fingers of both hands were apart and crooked downwards as if she had been trying to grip the soil. Her body was cold and stiff. Life was certainly extinct, although there was no blood visible and no sign of obvious injury. What was clear was that there had been something of a struggle, for the neatness of the ploughed field was roughed up. One set of tyre-tread sandals and one set of bare feet. All of that I recorded on my camera. A very careful examination of the ground around enabled me to find the imprint of one pair of tyre-tread sandals leading away from the body towards the harder ground of a local pathway, upon which I lost it. Returning to the body, Const. Bude and I carefully turned it over. When that movement was done, I took more photographs of the soil encrusted slightly muddy face and hands.

That turning over was the signal for an eruption of wailing and weeping from the onlookers as they saw her face. She was clearly well known to many of them. With no obvious injury in view, I carefully examined her neck and throat. I suspected that she had been strangled, but her face-down position puzzled me. Most strangulation victims I had seen previously had all been laying on their backs, with hands at chest or waist level. In this case, a close examination of the dead woman's fingernails showed no trace of flesh, blood or even cloth threads.

Once I was sure that it was safe, in evidence collecting terms, to do so, I had the body-box fetched from the Land Rover. The dead woman's body was lifted carefully into it, the lid clamped firmly down, and the coffin-shaped metal box loaded into the back of the Land Rover. I set Const. Bude to the task of finding an identifying witness and locating as many locals as he could who had been at the nearby beer-drink the previous evening, while I got on with the task of taking measurements and sketching on paper a rough plan of the scene and the pathways around it.

Routine investigations and a great deal of note taking over the next two or three hours gained us the names of necessary witnesses and outlines of their evidence. The home kraal of the immediate suspect, the man the dead woman had been seen to leave the beer-drink with, was a mile or two distant from the scene. There was no roadway of any kind, but there was a well-defined scotch-cart track which I was able to drive our Land Rover along in order to get there, so that was where we went.

One of the things that never ceased to amaze me in my years in Africa was the speed with which word of incidents, or the presence of strangers, spread. In this case, by the time I drew our clearly marked police vehicle to a halt at the edge of our target kraal, the kraalhead was already clearly expecting us. He was sitting on a traditional wooden stool, his badge of office on his chest. On one side of him, sitting on a large mat made of split bamboo were two village elders. Also seated, between those venerable gentlemen, was a clearly dejected adult male whose age I guessed to be about thirty. He was wearing a blue short-sleeved shirt and khaki shorts. He was barefooted. My suspicion, which proved to be correct, was that this was our suspect. He also turned out to be one of the kraalhead's own sons.

If I was going to gain the best co-operation from the kraalhead, I needed to ignore the suspect for the moment and go through the usual courtesies of arrival and introduction, so it was some several minutes after our arrival before we were able to speak directly with the villager we were interested in about why we wanted him.

In view of what we had learned already, the sorry-looking individual was clearly a suspect, so I had Const. Bude administer a formal Warn and Caution to him, in relation to a charge of murder. When he was invited to reply, he burst into tears and then confessed that he was responsible for the woman's death, although he had not intended to kill her.

He poured out his sorry story so fast that I had to ask Bude, who was translating for me, to stop him, several times, so that I could get down in English, on paper, the words he was uttering. Eventually, he finished. I read back to him, with Bude translating, what I had recorded in English. When he nodded his agreement, Bude asked him if he was able and prepared to sign the statement he had made. That he was prepared to do and did, signing in a laboriously slow and somewhat unsteady hand. In turn, Bude and I added our signatures to the handwritten document.

The story was simple and typical of other, similar cases that I had dealt with in the past. He and the dead woman had enjoyed each other's company at the beer-drink, He had made a proposition to her. Allegedly she had agreed, so they left the beer-drink together, to seek a quiet spot away from other eyes. Knowing of a cluster of rocks at the side of the tilled field, they started to cross. Half-way across, the woman had demanded payment. He and she argued. He grabbed her arm. She turned, started screaming about rape and tried to run. He grabbed her by the neck from behind to silence her. They fell. She was face down and underneath and he on top of her. He kept squeezing her throat to silence her screams. When she was silent, he tried to talk to her, but she did not reply. He walked away and went home to sleep. When he awoke, he heard rumour that the woman's body had been found the previous evening and that the police had been sent for.

It was always my habit, as investigating officer, to try to have somebody aside from us policemen and the suspect, to also sign as witness to the fact that any statement, made under Warn and Caution circumstances, had been made freely and recorded fairly. In this instance I asked the two village elders if they would act as such witnesses. Bude's spoken words in translation brought an immediate protest from the kraalhead himself: Why was I not asking him?

I explained that I was concerned that it would be painful for him to do so because I was going to have to take his son away, under arrest to face trial. The kraalhead's anger subsided, but, with a firm and natural dignity, he insisted that he too should sign the paper because a crime, a serious crime, had been committed. He, his elders and we in the police force were all part of the system of justice that kept peace in the area. It did not matter that it was his son who was the accused person. Although he sorrowed for that fact, he had a duty to do and wished to be allowed to do it. It was a reasonable viewpoint, fairly put, so, in the end, all three became witnesses to the recording of the warned and cautioned statement. The kraalhead and one of the elders signed their names. The other elder put his mark, a firm X, to the Warn and Caution document. In court, those three signatures proved valuable.

A simple question and a search of his bedroom produced a pair of tyre-tread sandals that the accused man admitted were his and were the ones he had been wearing the previous evening. Those became physical exhibits. I recorded brief statements from all three helpful villagers before heading back to Chibi Police Station, with the Land Rover full of body-box, accused person and essential other witnesses.

At the police station, after briefing my new boss about the case, I unloaded the witnesses and accused, prepared a Post-Mortem Request Form and made a telephone call to Fort Victoria Hospital to seek some indication of when one of the doctors might be available to carry out a post-mortem. "Not for a day or two," was the reply I received. There was nothing to do but to cart the body to Fort Victoria and leave it there, in the refrigerated mortuary, to await due process, so that was exactly what Const. Bude and I did. It was after dark when we finally returned to the police station at Chibi and took ourselves off to our respective quarters for something to eat and drink. Neither of us had any lunch that day, but, in the nature of the district police work we regularly did, that was just one of those things.

The following day, I formally charged the accused with murder. His reply on that occasion was that the beer must have contained evil spirits.

Over the next many days, the routine work of placing the accused on remand; arranging attendance at the post-mortem, taking statements, preparing plans, keeping the investigation diary up to date and arranging the photographic evidence, kept me quite busy. The aged Olympia typewriter in the Patrol Officers' office did sterling work as I thumped the keys up and down as fast as my unskilled fingers and too many thumbs permitted. Fortunately, the workload that came in during the remainder of that duty officer week was light. Two murders in the same week, or a murder and a fatal road accident, were not unknown. In that particular duty officer week, such was fortunately not the case.

The result of the post-mortem provided the cause of death as "Asphyxiation due to strangulation." Both hyoid bones in her throat had been crushed.

A couple of months later, in the next High Court sitting in Fort Victoria and clearly with some tutoring from other prisoners, the accused pleaded "Not Guilty" to a charge of murder. When he claimed that the warned and cautioned statement had been falsified and what had been recorded were not his words, the case entered a "Trial-within-a trial" situation.

Once Const. Bude and I had given our evidence, the kraalhead, the accused's own father, took to the witness box. Clearly anguished, but with a firm voice and great dignity, he supported what both Bude and I had said. In their turn, so did the two village elders. After due deliberation, the accused was convicted of the lesser charge of manslaughter and sentenced to seven years IHL (Imprisonment with Hard Labour). Job done! Case closed as completed. Not all such future events were as straightforward and simple as that one.

The station did have Patrol Targets that had to be achieved. So many days per quarter out and about in each quadrant of the district, creating a visible police presence on the ground. There were a few chiefs and headmen (sub chiefs, not kraalheads) to visit, store licences to be checked at assorted townships, wanted persons to be sought, witness papers to be delivered and random road checks to be carried out. There were also a series of Pioneer Graves that it was part of our duty to visit periodically, to ensure that the piled-up stones that marked them and the sturdy iron crosses at the head of each were clear of grass and bush overgrowth and had not been degraded by activities of grazing cattle or other agents, human or animal. The duration of each patrol was normally seven days. Transport was by the station motorcycle, with the Patrol Officer up front and a constable, or even a sergeant on the pillion seat. Often, we were able to base ourselves on one or other of the Intaf (DC's) Rest Houses, where basic facilities existed. Sometimes, it was a matter of being under canvas.

The first patrol that I was detailed off to undertake, was in October. The rains had started and the temperature and humidity were both way up and rising. It took me off station, out and about in Chief Madzivere's area, based at the DC's very commodious rest camp. That building was almost a replica of the mess at the police station. The oddest thing about it was that the wood-fired boiler that heated bath and tap water was directly behind the back wall of the toilet. In winter, that WC was a cosy place to sit. In summer it was a sweatbox in which nobody dallied. Mind you, having a proper toilet to use whenever out on area patrols was a luxury. When under canvas, it was necessary to use one or other of the bush areas close by, just as the African villagers commonly did. Kraals had strict rules. There were different areas of bush for men and women. Urinating one just did, decently out of sight. When defecating, it was expected that what was deposited was either delivered into a scrape in the ground and covered over, or at least covered with grass and leaves. That arrangement was of course much to the liking of a ubiquitous little insect commonly called a dung beetle. As its name implies, it loves dung, of any kind. It collects whatever dung is available, gathers it and shapes it into balls that will roll and pushes that food supply to its little burrow to provide nourishment for the next brood. It has been commented, wisely, that without the industrious activities of thousands of dung beetles, certain whole countries in the tropics would be un-inhabitable. Rarely, away from the townships, was there ever any form of privy. Where there was, they were usually built out of corrugated iron sheets and often placed on top of discarded ant hill mounds, which provided a natural form of septic tank. It was not advisable to use one when there were thunderstorms around. Later in my service I had the sad task of dealing with the sudden death docket for a constable who did just that.

A seven-day area patrol by motorcycle started with both the station motorcycle and Land Rover heading off together for whichever area was involved. The Land Rover carried a Hounsfield camp bed and sleeping bag for the European detail and a bedroll for the African police officer, as well as food supplies, a small gas cooker and all the basics that were needed for the time away. Once the heavier kit was in place, wherever, the Land Rover returned to base, leaving the patrolling pair to get on with the necessary work. At the end of the allotted days, the Land Rover would reappear to gather up the heavier gear and cart it back to the police station.

On this occasion, Const. Chisenwa, decided that the African quarters at the rest camp were too hot and airless for comfort, so he took himself off each night to sleep in one of the huts in a village nearby. Madzivere area was plagued by several troops of marauding baboon, so it was agreed that I would carry a .303 rifle with me, in case any opportunity arose to shoot one or two of them. My newly acquired Lee-Speed's long barrel made it an awkward companion on a motorcycle, when carrying a pillion passenger, so I took along one of the station's standard SMLEs instead.

Although I had the choice of any one of three bedrooms, I also felt they were far too hot and stuffy. I settled for putting up my Hounsfield camp bed in a corner of the broad and well-netted veranda, between the lounge and the veranda's external door half-way towards the bathroom. I leaned the .303 rifle against the inner wall near the foot of my camp bed and, as night fell, lit the Petromax oil lamp I had brought along. That item, placed on a wooden stand not far from the external door to the veranda, provided a good, strong light, by which I found it easy to make a simple meal and start to write up my day's activities in the Patrol Diary that I needed to keep.

With the writing done, it was far too early to think of going to sleep, so I settled back on top of the sleeping-bag on the camp bed, with my back against the lounge wall, watching the myriad of insects attracted onto the outside of the metal gauze netting of the veranda being picked off and gobbled up by a half-dozen geckos that were enjoying a bountiful feast.

Suddenly the external door to the veranda, the top of which door was also metal gauze, and which I thought I had fully shut, moved a couple of inches inwards. In through that open gap slid a snake. It kept coming, tongue flickering as it tasted the air, until I could see the whole of its seven or eight-foot length and the distinctive yellow band inches behind its head. It was another banded cobra, just like my unwanted companion from the top of the kopje behind the police station, but a bit smaller. That lesser size did not make its bite one bit less deadly. Very slowly I began to raise my knees and slide my still-booted feet back towards me, trying to set myself up for rapid movement whenever the time was right. Extended and not seemingly upset, angry or in a position to strike, the unwanted visitor slid across the veranda floor until it reached the inner wall. There it decided to turn towards me where I was sitting, carefully motionless. Apparently still unhurried and unworried, the scaly intruder slid nearer to me, its tongue still flickering and head low.

It slid under the .303 leaning against the wall and started to disappear under the bottom end of my camp bed. When three-quarters of its length was under my bed, I hurled myself forward, off of the foot of the camp bed and on to my feet. I grabbed the rifle, fled a few paces down the veranda and looked back. My sudden movement had upset the Hounsfield bed, moved it away from the corner of the veranda and alarmed the banded cobra. That reptile had backed into the corner where my bed had been, coiled itself, raised its head, looking towards me and flared its hood, ready to strike.

Grateful for the strong white light from the Petromax lamp, I rapidly worked a round into the breach of the .303 and, thanks to the fact that the cobra was holding its stance quite steadily, shot it where head and flared hood met. In the urgency of the moment, I forgot that any bullet going through a soft target and hitting a solid object behind it, will ricochet. My bullet bounced of two walls and a floor and slapped into my left knee, fortunately with only enough force to leave a bruise and a slight abrasion.

Ignoring the slap on my knee, I walked forward to the nearly dead snake, put my booted right foot on its neck and bashed its head flat with the brass butt-plate of my rifle. The body of the cobra was still writhing and I was still standing watching it, when Constable Chisenwa and a couple of villagers burst in through the veranda door. Chisenwa took in the scene at a glance.

"Ah, Ishe," he scolded me. "You must not leave doors open out here when there are lights on. The spiders, frogs, scorpions and snakes will all come to eat the insects attracted to the light."

I could only nod my agreement. It was another lesson learned!

One of the villagers with Chisenwa was carrying an axe. With the bladed end he gave the remains of the cobra a couple of prods. "Yafa," he declared firmly, meaning that it was dead. He uttered a few more words to Chisenwa who duly interpreted for me. "He wants to know if he can take the snake away, Ishe?"

"It's of no use to me and if you don't want it either, he is welcome to it, whatever he intends to do with it," I answered. Const. Chisenwa grinned. "He will skin it, Ishe. Then he and his family will eat the meat from it. After that he will sell the skin to a local witch doctor. It is a pity you broke both of its fangs when you hit it. He could have sold those to a witch doctor too."

That reminded me, that in Africa, nothing is wasted.

With the excitement over, Const. Chisenwa and his companions took their leave, carrying the snake's remains with them. I shut the veranda's external door very firmly after they left, fetched cloth and water from the kitchen, cleared the blood and bits of snake from the floor, plastered myself in insect repellent, put the light out and turned in.

One of the wanted persons we were required to make inquiries about was Kefasi Wuyayai Ndundu. Kefasi was, to my mind, a kleptomaniac. He was a loner, an outcast. He was also a one-person crime-wave. He was of no fixed abode but roamed the hills and bushlands of the area, stealing. Food, clothing, blankets, bicycles, cash and chitupus (Identity Cards) were all fair game to him. When any one of his itinerant campsites was discovered, or he was too hotly pursued, he would just abandon all that he had except what he was wearing, flee that area and set up somewhere else, promptly stealing whatever he felt he needed to set himself up afresh.

As far as I ever knew, he had had no schooling and could neither read nor write. That did not mean he was stupid. As I was to find out later, he had, not long back, spent a week in a bed in Chibi Clinic, recovering from an injury caused by falling off one of his stolen bicycles. His true identity he covered under a stolen name, backed by an equally stolen ID card, all the while having, in the bed next to him, a constable from Chibi Police Station who had a mild case of enteritis.

During the course of our patrol week, Const. Chisenwa came in one morning with an interesting piece of news. One of the local villagers, not a bad man, but one who occasionally set snares in order to put bush meat on the family table, had recently been out in the wild lands at the back of Ngomahuru Isolation Hospital, where he intended to set snares for dassies. He had seen foot spoor where none should have been. Following it cautiously, he arrived within sight of a cave. In that cave he had seen a man he recognised as Kefasi Wuyayai Ndundu. The poacher agreed that provided Kefasi did not find out that he was the one who had shopped him, he would guide us within sight of the cave. There he would leave us, to do what policemen do. Chisenwa and I deliberated. If we made a raid in full daylight, we might well find Kefasi away, out and about. If we approached the cave by night, our blunderings would likely alarm animals, warn our quarry and give him time to flee. The best chance we had was to camp rough, cold and quiet, overnight and to walk in on him as soon after dawn as we could. Our informant agreed to that plan.

That day we ate an early evening meal, put rainproof ponchos over our uniforms, for it was threatening to rain and set off to meet our guide some few miles away from the target cave. Through the last light of the evening, we walked to within a mile of that cave. In the lee of a small cluster of granite boulders we hunkered down for the night and tried for what little sleep we might get. As dawn approached and as soon as we could see well enough to progress silently, we moved on. Kefasi had no reputation for violence, but I carried the .303 rifle, just in case. We had gone barely a dozen paces when the rain started, heavy, persistent and noisy, drumming down on the trees, rocks and assorted grasses that we were walking through.

"The weather will help us, Ishe," Chisenwa observed quietly. "He will not hear us and he will not leave the cave until it stops."

I could only agree, equally quietly and push on, keeping my rifle as close to me and as dry as I could in the noisy deluge that was falling upon us.

Eventually, our guide stopped where the game trail we had been following crossed a small stream at the foot of a hill. In a whisper and with much gesticulation, he briefed Chisenwa on the precise location of Kefasi's latest shelter. Once he was happy that we would not get lost over the last hundred yards or so he wished us good hunting and left us, quickly vanishing along the way he had led us.

The cave was well hidden. The game trail we had been following led straight on around the base of the hill, some thirty yards downhill from where the cave was, above and behind a jumble of boulders. The rain and the soggy leaves and grasses allowed us to work our way cautiously and quietly upwards until we had sight of the mouth of the cave, no more than a dozen yards away. There was no one in sight and no signs or sounds of movement either. Abreast of each other, but a few feet apart, so as to prevent our quarry attempting to dash past us, we made it, undetected into the dryness of the front of the shadowy cave, where we paused to enable our eyes to become accustomed to the gloom within. The cave was about ten feet across and perhaps twelve or fifteen feet high. It appeared to go back a dozen or more yards. Some few feet ahead of us there was a small circle of stones with the ashes of a dead fire within. Scattered about were pots, pans and other clay and metal domestic utensils. A five-litre plastic bottle partly full of water was stood not far from the dead fire. Next to that was a sack of maize-meal. Stacked against one wall was a pile of dry branches and on the inside of that pile, a pedal cycle, complete with carrier rack over the back wheel. Stepping carefully around the dead fire we moved silently deeper into the cave until we heard some snores. I looked at Chisenwa. His teeth showed white in the gloom as he grinned hugely and pointed with a hand that was already holding a pair of handcuffs. Our quarry was fast asleep, clearly warmly wrapped up under several blankets, on a rush mat set close by one wall of the cave.

Const. Chisenwa was a policeman of considerable experience. His method of waking and arresting Kefasi was simple and effective. He grabbed the sleeping man's hair with his left hand, pulled and shook. Kefasi, who was sleeping naked under the blankets, cried out and reached upward with both hands. There was a click and our quarry was handcuffed by one wrist to the good sturdy wrist of an African policeman, before he was even fully awake.

Once Kefasi was fully awake and aware of what had happened to him he admitted who he was. All in all, he took his arrest very philosophically. Perhaps that was assisted by his firm metal linkage to Const. Chisenwa and the presence of the firearm I was carrying. Under careful watch, we allowed him to get dressed, before linking him to Const. Chisenwa once again by the handcuffs. After that, I lit a fire to help us look around the cave. In that flickering firelight I located a traditional African game-skin pouch. Inside it were a few cash notes and coins, along with four ID cards. That collection alone gave me sufficient reason to arrest him then and there, even forgetting about what else I knew he was wanted for questioning over. For the record, I warned and cautioned him concerning theft of Identity Cards and the pedal cycle. Kefasi shrugged and spoke briefly after Chisenwa had translated my words.

"He says he cannot remember where these things came from. He has had some of them for a long while, but he agrees they are not his."

I duly recorded what he said, but when I invited him to sign my notebook entry, he shook his head and explained that he never learned to read or write. He did agree to put his mark under my notes.

The rain by this time had started to ease. We loaded the sack of maize-meal, the game-skin pouch, the rolled sleeping mat and blankets onto the cycle, doused the fire and set off to walk the two or three miles to Ngomahuru Isolation Hospital. Const. Chisenwa led the way followed by Kefasi who was firmly handcuffed to the frame of the loaded bicycle that we set him to push. I walked a couple of paces behind Kefasi, who had been grimly warned that if he attempted to run away, I would put a bullet into him, which I never would have done as he was no real threat to anyone. Whatever he had got up to and no matter what kind of criminal nuisance he was, he did not deserve shooting.

The reception office staff at the isolation hospital were a bit surprised to see us, but they recovered their composure very quickly and permitted me to get on the party line telephone to speak with the police station at Chibi. Little more than an hour later, Reg Graham and Sgt Wuruyayi arrived to take charge of Kefasi and his stolen properties and to give Chisenwa and me a lift back to where we had left our own transport, so that we could finish our days out on patrol, which we did, without any more arrests or excitements from snakes.

What eventually happened to Kefasi Wuyayai Ndundu was a story in itself. He cheerfully pleaded guilty to every charge of Theft or Housebreaking that was put to him.

A score or more of unsolved cases were written off to his admissions, so much so that there was a serious concern that he was just admitting everything that was put to him, whether guilty of that offence or not. He certainly gave the station one of the highest crime clearance rates in the province that year. Sentenced to a few years inside, he was whistled off to Fort Victoria prison where he proved to be no trouble at all. That gained him the somewhat ironic status of a trustworthy prisoner, so he was allowed to work outside, under minimum supervision. He became one of that gang who regularly kept the internal affairs offices and gardens tidy. He proved to be such a dab hand with flowers and shrubs that when he was released, the DC Fort Victoria promptly employed him permanently, as a gardener.

Kefasi's arrest and the unplanned connection, in mid-patrol, with the police station, added a further task to our patrol duty list. Although most of Chibi Police District was purely Tribal Trust Land, there were a few ranches down in the south-east corner. The largest was Makorse River Ranch. It was owned by the Leibigs company, but they left it to be managed day by day, by a real character. Mr Williams was a single man, aged about 50 or maybe a bit more. He was an Englishman who had wandered the globe for years, until the end of WWII, in the position of ship's carpenter in the merchant marine. Just how or why he had ended up as manager of a cattle ranch in central Africa, nobody seemed to know, but there he was. He got on well with his black and white neighbours and was well respected as an experienced and capable cattle man. I had encountered him some weeks before, when a few of the ranch's cattle had been stolen. He was quick to discover they were gone, which allowed me to get on the trail of the thieves without delay, which led to a successful prosecution and the recovery of all but one of the cows; that missing one having been quickly killed, cut up and shared out, far and wide before any arrests were made.

On this latest occasion, Mr Williams had reported a sudden spate of snaring. His ranch-hands had collected a whole lot of snares, all allegedly made from quarter inch steel cable, before they could do any great deal of harm, but the ranch's prize Afrikander bull had been caught in one and injured. He requested a police presence and an investigation to stop the bout of snaring.

Mr Williams greeted us warmly when we arrived. He was dressed in well-worn but sturdy boots, khaki shorts and a similar short-sleeved shirt which rig appeared to be his everyday working dress. As usual, his shorts were not kept up by any proper belt, but by a length of half-inch rope, tied at the front with a large, complicated knot that seemed to be a combination of double reef knot, topped off with a sheepshank or something similar. Dangling from that rope belt, by a dog-lead clip, was a folding type of yard long carpenter's ruler, with brass hinges, swivels and terminals. It gleamed that much that I always suspected he polished it daily.

On his say-so Const. Chisenwa and I, me with my camera, climbed into his Land Rover to travel to see the injured bull and some of the collected snares. It was a journey of no more than a mile or so to the paddock concerned. For better control of the cattle and the grazing, the ranch, which was still thickly bushed and treed, had been divided into sections and paddocks by good firm barbed wire fencing and gates.

When Mr Williams stopped the Land Rover, we were within a couple of dozen yards of one of the largest Afrikander bulls I had ever seen. At first sight, it was browsing, partly hidden by bushes. From where I was, it appeared to be damned near five feet at the shoulder, amazingly flat-backed and rippling with muscle. It also had a pair of the most impressively broad horns that I had ever had cause to be wary of. Mr Williams at once climbed out of the vehicle and set off towards the beast, which raised its head and glared at our approach.

Something in its eyes warned me that we were heading for trouble. "Are we quite safe getting in close to him if he's injured," I inquired warily.

"He's alright," our guide assured us, leading us unhesitatingly forward, "he's big and strong, but he's never been nas… Look out!"

I am sure that the bull never before had been nasty. However, never before had he had a wire cable locked tightly round his front left leg, inches above the hock, cutting deeply and painfully into his flesh.

Three threatened men ran in three different directions – very fast!

For some reason, the pesky critter decided to go for me. Two things saved me from some serious injury. The snare, which was, to my amazement, still around the animal's leg and clearly hurting at every stride, slowed him down. Then, the nearness of a very handy mopane tree, sturdy enough for me to use to swing hard left and turn rapidly around. By the time our unfriendly bovine had charged past me, much too close for comfort and come to a three-legged halt, looking to see where I had gone to, I was back with my two companions, safely inside the cab of the Land Rover.

It appeared that there had been a bit of a communication gap between Mr Williams and the herd-boy who had found the bull with the snare round its leg. The bull's brute strength had clearly enabled it to tear the cable free from its anchorage and drag it about, but that effort had caused the snare to cut deep into its leg. Mr Williams, receiving the herd-boy's report at the ranch house had gained the impression that the snare no longer was around the animal's leg and had intended to just herd him to a nearby crush for some treatment to the wound.

The injured bull was eventually brought in, the snare was removed from the animal's leg and the wound treated. I collected a few of the snares, which were all of the same type, for evidence purposes, but we never did find the culprit in that case. I was just glad that nobody else had had a camera there, because my sudden, desperate and decidedly undignified, flight from that couple of tons of enraged bull with its massive horns, was not something I would have wished to have recorded on film.

Meanwhile, October rolled into November and the political situation became extremely tense. On the 11th November that year, 1965, Ian Lewis, Reg and I gathered together to listen over the radio to the Prime Minister, Ian Smith, read out, in measured words and sombre tone, the formal Unilateral Declaration of Rhodesian Independence.

Over the next few days and weeks, the international political world moved to voice its opposition to Rhodesia's UDI and declare its support for immediate black majority rule. To those of us who had experience of that situation, the thought of turning over the wonderfully well-organised, well-regulated and non-racial nation that was Rhodesia, to the kind of corrupt, tribal, lawless, repressive and inefficient style of government that was evident in the early independent nations of East and West Africa, was unthinkable. Aside from the fact that Rhodesia had been a self-governing colony under the crown since 1928, there were, as I have set down before, already 20 black members of parliament in the 100-seat house, with plans for that number to grow by 5 at each future election, until parity and then majority rule, could be safely established in years ahead.

There was an even greater reason for avoiding black majority rule for some years ahead. That was the historic division between the Ndebele and Shona tribes. The Shona were 85 percent of the black population; the Ndebele only 15. Despite that imbalance, until the appearance of the white man in numbers in the country in 1890, it was the Ndebele, with their fearsome fighting impis who ruled the roost, demanded annual tribute and took slaves from the several clans of the Shona peoples. As Mac McLeod had warned me in conversations in Mashaba, if majority rule put the Shona in charge, the first thing they would do would be to turn their guns on the Matabele people, in revenge for the oppression of past years. Then they would turn their attention to the whites and drive them out. After that they would enforce a one-party state and from within that, steadily run down and ruin the nation. Mac McLeod eventually proved to be right.

While the politicians of the world spouted hot air, trained terrorists began to infiltrate into the country from Zambia, from Mocambique and from Botswana and spout hot bullets from guns supplied by communist ruled countries. International sanctions and the Beira blockade came into being. Petrol Rationing appeared.

Police Anti-terrorist Units, both regular and reservist, began to take shape and training in counter-insurgency activities started to be stepped up, along with patrolling by African Ground Coverage details, operating in plain clothes.

Sadly for the BSAP, UDI provided an opportunity for a couple of score of white police officers, almost entirely all recruited from the UK, to escape from a job they did not like, should never have got into and would never measure up to the requirements of. They ignored the advice, from the UK Government, for all serving government officers to remain in post until the independence dispute was settled politically. They took what became known as the rat run, vanishing across the border in various directions, claiming that they had deserted "on principle." A couple were from Squad 9 of 1964.

While all that was going on, routine police work had to be sustained, so Ian, Reg and I simply got on with the job, as did every single one of our African staff.

Towards the end of November, I undertook another area patrol, by motorcycle, this time camped under canvas not far from Razi Township and the dam of that same name, in which lurked a known man-killing crocodile that the locals named "Majubeki." One of my patrol instructions was to kill Majubeki if I could do so safely. With that in mind, I carted my long-barrelled Lee-Speed rifle with me, instead of a police issue SMLE. Despite spending an hour or two watching the local fishermen and keeping an eye open for any chance to get a clear shot at the crocodile, all I saw of it over the first three days was a couple of ripples at a distance. Aside from that, Const. Peter and I simply went about our routine patrol tasks.

In the early hours of the third night, I woke up feeling anything but well.

Despite the heat and the rainy season humidity, my skin was dry and I was alternating between burning hot and shivering cold. I had a skull-splitting headache to go with it and my pulse was full and bounding. I had been taking my daily Paludrin tablet most carefully and regularly, so I should not have found myself going down with malaria, which was as I suspected what was happening. Const. Peter was not camped with me. He had gone off to see friends in a village nearby, where he was probably comfortably fast asleep.

Realising that I needed some medical attention, and that as soon as I could get it, I decided to get dressed and ride the motorcycle to Chibi Clinic, certainly an hour's ride away. At that clinic there would at least be a medical orderly and, perhaps more importantly, a telephone, because there was not one at or anywhere near Razi Township.

Getting dressed, sitting on my Hounsfield bed, was a struggle that took ages as I attempted to get properly into shirt, shorts, leggings and boots. Tying the laces of my boots was the worst thing. My fingers barely obeyed my mind and I had hardly enough strength to pull the laces even half tight. Getting upright was another major effort. I achieved that by getting on all fours and using my Lee-Speed rifle as a combined climbing-frame and walking stick.

As far as I recall, I did not even think about putting on my crash-helmet. I made it the few paces to the motorcycle, but, when I attempted to kick-start it, I found I simply did not have the strength to get that essential job done. With that failure I began to realise that even if I had been able to start the machine, I was in no fit state to ride a motorcycle over rough dirt roads for forty miles or so. Faced with that, I literally crawled back to my tent, dragging my rifle with me and collapsed onto my camp bed.

That was where Const. Peter found me shortly after full daylight. He took one look at me, tried to wake me and realised that I was barely conscious. He went and fetched one of the African store owners; one who, fortunately for me, owned a Peugeot 203 station wagon. I do not recall much of that, but, between them they loaded me onto the back seat of the Peugeot and drove me, with some haste, to Chibi Clinic. All I recall of that was having a thermometer stuck under my tongue by the medical orderly. My next memory is of Reg Graham appearing, loading me into the police station Land Rover and driving, like a bat out of hell, as he later informed me, straight to Fort Victoria Hospital. I learned later that I spent that journey in the front passenger seat of the Land Rover, with Constable Peter sitting in the passenger seat directly behind me, holding me upright by my shoulders as I kept on falling forward. My next brief recollection is of Reg opening the front passenger door of the vehicle and helping me out of it. What I do not remember is, apparently, telling Reg that I could manage the walk to the hospital front door myself, taking a couple of steps and falling face-down into the flower bed alongside the path.

The next thing I really recall is that I was dreaming I was in a coffin, but it was alright, because it was cold, so I couldn't have gone to Hell. Then the coffin turned into a bath, in which I was covered in ice.

When I next woke up, I was flat on my back in a hospital bed; linked to a drip and feeling as though I had gone ten rounds with a mincing machine and lost every round. One of the pinkies, the African nursing assistants, so called because of the colour of their uniforms, spotted that I was awake and called the ward Sister. That lady carefully checked both my temperature and pulse before speaking. Whatever the readings were, they seemed to meet with her approval, because she put away her watch and thermometer and said cheerfully, "Well, young man, welcome back to the world. Forty-eight hours ago, it was touch and go with you."

Shortly after that, Dr Ascough appeared. In answer to his inevitable, "How are you feeling?" I replied, "Wrung out and weak as a kitten. What hit me? Malaria?"

Doctor Ascough nodded. "Yes. Whichever strain it was, it was pretty aggressive. Your temperature was touching one hundred and seven when you arrived. It was a bit of a battle to get it down. However, you should be fine in a week or so. Until then, it's bed rest and recovery for you, right where you are."

A couple of days later, by which time I was feeling a whole lot better, Reg Graham came in to see me. One of the things that had been bothering me was what had happened to my Lee-Speed rifle and the rest of the gear that I had with me at the Razi Dam camp. On that score, Reg put me right, with just a trace of smugness. Once he had safely delivered me to the hospital, he had driven, with Const. Peter, straight to our patrol camp site, to recover everything there before anything, especially the rifle, might go missing.

He had found everything untouched. Seeing he was there, with a rifle and that Majubeki was a legitimate target, Reg had decided to see if the beast was anywhere to be seen, which it was, steady in the water and at a reasonable range. Reg informed me that his first shot had hit the crocodile exactly where he had aimed, just behind the eyes and blown off the top of its skull, much to the appreciation of the locals who had been there to witness Majubeki's demise. Reg offered his opinion that the Lee-Speed was a cracking rifle.

A week passed before Dr Ascough declared me fit and well enough to return to Chibi Police Station. There I was to spend a week on office duties only, before returning to full duties, out and about. Back on station, I thanked Const. Peter for his part in getting me to medical help so promptly. I also used that week of office duties to gradually collect two jerry-cans full of precious petrol along with a handful of equally precious petrol coupons, all of which I delivered personally a few days later, to the storekeeper at Razi Township who had kindly used his car to get me to Chibi Clinic.

It was shortly after that spell in hospital that our trusty motorcycle became unreliable. It let down both Reg and me more than once when we were out and about, resulting in quite some walking for us and our accompanying constables. Despite several trips to the Central Mechanical Engineering Department's workshops in Fort Victoria, it failed Reg once again. Ian Lewis put in a strong complaint and a request for a replacement. Chief Supt Briault was sympathetic, but, under present circumstances, was unable to provide us with a replacement, so we had to battle along with it. It eventually reached the point where nobody would use the machine. When our Dispol next came out on a station visit, Ian Lewis put the situation to him once more and pleaded for something to be done, because managing the station's workload with just the Land Rover as our sole item of transport was impossible.

Roy Briault thought about it for a while. Then he came up with a suggestion. If the motorcycle were to encounter an inadvertent accident, one which damaged it beyond repair, Chibi would merit some priority consideration for the delivery of a second set of wheels to replace it.

I never could work out whether I won or lost the drawing of short straws that followed a day or so later. Whatever, the journey was a legitimate one, to deliver a summons to a villager who lived in a remote location deep in the granite hills, not far from the banks of the Lunde River at the bottom end of the district, near to Hippo Pools. It was a walk of nearly eighteen miles to the main road from where the narrow hillside footpath that we were riding along "suddenly gave way under us" resulting in the station motorcycle tumbling twenty or more feet downhill onto rocks in a stream bed and both Constable Bude and I "…narrowly escaping following it down," as my subsequent written report recorded.

The recovery exercise that was needed to get the battered motorcycle out from where it came to rest was a considerable one. After that recovery exercise an inspection by a CMED supervisor in Forth Victoria resulted in the machine being formally written off. The inevitable board of inquiry, arranged and supervised by C/Supt Briault, found me to be blameless.

To the surprise of all of us, our replacement set of wheels turned out not to be a more modern and reliable motorcycle, but a Minimoke. It was made clear that it was being issued to us at Chibi on an experimental basis. The day it arrived, Ian took it out for a test drive and came back cursing and swearing. The vehicle's tiny wheels gave it hardly any road surface clearance at all. The result of that was that when Ian had followed the ruts created by the regular passage of a bus, not far from the butchery, the Minimoke had grounded on the crest of the ridge between the two ruts and had come to an ignominious halt, gently rocking from side to side.

We soon learned that when driving that machine, it was advisable to keep to one side of the dirt road or the other, so that the wheels on one side or the other rode on top of the central ridge created by buses and other heavy vehicles. Our new set of wheels could only accommodate four adults and it had no roof rack. However, we did learn how to strap a pedal cycle across the back. One advantage the vehicle had was that it could be easily lifted and carried by four strong people, which activity was needed every time it got bogged down in the deep muddy patches that developed along the dirt roads during the rainy season.

A month or so after we were provided with the Minimoke, a radio message from Provincial Headquarters asked for an opinion on how suitable the machine was for district station use. Ian Lewis replied with the laconic comment. "It is okay, but we have to switch on the headlights when we reach the bottom of the ruts."

Everyone, black and white, who owned a motor vehicle soon realised that fuel was going to be very limited for some time. Those of us at Chibi government encampment realised that we needed to take steps to ensure we had what we needed for our private use. One weekend, Brian Tullet, Bill Kennedy, Reg Graham and I drove two privately owned Land Rovers down to Beitbridge and across the border to South Africa, where we were able to fill up the several empty 44-gallon drums we carried there for the purpose. The hotel owners, where we stayed over on the Saturday night, treated us like royalty. We were representatives of a little country that was brave enough to stand up to the ill-conceived political aims of those in the international world who, without experience, or sensible thinking through of the "what if" of the issue, just trotted out the mantra of "Majority Rule."

Others based at Chibi followed our example in later weeks and months.

There was very little in the way of out-of-working-hours recreation and amusement in Chibi. TV transmission and reception was, in 1965, still limited to Salisbury and Bulawayo urban areas and short distances around those two locations. It was radios and record players that kept us amused and informed in camp. Given that situation, it was not uncommon for all of us European civil servants in Chibi to drive, fairly frequently, into Fort Victoria, where there was a drive-in cinema, a hotel, two motels and even a fish and chip shop, in addition to the recreation club at the rural police station camp. The travel took around an hour and a quarter of unhurried driving. That habit was fine as long as petrol for the mileage was available and affordable.

Despite the occasional trips across the border, those off-duty evenings and weekends in Fort Victoria dwindled greatly in number once petrol rationing came in shortly after UDI was declared. Set back upon our own resources and unable to travel as freely as before, we developed alternative methods of relaxation. Fishing, in one or other of the many dams around the area, became a regular pass-time. Most, if not all, of the dams had been, at one time or another, stocked with bream, mostly telapia or melana plura. Eels and barbel had appeared naturally.

In the dry, rain-deprived soils of the area, for the rainfall was short that season, worms were difficult to find. Ian Lewis, who was as keen a fisherman as any of us, had an idea. The garage for the Land Rover had once been a stable. It had a concrete feeding trough.

One of the station labourers was despatched to dig worms in the wetter lands in between the granite kopjes behind the police station. The concrete trough was filled with well-composted soil and the gathered worms were put into it. Hey-presto, an instant wormery!

With petrol rationing a real concern, the Europeans at Chibi shared vehicles and took turns at providing transport for those trips to the various dams. It was quite usual to have two off-duty police officers in the front of the vehicle and two or three off-duty internal affairs officers in the back, or vice-versa.

When fishing, any tiddlers we caught we threw back. The larger bream we kept because they made very tasty eating. Our African staff eagerly accepted any barbel that we caught, but they did not wish to know anything about any eels. Tribal beliefs were too strong. I have a photograph of Bill Kennedy, with an afternoon's catch laid out on the sloping top of a table soldier. In that photograph, there are a couple of dozen or more edible fish. On a later area patrol, once again camped beside Razi Dam, I caught so many fish early one morning that I filled both pannier bags of the motorcycle and, breaking the rules, rode as quickly as I could back to Chibi Police Station, where I split the catch between the mess and the Lewis family, so that the fish could be got into deep-freezes before they went off.

On one occasion, Ian Lewis decided to take himself, his wife Julie and their little daughter out to a nearby dam for a Saturday afternoon's fishing. At dusk, they started to drive home. Ian turned one fairly sharp corner in a grazing area thick with trees and scrub bushes and suddenly found that the track, which had been quite clear earlier that day, was blocked by a fallen tree. Ian came very close to driving into it. Only his careful driving, at slow speed, prevented that. Ian could not see anyone around, but, being unarmed and concerned for his family, he just rapidly reversed his car, worked his way around the roadblock, got back on to the track and finished his homeward journey without further incident, by which time twilight had gone and it was fully dark.

Because I was the duty officer for that weekend, I was the one who got the case to investigate, as an offence under the Law and Order Maintenance Act. There was nothing to be done that evening, but, early next day, Ian was determined to go out to the scene and start looking around. Ian's anger, which was entirely justified because it was clear that he and his family had been deliberately targeted, was something I struggled with. Whatever had occurred needed a calm, careful and thorough investigation, which I was determined to apply. I did not relish the presence of an angry, vengeful, senior detail out with me at the scene.

It just so happened that our Minimoke was in Fort Victoria for service, needing a minor spare part. Our Land Rover was the only station transport available. I got round my worry about having my boss at the scene by arranging, technically and for the record, to do an early morning road patrol, before dawn. I briefed Sgt Wurayayi, for whom I had a whole lot of respect, to come along with me and confided in him what I was up to. Catching on quick, that canny African policeman grinned and said, "He will scold you, Ishe." To which my reply was, "Not if we can find whoever did it."

Before dawn, Sgt Wurayayi and I were out of our vehicle, a half-mile clear of the scene and carefully closing in on it on foot. In view of the nature of the offence, I took the precaution of carrying my Lee-Speed rifle with me, slung across my back so as to leave my hands clear for my clipboard and camera. As soon as we could make out the fallen tree, thirty or forty yards ahead, we stopped to wait for full light. A few minutes later, we heard the sounds of cattle approaching from our right. They were heading straight for the fallen tree. Sgt Wurayayi and I moved rapidly to head them off. Our appearance was a bit of a surprise for both the dozen or so cattle and the two teenage herd boys who were driving them, both of whom were carrying axes over their shoulders, handles pointing forward as was normal. With waving arms, flapping hands and shouts, we two policemen turned the cattle away from their line of walk, until they began to mill around uncertainly. Behind them, the two herd boys were trying to urge them on. Sgt Wurayayi shouted at them, "Chenjerayi mafana. Iri Mapolisa pano." (Careful youngsters. It is policemen here!)

One of the herd boys shouted back something in Shona. He reached for the axe over his shoulder and brought it into his right hand.

Sgt Wurayayi translated the words as, "We have to drive the cattle this way. It is our proper path." I rather rapidly handed my clipboard and camera to the sergeant and brought my rifle off from my back and into my hands. Making sure that the approaching axe-wielder saw every move, I levered a round into the breach, thumbed forward the safety catch and swung the weapon up in line with him. He wisely chose to halt his approach.

My eyes took in both the nearest youth and his companion, who was further away, with his axe still over his left shoulder. "Tell them to find another way this morning," I bade my sergeant, "one that is far away from that fallen tree over there."

A bit of a heated argument ensued. It seemed that the two youths had received careful and precise instructions from their kraalhead. They would get into trouble if they did not obey. By then both youths had their axes in their hands and were gesticulating angrily. I decided that caution was required. Interrupting the argument between Sgt Wurayayi and the two youths, I said, "Tell them to put down their axes, please." A gesture from my rifle reinforced my words. Fortunately, neither of them felt foolish enough to take on the working end of a rifle in the hands of a grim-faced European policeman. The axes hit the ground.

Another gesture from my rifle encouraged them to back off. That allowed Sgt Wurayayi to put down my clipboard and camera and take possession of the two axes. A few minutes later, I had written record of who the two youths were, which kraal they came from, whose cattle they were driving and who had given them their instructions. They were adamant that they had to follow their given instructions. They claimed it would not be right to drive the cattle on any other route. Sgt Wurayayi let fly with a string of angry, emphatic words, gesturing at the cattle, which were idly browsing close by, at the tree across the track and then at me.

The two youth studied my expression, which I made as grim and hard as I could, having guessed what Sgt Wurayayi's words had been. The more aggressive of the two finally shrugged and, in very good English, asked if they agreed to take the cattle away, could they have their axes back. A few minutes later, the youths, both re-united with their axes and with their herd of cattle ahead of them were just distant sounds some way away.

As everyone had suspected, the downed mopani tree had not fallen naturally. The blade marks of the axes that had felled it were clear to see. So was the spoor of three bare-footed people, probably two adults and a youth. Sgt Wurayayi and I were able to pick up the spoor of the three and track them for about fifty yards, until we lost all trace under the hooves of the early moving herd of cattle driven by the two youths.

For a moment, both of us policemen stood looking at the cattle tracks and thinking. It was Sgt Wurayayi who spoke first. "Ishe, I know that kraal. The kraalhead is not a bad man, but he has a younger brother who is troublesome. He is a member of ZANU. All of our GC details know him."

While I was pondering whether to safeguard the tree or walk to the kraal about a mile or more away, there was the noise of a motor vehicle on the track. Returning to the fallen tree and the track, we waited until Ian Lewis, with Const. Bude, climbed out of his own private car, two feet from the fallen tree. Carefully keeping my eyes away from the sergeant's grinning face, I waited until my angry boss finished "scolding" me. Then I told him that if he and Const. Bude would kindly guard the tree until Sgt Wurayayi and I could get back with a large saw, I would solve the case for him, because we had some suspects already. If we got on with some careful forensic work and had just a tiny bit of luck, we would have the road-blockers in the cells within days; more than that I was not prepared to say right then.

Having vented his overnight anger on me, Ian Lewis was quickly in a far more relaxed and reasonable mood, so he and Const. Bude guarded the tree and its chopped end until the sergeant and I were able to get back there, with a suitable double-handed saw borrowed from internal affairs. While our sergeant and constable did some careful sawing, I told my boss exactly what had gone on. I pointed out that if the sergeant and I had not been out and about at the scene literally in the dark, that herd of cattle would have been and gone and so would every trace of spoor around the tree. We might still have had the chop-marks on the tree, but, collecting every axe within miles around for forensic comparison with the axe-marks would have been a logistical impossibility. Now all we had to do was to collect every axe in one single kraal and hope for a forensic match.

After that, the case became a routine one, despite everyone in the suspect kraal denying any knowledge of the affair. We gathered every axe in the suspect kraal, owner by owner, some dozen and a half of them and sent them and the chopped ends of the tree off to Salisbury. We received back, within ten days, the reports of two positive matches, one of which belonged to the kraalhead's younger brother, the known ZANU activist. When he was formally charged, his boastful reply was an admission. He did it to warn all Europeans that they were not wanted in the country. ZANLA would sweep them all away if they refused to go. His co-accused denied any involvement.

The forensic evidence was strong, ownership of the two axes was certain. The circumstantial evidence was useful too. Although the one politically motivated and boastful accused freely admitted the offence, he claimed that he had acted alone. When I was questioning the second accused villager, he simply refused to acknowledge the link between his axe and the felled tree. He was so confident that we would not convict him that he boasted about that fact. His confidence was amazing. That proved his undoing, because as I sat looking at him and the first accused, I recalled a case up in Nyasaland where an accused had similarly been faced with clear, strong evidence of his guilt but had steadfastly denied the case and been confident about his eventual release.

A wise constable had, in my presence, searched that man. The constable took away the bicep amulets he was wearing. Still the accused denied the case. He then took away the charm bands from around the accused man's waist and both calves. Still the man denied. Eventually, that constable searched in the accused person's hair. Hidden in the thick curly hair above each ear was a short piece of shiny twig. The accused's face started to crumple at the finding of his secret mutis. The constable at that time asked me to burn the man's charm twigs, which I did, right in front of him. That accused man then broke down, wept and admitted the crime he was guilty of.

As I studied the two accused, in the office at the police station, I realised that the kraalhead's younger brother was at least middle-aged and shiny on top. His co-accused was younger and blessed with a still thick and curly head of hair. He was also wearing a long-sleeved jersey. Acting on a hunch, I had him take off his jersey. Round his biceps were charms. He was not happy when I cut those away. Still he would admit nothing. A bit of further searching showed that he was wearing a single strand of beads around his waist. When I removed that, he protested that he would become ill without it. He still refused to admit any part in the roadblock crime. He was wearing shorts, so it was easy to see that he had no charms around his legs. Faced with his continuing denials, I carefully searched his hair. There I found what I was looking for. A single piece of matchstick-thick shiny twig, perhaps a couple of inches long, above each ear. The dismay on his face at my finding and removing them was evident. When I burned the charms in front of him in an ashtray, his admission quickly followed. The two instances were more than two years and many hundreds of miles apart, but the same African beliefs clearly spanned both time and distance.

A few weeks later, I prosecuted the case in court. Having been tutored no doubt by the political element in Fort Victoria remand cells, both accused persons denied any involvement in the case. Both accused me, the prosecutor, of torturing them in order to get their admissions. That had not happened of course. Nevertheless, it took a trial-within-a-trial to sort it out. Eventually, both accused persons went to prison for three years.

One of the saddest experiences of my first time at Chibi occurred when Reg Graham and I went out fishing together to Murenyi Dam, a few miles from the police camp. It was a bright, dry, pleasant day, without a cloud in the sky, which, for the time of year, was a disaster, for rain was desperately needed. The dam was a popular one for the African fishermen of all ages, so it was nothing unusual for us to be sharing a stretch of the bank, or the dam wall, with local villagers. Aside from the rare incident of political malice that I have set out in the few pages before this point, relations between everyone in Chibi Tribal Trust Land were good. Reg and I carried no weaponry aside from standard fishing tackle type knives while a few of the African adults carried much the same item. One or two of the elders carried axes by tribal habit rather than need, for the fishermen of all villages and races just got on and did what fishermen everywhere do: used their best wiles to catch fish.

For us two off-duty policemen it was recreation. We were out of uniform, not on call and just there to enjoy the traditional battle between us and our intended victims lurking below the waterline, all eager, we hoped, to gobble up any tempting ground bait or risk the worm on our hopefully hidden hooks. We fished with formal rods and reels, with painted floats of whatever size and shape that took our fancy. If no fish appeared interested in our carefully dangled worms, we would try a spinner of one kind or another. If we caught edible-sized fish, that was a bonus. If we went home with an empty keep-net, it hardly mattered. There was food in the fridge and the cupboards at the mess. For the Africans fishing all around us it was a very different activity. They were not there for recreation. They were there for survival. They needed to catch fish, of any size, to provide some tasty relish to eat with whatever sadza, rapoko, or other grain-based dish that might, or might not, be the bulk of their food for the day. If one of our hooks struck a snag and we could not free it, we simply cut the line and continued fishing with a replacement hook. If one of the local fishermen encountered the same problem, one of the local children who could swim, and a few could, would simply strip off and wade in to follow the stuck line and then dive down to release the hook from whatever was holding it. Hooks and line were precious. Reg and I were both in the habit of using line with a nine-pound breaking strain. On that, with a little skill, we could land much heavier fish, usually barble, if one chose to swallow our bait. The Salisbury ultra-lightweight tackle club used nothing more than two-pound line, but that was not for us. The African fishermen used whatever they could get hold of, preferably a line of twenty or more pounds weight breaking strain. That way, hooks could be pulled free from most snags and whatever the size of fish caught, it could be guaranteed to be brought safely to shore and clubbed to death to await transport to the cooking pot.

On the day in question, the fish were biting well and time passed pleasantly. Twenty yards or so along the dam wall, there was a young teenage local boy. He had no keep net. However, a small sack, half in and half out of the water, kept there and kept shut by a rock, served that purpose. Like the other locals around, his fishing rod was simply a straight stick, five or six feet long, with the few yards of line tied on to one end. His float was a small piece of carved wood. Where we were using worms from the station wormery, he was using grubs that he had dug at dawn. By the end of the afternoon, as dusk approached, Reg and I began to pack up. So too did the nearby youngster. He pulled in his line, fixed it carefully to his fishing pole, gathered his sack of fish, tied the neck of it carefully shut and turned away from the water. Half-way up the steep packed-earth bank that was the dam wall, he simply collapsed, face down, pole inert and sack wriggling beside him. He made no effort to get up.

Once we realised that he had not just slipped, Reg and I and others hurried across to him. There was no pulse and no signs of breathing. On realising that something was seriously wrong, one youngster was sent to tell the boy's family. As rapidly as we could we carried the stricken youngster up to the flat top of the dam wall. There, despite Reg's attempts at mouth-to-mouth resuscitation and vigorous pumping at his ribcage over his heart, we failed to revive him. By the time we finally quit, there was a crowd around. Through those there, the teenager's mother pushed her way. Sympathetic murmurs of "Yafa, Mai" (He is dead, Mother) greeted her. She took one look at her child on the ground and fell on top of him, weeping and wailing.

With the assistance of a local school-teacher whose English was excellent, Reg and I were able to explain that we needed to find out why the child had suddenly died.

It was agreed that we would take the dead child and his mother in my car to the police station in order to start that process of investigation. In that conversation I asked if the boy had been ill at all. The answer was a negative one.

As the small body was lifted from the ground by a relative, the mother ceased her wailing, much of which was to satisfy tribal custom, aside from genuine grief, long enough to ask if her son had caught any fish. The still damp sack, along with its contents and the boy's fishing pole were handed to her. She hefted the sack and said a few words before passing the sack and pole to a relative. Our helpful schoolteacher translated for me. "My son's life is not wasted. We have fish to eat."

The Sudden Death docket was straightforward. A post-mortem revealed that the cause of death was untreated double pneumonia.

If fishing was one recreational pass-time, hunting baboon was another. In Nyasaland there had been the occasional trouble with baboon. The first time I was invited to go on a baboon hunt I took along a police force .303 SMLE and a whole pocketful of cartridges for it. Pete Coetzee, one of the park rangers for the wild-life department in the area noted the amount of ammunition I had with me and simply fell about laughing. He assured me that if I got off two shots at them, it would be well done. If I got off three shots, it would be exceptional. If I killed any, he would buy me a beer for each one I downed. That hunt cost Pete Coetzee just one beer. It also educated me about how wary baboon were, how well they knew the difference between a walking stick and a rifle at two hundred yards and just how fast they could scamper across, up and down rock faces and vanish into crevasses in the rocks or behind trees and scrubby bushes.

It was that first baboon hunt that also taught me that a big dog-baboon could stand as tall as a man; run faster and bite a damned sight harder. When Peter Coetzee showed me, close up, the length of a baboon's eye teeth and the scissor arrangement of the teeth in its mouth, I suddenly developed a whole lot more respect for the animal than I ever had before. When he reminded me that those front top incisors were a great deal longer than those of a lion, that respect deepened even more. That day also increased my dislike of that particular animal. The reason for the hunt was that the particular troop had raided the grain stores of a village and literally helped themselves to half of what the villagers needed to survive until the next year's crops might appear. Left untouched, that troop would more than likely return for the rest. I have already set out how in my first murder case in Africa, it proved to be a baboon that had taken, killed and eaten most of the child victim, so perhaps the reader will understand my distaste and somewhat vengeful attitude towards this particular species of primate.

In Chibi, where the rains over the past year had been patchy and light, the DC had already begun a system of workfare. Those who volunteered to work for the DC without pay, were rewarded with work clothing, food and accommodation. At the end of each month, they were given a 200lb sack of maize meal, sufficient to feed the rest of their family for at least a month. One of the effects of that very reasonable arrangement was that many kraals were without their most active and robust male members. Baboon, particularly the troop leaders, were far less wary of women than men. A male villager who stood his ground, with an axe or spear in his hands, was something to be avoided. Such a person, maybe backed by a dog or two, could deter the raiders from raiding the grain-stores. Women were no such deterrent. One village matriarch, with her husband away on workfare attempted to defend what little corn-on-the-cob and rapoko the family still had in their grain store. The big dog-baboon leading the marauding troop bit her badly enough for her to need serious repairs in hospital. It then tore off the roof of their grain store allowing the entire troop to help themselves without further hindrance. When the story reached Mr O'Connor, it was a good enough cause for him to order and arrange a formal hunt, to nail that aggressive troop leader and thin down the size of what was understood to be one of the largest troops in the district.

To support the DC and his team, Ian Lewis and I joined the hunt, while Reg Graham held the fort at the police station as he was that week's duty officer. I armed myself with my Lee-Speed .303, just in case there was any long-range opportunity for a shot at the perishers. I also took the trouble to strap a handgun to my belt, a big, old Colt .455 revolver. My Nyasaland experiences had taught me that in heavy bush, a handgun with reliable stopping power was a very useful weapon. Ian decided to carry only one of the station's standard SMLE .303 rifles.

For this effort, the DC turned out his strongest team. Pete Visser, Brian Tunstall and Bill Kennedy, all suitably armed. With support from the local tribespeople by the hundred, a line of beaters was set up, at one end of a rocky ridge where the baboon troop had a favourite sleeping area. Ian Lewis and Brian Tunstall were tasked to walk with the beaters, to add modern firepower to the axes and spears being carried by the locals that day, with approval from the DC.

At the other end of the half mile long ridge, a curving stop-line of other locals was established, to try to prevent the troop breaking away across the flat lands at the foot of the ridge. Mr O'Connor took up the central position in the stop-line. Twenty yards or so to his right he placed Pete Visser, while Bill Kennedy was off to his left. He required me to stay close to him.

Without mobile phones, or portable radios, all the preparatory work had to be done by careful briefing, local knowledge and good map work. It was to the DC's credit that, as dawn broke, everyone was in position. Ian and Brian were briefed to each cover one side of the ridge. They were only to start the operation once there was sufficient light to accurately sight a rifle. Eventually, two spaced shots from the beater line warned us that they were moving. The African beaters started their drumbeats and shouts as the echoes of the two signal shots faded. Rising above those noises came the clearly alarmed barking of several mature baboons. Driven by the beaters, hastened along by an occasional shot from Ian or Brian, the baboon troop fled along the rising ridge until they reached the peak above us in the stop-line.

In his briefing, Mr O'Connor had indicated that he wished to be the person who shot the troop leader. It was pointed out to him that with several large male baboons in the troop, which was at least twenty-five or thirty strong and the speed with which baboon moved when being shot at or chased, making that happen might be difficult. Mr O'Connor countered that with an instruction that, Pete Visser, Bill Kennedy and I were not to fire a shot until after he had loosed off the first one.

The beaters' line was to link up with the wings of our stop line, which, we hoped, would give us a complete encirclement of the target troop. At that moment two sets of three shots were to be fired, one each from Ian and Brian, who, being on opposite sides of the ridge, could not even see each other. The beaters' line was then to cease forward movement, so that there was no chance of members of the stop-line shooting at them and vice-versa.

The ridge above us ended in a sheer rock face, perhaps a hundred feet high. On top of that was a cluster of granite boulders forming crevices and caves. At the base of the rock face, between it and us, carefully under cover some thirty yards back, were jumbled granite boulders and a thick cover of bush and grass, penetrated here and there by narrow game trails.

The first baboon to appear at the top of the rock face was big. It stopped, looked back and barked, deep-toned and loud. Other calls answered his. Mr O'Connor sighted on the brute, but held his fire, uncertain about whether this was the troop leader or not. Obedient to our briefing, Pete, Bill and I all held our fire. Three shots came from the left flank of the ridge. Part of the circle was linked up. The dog-baboon barked some more. Still Mr O'Connor held his fire. From one of the locals near to us came an urgent comment, in

English. "Shoot, Ishe. That is the boss one." At that, the DC fired and missed. His bullet smacked into the rock the baboon had been seated on and whined off into space. The baboon vanished among the boulders. Three shots came from the right flank of the ridge. More baboon appeared atop the rock face. Not the troop leader, but, both Bill Kennedy and I fired at the same time, possibly at the same beast, because the impact of one or more bullets lifted it and tumbled it backwards out of sight. One way or another, I was happy that one was dead.

For a few minutes, gunfire, drumbeats, whoops and ululations mingled with urgent calling from the baboon as they milled in and out of the rocks on top of the ridge. I picked off one more of the adult animals. Mr O'Connor certainly did hit another. Faced with a now noisy stop-line and four guns below them, the troop started to move back along the ridge. Ian and Brian promptly shot at them there so they turned back to the highest point once again, most of them going to ground in the crevices and caves. The big fellow made himself visible once more, directly in front and above us, barking frantically. "He's mine." The DC shouted, I think for my benefit. His bullet, this time, did strike home, causing the big baboon to pitch forward and down the rock-face. It vanished out of sight into the heavy bush and boulder tangle. "Got the bugger!" Mr O'Connor declared gleefully and launched himself forward into the heavy undergrowth, apparently in search of his victim.

I had seen the manner in which that baboon had come down. It did not fall limp, lifeless and tumbling, but with arms spread and hands scrabbling for a grip. I took off after the DC, shouting, "I don't think that one's quite dead, Sir. Be very careful!"

"Nonsense, young man," came the reply as the DC pushed on. "It's as dead as a dodo."

As sporadic gunfire continued, Mr O'Connor pushed deeper into the tangle of bush and grass. It was far too thick to wield a rifle, whether long-barrelled or short, so I carried the Lee-Speed vertically by my left side and fetched out the .455 revolver with my right hand, carefully thumbing forward the safety catch and then thumbing back the hammer.

Mr O'Connor's rash dash carried him in through the tangle of vegetation until he was close to the base of the rock face. He squeezed between two boulder that were six or eight feet high, with me barely two yards behind. As he cleared that narrow gap, following a very narrow dassie trail, his eyes were only for what was in front of him. He neither saw nor heard the wounded dog-baboon emerge from the grass behind and to the left of him. Silently, its vengeful attention solely upon the unsuspecting DC, it rose up and reached out towards that man's back. I noted the blood down the right side of its ribcage and saw it bare its fangs as its mouth opened to bite once it had a grip.

There was no time for shouted warnings. I needed to get in an instantly killing shot or the DC was in trouble. From barely four feet back, I had just enough angle to avoid shooting the DC in the back as I fired from the hip. The heavy bullet hit the unsuspecting baboon just behind its right ear, passed through brain and mouth and bounced off of the rock face ahead and to the left of Mr O'Connor. The forward momentum of the baboon and the impact of my bullet combined to pitch its dead form straight into the back of the DC's legs. Mr O'Connor tumbled backwards, on top of the inert and bloody carcass of the baboon. As he fell, his right hand tightened on the trigger of the Manlicher, which, fortunately was pointing upward. The inadvertently fired bullet wasted itself into space.

I helped the fallen DC to his feet. He was unhurt, but liberally splattered in blood and bits of baboon brain. I pointed down at the carcass with the .455 revolver. "Now it is dead, Sir."

Mr O'Connor looked at the dead baboon, tried to brush some of the muck and rubbish from his safari suit, looked at me and snapped, "Damn you, Sir!"

I never did find out whether that remark was because I had damaged his great white hunter opinion of himself, or because I had shot his fox, so to speak, or because I had caused him to become blood-stained. However, being the decent person he was, in a quiet moment later in the day, he did apologise.

That baboon shoot was a highly successful one. The troop had been scattered far and wide. Of their total number, whatever it was, twelve of them, including the troop leader, had fallen to gunfire, or spears and axes as they tried to break through the encirclement. Including that one round from my revolver, I had actually fired just four shots.

The carcass, of varying size and of both sexes, were handed over to the senior kraalhead for that area. The tips of the tails would be cut off and, in a few days, exchanged for a half-crown each at the DC's Office, that being the value of the bounty on them at that time. The skins would be tanned and made into karosses. The individual skins would be sewn together by using the sinews from the tails, after they had been carefully dried and separated into individual strands. That thread, called "rudzingo" was strong stuff. The hands and feet would be sold to practising witch doctors. The teeth might go that same way or be made into necklaces to be sold to tourists. Finally, the meat from the carcass would be eaten by those families which did eat baboon meat, which was a custom not all villagers followed.

The troop that plagued the area around Chibi Police Station and the DC's Office area suffered from the presence of numerous firearms, some of them in the hands of people a little more able to shoot straight than Mr O'Connor. The police station's several buildings were the nearest set of administrative buildings to the kopjes and rough country, so we got to do more of the shooting, whenever the troop made its presence felt. Our golden rule was that nobody went out alone, either clambering up to the water tank and pot-shotting at what was in sight from there, or walking around the high ground, using the footpaths and game-trails. Dry season shooting was a whole lot easier than wet season shooting. That was simply because, once the verdant growth of grasses, bushes and trees started to dry back, or was burned off by not always spontaneous fires, visibility improved markedly. That made the baboons easier to see. However, even in the wet season, their inclination to seek the highest point around, from where they could see danger early, did provide opportunities to cull them even during the rains. It was on one of those days in early January 1966 that Ian and I went for a late afternoon walk, weapons in hand, after hearing the usual noises of the troop on the move, somewhere in the rough country behind the police station. On this occasion we stuck to the footpaths and game trails as we attempted to quietly close in on our quarry to a distance from where we could get in a reasonably telling shot or two before the whole lot fled.

Despite our care, they detected our presence long before we saw them. Knowing full well what our purpose was, the troop moved off to put what they believed was safe distance between us and them. Eventually, after we had been tracking them for a half hour or more, they moved on to a particularly high kopje, better than a quarter mile distant and probably two hundred feet above us. From there the troop leader sat on the highest point, staring in our direction and barking warnings to the rest of the troop.

Ian shook his head and suggested we called it a day, as the troop was clearly not going to allow us to close in on them. When I told him that I was going to try for one shot from where we were, Ian suggested I was being just a trifle ambitious. However, by then I had some idea of just how accurate at long range my Lee-Speed rifle was. Its loading action was light and smooth to work and the trigger mechanism was the same. It had an open, "V" type back sight, not an aperture one, but I found that no disadvantage. Besides, my target was brilliantly outlined against the clear blue sky and was sitting quite still, watching us. As long as we were still, he would remain still, because, with quite a distance between us, he felt he was safe.

I also had the advantage of being able to lean on a very smooth boulder that was ideal as a firing platform. The crack of my bullet being fired was followed by the disappearance of my target and a chorus of coarse barking.

"You missed," Ian asserted with conviction.

"Uh-Uh," I countered. "The way he went backwards, he's dead."

"Not a chance!" was Ian's scornful opinion.

"Only one way to find out," I suggested. "Let's go for a climb and if he's not dead, I'll buy you a crate of beer."

"You're on," Ian agreed, "and if he is dead, I'll buy you a crate of beer." That climb was quite something, but okay as we took it steadily. Seeing and hearing our movements, the baboon troop backed further away as we progressed, until their barking was just a noise in the distance. Finally, when we had climbed the last few feet and reached the very top of the kopje, Ian examined the spot where the baboon had been sitting. "There you are," he said, "he's got away and you owe me a crate of beer."

Three of four feet behind where the baboon had been sitting, there was a crevice. I stepped that far, looked down and beckoned Ian over. As he looked down into the gap in the rock I said, "I think you owe me a crate of beer." Ian looked at the dead baboon and then at me. "I want to see where you hit him," he declared.

Between us we hauled the carcass up and out of the crevice. It was a very large and mature specimen. Probably the biggest either of us had seen in Chibi. My single shot had taken the baboon exactly where I had aimed, which was in the centre of the body, immediately under the ribcage. When we turned the animal over, there was no exit wound.

"I'm not using standard service rounds," I explained to my puzzled boss.

"I'm loaded with soft hollow-nosed rounds. My bullet would have spread on impact and gone through as far as the spine. When it impacted there, it has no penetrating capability, but a whole lot of clout. That's what lifted him off his feet and dumped him in that crevice. He was dead before he hit the ground." Ian looked at our dead quarry, looked down the long distance to the spot from where I had fired and shook his head. "If I hadn't seen it," he said with conviction, "I never would have believed it." He straightened up and looked around. From our vantage point we could see there was a far easier way down than the way we had come up. Ian pointed to it. "Let's tow this bugger back to camp, because otherwise nobody is going to believe the story."

Between us we hauled the dead baboon down the easier gradient at the back of the kopje. Once we reached flat ground, we broke off a couple of branches and created a very simple travoise with the inner bark as our string. It was crude, but effective. Back at camp, the dead baboon was something of a seven-day wonder. It certainly was big. Constables, witnesses and camp labourers all came to look at it. The story of my shooting it at a great range gained me the African nickname of "Magocha" which translated as "The hunter." In the warm weather of the rainy season, even if there were no rains, dead bodies of anything needed to be dealt with rapidly. Our senior camp labourer and I came to an arrangement. He would dispose of the carcass, if could he please have the bounty money on the tail.

Mention of the tail of that baboon brings a memory that clearly demonstrated how shrewd the rural African can be and the fact that he does not miss much. Just as at the police station where there was a "Wife of Member" position so that the wife of the Member-in-Charge could be paid for twenty-five hours of administrative work each week, at the DC's office there was an arrangement for one or two of the ADOs' wives to do something similar, by way of typing letters, doing some filing and helping to run the cash office. When baboons were snared and killed by villagers, the tails, as I have already set down, were worth money. One worthy African hunter soon noted that one of the ADO wives did not like to actually handle the cut-off tips of the tails of dead baboon. By the time they reached the cash office, they could be days old, blood-stained and very smelly. Not wishing to handle the gruesome items, she would simply sweep the offending thing or things into a waste-paper basket and hand the basket to one of the uniformed messengers to take away at once and throw in the deep rubbish pit at the back of the offices. She would then pay out the bounty money.

Our canny villager saw an opportunity. The next time he trapped and killed a baboon, he carefully cut the skin into short, narrow strips while it was still wet and wound them round thin, appropriately tapered, pieces of wood to dry. When dried, some careful brushing of the hair and a bit of daubing of blood, created a very fair semblance of the tip of a baboon's tail. As the story later came out, he first tried just one of his creations on the lady concerned. When she paid out on that, without even touching it, he went back with more. He did it for months, without being caught out. Eventually, his greed got the better of him. An additional uniformed messenger was taken on at the DC's office. His home was in the area where the apparently extremely successful baboon hunter lived. That new messenger ended up helping out around the cash office. He was aware his fellow local snared no more than one or two baboon each year. When he was asked to throw into the rubbish pit the several baboon tails that the man had just brought in, he smelled a rat. Not being squeamish, he took a good look at the several tails and soon realised what had been going on.

It was a classic case of fraud, which was not difficult to investigate. The accused admitted what he had been up to. When I outlined the facts, Mr Stainer said, absolutely straight-faced, "If I may say so Mr Prosecutor, that is quite some tale." Since the accused villager had no previous conviction, Mr Stainer handed down a relatively light sentence that gave the fellow three months' imprisonment with hard labour, with another three months suspended for two years.

In recording these events I do not wish to give the reader the impression that all we ever did was to hunt baboon. The station dealt, each month, with a fair weight of standard crime, from shoplifting to murder. The main road, upon which all too many drivers were inclined to travel far too fast, produced accidents of all magnitudes, right up to fatal ones, all of which had to be investigated and documented and, if any breach or breaches of assorted law was exposed, converted into statutory or common law cases to be further investigated and, hopefully, processed through the court system at the appropriate level.

Station monthly inspections came and went. Annual inspection loomed.

Offices and items of equipment were spruced up, uniforms made clean, tidy and sharply creased and leather-work was polished until it really was mirror-like.

A few days before we were due for annual inspection, one of the prison warders came into the patrol officers' office, carrying a small sack that appeared to contain something alive and wriggling. It turned out to be a raptor. It had got a bit over-ambitious and grabbed a large cockerel belonging to the warder. He had seen it and tried to knock it out of the air as it struggled to gain airspeed with its weighty prey. The result was that it flew into the wall of the prison and stunned itself. To stop it flying away when it recovered, he cut its flight feathers, stuck it into a sack and brought it to show us in case we wanted it.

Ian, Reg and I all studied the angry bird, which, at that time, had its legs tied. It appeared to be a young bird, in good health apart from the trimmed flight feathers. Ian Lewis suddenly had a thought. C/Supt Briault was a keen bird man. He never travelled far without carrying a large book on African birds of all kinds. He would surely appreciate a chance to see this raptor close-to. We thanked the prison warder appropriately and I took charge of our feathered guest. A two-inch thick branch was swiftly converted into a perch across one end of the mess veranda. Warily and making sure there was no way for it to escape from the veranda, I untied its legs. I set the bird down on the branch perch and rapidly took my hands away from it. It promptly tried to bite me and fly at the same time. Both attempts failed. It ended up on the floor, flapping its defective wings and screeching.

With my hands better protected by a pair of motorcycling gauntlets, I tried again, then again. At the third attempt, the feisty fellow stayed put on the perch, although every feather was standing out straight and its very viciously curved beak was wide open.

I collected some fresh meat from the kitchen fridge, cut it into chunks and, holding a piece in my gauntleted fingers, offered it to the raptor. Instead of its beak coming down to take it, as I expected, one of the bird's strong talons came up and grabbed, enclosing the meat and a couple of my fingers too. The strength in that grip was considerable. I managed not to snatch my hand away, but just let it pull my gauntleted hand and the piece of meat to the perch. When it was balanced to its liking, its head came down. That predatory beak tore off a portion of the square of fresh meat, which the bird eagerly swallowed. More pieces of meat went the same way, until I sensed that the bird was beginning to relax just a little. Very slowly I extracted my fingers from the bird's grip, so that it was sitting with both sets of talons firmly around the branch.

Over the next few days, we identified Hoppy, as we christened him, as a fairly-rare Ayre's Hawk Eagle. He really deserved to be flying free and wild, but, with his cropped wings, he was going to be flightless for quite a while. Getting water into him was an exercise, but he finally sorted out what a bowl of the stuff was for.

Fed and well cared for Hoppy calmed down considerably and I was able to carry him on my gauntleted wrists. In later life I rescued and raised, from a featherless blob fallen out of a nest, a pigeon. In the months before it found a mate and flew off for the last time, I sensed, from its behaviour, that it had a genuine affection for me as an individual. Not so with Hoppy. The pigeon would sit on my shoulder, gently try to groom my hair and softly tug at my ear if it required attention. If I had ever set Hoppy on my shoulder the only thing he would have done with my ear would have been to tear it off and eat it. However, Hoppy soon worked out that I was the source of food. Therefore, I was warily tolerated, but nothing more. If any of the many others who visited the mess attempted to approach him; Hoppy would lift one talon threateningly, open wide his beak and screech. Reg Graham, who had a great love for and affinity with animals, even failed to charm him.

That was how it was that a week or more later, when the day of annual inspection arrived, Hoppy, already fed and content, was left sitting on his perch on the mess veranda as we prepared for OC District to arrive to commence the annual inspection routines. The sun shone brilliantly, vehicles sparkled, brass, leather and glass gleamed as was essential and foot and arms drill passed off without any hitch. Paperwork was inspected and buildings too. When Mr Briault stepped into the mess, his final point of inspection, through the veranda door, Ian Lewis, Reg Graham and I were all close behind him. Hoppy immediately made his presence felt, by flapping his ineffectual wings and screeching. Our inspecting officer's interest in the building vanished. "Great Scot!" he exclaimed, his eyes wide, "What on earth have you got there?"

"No idea really, Sir," I replied untruthfully, with my fingers crossed behind my back. "It tried to take a chicken from the prison, flew into a wall when chased and the warder brought it to us. It seemed too fine a bird just to kill off so we intend to find it a home somewhere until it can fly properly again."

Mr Briault slowly walked closer to Hoppy. Without taking his eyes from the raptor, he gestured with a hand towards Ian Lewis. "If you'll be so kind as to let Mr Woolley run down to my car and fetch my book from the back seat, we'll soon identify our fine little feathered friend here."

At a nod from Ian Lewis I duly ran, reflecting that the words little and friend hardly accurately described any Ayre's Hawk Eagle or the size and attitude of our feathered guest. Back in the mess I handed the book on African birds over to Mr Briault. With his gaze switching from bird to book, he thumbed through the pages until he felt certain.

Displaying the coloured picture to us all, he declared with commendable certainty and, as we already knew, accuracy, "There you are. It's an Ayre's Hawk Eagle. Not a lot of them about. I have a friend in Salisbury who runs an aviary that is huge. He often takes in injured birds and lets them go once they've recovered. Would you like me to see if he would take care of this one for you?"

Three voices, as one, voiced "Yes, Please," and "Thank you Sir."

"How often do you feed him?" Mr Briault inquired.

"A couple of times a day, Sir," I assured him. "He'll be due for another feed shortly. Would you care to have a go Sir? If so, there's a pair of gauntlets over there on the chair. I'll get some meat."

Over the next half-hour, any inspection of the mess became forgotten. Hoppy did his best to tear off Mr Briault's gauntleted fingers with is talons and bite his equally well protected thumb with his beak. However, he did in the end condescend to accept an offered chunk of raw chicken, which he stood on and then tore to pieces with his beak before swallowing it, shred by shred.

Finally, Mr Briault stepped back, removed the gauntlets and turned to Ian Lewis. "I'm relying on you all to take good care of that bird until I get back to you about a home for him. If you need to cover the cost of feeding him, put him on the ration roll on my say-so. Got it?"

We all got it!

Mr Briault glanced at his wristwatch. "Good lord," he exclaimed. "It's time I was on my way."

Firmly clutching his book on African birds, he nodded to us, took a final glance at Hoppy and headed out, through the veranda door and away towards the offices and his car, followed closely by Ian Lewis.

The mess never did get inspected that year. The eventual Annual Inspection Report on Chibi Police Station was a very good, even kindly one. Forty-eight hours after his encounter with Hoppy, Mr Briault telephoned to say that he had made arrangements with his ornithologist friend in Salisbury to care for Hoppy until he could be safely released into the wild again. A few days later, when I, somewhat fortuitously, had to travel to Salisbury to give evidence in a murder case at the High Court, Hoppy travelled with me. I delivered him as instructed, safely into the custody of Mr Briault's friend, who was delighted to receive him.

As for the Annual Inspection Report, which arrived a few days later, Ian Lewis read carefully through it and then declared, "I'm still not sure whether it was our hard work in preparing for it, or more the presence of that bird, that got us this glowing report. Either way, the report is now on record." That evening, our boss joined Reg and I in the mess where he raised a full glass of beer and declared, "Here's to Hoppy."

It was a toast that Reg and I were only too happy to drink deeply to.

One of the things that both Reg and I appreciated was the fact that Ian Lewis pulled his weight as far as the weekly duty officer burden went. It mattered not whether it was a sudden death, a murder, or a road traffic accident of one severity or another, if it happened during his week on first call, then he dealt with it. The only area where he left it much to me, was on the court prosecuting duties. That was certainly not one of my favourite parts of policing, but Ian Lewis disliked it even more.

He was also a very active and direct person by nature. Shilly-shallying and prevarication were instant irritations to him. It was that nature, quickly recognised by our ever-observant African staff, along with the fact that he was tall and lean, which gained him the nickname of "Gumba Wa Checka", or "The Tin that Cuts."

As the dry season of 1966 kicked in Police Anti-Terrorist Unit (PATU) training and annual musketry courses began in earnest. I retained my marksman's badge and, in the annual inter-services shoot, shooting for the Fort Victoria Police Team, won the Fort Victoria Municipal Cup, awarded to the best police force shooter of the day. That put my name on the cup for the first time. It was not to be the last.

It was shortly after that, that an incident occurred that motivated me to make my next move. On a PATU training exercise, during a live ammunition fire with movement activity, a bullet creased the heel of my right boot. Fortunately, I was uninjured. Nobody admitted to loosing off that wild round and nobody was sure who it might have been, but it made me think that perhaps, if, as appeared certain, I was going to be involved in counter insurgency work of the flying hot metal kind, I needed to be among people who were dedicated full time to that work and who might be more reliable and safer to work with when under fire. In March, I submitted a written request for transfer to Support Unit.

In the early days of May, there were rumours of a terrorist incident along the power lines from Kariba to Salisbury in the area south-east of Sinoia Town. Despite that, I heard absolutely nothing more about any transfer, until the Viljoen family, resident at Nevada Farm in Hartley, was attacked by a group of terrorists in the early hours of the morning of 16th May 1966. Both adults were shot dead and the house shot up. Two infant children, in their cots, survived. No thanks to the attackers, because the cots and wall around were liberally sprayed with gunfire.

The following day, first thing in the morning, an urgent radio message arrived at Chibi Police Station. It contained orders for my immediate transfer, effective that day, to the unit often known as the black boots, based in Salisbury.

There followed a few hours of frantic activity. The first item was a hasty conversation with Shorty. For the second time in under a year, I had to explain my sudden transfer. Shorty had been very happy in Chibi, close to his home village and family. Now he had to decide whether to follow along behind me to Salisbury, or remain in Chibi, unemployed. I was aware that there would be many unemployed batmen in Salisbury, but Shorty and I got along well. He was good with uniforms and handy as a cook also. Shorty listened carefully to what I had to say about the sudden transfer and the choice he had to make, at unfairly short notice. This time there was no lighting up of his face at the mention of my next destination. Instead, he heard me out and then said simply, "Two days, Ishe. Then I come to Harare." I reckoned he had earned those two days off to say farewell to family and friends, so I made arrangements for him to receive bus warrants to get him to Salisbury, handed him a written note of Fife Hostel's address and a few shillings for food on the way and set him to start packing my gear while I sorted out other matters.

In rapid time I tidied up my cases on hand, typed notes of guidance and explanation for whoever might have to carry on with them, made a hasty visit to the District Commissioner's Office to make my farewells there, helped Shorty pack my last bits of uniforms and personal clothing, including a bagfull of items which required washing or ironing and stowed the lot into my Studebaker. With all that done, I drove the short distance to the offices, drew my Lee-Speed rifle from the armoury, said my farewells to Ian, Reg and the African staff and motored out of Chibi, quite literally in a cloud of dust, happy that I had a full tank of petrol, sufficient to see me to Salisbury and that my spare fuel supply of about 30 gallons was being taken over by Ian and Julie Lewis, with payment to catch up with me sometime later.

It was only when I was somewhere north of Chilimanzi that I realised that I had no proper Route Instructions for the journey, just a copy of the urgent radio message of that morning. I decided that would have to be sufficient and kept on driving.

Fishing, 1966
Hoppy the Hawk Eagle

Support Unit (1)

It was late in the evening when I arrived at the Fife Avenue Hostel for single European policemen in Salisbury. Evening meal was long finished, there was nobody in the hostel's communal dining room and the kitchens were quiet. The Member-in-Charge's office was likewise closed and dark. The only sign of life was in the bar, where a few off-duty patrol officers were drinking and chattering and in the snooker room, where all the tables appeared busy. In district uniform, clutching my privately owned .303 rifle and standing looking clearly perplexed outside the closed office, I immediately became a point of interest for a few members of assorted Town and Traffic Branch details who were preparing to leave the hostel to start their night shift duties.

"You just arrived?" one of them asked me.

"Yes," I confirmed. "As far as I know, a radio message was sent to warn i/c hostel that I would be arriving late and to have accommodation available, but it looks as though that message may not have arrived."

"Try the notice board," he advised helpfully, pointing to the far side of the foyer. "Keys for late arrivals often get pinned up there and if you need a late meal, try the drive-in. That's still open."

I thanked my friendly informant and walked across to the large noticeboard. Pinned to it in the bottom right-hand corner there was a manila envelope, boldly marked with my name, rank and number, under which was written, equally boldly, "Support Unit." The envelope contained a key to room number 17. Relieved that I would not have to spend a cold night huddled in my car, I pocketed the key and headed up the stairs to locate the room that was going to be my Salisbury home for probably the next two years.

Room 17 was, fortunately, on the first floor. I say fortunately, because it was quite an effort, single-handedly toting my tin trunk up that one flight of stairs and getting that item along with my issue kitbag and a few other items all safely stowed. The room was just about large enough for an iron-framed single bed, already made up for my use, a wardrobe, a small chest of drawers and a bedside locker. It was about half the size of my room in the mess at Chibi. A quick reconnoitre along the corridor located the communal bathroom, shower and toilet facilities. After that, it was a short car journey to the nearby drive-in, the location of which I knew well enough from my days in training in Morris Depot. With a generous serving of beef-burger, chips and peas inside me, washed down with plenty of strong hot tea, I returned to the hostel, showered and turned in.

The following morning, after breakfast in the dining room, I made myself as tidy and presentable as I could in brown shoes, stockings, shorts, tunic and cap and reported to i/c hostel office at 08:00hrs, firmly clutching my .303 rifle, which needed to go into whichever gun-box there might be on the premises. Through him I was also able to arrange for one of the batmen to help keep me in uniform and clean clothing until Shorty appeared.

With those essentials attended to, I climbed into my car and headed for Tomlinson Depot, wondering just what this first day with Support Unit might bring.

The first thing that it brought was a very tuneless and noisy close-range encounter with a small group of recruit constables who were being trained as buglers. Their allotted training location was under the canopy and around the trunk of a magnificent jacaranda tree that was just off of the pathway that led from the parking area to the single storey small office block which was Support Unit Headquarters. Squawks, squeaks and cracked notes of all kinds accompanied my every pace on that short march. I write "march," rather than walk, quite deliberately, because nobody "walked" when in uniform in Tomlinson or Morris Depots. Being suspected of "walking" by any instructor brought a swift bellow of, "Stop ambling and smarten yourself up!" or some equivalent warning. In Morris Depot it was the threat of a "Behind the Guard" punishment. In Tomlinson Depot it was standard for such defaulters to suffer an hour or so of "Pack Drill," with a few bricks in their backpack, out on the parade ground for their sins. With memories of Morris Depot still strong in my mind, I remembered to march as was expected, trying to ignore the awful racket created by the handful of enthusiastic beginner buglers.

Support Unit HQ building was adjacent to the larger HQ for the remainder of Tomlinson Depot. It was clearly marked and easy to find. What proved more difficult was finding anyone in the building, which seemed remarkably deserted. After standing at ease by the door for a quarter of an hour or so, without the appearance of anyone, I decided to make some inquiries at the main depot office. There, one of the instructors advised me that he had actually seen C/Insp. West, the unit's second in command and admin officer, in his office earlier that morning. He recommended that I just hang around until that person or another, might appear. He did comment that most everyone in the unit had left depot in an almighty hurry to get out and go operational once news of the Viljoen murders at Nevada Farm had reached them.

Fortunately, not long after I had returned to the Support Unit office block, C/Insp. West appeared. In his office I identified myself as being on transfer from Chibi, under instructions to report to Support Unit HQ, today.

C/Insp. West, I noticed, was wearing much the same uniform as I was, but his leather-work was all black, instead of brown. Half a dozen WWII medal ribbons added a touch of colour to his khaki tunic. He had clearly been around a bit.

"Route instructions?" he inquired of me.

I dug into the left breast pocket of my tunic and handed him my copy of the radio message that had caused my precipitate exit from Chibi. "It all got to be a bit of a rush, Sir." I explained, somewhat apologetically. "Proper route instructions got overlooked in the hurry to get on my way here."

He barely glanced at the radio message before tossing it into the "In Tray" on his desk. He reached for the phone and dialled a number he clearly frequently used. When his call was answered, he wasted no words. "I've got Patrol Officer Woolley here in my office. His number is 7207 and he's just arrived to join Support Unit. I'm going to send him over to you shortly. Can you get him kitted out, pdq, with everything he needs for the Unit? I want him properly uniformed for the Unit and out of here on his way to Zwimba just as soon as I can rustle up some transport for him. Is that okay with you?"

It clearly was "Okay" because C/Insp. West uttered a final "Thank you" into the mouthpiece of the phone, set the handset on its cradle and looked quizzically up at me.

"Wheels?"

"In the car park, Sir"

"Know your way to the Ordnance Stores?"

"Yes, Sir."

"Good. Get over there now. Get kitted out and report back to me here just as soon as you can. Off you go."

I drew myself up from at ease to attention, took a small pace backwards, remembering not to salute him because he was not officer rank, turned smartly about and marched out of his office, wondering just what the dickens I had let myself in for. Talk about "feet not touching the ground," I thought as I headed for my car. This is getting more like "The Bum's Rush!"

I parked my car in the first vacant bay I found outside the Ordnance Store building and headed smartly for the door marked "Issues." I had barely closed the door behind me before the European storeman behind the counter inquired, "Are you Woolley?"

At my confirmatory nod he lifted the movable part of the counter behind which he was and beckoned me through the gap. Lowering the counter-top behind me, he said, "Stand at ease here for a moment, while I run a tape-measure over you for some sizes."

I duly stood still while he wielded a tape-measure and made notes. His work was thorough, precise and swift. Eventually, he straightened up and said, "Right. You can relax now. Just stay put while I get what you need."

Put I stayed!

Before very long there was a pile of gear on the counter. It consisted of a poncho cape; additional pairs of trousers, soft blue; another blue bomber jacket, shirts, grey; one hat, soft blue and leggings, leather black (or rather raw leather yet to be polished black!). There was a further leather belt and brace, also of raw leather needing to be polished until black and shiny, and cap straps in ditto state. Hose tops, black woollen, pairs, were added to the pile, plus puttees, short and long, almost as an afterthought. On top of the pile were two pairs of Mars boots, straight out of their boxes. They were made as one-piece items with the soles welded to the uppers, not sewn. They were gloriously plastic. The uppers were pimpled as if to represent some form of textured or leather surface. Finally, on top of the lot, he thumped down a full set of army style 44 webbing, backpack, pouches and all.

As the store man balanced the webbing and boots on the softer stuff, he said, helpfully, "One pair of boots for parades and one pair for bundu-bashing. You sort out which for what." He suddenly seemed to realise that I had nothing with me in which to stow and carry away the pile of additional kit. To my relief, he reached below the counter, hauled out a part-worn blanket and in remarkably quick time had the lot all neatly tied into it. "That'll do you for now." He shoved a clipboard at me and tapped the record card on it. "Sign here, young man and then you can buzz off back to C/Insp. West and tell him he owes me a pint when next I see him."

I put my signature where he indicated it was needed, picked up the blanketed bundle, thanked him for his help and lugged my load of new kit to my car. Ten minutes later I was once again standing in C/Insp. West's office, my bundle of gear on the floor beside me.

There was a tray of mugs of tea on his desk. C/Insp. West gestured at the tray. "Grab yourself some tea, sit down and listen." It was an order, not an invitation. I duly grabbed, sat on, a chair and gave him my full attention.

Over the next twenty minutes or so C/Insp. West explained the structure of the five troops in the unit, designated from A to E and the fact that one was on duty at Vila Salazar in the lowveld, doing restriction camp guard duties, one was based on rotation, in Bulawayo and one was away covering restriction camp guard duties at Sikombela in the Midlands. Upon news of the terrorist murders of the Viljoens, the two troops then in depot had immediately been mobilized and sent off to a base camp at Zwimba Township, not far from Hartley, where a combined force of police, army and air force units were attempting to locate and capture or kill those responsible for the deaths of the Viljoens. The two Troops now at Zwimba were A and E. I was to join A Troop, commanded by Section Officer Reg Crayhart, working alongside E Troop commanded by SO Ginger Garland.

There would be a Land Rover and trailer with rations for the African members of the two Troops at Zwimba, leaving Tomlinson Depot at about 15:00hrs. I was required to be on it, in riot dress, all kitted out, packed and rationed for at least two weeks away. He reminded me that the Morris Depot Canteen would be able to provide me with all the tinned and dried foodstuffs that I might need for the time I was away and suggested that I get there asap in order to make whatever purchases I felt I needed.

When he asked if I had any questions, I had just one. "Would someone please arrange for Shorty, Mujere Mapuvire, my batman, to be accommodated somewhere until I get back, whenever that might be?" To my surprise, C/Insp. West replied, "The others have taken batmen with them. Yours can join you there. I'll see to it for you."

I am not sure whether I left that office in a mental haze, or a mental daze.

Events were moving at a pace at which routine had vanished and reality suddenly seemed to have blurred edges. Fortunately, I had sufficient funds in my wallet to allow me to prowl rapidly around the Depot Dry Store, stocking up on tea, coffee, sugar, powdered milk, rice, tins of chopped ham, stewed beef, tins of vegetables and so on, not forgetting a few blocks of dried fruit and several sticks of biltong.

The matter of being sent out "On Travel and Subsistence Allowance" was no great irritation. The daily allowance at that time, of seventeen shillings and sixpence per twenty-four hours, was quite adequate to live on, provided people did not, daily, booze away a total sum greater than the T&S Allowance, plus standard pay. Regrettably, many police officers, not only the single ones, did just that, as I was to discover.

Back at Fife Avenue, I rapidly explained to i/c hostel what I was about and pointed out that in the rush that I was in, leaving a tidy room behind me was not going to be possible. He agreed to safeguard my room key while I was away and arrange for one of the staff to do some tidying-up after I had left for Zwimba.

Sorting and packing and climbing into what, in effect was really a uniform designed to handle urban riots, knowing that I was heading off to possibly, if not probably, get into a firefight with terrorists, was a wee bit surrealistic. However, that was the way it was. One pair of my Mars boots went into my wardrobe and the other went on to my feet. Neither had seen a polish brush or cloth. Nor had my trousers and shirt seen any washing or ironing, either. Not that it would matter I judged.

Part way through all the activity, I realised that I was late for lunch: Too late in fact for any main course, but just in time for a plate of dessert. A sympathetic cook made it a double portion. That was how it was that reasonably well fed on apple pie, custard and tea, I packed my 44 webbing, my service kitbag and my bedding roll of two blankets around a pillow and headed back to Tomlinson Depot.

It was only when I was getting ready to clamber into the Land Rover's front passenger seat, that something suddenly struck me. I turned to C/Insp. West. "Excuse me, Sir, but if I'm off to hunt terrorists for a couple of weeks, it might be useful if I took a firearm with me?"

A few minutes later, I had drawn a standard .303 SMLE No.4 rifle, a 9" bayonet and scabbard and an adequate supply of clips and ammunition from the armoury and was being driven by one of the African drivers out of depot on the way to link up with what became familiarly known as The Zwimba Gang of The Black Boots. The top item in my 44 webbing backpack was my camera.

Zwimba Tribal Trust Land bordered the Hartley European ranching and farmlands. Support Unit had established a tented camp near by the small cluster of buildings that was Zwimba Township, close to but not quite alongside elements of Army and Air Force.

I was not expecting anything like a formal welcome to the Support Unit element at Zwimba, which turned out to be a good thing, because once the Land Rover I was in drew to a halt by the tents and the few police Land Rovers parked in line near them, I fast became convinced I was both invisible and, in the scheme of things at that moment, highly unimportant. The reason, as I was soon to learn, was that the two Troops of Support Unit had been sent out from depot two days before in the utmost haste and in a state of total unpreparedness. One of the expectations, so I was to learn, had been that there would be no difficulty in rationing the African police from provisions purchased at their destination. Bad thinking! The result was a decided shortage of rations for the constables and sergeants in the first forty-eight hours. The trailer load of bread, maize-meal, sugar, tea and so forth that had arrived with me was of far greater importance than the addition of one more patrol officer.

The result of that was that I sort of just stood by until the issuing of rations, section by section had been completed. Only when that hurry-scurry had abated, did the three-bar types find time to introduce themselves to me. 4912 "Reg" Crahart, who had signed on in 1952 as Redvers William Crahart, and who was to be my troop commander for a while, came across and stuck out his hand. "You must be our newest member," he surmised somewhat obviously. "Welcome to the war zone." A gesture of his hand encompassed the whole camp. He pointed at a couple of green canvas 10' x 8' ridge tents nearby. "You'll be sharing that furthest tent with Terry Rowlandson. Willie Wielopolski's in the nearest one, with me. You can meet up with the rest of the gang when we have some grub a bit later. For now, let's get your stuff stowed into your tent."

It did not take long to get my ration trunk, kitbag and webbing stowed inside the tent and to have my bedding roll laid out on the unoccupied

Hounsfield camp bed. In that time, Reg inquired if I had had any briefing before leaving Salisbury. On getting a firmly negative reply from me, he took time to bring me up to date. What he set out told me that it had not been made totally public, but as he put it, "The first shots in Rhodesia's Terrorist War have recently been fired." He went on to explain that over the past couple of days, he and the rest of the team at Zwimba had been briefed by Special Branch. The outline was that sometime, in the late days of March, or early days of April, there had been a penetration into Rhodesia, from across the Zambezi from Zambia, of 47 well-armed male members of ZANLA, (Zimbabwe African National Liberation Army). That gang had worked their way southwards until they were north-east of Sinoia. There the group had split into two. One group of seven, code named Armegadon, had, on 28th April, 1966, made a bungled attempt to blow up a pylon and bring down the main power line from Kariba to Salisbury, a half-dozen miles or so southwest of Sinoia. Regular members of the Police, along with Police Reservists, supported by elements of Air Force had responded rapidly. In that combined operation, they caught up with and eliminated every member of that group.

The second group led by Gumbashumba made their way to the Hartley District. Once there, they infiltrated themselves into the Zwimba Tribal Trust Lands and commenced to build a network of contacts and supporters. Despite the presence of Ground Coverage details operating there in plain clothes, their presence remained undetected. Whether it was for revenge, having learned of the demise of their fellows, or purely to terrorise the European farmers, in the early hours of 17th May 1966, several members of that group carried out an attack on Nevada Farm. They shot dead the farmer, Johannes Viljoen, when he opened the door to a knock at one o'clock in the morning. They then entered the house and shot dead Mrs Viljoen. The two Viljoen children, Tommy (aged 3) and Yolanda (aged nine months) were both asleep in their cots at that time. After killing both adults, the members of the group ransacked the house. They sprayed every room, including the bedroom in which the two children were sleeping, with gunfire. Fortunately, both of the infants survived unscathed.

Our task, as Reg informed me, was to undertake both foot and mobile patrols of the TTL and farming area, seeking information about, or traces of, the three dozen or more terrorists who were so far unaccounted for from that group of 47, especially those who had murdered the Viljoens. Ground Coverage, CID and Special Branch details were out and about also. At that time, there was no information as to whether those responsible had left the area or whether they had simply gone to ground.

With that helpful background information provided, Reg went on to inform me that I would be taking charge of number one section of A Troop the following morning. Just what I might be required to undertake on the morrow or in days ahead would be made known after a briefing due for 09:00hrs next morning.

The catering system for the camp was simple. Two cooking fires had been established for each Troop: One fairly large one for the African Police and a much smaller one for the Europeans. It was not a racial division. It was merely the recognition of greater and lesser numbers and the fact that camp kettles and bulk cooking were sensible arrangements for African policemen on wet rations when in a base camp, whereas the European element cooked individually using issue mess-tins or left it to the batmen they had brought along with them. Since most of those were anything but "cooks" in European domestic terms, some of the offerings got to be quite interesting while others were definitely inedible. Until Shorty, who was a decent cook, joined us, I cooked for myself.

That evening, I met the other two European members of A Troop. They were, 6918 Terry Rowlandson, who more properly was an "Allan-Rowlandson" and 6764 "Willie" Wielopolski. The latter answered to "Willie" because his real Christian names were Leszek Conrad, neither of which he liked. The others alongside us were 6603 Kerry Croasdell, 5998 Ian "Dumpy" Dunbar and 6074 "Chimp" Webster. The latter had joined with the Christian names of Barry Keith. Somewhere along the way he had adopted a shaven-headed hairstyle. That and the fact that he was, by build, a stocky fellow with longish arms, promptly earned him the nickname of "Chimp." After a while he decided he was quite happy with that, so he eventually had, so the story went, changed his Christian name, by Deed Poll, to "Chimp." In the time I knew him, I never heard anyone refer to him as Barry or Keith.

In the middle of May, the weather was cool and dry, so the warmth from a fire was welcome. It was not long before a few bottles of beer appeared. My alcohol intake had ever been light. I enjoyed a pint after a game of cricket or tennis and a social pint or maybe two were fine on an evening out, but there was no way that I was going to keep pace with the individual rate and volume of consumption that was going on around the fire that evening. Entirely to ward off the chill you understand. Reg Crahart had a couple of beers and then switched to his favourite tipple, which was brandy and lemonade, which he consumed at a quite amazing rate. Reg noted my slow rate of consumption and urged me to drink up because I was now a member of a real police force, where everyone drank beer, whiskey and brandy, not cissy stuff like the pink gin that the Colonial Police Forces all floated on. The words themselves did not trouble me, but the way it was said did. I got a nasty sensation that relations between the troop commander and me could easily become strained.

Setting aside Reg's snide remarks, the conversation was broad ranging. There were concerns about being in riot gear, with bolt-action .303s as our weaponry, to go chasing after and perhaps catching up with, terrorists who were believed to be equipped with AK47 semi-automatic rifles, RPD light machine guns and Rocket Propelled Grenade launchers. The comforting belief was that the terrorists had most likely split into smaller groups, for the purpose of better avoiding detection. It was assumed they were unlikely to be wandering around with full packs and weaponry on display in daylight. Defence force units were actively patrolling by day and moving into static ambush positions by night, hoping to encounter terrorists through those activities and capture or eliminate them. The general feeling, with which I agreed, was that the more we walked, the better it would be, because standard police Land Rovers, with or without riot screens in position, were no protection against bullets or the landmines that were rumoured to be in the hands of the terrorists.

There were also concerns about the broader and longer picture. Would the sanctions recently imposed by the UN, following Rhodesia's Unilateral Declaration of Independence in November of the previous year, force an early political capitulation? How many terrorists were there in training abroad? What was going to be the effect of the existence of not only ZANLA, the military wing of the Zimbabwe African Union (ZANU) supported from within the Chishona and Kalanga tribal elements in the country, but of ZIPRA (Zimbabwe Indigenous Peoples' Revolutionary Army), the military wing of ZAPU (Zimbabwe African Peoples' Union), drawn from within the Matabele Tribal Group. Everyone around that campfire was agreed that there would inevitably be conflict between those two forces. Depressingly, the general opinion was that a political settlement with the UK Government was unlikely without an immediate and catastrophic hand-over to black majority rule.

It was Reg Crahart who pointed out that A Troop's Troop Sergeant, Isaac, was actually a Zambian who had left that country to join the police in Rhodesia a couple of years after Zambia became independent. Apparently, Sgt Isaac's view on corruption, incompetence, tribal preferences and so on were of the kind that, politically, would put him somewhere to the right of Genghis Khan. That raised the issue of what would happen if, as and when any of our sticks might encounter armed opposition. The general feeling was one of total confidence that the African members of the unit were one hundred percent loyal and reliable. Several of them were ex-members of the King's African Rifles. Some of them had seen service in Malaya. They knew full well which end of a rifle was which and just what a bayonet was for. With that comforting thought to escort me, I made my personal excuses at a reasonably early hour, sought guidance as to where the communal latrines had been dug and then took myself off to bed.

It was only when I awoke a few hours later that I had the sudden thought that nobody seemed to have even mentioned night guard duties. Having pondered on the problem for a few minutes, I decided that, as the rookie in the outfit, I needed, for a while at least, to keep my eyes and ears open and my mouth shut. I made sure that my newly issued .303 rifle was within easy reach, that it was loaded and cocked and set with the safety catch on. With that much re-assurance to satisfy me, I turned over and went back to sleep.

I was up that morning with the dawn. The only other person moving about then was a patrolling constable, armed and alert. That, to some extent answered my early morning concerns over guard duties. A bit of investigation quickly revealed that whoever had chosen the field as a base camp site, had not got round to thinking about a supply of good clean fresh water. For the moment a few Gerry Cans, refilled as needed from a local borehole and pump, provided what was needed. There was a camp kettle full of hot, if not boiling, water on the fire. A mess-tin full of hot water, placed on the flat wing of the nearest police Land Rover served for a washbasin and canny use of the wing mirror made a semi-civilised shave possible. By the time I had got that much prepared for the coming day, others of my European comrades were stirring, one or two of them a touch bleary-eyed. I gathered it had been about midnight when they decided to call it quits for the evening.

I also ended up on the receiving end of one or two peculiar looks when, after shaving, I sat down, stripped and thoroughly cleaned my .303 rifle.

A bugle call at 06:00hrs signalled Stable Parade. Dress order was casual, to say the least. There were three Land Rovers to each Troop. Every vehicle was thoroughly checked over, just as it would have been in depot or on a station. That was just as well, because out and about in the Tribal Trust Lands there was not much in the way of garages or repair facilities and standard VHF radios, of the kind we had in the Land Rovers did not reach very far. Not that they had, until now, been called upon to do so. The equipment had, after all, been perfectly good for years, for dealing with riot situations in the major urban centres. Armed insurgency situations had not yet appeared in the forward budgeting processes, so, for the present while at least, those of us engaged at the sharp end would just have to get on with what we had to work with and innovate and compensate as and when necessary. There was a general feeling that we were a wee bit under-equipped, but there was also an over-riding determination to just get on and do the job in hand, using the tools we had presently available.

Breakfast that morning consisted of tinned grapefruit, tinned baked beans and a couple of slices of bread, washed down with a large mug of tea. I did notice that a couple of the gang went for large mugs of coffee only.

As Reg had warned, there was a briefing at 09:00hrs. All the Patrol Officers and above were required to attend it. Apart from a repeat of what Reg had already told me, the briefing confirmed that following the murder of the Viljoens, those responsible appeared to have vanished from the face of the earth. The Special Branch officer pointed out what we were already aware of, which was that the government's African Registration Certificates, or Situpas, which all adult male Africans were required to carry, was pretty useless when trying to establish an identity for certain. There was neither any photograph nor fingerprint upon it. Only personal information which had been hand-written by whichever issuing officer at some DC's office. Multiple Registration Certificates had been found on recently killed and captured terrorists. Those promptly providing them with an ability to simply blend in as one of the local African village people once they had hidden their weaponry and packs. Until some intelligence was forthcoming, the only tactic we could use was to carry out day patrols and night ambushes across as wide an area as we could.

The lead units in that effort would have to be the police Support Unit elements, with elements of the Rhodesian Light Infantry waiting in base camp, with Air Force helicopters available for rapid deployment, if contact was made. For operational convenience, the TTL was split into two halves. A Troop would cover one half, while E Troop would cover the other. Day and night activities were to commence immediately. The strength of each patrol was to be at least ten men. When the briefing officer asked if there were any questions, I had one. "How are we to manage when we are away from our vehicles, because presently we have nothing by way of portable radios, only the VHF sets which are fixed in the vehicles?"

The answer was not very reassuring. "Gentlemen, getting into sustained firefights with terrorists is not your primary task. We have the RLI units with us to do that, if it comes to it, which we hope it will. Your primary tasks are several. You are here to create a police presence and to gather information. You are required to carry out spot checks on people and vehicles and undertake night-time ambushes. As for communications once you are away from your vehicles, we recognise the problem, but, until we can get some suitable radios, you'll just have to do the best you can. That's why we have specified at least ten men to a police stick. With that number, you should be able to handle any group of terrorists you come across, especially if they walk into one of your ambushes. Good luck to you all."

With that, the briefing was over. It was time for the two Troops to fall in and for me to formally meet the men of number one section of A Troop.

Once the troop was formally "On Parade," without firearms, SO Reg Crahart ordered them to stand at ease and introduced me to the assembled African policemen. "This is Patrol Officer Woolley. He's now in charge of Number One Section. Today we are going to carry out a daylight patrol, in strength, through the TTL. This evening we will be moving into night ambush positions that we will be given later in the day. If there are no questions, I want you back here in one hour, all ready to move out. Are there any questions?"

The Troop's Sgt, Isaac, had one. "Ishe, what about our rations? The wet (bulk) rations are good while we are here in camp altogether, but not if we have to patrol on foot."

It was a very fair question: One with which Reg Crahart clearly struggled. After a long pause he replied, "We'll keep the day patrol short so that we can all get a decent meal inside us before we head off to our night ambush positions." He turned away from Sgt Isaac and addressed the Troop directly. "Troop dis-miss! Fall in again here one hour from now."

I noticed that some of the African police did bother to draw themselves up from "At Ease" to "Attention" before turning right, taking the regulatory three paces and then breaking ranks. Others were not so well trained. They just strode off. My thoughts dwelt briefly on my troop commander's demonstrated absence of militaristic skills in dismissing the parade from an "At Ease" position.

Just on 11:00hrs A Troop's three Station-Wagon styled Land Rovers drove out from the grassy field that was our base camp and turned on to the gravel road that linked Gatooma with Sinoia. The day was bright, dry and still. The dust lifted by our speeding wheels hung on the roadway like a reddish-brown mist. My reward for being the junior patrol officer was to be positioned at the rear of the column, where the dust was thickest. My allotted vehicle, PR242, had been sparkling clean after Stable Parade. That condition did not last long as tail-end Charlie in a three-vehicle convoy driving in decently close order. Back at camp we had left sufficient men to carry out guard and cooking duties so that there would be a hot meal for the African police on return to camp later in the day.

Reg insisted on driving the lead vehicle himself, with Terry as his front seat passenger. I was content to leave PR242 in the experienced and capable hands of Const. Kisimis, one of our trained driver-constables.

After a dozen or so miles of travel along the main road, our vehicle radio crackled into life as Reg warned us to be ready for the left turn that would take us into our allotted patrol area. Shortly after making that turn, Reg halted our column because he wanted to position a couple of constables on top of each vehicle, from where they would have a much better view of the countryside and its occupants than those of us at lower level inside the vehicles. With those details posted atop the vehicles, one hand tightly clutching their rifles and the other, probably more tightly, clutching the sidebars to the roof-racks within which they were seated, we pushed on, although the pace of the column slowed considerably. It was also necessary to halt every half-hour or so, in order to change over the constables allotted to the roof-carrier positions. Being perched up there was an extremely uncomfortable experience, as a short, experimental, few miles in that position quickly taught me. It also taught me to follow the sensible example set by those constables who had been up there before me and slacken off the sling to my .303. That way, I was able, like them, to loop the sling around my wrist, so that when any particularly sudden and vicious pothole or rut threatened to unseat me, I could get a second handgrip on the roof-rack without fear of losing my rifle or being pitched off myself. I also discovered that the car commander being on top of the vehicle created all sorts of problems when the radio burst into life and Reg, leading the column, wanted to speak to me. The microphone lead was far too short for that kind of positioning, so down I clambered and down I stayed.

Shortly after having come down from that position, rubbing my battered backside and wondering about the real tactical worth of the details on top of the vehicle, I took a photograph of PR242, with two constables on top, perhaps as a record of just how green and ill-prepared we were at that time.

After about an hour or so of swallowing each other's dust, Reg decided we would cover much more ground if we split our column into single vehicle units. Reg, Willie, Terry and I put our heads together over our sets of maps, agreed a rendezvous point for later in the afternoon and set off. Over the next few hours, we visited kraalheads, two of the local schools and an assortment of townships and isolated individual stores. There was no need, as we soon discovered, to tell the local people why we were there. Word of the murder of the Viljoens was everywhere, well ahead of us. Everywhere we went, the story was the same. Nobody had seen or heard of any strangers in the area, let alone anyone carrying weapons or recruiting people for external terrorist training, or plotting acts of violence against farmers, ranchers or the civil administration or security forces.

Outwardly, there was no hostility towards us policemen. A few locals waved or called greetings as we drove unhurriedly along. Others carefully turned away or kept their heads down until we had passed by. The locals were quite used to police officers in standard District uniform, both on foot, with cycles, or moving about in vehicles, but the two clearly armed constables on the top of our vehicle, in greys and blues, with soft hats, were a genuine novelty. They provoked a few words of puzzled but good-humoured banter from some of the bolder elements of the population.

As arranged, I reported every half-hour by radio to Reg, giving him our location in map reference terms and passing on the news that while we were generally being well-received, nothing by way of useful information was being gathered. That, of course, was exactly what we had expected. Our vehicle radios, needing line of sight for best transmission and reception, were intermittent in performance. Hills, folds in the ground and even heavy tree cover, all degraded voice quality to a greater or lesser extent. Very clearly, improved radio communications had to be high on the list of priorities.

On the matter of being green and inexperienced, we in Support Unit were not alone. At one of the larger stores we visited, there was a generous veranda, with a tailor busy working at a treadle-powered Singer sewing machine. Lounging around on either side of him were three or four local adults, dressed in the usual assortment of clothing, older or newer, that rural villagers commonly wore. One or two of them were customers waiting for their personal clothing repair to be completed, others were just passing the time of day.

As per our briefing, we moved towards them, intending to request the production of their registration certificates, in order to properly identify them. As we closed in on them, I spotted something that made me say to Sgt Thomas, "Don't ask for their situpas here and now as a group. Escort them one by one to speak with me on the far side of our Land Rover, out of hearing."

Sgt Thomas looked suitably puzzled, but, as I retreated to the far side of our vehicle, motioning for Const. Kisimis to join me, Sgt Thomas did as I had instructed. One by one, the adult males, including the tailor, were sent across to where I could have a word and check them out. The first three were routinely identified, questioned briefly and sent back to the store veranda. The fourth one was the one I needed a serious word with. He was aged somewhere in his middle twenties. He was dressed in tyre-tread sandals, well-worn khaki shorts and a green T-shirt under an equally well-worn short sleeved white nylon shirt with a pocket over the left breast.

"What's your name Constable?" I asked him quietly once he was on the side of the vehicle away from the store. "Ah!" he exclaimed worriedly, clearly perplexed. "You know me, Ishe?" he asked, equally quietly.

I shook my head. "No, but I know the crest that's showing through the nylon of your shirt pocket. If I can see it, so can everyone else. If there are any terrorists in the area, that police notebook in your pocket could cost you your life."

The ground coverage constable's face paled. His right hand went up to cover the offending article. "You can see it?"

I turned to Const. Kisimis. "What can you see Kisimis?"

"It is a police notebook, Ishe," Const. Kisims confirmed, without hesitation.

A couple of minutes later, the Ground Coverage detail, like the first three, was sent back to the store, to all intents and purpose having been treated just the same as everyone else. However, while Kisimis and I checked out the remaining few loungers, one by one, our plain clothes police comrade unhurriedly mounted his cycle and pedalled away, to continue his essential and risky work elsewhere, just a little wiser and certainly a lot safer, because his shirt's breast pocket was empty.

At 16:00hrs we rendezvoused as arranged and made the return journey back to Zwimba Base Camp, for a hasty debrief to the Special Branch (SB) officers, a rapid briefing and issue of map locations that were to be the sites of our night ambush duties and then a hurried meal, one that would have to see us through until we returned to base camp the next day.

As dusk was setting in, we set out. The troop commanders plus a number of cooks and camp guards remained in camp. For the rest of us, each Land Rover had a dozen details in it. Of that number, the driver and one constable would return to base once the other ten had been set down within walking distance of their allotted ambush location. At sunrise the ambushes were to be lifted and each stick was to be uplifted by Land Rover from the point at which they had been set down. If suspected terrorists walked into any of our ambushes, it would be up to the stick leader to initiate the contact. The only guidance from SB was that if we clearly saw weapons being carried, we should not hesitate to open fire. Without weapons being visible, we should exercise extreme caution before firing, because normal tribal trust land activity was on-going and many local people would be moving around, perhaps late into the night or early hours of the next day as they attended beer-drinks and other social activities. Nobody wanted any innocent African civilians killed in error in any of our police ambushes.

Moving on foot, after dark, into an ambush position that I had not previously surveyed broke several of the rules I'd had ingrained into me in my years as an Army Cadet at Grammar School. Not knowing precisely where other defence force units were was also uncomfortable and not having any radio communications once we had been set down from our vehicles did not help either. Nevertheless, we had our allotted task to accomplish, so we swallowed our concerns along with our hasty but filling meal and went about the business of preparing for that night's activities. 44 webbing packs and pouches were loaded with our necessaries and bedrolls were strapped into place. Rifle magazines were charged and fitted in place and rifle slings removed and stowed to avoid them snagging on branches and fronds as we walked.

As our vehicle drove off, heading back to base camp, I gave the order to load and make safe. Rifle bolts slid back and then forward and safety catches clicked on. In close order and single file, I set Constable Peter as our point man, with Sgt Thomas in support behind him. For best control, I positioned myself in the middle of the remaining details. From that position, I gave the order to move out.

Fortunately, the school that my stick was tasked to ambush was no more than a couple of miles from the main road. Equally fortunately, there was sufficient grazing land and wooded cover for us to work through, without having to follow any of the well-used footpaths and cattle tracks that would have taken us so close to village huts, where an inevitable canine chorus would certainly have marked our passage and brought inquisitive eyes to bear on us.

An hour or more after full dark, we came within sight of the school, which consisted of a brick under corrugated-iron classroom block, with three small houses of similar build set in line fifty yards or so from the classrooms. The ground between classrooms and living quarters was one clear, flat, open space. A 360-degree circuit of the cluster of buildings, at a discreet distance, revealed a track broad enough for a car or scotch-cart. Twenty yards or so from where that track joined with the open ground there was sufficient grass and bush cover to enable us to go to ground with a commanding view of the track, the open ground and the three houses, all of which had candle or oil lamp light shining from within.

In quiet whispers I set out fields of fire, paired off the stick members and set my ambush line, each man within easy arm's reach of the next detail. Two details to be awake and on guard at all times, hour and hour about. Those not alert could sleep until it was their turn. All details to be awake, alert and ready to move out before dawn. Once we were settled, nobody was to leave his position. If anyone needed a leak, he was to do it lying on his side, clear of his bedroll. The dry ground would rapidly act like a sponge. If anyone on guard duty saw or sensed anything suspicious, the entire stick was to be wordlessly awakened. Nobody was to open fire until I gave the order or opened fire myself. Once I was certain that everyone knew the routine, I unrolled my groundsheet and blanket on the left end of our line, set my pack where I could use it as a pillow and began my first hour of guard duty, rifle in hand. Over at the right end of the line, Sgt Thomas did the same.

The night was moonless, but the stars were clear and bright and the air cool. In that first hour I sat up, knelt up, changed my laying position a dozen times and tried not to look at my wristwatch too often. The only movement was when individuals from the houses left them to visit one or other of the latrines built a score of yards or so behind the houses. One by one the soft lights shining from within the dwellings were extinguished and darkness tightened its grip.

The night passed uneventfully, apart from the feeling that the stars moved more slowly as the night went on, that the ground grew harder the longer I lay on it and nearly everyone, including me, snored at some time or another and had to be nudged into silence or wakefulness.

As dawn approached, I passed word for everyone to pack, two by two in turn and be ready to move out. When every detail was set and ready, we moved off, heading back towards the main road and a rendezvous with our transport back to base camp. We were out of sight of the school before anyone was up and about, but, with the school a half-mile behind us, Const. Peter, ex-KAR, signalled that there were people ahead. As the rest of the patrol faded into the nearby bush for cover, I moved up to Peter's position. A couple of hundred yards ahead of us were half a dozen cattle, busy grazing and browsing. Close by them were two children and a male adult. The children were pointing at the ground and talking animatedly. "They have found our spoor Ishe," Const. Peter said, stating the obvious. "They will follow it and know where we have been and what we have been doing. If they are friendly to the Gandangas they will tell them."

Const. Peter was quite right. Local people knew the normal movements in and around their area. Any sign of a strange presence was quickly picked up and word passed around rapidly. There was little doubt that the school's teachers would soon learn that their school had been under surveillance overnight. My answer was also a statement of the obvious. "There's nothing we can do about our spoor, Peter, so let's just step along and talk politely with them. Besides which, the whole TTL is crawling with police patrols and everyone living here probably knows it and the reasons why. Just go on ahead and offer them a friendly Mangwanani. Let's see how they react."

Peter nodded, rose to his feet and moved forward. I signalled for the rest of the patrol to move on and assumed my place in the line as we did so. When the three locals ahead of us noticed our presence, Const. Peter shouted a good-morning greeting, which was answered promptly and politely. Typically, as the distance between them and our patrol diminished, the conversation simply kept going, until Sgt Thomas and I reached where they were. I decided that it was time for a little direct conversation with the local people, so I called a brief halt. With my sergeant interpreting, I discovered that the local male adult was a government pensioner. He had served as a DC's messenger for many years. He and his two sons were out early because one of their herd of cattle had not been found and brought in to be penned the previous evening. They would normally have just kept on looking, but with the area buzzing with news of the killings at Nevada Farm and armed soldiers and policemen all over the place through day and night, they had waited until dawn to start to look for the missing animal. They had seen our spoor and wondered whether it was Gandangas or security forces. Now he had seen us, he was happy.

There had been a puzzle in my mind ever since I had arrived at Zwimba. It related to why the Viljoens, who were apparently relative newcomers to the area, were selected as a target, rather than one of the other white families, longer established and wealthier, in nearby farms and ranches? I put that question to the villager we were speaking with. Before he answered my question, the villager sent his sons off to continue herding their cattle and to look for the missing one. When they were out of earshot he replied, at some length. Before the killings, he had heard nothing of the presence of the armed terrorists, probably because of his past government service. In the days since the killings and the arrival of security forces, people had started talking, but carefully and quietly, only to others they trusted. Nobody he had spoken with had, according to them, actually seen or spoken with the armed intruders, but they had heard of people who had. As for why the Viljoens had been targeted, he and other locals had discussed that subject. The word in the villages was that it was because Mr Viljoen was very harsh. Reputedly, he was very rough with his tongue and very quick with his sjambok. He worked his employees harder and for longer hours than others and paid them less. Other white bosses had built small medical clinics and even schools for the children of their employees, but not Mr Viljoen. When asked, he had bluntly refused to do so, telling his employees that they were "Kaffirs" and did not need education, but just to do as they were told.

With one eye on my wristwatch and thoughts of our rendezvous with our transport in my mind, I thanked our informant for his time and his words, exchanged a handshake and moved the patrol on.

Back in base camp, having stood down my patrol members, I discovered that Section Officer Crahart was not yet up and about. When I quietly checked his tent, he was in there, fast asleep and snoring gently. There was a distinct odour of stale alcohol within the canvas walls, so I just left him to sleep and went off to find one of the SB details, one who was up and about, to provide a verbal debrief. After that, it was time for me to get washed, shaved and breakfasted, to enable me to be ready for whatever the rest of the day might bring. I was half-way through breakfast before any of the other patrols returned. It was about then that Reg Crahart finally appeared. He declined the cook's offer of breakfast. While Reg sat and sipped gently at a scalding hot mug of coffee, I gave him a condensed version of number one section's overnight activities and advised him that I had already debriefed to SB.

For some reason, that annoyed him. He told me that I was under his command and that I should report directly to him before going anywhere near SB. He also pointed out that I should remember that I had just one bar on my shoulders now, not the couple of pips I had had in Colonial Police. When I pointed out that I had tried to do just that but had found him still fast asleep in his tent and just left him in peace to sleep a while longer, I got an earful for not waking him. I listened to his instruction to report first to him, in future, or else, without answer, other than a nod. Having an argument, in front of African staff and a batman or two, with my troop commander, was not, I judged, a sensible thing to do. Leaving Reg to finish his coffee, I found reason to be elsewhere, hoping as I went that it had just been a hang-over talking and not the real, sober, Reg Crahart.

A little later that day, in a quiet moment, I mentioned Reg's snappishness to Terry Rowlandson and asked him if our troop commander was usually that grumpy in the mornings. What Terry told me gave me some cause for concern. It was a tragic tale all round. Reg had once been happily married, with a charming wife and a child. A few years back he had been stationed in Umtali, where he rented a private house with a swimming pool. One afternoon, when Reg was off duty, his wife had gone out of the house and left him in charge of their two-year-old kiddie. Relaxing at the poolside, Reg had had a few beers and dozed off to sleep. His wife had returned to find Reg fast asleep at the poolside and their kiddie floating, lifeless, in the swimming pool. After that incident and the divorce that followed, Reg had started drinking a bit more than he apparently already did. Terry also informed me that it was common knowledge that I had held the rank of Inspector up in Nyasaland, about which Reg had apparently commented, when first he learned that I was to join A Troop, that I had better not try to pull rank over him.

Two days later, Shorty arrived at Zwimba. Two improvements promptly occurred. I had cleaned and ironed uniforms to change into on a regular basis and when we section leaders and Reg were all together as a group in camp, the quality of our meals improved markedly. Shorty took amazingly well to base-camp life. There was only one point that annoyed him. Being a cleanly individual, he did not like the absence of ample hot water and a bath. He did, however, do the best he could, daily, with a bucketful of water heated over the open fire, a massive bar of green soap, a sponge nearly as big as he was and a huge multicoloured towel.

We European police officers, when not out and about on patrol or ambush duty, wangled trips to Hartley or Gatooma, for rations and other legitimate purposes. On those occasions, we visited the single quarters and took the opportunity to grab a quick shower or bath. For the next two weeks or more, our duties varied, from roadblocks, to day patrols in vehicles or on foot and night ambushes. As our Ground Coverage details and Special Branch members began to obtain information, targeted searches commenced. Each of those aimed at kraals wherein lived known politicians or whom other locals gossiped about as being terrorist sympathisers.

Our pattern of activity when undertaking such a search was to leave our vehicles under guard at a safe distance, then to walk into our target, establish a cordon around it and once that was in place, carry out our search. It was on one such exercise, nearly two weeks after our arrival in Zwimba, that Constable Mapfumo's sharp eyes and knowledge of village life combined to give us a very positive and interesting result to our search.

Working alongside two African SB details, we diligently searched the target kraal. We started by carefully identifying the half-dozen or so male adults who were present. The SB details had the lists of residents of the kraal, from the DC's office. They established that three adult males were not present. The kraalhead told us that they were all away. Two were working on local farms and the third one, a teacher, was in Harare (Salisbury). Having accounted for the adult males, we then worked from hut to hut and from floors to thatched roofs. We shifted grain in the grain stores, we dug through the piled-up cattle-fodder on its racking eight feet or more above ground. We searched beds and bedding, a couple of suitcases and the few bits of European style furniture that were there. We paid careful attention to the shell of an old car that was being used as a chicken roost. After a couple of hours of careful work, all the while under that apparently nonchalant gaze of the adult males, who sat in the sun in a group and watched us, we had found nothing suspicious. The SB details and I agreed that there was nothing to be found. With that decision made, I called in the members of the cordon around the kraal. One of those who walked in was Const. Mapfumo. His route took him past the kraal's rubbish pit, located in the bushes just at the edge of the swept clean area surrounding the huts themselves. He paused as he passed it, then walked over, unhurriedly, to where I was. "Ishe," he said quietly, "the rubbish is not right. The hole is not full, but the rubbish is old. I will show you."

Mapfumo was right. The pit was a rectangular one, six foot by eight foot in dimension, probably originally about eight feet or more deep. It was filled with all sorts of the normal animal and vegetable detritus that arises from a village family of two dozen persons or so. The soil that had been excavated in the digging was banked up on all four sides. The usual custom was that once the pit reached natural ground level, the original soil would be piled up over the filled hole. As the vegetable matter rotted down, the piled soil normally sank until only a modest mound remained, marking the location of the pit. Naturally, day by day, fresh waste material ended up forming the top surface of the rubbish in the pit. However, as Mapfumo's sharp eyes had noted, the top layer of this village pit, still some two feet or more below the natural ground level, appeared to be of well-rotted animal and vegetable matter, suggesting that no fresh material had been added to it recently.

For the past couple of hours, my concentration had been on the huts, grain stores and the animal feed lot. I had paid scant attention to the perimeter of the cleared ground. Leaving Mapfumo to safeguard that one rubbish pit, I called over one of the SB details and took that man and Sgt Thomas with me on a tour of the perimeter of the cleared area. It did not take us long to find that there was another, newer, rubbish pit at the far end of the kraal. The topmost rubbish in it was recent stuff.

The SB detail called over the kraalhead, who offered the simple explanation that the other pit was full, but they had not yet got around to covering it over. His answer was plausible, but his body language was uneasy and his eyes looked everywhere but at us as he spoke. The SB detail looked at me and gave a slight shake of his head. He too felt that something was not quite right.

Taking the unhappy kraalhead with us, I asked for a badza (hoe) and returned to where Mapfumo was standing by the old rubbish pit. Through the SB detail, I told the kraalhead to get into the rubbish pit and dig the rubbish over. When I shoved the badza at him, he refused to take it, protesting that the pit was an evil place to go. It was full of spiders, scorpions and centipedes. The beads of sweat on his forehead, in the cool of a dry season day, spoke volumes. I turned to Sgt Thomas, "Tell him that he can get in there carefully and dig over the rubbish, or we'll throw him in and pile the earth on top of him. Make it sound as though we mean it."

A positively evil grin appeared on Sgt Thomas's face as he turned to the unhappy kraalhead. Wordlessly, his left hand brought his bayonet out of its scabbard at his belt and fitted it onto his .303 rifle. With the now terrified kraalhead's eyes wide and staring at him, Sgt Thomas carefully tested the point of his bayonet with the thumb of his left hand before he absolutely snarled a dozen or so words of Chishona at the now quivering figure in front of him.

As Sgt Thomas stopped speaking, I shoved the badza at the kraalhead once again. This time he repeated his refusal, but having started to speak, he just kept going. When the SB detail asked him a question, he pointed to a spot in the pit. The SB detail climbed carefully into the pit and raked over the rubbish where the kraalhead has pointed. A few inches down there appeared a battered old saucepan lid. The SB detail carefully cleared the lid of rubbish and lifted it. Buried in the rubbish pit below that tin lid was a very large locally made clay pot. The neck was about eight inches across. The body of the pot proved to be about two feet deep and at least two across. Before he ventured to put a hand into the pot, the SB detail asked the kraalhead what was in it and who had put it there. The kraalhead claimed he did not know, but that he had only been told about the pot by his younger brother, the teacher in Harare, when that man last visited his home kraal a few weeks ago.

Warily, the SB detail knelt down and reached deep into the pot. When he withdrew his arm, there was a slab of explosive material in his hand. The eventual tally from that pot was over a kilogramme of explosives, four hand grenades of Chinese manufacture and a couple of hundred rounds of 7.62mm cartridges, usable with an AK or SKS rifle. Thanks to Const. Mapfumo, this time our search had not been a total waste of time. A radio call from our Land Rover quickly brought more CID and SB details, all bristling with weaponry, to the scene. Once they were there in strength, us black-boots were no longer needed, so we were released, to return to base-camp. Remembering Reg's admonishment, I tried to find him. He was away on a ration run in Hartley. When I caught up with him the next morning, he already knew all there was to know of our modest success. It was not only the Africans who had a bush telegraph system!

About two weeks later, there was an early morning encounter between a couple of armed game rangers and what was at first believed to be a gang of poachers, on the southern escarpment of the Zambezi Valley, north-east of Karoi. Some good work by Game Department Trackers and elements of the RLI resulted in a contact in which four ZANLA terrorists were killed and one wounded and captured. Two others were believed to have got away. Word eventually filtered down, that from the wounded terrorist and documents that had been recovered after the contact, it was confirmed that they had been part of the group of 47 who had infiltrated Rhodesia from Zambia some two months or so before. That group had split into smaller units to try to avoid detection. While other small groups had pushed on, this group had remained to subvert the Zwimba area and recruit locals for overseas training. They had also been involved in the Nevada Farm killings. After that action they had at first simply gone to ground, relying on false identities to avoid detection. When a couple of their civilian contacts were arrested and detained for questioning, they had decided to head north, with the intention of re-crossing the Zambezi, to the safety of Zambia. The intelligence gathered made it certain that there were no active terrorists left in the Zwimba area. The 33 terrorists unaccounted for would have to be sought elsewhere. Operation Nevada clearly needed to be wound up. For our final couple of days at Zwimba, camp procedures were still maintained, with guards on duty as usual. Apart from that, there was a distinct air of relaxation. A vehicle run was arranged in order to allow us to return items of kit and equipment borrowed from Midlands Province HQ, including a water bowser. Reg Crahart started celebrating somewhat early in the day and decided not to undertake the journey himself. That task he delegated to Terry Rowlandson and me. Our instructions were not to come back without a good supply of bottles of Castle and Lion beers. During the journey the conversation arose about the fact that the Europeans were able to have a few ales in celebration, but there was no beer hall near Zwimba for our African staff to get hold of a pint or two of Chibuku. Terry and I agreed that that situation was unfair. The result of our agreement was that when we left Hartley later in the day, we had liquid refreshments for both African and European policemen in our Land Rover. A couple of pints apiece for our constables and sergeants was not going to make them motherless, but it would at least show them that we wanted them too to have a relaxed last night on Operation Nevada.

When we returned to Zwimba, Reg Crahart took exception to the fact that we had brought back a supply of Chibuku for the African policemen. Reg had a go at me, but had to back off when Terry Rowlandson, somewhat generously, claimed that as senior man it had been his idea, not mine. When SO Ginger Garland pointed out that technically, we Europeans were all going to be drinking on duty, just as we had done nearly every evening of the operation, Reg grudgingly agreed that the African police could have their Chibuku. Sgt Isaac, as senior Troop Sgt duly took control of the Chibuku, to ensure it was shared out fairly. After our evening meal, what should have been a pleasant and relaxed final evening at Zwimba was somewhat spoiled by the clear atmosphere between Reg and myself, so, after one beer and some speculative conversations about where next our troop might be sent, I left the others to continue with their imbibing and took myself off to my waiting and welcome Hounsfield camp bed.

Back in Salisbury, a debriefing was arranged. It was then that I met Supt Bert Freemantle, Officer Commanding Support Unit, for the first time. At first sight of him, I wondered how the heck he had ever got into the BSA Police. Even allowing for a bit of shrinkage as the years roll by, my new commanding officer was diminutive. As I learned, I was not the only person with that thought, because the African members of the Unit had long ago given him an African nickname. They called him "Chikuswani" which literally translated meant "fag end." As I also learned in future days, they did not use that nickname in any derisory way, for they all had a lot of respect for him and quite a lot of affection too.

The medal-ribbons on the bar above his left breast pocket spoke of active service in WWII. It was common knowledge that he had been among those parachuted in to capture and hold the bridges at Arnhem, in which battle he was taken prisoner by the Germans and spent the last months of the war behind the wrong kind of barbed wire fence.

The de-briefing session, led by Bert Freemantle, with C/Insp. West taking careful notes, was interesting. SO Garland spoke first. He had comments about the problems of bulk rationing for the African Police and the problems of having to cart bulky bedding rolls during overnight activities. He also pointed out that acacia thorns went straight through the soles of the Mars boots we had all been issued with. He was also of the opinion that without better radio communications, we could not be fully effective, especially if any contacts occurred in thick bush, where visibility was very limited. He also represented strongly the feelings of both African and European members of the unit that our blue and grey riot gear was not suitable for counter insurgency work out in the bush, where we stuck out like sore thumbs.

When our OC asked Reg Crahart, "What about your troop Reg?" His non-committal reply was, "We managed alright!" I glanced at my watch. The time was close to 17:00hrs. Having asked the senior men, our OC got around to asking us patrol officers, one by one, what our views were. There were comments on driving upon bush tracks with vehicles equipped with tarmac road tyre treads, resulting in too many punctures. Also, the difficulties of changing tyres and the matter of a certain lack of tools to allow us to carry out even the simplest of repairs. It was commented also that patrolling in vehicles might be alright for showing the flag, but by working from a fixed base camp, we were very vulnerable to being ambushed in the late afternoon or early evening, when returning to camp. That also raised the issue of how thin-skinned our vehicles were and for that matter how vulnerable they would be if one set off a landmine.

What impressed me was Bert Freemantle's genuine interest in getting as much feed-back as he could. He was clearly concerned to learn of our overall strengths and weaknesses and determined to try to do something about the latter.

I pointed out that the matter of weaponry and firepower had to be considered. We had been patrolling ten-strong, to give us some firepower, but, what if we needed to move around in a hurry. That could be done only by using the Alouette helicopters. They could only carry six men and their equipment. If a six-man patrol came into contact with even the same number of Gooks, let alone a larger one, life could get interesting. I also pointed out what the African members of my section had told me. They had had no training on ambush techniques, nothing on map or compass work and no first aid training on how to deal with battlefield casualties. They had no understanding of what "Fire and Movement" was, or a "Flanking Movement" in battlefield terms. Prior to Zwimba, their training had been directed towards town anti-riot work. In addition, I supported SO Garland's observations about wet rations in bulk, which were fit for a base camp, but not for bush patrol work. I raised the need for individual gas-powered and smokeless camping cookers, which had been on the market for years, aligned with individual ration packs, which combination would improve greatly on what we had encountered at Zwimba. I ended by pointing out that even the one single water-bottle we had on issue was incapable, on its own, of providing sufficient water for both cooking and drinking over a 24-hour period.

As the debriefing continued, I was not the only one who noted that Reg Crahart was remarkably quiet, but kept looking, every few minutes, at his wristwatch.

Somewhere towards 18:00hrs, we all ran out of topics of concern. Our OC had a clear idea of the problems we had encountered and our limited operational ability, created by kit that was never designed for countering well-armed Gooks out and about in the bush. C/Insp. West had a lengthy set of notes as a basis for a comprehensive report and Reg Crahart had the mutters. As we headed towards our private vehicles, he took a parting shot at me. "If you weren't so effing verbose, we'd have been out of there an hour ago!" His temper did not improve when he discovered that his car had a flat battery and refused to start. Terry Rowlandson gave him a lift to Fife Hostel. There Terry remarked later, he promptly headed off towards the bar.

After a few days of depot routine, where time was split between parade ground and classroom, our OC arrived at our tea-break gathering with a smile on his face and good news to pass on. He had been able to obtain proper sleeping bags for the whole unit. Each troop would be issued with them as they rotated back to Salisbury from restriction camp duties at Villa Salazar, covering Matabeleland Province from Bulawayo Camp, or doing guard duties at Sikombela, better known as "Wha-Wha" restriction centre in the Midlands. There was, he advised, a good chance of getting individual "Gaz" Cookers and additional water-bottles before long. It was clear that Mr Freemantle had taken up our debrief comments and had represented them upwards as strongly as he could.

A couple of days later, the sleeping-bags duly arrived. They were distributed to everyone in A and E Troops. They were made from a linen material, sewn into four-inch squares, in order to prevent the padding, which was kapok, from simply sliding into one corner or another, in one clump. The first thing we all observed was that the sleeping-bags did not have any form of waterproof groundsheet built in. The second was that the zip was somewhat short, making getting in and out a bit of a wriggle, especially when in uniform and with boots on. The third thing was that they seemed a wee bit lightweight and flimsy, bearing in mind that this was the middle of the dry, cold season of the year, during which temperatures could plummet once the sun had gone down and in which heavy dews and morning mists were not unusual up on the high veldt. The big question was, how would the sleeping bags perform out and about in the bush?

There was only one way to discover that, so, a three day and two nights long exercise was arranged, in the area of the Nora Valley, at Goromonzi.

Over that period, we would all develop our compass and map-reading skills, practise formation and silent signal activities and our ambush and counter-ambush procedures. Ration packs had been delivered, but no Gaz cookers, so open fires would be the order of the day.

In order to fully test the efficiency of our nice new sleeping bags, the instruction was given that nobody was to be allowed to take any blankets with them on the exercise.

After an early morning parade, on a bright but chilly day, the troop duly embussed into, or rather, onto, a couple of open backed 5-ton lorries and set off for Goromonzi Police Station, where the Member-in-Charge gave us a cautious welcome and two warnings. If we caused any grass fires, there would be hell to pay, because grazing was short this year and that there was to be no "Shooting for The Pot." Anyone caught poaching would be prosecuted!

With that cautionary welcome to cheer us on our way, we set off for our exercise area. As arranged, we set up one large troop-sized overnight camp, where we put down our packs and sleeping bags, in a properly defensive pattern, before starting on our assorted training activities, in order to get as much operational training as we could before nightfall.

The Nora Valley has steep sides, which are cut into at irregular intervals on both flanks by tributaries of the stream that meanders its way along its length. The terrain is broken and uneven. It varies from a few small, open and well-grassed clearings, through patches of scrubby bush and occasional stands of mature trees, to granite outcrops and jumbles of boulders of all sizes, from footballs to houses. As a practical training ground, it was ideal for our purposes. For the remainder of the day, we worked diligently. At times as individual sections and at others as a whole troop. We read maps, worked on compass bearings, walked, crawled and slithered on our bellies and tried to make silent signals work. Sections ambushed each other, counter-ambushed each other and attempted all sorts of camouflage ideas in order to see how best we could hide our grey and blue uniform colouring. In trying to establish what patrol formation best suited which type of terrain, we temporarily lost contact with various troop members, both black and white and managed to lose Willie's entire section for a while.

When the shadows began to deepen, Reg decided that we had done enough for that day. We made our way back to our base-camp area before full dark and settled in for the night. We four Europeans held the centre of our camp circle, with each section taking one third of the circle around us. Despite not being in a danger zone, we set a rota of guards for the night. We also established a fireplace for each section and one in the centre of the camp for section leaders and our troop commander. The fires which we lit, carefully within stone circles, were not large. Troop members cooked individually, using their mess-tins and the metal cups into which our water-bottles fitted when in their webbing cases. At each of the four fireplaces, a few careless fingers got burned, a few glowing embers burned holes in uniform items and a few recommended rack-pack meals proved to be anything but tasty.

Eventually, the eating of our evening meal was done. Mess-tins and here and there a tin plate, were cleaned with water, grass and sand and everyone began to roll out the experimental sleeping bags. I positioned myself so that my feet were a good yard or more from the fireplace, placed my pack to act as a pillow and wriggled, feet-first, into my sleeping bag, drawing it up so that it allowed me to sit up and talk for a while with Reg, Terry and Willie, as we sipped hot tea before getting our heads down. Quietly running through our activities of the day, we agreed that without suitable radio communications, we were going to be heavily handicapped. In thick bush, we could be ten feet from each other, yet not be able to see each other at all. That meant that even communication by silent signals was impossible. Calling out could be fatal in a close encounter with terrorists. Radios with throat microphones would be ideal, but even ones with open microphones, which we could use at a whisper, would be an improvement on nothing at all.

Gradually, as we talked, the temperature sank steadily. The stars were a beautiful sparkling canopy over us, but their bright twinkle presaged a cold night. It was not long before we all decided to get our heads down. There was no suggestion of taking off any of our uniform for the night. We just hunkered down in our nice new, but decidedly experimental sleeping bags, set our blue bush hats over our heads for a bit of warmth and tried to relax into sleep.

Somewhere towards midnight, a steady, cool breeze began to establish itself and the temperature sank some more. The thinness of the sleeping bag material made sure the breeze cut right through it. Our riot-gear uniforms were not made of wind-proof or damp-proof cloth, so the cool breeze soon cut through our uniforms as well. A great deal of wriggling and shuffling occurred, as, all around our camp, for European and African Policemen alike, the biting cold wind defeated any attempt to relax and sleep.

Cautiously, in case anyone was sleeping, I sat up slightly and looked around. I was just in time to see Reg take a good long swig from a bottle of brandy before stowing it back into his pack.

I decided that the only way to combat the cold creeping in from outside was to get some warmth into my insides, so I wriggled my way out of my sleeping bag and set about raking over the ashes of our fire, to heat some water for a cup of tea. While the water in my mess-tin over the fire was heating, I stepped quietly around the camp, to check that we did have guards awake and alert. I soon discovered that I need not have worried. The entire camp was awake, simply because everyone was so cold.

When I returned to our section leaders' location, Reg, Willie and Terry were all sitting as close as they could get to the fire, with their sleeping bags wrapped tightly round them. I noticed that my mess-tin of water was not the only one heating on the fire. When tea for all was ready, Reg declined to have any, commenting that he would rather stick with the brandy and lemonade that he was sipping from his water bottle cup. I suppose that in order to be more accurate, I should record that Reg's favourite tipple was not brandy and lemonade, but brandy and lemonade powder. That way, as he explained, he got the flavour of lemonade, without the diluting effect of the carbonated water. When Terry commented that if he had known how cold it was going to be he would have brought a bottle along himself, Reg dug into his pack and fetched out a second, unopened, bottle of brandy.

"Stick some of that in your tea," he offered. "It'll help warm your belly-buttons." Nobody refused Reg's kindly offer.

Despite our alcoholic fortification, the seeping cold continued to kill off any thoughts of sleep. Reg gave permission for everyone to smoke if they wished and for the fires to be built big enough to allow everyone to sit down-wind, so that they were receiving some warmth. Fortunately, there was no shortage of dead wood around and about at that time. Soon, four bonfires, rather than normal-sized campfires, were burning and a few more holes appeared in uniforms and also our flimsy new sleeping bags too, as hot embers flew about in the wind.

For several more miserable hours, we huddled, sipped hot drinks and talked in order to while away the time. From several mouths, the phrase, "I wish that xxxxxx wind would stop," was uttered. Everyone agreed. Regrettably, it became a classic case of, "Be careful what you wish for, because sometimes, you get it!"

An hour or more before dawn, the wind did die down. However, as it did so, the dew began to form and thicken. Leaves and branches glistened and dripped. Spiders' webs took on a fairy-tale form as they collected water droplets that glistened and twinkled as they reflected the firelight. As the dew deepened, our nice dry new cloth sleeping bags began to absorb the ample supply of fine water droplets. By dawn, they were totally sodden. Worse still, the kapok filling within the four-inch sewn squares also absorbed as much water as it could take. The effect was that the kapok welded itself together in a single wet lump in one corner or another of each square, deepening our misery and discomfort. The language, from Africans and Europeans alike, about the worthlessness of the sleeping bags, would have formed a new encyclopaedia of invective, had it been gathered and collated.

Once breakfast had been consumed and the sun lifted over the valley rim, the camp turned into the nearest thing I had seen in a long while to the drying room in a Chinese laundry. There was no way we could roll and stow the sodden, lumpy material of our issue sleeping bags. It had to be dried out first and the nearest drying rails were the trees and bushes all around. For the remainder of that day we pushed on with our scheduled training programme and made the most of the sunshine when it appeared over the valley rim. Late in the afternoon we headed back towards our base camp just a little earlier than we might have done had we had our usual bedding rolls with us. As it was, we used the last hour of daylight to re-stock our overnight woodpile, because we sensed another cold, cold night ahead of us. As it turned out, the cold breeze did not appear. The downside of that was that the dew began to settle in the early hours of the morning and, just before dawn first showed, Reg's supply of brandy ran out. I am not quite sure who was most aggrieved, Reg, or those of us who had shared his liquor with him.

Once again, with a good breakfast inside us, we left our soggy sleeping bags draped all over in a vain attempt to get them as dry as possible as quickly as possible. That morning we were particularly careful with our weaponry, because we intended to repeat some of our ambush and counter-ambush activity, using blank ammunition and we wanted no accidental mixing of live and blank rounds. The wisdom of our thoroughness was flagged up a little later in the day when Const. Phineas stumbled over a tree root. He loosed off an unintended shot, the blast of which burned a hole in Sgt Thomas's blue trousers and, just a little bit, his backside as well.

Once we had our lunch inside us, we began to dismantle our temporary home. We carefully burned every scrap of used material that was burnable, before making sure that our fires were totally out. We were equally careful in scattering the rocks that had formed our fireplaces. We dug a pit for the crushed, empty tins of food we had consumed and covered it with a weight of rocks heavy enough to deter any small carnivores that might get a scent of bully beef or chopped ham. Then we rolled and packed our still-damp sleeping bags and completed the one last task which we certainly needed to do before starting the two-mile or more walk to rendezvous with our transport. That last task was not to fill in our latrines, for we had dug none during our stay, preferring to allow each man to do his own thing, adequately distant from camp, as need arose. Instead, it was to gather the collection of string, wire and cable snares that we had encountered, sometimes the hard way, as we had moved around the valley. A couple of hours later, we checked out as it were by reporting our departure to Member i/c Goromonzi. Remembering that man's comment about not shooting for the pot, Reg took some pleasure in dumping our collection of nearly three dozen snares on his desk and commenting as he left, "We didn't shoot anything for the pot. With that many snares being set, there's bugger all left to shoot!"

We got back to Morris Depot a wee bit late for anything like a decent debrief that day, so it was a case of everyone debussing and disappearing, without need for any formal parade. Back at Fife Hostel, all four of us Europeans headed for the bar for a late sundowner, before looking to get cleaned up and eat a meal. In grateful return for him sharing his precious brandy with us over the past two nights, Terry, Willie and I each stood Reg a couple of large double brandies before we three headed to our rooms, leaving our troop commander to ponder upon the serious decision of which end of the row of drinks before him he should start on first.

The following morning, we had a discussion with Supt Bert Freemantle and C/Insp. Eric West about the sleeping bags and their poor performance during the field trials. Unanimously, we chorused our recommendation that this particular make and type of sleeping bag was totally unsuitable for our requirements. There was a long moment of silence before our OC looked at each of us in turn and then said, "That is most unfortunate Gentlemen, because headquarters have already purchased four thousand of them!"

We also represented strongly for the issue of camouflage clothing, purely for use whenever we were directly engaged on duties outside of urban areas and in direct likelihood of encountering armed opposition. The answer we received was that the request had been put already to Compol (the Commissioner), whose reply had been an emphatically negative one. He had apparently declared that nobody in his police force was going to be allowed to wear camouflage clothing as long as he was Commissioner.

In the days that followed, we all trained hard to convert our riot police troop into an effective counter-insurgency team. One small step forward, at least for us European members of the unit, was the decision to issue each of us with a semi-automatic 7.62mm FN rifle to replace our issue .303s. Although the entire troop was one large team, there was a keen sense of rivalry between the three sections. On the days when we were able to get out to live firing exercises and target work, on the Woolendale Rifle Range, it soon became clear that the order "Ten Rounds Rapid – Fire!" resulted more in fire than rapidity, to say nothing of the remarkable level of inaccuracy. Figure 11 targets at three hundred yards were often left unscathed, despite a hundred rounds or more being hurled in their direction. With the ever-present worry of fire-power nagging in my mind, I taught my section how to use a trick taught to me during army cadet training in grammar school. Standard operation of a .303 bolt action rifle dictated that your thumb went on top of the small of the butt and your index finger pulled the trigger. That meant that when you needed to eject the fired round and re-load, you let go of the small of the butt and grasped the knob of the bolt between thumb and forefinger. You then worked the bolt arm upward and then slid the whole bolt backwards, thus ejecting the spent cartridge and, upon sliding the bolt forward again and then the bolt arm downwards, still using thumb and forefinger, you shoved a fresh round into the breach and locked the bolt safely home before firing. However, it was possible to work the bolt with thumb and forefinger and pull the trigger with the second finger of your hand. That increased the rate of fire. It took a bit of dry run training before the African policemen really got the idea, but, once they had become used to it, the faster rate of fire was noticeable. In a rapid firing competition with the other two sections, my section came out on top, for both speed and accuracy. That brought broad smiles to their faces; perhaps because we section leaders had bet a crate of beer for our sections on the outcome.

In the middle of August 1966, A Troop members received advice that we were to be the next troop to undertake restriction camp guard duties at Vila Salazar, a remote police post in the lowveld, on the Portuguese border close to Malvernia, the small town just across the border. We were to be flown out from New Sarum, the Rhodaf base in Salisbury, in a Dakota, to Boli Landing Strip, a few miles from Vila Salazar. On landing there, we would be met by vehicles used by the outgoing troop and proceed in those vehicles to Vila Salazar. There we would relieve the guards on duty, so that the entire outgoing troop could emplane in the waiting Dakota, for their return journey to Salisbury. We were to take sufficient kit, equipment and rations for a six-week long stay at Vila Salazar. Willie Wielopolski listened carefully to that arrangement and then pointed out that he was due to go on a month's leave, starting on Saturday, 20th August 1966. It was too late to make alternative arrangements, so it was left that the troop would proceed to Vila Salazar one Patrol Officer short and that a replacement would be sent down as soon as possible.

A week or so later, Friday, 19th August 1966, our departure day, was a cold, bright and clear one. The troop paraded early, alongside a mountain of personal kit and boxes of essential supplies. Once everyone and everything necessary had been accounted for, we climbed aboard our waiting transport and set off for New Sarum. Once we had been cleared through the gate, we were directed to a hard-standing area where our aircraft awaited us. There was no haste, fuss, or palaver. The air force ground staff were clearly experienced, efficient and utterly unflappable. Heavy tin trunks and supply boxes were loaded into the Dakota first and placed at the centre of gravity. Lighter kitbags and webbing sets were distributed fore and aft of those down the length of the fuselage and the whole lot secured with nets and strappings before the order was given for us all to remove magazines, make weapons safe and emplane. In single file, section by section, we clambered up the short ladder and made our way along the fuselage, settling down on the seats along either side of the fuselage.

After an uneventful take-off, spot on 09:00hrs. and a period of steady climbing, our aircraft settled down to cruising speed at ten thousand feet, which was perfect as far as I was concerned, both for sheer enjoyment of the changing panorama gradually unrolling below us and for me to take a photograph or two of the interesting places along our route. In the calm, steady atmospherics of the cold season, the nearly two-hour long flight was smooth and uneventful. Even those of our African members who had never flown before and who had been a wee bit jittery before take-off, began to relax and enjoy this view of the countryside that they had never seen before. I could not help but notice, as I had during the train journey from Salisbury to Umtali and back, the stark difference in tree coverage between the Tribal Trust Areas and the European Farming Areas. Once south of Triangle, a member of the aircrew came back to warn us to make ourselves ready for landing as we would shortly be arriving at our destination. On this occasion, our pilot took us down slowly and steadily. The rumble of the aircraft's landing gear dropping into place warned us that we were nearing the end of our journey. At this time of year, the grass cover on Boli Airstrip was short and the ground dry and solid. On this occasion there were no wild animals grazing on the landing strip either, so our touch-down was gentle and the run down to a halt was more a matter of vibrations rather than bumps.

The first thing we noticed after leaving the Dakota, was the relative heat, compared with the temperature in Salisbury when we left. Cold season or not, this lowveld location was several degrees hotter than up on the highveld. The camp that Support Troop occupied at Vila Salazar was set a few hundred yards distant from the Police Post. It consisted of a number of rondavel style huts made entirely from sheet steel. They were water and wind proof, but, as we discovered, they fast became bake houses in the daytime sunshine and refrigerators at night. There were at least some decent toilets and shower blocks available, with water piped in from a pan not too far away. There were a couple of the rondavels that acted as kitchen and dining rooms for us European details and similar arrangements for our African details. Within our camp area there was the large, thatched building, made of upright poles with a sort of wicker interweave to provide walls that Joshua Nkomo had used as a meeting room, before the tighter controls over the restrictees had come into force a few months back.

Within a couple of hours, the handover was all done and dusted, the outgoing troop had been transported to Boli and been flown out and A Troop guards had been established at each of the restriction camps. In

Willie's absence, our troop commander became leader of No. 3 Section. That way we intended to work a rotating pattern of 24 hours on duty followed by 48 hours off. The on-duty section being divided between the restriction camps, with the two other sections being off duty in our main camp at Vila Salazar. We found that our transport, for getting around and about in the area, was not a fleet of Land Rovers, but a few Ford 4x4s. These lumbering brutes had a body divorced from the engine and driver's cab portion. The body portion had a passenger section close behind the driver's cab and a load-carrying section accessed from the back of the vehicle behind that. The four-wheel drive was engaged not by any lever in the driver's compartment, but by climbing out and altering the adjustable settings on the front wheel hubs. The vehicles were also equipped with standard roadster tyres, totally unsuited to the ground in that part of the lowveld, which alternated between rich black soil associated with the heavy mopani woodlands and scrub and the rough, rugged basalt rock formations that broke the surface in numerous places and rapidly deteriorated into thick sand.

Vila Salazar was the point at which the Maputo to Bulawayo railway line crossed the border. It was a customs and immigration point, with presence of Animal Health Department staff, police and a medical assistant who ran a small clinic. It was also surrounded by the Gona Rezhou game reserve, a large area of land given over purely to the natural wildlife of the area. The border itself was very clearly designated by a game fence that many of the antelope species just jumped over and herds of elephant simply pushed against until it broke and fell down, allowing them to simply walk through. Repairing the game fence was a task that kept a whole gang of the Game Department regularly busy.

In the very early 1960s, active and rabble-rousing ZAPU nationalists; those who caused political troubles in the townships and in the tribal reserve lands, were originally simply banished from the urban or reserve area they had become a nuisance in, to live, almost totally unsupervised, in the area around Vila Salazar and the game reserve. After a couple of years or so, it had become clear that they were adversely politicising the nearest villagers, recruiting some for external training and freely communicating across the border with the nationalistic elements in both Mocambique and South Africa. The decision was eventually made for tighter control within formal encampments, with a police guard present, to keep the activists from interacting with the population of Beitbridge, Nuanetsi and Triangle, which police districts bordered on the Gona ReZhou game reserve.

The numbers of restrictees grew until there were four camps, each the size of a football field. There was a fifth, smaller, camp that was home to the leaders of ZAPU, Joshua Nkomo, John Fiendo Mpofu and a dozen or so others. They were housed in a fenced area containing a small cluster of metal rondavels, identical to those of the Support Unit encampment. The other four camps were each ringed by a simple coiled barbed wire fence around an oblong area almost the size of a football field, in which there were quite large wooden dormitories with corrugated iron sheets as roofing material. The barrack rooms each had kitchens and latrine buildings nearby. The camps were spread out over a distance of about a mile and a half, with sufficient tree and bush cover between each camp so that they were out of sight of each other.

Our task was to ensure that there was no communication between the camps, or between inmates and outsiders, unless it had been properly authorised. Tents existed for the use of the guards on duty, sited close by the gateway to each camp. The tents at least offered some protection from sun, wind and rain. Every hour or so, guards from the tent would make a circuit of their respective camp, to ensure that the coiled barbed wire fence was intact and that there were no signs of unauthorised entry or exit of persons. Each camp had an official spokesperson, with whom the guards were permitted to communicate. Apart from that one individual, no communication was permitted between Support Unit members and the inmates. To make sure that all was well, we section leaders worked shifts with the guards, periodically driving up and down from camp to camp, checking that the few guards on duty at each were all okay and taking the occasional walk around the perimeter of each camp ourselves, with or without one of the guards on duty.

My introduction to guard duties at the camps was not a propitious one. Standing up to stretch, in the tent at No. 4 camp, I gave the canvas wall an inadvertent knock. That knock dislodged a small, red, scorpion, which dropped from the ridgeline, landed on my left forearm and stung me. I promptly knocked it off of my arm onto the floor and crushed it under my right boot, but by then the damage had been done. By the time I had driven back to base camp, I had a thumping headache and the glands under my left armpit were swollen and painful. The medical orderly at the clinic listened to my report, checked my temperature, pulse and blood pressure, stuck an Elastoplast on the entry point of the sting and ordered me to rest for 24 hours and not to drink any alcohol in that same period.

Reg Crahart was highly annoyed with me for disrupting the arranged schedule of work. However, he was, over one point certainly sympathetic when I reported the situation to him, "Twenty-four hours without alcohol?" he queried. "That's rough!" What was even more rough was the way my body felt for at least half the 24 hours as my immune system attempted to counter and overcome the venom from the scorpion, which, fortunately, it managed to do.

The routine boredom of guard duties was, during off-duty hours, relieved by visits to the swimming pool at the police camp, games of tennis at the tennis court beside the swimming pool and by visits to the bars and restaurants across the border in the small town of Malvernia, as well as by patrols by vehicle up and down the border fence. Relations with the Portuguese authorities across the border were excellent at that time. Once our faces had been noted and we had become part of the community, we were permitted to move to and fro across the order quite literally as we wished and without formality.

I had already learned, from working with the Portuguese authorities on the borders in Nyasaland, that the basic difference between us and them was that Rhodesians really wished to develop and grow the nation for the good of all. The Portuguese in Mocambique regarded themselves as there purely temporarily, in the long or short term. Officials, whether military, police or customs, were there to see out their official period of service, greater or lesser and return to metropolitan Portugal just as fast as they could. Those who were in business in Mocambique were purely interested in making profit as fast as they could. Not profits for the development and growth of their activities in Mocambique, but purely to salt away in savings or in the purchase of property back in their homeland. They truly were colonizers, not settlers. In some ways, that paralleled my view of British control of Nyasaland and the attitude of the colonial office appointees there.

The two locations across the border which we frequented most were the railway restaurant and bar and the motel. The railway restaurant and bar was a natural development once the railway and the station appeared. However, the motel had come about because one of the early traders in the area quickly realised that with hardwoods like mukwa, marante and teak each growing in profusion over a great area, all he needed to do was to cut them, haul them to the railway line and send then down to Maputo, to ships that would carry the quality hardwoods to Europe, where they could be sold for considerable profit. His first business permits were granted without any great fuss. However, within a year or two, the wealth he was accumulating, from his very simple business activity, became glaringly obvious. So, according to the story told to us, when he wished to renew his permits, it was suggested by those in authority on the Portuguese side, that to avoid any problems with the renewal of his trading permit, he might wish to "do something for the town" as it were.

Swiftly realising which way the permit wind was blowing, the businessman promptly sat down with the great and the good of the small town and asked them what was needed. The decision was that there was a need for a motel for travellers and a bowling green for recreation for the town's more permanent governmental service residents. Both developments quickly appeared and his permits for cutting and hauling hardwoods were duly renewed. The irony, so we were told, was that the businessman made another small fortune over the years, from the motel and the restaurant. I have a photograph of one of the heavy flat-back lorries hauling hardwood tree-trunks, so the business was still going strong in 1966. However, the bowling green became the cause of "an incident" one Christmas when, because of a dare, late one dark evening, a rather inebriated Rhodesian Policeman drove his Land Rover right across the centre of it, leaving tell-tale tyre marks and a great deal of damage behind him. Fortunately, that incident was not perpetrated by any of our A Troop personnel.

We had been in the lowveld about two weeks when a team of government geologists and surveyors appeared and set up a temporary camp close by the police station. They were there to take soil samples as part of a nation-wide search for oil. They required guards to ensure their safety. A Troop was ordered to provide this. The pattern of their search was simple. At half-mile intervals, along a thirty-mile stretch of the border fence, a half-dozen soil samples were to be taken. They were not to be taken at the border fence itself, but at fifty-yard intervals along a quarter-mile line set at right angles to the border fence. At each of those selected and measured spots a hole was to be dug, eighteen inches wide and two feet deep. A sample of soil, weighing at least one pound, was to be taken from the wall of each pit, at the bottom, making sure no contamination from surface soils occurred. Over a period of a week or so, Reg, Terry and I all got involved in that survey and soil sampling work. As well as being the armed guards, we helped to clear trees, cut scrub, bush and grass. We also dug holes and took and bagged soil samples as needed. Our efforts certainly helped to get the project completed on time. We all hoped the results would be positive, because finding oil reserves under the ground within Rhodesia would be a most welcome discovery.

With the survey team gone, the relative monotony of the daily routine at Vila Salazar rapidly re-established itself. The railway brought fresh supplies on a regular basis, every week, not only for us, but for the restrictees also. Sacks of maize, rice, potatoes, onions, fresh and dried meat and assorted vegetables too. It was our task to transport them from the siding to the various camps. One early grouse from our own constables and sergeants was that the detainees were getting better rations, in greater quantities, than they were issued with.

Handing over the supplies was a very formal and meticulous procedure. The calculations of numbers and their ration entitlements were made, the figures were agreed upon and sacks and boxes checked. Our instructions were simple. We were to err on the generous side and to avoid any allegations of short rations. During that first tour of duty at Salazar, there was just one incident over the rations. For some reason, sacks of broken rice appeared, instead of the usual whole-grain rice. Every camp refused to accept it and threatened to go on hunger strike. Urgent messages flew from us to the police post and from there to Fort Victoria Provincial Headquarters. Sacks of the real item appeared on the next train. A query about what to do with the broken rice resulted in an instruction to give that to the restrictees too, because HQ did not want it sent back to them. Notably, when we put it to the detainees that they could have both the whole-grain and the broken rice, they no longer refused to accept that latter item. That caused further mutters from our African police because they felt that as the restrictees had refused initially to accept the broken rice, once the whole-grain replacement appeared and headquarters had indicated they did not require the rejected rice to be sent back, it should have been given to them.

As we slowly discovered, each of the camps had its own individual nature. Camp 1 was never any problem, while Camps 2, 4 and 5 managed at least civil, if never friendly, relationships with the guards on duty, whether black or white. Camp 3 was another story. There the relationship varied, day by day, from antagonistic to downright venomous. It was not uncommon, when carrying out a perimeter check, to be paralleled in movement on the inside of the fence by a small group of inmates, all busily relating, in English, in rather loud voices, what was going to happen to all Europeans and particularly us white police officers, when black majority rule came about. Being expelled from the country was one of the more civilized and less painful options they talked over. Occasionally the odd stone would be pitched at us. It was necessary to ignore the harassment and just get on with our job. Our African staff suffered much the same abuse, frequently being called "Sell-outs."

My first patrol of the perimeter of Camp 4 and what I found myself looking at on the ground, gave me some cause for concern. As related earlier, in Nyasaland I had worked a lot with the game department staff, both black and white and had enjoyed many hours of tutoring on how to track and read signs in the bush. Added to that, my hobby of archaeology tended to keep my eyes on the ground out in the bush, doing personal ground surveys. Whichever it was, my eyes noted clear evidence of movement of people into and out of Camp 4. Without saying anything to anyone, right then and there I made it my business to undertake casual routine patrols around the perimeters of Camps 2 and 3. Each displayed the same tell-tale traces of movement in and out, other than formally at the gate. My prompt verbal report to Vila Salazar Police Station of my suspicions was met with the somewhat deflating and casual response that such activity was well-known and under observation and consideration.

Towards 05:30hrs on Sunday, 4th September 1966, I drove VPF 22 from our main camp, in order to change over the guards on duty and start my turn on guard shift. Within a few hundred yards I realised that there was a problem with the vehicle's clutch and gearbox system. I found that by using the old-fashioned system of double-declutching, I was able to make the system work, but that was all. It was clear that the vehicle was going to need some repair, either at Rutenga or even in Fort Victoria. In the meantime, because I could keep the vehicle functional at least, I decided to push on with the changeover. In relieving SO Crahart and his No. 3 Section, I reported to him the mechanical problem with VPF 22. Reg simply nodded, said, "Let me know if it breaks down completely" and returned to our base camp in VPF 23. Once I was settled in as I was there for the day, I did what I usually did, which was to pick one camp at random and simply walk the perimeter, in company with one of the constables or sergeants. At Camp 3, the logbook of activities at the guard tent recorded that the last night patrol had been carried out at 04:00hrs. The notation recorded all was well at that time, quiet and normal. Taking Sergeant Isaac with me, I set off. Somewhat strangely, there was not a single detainee anywhere to be seen. Despite that, all else appeared normal until we reached the corner at the far end of the staked down coils of barbed wire that formed the fence all the way round. The side fence, over its entire length, had been dislodged from its anchoring stakes and pushed out, very neatly, about six or eight paces. Some of the stakes had been pulled out and cast aside, others were still in situ. When I looked from the dislodged fence to the barracks hut, it was clear that there were many pairs of eyes closely watching our progress. The next ten minutes of patrolling revealed that the coiled barbed wire fence on both sides and at the rear of the camp had each been uprooted and pushed outwards. In two locations, firewood piles had been dumped in the newly claimed ground beyond the old line of the fence.

Sergeant Isaac was astounded. I was impressed, but also concerned in equal measure. I had no reason to believe that the recorded 04:00hrs perimeter check had not been properly done or factually recorded. That meant that the inmates had to have pre-prepared the untying and loosening of the anchoring stakes and carried out the re-location of three sides of their camp fence the moment that patrol activity had ceased. It displayed common purpose and sound organisation, carried out in complete silence and at no small risk, for if the guards had become aware of their activity, they might well have feared a mass escape attempt and opened fire at those moving the fence.

For the scores of inmates, the pushing outwards of the fence on three sides of the camp, provided that the preparations had already been done, would not have been a mammoth task. Putting the fence back to its rightly position was clearly going to need more hands than the few guards available at the front gate. There would have to be some discussions with the inmates first, the creation of an unarmed working party and the presence of armed guards, all in sufficient number to dissuade the inmates from any attempt to stop the corrective work from being carried out, which, I sensed, was a quite likely event.

By the time I got back to the gate there were one or two of the inmates outside of their hut. I called for the camp's spokesperson, intending to ask him why the fence had been moved. Camp 3's official spokesman, Mr Chirongomo, was, as usual, not presently available, but I was advised that he would appear shortly. That situation did not surprise me. It was just one of their ways of not co-operating. "Shortly" could mean anything from five minutes to several hours.

Now that the inmates were well aware that their unauthorised adjustment to the position of the perimeter fence had been noted, without any great reaction, more of them appeared from the several dormitory huts and normal routine began to establish itself.

Firewood began to be cut, a few of them started kicking a football about while others engaged in group conversations, or educational classes run by some of the many teachers who were among those within the camp.

When I had waited for nearly half an hour, without any appearance from the camp's spokesperson, I got on to the radio in VPF 22 and made a detailed report, direct to Reg Crahart at our Support Unit base and to the police station, about what I had discovered. The Member-in-Charge, Inspector Ron Pilborough, promptly instructed me, over the radio, to see that the fence was put back to where it should have been. Without waiting any further for the elusive Mr Chirongomo to appear, I set off in VPF 22 for Camp 4. There the fencing was all in standard order, as it was at Camps 1 & 2 when I checked those locations. It was at least a small degree of comfort to know that we were not facing a united act of rebellion, common to each of the camps.

The verbal instructions I had received, at about 07:30hrs, were clear and concise. Take a working party to Camp 3 and put the fence back where it should be, without delay. I bothered to ask Ron Pilborough what he wanted me to do if I encountered any serious opposition, because at Camp 3 they could muster a whole lot more people than we had guards, even if we used everyone rostered as off duty for the day. Was I to play it softly and back off or stand my ground and get the job done regardless? Ron Pilborough's response to that query was unequivocal. "They won't tackle a working party backed up by three or four armed guards. Get that fence back where it should be and let me know once that has been done. If we give any ground over this one, we'll have the other camps doing the same thing and that is not on."

With those clear instructions ringing in my ears, I drove back to our Support Unit Camp, further briefed Reg Crahart and asked him how many men I could have and did he want to come along, just in case there was any problem. Reg decided he did not wish to. As for manpower, I could have four men as a fatigue party and could use the off-duty guards at the tent as my armed escort. Reg felt that should be quite enough. When I commented that I thought a greater show of strength might be safer, Reg disagreed and told me to just get on with the job and stop arguing.

I duly rounded up Sgt Servester and Constables Ephraim, Kaunye and Tirivaviri, briefed them on the task ahead and drove us all to Camp 3, this time in VPF 23. There I made a further request for Mr Chirongomo to speak with me and received the usual reply that he would come along shortly. I used the waiting time to brief the armed guards on duty, all six of them, as to what was about to be attempted and chose four of them, Sgt Isaac and Constables Peter, Manklumo and Chenjerayi, to act, with me, as an armed support group to the four unarmed members who would be doing the physical work needed.

Sgt Isaac, for whom I already had a whole lot of respect, expressed everyone's concern. "There are not enough of us, Ishe. They will try to make trouble when they see we are so few."

At that point the elusive Mr Chirongomo appeared at the gate, with his usual entourage a few paces behind him, listening keenly. With Sgt Isaac close by me, I explained that I was there under orders to put the fence line back to where it properly should be and that I would appreciate it if he would work with us to ensure that the job was done without any trouble being started. That invitation he declined, claiming not only that he had many other tasks to attend to, but that we had no right to do anything to the fence because this was their land, not ours. When he started in on telling me that he would remember me and see to it that once ZAPU was in charge of the country I would be dealt with, I thanked him for speaking with me and turned away, leaving him with nobody to rant at.

Back in the guard tent, I made sure that my own FN rifle was safe, with full magazine in place, but breach empty and safety catch on and that the four guards with .303s accompanying us had the same situation with their rifles. Then I gave the order for bayonets to be fixed, but for there to be no shooting unless I ordered it.

Working anti-clockwise round the camp and keeping all of us police details on the outside of the barbed wire coils of the fence, we moved slowly and cautiously to accomplish our allotted mission. We five armed details formed a wary and sharp-eyed semi-circle a few yards back from Sgt Servester and his unarmed details as they lifted and shifted section after section of the misplaced fence, securing it to those stakes of the original fence line that were still standing. The camp inmates had piled firewood, logs, scrub poles and rushes in several locations just inside the expanded fence, which, if we had just lifted the fence over them, would have been outside the replaced fence and thus denied to them. To prevent that potential irritation and what might flow from it, where there were inmates nearby, we politely asked them if they would please move the materials back within the original boundary. Three such groups did, somewhat to our collective surprise, although they too maintained the continual litany of verbal hatred, in English, Chishona and SiNdebele, directed towards us and me in particular. Where there were no inmates nearby, we lifted the fence over the piles and, once it was secured in its proper place, pitched all the woodwork over the fence so that the inmates still had access to it.

Close by the north-west corner of the camp, there was a large pile of logs, each six to eight feet in length and a foot or more across, topped off with brushwood and rushes, to a height of eight feet or more. The larger tree trunks had been carefully laid at right angles to the line of the fence. To the right of that pile, some ten yards or so distant, was a group of a dozen inmates, all jeering and shouting assorted insults. Two more were actually sitting on the inner end of some of the larger logs. In English and Chishona we asked them if they would kindly move the woodpile inwards so that we could put the fence back in its right place. One of the two shouted a reply, in perfect English, "We will not do it. It is your fence that you are moving. You can move the wood as well." His raised voice stirred up the gang by the nearest hut and attracted others too. A small crowd began to gather, sensing a confrontation building. The two seated on the inner end of the logs refused further requests to please move. I then caused the fence coils to be brought up to either side of the wood pile and had my four fatigue details start pulling the lighter brushwood and rushes out towards us. My intention was to get to the larger logs and have the fatigue details lift them one by one, by their outer ends and tumble them end over end inwards, until they were within the old perimeter line. Pulling the lighter stuff towards us immediately caused the onlookers to set up howls of anger from the several dozen now around, that we were stealing their wood.

At that point one restrictee, obviously one of the camp committee, pushed his way to the front of the crowd, walked to the inner edge of the woodpile and demanded to know what I was doing stealing their wood. Ignoring the jeers and catcalls from all around, I directed Sgt Isaac to watch my back and stepped onto the edge of the woodpile so that he and I could speak and hear each other. To him I carefully explained my intention to relocate the woodpile inside the old fence line and secure the fence outside of it, so as not to "steal their wood." That senior fellow listened without argument to what I had to say. He then told the two seated individuals to move and for them and others to begin shifting the woodpile back to where I required it to be. His instructions were met with action to obey by some and with jeers from others. I stepped off from the woodpile poles that were about to be moved so that they could be lifted. As I did so, two of the group on my right simply charged at me. One grabbed me by the waist in a sort of rugby tackle and the other grabbed my FN rifle and tried to pull it from my grasp.

I am not a giant, but, at better than six-foot tall, and around 180 pounds in weight and literally fighting fit, I was not an easy mark. Besides that, my early years had been spent on the bomb dumps of the East End of London, where you learned, amid the gang-fights, to never use your fists until your feet were tired and you always used your head, preferably on the other fellow's nose, before he did that to you. The man who had grabbed me round the waist dropped to the ground, howling. Sgt Isaac, who had been carefully guarding my back, put the butt of his rifle firmly into the ribs of the fellow trying to pull my FN from me. That man tumbled over backwards, picked himself up and bolted. Whether to help their grounded friend, or to try to get at Sgt Isaac and me, the onlookers, shouting, started to surge forward. The crack of a .303 rifle and the spurt of dust the shot kicked up from the ground in front of them suddenly changed their minds and the direction of their movement. Except for those at the woodpile, the crowd scattered in disarray.

A quick look back at my guard team revealed just one, Const. Peter, with his rifle aimed from his shoulder towards the disappearing crowd. I bellowed, "Hold your fire!" at which he lowered his weapon to a wary port arms position. At that point, Mr Chirongomo appeared, at a run. He motioned at the still groaning individual lying on the ground. "Why have you killed him?" he demanded angrily.

Before I made any reply, the helpful senior inmate answered him. He too gestured at the man on the ground. "This one and another tried to take the Murungu's rifle from him. They could have got us all shot. They were stupid." If I could have given that man a medal, then and there, I would have done so, because those words, coming from one of his own kind, clearly took the wind out of Mr Chirongomo's sails. Perplexed and needing time to think, he bent down, helped my assailant to his feet and sent him away, then stood, grimly silent, looking around, as the situation was explained to him. Eventually he looked directly at me. "This shooting I will report to the Red Cross," he stated. "That's fine by me," I assured him, "Because I too will of course report the incident to my superiors. In the meantime, I have a task to finish, with or without your co-operation."

Mr Chirongomo thought about that for a moment. Then he called to a few of the inmates who had been watching our conversation from a safe distance. He snapped a few phrases at them in SiNdebele, before turning to me. "I have told them to move the firewood piles back. If you give us time to do that, there will be no more trouble. My friend here will see to it." He gave a nod in the direction of the helpful inmate and walked rapidly away.

I never did discover the name of the helpful inmate, but, with him on the inside of the fence, working along with us, the remaining wood piles were moved back to where they had originally come from and the fence line returned to its proper position without further trouble. When the final section was secured, I turned to him and said, "Thank you. I appreciate your help." He just shrugged and strode off.

I took a moment to recover the one spent cartridge from Const. Peter, who was a bit worried over whether or not he would get into trouble for having fired that warning shot. I carefully assured him that although his shot might have been a little premature and he had, technically, disobeyed my order not to shoot unless I instructed it, there would be no repercussions for him. He had, after all carefully put his bullet into the ground and had only fired it because he felt I was in trouble that could have got worse. To prevent any demonstrations against him during the remaining hours of his duty shift I drove him back to Salazar, with the four men of the fatigue party.

My efforts to find Section Officer Crahart and Insp. Ron Pilborough were unsuccessful. I was advised they were both over the border carrying out a working lunch and liaison visit. In the absence of both those individuals, I delivered a detailed verbal report to SO Felix Kutner. Being just a little wary of what might arise from the incident, I made sure I had PO Rowlandson with me. SO Kutner listened in silence until I was finished. For the record and as was customary, I handed the expended cartridge to him and asked if he wanted a written report in addition to my verbal one. That offer he declined, although he warned me that Insp. Pilborough might require one once my verbal report had been passed on to him.

The remainder of that day passed without further incident. I took some time to compile a formal, written, report of the incident at Camp 3, while the events were still clear, in detail, in my mind. 18:00hrs came and went. It was Reg Crahart and his section who were due to replace me and my team. It was not unusual for Reg to be a wee bit late. Experience had taught me that he was not the best timekeeper in the world.

At 18:17hrs, SO Crahart and his section arrived for duty. The changeover of guard shifts should have taken place routinely. However, already having been verbally briefed by someone, possibly SO Kutner, about what had gone on and the fact that a shot had been fired, my troop commander arrived loaded for bear. Tumbling unsteadily out of VPF 24, in front of our African staff and well within hearing of a handful of restrictees lurking near the gate to Camp 3, he promptly accused me of deliberately provoking a situation whereby tempers had been lost and shots fired. "There's going to be hell to pay and it's all your f---ing fault!" he fumed. His verbal fuming was matched by the reek of alcohol about him and the patently obvious wobble in his walk.

Keeping my voice as low as I could, I fired back, "I think we need to have this conversation when we're alone and when you have not got a skin-full under your belt. Take a look at yourself. You can barely stand up!"

Without further words, I gathered my team and headed for base, changing guards at the other locations as was needed. Back in our base camp, I had a word with Terry Rowlandson and asked him if he had seen the state in which Reg had gone on duty. Terry confirmed what I had suspected, which was that our boss had spent the day in Malvernia and returned late, reeking of booze. So much so that Terry had offered to drive him round for the changeover of guards. Reg had declined that offer.

Terry Rowlandson relieved Reg Crahart at 06:00hrs the next day. Reg carefully ignored me and went off towards the police station. At 07:30hrs, I was summoned to the police station, where Inspector Pilborough required me to submit a detailed, formal, report of all that had gone on at Camp 3 the previous day. An hour or more later I left the detailed report with him to study and returned to our base camp to pick up the routine of vehicle checking, cleaning and camp maintenance. When I returned to our Support Unit Camp, I found Reg fast asleep on his camp bed. I left him to sleep.

At 17:40hrs that day, I went on night guard duty, with my team. All was routine until I drove in to relieve the guards at Camp 3, where most of the inmates appeared to be assembled just inside the gate. As I climbed out of VPF 23 my arrival was greeted by yells of wrath and jeers and a few stones, thrown by unseen individuals at the back of the mob. Mr Chirongomo was conspicuous by his absence. Being fairly sure that the demonstration was against me and not the African staff I had with me, I simply ignored the noise, carried out the necessary changeover and drove away. I learned later that once I was gone, the crowd promptly dispersed.

At Camp 4, where SO Crahart just happened to be, I told him what I had been greeted with at Camp 3. He instructed me to carry out no perimeter checks at Camp 3 and to limit my checks on the guard tent to just one either side of midnight. The rest of that shift passed off quietly.

On the morning of Wednesday, 7th September, I was instructed by SO Crahart to escort Driver Constable Mutandwa, in VPF 22, to Rutenga and Matibi, to see if local repairs could be carried out on the vehicle's troublesome gearbox. I was also to collect rations for our Troop. In accordance with those instructions, we left camp at 10:20hrs. With the gearbox misbehaving and despite the gravel roads not being in too bad a condition, it took us three hours of steady driving to reach Nuanetsi Police Station. That put us an hour or so behind schedule, so I took the trouble to step into the radio room there, intending to advise Salazar that we might be back later than expected. Quite unintentionally, I found myself listening in to a radio conversation between Inspector Ron Pilborough and OC Province, Peter Sherren. The subject of their conversation was the uprooting of the fence at Camp 3 and what had caused the shot to be fired. The Red Cross were demanding answers. I listened to Inspector Pilborough claiming that he had known nothing of the incident until it was all over and done with. He put the blame for the incident squarely on my shoulders for not telling him about it and not seeking to take sufficient armed guards and a large work detail to put matters right or giving him the chance to negotiate the return of the fence to its correct position with the camp committee. His final criticism was that I had stupidly walked inside the camp fence line, alone, into the middle of a crowd of angry restrictees with an FN rifle loosely held in one hand, so it was no wonder that one of the inmates had tried to grab it. He ended by commenting that I was lucky one of my constables had had the wit to fire a warning shot, because that had probably saved my life. When Propol broke off the conversation, I immediately called Salazar and identified myself. Only the radio operator answered. My words were controlled and few. "Kindly ask Member-in-Charge to tell SO Crahart that I am behind schedule and will be back later than expected. You might also advise him that I have been standing here listening to his conversation with Propol. I'll have a few words with him about that when I get back."

A few minutes later I received a summons to Member-in-Charge Nuanetsi's office. He was speaking on the phone when I entered. He pointed at a chair and said into the phone, "He's here now Sir. I'll put him on." Handing me the phone, he mouthed silently, "Propol."

"Good afternoon, Sir," I said into the mouthpiece. "You wished a word with me?"

Propol did not beat about the bush. "Good afternoon Mr Woolley. I take it you perhaps disagree with what you heard over the radio?"

"That's to say the least of it, Sir."

"Did you submit a written report of the incident?"

"Yes, Sir."

"Do you have a copy you can let me have?"

"I do, Sir."

"Good. Get a copy to me. Mark the envelope Private & Confidential and get it to me discreetly, just as soon as you can. Got that?"

"Yes, Sir."

"One last thing. This conversation never took place. I can rely on you for that?"

"Absolutely, Sir."

"Good. Now put Member-in-Charge back on the line, please and you can go about your other business."

I handed over the phone, offered an "Excuse me, Sir" to Member-in-Charge and left, feeling a great deal better than I had been feeling a short while before.

It was after 21:00hrs when Const. Mutandwa and I eventually got back to Vila Salazar. Reg was on shift, but Terry Rowlandson was in camp. He promptly told me that at shift changeover this evening, there had been a crowd of what appeared to be all the inmates of Camp 3 at the gates. As the incoming vehicle drove in they greeted it with jeers and boos, but once they saw that the incoming officer was not me it all quieted down. Terry reckoned that when I did appear again, there could be a problem. On that cheerful note, we both headed off to clean up before going to get our heads down for some sleep.

Early the following morning I paid a brief visit to the home of Dave Williams, the resident Animal Health Inspector, whose remit ensured he drove far and wide around the entire lowveld. He was also someone who had had a clash or two with the present Member-in-Charge of the police station. That visit started a copy of my detailed written report on the warning shot incident going discreetly on its way to Officer Commanding Police Victoria Province, as requested.

Although the restrictees were limited in their ability to move about without prior agreement, there was no shortage of visitors to the various camps. Apart from relatives and friends, there were visitors from all sorts of organisations from churches to Amnesty International and the Red Cross. One of those periodic visitor groups were the priests from Gokomera Mission. When one of their Land Rovers drove into our camp mid-morning of 8th September 1966, I wondered what the purpose of the visit was. When I got close enough to see the face of the reverend father driving the vehicle, I began to make a shrewd guess, because that man's right eye was closed and blackening fast and there were traces of blood on his clearly grazed right cheek. His story was simple enough. This was his first visit to the camps. He had been to Camps 1 and 2, where there had been no difficulties at all. However, when the guards had let him inside Camp 3, there he had been poorly treated. They had not been interested in holding any form of service. All they had demanded was that he should make the authorities give them a larger area of land. When he pointed out that he could speak with those in charge of the camp but could not give them orders to do this or that, an argument had started. During the course of it he had been roughed up and thumped by one or other of the inmates of Camp 3. He wished to report the incident to the proper authority. Terry and I listened to his story, offered our sympathies and directed him to the police station, where he could formally register his protest.

Terry and I watched the mission vehicle drive off towards the police station and had a conversation about what might happen when I went on duty at 18:00hrs. Our decision was that Insp. Pilborough needed at least to be made aware of the potential for trouble. I took myself off to see Ron Pilborough. He made no mention of yesterday and neither did I. The result of our conversation was that when I went on guard duty, with Sgt Servester and his section and reached Camp 3 at 17:45hrs, Patrol Officer Butler was already there, sitting in one of the police station's own vehicles, watching and waiting.

As soon as I was recognised, the inmates started to gather in small groups outside their allotted huts. Although they were very vocal and full of interesting ideas and views about my past, present and future, none of them approached the gate and no stones were thrown. The moment I drove off towards Camp 4 to relieve Reg Crahart, PO Butler also left, heading towards the police station. I duly relieved Reg Crahart, gave him an up-to-date briefing of recent events and watched him head off towards our Support Unit Camp and 24 hours off duty, leaving me to see through what turned out to be a very routine and peaceful night.

Friday 9th September 1966 proved to be one of those days that started with a clear blue sky, a sun that blazed brilliantly and not a puff of wind and simply went on like that. From my base at Camp 4, I made the periodic checks on the camps, patrolled perimeters and checked in by vehicle radio with main camp, to let them know all was well. Just after lunch, when I climbed out of my vehicle at Camp 3, a small group of restrictees walked towards the gate, from where they called a request to speak to me. One of them I recognised as the helpful fellow of a few days back. Their request, for which he was the spokesperson, was a simple one. They needed more malala palm leaves. Would I permit a few of them to leave camp for a while to search for and gather a fresh supply of the leaves? I was well aware that the dried and shredded leaves of the malala palm made perfect raffier type strips that they used to weave into hats, some of which they wore themselves and some of which they sold to visitors and even their police guards. They also stained the dried strips of leaf, using urine of assorted strength, created purely by evaporation, so that they had different shades of brown with which they could create patterns in their weaving.

Having listened to their request, there were a couple of things that puzzled me about it, so I politely asked why was Mr Chirongomo, the official spokesperson, not making the request and how come it was being made to me, with whom they clearly had issues and not to SO Crahart or PO Rowlandson?

The answers were straightforward. Mr Chirongomo felt I would say "No" to him because of recent bad events and they had asked SO Crahart the previous day, but he had said, "No" to them.

I gave their request another moment of thought. There were no radios allowed in the camps and very little else, apart from newspapers or magazines that were inevitably days or weeks old when they got to them. Some of them had been there for a couple of years or more. I could think of worse things for them to be doing than staining dried leaves and weaving hats. I looked directly at the helpful inmate. "Alright," I advised him, "but there are three conditions. No more than six of you. You are to be personally in charge of them and you will all have to be back within the camp before 17:30hrs which is when I and my team are due to go off duty. If that is agreeable, you can start as soon as you are ready."

The helpful restrictee nodded and spoke briefly to his companions in SiNdebele. When he was done there were nods of agreement from all of them.

A few minutes later they were gone, carrying only some yards of string to tie the collected leaves into bundles and a couple of bottles of water. I turned to Sgt Thomas as they vanished into the bush. "Do you think they'll all come back?"

"Yes, Ishe," he replied with total conviction. "You have been kind to them. They will be too ashamed to cheat on your kindness."

As it turned out, Sgt Thomas was right, but before they reappeared, other events surfaced. Motoring between Camps 3 and 4, I encountered PO Butler, trudging along towards Salazar on foot in the heavy sandy conditions. The police station's Thames Trader flat-back lorry was stuck in the sand some few miles away and needed rescuing. I drove him to the police station, where neither Insp. Pilborough nor SO Kutner were locatable. Inquiries there revealed the station had neither a towrope, nor any chains which we might use. I carted PO Butler off to our own camp, where I discovered that SO Crahart too was missing. Terry Rowlandson had not seen him since early morning. Hearing our conversation, Sgt Isaac informed us that he had seen our troop commander in Malvernia a little before lunchtime. He thought he was still there. With time pushing on and shift changeover in mind, I helped locate a couple of tow-chains and handed responsibility for rescuing the police station's vehicle over to Terry. The consideration was that it might need the towing power of two vehicles, so I gave up my transport to assist in the rescue and waited at camp so that I could travel in SO Crahart's vehicle back to Camp 4, when he arrived to start his duty shift.

At 17:30hrs, SO Crahart appeared, apparently having walked across from the police station. He was noticeably unsteady on his feet, reeked of alcohol and, on seeing me at our camp, promptly demanded to know what the f--- I was doing there instead of being at Camp 4 ready for handover. His words, although delivered in a clearly angry tone, were careful and slow. Sgt Isaac, standing behind him, looked at me and shook his head. His message was clear. There was no formal parade of the on-going duty shift that evening. Our troop commander simply ordered everyone into the vehicle and set off.

Later that evening, with Terry Rowlandson still not yet returned, I received a message from the police station. 6895 Patrol Officer Kenneth Gordon Stewart was on board the evening train. He was under orders to join A Troop for the rest of our stay at Salazar. At 22:00hrs, only just after Terry Rowlandson had returned from his vehicle rescue mission, I met the evening train at Malvernia Station, collected the newest member of our troop and got him settled into camp for the night.

Saturday, 10th September 1966, brought two incidents of the kind that were entirely avoidable and undesirable. Shortly after lunch, when I was showing Ken Stewart around the camp, SO Crahart drove in, far faster than was needed, or safe. Even before the vehicle's wheels had stopped rolling, he had the door open and was bellowing, "Where's f---ing Woolley?"

It transpired that he had noticed some of the inmates of Camp 3 sorting and splitting malala palm leaves. When he learned of my decision of the previous day and saw the entries in the gate logbook, he was furious. He stormed off to his vehicle, shouting loud enough for all to hear that he was going to have my f---ing guts and drove away, wheels spinning.

Reg decided, quite stupidly, to tackle me out in the open, in front of Terry and Ken and with half our African members within sight and sound. One of Reg's difficulties in confronting me was that I was a good couple of inches taller than he was. It is never a good idea to try to threaten and dominate anyone both taller and bigger than you are unless you are perfectly sober, in full control of yourself and on absolutely certain ground. I knew very well Reg was way out of order, on more than one point.

He ended his slurred tirade at me with the advice that I was confined to camp, until he could get me on to the next train out of Malvernia, back to Salisbury and up before our OC on disciplinary charges as he had had more than enough of my continual troublemaking.

I waited until he had run out of steam and foam-flecked words before I made any reply. Then I said, quite conversationally, "Section Officer Crahart, you are, with all due respect, out of order, on more than one point. First, you have reminded me, a couple of times in the last few minutes, that I am no longer an Inspector of anything, but just a Patrol Officer. I need to remind you that that even a Patrol Officer is not to be dressed down, shouted at and demeaned in public, in the presence of junior ranks, by anyone, no matter what their rank, or the condition they are in."

"Secondly, when you set up our operational pattern after we arrived here, you expressly stated that you did not want us, Patrol Officer Rowlandson and me, referring every tiny problem to you when we were in charge of the guard shift on duty. Your reason was that if we did that, you would never get a moment's peace. You told us to deal with any day-by-day problems and that matter of the malala palm leaves was just that, a day-by-day problem.

"You made your decision when you were guard commander. I made my own decision when I was in that position. That they were different is irrelevant. And if you cannot remember what instructions you gave us about three weeks ago, I am sure that Patrol Officer Rowlandson probably can, just as much as me."

SO Crahart's angry certainty started to crumble. He looked at Terry, who said, just as conversationally as I had been speaking, "That's what you said, Reg. You wanted us to make decisions for ourselves."

SO Crahart's shoulders slumped. His lips tightened. "Get that rubbish pit finished before dark," he snapped, before whirling rather uncertainly about, climbing back into his vehicle and driving off.

Terry and I exchanged wordless glances. Ken Stewart looked at each of us in turn. "What the hell was that all about?" he inquired. "And what's all this about a rubbish pit?" Terry explained. "We started digging a fresh rubbish pit this morning. It's got to be ten by ten by ten and that takes some digging with just picks and shovels, even with all of us taking turns. As for the rest of it, let's grab a cup of tea and we'll tell you a story. A damned sad one."

It was an hour or so later that Sgt Isaac appeared. Addressing Terry as the senior detail he reported that the rations that had arrived by train the previous day and which had been, as usual, stored in the big cold room at the police station, ready for issue today, appeared to be short. All three of us Patrol Officers walked across to the pile of boxes. It did not take long to establish that the week's rations for our African staff were not up to full measure. There were only 82 loaves instead of 90. The fresh meat ration was short and so was the number of tins of corned beef and chopped ham. Further shortages appeared to exist in the rations of tea, sugar and powdered milk.

The rations for our African members were, nominally, a regular weekly order, shipped from Bulawayo. More often than not, the order arrived piecemeal. Bread would arrive one day, the fresh meat the next and tea, milk powder and sugar two days later. Just occasionally, the entire week's order did arrive in one delivery. Because of that, every incoming delivery was supposed to be checked out as it was unloaded at Malvernia Railway Station, signed for as correct and brought across to our side of the border, where the perishables were stored in the cold room, ready for distribution to the African members of the troop. It was section Officer Crahart who had supposedly performed that task the previous day. A discreet pow-wow between Ken, Terry and myself resulted in Terry, as senior PO, accepting the job of informing Reg that there was a problem. When Terry did just that, SO

Crahart simply told him to tell me to sort it out. A couple of hours of effort the next morning, in company with Sgt Isaac and a bit of to-ing and fro-ing across the border revealed that there was no consistency between the quantities ordered, the invoice relating to the order and the consignment note, which our troop commander had signed off without even opening any of the sealed boxes. I spent a while with Insp. Pilborough, outlining the inconsistencies and arranging for the shortages to be provided, urgently. Somehow, he and I managed to stay away from any discussion of other recent events. Back at camp, Sgt Isaac and I held an informal briefing for the African staff so that they understood they were not going to be short-changed on their ration entitlement. My subsequent verbal report to SO Crahart delicately avoided pointing out who had signed for what without properly checking that all the items listed were there and in the correct quantities.

There was of course no limit on movement across the border by our off-duty African staff. Once they had obtained verbal permission from whichever one of us was duty officer for the day and signed out in our camp's activities and movement logbook, they too could move to and fro just as we Europeans did. To their credit, very few problems ever arose. However, on the morning of 12th September, Consts. Ben and Mawire were missing. They had booked out of camp the previous afternoon, to visit Malvernia and had not returned. PO Stewart and I set off to find them. We checked the usual bars on the fringes of the town, which were the favourite haunts of our African staff, without success. To some extent, it really was like looking for a needle in a haystack. We were about to give up when an empty timber lorry drove into the main square and stopped. Down from the back of it climbed our two missing constables.

Their story was simple. They had crossed the border with thoughts of a little bit of drinking, followed by a whole lot of womanising. They had learned of a very entertaining professional lady who lived in a village a dozen miles or so out of town. A friendly lorry driver had offered them a lift there, with a promise of a lift back late in the evening. With that all sorted out, off they had gone. The friendly lorry driver's information had been, according to them both, absolutely right. Sadly, the lorry driver himself had got too drunk to drive them back, so they had to wait until morning when he was once again fit to drive.

Back in camp, I related their story to SO Crahart. His decision to give them a couple of extra hours digging in the new rubbish pit was a sensible one.

That matter of entertainment by professional ladies was not confined to the Africans in the area. One of the regular habits, or customs, call it what you will, of the Portuguese menfolk, after the end of the weekly Friday evening social and dance, was to send their ladies, whether wives or girlfriends, off to their homes, while the men went off for some dallying with the local Mahuris. They were quite open and casual about it and were forever puzzled because we Europeans from the Rhodesian side always declined their warm invitations to accompany them.

That behaviour contrasted sharply with the severe eye that the Portuguese mothers and grandmothers kept on the young girls in their families. At weekends, the police camp's swimming pool was often the centre of braaivleis (barbecue) parties, sometimes attended by family groups from the other side of the border. On such occasions, the "Duenas" did, quite literally, park their chairs two inches from the water's edge, from where they kept close eyes on their nubile charges and just how close they got into contact with any young gentlemen in the water, whether Portuguese or Rhodesian, during games of water-ball and the like.

The next couple of days passed without notable incident. Ken Stewart proved to be a reliable and sensible colleague. He had a good sense of humour, got on well with the African members of the troop and pulled his weight whenever work tasks were there to be performed. He drank only in moderation and never mixed drink and duty, much to the relief of Terry and me. However, it was not long before he came off from one duty shift and promptly asked if he could have a quiet word with us both. He had been relieved by SO Crahart, who had been carrying, by its straps, the backpack part of his 44 webbing set. Between the vehicle and the guard tent at Camp 4, which we Europeans used as our base when on camp guard duty, SO Crahart had stumbled and dropped to his knees, knocking the webbing pack as he did so. The sound of clanking glass bottles came across loud and clear. Ken wanted to know what would happen if any of our African staff paraded reeking of alcohol or with alcohol in their packs. As Terry Rowlandson advised him, there was little we could do about it, except hope and pray that situation would never crop up.

Wednesday, 14th September 1966 dawned dry and bright. Our troop commander was off duty, so he headed for Malvernia early, leaving Terry Rowlandson on guard duty with his section and Ken and me to get on with daily camp routine. Rations were issued at 07:00hrs. When fatigues parade was called at 09:00hrs, Const. Edward reported a problem with his .303 rifle. The bolt was jammed open and would not slide shut. I took a look at it, gave him full marks for having stripped and cleaned the weapon before coming on parade and flipped the safety catch ALL the way off, after which the bolt slid to and fro quite readily.

Shortly after that, word reached us that water supplies for Camp 2 and the police station had failed. Inspector Pilborough sent word that he and his staff were fully occupied with visiting external officials and for me to sort out what was wrong and get it put right, rapidly. Leaving Ken to care for the camp, I headed for the water-pumping station, where I learned from the African artisans that one of the three pumps had failed. Normally there were two in operation, with the third available to allow for servicing and breakdown cover. On this occasion, while one of the pumps was stripped for a routine service, a second one had failed. Repairs would take about ten to twelve hours. I did a very quick tour of the camps to check on the water supplies at each. Camp 2 was, as reported, already out of water. Camp 4 was down to a few inches in their header tank; too little to see out the day. The other camps would, with care, have sufficient for the day.

When I reported that situation to Insp. Pilborough, who was still awaiting the arrival of the party of external officials, his language was colourful to say the least. Dignitaries arriving to find a camp or camps without water supplies, would be a disaster, but, as he pointed out somewhat defensively, he could not stop pumps from breaking down, no more than the water board staff could and if the pump needed twelve hours for repairs, that was that. The camps would have to manage as best they could. At least the dignitaries would see that the police camp was in the same boat as Camp 2, so they would not be able to say the restrictees were being deliberately victimised.

I had to repeat my comment that there was one solution, before he took it in. Even then I had to repeat it a third time for him. There was, not far distant, a disused army camp. It was kept on standby in case of serious trouble at the camps. It had a water tower with a tank on top that should be full. We had a 500ltr water bowser at the Support Unit Camp. It was empty, but, if filled from the old army camp, it could be put into Camp 2 as a holding measure. Similarly, we had an assortment of water Gerry-cans associated with our transport fleet. We could collect and fill those too so that, at worst, the camps would all have sufficient water for cooking and drinking until supplies returned to normal.

Once he fully registered what I was getting at, Insp. Pilborough told me to get on with it. He pointed out that there were keys to the army camp on the board at the police station, so I would not have to waste time breaking-in to the place. I hastened back to our Support Unit Camp, hurriedly briefed Ken Stewart and set him to rounding up every water Gerry-can he could lay hands on, anywhere in the area. Fortunately for my bright idea, there was water in the 1000ltr header tank at the army camp. Within a couple of hours, Camp 2 had ample water for its essential needs for the day, as did the other camps, even though Camp 4 needed supplies from our Gerry-cans before full pumping power returned just after dark.

At evening changeover of guards, Ken relieved Terry and the frenetic activity of the day slowed to a more normal pace. SO Crahart returned to camp from Malvernia late in the evening. Before he collapsed on to his camp bed, to sleep off his day's drinking, he enquired whether everything had been quiet through the day. Terry and I looked at each other. An unspoken message passed between us. Almost in chorus we assured him that it had been just one of those routine days and that there was nothing for him to worry about.

By the time Reg surfaced the next day, the water supplies were back to normal, our water-bowser was back where it had always been and assorted water Gerry-cans were back with the departments we had borrowed them from. If Reg Crahart did ever discover what had gone on, he certainly never mentioned it.

On Friday 16th September 1966, the Geological Survey Team arrived again, to take more soil samples. I was due on duty that evening but was able to help them, once again, for most of the day in their careful collection of the necessary soil specimens. That activity certainly provided a bit of light relief from the usual daily routines, trials and tribulations of our stay at Vila Salazar.

Having relieved PO Rowlandson and his section and established my team on duty at each camp by 18:00hrs, I decided to take make a circuit of the perimeter fence at Camp 3. I found that one short section of the back fence-line had been flattened by a pile of firewood logs that had clearly been dumped quite deliberately right on top of it. From out of sight behind the nearest hut, one of the inmates yelled, "Shoot the logs, Murungu. That will move them." At that there was some laughter from other unseen inmates. Back at the camp gate I called to one of the inmates nearby and requested a word with Mr Chirongomo. For once that man appeared almost immediately. When asked about the woodpile and the short stretch of flattened fence, he of course, knew nothing about it. He did, however, assure me that if I gave him a few minutes, he would see to it that the wood was removed from where it now was and the fence put right. He was exceedingly co-operative and pleasant, which was just not his style. I did of course reciprocate in kind. I informed him that I would be back in a couple of hours or so and would be most grateful if I found then that the fence was upright and the woodpile back on the inside of the wire.

Once I was out of sight and hearing of the camp spokesperson, I used my vehicle radio to report the incident to both Support Unit Camp and to the police station. To SO Kutner, at the police station, I expressed my suspicions about Chirongomo's suddenly friendly and helpful attitude and suggested it might be interesting to have a snap rollcall at the camp, not right then in the dark of evening, but perhaps the next morning. I left him to think about it.

Two hours later, not only was the woodpile back where it should have been and the fence, just a little battered, restored to roughly its right shape, but Mr Chirongomo was at the gate to greet me and personally show me that all was right and proper as promised. My suspicions deepened.

The following morning, Insp. Pilborough arranged, as he was entitled to do, a snap rollcall of the inmates at Camp 3. Such rollcalls were not popular. It took a while to gather the restrictees, organise them into some form of order that could be reliably counted and whereby they could not "double-up" in order to cover anyone who might be missing. The barbed wire fences that existed around the camps were so nominal a barrier to clandestine movement in and out that they were, in reality, just a token gesture. Both sides of the engagement understood that and, as long as the camps appeared to have their correct quota of inmates, no action was taken. The snap rollcalls were simply a way of reminding those on the inside of the enclosures that it was those on the outside of the enclosures who were in charge. The result of the rollcall at Camp 3 on this occasion revealed that there were five restrictees unaccounted for. Mr Chirongomo, as usual, knew nothing about the missing persons, individually or collectively. Insp. Pilborough, asked Mr Chirongomo, very politely, if he had any information about the whereabouts of the missing men. Mr Chirongomo told Insp. Pilborough, equally politely, that he had not the faintest idea where the missing men were, or how or why they had left the camp. It was of course possible, he suggested, that they had taken themselves outside to collect herbs or perhaps to find a particularly fine piece of wood for carving. He assured Insp. Pilborough that he would of course advise the guards the moment any of the missing men returned and hoped that the guards would not be so unreasonable as to shoot at them if they should see them trying to re-enter the camp. On completion of the usual insincere pleasantries, the roll-call parade was terminated and the guards and the guarded returned to their normal daily routine.

14840 Const. Mutandwa was, under normal circumstances, a very reliable member of the troop, with a clean disciplinary record. Sadly, when he paraded for guard duty at 17:30hrs on Monday, 19th September 1966, he was in no fit state for anything. He was, to give him his due, splendidly turned out and in good time for the formal calling of the parade, but that was where the positives ended. He was happily and gloriously drunk. He was dangerously wobbly on his feet and incapable of coherent speech. Sgt Isaac and I were both certain that he was far from fit to be on duty. I removed his rifle from him and drove him to the police station, where I left him in the hands of Sgt Zwenyika, to be placed in the cells overnight. I was unable to report the incident to SO Crahart, because he was over in Malvernia.

With that necessary disciplinary chore attended to, I proceeded with my duty section, to relieve PO Rowlandson and his section. In the middle of that handover, there was an urgent radio call from the police station. It was a request for me to get down there as fast as I could, because Const. Mutandwa was refusing to go into the cells and threatening to fight anyone who tried to put him there. At the police station I found Const. Mutandwa backed firmly into one corner of the charge office, where he had two walls to help him stay upright. Both his fists were aggressively up. 7245 PO Robert Preller and Sgt Zwenyika were trying to explain to him that it was in his interests to take off his boots and give up his belt and wristwatch so that he could be recorded as correctly detained in the cells, but he was having none of it.

When he saw me, his fists dropped. He pulled himself into a decidedly wobbly parody of the parade-ground attention stance. All I said was, "Follow me please, Mutandwa." I walked slowly out of the charge office, into the cell block and straight into the first empty cell. Const. Mutandwa followed, unsteadily, but uncomplainingly. I gestured at the bunk type bed. "Make yourself comfortable on that while I go to get you a pillow and some blankets." When I returned a couple of minutes later, he was, as I thought he would be, flat on his back on the bare boards, sound asleep.

Two minutes later, his boots, belt and wristwatch were in a property box in the charge office, the detention records were all correct and Const. Mutandwa was left to sleep it off, head on a firm pillow and covered by a blanket. Back at our Support Unit Camp, SO Crahart was still absent, so, for the record, I made a formal report to PO Rowlandson and drove back to Camp 4 to resume my 24hrs on guard duty.

At 06:00hrs on 20th September 1966, while I was making a circuit of the perimeter of Camp 3, I received a report that one of the restrictees, while chopping wood for the breakfast fire, had cut himself with an axe. A look at the injury showed that he had quite a nasty wound to the outer edge of his right foot. The camp's designated first aider felt it needed stitching. I agreed. I drove the injured man to the clinic at Vila Salazar, left him there to be attended to and drove to our Support Unit Camp where I briefed SO Crahart, in relation to Const. Mutandwa and the injured retrictee. SO Crahart ordered that Mutandwa be left a while longer in the cells, so I picked up the injured restrictee, returned him to Camp 3 and once more resumed my interrupted guard duties.

Just after lunch that day, SO Crahart radio'd through to me at Camp 4 to pick up Const. Mutandwa from the police station and return him to his rightful position in the guard team at Camp 3. On the journey back to Camp 3, Const. Mutandwa apologised for getting too drunk to go on duty. According to him, it was all the fault of the Mahouris in Malvernia. They slipped muti into their customers' beer, so that they could not make jiggy-jig properly. One of the Mahouris he had been with during the day must have put something into his beer, because he had only drunk his usual amount of beer for the day, so it should not have had the effect it did. "One of the

Mahouris?" I commented. "Ah, yes, Ishe. I am a man!" There I let the conversation lapse.

The remainder of that guard shift passed quietly. At 17:50hrs the routine shift changeover took place. I handed over the guarding responsibility for the next 24hrs to PO Stewart and his section and drove my team back to camp.

At 20:00hrs, there was an emergency call-out. PO Stewart reported by radio that he had been beaten up by two African men he had found outside the wire at Camp 4, attempting to work their way into that camp. While escorting them towards the guard tent at the gate, they attacked him and, after beating him to the ground, fled. Insp. Pilborough and SO Crahart were both over in Malvernia. SO Kuttner assumed command of all readily available manpower and drove them to the entrance drive to Camp 4. Even though backed by the presence of more than thirty armed police officers, SO Kuttner, wisely remaining outside the gate requested that the camp spokesperson should speak with him. That man, Mr Malembo, duly arrived on the inside of the gate and the usual kind of conversation took place through the wire. Mr Malembo had no idea who the two men who had assaulted PO Stewart might have been. Neither he, nor anyone else in the camp had seen or heard anything of the arrest, the struggle, or where the men might have gone to. He flatly denied that they might have been inmates of Camp 4. While Malembo and SO Kuttner were talking with the camp committee of a half dozen inmates standing within earshot, others in the camp slowly began to emerge from the huts and gather in a semi-circle a few yards behind Mr Malembo and the committee members near the gate. Not a word was spoken. No orders were given, but each hut's occupants stayed closely together. In a very few moments, that semi-circle numbered more than 150 men, all standing in total silence, listening to the words being exchanged through the wire at the gate. Every single one of them was carrying either an axe or a heavy-weight knobkerrie. The air of tension was palpable.

SO Kuttner did not fail to see what I had seen. "I see your men are carrying weapons. Why is that?" he asked, in a carefully non-aggressive or provocative tone.

Mr Malembo shrugged. "It is night-time. We Africans always carry an axe or a knobkerrie when we walk out at night. It is our custom."

SO Kuttner considered that for a moment before he replied. Then he said,

"Very well. Perhaps we should all go into our quarters, where nobody needs weapons and we can sleep for the night. There will be time to talk some more in daylight."

Mr Malembo nodded his agreement and turned away from the gate. Without a word said, the semi-circle of silent armed men faded away into their respective huts. Fortunately, PO Stewart was more shaken than hurt by his encounter, in which no attempt had been made to relieve him of his rifle, so he volunteered to remain on duty to complete his shift. Just for safety, we doubled the guard on the camp and issued instructions for guards to patrol in twos for the rest of the night, which passed off without further incident.

The following morning there was a somewhat informal gathering of all of us European police officers, in Joshua Nkomo's meeting hut in our Support Unit Camp. It was the common view of all of us that something was stirring. The sustained insults being hurled at me and other guards at Camp 3, the missing men at Camp 3 and the assault on PO Stewart at Camp 4 were oddities. Of more concern was the silent parade of more than 150 men at Camp 4, every last one of them carrying an axe or knobkerrie. Insp. Pilborough informed us all that the Ground Coverage and Special Branch details operating in the area were hearing stories of restrictees allegedly coming and going at will, both between the camps and across the border.

Snap searches of the camps were discussed as were more regular rollcalls. It was agreed that there was little or nothing that could be done to make the camp fences less porous. The coiled barbed-wire fences never were designed as anything much more than perimeter markers. They could be wriggled through with little effort, lifted, flattened and generally made a nonsense of at any time, particularly during night-time.

The outcome of the pow-wow was that Insp. Pilborough would send a detailed report to Fort Victoria Provincial Headquarters, advising them of our concerns. Locally, discreet patrols would be undertaken by Support Unit personnel, to check on any signs of unauthorised movement between camps.

Much of the rest of that day I spent writing reports relating to Const. Mutandwa and his episode of drunkenness.

After going on duty at Camp 4 as usual at 18:00hrs on the evening of the 22nd, I left Sgt Servester in charge and slipped quietly away on my own to lay in ambush on a game-trail that passed close by both Camp 4 and Camp 5. Four hours of patient waiting produced no signs of movement, so I returned to my tent at Camp 4, to get a few hours of sleep. At 04:00hrs, I repeated the exercise, this time between Camps 3 and 4. Once again, nobody appeared, but, in those few hours of solitude as dawn broke and the sun rose over the horizon, I was able to just lay and enjoy the marvel of that amazing time of year when the first rains begin to make their presence felt after several months of dry weather. It never ceased to amaze me, how the first rains wiped the skies clear of dust, making everything seem closer and in sharper focus. Sunlight brought with it the morning chorus of myriads of cicadas up in the trees and silenced the night-time calling of thousands of frogs, but not before most of them had managed to grab a good mouthful or two of the sausage flies that always seemed to spend more of their short lives buzzing around in circles on the ground rather than flying about on their relatively small translucent wings. When I gave up my solitary ambush position and carried out a perimeter patrol of Camp 3 at about 08:00hrs, one particularly vociferous group of eight or so individuals, all from the hut nearest the south corner of the camp, greeted my presence with a particularly noisy chorus of jeers and derision. It crossed my mind that that kind of performance was certainly one way of warning others of the presence of a patrolling guard.

Later that day, SO Crahart, on a discreet patrol with a couple of constables between Camps 3 and 4, detained two African men who claimed to be out from Camp 4 just looking for herbs. To avoid any possible demonstrations from Camp 4 inmates, he just drove them to Vila Salazar Police Station, where he handed them over to uniform branch personnel. Word eventually filtered back that they were not Camp 4 restrictees.

The day after that, in mid-morning, when I was checking the camps, Const. Mchengu reported that while he was patrolling the fence at Camp 4 just after lunch, he had seen a man walking towards the camp from the direction of Camp 5. When he challenged him, that individual fled into the bush and vanished from sight. With Sgt Thomas and Const. Mchengu, I picked up the tracks of the man Const. Mchengu had challenged, at the point where the encounter had occurred. Backtracking showed that the man had come from Camp 5. Following the tracks forward established that they led, without a break, straight back to Camp 5. As required, the incident was reported back to SO Crahart and Insp. Pilborough.

Over the next few days, the game of catch-as-catch-can continued. Nobody got hurt, because our instructions were firm that we were not to shoot at anyone we found outside the various camps, but to arrest them if we were able to. Gradually, the unauthorised movement between camps slowed, but it took a meeting at Camp 4, addressed by Joshua Nkomo himself, to finally bring it to a halt.

On the 28th September, when driving between the camps to check on the guards, I noticed something fluttering on the ground in the track some twenty yards or so ahead of me. Driving up close to it I realised it was a bird of about 8 or 9 inches in length with a very dark blue and shiny colour to its plumage and a decidedly long pair of tail streamers. Its struggles at my approach once I had left the Land Rover clearly indicated that it had suffered some kind of damage to its left wing, probably from being hit by a vehicle. Knowing that John Williams, the veterinary officer had the habit of taking in, caring for and later releasing injured birds, reptile and animals, I carefully gathered up the injured bird, placed it in the back of the Land Rover and went on to complete my routine checks on the camps. Once that was done, I headed for John Williams' bungalow in order to hand the injured avian over to him. He took one look at it and promptly identified it as a Blue Swallow. He went on to inform me that it was one of the birds of Africa which was regarded as endangered and certainly worth trying to save and rehabilitate if he could.

On the 29th September 1966, we were advised that A Troop would be returning to Salisbury on the 3rd October. That news cheered everyone, Africans and Europeans alike. The next few days proved to be edgy ones, because the first rains decided to appear. As was often normal, the first rains came with a violent thunderstorm that crackled, banged and flashed for an hour or more, while the welcome rain it had brought poured down as though it was never going to end. After the storm had gone, the roads were awash and the surface of the ground, previously so dry and dusty, was suddenly soft, soggy and slippery too. While the rain was welcome and needed, it gave us some concern. The state of the airstrip at Boli was a worry. Landing a Dakota or light aircraft there in the dry season was fine, but once the rains started, it was a day-by-day affair, or perhaps, to put it better, a downpour-by-downpour affair. To land and lift off safely within the limited distance available, the Dakota needed ground that was firm enough to allow a Land Rover to motor on it at a minimum of 60 MPH. If that speed could not be achieved, from a standing start at one end of the airstrip, before running out of room at the other end, the landing of the Dakota, with our relieving troop on board could not take place. If that safe landing could not take place, we would have to stay a few more days, while a changeover by road transport was organised. That was of course something none of us wished to see happen.

SO Crahart handed the task of monitoring the ground conditions at Boli to me. Every time a rain shower appeared that might have impacted the airstrip, off I went, duty bound to carry out a test run. Over the last three days of that tour of duty at Vila Salazar, I discovered the amazing speed at which green shoots of grass could spring from parched ground once the necessary few drops of rain descended to encourage them. I also discovered just how fast an amazing assortment of grazing animals could appear to enjoy nature's greening bounty. Before even thinking of making the necessary test run along the length of the grass runway, a slower drive became needed on each occasion, just to clear the menagerie of grazing antelope. There appeared to be everything from duiker through to impala, zebra and kudu. On one occasion, there was a very rare nyala among the throng. That animal was a delight to see. On another occasion it was a large troop of baboon, all busy scrabbling away at the ground, digging into every hole and turning over every stone in their hunt for spiders, scorpions, beetles, millipedes and the like, which were their staple diet. On each visit to the airfield, once I had completed a gentle, precautionary drive along the whole length of the landing strip, I lined up on the centre line of it and set off, working my way as fast as I could up through the gears, while pushing the acceleration in each at a steady, but forceful rate, until my vehicle reached that all-important 60 MPH. At the end of each check run, I was able to radio through to SO Crahart, directly or via a messenger, that all was well. The all-important landing strip proved fully usable when needed and the changeover took place on schedule.

Before dark on 3rd October 1966, the entire troop was safely delivered back to Tomlinson Depot. A couple of hours of carefully organised mayhem followed as weaponry was made safe, cleaned, inspected and returned to the armoury, lost and damaged items of kit and uniform were recorded, replacement orders were duly submitted, almost smack on closure time for Ordnance Stores and the entire troop was given the next three days off duty.

The Zwimba Gang, 1966

From left to right:- Chimp Webster, Willie Wielopolski, Reg Crahart, Terry Rowlandson, Kerry Croasdale, Jock Baker, Arnold Woolley (The Author)

More Time With Support Unit

At 09:00hrs on Friday 7th October 1966, after a three-day break, A Troop paraded at the start of what we then believed was going to be a few weeks of training in and around Tomlinson Depot. That belief was shattered in more than one way on that first day back. Willy Wielopolski's return to us from leave resulted in Ken Stewart vanishing to another troop, because with four European members A Troop was a bit top-heavy. That much we had expected. However, at tea-break that first morning, C/Insp. Eric West broke the news to Reg, Terry, Willy and me, that A Troop was to leave, by road, the next morning, for a spell of duty based at Makuti Police Camp. The name meant absolutely nothing to any of us. Seeing our blank faces, C/Insp. West explained that it was a recently established patrol base, thirty miles or so beyond Karoi Police Station, on the main road north to Chirundu. It was located close to where the road to Kariba turned off from that main north road, before the start of the drop down the escarpment into the Zambezi Valley itself.

C/Insp. West cheered us up even more by answering Reg's questions about how long we were going to be there, what we were going to do there and what facilities were there by responding along the lines of, "As long as you are needed. You'll be fully briefed when you get there," and, "I believe the Ops. Room is a caravan, but there are sufficient tents scattered around it to accommodate all of you."

Reg's somewhat acid comment was, "Char bloody ming! We've just done the best part of two months at Salazar, had only three days off and now we're going back out into the bush again."

C/Insp. West chose to ignore that and went on to tell us that the place had been chosen because it had two advantages. There was a reliable borehole, so we would not be short of water and, it was only a mile or so from the Makuti Motel, which had a restaurant, a bar and a swimming pool that we could use during off-duty hours. Reg cheered up a bit at the mention of the bar. Terry and I exchanged meaningful glances. When we passed on the news to our African staff, they greeted the news with typical African pragmatism.

Sgt Isaac commented quietly to me, "It will be good if we go down into the Valley for patrols, Ishe. Plenty nyama there." (Lots of meat.)

That afternoon, Const. Mutandwa was marched in before Supt Freemantle to be dealt with for being unfit for duty through drink during our stay at Salazar. He dutifully pleaded guilty. I was called in to give brief details of the offence, which I did. Somehow, I managed to get it across that he had paraded properly dressed and wanting to go on duty. However, somehow I forgot to mention his refusal to go into the cells and his wish to punch the lights out of the whole brown boot contingent at Salazar Police Station. I also managed to point out that he had not, due to pressure of our workload, been released from the cells as promptly as he should have been as soon as he was fully sober next morning. I further pointed out that he was, usually, a very reliable member of my section and any sentence of imprisonment would mean he could not leave for Makuti with the rest of A Troop the following day. One way and another, the result was that he received a ten-shilling fine and a warning that any next instance such as this would guarantee him a few days in the cells, with loss of pay and probably a greater fine on top.

At 07:00hrs on 8th October 1966, A Troop paraded at Tomlinson Depot. It was one of those days when the rain came with the dawn. It deluged down briefly and then cleared off, leaving the rising sun to warm us, dry out our uniforms and kit and raise clouds of steamy water vapour as it did so. Once everybody and everything was accounted for as all present and correct, C/Insp. West handed our Route Instruction documents to SO Crahart, wished us a good patrol and safe return and walked away to the offices. Reg gave the order to embus and forty-two armed policemen, all dressed still in blue and grey riot uniform, topped off by "Hats Soft Blue" climbed into the waiting assortment of vehicles.

I mention the assortment, because that was just what it was. Reg led the way in a Land Rover, followed by four Ford 4x4s, with a Bedford 5-ton flat-back lorry piled high with our kit and katundu. Terry, who was an authorised heavy vehicle driver, took the wheel and Willy and I shared the cab with him, our FN rifles between our knees.

October in Rhodesia meant heat, dry and dusty if the rains stayed away, or steamy and muddy if they arrived on time. Our journey was one of showers, bright patches, steamy tarmac and hundreds of frogs and toads all seemingly eager to commit suicide under the wheels of assorted vehicles including ours. The carnage that was created was welcomed by every flesh-eating bird within flying distance of the roads. Inevitably, some of those unwisely stayed too long to tug at this or that tasty morsel of flattened flesh and became flattened themselves. Their fleeter fellows seemed to have no compunctions about gobbling up bits and pieces of the crushed avian casualties along with bits of frog and toad.

We arrived at Lomagundi District Headquarters in Sinoia, at mid-morning. There we duly made a courtesy call to let our presence be known and took time for a much-appreciated leg-stretch and comfort break, before pushing on northward, past Karoi Police Station. A couple of miles short of our destination we came across a formal roadblock, manned by regular and reserve police from Karoi. Their objective, so they advised us was to check and inspect all traffic travelling southwards. From the roadblock it was a short run on to Makuti Police Patrol Base, situated just off of the main road on the western side. Once our vehicles had turned into the recently established Makuti site, we found it to be very much as C/Insp. West had prepared us for. There were a score or so of tents somewhat randomly placed around a small caravan, alongside of which was one metal rondavel type of hut that we were quite familiar with from our Vila Salazar stint. As we discovered, the caravan acted as control room and the rondavel as a store. Overlooking them was a water tank on a tower and a modest radio mast that carried both SSB and VHF antennae. Some few score yards distant there was an area of cleared land marked out as a helicopter landing zone. A short way off, there were hessian enclosed areas demarcated for pit latrines and cold-water showers, fed from a small water tank. Willy summed it up pretty well as we debussed. "Now I know what primitive means." Nobody argued. As required, we reported to Supt Holt, whose positional title was Border Control Officer, North-East. Like all the other BCO's, he used the radio call-sign "Rampart" which seemed pretty appropriate. His greeting to us was heartfelt and genuine, "I'm damned glad to see you here. There's a mountain of work to be done and not many of us to do it. Can you be operational by first light tomorrow?"

Reg's response was a somewhat wary, "We could be, Sir, but what for?"

"Anything and everything, if I'm honest with you," Supt Holt advised. "Our maps are lacking in a whole lot of detail, especially on where there is water. We don't even know which areas we can and cannot get radio signals to and from. All of that means a real need for both vehicle and foot patrol work. We know that ZIPRA insurgents are penetrating the valley, coming across the river from Zambia. That means we need day and night ambush work doing down on the valley floor. Then we have the tsetse fly fences east and west that need patrolling and checking for spoor. Added to that, the roadblock must be manned twenty-four hours a day. I'll be wanting four of your African details down there, alongside the roadblock itself, all the time, to provide fire power in case of trouble." He paused and took a long, deep breath before going on. "If you guys make contact with Terrs in any significant numbers, don't try to be bloody heroes. Stay in touch with them if you can and get a radio message back to me, on the turn. I'll do my best to get some back-up to you just as quick as I can. For the moment, take yourselves off and get your troop settled in. I'll see you four back here at 16:00hrs for a briefing about tomorrow."

Getting settled in was not a complicated affair. Reg took one tent, Terry, Willy and I took another. One tent became our dining room, while others were allocated to our African police and one became the sleeping quarters for our batmen. Kit was moved in, vehicles parked, guards allocated for necessary duties and all others were stood down but confined to camp. In short order, fireplaces were sorted out, cooking processes started and tea was produced. Over that tea-break we four European policemen agreed that it would be daft to have our personal batmen cooking individually for each of us, so we would pool our resources and mess together when in camp. A quick wander around the encampment confirmed my first impression, that there was no facility for a hot shower or a hot bath. There was also no perimeter fence. Nobody appeared to have considered clearing any of the bush and scrub surrounding the cluster of tents, which appeared to have been put down haphazardly and certainly not in any tidy, orderly fashion. Given that the rains had already started, there was no sign of any attempt to drain the rainwater away from the tents, individually or collectively. Clearly there was much work to be done if the camp was to be even half bearable and safe as a base for longer than just a few days.

At the appointed hour, we four European members of A Troop gathered in the command caravan. Supt Holt provided us with 1:50,000 scale maps of the area and pointed out to us on the control room map the locations of our tasks for the morrow. Those tasks began with a repeat of his stated need for four of our African members to be at the floating roadblock on the main road, for all 24 hours of each day. He wanted us to start assisting the roadblock crews as of 06:00hrs the next day. He also required a supply run to Sinoia for assorted needs, from maps to gas bottles and further supplies of ammunition. Two daylight patrols, with overnight stops out, were also on his list, the first to Rekometje Tsetse Fly Research Station in the Zambezi Valley, the other from the main north road along the game fence to the Nyaodza River Mouth on the shore of Lake Kariba. Both patrols to be carried out by vehicle, checking for terrorist spoor along the way, staying out overnight and returning the following day, carrying out further checks for spoor on the way back. Reg decided he would take on the Sinoia run, Willy would remain at Makuti to supervise the roadblock support work, while Terry would do the Rekometje Mission patrol and I would take on the patrol to the Nyaodza Mouth and back. It was also agreed that because the game fence track to the Nyaodza Mouth was somewhat rough, I would have the use of our Land Rover. Once Rampart's briefing to us four was completed and we were dismissed, we briefed our African policemen on the assorted pieces of work that had been handed to us. Reg allotted men to each task for the morrow and stood down everyone except for those allocated as the patrolling guards.

That night, none of us slept well. Raging thunderstorms came and went although the rain seemed constant. Making a trip to the latrine block in the middle of the night meant first getting your boots on, then attracting the attention of the patrolling guard, before slogging your way through the mud, well wrapped up under a poncho cape, to the latrines, where the box-type wooden seats were soaking wet and cold and the rain lashed continually down.

At 05:00hrs, along with Terry and Willy, I was up and about. Shorty produced bacon and egg sandwiches and tea for all three of us, before we went our separate ways. I had decided I would not drive the Land Rover but would assign that task to Const. Kisimis, so that I could occupy the left front passenger seat and from there concentrate on map-reading and using my eyes more widely than just on the dirt track ahead, once we left the metalled surface of the main north road. Normally, we would have stowed our backpacks on the carrier on the roof and lashed them down there, but with the rain pouring down and thunder and lightning frequently crackling and rumbling, we chose to stow them inside the vehicle, where they had a chance of staying reasonably dry. Once we had our packs on board and had cleared and made safe our weapons, we embussed and set off, heading southwards, through the roadblock on the main road and on a further few miles until the game fence came into plain view. At something like eight feet high and of sturdy construction, it was easily visible. The fence itself took a straight line from start to finish. It simply cross-grained up, down and over, directly through some very rough and broken country. The drivable track paralleled it, on the northern side, often within touching distance where it could, but veered away every so often where the terrain alongside the fence was simply not drivable.

Our progress over several miles could best be described as slow, bumpy and soggy. Each time we detected a game trail of any sort joining the track from the thick bush on our right, we stopped long enough to check a few yards of it for spoor. With rain teeming down, intermittently if not steadily, it soon became clear that there was very little chance that we would locate spoor of any kind because the rain was washing our own boot-prints away almost as soon as we made them. With ponchos draped over us and our weapons, we were dry enough, but, once we had climbed in and out of our vehicle a few times, the interior of that was almost as wet as the outside. The map I was trying to follow as we slowly progressed soon became sodden and in danger of falling apart, so I folded it and put it away. A couple of experimental calls on our VHF radio confirmed what I had expected, which was that because of the terrain, we had no signal getting in or out, other than when on a few high points along the fence line.

At about ten miles in from the main road and in the middle of some bursts of thunder and lightning that were so loud the storm must have been almost overhead, our Land Rover, which was grinding slowly along in second gear in 4-wheel drive, topped a rise which gave us a clear, elevated view of the game fence dropping away into a dip between two ridges, the bottom of which was about fifty yards ahead and fifty feet lower than us. In the bottom of the dip there were four African men. They were all wearing assorted civilian clothing, carrying firearms and backpacks. Three of them were on the far side of the fence. The one on our side of the fence appeared to be in the act of passing an SKS rifle through the fence to his comrades, because most of its length was on the far side of the fence. The yells from inside our vehicle told me that several of my companions had seen ahead of us precisely what I had seen.

Every time I conjure up that freeze-frame moment in my mind, I grow more and more certain that Driver Constable Kisimis had already changed gear and set our vehicle moving backwards even before I had time to bellow the order for him to do so. It took just a few seconds for our vehicle to back off and drop a few feet below the ridgeline, taking us safely out of any direct line of fire from the obviously terrorist group. What concerned me, as I flung open the door to get out, was whether it was just the four we had seen, or were there more around and if so, how many. The sound of a brief burst of gunfire from the direction where we had seen the terrorists caused me to pause just long enough to swiftly cock my FN and then I launched myself out of the vehicle, intending to get to the ridge-line crest in order to engage the enemy. In my haste, I put my booted right foot on a slippery root and went crashing to the ground. The result of that was that my team were nearly all at the crest of the ridge and had opened fire before I was in position to do so myself. My second view of the scene in front and below me showed me that the one terrorist who was on our side of the fence was down on the ground, weapon-less, while those who were on the other side of the fence were fast disappearing southwards into the bush. Some wild and erratic gunfire came at us from one of the fleeing men, who was triggering bursts from an AK rifle which he had pointing backwards at us over his shoulder as he was running. I managed to get off just a few hastily aimed but apparently ineffective shots at the fleeing terrorists before they vanished completely. With no more gunfire coming at us I bellowed an order for my section to cease fire and relative silence descended. I say relative because the rain, the thunder and the lightning were themselves far from silent.

Detailing four of my section to remain atop the ridge to give us cover, I led the rest cautiously down towards the fallen terrorist, who proved to be still alive but somewhat damaged, to the extent where he made no effort to use any further the SKS rifle laying between him and the fence close by. A simple feel of the barrel and sniff at the muzzle told me the weapon had been very recently fired. Its empty magazine and fired cartridges on the ground around confirmed that. Once that weapon was under control and made safe, we eased the pack off of the wounded terrorist's back and set it down safely away from him. A rapid frisk showed he had no weapons or grenades hidden about him. It also revealed that he was wearing four layers of clothing above the waist and three set of trousers below. That discovery was in line with reports that terrorists frequently wore several layers of clothing, so that if they were spotted by security forces and managed to get away, they could rapidly discard and hide weapons, pack and outer layer of clothing, to confuse pursuers. A quick physical examination revealed that he had been hit thrice. His right forearm was broken and there were two clean but bloody bullet wounds in his left thigh. Efforts to get him to talk, in English, Chishona and SiNdebele met with a determined silence and the kind of looks that yelled "HATE" in capital letters. Some crude but effective first aid, involving a splint, some wound dressings and yards of bandage, stemmed our prisoner's loss of blood. A quick look in his pack revealed a Togarev pistol, slabs of explosives with Cyrillic writing, a couple of Russian hand grenades, some hundreds of rounds of ammunition and a whole sheaf of papers, as well as several items of clothing.

Efforts to make wireless contact from our vehicle proved completely unsuccessful, so we marked the location of the encounter with a cairn of stones, found a spot close by where we could turn the Land Rover around, loaded our groaning prisoner and ourselves into the vehicle and set off, back towards the main road. A mile or more back along the track I was eventually able to get a radio message through to Makuti Base Camp, so that by the time we reached the main road there was quite a welcoming party there. In short order we were relieved of our prisoner, his SKS and his pack by SB details who whisked him away. I and my section were required to lead a couple of vehicles full of PATU details back to the scene of our encounter, while a helicopter provided top cover for us. The cairn of stones allowed us to pinpoint the location we needed without too much difficulty. Once we had done that, we were instructed to carry on our interrupted patrol, leaving the PATU boys to clamber up and over the game fence itself, just as the terrorists had done, in order to try to follow the three who had fled southwards.

Where we had all been alert prior to our sudden encounter with that fortunately small group of terrorists, for the rest of the day we were all hyper tense, far more aware that we could again suddenly encounter further armed insurgent elements, of whatever group size, during the rest of our patrol. Our eyes darted everywhere. At each ridge we crested, as the bonnet of our vehicle sank and we were able to see down into the next dip, hands moved closer to rifle triggers and only relaxed as each new vista proved to be without any terrorist presence. At each stop, there was no need for orders. Safety cordons were quickly established while others of us checked the ground. Raindrops and thunderstorms came and went. Our ponchos streamed and dripped, but our eyes and attention remained solely on the bush about us, until we finally left the last of the broken county behind us and moved on to the flatter land of the Nyaodza estuary.

The rain and the thunderstorms eased and vanished into the distance as we reached the flatter terrain and came in sight of the expanse of water that was part of the huge Kariba Dam. Following the track northwards, away from the game fence, I was looking for a suitable night camp site before daylight faded. I had barely instructed Kisimis to take it very easy on our speed, when we rounded a bend and what I saw caused me to yell, "Hold it, Kisimis. Lions!" My warning brought our fortunately slow progress to an abrupt halt. Less than a hundred yards ahead of us were a pride of a dozen or so adult lions. They were all laying down, either on one side or the other, or on all fours, gazing in our direction, with an air of interest rather than concern. They were not bothered that they were all over and on either side of the track we were driving on, even if I was. Disturbing them and then camping not far away was hardly a sensible thing to do, so, once again, it was a case of reversing a safe distance, turning about and finding a suitable night stop location a few hundred yards away, well clear of the track itself, but from where our night guards could see what was moving along it. Once we had our overnight gear out of the vehicle, we set our sleeping places in a circle around the Land Rover, established double guards and lit three small fires for cooking purposes, rather than one large one. Under normal circumstances, cooking fires alight after dark in an operational area would have been a total no-no, but it had been a long day and a long while since our early breakfast and, despite our best efforts to break up the sharp outlines of our vehicle, by using some dead branches, it still stood out like a sore thumb, for anyone with sharp eyes. The fires were also a bit of a deterrent to the pride of lions, whose occasional roars throughout the night sounded far closer to our wary ears than they probably really were. Once everyone had eaten, I produced my roll of four-by-two and carefully cleaned and oiled my rifle. Once it was re-assembled and back in operational order, I passed the roll of cleaning cloth on to the detail nearest to me, who then cleaned his rifle. That way, only one rifle at a time was inoperable.

Inevitably, as we went about our routines, we talked over our first, albeit brief, encounter with ZIPRA terrorists. Sgt Thomas and the others were remarkably pragmatic about the encounter. They brushed aside my apologies for falling flat and being the last one to get a gunsight on the enemy. They also agreed that it was fortunate that we had encountered only a very small number of ZIPRA and under circumstances that, thanks to Const. Kisimis's capable driving and prompt reactions, favoured us.

Once everyone had eaten and had their fill of tea, we let the fires die to glowing embers. Those of us not immediately on guard duty scraped a hip-hole, wriggled ourselves into our un-loved sleeping bags, checked that our weapons were ready to hand and settled down to sleep until it was our first hour of guard duty, each in turn. In circumstances like we were in, safety dictated that our guards should be static, with their backs to something safe and solid and within easy reach of others. To accomplish that, I positioned one guard to sit on the front bumper and the other to sit in the opening of the open back door to the vehicle. From those positions, the guards, including me, could not be jumped from behind by humans or animals, but had easy eye and ear cover of a full 180 degrees each for each of the hours, turn by turn, of staying awake and alert.

That night camp raised once again the issue of snoring. It is a distinctive human noise. One that varies in volume from a quiet rumble to a stentorian roar, capable of being heard hundreds of yards away, so those on guard duty had orders to waken any culprit and have them change their sleeping posture, in the hope that that would silence their noise.

That I had to do for a couple of details in my arc of responsibility as the night progressed, fortunately uneventfully, until the first glimmers of dawn showed. Then it was time for morning stand-to, with everyone lying awake and alert, weapons to hand and ready in case of any dawn attack on our overnight camp.

Once the sun was clear of the horizon, we re-kindled the fires, brewed tea, cooked and ate our assorted breakfasts and prepared for our return journey along the tsetse fly control fence. Given our low-level position, just a few metres above the tranquil surface of Kariba Dam's water, it was more in hope than expectation that I tried the VHF radio in our vehicle. To my pleasant surprise, I found Kariba Police Station on the air and coming through loud and clear. Via that location I was able to advise Makuti of our quiet night and our intention to set off shortly on the return journey. My inquiry as to whether or not there had been any further activity anywhere along the fence brought a gratefully received response that all had been quiet.

Our return journey to the main north road was an uneventful one, even if a slow and wary one. At the point where we had had our lively encounter the previous day, Sgt Thomas asked if it was alright to stop for a moment. Once we had halted and had our scouts out, I watched with curiosity as each member of the stick pocketed a small stone from the area around the crude cairn of large stones that we had used to mark the spot. Sgt Thomas saw my puzzled look. He held out the stone he had in his hand so that I could see it. "It is for the future, Ishe. Mwari was kind to us yesterday. It is good that we carry that kindness with us, to let him know we have not forgotten his help." He placed the small stone, no bigger than a walnut, very carefully, into the left breast pocket of his uniform grey shirt. One or two others I noticed wrapped theirs in handkerchiefs or pieces of four by two and put them away equally carefully, into pockets or packs, before we continued on our way. As I watched them, I suddenly remembered the small and much worn silver St Christopher medallion that had been in my wallet for more years than I could remember. Discreetly, I patted the bulge of my wallet within my trouser pocket and offered a quiet word or two of thanks upwards before I took up my own position in the Land Rover and directed Const. Kisimis to drive on.

It was mid-afternoon when we reached Makuti Base Camp. After standing down my section, I made my way to the caravan, where I formally logged back into camp and made my verbal report to Supt Holt. He, in answer to my question, advised that there had been no positive result, so far, from the follow-up after yesterday's brief encounter. Once my debrief was done and placed on record in the typewritten activity log, I was free to relax for a while. One of the Special Branch details, Eddie Boddington, was kind enough to show me and allow me to photograph the contents of the wounded terrorist's pack. Aside from the hardware and clothing, there was a well-thumbed copy of Mao Tse Tung's infamous *Little Red Book* full of anti-Western propaganda and pro-Communist boastings.

In the mid-afternoon heat and high humidity, I decided that a shower, even if a cold one, would be welcome, so I stripped off in the tent, wrapped a towel around me and went off to get cleaned up. The cold water was something of a shock, although an agreeable one and at least I was able to come out of the enclosure feeling a whole lot cleaner than when I went in, but I still had the niggling feeling that it would be great to be able to relax in a hot bath and soak for a while. Sadly, without a bath and hot water system, that luxury was not available.

That evening, when it was time to eat, Willy, Terry and I sat down in our makeshift mess and enjoyed a civilised meal. When I inquired where our troop commander was, Willy gestured, theatrically, to the north. "Having a meal at the Makuti Motel," he declared. "He gets paid more than we do!" Little more was said on that subject, but they were both keen to hear the story of yesterday's encounter on the fly fence. Both were kind enough to be just a little sympathetic over me slipping on the wet tree root and ending up on my backside, entangled in poncho and rifle sling, when the brief firefight started. It was certainly not the most heroic and glorious way of leading men into a combat situation. What I was able to do was reassure them that even though I was, if only briefly down and out of it, the members of my section, one and all, had acted competently and admirably, entirely on their own initiative. That was a powerful plus point for us all.

In the light from a Tilley lamp, we washed our meal down with a couple of beers and then, by common consent, headed for our camp beds. That proved to be a good thing, because we had at least had a few hours of sleep when we were woken. It was just after four o'clock. An army call-sign had initiated an ambush in the valley, not far from the base of the escarpment. They had reported three kills and that perhaps the same number had got away. We were needed to be up and out at first light, to link up with the army call-sign, carry out a sweep of the ambush area and undertake any follow-up that might be needed.

Reg Crahart was not at all amused at the sudden and early call. He declined to share our early and hasty breakfast, consoling himself with a couple of cups of coffee only.

He decided to leave Willy and one section in camp to cover the roadblock and other camp routine duties and led the rest of our troop out and northwards as dawn began to break. One Land Rover, with three Special Branch details tagged along with us. Makuti lies at about 1400 metres above sea level, while the valley floor is about 600. That descent, of about 800 metres, down the escarpment, in the distance of a few short miles, is a spectacular drive. It is one that, for best effect, needs to be taken slowly, with several, if not many, stops to enable one to enjoy the view far out and away across the treetops and the majestic hills of the escarpment fading away on either side. We had no time for such touristic pleasures. Ours was a non-stop, hasty and occasionally hair-raising dash, until we stopped, left the vehicles under guard and set about walking the few miles eastwards to link up with the army unit. Much to our relief, a Police Reserve Air Wing light aircraft was already up and providing top cover and tell-star functions for us footsloggers, so locating and joining with the army unit was made easy.

Back-tracking of the terrorist group suggested that they had been certainly six and maybe eight in number. Cross-wise sweeps of the area soon located both foot-spoor and a trail of bloodstains. Leaving the army stick and the SB details to deal with the dead terrorists and their packs and weaponry, we set off to follow the boot prints and bloodstains.

On this occasion, if we were reading the signs correctly, we had numerical superiority. Our quarry numbered perhaps four, of whom at least one was wounded. On our side we had some two dozen. Once away from the ambush site, the bush thickened, to the point where it was possible to progress no more than two abreast, or in stretches, only in single file, following a clearly demarcated game trail that the fleeing terrorists appeared to have decided, or been forced, to follow as they fled from their ambushers in the dark of night.

An hour or more after we had left the army unit and SB details and something in the order of three miles on, we were still cautiously following boot spoor and periodic spots of blood, when our top-cover radioed that they had sighted what they believed was a person, possibly a terrorist, stationary, a few hundred yards ahead of us, at the base of a large baobab tree beside the game trail. The thickness of the bush and tree canopy prevented them from being certain whether the individual was alive or dead, but he was certainly in a position where he could put gunfire down the game trail if he intended to. Reg called a halt to our progress.

"If that bastard is waiting for us, he'll open fire the moment he sees us. There's no sense in walking straight into that situation."

Terry and I looked at each other. We were clearly thinking the same thing.

"How about if we crawl?" Terry asked, remarkably innocently.

"We?" Reg queried, warily.

Terry grinned hugely. "Arn and me, Reg. Our knees are younger than yours."

Reg thought about it for a long moment. "Okay. Stay on radio and give us a sitrep every hundred yards or so. We'll move along behind you but back a bit. Just don't stick your necks out. That's all."

We both assured him that we had no intention of sticking our necks out. It was just that we had to make progress along the game trail, following the boot and blood spoor before the traces disappeared.

With the twists and turns of the game trail preventing us from seeing much more than twenty or thirty yards ahead most of the time, once we were out of sight of those behind us, we decided we were safe walking carefully but upright for about three hundred yards. After that, we would need to be very wary indeed until we sighted the baobab tree that might, or might not, be hiding a Gook.

Every hundred paces, Terry radioed back to Reg. We set crossed sticks in the game trail to inform those behind us where next they should move up to. After the third marker, we both decided to stay upright, but drop to our knees at each bend, in order to peer along the next visible stretch of the trail from under the trail-side bushes. Bend by bend and yard by yard, we moved forward, stepping as quietly as we could and silently cursing every bird that we disturbed, until Terry, peering forward from under a Jesse bush, slithered cautiously backwards and whispered, "Up ahead. The trail seems to widen and there's a baobab tree with what looks like a k-factor sitting on the ground and leaning back against the trunk. Can't see any weapons and he's not moving. You take a look."

Easing past Terry, flat on my front and staying close into the root system of the trail-side bushes, I wriggled forward until I too was able to see what he had seen. No more than thirty or forty yards away there was a figure just as Terry had described. Clearly an African male adult. He was wearing a blue denim bomber jacket and jeans. He was bareheaded, sitting on the ground between the roots, leaning back against the trunk, with his arms down by his sides. I let my eyes roam upward to scan the branches of the huge baobab tree until I was satisfied that there was nobody hiding up there. Just as Terry had done, I slid backwards out of sight until he and I could hold a whispered conversation. It would have been remarkably easy for us to have put a couple of bullets into the individual, but Special Branch wanted live prisoners rather than dead bodies and the man ahead did not appear to be much of a threat to us. We decided to put into practice some of our recent training in the "Buddy-Buddy System." On our stomachs, we took turns to slither forward a few yards while the other held a steadily aimed rifle on the unmoving figure seated at the base of the baobab tree.

By the time we had covered half the distance, we were able to detect that there was some dark staining all down the individual's right side. It was also clear that his eyes were closed and that there was a backpack against the tree trunk a few feet from him. Not far beyond the baobab tree the game trail made another bend, beyond which it was out of sight. I decided that the location was not a good place for an ambush and whispered as much to Terry. He nodded in agreement and we both rose to our feet, weapons ready for instant use, our eyes darting between the silent figure against the tree and the thick, impenetrable bush around. No gunfire or other obvious threat greeted our movements and as the seconds passed, we began to relax, just a little and breathe more normally.

A quick check on the blood-stained figure showed that he was still alive, but not by much. As I checked him over for weapons and found none, Terry radioed for Reg and the others to come forward to meet us, which they did a whole lot quicker than we expected. Reg took one look at our unconscious prisoner and set to himself, with our troop first aider, to try to keep our prisoner alive. In quick time, a drip was set up and the gunshot wounds to his right shoulder and left wrist were dressed and bandaged and a radio message passed, via our top cover, to Makuti, to advise them of our capture.

Leaving Reg with Terry and most of the others, I took Sgt Isaac and two other details with me, to scout a little way along the game trail beyond the baobab tree. Without the helpful blood spoor from the wounded man, all that was left was the boot spoor of the others. Twenty yards or so beyond the baobab tree the game trail not only turned but divided. The faint signs we were following all appeared to continue down the left branch of the fork. I was about to turn back to go and report our finding to Reg, when I caught sight of movement on that trail, coming towards us, fast. Even as I instinctively brought up my FN, all ready to fire, my eyes and mind registered that it was not a terrorist approaching, but a rhinoceros. It took one look at us who were barring its intended route, snorted loudly, put its head down and charged. I was fortunate because I was standing just about where the game trail divided. I yelled a warning and dived out of the way of the oncoming beast. Somehow my three companions also managed to hurl themselves aside, although Sgt Isaac ended up deeply entangled in a hook-thorn bush, from which he needed a bit of careful and patient extraction a few minutes later. The yells and screams from those by the baobab were brief, but deafening. Terrorists held no fears for our African policemen, but they all knew, like me, that there was only one thing to do in the face of an angry, oncoming rhino and that was to get out of its way, fast! Thankfully, nobody got hooked by the beast, but a few suffered bruises and abrasions as they were unceremoniously knocked out of the brute's way.

Once some calm and normality had been re-established, it became clear that the chances of tracing the fleeing terrorists any further had become impossible as their spoor had vanished under that of the rhino. The upshot of it all was that we aborted the follow-up, constructed a crude stretcher to carry the wounded terrorist and made our way back from whence we had come, until we were able to hand our unconscious but still alive prisoner and his pack over to waiting Special Branch details and make our own way back to Makuti.

That evening, while our main meal of the day was being prepared, we took ourselves off to the Makuti Motel for what we considered was a well-earned sundowner. We settled down at a table on the veranda from where we could watch the aquatic antics of those splashing about in the pool and, somewhat naturally, talk through the events of the day. After an hour or so, Willy suggested it was time to get back to camp for our evening meal. Terry and I were happy enough to do just that, but Reg decided he needed another drink or two and would make his own way back to camp later. As there was a constant flow of traffic between our camp and the motel, that arrangement seemed perfectly reasonable, so we three made our farewells to Reg and back to camp we went. The wheels of our vehicle had barely stopped turning before we received a verbal message that Rampart wished to speak with SO Crahart. In the absence of our troop commander, all three of us decided to go along to the command caravan, where we found Supt Holt poring over a set of maps.

Rampart's instructions were simple. He wanted two sections out of camp early next day, for a week of duty down in the valley. The first one to make a patrol base camp at Marongora Dam, from which to carry out night ambushes and day patrols, while the second section was to base up at Rekometje Tsetse Fly Research Station. That section's task was to provide reassurance and protection for the two European research scientists based there and to also carry out day patrols and night ambushes. Our third section and troop commander were to remain at Makuti in reserve in case of need.

In Reg Crahart's absence, we sorted out for Terry to do the Rekometje Mission task, for me to undertake the Marongora Dam work and for Willy and his section to remain in reserve at Makuti. With an early start indicated, we briefed our African policemen, ate our evening meal and headed for our camp beds relatively early.

At dawn on 12th October 1966, with Reg seemingly nowhere around, the rest of us got up and got on with attending to the tasks Rampart had given us. It was a bright, already warm and glorious day, without a single rainy season cloud in the sky. With a vehicle for each section and static camps to work out of for the week, we loaded a bit more gear than we would have otherwise done, starting with camp kettles that would hold sufficient for each section's African policemen to cook and eat communally, rather than individually. The two Ford 4x4s were cumbersome vehicles and highly visible, but they at least had the advantage of having VHF radios in them, which, with a touch of luck and fair-weather conditions, meant that if we encountered anything interesting, we could at least report back to whichever defence force station we could get signals to and from.

With Terry's vehicle leading, we left Makuti Base Camp and headed north at a steady, unhurried speed. I noticed a civilian Peugeot station wagon pass us heading south, not long after we left base camp, but otherwise took no notice of it until the radio crackled into life with a message from Terry for my call-sign. Terry requested a change of channel. With that made and a little privacy in our conversation, he wanted to know if I had got a good look at the passenger in the vehicle that had passed us going south. I had to reply that I had not and inquired why the interest. Terry's reply was that he thought the driver was a lady and the passenger was Reg and offered the thought that our troop commander had probably spent the night at the motel. My reply that it was his hangover and at least he would be back at camp in time for day duties and to get a briefing from Willy brought agreement from Terry and the end of that particular radio conversation.

Because of our visits to the motel, it was not until we were north of that location that we were in country that was still fairly new to us. The junction, a few miles north of the motel, that was the road to Kariba, brought a comment from Const. Kisimis, who was driving our vehicle that he wanted to see the lake before we returned to Harare, because he had heard so many stories about it over the years. My reply of, "You and me both, Kisimis. You and me both," brought a huge grin to his face.

Beyond Kariba Gorge, the Zambezi River flows through a wide and game-rich floodplain, with up to a 30ft depth of rich soil. The valley floor is hemmed in by towering escarpments in both Zimbabwe and Zambia. Despite the presence of terrorists, the shoreline of the river was still open to fishing safaris. Both photographic and hunting safaris were still functioning, based in one or other of the permitted safari areas and in the Mana Pools National Park, where the population of elephant, buffalo, lion, leopard, large antelope species and smaller mammals grew each year to extraordinary numbers as water holes elsewhere in the valley gradually vanished as each year's dry season progressed.

Although we were operational, with weaponry at hand and eyes very much open, there was a certain air of excitement and interest among all of us in the two vehicles which had nothing to do with the insurgency we were on duty to counter. Our previous rapid dash down the escarpment had been at a fast pace, with no opportunity at all to take in the splendour of the scenery. This time, travelling at a much lower speed was brilliantly different. Every next twist and turn of the broad, modern 22-foot wide tarmac road opened fresh vistas of the southern escarpment itself and the seemingly unending and unbroken miles of treetop foliage on the valley floor, extending to the far horizon. Just here and there were a few small gaps, suggesting open areas, but they were few and far apart. At one particularly spectacular viewpoint, Terry pulled over to the side of the road and stopped, so that everyone could get out and take a good look at the scenery ahead, around and below us. It was an opportunity I did not waste, because, as ever, my camera was close to hand. Halfway down the escarpment road was the headquarters of the Game Department, close by a small dam which was known as Marongora Gate Dam that guaranteed their water supplies all year round. Prior to the insurgency, every visitor to the valley was required to book in and out of that location. That was no longer the case for those of us on operational duties. From that central location, the dedicated members of the staff, black and white, had always done a splendid job in attending to the welfare of the valley and the safety of those moving around within it. The tourist attraction of the Zambezi Valley cannot be understated. Camera and shooting safari expeditions were strictly controlled and poaching was prevented as far as humanly possible, given the vastness of the area. Fortunately, relations between the game rangers and the defence forces, particularly the police, were excellent. Without stopping, we exchanged a friendly wave with the uniformed rangers on duty at the entrance to their establishment and continued our steady descent to the flat land of the valley floor.

When we reached the dirt road turn-off to the right that was signposted "Mana Pools" and "Rekometje Tsetse Research Station," Terry again halted, to give everyone a chance for a comfort break and leg-stretch. Together we studied our maps and then looked back at the escarpment towering majestically above us to the south. There was not a breath of wind and both of us were sweating profusely, although we were, quite literally at that moment, just standing around. Terry bent down, picked up a handful of the dry, dusty roadside soil and let it dribble slowly through his fingers and back to the ground. "What the heck is this place going to be like once the rains set in and the humidity rises?" he mused.

"Pretty steamy and uncomfortable would be my guess," I replied. "And that's even before we start to think of carting packs, rifles, ammunition and water around on foot."

Terry studied his map some more and then took a long slow look at the countryside around us, which, to me, looked a little less thick and impenetrable than the area beside the Nyakasanga River where we had been only a couple of days before. "This place makes Vila Salazar look and feel like a holiday camp."

"Yeah," I agreed. "And there's no Malvernia to go to either."

Terry laughed, folded his map and called for everyone to embus. "You peel off to the right about a mile along this track. Happy hunting!"

With that, we both climbed into our respective vehicles and set off once again. We had maintained a steady distance of about thirty yards between vehicles on the clean, clear tarmac of the main road, but almost immediately it became clear that that was not possible once we set our turning and churning wheels onto the gravel surface of the side roads of the valley floor. Like the gravel roads in the populated farm and tribal lands of the highveld, the regularly used valley floor roads were graded and maintained, but, despite the fact that there had already been some heavy rainstorms, the track, rather than road, we were on was still corrugated, rutted and inches deep in the dusty sand or soil which formed a thick plume of dust behind each vehicle. Const. Kisimis was an experienced police driver, so he promptly let the distance between the two vehicles increase, until he could clearly see far enough ahead for safe driving and we could leave the air vents and windows open without being plastered in dust inside the driving cab of the vehicle. Helpfully, Terry radio'd back that he had just passed the turn-off to Marongora Dam and warned us to look out for it. With that much guidance, we made the turn without problem and, at a slow and steady speed, continued until we reached the dam's earth bank wall.

The dam itself was the size of about six or eight football pitches. Behind the retaining wall there was a broad expanse of water, with two inlets running out to form a slightly uneven Y in general shape. With a long dry season behind us and the real rains hardly yet begun, we were not surprised to see the dam only about half full. What did surprise us all was the abundance of wildlife, most of it taking not the slightest notice of our intrusion. A herd of impala were nibbling daintily at greenery on the ground and in the bushes. A lone kudu bull was watching a family of giraffe warily drinking in the very shallow water of one arm of the dam, while in the deeper water of the same arm, the backs of a family or perhaps a small herd of hippo could be clearly seen. Sgt Thomas flung an arm up and pointed. "Chenjerai Ishe. Ma Crocodile!" Three sizeable crocodiles, all about 14 to 16 feet in length were basking in the morning sunshine on the bank between the present water line and the clearly definable highwater mark once the dam was full. I took a long hard look at the lurking shapes. My mind flicked briefly back to Mushandike Dam and a picture flashed across the screen of my memory. Taking heed of it, I gave the first order for our stay at the dam that week. "Nobody is to go for water on their own as long as we are here, Sergeant. Two men at least. One armed and ready to cover the other, please."

Sgt Thomas rattled off a burst of Chishona at the rest of the stick. Over the next week, nobody broke that rule.

I left Sgt Thomas, Const. Kisimis and three other details to guard our vehicle and set off with the remainder of the section on a foot patrol around the dam, to check for human spoor and seek an accessible but defendable location for our base camp for the week. Eventually, I decided that the best place was on the slight ridge that separated the two arms of the dam. Getting there meant a wee bit of careful driving by Const. Kisimis and just a small amount of bush clearing too, but it was worth the effort. The waters of the dam protected us on three sides and a bit of branch cutting and decorating soon made our vehicle, parked within the perimeter formed by our sleeping positions, a whole lot less visible to any terrorist onlooker.

Obedient to my operational instructions from Rampart, I split my stick into two. I allocated four of the constables to work with me and four with Sgt Thomas. By alternating each sub-section between night ambush and day patrol activity, the task we had been set could be carried out without too much stress and strain or sleeplessness.

For that first night in the Zambezi Valley, I left Sgt Thomas and his sub-section in camp and set off on foot with my four men to find a suitable position from which to ambush any insurgents moving along the road to Mana Pools. The position I chose covered the junction where the track to Marongora Dam joined that Mana Pools/Rekometje road.

On the southern side, some thirty yards or so from the road junction there was a fallen msasa tree with plenty of room behind it for five firing positions and nothing but short, burned-off grass between it and the roadway. We had the promise of a hot, dry and star-lit night ahead, which was perfect for our purpose. With our sleeping bags to lie on and packs as our pillows we settled down to our task. Dusk mellowed into total darkness and the stars began to display their full glory as they marched their steady courses across the night sky. Owls and bats flickered their silent ways into and out of my line of vision as I took the first hour of watchfulness while the others did their best to snatch some sleep. Beetles and moths crawled, whirred and fluttered by as they went about their activities. The night was full of small animal and insect noises, although the distant roar of a lion and the far-off shrill trumpeting of an elephant acted to remind me that there were far larger creatures in the valley. That first hour passed more quickly than I thought it would. Quietly I awoke the constable laying to my right and only when he had knelt up and appeared fully awake did I then unsheathe my bayonet, dig a comfortable hip-hole in the soil and settle down to sleep away my four hours off watch. It was during my second turn as watchman that I sensed small silent movements against the canopy of stars above me. They were not the movements of birds or bats and at first I was puzzled. Then my eyes better caught one of them. Although we were positioned directly behind the trunk of the fallen msasa tree, there was the great trunk of a living baobab tree some several feet behind us. Its weirdly shaped, spindly arms stretched out far, the tips of one of them being right over us. What I was picking up was the silent bursting open of the flower pods on that tree, provoked by the few small first rainy season showers of recent days and the promise of more soon to come. Before long, each flower was abuzz with insects, attracted by the pollen and the distinctive scent wafting about. Their movement from tree to tree would do the job nature was setting a start to, just as they had been doing for millennia. I felt so privileged to be there at that moment.

The rest of the night passed without incident. Once it was light enough for safe movement I lifted the ambush and we set off to return to our base camp at the dam, where we were quite properly challenged by the guard on duty as we approached, even though we were exactly on time and on the line arranged. I would have been far more concerned if we had not been challenged.

Sgt Thomas and his sub-section had found a few stones which they used to rim the communal fire-pit and had also set up a triangle of cut branches that permitted one of our camp kettles to be suspended over the fire. One of the lessons we had learned from our Op. Nevada activities at Zwimba was that trying to keep to three cooked meals a day when out and about in the bush was simply not a practical habit. We all rapidly developed the routine of starting the day with a good hot cooked breakfast, finishing it with another good hot cooked meal as dusk set in and managing through the time in between with cold food nibbles such as dried fruit, dry biscuits, mixed nuts and the like, just to stave off any gnawing hunger pains.

With a good solid breakfast inside me, I headed to our vehicle at 08:00hrs to call in and provide a situation report. It was then that I learned of the tragic deaths of Supt Wickenden and three members of the SAS unit he had been operating with, in an accidental explosion near Chirundu. That radio conversations brought to light that Terry Rowlandson's section had managed to leave half their rations behind in Makuti. That situation was fairly easily resolved because there happened to be an army vehicle moving, early, between Makuti and Chirundu. That vehicle would carry the missing rations, a mixture of fresh meat, fresh bread, vegetables and rat-packs, as far as the

Mana Pools/Rekometje turn-off. My section was to collect those rations and deliver them to Terry and his men at Rekometje.

Leaving the rest of my subsection in camp, I joined with Sgt Thomas and his men, cleared the tree-branch camouflage from VPM 23 and set off in that vehicle to make the rendezvous with the army vehicle on the main road. Perhaps more by luck than judgement, both vehicles reached the RV just about together. The transfer of packages was swiftly accomplished, with only a little ribald banter between the two sets of uniform and then each vehicle went on its own appointed mission for the day.

One of the first points of learning for drivers and passengers using the gravel roads throughout the valley floor was that while the roadside signs might not be strictly as per the Highways Book of Rules and Regulations, each meant exactly what it said, no matter what the colour of the board or the paint, or the crudeness of the lettering. On the Mana Pools/Rekometje road, just beyond the turnoff to Marongora Dam, the road traverses the Marongora River. On either side of the watercourse, the bank had been cut away to lessen the steepness of the slope. On the approaches to each cut-away, there were identical hand-painted warning signs. Each consisted of a well-embedded six-foot high wooden pole which carried a two-foot square wooden board facing the traffic approaching the river. Each board carried a caricature of an open-topped Land Rover flying through the air. The driver was clutching the steering wheel with one hand and holding his hat on with the other, while his passengers were depicted several feet above the vehicle. The single word written in big, bold lettering read, "BUMP."

Const. Kisimis's somewhat energetic first ever approach to that stream crossing resulted in us emulating the cartoon on the boards. The crash of the vehicle landing, stalling and halting was drowned out by the wails of anguish and multi-lingual cursing from the constables in the passenger compartment behind us as they were first sent rocketing roof-wards and then brought back down with a vengeance as gravity asserted its authority.

Suffice to say that the gash in my eyebrow, caused by the front sight of my FN rifle and Const. Aaron's twisted and swollen ankle both healed well. A quick check on the luggage compartment revealed that the fresh meat, loaves and ration packs had each escaped from their orderly individual boxes and re-distributed themselves to the eight corners of the compartment. It took us a while to make good the damage caused by the shaking we had received, make the supplies look just a little more presentable and think about moving on, which was the point at which we discovered that even though our vehicle had four-wheel-drive capability, the standard tarmac road tyres that it was equipped with just spun uselessly in the deep soft sand of the stream bed. Fortunately, there was a tyre foot-pump among the tools behind the driver's seat. That allowed us to deflate all four tyres, which spread and increased the contactable rubber tyre surface and allowed me to gently ease the vehicle forward until it was on firm ground, at which point I handed the driving back to Const. Kisimis, who was himself somewhat battered, bruised and more inclined to take greater note of the informal road signs. Once we had re-inflated the tyres we pushed on.

A couple of hours of steady, cautious driving brought us to Rekometje Tsetse Fly Research Station. As such locations go, it was not a large place. It consisted of a bungalow for the two European Researchers, Glyn Vale and Andy Devine, half a dozen brick under iron houses for the African staff and servants, a garage/workshops/store building and a modest laboratory complex. The importance of the work carried out there was, however, significant in the ongoing battle to control and, if possible, eradicate the pestilential tsetse fly, which troubles much of Sub-Saharan Africa. The human form of the infection that the fly carries is trypanosomiasis or sleeping sickness while that same condition in cattle is called nagana.

Sleeping sickness is caused by two germs, Trypanosoma brucei rhodesiense and Trypanosoma brucei gambiense. The more severe form of the illness is caused by T. Rhodesiense. All tsetse flies carry the infection. When an infected fly bites you, the infection spreads through your blood. If untreated, it affects the brain, causing drowsiness, lethargy, coma and death, usually within six months. Huge swathes of central and east Africa are infested and deaths from sleeping sickness in humans and cattle are as much a fact of life now as when I made my first visit to Rekometje, better than half a century ago.

Glyn and Andy were able to steer us the short distance between the research station itself and where Terry Rowlandson had established his temporary base camp, in a defensive half-circle, on a bluff overlooking the nearby river, which was still just a broad expanse of sand, as the real rains had yet to arrive in the valley or the river's catchment area in the high land above the escarpment. He and the half-section in camp when we arrived greeted the appearance of their missing rations with some relief and only a casual question or two as to their rather disorderly condition.

Having made our delivery, I chose not to linger there, but to quickly start out on our return journey. This time stopping to check out several of the greater game trails that criss-crossed the road we were using, to try to find traces of terrorists moving on them. The process of checking was simple. At each likely trail we parked our vehicle twenty or thirty yards beyond it and left two details to guard it while I and the others walked a short distance along each game-trail on either side of the road. On this particular journey, we found only the spoor, both old and very fresh, of game animals large and small.

There was not much daylight left by the time we reached Marongora Dam and re-positioned our transport in the middle of our small base camp, so it was a case of getting a good meal cooked and consumed without too much wasted time. Conversations during the day, in which Sgt Thomas had expressed some concerns at being sent off on a first ever night ambush duty without a more senior detail present caused me to decide to add myself to his stick for this one night. The rest of my sub-section could remain in camp. With dusk falling it also made sense to head for the same ambush position as the previous night, so that is just what I did. As was wise, we were safely in position before full dark and with Sgt Thomas in place next to me, we began a second night of ambush duty in the Zambezi Valley.

My habit when on such night ambushes, was always to take the first hour of guard duty. That inevitably led to a second hour sometime before dawn, but it had the effect of pre-empting any arguments between those who were fortunate enough to collect only one hour of guard duty and those who found themselves doing two on any given night. It was towards halfway through my first hour on guard that I began to hear a sound that I could not place. It was a dry rattling noise, rather like wooden sticks being tapped together. It was also definitely not coming from the road, but from the bush, a short distance away to our left and it was drawing steadily closer. Eventually, a dozen or more buffalo, with a couple of last year's youngsters among them emerged from the bush, stepping out cautiously into the flat grassy area of our demarcated killing ground. In the vanguard was a huge old bull with a massive spread of horns. Like the other adults behind him, he was carrying his head up, nostrils flaring, as he tested the air for scents that might forewarn of danger. There seemed to me to be a lot of head and tail movement. I gained the distinct feeling that they were decidedly agitated and wondered whether they had got wind of us. I gave a thought to the fact that the small herd would surely take off and head elsewhere if they did get wind of us humans and pondered upon how far our scent would be detectable in such a still, hot night in which there was not, so far, even a breath of wind. The small herd's forward progress out from the bushes into the grassy area brought a lessening of the strange clicking I had heard. Then I realized that it was caused by the horns of the beasts rattling against the dry branches of the foliage they were moving through. Out on open grass, there was nothing to make the noise, so it vanished.

Within a couple of minutes, the buffalo crossed the grassy area and the rattling began again. Somewhat puzzlingly, the buffalo did not head off and away in a straight line, but gradually circled around us at a distance of probably fifty yards or so. By then, all of us were sitting or kneeling up, listening and peering into the darkness of the thick bush the herd was pushing its way through. Eventually, the buffalo completed a full circle of our ambush position and came out once again to our left, onto the open grassy area between us and the road. Then, led without hesitation by the magnificent old bull, they closed in on the fallen tree shielding us from the roadway and, one by one, settled down, not half a dozen paces from us. It became obvious that they were settled down for the night, slap bang in front of us and so close that, as Sgt Thomas and I agreed in a whispered conversation, they had to be aware that we were there.

I spent most of my second hour of guard duty wondering what on earth would happen if any terrorists appeared, moving along the roadway beyond the bulky shapes of the resting buffalo and gunfire erupted into the night. As it turned out, no such event happened. At first light, the buffalo began to waken and stir, but they made no effort to get up and move off. Motioning for my men to stay in place, I permitted a full half-hour of daylight to pass before I rose, slowly, without my rifle in hand, so that I was clearly visible to the buffalo, not knowing quite what to expect from them. At my movement, the old bull, the nearest one to us, raised his head and looked at me. Unhurriedly, he rose to his feet and, just like a dog, shook himself thoroughly, although his eyes seemed firmly fixed on me. Following the example of their leader, the remainder of the small herd stirred and rose, before moving off just a few paces, where they began to nibble at whatever was of interest in the grass. The old bull sniffed the air and gazed around before turning once more to face me. Our eyes met for a second time and I had the strangest feeling that a message passed between us. Each of us understood that we were no threat to the other. I felt myself nod twice, slowly and clearly, without any conscious thought to do so. The old bull uttered two long, soft snorts that had no aggression in them, then he turned and led his group unhurriedly away in the general direction of the dam.

Sgt Thomas, who, like the others, had been peering over the top of the fallen tree, stood up and said quietly, "Ishe, he was talking to you."

"Strangely, Sergeant, I got that impression too, although I've no idea why."

With that, we both began to pack our gear, ready to move off. A short distance from our ambush point, we noted the spoor of the buffalo as they had circled around us. Then it became clear why the buffalo had sought us out. Superimposed upon the spoor of the small herd of buffalo was the clear, fresh spoor of two adult lions, the best night-time hunters in the entire valley.

Our return journey to base camp at Marongora Dam was uneventful, although we all kept a wary eye open in case we had more than just a couple of lion prowling around the area. Our base camp details had a less eventful night than we had, except for the fact that as soon as I appeared, Const. Mutandwa reported to me that Const. Aaron, when wakened, had refused to take his turn of night guard duty. Const. Aaron's answer to my question as to why he had refused to take his turn of guard duty was typically African. "I was dreaming, Ishe. It was my spirits that told Mutandwa to go away, not me." "Very well," I advised him, with Mutandwa listening carefully to our conversation. "When we get back to Harare, your spirits will lose one day's time off and carry out fatigues instead and so that they will not feel lonely, you can keep them company for the day." Const. Mutandwa's broad grin told me that I had dealt with that little situation about right. As the two constables moved away, conversing quite amicably, I offered a mental "Thank you!" to Mr Stainer.

After taking time for a decent meal, that morning, Friday, 14th October 1966, I led half the section off on foot at about 08:00hrs to establish a daytime ambush on the junction of a notable game trail with the track to Rekometje Tsetse Fly Research Station, about two miles east of our base camp. That ambush was routine and uneventful. By 17:00hrs we were back at base camp, in time to prepare and eat our second meal of the day, prior to me moving off on foot once again, with half the section to carry out a full night ambush on the same location, while Sgt Thomas took the remainder of the section to ambush another game trail a little closer to the dam. Leaving our vehicle unguarded was a calculated risk, but one I felt justified in taking, given all the circumstances. Both of those ambushes passed off without incident, allowing my section to re-assemble as a whole unit, shortly after dawn on Saturday 15th October and proceed back to our base camp location for a meal and a routine radio call to Makuti. That radio call resulted in an unexpected and somewhat weird instruction, from SO Crahart for me to return immediately to Makuti for a special task that needed doing, details to be advised when I reached Makuti. Somewhat puzzled, I gave orders for the section to break camp, make safe our fireplace and clear the camouflaging greenery from our vehicle so that we could load it and get under way.

By 07:30 we were moving, carefully and slowly at first, as Const. Kisimis threaded a way between trees and bushes until we had at first a track to follow and then a recognised road and eventually the hard-topped main north road, all the way up the escarpment, past the Makuti Motel and on to our main operational base that we had left four days previously. During that journey, Sgt Thomas, Const. Kisimis and I compared thoughts about what we had encountered and what we had learned from our brief stay in the valley. In general, our thoughts were the same. The valley was an incredible and unique place. The game was plentiful and wonderful to see at such close range as we had encountered it. The valley was uncomfortably hot already, even before the hot season had really got going and the mosquitoes and tsetse fly were troublesome. The single one litre water-bottle per person that we carried on our belts contained too little for us to survive on, even for just one day, if we were away from a source of water for re-supply. We needed mobile radios of some kind so that sub-sections could talk to each other and to other stations when away from our vehicles. Our vehicles were not suited to the poor roads of the valley and the ordinary roadster tyres they were fitted with were not good in the dry, dusty sand on the roads and would be worse when the rainy season really turned the road surfaces to mud. The uniforms we were wearing were all wrong for work in the valley and our issue sleeping bags were worse than useless. The 44 webbing, packs and pouches were alright for day or overnight patrols but would not be adequate for longer patrol periods out and about on foot. Our "Mars" boots, moulded as one unit, so as theoretically to be waterproof, were cracking across the sole at the ball of foot point because the compound used was too brittle, so better boots would be needed, preferably the ankle-high type that might allow us to wade through a few inches of water yet still keep our feet dry.

By the end of our journey, I had a headful of serious points to deliver at the debrief I expected to encounter. That debrief never took place. Instead, having used the vehicle radio to keep Makuti advised of our progress, I found Reg waiting for us in the parking area, with a requisition book in his hand. While the members of my section started to unpack our personal gear from the vehicle, our troop commander thrust the requisition book at me and said, "When your vehicle is clear I want you to go into Karoi and pick up the list of supplies that is written up in this requisition book. The list has been sent on ahead of you so it should be waiting. Check it out and get it back here as fast as you like. When you've unloaded it here, you can get back to the valley for a few more days down there." Having delivered the book into my hands, he simply turned away and walked off in the general direction of the HQ caravan, leaving me somewhat speechless.

Wondering just what the dickens was going on, I went in search of Willie Wielopolski. I presumed he was around somewhere because his section's vehicle was standing next to ours in the parking area. I found Willie sitting in our dining tent, finishing a late breakfast. He had no idea why I had been called up out of the valley to do a supply run to Karoi, other than the fact that the previous evening SO Crahart had told him to take today off and just relax. He had no idea what the urgent need for a ration's re-supply was all about, because there appeared to be no shortage in the store tent. He also had no idea what Reg had meant by "a few more days down there." It took me just a few minutes to find Sgt Isaac, our troop sergeant, who confirmed that there was no shortage of rations that he was aware of.

Keeping my thoughts to myself, I called my own section together and explained to them the orders I had received from our troop commander. They were not impressed. Sgt Thomas shook his head in disbelief and muttered "Ari Penga!" (He's mad!) When I gave them the choice of remaining in Makuti Camp, or all of them coming with me on the Karoi stores run, not one of them hesitated. They would all welcome even an hour of free time in Karoi, which is what I had rather expected.

By 09:00hrs we were on our way to Patel's Emporium in Karoi. There were only two short delays on the way. The first was at our own routine police roadblock. The second was when we had to enter the Tsetse Fly Control Shed, through which all southbound traffic had to go. It was a vast barn-like structure with sliding doors at each end. Within it, once both doors were closed, vehicles of every shape, size and type were checked to ensure they carried no unwanted passengers of the tsetse fly type. Wheels and wheel arches were sprayed, before the unfailingly friendly and cheerful Tsetse Department staff slid back the southerly door so that the theoretically cleansed vehicles could continue their journey. We, although in a government vehicle, were no exception to the rules, so our Ford 4x4 was duly checked out, sprayed and worked over by one of the staff wielding a small version of a butterfly net with which to capture any real live tsetse fly that we might have carried with us out of the valley. Just for good measure, a generous puff of insecticide went into the empty goods compartment of our transport, before we were declared safe to proceed. The reek of that chemical compound swiftly permeated the whole vehicle, resulting in every window being fully open for the rest of the journey.

The staff who worked at Mr Patel's Emporium were friendly, efficient and well prepared for our arrival. I handed over the necessary government paperwork that would ensure payment for the goods would appear in due course. The several sacks, boxes, packets and parcels were all itemised and counted off and the duly ordered and now supplied rations, from fresh bread to powdered milk, tea, coffee, sugar, fresh and tinned meat and fresh vegetables were all loaded into the goods compartment and on the roof rack of our vehicle in a commendably short space of time.

That allowed me to provide my sergeant and constables with an hour of free time in which to do any personal shopping they might require, for items such as toiletries and cigarettes, while I enjoyed a leisurely cup of tea and a chunk of home-made coffee cake at Peter Veck's café, and kept a close eye on our transport with its cargo of stores and our personal firearms, which were stowed under lock and key and well out of sight. Just before my section's members took off like a bunch of happy, chattering schoolboys, I had issued two instructions. They were not to be late back and that they were limited to one single pint of beer each. That latter instruction brought smiles to the faces of several of them. Technically they were on duty and drinking on duty was a disciplinary offence. My words carried the un-stated message that I would not make a fuss if any of them returned with a slight taint of alcohol about them, but it had better be a slight one. That much relaxation of the rules I felt would help rather than hinder the maintenance of discipline and unity within our small team. With about ten minutes to go, I took myself out to our transport, unlocked the driving cab and the passenger compartments and waited. In twos and threes the entire section made it back on time, all clutching brown paper bags containing their purchases and with just some of them smelling slightly of alcohol. Right on time and in high spirits, we set off once again on the road northwards to Makuti, where we arrived at about 14:00hrs. Leaving my team to unload the rations at the store tent and then see to the refuelling of our vehicle, I went in search of SO Crahart, who proved to be nowhere around. Willie Wielopolski advised me that Reg had gone to the Makuti Motel for lunch and had not yet returned. He also advised me that there was word out from the HQ caravan that relatively fresh spoor of two large terrorist groups had been located by our forces patrolling the Zambezi riverbank in the area of the Chewore river mouth. There was a need for us operating in the valley to be even more vigilant. He suggested that I needed to get a briefing from Rampart before heading back down into the valley. Looking at my watch and thinking of travel time and daylight hours left, I took myself off somewhat rapidly to see Supt Holt in the command caravan. Supt Holt seemed surprised at my appearance. His response to my formal salute was a brief flicker of his hand towards his head. "I thought you were on patrol down in the valley?"

"So I was, Sir, but Section Officer Crahart sent a radio message this morning for me to break camp and report here with my section for a special task. That turned out to be a ration run to Karoi." Rampart's eyebrows raised a little, but he said nothing, so I continued. "That task I've just completed, Sir. Now I am informed SO Crahart wants me to return to resume my patrol and ambush duties in the valley, but PO Wielopolski tells me there have been some developments I need to know about and suggested I spoke to you, Sir, for a briefing before I left."

Supt Holt nodded. "Sound advice. I was not aware that Crahart had called you up from the valley. Have you spoken to him today?"

"Only long enough to receive from him the purchase requisitions for the supplies, Sir. I need to be on my way as fast as I can so that I can get back to the valley floor and re-establish the camp I left from this morning. If my section is to do any ambush work tonight, we need to get a meal inside us and get out and into position before it is too dark to move safely. There's not a lot of time left to do that, Sir, with all due respect to SO Crahart and his orders."

Supt Holt nodded again. "I take your point, Woolley. I don't know why Crahart called you back here. Meanwhile, take a look at the map." I duly looked at the large map of the valley and escarpment, in 1:50,000 scale, that decorated one wall of the caravan.

Rampart's hand indicated a spot on the river. "Late yesterday afternoon, an army patrol found two sets of boot spoor of terrorists, recently arrived from Zambia. They landed about a mile apart, just east of the Chewore mouth. Each group appears to be about two dozen strong. If they follow their usual habit, they'll push southwards to make their way up the escarpment anywhere between the Rekometje Gap and the main road. There are units trying to track them, but you and Rowlandson need to know of that presence because they are likely to be moving through the area that you two are covering. I know what your original orders were, but as of now there are to be no more split strength patrols or ambushes. You're to operate only at full section strength. Understand?"

"Completely, Sir."

"Good. Now that you've appeared right out of the blue, I have a special task for you. Rowlandson's not been on radio for the past 24 hours. Nothing more than radio failure is my guess, because we know the research station itself is okay and the staff also. What I want you to do is to get to Rowlandson as fast as you can. Update him on the two incursions and pass on my orders to stop the split ambushes and patrol work. Is that clear?"

"Abundantly, Sir."

"Right. You get on your way as fast as you can. Try to stay in radio contact and send a message back once you've briefed Rowlandson. Off you go!" A wave of his hand reinforced that last instruction. I saluted, turned about and hastened to A Troop's set of tents, where Willie confirmed that Reg was still absent. I gave Willie a short version of my conversation with Supt Holt, chased up my section, saw to the loading into our vehicle of all the gear we had removed a few hours earlier and the men themselves and, with Const. Kisimis at the wheel, headed out of Makuti camp and northwards.

As we travelled, I briefed Sgt Thomas and Const. Kisimis on the two recent penetrations by insurgents and urged our driver to push along as fast as he felt safe enough to go. By 15:00hrs we were passing the turnoff to Marongora Dam and our recent camp site and by 16:45hrs we were at Terry Rowlandson's patrol camp, from where I was able to use our vehicle radio to confirm for Rampart that I had briefed Terry as required and confirmed also that it was only a radio defect that had kept his section off the airwaves. Leaving Terry to re-organise his activities as directed by Rampart, I set off with my section to return to Marongora Dam. By 18:30hrs we were back re-occupying the camp we had set out from barely ten hours earlier. With no time to get a decently going full fire fit for cooking on before full dark, we camouflaged our vehicle as best we could and made do with a meal of tea and fresh bread before I set up a double guard rota, one tasked to guard our landward side and one tasked to keep observation on the dam itself, in case any of our recent insurgents decided to visit the place for water. In view of the previous problem with Const. Aaron, I arranged matters so that it would be me who woke him. When the time came, there was no problem that night, which passed routinely.

The following morning, Sunday 16th October 1966, I called "stand-to" as usual as dawn broke. Only when daylight was fully upon us did I then permit a proper cooking fire to be lit and a satisfactory full meal to be prepared. At about 08:00hrs I left two details to guard the camp while I set off with the remainder of the section to make a complete circuit of the dam to check for any insurgent foot-spoor, of which we found none. What we did find was the spoor of a great deal of wildlife, large and small. Moving quietly and cautiously, with weapons constantly at the ready and eyes roaming everywhere, it was not surprising that we actually saw not only their spoor, but the animals themselves. In our slow, steady and cautiously silent circuit of the dam we had sight of kudu, impala, bushbuck, giraffe, buffalo, warthog and one lone bull elephant with a huge pair of tusks and an impressive scar on his right shoulder. The scar, clearly over a healed wound, was still fairly fresh. It caused some discussion among the constables as to how it had been occasioned. One or two suggested that it could have been caused by a fight with a younger bull, which this old fellow had lost and then been driven out of the herd to roam on his own. Others thought it more likely the wound had been caused by a deadfall trap set by poachers, whose method was to embed spears in a heavy log, haul it up high in the trees over an elephant trail and set a trip-line which, when triggered would cause the weighted spears to drop on top of any passing elephant, hopefully with crippling or fatal effects. Whatever the cause of his healed wound and the reason for his apparently solitary existence, we skirted well clear of the grand old fellow and left him to his browsing as we pushed warily onward.

Our cautious patrol around the dam, walking all the way just a few yards into the bush and scrub tree line that marked high water and checking out every game trail that we crossed, took us over three hours, but it enabled us to get on to our vehicle radio and report that, so far, there was no sign of any insurgents from the two recent incursions having the dam as a watering point. I had completed my report to the radio operator on duty at Makuti and was about to book off the air, when Reg Crahart came on the air. His message was short. "Pack up and return to Makuti. Acknowledge."

My single word response of "Acknowledged" brought "Roger, out!" from the other end. I stowed the microphone into its clip on the dashboard, shook my head in sheer wordless disbelief and turned to give the necessary instructions to the men of my section. The expressions on the faces of the two men nearest to me, those of Sgt Thomas and Const. Kisimis, both of whom had clearly heard our latest orders, reflected my own feelings. "That boss is no good, Ishe," Sgt Thomas muttered. "He is wrong in the head."

For the second time in twenty-four hours, we packed our kit, made safe our fire pit, buried our rubbish, climbed aboard our vehicle and set off once again to return to Makuti, where we arrived at about 13:30hrs. After standing down my section, I duly reported my return to Supt Holt in the command caravan and then went in search of my troop commander, who was, once again, nowhere to be found. What I did find was Willie Wielopolski, who was busy loading his section's Ford 4x4 with personal kit, rations and section cooking gear. He informed me that he was preparing to set off, under orders from Reg Crahart to re-supply Terry Rowlandson and his section and then to set up camp at Marongora Dam to undertake the same kind of patrol and ambush duties that I and my section had been undertaking for the past several days. His understanding was that I was to replace him and his section, carrying out local patrols from Makuti Camp for the next week or so. He had no idea why I had been called up from the valley, rather than Terry and his section. I looked at the daylight, gave a thought to travel and time and suggested that he might bed down with Terry's section rather than do an evening drive back to Marongora during ambush hour when we knew there were insurgents in some numbers in the area. Willie was a bit wary of not being where Reg had told him to be for the night, but when I pointed out that it was not Reg's hide that would feel the pain if Willie's section was ambushed on the way back to Marongora, he agreed to play it safe.

Having seen Willie and his section off, I went to my tent, stripped off my clothing which had not been changed in a week, wrapped a towel around me and headed off to the shower. Supt Holt was coming out of the hessian enclosure as I went in. As we greeted and passed each other he commented, "If I'm sent up here in the cold season, Woolley, I'm going to demand they put in a hot water system and a bathroom before I arrive."

Rampart's comment set me thinking as I stepped on to the wooden duckboards that served to keep our feet out of the mud, hung up my towel and turned on the tap. The cold water was a bit of a shock at first, but the good, vigorous lathering and scrub down which followed cleansed off the dust and sweat of the past few days and that was very welcome. Feeling refreshed and clean, I returned to my tent, where Shorty had laid out a full set of fresh underwear and uniform, with a large mug of tea right close to hand. I dressed myself in the welcome change of clothing and spent the next while sitting in a camp chair outside the tent, sipping cautiously at the scalding hot tea and thinking about bathrooms and hot water systems. Slowly, the glimmering of an idea began to form in my mind.

It was starting to get dark when my troop commander appeared, from precisely where I had no idea. My dutiful "Good evening Reg," brought a brief nod and an instruction to be up and about early on the morrow because there was a lot of work to be done. With that admonishment delivered, he took himself off in the direction of the HQ caravan. A little while later, Shorty advised me that the evening meal was ready. He presented me with a plateful of fresh venison and vegetables, set on a bed of rice. It was a very pleasant change after a week living on corned beef, chopped ham and maize-meal, prepared and eaten out of a set of mess-tins. A couple of hours later, with Reg nowhere in sight, I turned in. The comparative luxuries of a Hounsfield camp bed to sleep on and no guard duties to perform, sent me off into a good night's sleep, wondering briefly before I nodded off, just what my troop commander might wish me to do the next day.

On Monday, 17th October 1966, I was up, dressed and operational by 06:00hrs when my section fell in to undertake "Stables Parade" as per usual routine. Reg's Land Rover and my section's Ford 4x4 received a thorough going over, mechanically and in terms of presentation too. Somewhere towards 06:30hrs Reg appeared. When I asked him what he wanted us to do for the rest of the day, once Stable Parade was over and breakfast had been eaten, he grinned broadly, pointed to an as yet undisturbed patch of ground on the edge of the camp and advised that Rampart wanted another set of pit latrines to be dug. Four more "thunder-boxes" had been delivered to the camp the previous day, but they needed latrine pits digging before the commode-like boxes could be set over them and surrounded by hessian walls to provide a modicum of privacy.

By the end of that day, thanks to the combined efforts of the whole section, including me, the task was completed and Rampart had his additional latrine area. It was five yards long, a yard wide and eight feet deep, covered by wooden logs scavenged from suitably sized trees nearby and surrounded by the necessary hessian modesty screen. Reg spent the morning between supervising the construction work and visiting the HQ caravan. When I called time for a lunchbreak, Reg took himself off in the troop Land Rover, without saying where he was off to and only re-appeared half-way through the afternoon, in good time to oversee the finishing touches to the project and call Rampart across to inspect the fruits of our several hours of labouring. Supt Holt duly admired our handiwork, but graciously declined Reg's invitation for him to be the first user of the new facility.

When Reg vanished again in his allocated vehicle at dusk and did not appear for evening meal, I asked Shorty if our troop leader was eating with us and how his meals were being kept hot until he arrived. Shorty shook his head. "That boss eating in another place somewhere. He only wants coffee in the morning. No eat food." That information confirmed what I appeared to be seeing. However, if Reg wanted to eat elsewhere, that was his choice. He was the one who would be paying the cost. What concerned me more was the fact that I had absolutely no idea what my orders for the following day might be and no way of properly preparing myself or my section for the next day's activities.

317

Next day, Tuesday 18th October 1966, Reg was up and about at 06:00hrs, supervising Stables Parade. When I asked him whether he had any particular orders for me for the rest of the day, he advised me that Rampart wanted a vehicular night patrol carried out of the fly fence to Kariba. For a moment I just stared at him. Then I pointed to our Ford 4x4. "You want us to do a patrol in that vehicle, after dark, between the main road and the Nyaodza river mouth? Any terrorists in the area will see and hear us coming from a mile away. That could drop us in some serious dirt!"

"I don't want you to do anything," Reg snapped. "Rampart has given the orders and you had better damned well obey them, but you can take the Land Rover if you want to. I can use your Ford for running around here." At that, he simply turned and walked away.

When I briefed my section on our latest tasking, there was much shaking of heads in sheer disbelief. Precisely as instructed, at 18:00hrs, with each of my section carrying only "battle belts" with water, hard-tack rations, a rolled poncho and ample ammunition in case of a contact, we set off. I had considered taking over the driver's role myself for this trip, with its need for low revs on the engine, quiet running and driving on sidelights only, which was my intention. However, that might have given Kisimis and the others the feeling that I did not rate our trained driver constable as a competent driver. That could be very damaging as far as his own confidence and the team's morale was concerned, so we set off with Kisimis behind the wheel as usual and me in the front passenger seat. Dusk was just beginning to set in as we cleared the gate from the main road and set off along the fly fence. Two miles in, on a fairly steep incline, when Kisimis pushed down on the accelerator for more power, there was a "clunk." Our vehicle lost power. Kisimis swiftly pulled hard up on the handbrake to prevent us rolling backwards, looked at me and muttered, "Half-shaft Ishe!"

"Yes," I replied, confirming the obvious. I ordered everyone out to take up defensive positions while Kisimis and I set the vehicle into four-wheel drive and reverse gear and slowly eased it back down the incline to level ground, from where we tried to make radio contact with Makuti or any other call-sign that might be able to relay a message for us. After a quarter-hour or more of fruitless effort, I made the operational decision to abort our mission. After a five or six-point turn in the very limited space between fly fence and thick bush, Kisimis had our vehicle pointing in the right direction and my section's members re-embussed. In four-wheel drive and on full headlights, we crawled noisily back to the main road and returned to our base camp at Makuti, where I stood down my section for the night and, noting that my section's Ford 4x4 was not present, went in search of Supt Holt, only to find that he too was away, having stated an intention to go for a drink at the Makuti Motel.

Working on the probability that I would find both Rampart and Reg enjoying a quiet, off-duty drink at the motel, that was where I headed to next, driving the Land Rover somewhat carefully, in four-wheel drive mode. I found them as I expected, at a table on the veranda overlooking the swimming pool, enjoying a cold beer. Reg was not at all happy to see me there and made that quite plain. When I explained about the broken half-shaft, his immediate challenge was, "Who was driving?" His unstated allegation was not missed by me, or by Rampart, from the look on that officer's face. My reply was, "Driver Constable Kisimis and he didn't do it deliberately either." As Reg scowled and thought about a reply, Supt Holt chipped in. "Better get along to CMED tomorrow and see if they can do a repair job quickly. We have all too few vehicles up here anyway, particularly Land Rovers."

That silenced whatever it was that Reg appeared to be building up to say. I replied, "Very good, Sir," to Rampart, wished them a good evening and took myself back to camp, where much to my surprise, I found Terry and Willie, who explained that they had been called back out of the valley that afternoon by our troop commander. Neither of them knew exactly why.

The next morning, Wednesday, 19th October 1966, all three of us Patrol Officers and our African details were up and about in time for Stable Parade. It was the first chance in some days to check over all our vehicles together. VPF 21's spare tyre was not only deflated; it was ruined. Our troop trailer, MJN34T, had a canvas covered spare wheel that had not seen the light of day for some while. When we removed the cover, the spare wheel itself was flat. Closer inspection showed cracks in the wall of the tyre and a brittleness in the fabric that suggested that particular tyre was way past its sell-by date. VPF 29's spare tyre was nice and new, but it too appeared deflated. A careful examination revealed an acacia thorn deeply embedded in the tread. Some careful work with a pair of slim-nosed pliers extracted the offending thorn, which proved to be almost three inches long. It had clearly penetrated both tyre case and inner tube too. Our collection of defects was added to when we discovered that four VHF walkie-talkie sets had been allocated for use by our troop a couple of days before but had not yet been passed down to us because at least two of them did not appear to be functioning.

The collection of spare wheel problems, the Land Rover's broken half-shaft and the VHF radio sets problems all indicated a need for a journey to the District Police HQ, in Sinoia, where all the items listed for repair could be attended to. Willie and Terry did not appear to be keen to do the trip, so when I volunteered to undertake it, if Reg approved the journey, my offer was promptly taken up by my fellow POs. With that decided, we all went in search of our troop leader, who was nowhere to be found. That left us with a wee bit of a dilemma. However, when I related to Terry and Willie the conversation I had had with Supt Holt and SO Crahart at the Makuti Motel the previous evening, they too agreed that it was safe to take Rampart's instruction to get on to CMED as an authority to make the trip to Karoi which was where the nearest CMED unit was and then on to Sinoia if necessary for the radio repairs.

After a decent breakfast of maize-meal porridge followed by scrambled egg and beans on toast, we set off to drive our Land Rover southward for repairs. I drove the vehicle myself, with Sgt Thomas in the front passenger seat and our trailer hitched on behind, carrying the assorted spare wheels for the Ford 4x4's and the trailer, along with the defective radios.

Thanks to a few radio messages already passed from Makuti to Karoi, the CMED mechanics were expecting our arrival. They could not have given us better service if we had been Compol. It was their helpful attitude that encouraged me, over a cup of tea in their office, to explain the lack of any means with which to have a hot bath at Makuti and my thoughts about correcting that situation, on the basis of one good turn deserving another. A few telephone calls later, I had assurances of an old, but usable iron bath, complete with taps, an unwanted wood-fired boiler from the Department of Public Works in Sinoia, a spare tent from Karoi Police Station and the promise of a day's use of an African plumber and the necessary piping. With our Land Rover's half-shaft speedily replaced and assorted other bits and pieces repaired or replaced as necessary, I set off for Sinoia, where the radio room's workshop staff promptly got stuck in to make the two VHF sets workable, which permitted me to set off to collect the promised gash items that I needed to create a tented bathroom at Makuti Camp.

It was getting dark when Sgt Thomas and I returned to Makuti with our vehicle and trailer crammed with repaired spare wheels, a much patched but very usable tent and fly sheet and the bath, boiler and piping. As pure luck would have it, the first person to set eyes on us as I drove into the parking area happened to be Supt Holt. He took one look at our cargo and inquired, "What the heck have you got there, Woolley?"

"The makings of a bathroom I hope, Sir," I replied innocently.

Supt Holt studied the strange assortment a little more closely for a moment or two, in silence. Then he gave me a decidedly wary look and said, "I think it best if I don't ask exactly what you've been up to Woolley, but if it works, I want first go, got it?"

"Yes, Sir," I replied smartly. At that he turned and walked away, leaving Sgt Thomas and me to summon up a few details to give us a hand with the unloading of our assorted winnings.

When Shorty called us for evening meal, Willie, Terry and I sat down to a table laid for four. "Anyone got any idea where Reg is?" I inquired. Two shaking heads gave me my reply. Over our meal we exchanged experiences of our assorted patrols in the valley and the limitations of our decidedly unsuitable transport, weaponry, uniforms and radio equipment. It was a lengthy discussion.

Late that evening, with Const. Kisimis driving, I booked out of camp on a routine night road patrol. A few hours later we returned, having proved that there were lots of small game in the area and that the "V" site of a .303 rifle works well with strong torchlight. The next day Thursday 20th October 1966, the African plumber I had been promised appeared bright and early. By mid-afternoon, the new tent was up, the bath was in it, the boiler and piping were both working well and Supt Holt had his much longed-for hot bath. When the very efficient African plumber climbed into his Land Rover to head off southwards, he did so with a broad smile on his face. Part of the smile might have been the conclusion of a successful task, but I guessed that much of his smile had something to do with the very ample supply of venison in the back of his vehicle, to be shared between him and the other friendly and helpful individuals I had encountered in Karoi and Sinoia the previous day. After all, one good turn certainly does deserve another one and a promise is a promise.

Friday, 21st October 1966 started off with a real monsoon deluge that looked as though it would go on all day, which it did. SO Crahart appeared for Stable Parade, which caused strange looks and shrugs to pass between us three Patrol Officers. Nobody asked what time he had arrived back in camp, or from where. When he eventually got around to noticing the additional tent and the boiler and discovered that I had been behind its appearance, he demanded to know where I had got the materials from and who had authorised it, because he had not. He was not over amused at my somewhat short answer that it was all scrap material, rescued from assorted locations at no cost to anyone and greatly approved of by Rampart who had been the first to test the bath's working efficiency. That conversation ended with Reg barking, "You're always buttering up to senior officers, aren't you!" and marching off.

As usual, Willie, Terry and I ate breakfast together in our mess tent. Reg had coffee delivered to his tent.

At 09:00hrs the full troop paraded, shielded from the rain under glistening and streaming ponchos and then stood easy while Reg went off to see what task Supt Holt had for us for that day or for the next while. When he returned, it was with instructions that Terry and Willie were to go back down into the valley, at once, to do day patrols and night ambushes, one to the east and one to the west of the main road. I was to stay in camp. On Sunday Terry and Willie's sections were to return to Makuti and I was to be ready to deploy to the valley, for an indefinite period.

While the bulk of our troop was busy getting ready to depart as ordered, I decided that a mid-morning cup of tea was called for and headed for our mess tent. I was still waiting for tea to appear when Reg came in and told me that the communal messing arrangement that we four had had since we arrived at Makuti was finished. He alleged that both Terry and Willie had complained and that he was not happy with it either. The mess tent was to become a store-only tent and we were to eat individually in our own or shared tent.

When he had gone, I hurried out to have a quick word with Willie and Terry who were just about ready to leave. A direct question to each brought the same answer. Neither had been aware of what Reg had just come up with and neither of them had complained. As far as they were concerned, when they returned from their present taskings we would all ignore Reg's latest piece of nonsense and carry on as usual with communal messing. I saw them both off with a wave and the thought in my mind that I was pretty sure I knew just who was telling porky pies.

As it was, any argument that might have brewed was scotched by the sudden arrival of an A Reserve Patrol Officer from Salisbury, directed to Makuti to do duties on the floating roadblock. Supt Holt, knowing nothing of Reg's intention to disband our mess tent, instructed Reg to find him a tent to sleep in and make arrangements for him to mess with us. Reg was in a particularly foul mood for the rest of the day, until he took himself off, at a relatively early hour of the evening, as usual, to the Makuti Motel.

By 06:00hrs on Saturday, 22nd October 1966, the rains of the past 24hrs had eased, leaving a hot sticky atmosphere in which clothing stuck to your skin and every footfall was a muddy and slippery one. In the absence of our troop leader, I organised the checking and cleaning of the vehicles still in camp and when that was done, called a snap weapons inspection, which resulted in some time spent later in the day, with constables pouring lots of boiling water down rifle barrels, followed by much energetic use of ramrods, gauze and cloth patches and oil, until I was happy to declare their weapons rust free and safe for use if needed.

Just on 07:00hrs Reg appeared from the direction of the HQ caravan. He passed on word from Special Branch that a major incursion of terrorists was expected to take place from Zambia, sometime on the next day. After breakfast, just on 08:00hrs, Reg instructed me to drive to Karoi for rations. Included in the list of necessary items was "Mantles, Tilley Lamp, several." After the foodstuffs, that item became a priority, because although we had candles and a few Hurricane Lamps in our stores, the Tilley Lamp was the item that lit our evenings and night-time hours and did so very efficiently. I managed to find a few dozen at stores around Karoi and promptly bought the lot. That trip took me until lunchtime. When I was back at Makuti I found that I was just in time, in the absence of SO Crahart, to sort out an argument among our batmen over who should be on work and when they should be on time off. Working with them all, I created a duty roster that ensured that one of them was on duty, for eight hours to a shift, with cover from 06:00hrs to 22:00hrs daily. That allowed reasonable days off for the spare servants, even if there was nowhere close by for them to go.

When Reg did appear, it was early afternoon. Thinking about my forewarned instructions for the morrow, I asked him what time he wanted me and my section to be on our way down into the valley and whether there were going to be any specific orders, or just general guidelines for what we were to do. When it became clear that he had no idea about what was required of us, I suggested I went to have a talk with Rampart and the duty Special Branch detail. Somewhat to my surprise, Reg approved of that suggestion without argument, so off I went. The control room map of the valley was far more crowded with pins and tags of assorted colours than I had seen it so far. Supt Holt and the duty SB man listened politely to my inquiry about the next day and what might be required of us. At Supt Holt's request to be reminded where I had been based when last in the valley, I tapped a finger on Marangora Dam. Supt Holt rubbed his chin between finger and thumb and glanced at the SB man before saying to me, "Get a base camp set up there again tomorrow. You can do random vehicle patrols between the Research Station and the main road during daylight hours, checking for terrorist spoor and set up night ambushes on the roads and game trails around and near that dam." He tapped the red tag on the map nearest to the dam. "Game rangers reported probable terrorist spoor there two days ago, heading south of course. That group appeared to be eight or ten strong as far as they could tell, so keep your eyes open and your wits about you. If you do run into anything nasty in daylight, don't be afraid to cut and run. I don't expect battle tactics from you people. You're not trained or equipped for that. Got it?"

"Yes, Sir," I agreed, without feeling at all upset by Rampart's remarks. It was in fact reassuring to learn that he had a realistic view of our capabilities and our limitations.

"Do you want us out of here at any particular time, Sir?" I asked. Holt thought about that for a moment before deciding, with just the glimmer of a smile on his face, "Let's say 09:00hrs. That should give you time for breakfast and a bath before you go."

Following those orders from Rampart and with me well breakfasted and bathed, my section and I left Makuti Base Camp in our Ford 4x4 at precisely 09:00hrs on Sunday, 23rd October 1966. Some way down the escarpment and within ten minutes of each other, we passed A troop's other two sections, travelling uphill and southwards.

When the valley floor came fully in to view, it was clear that the recent heavy rains had had a startling effect. What had been brown, grey and hazy was now green and clear as a bell. Here and there patches of dark clouds stood atop opaque pillars of falling rain.

Dvr. Const. Kisimis looked at what awaited us and shook his head. "The roads are going to be no good, Ishe. Too much trouble!" I knew exactly what he was thinking but took a certain degree of comfort from the fact that there were now two shovels and an axe stowed behind the back of the bench seat we were sitting on.

It had been my intention to carry out a patrol through to Rekometje Research Station, checking for spoor, before returning to Marangora to re-establish our base camp there, but the heavy rain that descended upon us a few miles in, made any checking for spoor pointless. It also reduced our progress to a crawl. Peculiarly, the rains had not yet put enough water into the streams flowing from the escarpment, across the valley floor to the Zambezi, so those gave us no great problem. What did bring us to a halt were a few patches of heavy black soil into which our roadster tyres sank deeply and even after engaging the four-wheel drive mode on the vehicle, we could not overcome our bogged-down situation without additional support. That additional support came by way of us cutting tree and bush branches and laying short stretches of wooden causeway that gave the roadster tyres something to grip on until firmer ground was reached. Each time the vehicle ground to a halt it was a case of setting up a security screen of four details to guarantee that we were not caught off-guard by any terrorists, while the rest of us shovelled mud, or cut and carried branches and brushwood until Kisimis could get the vehicle moving forward once more. It was hot, wet, muddy work, made more uncomfortable by the need to keep our rifles free of the mud we were struggling with. The only way to do that was to carry our rifles across our backs, with the webbing slings across our chests, which was fine until a downpour hit us as we sank and ground to a halt in one particularly sticky mud-patch, when we rapidly found out that rifles slung in that fashion were not compatible with wearing a poncho cape to keep the rain off. The only thing to be said about that rainfall in the Zambezi Valley in October was that it was at least warm, so although we were rapidly soaked and mud-covered before we had gone many miles, we certainly were not cold.

At the research station, we stopped just long enough to check that Andy and Glyn were okay and to pick up any information from them and any gossip from their African staff. From Andy and Glyn I learned that they had been contacted by radio from their own HQ and warned to expect an army presence at their location in the very near future. When they heard our vehicle, they thought we might have been that unit arriving. That information puzzled me somewhat as Rampart had not mentioned any army presence in the area. They also advised that their African staff had spoken of seeing in the past couple of days certain spoor that could only be attributed to poachers or terrorists. That information they had passed back by radio to their own headquarters.

Much to their credit, neither of them was particularly concerned at the evidence of incursions and likely terrorist movements nearby. They were well aware that the terrorist groups' purpose was to get across the valley and move southwards as clandestinely as they could. Attacking the research station would be counter to that main purpose. They were also both realistic enough to accept that among their dozen or more African assistants there might just be one or two who were sympathetic to the terrorist cause. Unlike the unfortunate Viljoens at Nevada Farm in Hartley, both Andy and Glyn treated their servants and the African staff of the station with fairness and concern. As a result, they had excellent relations with their African assistants, which I found reassuring.

In the early afternoon, we left the research station and set off to battle our soaked, soggy and muddy way back to Marongora Dam, where we warily re-occupied our original temporary camp. This time, with the knowledge that terrorist spoor had been found less than five miles from the dam, although a few days ago, I made the individual positions somewhat more attack-proof by a judicious amount of digging and banking of earth and the placement of dead tree trunks and branches of sufficient thickness to stop a 7.62mm bullet or a piece of shrapnel from rifle grenades or mortar bombs, both of which we knew the terrorist groups carried. We also worked out and cleared an alternative pathway in and out for our vehicle. Being creatures of regular routine and habit was neither wise nor safe in the situation we were in.

After an early evening meal, I left four details to guard our camp and vehicle and set off on foot to the ambush position we had used before on the junction of the Old Mana Pools and Rekometje roads. By 18:00hrs the ambush was in position, under a clear starry and moonlit sky, without any hint of cloud or raindrop to be seen. The brightness of the night was such that I was able to watch the myriad of spiders, beetles, millipedes and moths that went about their routine nocturnal activities. It also enabled me to spot the movement of a large black scorpion that seemed determined to use my recumbent form as a viewing platform. The first time it tried, I used a piece of dead wood to flip it several yards away. When it promptly scuttled back and made a second try, I flattened it with my rifle butt.

Apart from the unwanted attentions of that scorpion, the night ambush was uneventful, the stars and moon moved in their ageless rhythm, owls and bats flew and, not too far away, lions periodically roared and elephants occasionally trumpeted as they too went about their habitual nocturnal activities. As dawn drove the night away on Monday, 24th October 1966, after our usual dawn stand-to, I lifted the ambush and led my men back to camp for breakfast and, two by two, a careful weapon cleaning exercise. By 08:00hrs I took my section off for another road patrol to Rekometje, this time in fair weather that allowed us to carry out our basic purpose far better than conditions had the day before. Patiently and diligently, we stopped long enough to investigate each game trail and track, not just where they met the Rekometje road that we were on, but also for a hundred yards or so, on either side of that road.

About half-way to Rekometje our efforts were rewarded. Const. Aaron spotted something quite unnatural and called me to see it. The surface of the roadway had been brushed. The game trail on either side was marked by the tell-tale track of a cut-off bush having been dragged along it, sometime after the rain of the previous afternoon. It was not unusual for poachers to tow a bush behind them as they walked, or to brush out their tracks as they went. It was highly likely that the insurgent groups had been briefed to do the same. Quite obviously, the unnatural markings themselves, on the road and game trail, instantly became an item of interest, just as much as the sight of a clear figure of eight boot tread pattern in the surface of the trail would have been.

With weapons cocked and safety catches off, we cautiously followed the brush marks southward from the main dirt road. What very quickly became clear to us was that there were tracks of birds, lizards and small game superimposed on top of the brush marks, suggesting that the sign we were following was probably at least a few hours old. Thirty yards or so along the trail we found the discarded bush that had been used to sweep the trail of boot marks. Beyond that point there was clear evidence of boot spoor, at least a couple of them clearly being the figure of eight pattern we knew to be associated with insurgents. We followed the signs for another fifty yards or so, carefully trying to distinguish individual boot-prints, one from another. By then our collective thinking was that the group was certainly more than eight and maybe as many as a dozen strong and that the tracks had been made sometime during last night, which meant they were more than likely a dozen miles distant when we located their sign.

Back at our vehicle I got on to the radio. Makuti Base Camp did not respond, so I called Chirundu Police Station, whose response was prompt. Via that location I passed on the details of what we had just found and exactly where. A few minutes later, Chirundu relayed instructions from Makuti, for us not to attempt any follow-up of the group whose tracks we had located, but to continue to follow our present orders.

Obedient to our orders, we made safe our rifles, climbed back into our vehicle and carried on, uneventfully, until we once again reached the Tsetse Fly Research Station, where we paused long enough for a brew of tea, kindly provided by the station's staff, before setting off on the return journey to Marongora, where we stopped short of the dam and our camp, rested for an hour and then set off to repeat our patrol to and from Rekometje. That further patrol was uneventful and produced no further sign of insurgent movement. It got us back to Marongora, as was my intention, in time to prepare and eat a meal, before heading off to carry out another night ambush. However, at Marongora we found Terry Rowlandson with his section, in their vehicle, waiting to pass on a written note from our troop leader. The message was that we were to cease any movement on foot or night ambush work, because there was an army presence in the area. We were to confine ourselves to day patrols in our vehicle. While that was the official message, Terry also confided that there appeared to have been a bit of an argument in the HQ caravan at Makuti, between the army officers and the police. The army regarded us Support Unit details, white and black, as ill-trained, ill-equipped and unreliable, starting with our radio communications.

The latter point proved itself, with Terry having to do the drive to brief me, because of Makuti's inability to get a radio message through to me, even via Chirundu.

Terry and his section had barely departed when rain began to fall, causing us all in camp to swiftly erect our ponchos as individual bivouac tents, with the aid of a few bits of wood and string. The rain was, at first, that heavy that it threatened to put out our cooking fire. Eventually the rain eased off and then finally stopped, so we revived our flagging fire, ate a hearty meal and prepared for a night in camp, with guard duties all fairly shared out, me included.

After an early wakening on Tuesday 25th October 1966 and the usual pre-dawn stand-to, we took time for a breakfast meal and then set off once more on our allotted duties along the road to Rekometje Tsetse Fly Research Station, where Andy Devine reported that all was well and quiet although the promised army presence had still not yet materialised. I brought him up to date on our latest instructions, although, at that point, we too had seen or heard nothing of any army presence in the area.

Back at Marongora towards noon, there was a further surprise for me, because Sgt Zwenyika and the vehicle and constables of number three section were there waiting for me. All Sgt Zwenyika could tell me was that he had been instructed by PO Rowlandson to drive down to reinforce the troop's presence at Marangora.

Totally confused and a bit wary of just what was and was not going on around my base camp at Marongora, I took it upon myself to drive to Makuti, to sort matters out. Leaving Sgt Zwenyika in charge of the camp, I took Const. Kisimis and Sgt Thomas and drove our vehicle myself to Makuti, at some speed, or just as fast as the up-gradient and severe turns allowed. When we reached our Combined Operations Base Camp at Makuti at 13:00hrs, I was not surprised to find our troop commander away, out at the motel, apparently having lunch there. Fortunately, Supt Holt, an SB detail and an army officer were all in the command caravan when I appeared at the door with my question as to what the heck was going on. Supt Holt was a little baffled at my appearance there. "Has your troop commander not briefed you?" At the negative shake of my head, he went on, "A fairly powerful Crusader (Army) stick has been dropped off between Marongora Dam and Rekometje to undertake day patrols and night ambushes on the game trails where we have note of terrorist movement. We didn't want any unfortunate encounters between your section and them. That was why we pulled off your own night ambush work. That second section from your troop was sent down to be stationed at the Research Station, under your control until you are relieved. Does that give you a clear picture?"

"Yes, Sir, it does, but, with respect, Sir, Sgt Zwenyika appeared convinced that his briefing was just to join me at Marangora. With your permission, I'll get back down there and get him and his section over to Rekometje as fast as I can."

At Supt Holt's, "Right, Woolley, off you go then," I left the caravan and went in search of Terry Rowlandson, whose story was simple. He had been briefed by our troop leader, apparently on orders from Rampart, precisely as he had passed on to Sgt Zwenyika. According to him, there had been no mention of Rekometje Research Station, let alone basing Sgt Zwenyika and his section there.

By 15:00hrs I was back down in the valley at Marongora, where I briefed Sgt Zwenyika and escorted him and his section to Rekometje, where I briefed Glyn and Andy on latest developments before driving back to Marongora to once again remain in camp for the night.

About midnight, I was awakened by Sgt Thomas who was doing his turn at night guard. "There is shooting, Ishe. Listen!" There was certainly a random scattering of shots. What I heard lasted no more than a minute or two, a few miles distant to our east. Sgt Thomas explained that he had heard a lot of shooting that was over quite quickly, just before he woke me. It was the typical gunfire pattern of a sprung ambush. Quietly we woke the rest of our section and briefed them on the gunfire we had heard. After that I doubled-up the guard for the remainder of the night, just in case. At first light there was a short period of helicopter movement to our east, but it was days later that I learned for sure that the army unit had indeed sprung a successful ambush upon a group of insurgents, killing three and wounding two more on a game trail upon which we had reported seeing terrorist spoor in daylight. When I explained that to the African members of my section, it brought on a smile or two. They, like me, began to feel that our hours of daylight patrolling had not been totally wasteful ones.

On 26th October 1966, Terry Rowlandson brought down fresh rations for those of us at Marongora and Rekometje and fresh orders for me. I was to extend my area of road patrols and checking for spoor, right out to Mana Pools and the Zambezi River and to resume my night-time ambushing of likely terrorist routes.

For the next 48 hours I took my section on day patrols and night ambushes, without any positive result at all, apart from all of us seeing more wild game of all kinds than any of us had seen before in our entire lives. It was during those two days that I first encountered the strange habit of antelope, greater and lesser, singly or in herds, of being determined, once they observed us, to race ahead and cross the tracks we were motoring on, ahead of our vehicle. That strange compulsion led to us seeing kudu, impala, bushbuck and even lumbering warthog at very close range indeed. Those mad-cap dashes by antelope of all sorts, barely a few feet in front of our vehicle were sights never to be forgotten by me, or by my African companions.

On Friday, 28th October 1966, with radio communications for once working well, I received instructions, at 10:40hrs, from PO Rowlandson, to order Sgt Zwenyika and his men to uplift from Rekometje and return to Makuti. At 11:50hrs I was in the middle of instructing Sgt Zwenyika and his section to break camp and return to Makuti, when PO Rowlandson came on the air again, this time with instructions for me and my section at Marongora to also break camp and return to Makuti, without delay.

By mid-afternoon, both sections were back at Makuti, where I discovered that our troop leader had decided to take a few days off on Local Leave, leaving Terry Rowlandson as senior detail in charge of the troop. I also discovered that the reason I had been called back from the valley was that, according to a radio message from Salisbury, Special Branch wanted me to give evidence in a court case against a captured terrorist. I was required to report to Crime Sabotage offices in Salisbury, early on Monday 31st October, ready to give evidence in court. Beyond that, there was no detail about which terrorist or where he had been captured.

Although a little uncertain about whatever evidence I was being called upon to give in Salisbury the next week, I set that problem aside, enjoyed a leisurely hot bath and a shave and then a change into fresh uniform, before joining Terry for a couple of sundowner drinks at the motel. Having been instructed to be on a vehicle that was one of a small convoy leaving Makuti for Salisbury at 04:00hrs the next day, my stay at the motel was a relatively short one, because I certainly felt I needed a few hours' sleep.

The convoy left on time early the next morning, Saturday, 29th October 1966. By 08:00hrs I was in my room at Fife Avenue and by 09:00hrs I was at Support Unit HQ in Tomlinson Depot, where my appearance was a bit of a surprise to C/Insp. West and the others who were on various depot duties at that time. What then took place was a sort of extended de-briefing, as I took full advantage of C/Insp. West's invitation to tell him what I had encountered over the past three weeks. C/Insp. West listened and made notes, ordered a tray of tea, listened some more and made some more notes. He also asked several very shrewd questions about vehicles, weaponry, transport, radios and the present ration regime. He agreed that hauling fresh meat, vegetables and bread around, out and about anywhere was unsatisfactory and doubly so in the valley. It was quite clear to me by the end of that debrief that the string of WWII medal ribbons which decorated his uniform had not been earned doing office duties.

At the end of that debriefing, C/Insp. West sent me off duty for the weekend, with a reminder not to be late attending at the Crime Sabotage Unit's office the next Monday.

After three weeks away at Makuti, it was pleasant to have a weekend off back in Salisbury. The only minor problem was that Shorty, my personal batman, was still in Makuti. However, a friendly word with one of the other members and a little crossing of a batman's palm with silver soon sorted out that temporary problem. That particular Saturday, the rains took a day off, so I took myself to the Police Club's tennis courts, where a few sets of tennis kept my mind off other matters for a while at least and helped give me an appetite for my evening meal at Fife Hostel.

Having taken the day off on the Saturday, the rainy season made up for it the next day by delivering several days' ration of rain all in one go, so whiling the time away was a matter of listening to the radio, reading newspapers and books, playing a game or two of snooker and writing a probably long overdue letter to my mother and brother back in the UK. On the basis of accepting that a change is as good as a rest, my weekend back at Fife Hostel certainly saw me well rested, refreshed and ready to deliver whatever evidence it was that had been the cause of my rather sudden and unexpected summons back to Salisbury.

In tunic, shorts and cap, with leather boots, leggings, belt and brace all in meticulously polished shiny black leather, I duly presented myself at the offices of the Crime Sabotage Unit at 08:00hrs on Monday, 31st October 1966. There, the duty detail, who had, coincidentally, until a week before, been doing a spell of duty at Makuti, took one clearly surprised look at me in all my parade finery and promptly let fly with, "What the hell are you doing here, Woolley, especially all dressed up like a Christmas tree?"

It took about a quarter of an hour to sort matters out, but the long and the short of it was that there had been a cock-up somewhere which had resulted in me being called on to give evidence relating to a captured terrorist, instead of the correct detail involved in that particular action. The cock-up had allegedly been realised and a radio message had been sent to Makuti on the afternoon of 27th October. How that cancellation message had never been acted on was a mystery to everyone.

By 09:00hrs that day, I was back at Support Unit HQ, somewhat more appropriately dressed in blue and grey and equipped for a return to Makuti. The only problem was that there appeared to be no transport heading in that direction. The plus point of that morning was the advice that waiting for my collection at Depot Armoury was an FN rifle, BSAP No 105, which I was able to go and collect without delay. Once back at Support Unit HQ, an hour or so of telephoning around eventually revealed that radio branch had a vehicle headed to Chirundu, sometime later in the day. It was arranged that the vehicle would stop off at Tomlinson Depot to uplift me. That loose arrangement left me kicking my heels all through the rest of that morning and through the afternoon as well, until just on 17:15hrs, when the vehicle finally arrived. The radio technician driving it was pleased to have company on the long journey. As he drove us along, he explained that the vehicle was carrying radios and spares needed at Sinoia, Makuti and Chirundu and that he was not expected to get beyond Karoi or perhaps Makuti that night, so he had overnight gear with him. Our conversation soon established that neither of us had consumed anything since breakfast other than tea and biscuits, so we agreed that a break at Sinoia, just long enough to eat a decent evening meal, would be a wise move. In the end, we arrived at Makuti at 22:40hrs.

Having climbed somewhat stiffly out of the radio branch Land Rover, we were promptly challenged by the constable on night guard duty, which impressed both me and the radio technician. With our troop commander away, I put the radio technician into his vacant place, reported our arrival to the duty detail in the command caravan and took myself off to my own tent get some sleep.

The following morning, Tuesday, 1st November 1966, started off with me explaining to Terry Rowlandson, as acting troop commander, the story of my abortive trip to Salisbury and being issued with an FN rifle. We decided there was no point in trying to sort out who had got what wrong, so we just put the incident behind us and got on with more pressing needs. Terry brought me up to date with the latest information on the sections he had deployed into the valley while I had been away. After providing a decent breakfast for our overnight guest and seeing him safely on his way to Chirundu, Terry and I set off to search for a place in the nearby wilderness, in which we could establish a jungle alley to use for live fire weapons training for our own people and anyone else short on weapon handling and live firing. We needed a place that would be reasonably close to Makuti, not too far from a vehicle track, with scrub, trees and rocks, in a curving gulley, with or without a watercourse. Only with that kind of configuration could we guarantee that any stray shots would not fly free and cause danger for anybody around. Despite a whole lot of walking and searching, we found nothing suitable that day. What we did find was a sudden thunderstorm when we were a mile or more from our vehicle and without our ponchos, so it was a decidedly saturated pair of Patrol Officers who eventually climbed into our vehicle and dripped our soggy way back to Makuti.

Our search for a suitable live firing location had to be set aside the next day because of a need for a ration run to Karoi and then a round trip to Marongora and Rekometje to deliver the fresh rations to the sections operating in the valley. With Willie down in the valley and Terry needing to remain in Makuti, the ration-run fell to me. That round trip took almost the entire day. Apart from having to dig and push our vehicle out of the mud twice, the trip was uneventful, although, to me, it was remarkable to note how fast the valley's assorted foliage had grown, greened and thickened in the very few days I had been away from it.

The next day, Thursday, 3rd November 1966, Terry and I resumed our hunt for a safe site for our jungle alley. It was not until late in the morning and after quite a deal of walking, that we eventually found what we were looking for, a one hundred and fifty yard long and gently curving gulley within easy reach of a vehicle track and only a mile or so from Makuti Camp itself. Not wanting to waste time, we returned to Makuti, ate a hasty lunch, gathered a work party, an assortment of figure 11 targets and necessary tools and set off to construct our jungle alley, which work we managed to complete before darkness set in.

Early the following day, there were problems trying to contact Willie and Sgt Isaac, in charge of their respective sections at Rekometje and Marongora. Terry wanted a changeover of men to take place the next day, but, without some pre-arrangement, there was no guarantee that the sections now out on the ground would be all together and in their respective campsites when the relieving sections arrived. To make sure that the following day's intended change-overs would be smoothly achieved, Terry decided that I should carry out a vehicle patrol to both locations in order to verbally pass on the necessary information. I was also tasked to attempt to locate and ensure the integrity of the grave of a European hunter killed in the valley in the early 1900s. He had apparently been killed by a lion, not far from Mana Pools. His details and the location of his grave were on record in the Pioneer/Isolated Graves Register at Chirundu Police station, but the grave had not been checked and confirmed as having been visited and as being in good order for the last two years. Officer-in-Charge of Lomagundi District had detected that failure during the last annual inspection of the station and had instructed a visit to the gravesite should be made. Given the present operational situation in the valley, Insp. Baird, the present Member-in-Charge at Chirundu had asked if somebody out on patrol from Makuti could try to find the grave and make sure it was cleared, cleaned and made tidy, so that Chirundu's Pioneer Graves Register could be annotated and OC District's instructional comment from the annual inspection could be marked off as attended to.

Being convinced that we had a full day's activities ahead of us, I made sure that everyone coming out with me had eaten a good morning meal before we set off. With the thought that the Game Department's staff, African and European had years of experience of patrolling the valley, in vehicles and on foot, I called in at their HQ part-way down the escarpment road. A quick question or two brought to light that one of their African staff knew exactly where the grave was. My request for him to be allowed to come with us for the day was granted without hesitation, for which I was most grateful. The result of that piece of inter-departmental co-operation was that once the necessary messages had been passed to Willie and Sgt Isaac, we were able to make our way on towards Mana Pools to hunt for the missing grave. Thanks to our borrowed guide, we were able to save a great deal of time searching for the grave, which proved to be located somewhat distant from the map reference supplied by Chirundu Police Station. We re-erected the Pioneer Grave marker, which had been flattened, probably by elephant or rhino, cleared an amount of encroaching bush and re-stacked the scattered stones into a recognisably grave-shaped mound, before paying a moment of silent respect to a fallen, if distant, old comrade. With all the tasks satisfactorily accomplished, at about mid-afternoon we started on our return journey to Makuti, pausing on our way at Game Department HQ long enough to drop off our very helpful guide. The result was that we arrived at Makuti Camp almost on the dot of 17:00hrs, when I was able to stand down those who had been with me and send a radio message to Chirundu to allow the records to be updated with the visit we had made to that isolated grave.

Terry's arrangements for Saturday 5th November 1966, as discussed during the previous evening, started with me taking No. 1 Section out for a live firing training exercise once we were done with Stable Parade and breakfast. In calendar terms, it might have been the traditional Guy Fawkes's Day, with thoughts of fireworks galore, but on this occasion the rainy season decided that it should be a very damp squib of a day, because dawn brought a deluge. It was a real rainy season downpour that went on for a couple of hours and left the ground treacherous underfoot and the tarmac surface of the main road gently steaming. It also put about a foot of water into the gulley we had chosen for our jungle alley. To add to the fun of that day, when it was time to embus to drive to the jungle alley, Const. Efeti appeared to be behaving like a real stumblebum. He missed his footing completely when trying to get into the passenger compartment of the vehicle and had to be grabbed quickly by two of his companions to prevent him falling flat altogether. I put that down to the slick, slippery conditions.

Once out at the jungle alley, I explained to the section's members the purpose of the training, which was to test their powers of observation, reflexes and weapon-handling abilities. I told them that I would walk directly through the target area close behind them, one by one, telling them when to apply safety catches and when to ease them off. That "Safety Catch Off!"

order would be the only hint that they were approaching the point where one or other of the targets, to left, right, or ahead, at whatever height, would become visible. Once I was sure they had all understood the process, I ordered them to load a full magazine and apply safety catches. It was in attempting that that Const. Efeti dropped his loaded magazine.

He picked it up rapidly, but, when he appeared to intend to just slap the muddy magazine into place in the rifle, I bellowed an order for him to stop and strode over to check that the magazine was clean and clear of dirt, grit and water before he slotted it into place, let alone attempted to put a bullet up the spout. That intention brought me close to him, at which point I realised that he reeked of alcohol, was decidedly wobbly on his feet and totally unfit to be on duty, let alone in charge of any loaded firearm. I duly removed his firearm from him, told him to sit down and stay put in that one place and then got on with the training, which, thank heaven, passed off without any further untoward incident.

Back at Makuti before lunchtime, I confined Efeti to his tented quarters, reported verbally to Reg Crahart, now back from his local leave, what had gone on and then sat down long enough to write the brief but necessary report on the incident. I was in the middle of that activity when Terry arrived, to tell me that Chirundu Police Station had sent their thanks for finding the grave and, in view of that success, would we kindly try to find another one, not far from the Sapi River, if we had any patrols covering that area. Rampart, having of course been made aware of the latest request, had looked at the map, decided that nobody had checked that area of late and added that task to our workload once the changeover was completed. Terry and I had a quick word with Reg, who decided that it would be wise to carry out a combined sections patrol to tackle that particular task.

By 15:00hrs Terry and I had loaded our respective sections into their allotted vehicles and set off for the valley, to carry out the necessary changeover of personnel. I was not too happy at out late departure, but the general wisdom of the day then was that ambushes on security forces travelling at dusk was something not on the terrorist's agenda. As it was, we made the changeovers without any drama. Terry and his stick based at my old camp at Marongora and I took my team on to relieve our Rekometje Research Station team, being careful to make prior communication with the army unit not far away.

In the early hours of Sunday, 6th November 1966, about five minutes after I started my turn of night guard duty, there was a sudden and monumental flash of lighting, followed immediately by a great rumble of thunder that warned of a storm initiating almost directly overhead. Forewarned by nature's lightening display I rapidly rolled my sleeping bag and groundsheet, strapped them to the bottom of my pack and dismantled my poncho bivouac tent so that I could use it for its original purpose. Being pretty sure of what nature was about to hand to us, I quickly shoved my pack and shoulder webbing into our vehicle and made sure all the windows were tight shut. Within a few seconds of my completion of that hasty re-arrangement, the rain began, at first moderately heavy and shortly after that, very heavy indeed. It is meteorologically correct to state that thunderstorms, although having a general direction of travel, in reality move in circles, greater or lesser in diameter. That particular storm seemed to have taken a distinct fancy to the Research Station and the two small defence force base camps close by. It snapped, crackled, rumbled and popped out its considerable load of moisture all over and around us for a couple of hours before drifting slowly northwards towards the Zambezi River. When my hour of night guard duty was nearing its end, I woke Const. Phineas, whose turn it was for an hour of guard duty. His poncho bivouac was only a few yards from our vehicle, so in order to keep his sleeping place dry, I had him literally crawl out of his sleeping bag, clutching his rifle and come up under cover of my poncho. We then did a quickstep over to our vehicle, where I opened the front cab door, shoved my FN rifle in and then slid out from my briefly shared poncho and into the dry of the cab, where I settled down to get a few hours' sleep until dawn. Const. Phineas, at the end of his hour of guard duty, woke his relief and carried out the same sort of double-up under cover until he could slide back into his own piece of dry ground under his own bivouac, leaving his relief detail to wear my poncho while his bivvy stayed in place and intact. Towards dawn, with the storm just a far distant flicker and rumble and the rain almost stopped, I recovered my poncho from the guard and called the section on to dawn stand-to. A half-hour or so later, with full daylight established and one detail on guard, we set about resurrecting our very dead and soaking fire-pit so that we could eat a decent breakfast before heading out to rendezvous with Terry Rowlandson's section and then carry out our search for the indicated grave and make some checks on the game trails and tracks west of the Sapi River.

At 09:00hrs, on time and place, as arranged, our two sections met up and started on the drive towards the Sapi River. There was an early warning of what the day was going to be like, because the Rekometje River was flowing. Fortunately, not in full flood, but there were two channels to cross, both of which gave us trouble as our thoroughly unsuitable Ford vehicles with their tyres designed for tarmac only, sank and stuck in the softened sand. Eventually, we got both vehicles across and onto the track to the east of the river. At noon we were still battling the road conditions, made awful by the heavy overnight rain. When Terry's Ford, which was the front one of our two, bogged down again, we set to once more with axes and shovels, to dig and push it forward on to a drier stretch of track. With all hands to the effort and the vehicle static, I leaned my nice new FN rifle against the nearside of the vehicle so that I could use both hands to shove cut wood under the rear tyres. Two of my constables did the same with their .303 rifles. Terry, who had decided to drive the vehicle himself that day, tried to move the vehicle forward before we had finished shoving the cut wood under the wheels. To give him his due, Terry got the vehicle moving forward, but before any of the three of us could grab our firearms. The result was that the three weapons toppled over. The rear nearside wheel found a bit of unexpected purchase as it rode over all three, before Terry heard our yells for him to stop.

Interestingly, the two Lee-Enfields simply needed cleaning and clearing of the mud they had been pushed down into. Other than that, they suffered no harm. However, the bakelite fore stock of my FN was shattered as a result of the wheel going over it. Once I had cleaned it of its share of the roadway mud, I found that it was fortunately still functional. However, that was only with my face-veil wrapped around the barrel and gas-chamber, to prevent my left hand being burned when the weapon was fired. Some days later, the Depot Armourers put right the damage, but it cost me a £2:41 deduction from my next month's pay, which rankled.

That day, it took us eight hours to travel the thirty miles to the Sapi River, which we finally reached just before dusk. Then it became a race to get a defendable camp set up and a fire going before full dark. Having had nothing to eat since breakfast and with a long tough day behind us, we kept the cooking fire going later than we normally would have done, until everyone had been properly fed. After that, we went into night routine, with two guards on duty each hour, including both of us POs. For once, radio communication was good, so we were able to inform Chirundu of our overnight location, which they then relayed to Makuti for the information of both Rampart and our troop commander.

That night was a hot and very humid one. We all slept on top of our sleeping-bags rather than inside them. We were, of course, fully dressed, with weaponry close to hand. Once full daylight came, we were happy to see that Monday, 7th November 1966, looked like being a dry day. After the usual dawn stand-to and a refreshing breakfast, washed down with plenty of tea, we left six details to guard our camp and vehicles and set off on foot with the rest to check the game trails and search for the pioneer grave for Chirundu.

The grave we were hunting for we never did find. However, after some three hours or more of steady walking and searching, what we did discover was the very clear boot spoor of a terrorist group heading southwards. They were not following the main riverside game trail, but a lesser one that appeared to run parallel to the river somewhere near a mile from the actual watercourse. The indications were that the boot-prints, some of them of the well-known figure-of-eight configuration, were about 8-12 hours old. What was of some concern was that there appeared to be a lot of them. The discovery of those tracks created a need to get the information back to Makuti just as fast as we could. I was fairly certain of our map reference position. That I was able to work out, because a couple of back-bearings from prominent features on top of the escarpment and our known distance from the river gave me a good fix. However, there was one small problem. The VHF radio sets we had recently been issued with had screw-on aerials that were about fifteen inches long. The aerials were in the shape of a slim tapering cone. They were made of some kind of reinforced cardboard with the aerial wire spiralling up and around on the inside. They were, unfortunately, incredibly brittle. With us bending, ducking and weaving through thick bush, both aerials had caught on branches, promptly snapped and become useless as we discovered when we attempted to use them to report what we had found. Terry and I had a quick conversation and agreed that our proper course of action was to head back to the main game trail alongside the river and use it to move swiftly back to our camp, from where we could use one or other of the vehicle radios to pass on what we had found.

A couple of hours later, having moved along a little bit faster perhaps than was strictly safe, given the circumstances, we were back with the vehicles. For once, radio communication direct to Makuti was good. Terry was able to speak directly to Supt Holt who took down map co-ordinates of our find and left us to stand by while he and the control room staff plotted the information on to their map and decided what was to be the response, if any. A few minutes later, he came back on the air. The information we had passed back to Makuti had been relayed to the Crusader Unit at Rekometje. We were required to take no further action in respect of it. Additionally, Terry and his section were to return to Makuti, while my section was to re-occupy the camp at Marongora, from where we were once again to revert to day patrols and night ambushes in the vicinity of the dam, until we were otherwise instructed.

In the early afternoon we set of on the return journey towards the main tarmac road from Karoi to Chirundu, via a short stop-over at Rekometje, where we advised the Crusader unit of our intended movements and confirmed that they had been briefed on what we had found. Fortunately, apart from a couple of enforced stops and some digging and cutting of branches, we made good time and managed to get to the turn-off to Marongora Dam while there was still some daylight left. However, there we found a surprise, in the form of a Crusader vehicle out of Makuti, under command of Lt Dyke. With his army details he had Const. Mutandwa and two others and a set of instructions that he was to liaise with me and my stick for the purpose of carrying out a combined night roadblock on vehicles travelling south on the tarmac main road. The Crusader vehicle was carrying drums, poles and signs suitable for the task.

Terry Rowlandson listened to the story, shook his head in wonder and, by agreement, headed off with his section to continue to Makuti, leaving Lt Dyke and me to deal with the matter of asking details who had already done a full day's hard work to continue with another overnight activity. My request to Lt Dyke to know who had set up the arrangement brought up the name of our A Troop commander, who had, apparently, when asked for a police presence on the intended roadblock, promptly nominated me and my section. With night falling fast, it was no time for arguments. I sent my section off to occupy our established camp at the dam while I added myself and my patrol gear to the Crusader vehicle's existing load and set off along the road to Chirundu to find a suitable place to establish the roadblock.

We needed a bend that would prevent any oncoming vehicle seeing us so far ahead that it could stop and enable unauthorised passengers to clear off while still out of range of effective gunfire yet permit a safe braking distance for law-abiding drivers. It also had to have adequate tree cover close to the road wherein the army details not directly out on the road with the police details could be located out of sight, but well able to cover and support those details on the road. Eventually we found a suitable location and set about putting up the drums, poles and reflective "Police Ahead" signs. It was not as if we were difficult to see, because the only safe location for the army vehicle was within the roadblock area. It certainly created an interesting chicane effect.

It was at that point that it became apparent that nobody up at Makuti had even considered the need for torches as part of the necessary equipment for a night-time roadblock. Neither had they considered that there might be a need to deal with routine traffic offences that could just call for the issuing of routine paperwork to produce vehicle documents or drivers' licences, or even to issue an invitation to pay a deposit fine. It was perhaps unlikely that any such paperwork would be needed, but there was a fair chance that it might be. Lt Dyke of course had no idea about such things. He and his section had been tasked to support a police-controlled roadblock overnight and directed to use an army heavy vehicle to carry the equipment. Const. Mutandwa and his two companions could only advise what they had stated already. Nobody had discussed with them any matters of torches, routine Road Traffic Act paperwork or anything else.

With twelve hours or so of roadblock work ahead of us, it was decided that Lt Dyke and I would cover all twelve hours, with one constable and one army detail on four hour shifts with us. Two other army details were to stay awake, turn and turn about to back us up if needed, while everyone else was to try to get as much sleep as they could.

There had already been incidents when terrorists had secreted themselves within the back compartments of heavy goods vehicles travelling south from Chirundu. Some drivers had willingly assisted them; others had been coerced at the barrel of a gun. Opening the rear doors of any lorry possibly containing armed insurgents was an activity not to be undertaken lightly or carelessly, just in case. With the roadblock in position and radio communications having been established with Chirundu Police Station, we set about waiting for the first vehicles. That wait took nearly three hours. Eventually, two heavy vehicles appeared, travelling south, one close behind the other. Both drivers slowed their vehicles appropriately once they saw our warning signs at the roadside and stopped when signalled to do so. Both drivers were surprised by our presence, but quite happy and cheerfully cooperative when we asked to inspect the interiors of their wagons. We stood warily to one side as each driver loosened and then swung open one half of the twin rear doors, to allow us to see the loads inside. The first was packed so tight with huge cardboard boxes containing office supplies and paper that the possible presence of unauthorised passengers could be ruled out immediately. The second one was packed with a jumble of mining and agricultural machinery, with plenty of spaces for unwanted passengers. In the absence of torches, we were able to inspect their manifests and driving licences by the glow of their headlights, before sending them on their way.

From there on the flow of vehicles, large and small was slow, but steady enough to prevent the night from being a totally monotonous bore. The constables and army details rotated as each four hours passed, while Lt Dyke and I remained on duty, to lead the checking activity and to lead any firefight that might erupt if we disrupted the intended journeying of any armed insurgents, which, perhaps fortunately, we did not. Eventually, the night gave way to dawn, dawn turned to full day and Lt Dyke radioed to Chirundu, for relay to Makuti, that we were lifting the roadblock.

By 06:00hrs on Wednesday, 9th November 1966, I was back with my own section at Marongora Dam, having been on the go for an entire 24 hours and Lt Dyke and his vehicle full of men and equipment were well on their way back to Makuti. I was in the process of instructing Sgt Servester to take a foot patrol out to check round the dam, while I snatched a few hours' sleep, when I received a radio message that instructed me to get Const. Kisimis back to Makuti as fast as I could, because he had long leave starting this date and to re-ration for my African staff while I was there. I questioned whether they needed me to uplift my entire section for return to Makuti, or whether I should leave half to maintain our camp at the dam until I returned. I was promptly told to return to Makuti with my entire section, ready for redeployment. Obedient to those latest instructions, we again made safe our fireplace, packed our gear, loaded ourselves into our vehicle and started off on the steady grind of a drive up the escarpment. I must confess that that was one journey when the majestic grandeur of the scenery failed to impress me, for the simple reason that once our vehicle, with Const. Kisimis driving it, reached the smooth surface of the main road, I simply fell asleep until Sgt Servester nudged me into wakefulness as we approached Makuti Camp.

As was customary, I went directly from the car park area to the control caravan to book my section and I as being back in camp. Supt Holt took one look at me and commented, "You look shattered, Woolley. Are you going down ill or something?"

My reply of, "Just no sleep for 24 hours or so, Sir. Nothing more," brought a frown and a request to know what I had been up to. When I recounted the events of the past day or more, Supt Holt's face tightened. "You were not supposed to have been involved in that roadblock, Mr Woolley, but leave that to me. Meanwhile, I gather that your troop is a bit short on drivers, so you'll need to be your own driver for a while. Just to keep you up to date, E Troop will be replacing A Troop on the 15th of this month, until then, I want you and your section to remain based at Marongora Dam, doing day patrols and night ambushes just as you have been doing. Get yourself and your section provided with enough rations to cover those next few days and off you go, carefully. Understand?"

"Yes, Sir," I replied, saluted and left the caravan, to go in search of my troop commander or Terry or Willie. Reg was nowhere to be found, apparently out doing a farm patrol or some such. However, Terry was in camp. From him I discovered that Willie and No. 2 Section had left at crack of dawn that morning, to provide some presence at Rekometje as the Crusader Unit there had been withdrawn to go elsewhere. The problem was that they had, once again, left half their rations behind, which had only just been discovered. The solution was for me to again deliver their overlooked rations to them.

I called my section together, briefed them on our latest orders and gave them two hours of free time before we needed to set off for the valley once more. Shorty, my batman, produced tea, fresh clothing and a hot meal in rapid time, after which I felt just a bit more awake. At 14:00hrs, fully rationed, re-supplied and a little refreshed, I drove my section out of Makuti and headed north once more, driving perhaps just a little faster than I should have been, in order to get to Rekometje and back to Marongora Dam before full darkness set in. That night's ambush proved to be a very uncomfortable one, because it began to rain heavily before we reached our chosen spot and continued raining heavily all night long. By dawn we were all soaked through, despite huddling under our supposedly waterproof ponchos, the seams of which proved to be anything but waterproof. That rain was so heavy that it drowned out all the other noises of the jungle night that we had become used to. It was that bad that when I wrote up my notebook for the day I recorded, "Thursday 10th 05:00hrs. Ambush Floated," instead of Ambush Lifted. There was no way that any open fire was going to survive, so I made the decision to walk half my section at a time the couple of miles to the Game Department's stone-built, unoccupied, Gate House near the main road. There we lit a fire in the middle of the one room building so that a hot meal for everyone could be cooked.

It was during my walk with the second half of my section that 18182 Const. Simon suddenly gave a yelp and hopped to a one-legged halt. On careful examination, it was clear that one of his pair of issued boots, manufactured by "Mars" Footwear, had split right across the sole, allowing a thorn to penetrate his foot. In the next few days, several more pairs of boots failed in similar fashion, including my own. I made a report of the failings to Makuti, over the vehicle radio, via Chirundu. Reg Crahart's reply was to do the best we could and if necessary, to patrol barefooted.

For the next four days, with the rainy season well and truly set in, we remained based at Marongora Dam, carrying out our day patrols and night ambushes, without incident, until early on Sunday 13th, when we were ordered back to Makuti to prepare for the Troop changeover. On arrival back at Makuti, I tackled Reg Crahart over what was to be done about the cracked boots, which were basically unwearable and asked what Support Unit HQ had said about the problem. To my utter amazement, I discovered that he had not even informed our HQ, or anyone else, of the problem. His reason being that it could wait until we were back in Salisbury. I waited until Reg took himself off to the Makuti Motel for Sunday lunch and no doubt an ale or two, then I collected a few pairs of the failed boots and took myself off to speak with Supt Holt, because, in my view, it was essential that our HQ were made aware of the defect so that E Troop, equipped with boots identical to ours, might have an opportunity to bring with them at least some spare boots.

Supt Holt listened to what I had to say and then carefully inspected three pairs of the offending boots. Having taken a good look at them, he motioned me to sit down and reached for the telephone on his desk. A few minutes later he was speaking with C/Insp. West to whom he outlined the story of the failed boots and made two requests. The first being that before E Troop left Salisbury, a particularly careful inspection should be made of their Mars boots, to weed out any that might already be showing signs of cracking across the sole. The second request being that a few pairs of the commonest sizes of boots in use should be added to the supplies that E Troop carried with them on leaving Salisbury.

When his conversation with C/Insp. West was over, Supt Holt set down the phone handset on its cradle and looked directly at me. "Usually," he said, with some emphasis, "I disapprove of anyone carrying tales behind the back of a senior detail to report to a more senior person about some fancied misbehaviour or failure." Having said that, he paused for a long moment before continuing, "However, in this case, I am prepared to make an exception, which is why I let you hear the conversation I have just had with C/Insp. West. I shall also need to have a word with SO Crahart about this, which will not do anything to help with what appears to be something of an atmosphere between the two of you, if I may put it like that?"

"We do appear to have different opinions about some things, Sir," I agreed.

Supt Holt acknowledged that remark with an inclination of his head. "Just try to keep a lid on it, please, at least until the day after tomorrow, when you should be out of here and on your way back to Salisbury. Do you think you can manage that?"

"I'll do my very best to, Sir," I assured him.

"Good. Let's leave it there."

That of course was just what we did.

Late in the afternoon, Terry, Willie and I decided it would be a good idea to go for a drink at the motel, as a sundowner before evening meal. When we walked into the motel, we noticed Reg Crahart seated at a table on the veranda, deep in conversation with a lady of about his own age. Anxious not to intrude into his privacy, we chose a table well away from the conversing pair and sat back to enjoy our chosen beverages. The main topic of conversation was our individual experiences during our time at Makuti. We were all certain that this would not be the last time we would find ourselves operating in this part of the country and equally certain that we had a whole lot to learn as far as training, tactics, uniforms and weaponry were concerned. After a relaxing hour or more, with a couple of ales inside us, we left the motel, noting as we did that Reg and his companion were no longer at their table. Neither was Reg anywhere to be found when we returned to Makuti Camp.

Just after lunchtime on Monday, 14th November 1966, Section Officer Garland arrived at Makuti, in company with C/Insp. West and the routine of changeover commenced. A couple of hours later, in pouring rain, the main body of E Troop personnel arrived. By the time we had checked through the necessary inventories and handed over all the equipment, ammunition and supplies that needed to remain at Makuti, it was late in the day. It was also still pouring with rain, so it was decided that we would remain at Makuti overnight and leave in the morning. The personnel for the two troops set about squeezing into tented accommodation meant for just one troop, which proved to be an interesting exercise. Even the cabs of assorted vehicles became temporary sleeping quarters.

At 09:15hrs the next day, Tuesday, 15th November 1966, A Troop personnel, all in high spirits at the thought of Salisbury and a few days of time off, boarded our vehicles and followed closely behind as Reg Crahart led our convoy out of camp and southwards. On our way, we exchanged a few ribald words with the Brown Boots manning the roadblock and then filtered, vehicle by vehicle, through the tsetse fly control shed. After that, it was just steady driving, in convoy, with comfort breaks at Karoi and Sinoia. The rain remained steady as the miles rolled by, until we rolled into Tomlinson Depot at 15:20hrs. There we parked our vehicles neatly in the carpark, lodged our weaponry into the armoury and paraded formally for dismissal and a whole week of time off for everyone.

It was only part of a conversation in the bar at Fife Avenue Hostel, later in the evening that reminded me that the first anniversary of UDI, on 11th November 1966, had come and gone without any of us in A Troop even realising or mentioning it.

With the prospect of a whole week of free time ahead of me, there were three things that needed to be attended to immediately. The first was to provide Shorty with funds for bus-fares to and from his home in Chibi, so that he too could have a few days off. The second was to fill out and submit my claim for Travel and Subsistence Allowance, at 17/6d per day, for the time I had been away. The third was to sit down and write a letter to mother and brother in the UK, to let them know something of my activities since the last time I wrote, some several weeks back. Mothers naturally worry about their offspring, even if they have become adults and mine was no exception. The correspondence waiting in my postal pigeon-hole was guaranteed to contain at least one letter from my mother. If as did happen, my time away from Salisbury was lengthy and the silence from me long, there were likely to be comments like "Urgent!" written in large red letters above my address. At least I had a mother who cared about her youngest offspring, even if he was more than 5,000 miles away from home.

Nora Valley Training
Left to right: Sergeants Servester, Watson, Isaac

Sikombela and Beyond

On Tuesday, 22nd November 1966, at 09:00hrs, A Troop paraded for duty at Tomlinson Depot, with all of us, at whatever rank, wondering what duties might be waiting for us. We three Patrol Officers got there deliberately somewhat early, in the fond hope that perhaps SO Crahart had received some early indication of our next tasking, wherever. We might as well not have hurried, because there was no time to ask Reg about it, as he arrived barely in time to avoid being late on parade.

As it turned out, all that was required of us, until further notice as C/Insp. West eventually advised us, was to undertake routine depot duties, which comprised of lecture and parade-ground work, as we all attempted to improve our own skills and those of our junior ranks, in the intricacies of map references, compass bearings, back-bearings, stripping, cleaning and re-assembling our assortment of weapons and, not least of all, how to get the best brightly bulled surface onto our proudly-worn black leather-work, which distinguished us from our brown-leather clad standard duty uniformed colleagues. We spent many hours learning and teaching the current phonetic alphabet and proper radio procedures so that every member of our troop was at least capable, in a basic form, of transmitting and receiving messages over the somewhat improved portable VHF radio sets that were slowly trickling into our possession. The best improvement on those was that the fragile conical aerials of moulded cardboard with wire aerial inside, had been replaced with half-inch wide aerials of solid, but flexible metal. Another plus point was that there were FN rifles issued to Reg, Willie and Terry.

One of our more enjoyable days involved learning to work with "top-cover" provided by our Police Reserve Air Wing members. Such pieces of directional advice to assorted pilots of, "left a bit more!" seldom worked well. It took us all a while to get the hang of, "Change course ten degrees to starboard," or whichever the correct line was to bring the aircraft overhead. A great part of those training days was activities by trial and error. Some of the errors we learned very quickly not to repeat, such as not to pitch signal flares for the aircraft upwind of ourselves. Choking on dense orange smoke distracted somewhat from paying any attention as to whether the air-wing aircraft had homed in on the flare and was passing directly overhead as intended, or not.

It was also a welcome period of not having to worry about rationing and cooking for ourselves, because our three meals a day were all ready-made and waiting for us at the set mealtimes when the Fife Hostel Dining Room was open. All that was needed of us at mealtimes was to take our place in whatever length of queue existed, then present ourselves at the service counter, indicate our choice from the day's menu to the counter staff and cart our generously laden plates to the nearest vacant place at one of the refectory-type tables, where we could plant ourselves onto a bench-style seat and get munching. Us "black-boots" had little time for the many Town Police and Traffic Section members who frequently bemoaned the lack of variety on the menu, or that the vegetables had been overcooked. We invited them, sometimes politely, to join us for a few weeks of cooking for themselves in mess-tins over wood fires. Our stout defence of the cooks and serving staff did not go unnoticed by the catering workers who quite often made sure that those of us who wore black leather received a little more than our fair share of the breakfast eggs and bacon and some of the more tasty and appetizing main dishes and desserts at lunch and evening meals.

Those days based in Salisbury were only slightly marred by our troop commander's persistent snide remarks about colonial police activities and the rank I had carried when in Nyasaland. I was informed, helpfully or unhelpfully, that when I was out of earshot, Reg frequently referred to me, somewhat sarcastically, as "The Bwana." For my part, I simply tried to stay as distant from him as daily activities allowed.

It was perhaps no great surprise to me when C/Insp. West called me in to his office mid-afternoon on Thursday, 1st December 1966, when SO Crahart was somehow absent from Tomlinson Depot, for whatever reason, to inform me that our troop commander had nominated me and my section for a month-long tour of duty at Sikombela Restriction Centre in the Midlands Province not far from QueQue. We were to be given 24 hours off and were required to parade the next evening at 20:00hrs, all packed up and kitted out for a month at Sikombela, perhaps better known as "Wha-Wha." We were to travel to QueQue on the overnight train to Bulawayo. Detailed route instructions would be made available when we were ready to leave for Salisbury Railway Station next evening at 20:00hrs. The added piece of information that it was in order for me to take my batman along for the month did little to ease the irritation which I felt on behalf of my section who were, to my mind being picked to be away over Christmas and the New Year, because of SO Crahart's dislike of me.

As quickly as I could, I called my section together, briefed them on our latest tasking and expressed my regrets that they would be out in the bush, away from friends and families over Christmas. I was grateful for the comment from the ever-cheerful Const. Mapfumo, who promptly said, "It is okay, Ishe. We shall have free food while we are away. The ones who stay here will have to pay for theirs!" Noting the nods of agreement from others, I felt at least a little more cheerful as I left Support Unit HQ and headed for Fife Avenue Hostel, to start making the necessary preparations for another month away.

By the time that I settled back into my allotted seat on the overnight train to Bulawayo the next evening, I was at least a lot better informed about what I was headed into for the next few weeks. Wha-Wha Restriction Camp was, to the activists of the Shona/Kalanga element who formed the Zimbabwe African National Union, (ZANU) what Gonakudzingwa Restriction Camp was to the Ndebele activists who were members of the Zimbabwe African People's Union (ZAPU). Both camps were for those of political bent who had not been convicted of any offence on the statute book, but who were, in the opinion of the government, likely to stir up trouble in political terms, whether for the Europeans of the nation, or for their political opponents in tribal loyalty terms.

The Sikombela Restriction Camp was located some 50 or so miles northwest of QueQue (now KweKwe) in Midlands Province. It was there that the senior ZANU figures, such as Ndabaninge Sithole, leader of ZANU until overthrown by the Mugabe element, Mugabe himself and his supporters, such as Simon Muzenda, Edgar Tekere, Enos Nkala and Edson Zvobgo, were all at one time or another after 1964, sent to in order to supposedly get them out of the way. In many ways, lumping them all together with plenty of time on their hands and nothing much to do, simply guaranteed that they would get their heads together to plot, plan and better arrange the downfall of the white minority government of Rhodesia.

That was how it was that those I have listed above were all participants in the formulation of what later became known as The Sikombela Declaration, which was a lengthy dossier outlining and indeed ratifying the strategy for an all-out armed war of independence. The fact that there was not a single Ndebele tribesman involved in formulating that dossier spoke volumes about the attitude of ZANU towards their ZAPU counterparts. The purpose behind ZANU in forming ZANLA, the Zimbabwe African National Liberation Army was twofold, not just singleton. Firstly, it was to get rid of the white government and "recover the land for our people." Secondly, to take revenge upon the Madzviti, (meaning Pestilence) which was how most Shona/Kalanga people still regarded the Ndebele, for the many years of annual slaughter, cattle raiding and slave-taking that the Ndebele Impis inflicted upon their neighbours prior to the arrival of the Pioneer Column in 1890. As became known in later years, the dossier was hidden well away from the irregular searches of the barrack blocks that uniformed and Support Unit police personnel carried out. The dossier was hidden from prying eyes within an anthill, where it remained undiscovered by the authorities even after Sikombela was closed a year or more after our stint there, when the inmates were moved to the Remand Prison in Salisbury.

It is probably appropriate at this point in my narrative, to record that it took some three decades after its closure and twenty-six years after Independence for Zimbabwe, for the ZANU Government to remember, in 2006, that Sikombela had existed, had played a significant part in the then struggle for independence and declare that location a National Monument designated as being of significant historical value.

That of course was still to be in future years as our train slowed and stopped, somewhere close to midnight, at QueQue Railway Station. As arranged, we were met there by "Chimp" Webster and the sergeant of his section, in one of the force's Ford 4x4s. Even now I recall vividly the blazing thunderstorm and teeming rain which greeted us on our arrival. That rainfall seemed to intensify as we headed for Sikombela. Chimp drove our vehicle in what I can only describe as something of an over-enthusiastic hurry, given the fact that we were on a dirt road, which was fast turning into a mudslide. When Chimp's driving put the vehicle somewhat seriously canted over onto two wheels for a second time going around one of the many bends, I felt it necessary to point out to him that if he turned us over, his chances of making the mid-morning train to Salisbury would vanish and heaven alone knows when he would get away, back to civilisation and Fife Hostel. Whether or not my remarks got through, I know not, but after that Chimp managed to keep all four wheels of our vehicle on the road until we reached our destination, which was a District Commissioner's Rest House, a mile or so from Sikombela Restriction Camp itself. By kind permission of the DC, the guarding section was permitted the use of the brick-built and corrugated-iron roofed Rest Camp, which made the stay at Sikombela a whole lot more comfortable than if we had been under canvas. There were proper washrooms, toilets and a kitchen available to us, which were much appreciated. It did not take long for Chimp and me to complete the essential hand-over documentation and make the necessary arrangements for my section to assume guard duties at the camp itself as of 06:00hrs that morning. Fortunately, it was possible, with me adding myself to the numbers available, to work a pattern of duty of eight hours on and sixteen off.

Having got the basics of changeover completed, we all settled where we could to grab a few hours of sleep before setting off for the 06:00hrs changeover and my first actual sight of the restriction camp itself. Pleasingly, the rain had eased while we were sleeping, so my first view of the fenced enclosure was in bright, clear sunlight. The camp itself, within the perimeter fence, consisted of six distinct rectangular wooden barrack-type huts, set upon concrete bases, each measuring approximately five yards by nine yards in size. The six barracks huts were set in two rows of three about 40 yards apart, with about 15 yards between the two rows. Within the fenced area were other buildings that functioned as washrooms, toilets and a kitchen and canteen building. Outside of the fenced area, by the gate there was a tent for the use of the guards who happened to be on duty. Having done one tour at Gonakudzingwa, there was a certain familiarity about what I found myself looking at as we uplifted Chimp's constables, replaced them with mine and Chimp and I made a quick circuit of the place, during which he voiced the opinion that where the ZAPU restrictees at Gonakudzingwa were openly hostile, this lot were sullen and contemptuous of us on the outside of the wire. By the time I eventually finished my one and only tour of duty at

Sikombela a few weeks later, I felt I had no reason to dispute Chimp's cautionary observations.

With the changeover completed and that brief introductory tour around, it was time to get Chimp and his men back to the rest camp and then to drive them to QueQue in time to catch the Salisbury train, all of which was accomplished in good time and in cheerful spirits. Driving back towards Sikombela, I was reminded just how wild and untamed the local countryside was by the sudden effort of an ostrich to first race alongside and then attempt to cross the road in front of me. Not wishing to arrive at Sikombela with a set of feathers decorating the bonnet, I eased my foot off the accelerator and let the hurrying bird go safely on its way.

Of the next month at Sikombela, there is little to interest any reader of this narrative, except for mention of one incident which occurred half-way through our stay there. I was on guard duty, in the middle of morning shift which ran from 06:00 to 14:00hrs. The weather was hot and dry. I was up to date on patrol circuits of the camp and had settled down seated on a metal and canvas folding type of camp chair, tilted back slightly against a tree by our tent at the gate, reading my way through a typical wild west of America cowboy book. I was comfortable, relaxed, silent and motionless, which was just as well, because out of the corner of my left eye I sensed as much as saw a flicker of movement. The nature of that movement was unmistakable. It froze me into total stillness, because it was the flickering tongue of a snake, testing the air around it.

In the next moments, which seemed like a lifetime to me, the snake's head, swaying from side to side, came into my vision, a few inches left of my own head. Its mouth was shut, its tongue sliding in and out, tasting, analyzing. The egg-shaped head, bright green top and lighter green lower part, with large round eyes, identified it as a boomslang, or tree-snake in Afrikaans and local languages. Without any hint of worry, haste or concern, the snake let more of its light weight descend upon my left shoulder, before wrapping itself around my left bicep and then my left forearm. Its tongue tested the air over my left hand and investigated the book held open between my still hands. Satisfied there was no threat there, it slid downwards, on to my blue riot trousers, curled around my left calf and down onto the ground. Once all of its approximately 5' length was at ground level, it slithered away, quite unhurriedly, into the brush alongside the fenced camp, at which point I brought all four feet of my camp chair on to the ground and started breathing again. Boomslangs are not normally aggressive unless threatened. They are back fanged, but their venom, although slow to take effect, is highly toxic, causing massive internal bleeding, which is usually fatal, despite hospital treatment.

My own wariness of snakes came from an encounter in Nyasaland, when I was still very much a learner of African ways and habits. On that occasion, I was called to a kraal to deal with an allegedly rabid dog. At the village, armed with my police issue single-shot greener shotgun, there appeared to be no immediate sign of any of the several local village dogs within sight behaving anything other than normally. At my constable's interpretation of my question as to where the allegedly rabid dog was, the kraalhead thought for a moment, looked around, carefully selected one large male dog sitting peaceably under a nearby tree and stated "Uyu!" meaning, "That one!" Thinking that the dog in question did not look very rabid to me, but accepting the kraalhead's indication as accurate, I duly shot and killed the dog which he had pointed to, avoiding damaging its head. I stepped toward the dead dog, levered open the breach of the shotgun, to eject the spent round, picked that up and closed the breach mechanism on the empty chamber. After all, I saw no need to re-load, having done the job I was sent out to do. Had I been longer in Africa and more aware of the customary politeness of always trying to provide a visitor with a positive answer to any question, I might have avoided what followed. While I was standing holding an empty weapon, the genuinely rabid dog appeared and headed straight for me. I brained it with the butt of the empty Greener shotgun, but not before it had bitten me in the leg. That episode resulted in me having to have a whole session of eleven quite painful injections of anti-rabies serum and learning another morsel of local custom.

It also created a little bother for my then Provincial Commanding Officer, Ass. Comm. John Le Mesurier. Perhaps because of my involvement in Cadet Corps at Grammar School, I seemed to be able to manage better than most on any formal parade ground, which fact had been noted by my OC Province, who had decided that I was to be parade commander for the then looming Queen's Birthday Parade. That meant full Sam Browne Belt and of course, carrying sword and scabbard. Customarily, the eleven necessary daily injections for rabies serum were placed in a circle around one's bellybutton.

Twenty-four hours after the first injection, readying for a parade rehearsal, I found I simply could not take the pain created by the tightness and weight of leatherwork, sword and scabbard, directly on top of the injected spot. When Mr Le Mesurier discovered I was about to drop out of the parade, he promptly stepped in to sort it out. I believe it is likely that I am still the only person who has ever had his rabies serum jabs stuck in turn into both buttocks, both thighs and his left arm until the sequence was completed, the day before Queen's Birthday Parade, which I duly commanded, very much, I am pleased to recall, to the approval of OC Province. For those sharp-eyed readers who have spotted that my right arm was left free of its fair share of the jabs, that was to guarantee that my ability to apply the several movements of sword-drill, required for the parade, were not threatened by a stiffened and painful right bicep.

However, picking up on why I was wary of any encounter with snakes, which I mentioned half a page back, that encounter with the anti-rabies serum carried with it a stricture from the doctors that in future I should avoid falling victim to any snake-bite, for the simple reason that were I to need any anti-venin injection to counter a snake-bite, that would send me into instant anaphylactic shock, which I would be unlikely to survive unless I was in a hospital with fully trained staff and essential equipment close to hand.

Apart from that all-too-close encounter with a very venomous snake, a couple of snap searches of the barrack blocks and a weekly ration run to QueQue, there was little or nothing to break the routine boredom of restriction camp guard duty. When 8th December 1966 arrived, any pleasure I might have felt at having completed two whole years in the BSAP simply vanished at the thought of another day at Wha-Wha and in wondering just how long I and my section were going to be stuck there. Readers can perhaps judge the level of boredom suffered by all of us, from the fact that we really did welcome the occasional heavy downpour of rain, with or without the thunder and lightning which sometimes came with it. Even Christmas and the New Year passed by as just other days on the calendar. Finally, on 3rd January 1967, there came the welcome news that we were to be replaced, the very next evening, by elements of D Troop. When I broke that news to my section, there were smiles on all faces and much clapping of hands all round.

It was clear that they disliked being on duty at Wha-Wha just as much as I did.

On our arrival back in Salisbury Railway Station, on time, early on the morning of 5th January 1967, it did not take long to discover that there appeared to be no transport of any kind waiting to carry us to Tomlinson Depot. A quick, short walk to Mashonaland Provincial HQ, fairly close the railway station and a phone call that put me in touch with C/Insp. West, brought to light that our troop commander was supposed to have organized the transport for us. The lack of transport waiting for us was put right without too much delay by C/Insp. West, so by mid-morning we were back at Support Unit HQ at Tomlinson Depot. There, I discovered, to my amazement, from C/Insp. West, that the remainder of A Troop had left depot the day before, called urgently back to Makuti for another stint of counter-insurgency activities in the Zambezi Valley and that SO Crahart had asked for me and my section to be transported to Makuti as soon as possible. Having delivered that much information to me and perhaps noted the incredulous expression on my face, C/Insp. West leaned back somewhat in his chair, and said, with just the trace of a smile on his face, "No need to say it, Mr Woolley. The OC and I have talked this one over and decided that you and your section have earned a few days off after your month or more down at Sikombela. You are all stood down as of now, for a four-day break. Brief your section to be available back here after that time off at 08:00hrs on the 10th January all kitted out and ready to climb aboard whatever transport happens to be heading to Makuti or Chirundu on that day. Does that make you feel better?"

"Very much better indeed, Sir," was my relieved reply. "My grateful thanks to you both for amending SO Crahart's orders for us." It was with a decided sense of relief that I imparted our latest orders to Sgt Servester and the rest of my section and took myself off to Fife Avenue Hostel, to catch up with Shorty, my batman, who we had dropped off there earlier, in order to warn him of the latest orders and departure date and time.

Five days later, in the middle of the afternoon, amid a thunderstorm and torrential rain, my section and I arrived once more at Makuti camp, where I discovered that SO Crahart was not present. At that piece of information, I took myself off to the command caravan, where I duly reported my presence to Rampart, Supt Holt, who read very carefully through my route instructions, waved me to sit in a spare chair and said, somewhat wearily, "I have enough problems, Woolley, without having to worry about warfare between you and your troop commander, who, when last I spoke to him, was intent on putting you on a charge for being AWOL, because he said that he left orders for you to be here some days ago." He paused, tapped my route instructions and went on, with a somewhat concerned shake of his head. "These papers tell me a different story." He paused for a long moment, staring at my route instructions and clearly doing some thinking. "Right," he said, breaking the thoughtful silence, "You and your section get yourselves sorted out to bed down for an early night here, because I want you up and about and on your way to Marongora Dam at first light. We have not had the manpower to cover that area for a while. I'll leave the day-by-day details to you as I know you and your section have been based down there before. Make it up from OPs (Observation Posts) day patrols for spoor and some night ambushes. No need for vehicles. I'll arrange transport to get you down there. Take rations for two weeks, but I shall try to get you back here in about ten days. Meanwhile, I'll have a word with Crahart. I believe I know where I can find him."

At first light the next day, it was a couple of army vehicles that provided transport for us, setting us down at my request where the track to Marongora Dam joined the road to Rekometje Research Station. The valley was lush, green and muddy after the recent heavy downpours and the noise of vehicles grinding their way in low gear right to the dam would have been heard miles away, potentially by unfriendly elements. That advantage was one I did not intend the opposition to gain. Once within sight of the dam, I headed my section in a careful broad circuit of the location, checking every game trail for signs of human footfall, of which we found none, although signs of wild-life, greater and lesser, were abundant. With that safety sweep completed, I steered my section back towards the same thicket from which we had operated previously. Again, that re-occupation was not a matter of just blundering in, but one of careful and wary inspection, yard by yard, because there had been a couple of previous episodes of ZANLA elements booby-trapping previously used but empty defence-force bush camps, hoping to create casualties if they were re-occupied. Fortunately, our previous position appeared to be just as we had left it, with no nasty surprises awaiting us.

Although we were without any vehicle with a radio in it, we did have our latest make of mobile VHF set, with its much-improved flexible aerial, which, when conditions were decent, at least allowed us some communication with Chirundu Police Station and, quite often, directly with Makuti Camp itself.

For the next week or more I and my section carried out the duties we had been assigned to, without any great excitements arising. That is not to say that the patrol was without incident or interest. Completing one of our sweeps around the damn, late one afternoon, we encountered a huge bull hippo demarcating his territory by defecating generously and distributing his faeces broadly by some energetic fanning of his tail, as was usual for his kind. On another day, Sgt Servester, on point, very nearly triggered a shot at a rustling in the grass close by him, which turned out to be the wiggling of a large and adventurous catfish (barble) seeking a new watercourse home. A quick smack from the butt of his .303 rifle provided the sergeant with an unexpected but welcome addition to his dry rations. As for those dry rations, one of the most difficult problems was that of cooking a hot meal, without creating rising columns of thick smoke which might be seen, or even smelled, from miles away. It was one of those issues which clearly separated those of my section who were village-raised from those who had been township bred. Smokey fires inside a kitchen hut were intolerable, so village children learned at an early age which smoke-free wood to burn, while township-dwellers had the availability of electricity, which most of them used the light from to cook by. That difference resulted in the town-raised members of the section, like me, having to clamber up a steep learning curve over the issue. Eventually, as the insurgency continued, the routine issue of GAZ cookers resolved that particularly troublesome problem; but in those early days, we learned such niceties the hard way. Fortunately, my own section was never a victim of an attack from insurgents who had seen and zeroed in on smoke rising from a security forces campfire.

One of the major problems during that patrol became that of trying to stay dry. We carried our waterproof capes, habitually referred to as "Ponchos" which, once set up with four or six pegs, two vertical sticks and a few feet of twine, doubled as night-time bivvies. That improvised tent provided just sufficient roughly dry space for a sleeping bag in my case, or a bedroll in the case of the rest of my section. Getting to sleep, fully dressed, with boots on, rifle by my side and using my 44 webbing pack as a pillow, with my face-veil over my bush hat and tucked firmly into my buttoned-up grey shirt to keep the mosquitoes off, was a skill not easy to master at first.

The dodgy days were those when it was teeming with rain as dusk descended and a personal decision had to be made to remove the cape from around our shoulders in order to turn it into an overnight bivvy and risk getting soaked by the heavy rain in the process, or to simply hunker down wearing the cape, with our backs to a tree and see the night through by dozing as best we could in between guard-duty turns. I made it clear that it was a personal and individual decision as and when needed, for each section member to make for themselves. That was a decision which worked well. When the weather was fine and the stars were bright, we needed no shelter, so just rolled out our sleeping bags and bedrolls and slept in the open, with weaponry ready for instant use if needed.

After eight days out, just after breakfast in the early morning, the sound of a motor-vehicle approaching the dam on the well-used track brought us all to our feet. I had deliberately chosen a campsite well away from that track, but one from which we could easily monitor both that rough track and which gave us a good broad view of much of the dam and shoreline. We watched with interest as an RLI Land Rover came into view and stopped where the track virtually ended, just where tree and bush growth did the same. The half-dozen camouflaged occupants fanned out and took up defensive positions, which was commendable, but then simply remained there. It was clear they had no webbing and packs with them, which suggested they were on a day mission only. Whatever they were about, it was clear that they needed to know we were operating in the vicinity at and around the dam and we needed to know why they were there. Sgt Servester and I stepped away from our screening bushes and walked down towards the water's edge, from where we gave them a wave and a shout. There was little fear that they would think we were terrorists, because our riot gear of grey shirts and blue pants was very easily distinguishable. With visual contact safely made, Sgt Servester and I walked around the water's edge until we were at their location. The corporal in charge had verbal instructions for us which were simple enough. We were to walk to the main track, wait for the incoming section, which would be with us by mid-morning and return to Makuti in the relieving section's transport. Having delivered their message, the RLI unit boarded their vehicle and drove back the way they had come, while Sgt Servester and I returned to our temporary camp, informed the rest our section what was about and got ready to break camp. With happy smiles on our faces, it did not take us long to make our fireplace safe, pack and don our 44 webbing and set off to cover the short distance to our appointed rendezvous, where we set ourselves down out of sight to await the appearance of the relieving section.

A couple of hours after we had settled out of sight close to the junction that was our rendezvous point, we heard the noise of vehicles approaching and then watched as two police Land Rovers came into sight. Breaking cover, I moved my section out onto the track and into plain view, fully expecting to see either PO Rowlands or Wielopolski leading the incoming section. To my surprise, it was Reg Crahart who stepped out from behind the wheel of the first of the two vehicles. My surprise must have showed, because, before I could ask the obvious question, Reg said, somewhat sourly, "Don't ask." Then he promptly answered the unasked question by continuing, "Willy's down with a Gyppo gut and a bit of a fever and Terry's already out, so I'm down here for the next week or so. Anything doing locally that I need to know about? By the way, I'll need your maps of the area. They've run out of them at Makuti, so I have none with me."

While Reg sorted himself out and donned his webbing and our two sections exchanged the usual light-hearted banter common between sections at hand-over times, I extracted my map-case from my webbing, orientated the most local map and pin-pointed the location of the rendezvous site and our recent camp for the past week or more for Reg's benefit, before handing the maps and their case over to him. My verbal briefing that the area appeared quiet seemed to please him. In return, Reg advised me that the whole valley appeared quiet, with no incursions having been reported for a week or more.

With Reg and his section settled into patrol order and my section settled into the two vehicles, with me driving the one and Const. Kisimis driving the other, we waved our final farewells and parted company. The drive to the tarmac of the Great North Road did not take long and the climb up the escarpment to Makuti Camp went without hitch. At Makuti Base Camp, I stacked my patrol webbing in the tent allotted to me, commiserated with Willie Wielopolski over his upset insides and went off to report the completed changeover to Rampart and find out what he had in store for me and my section and when. Possibly as befitted a period of quiet, Rampart had no immediate patrol work for us to do down in the valley. All he had for us was to take over the routine camp guard duties and hold ourselves ready should there be, as he put it, any eventualities.

Three days later, the eventuality cropped up, but hardly in the fashion any of us would have expected. Willie was still not fully recovered from his upset stomach and bit of a fever, so it was no surprise when I was summoned to the control caravan where I learned from Rampart that the latest intelligence reports from Special Branch had indicated that a crossing had occurred a few days before. The spoor of the group had been located close to the Zambezi, just a few miles east of Chirundu. Past patterns of behaviour suggested that the group, numbering about 24, were unlikely to remain together. They were far more likely to scatter into smaller groups to avoid detection. Rampart went on to say that he had attempted to get that information through to SO Crahart and his section based at Marongora Dam, but, for whatever reason, attempts to make radio contact from both Makuti and from Chirundu, had not succeeded. Rampart put that down solely to radio problems and nothing more dreadful. However, he wanted me to make a careful visit to Marongora Dam, locate Reg and his section and brief them on the latest incursion and the need to concentrate on ambush work rather than patrols, until the terrorists were accounted for. He repeated his quiet word of warning for me to go carefully and sent me off to gather my section and get under way.

Word of what we were about circulated rapidly among the African members of A Troop who were in camp. Our very able troop sergeant, Isaac, listened in as I briefed my section on the task ahead. He promptly requested that he should be allowed to change places with Sgt Servester, because it was too long since he'd had any patrol work to do. With that change made, my section's members and I loaded ourselves into our two Land Rovers and set off. By noon we were as close to the dam as I judged wise for vehicular travel, so it became a matter of driving our vehicles just out of sight of the road, leaving four details to guard them and starting off on our approach to the dam on foot in a carefully spaced foot patrol order. A little over an hour of wary walking brought us within sight of my section's campsite of a few days before. A cautious approach to it indicated no signs of human presence or activity. Reg and his section had clearly set up camp elsewhere.

As we all stood within the cover of the bushes, looking out and wondering, it was the sharp eyes of Const. Phineas which came to our aid. His low call of "Ishe, smoke!" and his pointing arm steered our attention. Given what we knew of the latest incursion, it was with a great deal of care that we made our way around the dam until we were able to make safe contact with our A Troop comrades. Apart from the fact that their chosen campsite was far closer to the vehicular access track than I would ever have chosen, the other point of concern was that SO Reg Crahart simply was not there. A quick question brought to light the startling information that Reg had been collected, the day after he and his section had set up their patrol camp, by a European lady in a civilian Land Rover. According to his section sergeant, he had instructed his section to remain in camp where they were, carrying out observations of the dam, until he returned in a few days. As I listened to that quite incredible story, my eyes met those of Sgt Isaac, who just shook his head and muttered, "His brain is no good!" To my mind, that was the understatement of the year. A quick check revealed that the section's VHF radio was present, but simply switched off.

Having passed on the latest information from Rampart and leaving Reg Crahart's instructions to his section to stand, I steered my own section, possibly a little faster than wisdom dictated, back to our vehicles and got on the airwaves to speak briefly with Chirundu. My words were carefully chosen in asking them to inform Rampart that I had briefed the Marongora section and was on my way back to Makuti. On the journey back, Sgt Isaac and I, alone in the relative privacy of the cab of our box-body styled vehicle, had a conversation about what we had encountered. Unsurprisingly, Reg Crahart's over-indulgence in alcohol was clearly well known to the African staff as much as it was to us Europeans. Surprisingly, it seemed that Sgt Isaac and all of our African staff in Support Unit knew of the tragic death of his infant son and the break-up of his marriage, both of which upsetting events had clearly deepened his dependency on liquor to shut out the gremlins of troublesome memory. What neither of us could fathom was the thinking of whoever the woman was who had uplifted Reg Crahart.

During that journey, I pondered hard on exactly how best I should deal with my face-to-face report to Rampart. Running through my mind was the damage it would do to Support Unit's reputation if the full story got to the ears of the brown boots or perhaps worse, to the army elements we were trying our best to work with. On top of that, Reg Crahart clearly needed professional help to clear his head of the personal demons he had lodged there. Him ending up on a formal disciplinary for deserting his post would just add to his burden. Eventually, my report to Rampart was exactly as I had relayed by radio to Chirundu. Nothing more. The report I delivered was factually accurate. That it was just a wee bit economical in relation to one fact was something else. It was also something which I chose not to mention to either of my fellow POs. A few days later, with Willie Wielepolski back on full duty once more, further changes of task brought Reg back to Makuti, where he took the first opportunity to have a discreet conversation with me about his recent dereliction of duty.

"You found out I was not down there at Marangora. What have you said about it?" was his almost snarled question. My quiet reply was, "Nobody aside from me, the section you deserted and Sgt Isaac, knows whatever you got up to. As far as I am concerned it stays within Support Unit, but when we get back to depot, I intend to have a conversation with C/Insp. West and Bert Freemantle, because you clearly need some help in sorting out the personal problems that are making you unfit to command any operational unit whose lives may well depend upon you being wide awake and clear-headed at all times, got it?"

Whether Reg actually "got it", or not, I never found out. His lips tightened together, then he just turned away and took himself off towards the vehicle park. The noise of a vehicle leaving the camp suggested he was on his way once again to the Makuti Motel.

Although as a troop, we were expecting to remain at Makuti, engaged in Zambezi Valley duties, for at least another couple of weeks, that was not what happened. The day after Reg and I had our little conversation, messages reached us to be ready to return to Tomlinson Depot the following day. Puzzled, but happy, we handed over to the incoming troop and set off for depot in Salisbury, which location we reached about midday. While the others attended to the routines of stand-down, I headed straight for the main offices, where, to my relief, both C/Insp. West and Supt Freemantle were available. To the credit of both, my request for an immediate and confidential conversation with the two of them was accepted. When my somewhat lengthy story was done, Bert Freemantle asked, "Why did you not tell Supt Holt that you had discovered Crahart absent from his duty and probably dallying with a merry widow?"

"I'm not entirely sure, Sir. Partly protecting the unit's reputation. Partly because despite wanting at times to knock his blasted head off, I think he needs help with his personal problems. Losing his infant child and creating a marital bust-up because of a drinking problem suggests a need for some help, rather than a serious disciplinary charge. It seems to me, Sir, that a transfer to a town posting and some professional help would appear to be what he needs. If that is not possible, then transferring me to another troop might be an answer, because part of the problem seems to be that he deeply resents the fact that, in my Nyasaland Police service I ranked as Inspector, basically senior to the rank he holds."

"Transferring you would not help solve Crahart's personal problems, would it?" was my CO's shrewd reply. He glanced at C/Insp. West. "If it is any consolation, Woolley, I think you've done the right thing in handling this the way you have. Now be a good fellow, enjoy your three days off and leave this to us to sort out." His right hand gestured towards the door, so I came to attention, saluted, turned about and marched out.

Three days later, when I reported for duty once more, along with Terry Rowlandson and Willie Wielepolski, I was not surprised when all three of us were called in by C/Insp. West, who did not beat about the bush. After his formal instruction of "At ease, please, gentlemen," he went on directly, "I've called you three in together to inform you that Section Officer Crahart has been transferred to other duties. He will be replaced as your troop commander by Section Officer Van Wyk, who will be joining the unit at the end of the week. His background is Town Branch and Traffic Section, so he will need a bit of support from you three until he finds his feet in the unit. I'll be relying on you three to make him welcome and bring him up to date on what you've all learned over the past few months of chasing terrorists since the Viljoens were butchered in Hartley." He paused for a moment, just long enough to let a wry smile flicker across his face. "What the unit has been involved in lately has been somewhat different from the urban riot control work it was originally set up to deal with." He pointed a finger at Terry Rowlandson. "Until Van Wyk gets here to take over, you'll be acting troop commander. Any questions?"

The three of us standing at ease in front of his desk glanced briefly at each other before our collectively chorused, "No, Sir," brought about our dismissal from his office and an opportunity to talk over Reg Crahart's sudden disappearance from the Support Unit scene.

It was only then that I felt it appropriate, out of respect to both Terry and Willie, that I should bring them up to date in detail about Reg's absence from his post in the valley and my subsequent actions and conversations. When I finished the story, there was a moment of silence as they both mentally digested what was an almost unbelievable picture. "Let's hope they can dry him out, wherever he's been shifted to," was Willie's thoughtful observation, "Because somewhere under his personal demons and the alcohol there's a decent bloke." That about summed it up, so we left it at that and got on with the daily routines of depot activity, starting off with telling our African staff of Section Officer Crahart's departure, of his replacement's impending arrival and of the fact that until that man arrived, Patrol Officer Terry Rowlandson was in charge of A Troop. It was news that was very well received by all our African members of the troop.

Section Officer Moebe Boemsma Van Wyk, duly appeared mid-morning on Monday 16th of January 1967. That his transfer had been arranged at rather short notice was suggested by the fact that he appeared in standard hot season dress, wearing brown leather. He was big, blond, blue-eyed and cheerful. Something of a total contrast to our previous troop commander. C/Insp. West brought him into the communal tea-room, introduced him all round and thoughtfully departed, leaving us three section leaders to bring our new troop commander up to date on events over the past several months. Moebe proved to have a quick and agile mind and was clearly able to absorb and retain information at a rapid rate. When Terry offered to call the troop together to allow our new commander to introduce himself, I expressed the view that it might be better to wait until he was properly dressed in grey shirt, blue trousers and black leather-work instead of standard uniformed branch brown. That remark led to a rapid visit to the Ordnance Store and a swift transformation into proper attire for a Section Officer in Support Unit, even if there was a certain lack of shine to the black leather. By then it was time for lunch, so we adjourned to the Fife Hostel Canteen, where we continued our introductory chattering over our meal. By the end of that day, Terry, Willie and I were certain that our new troop commander was somebody we could all get along with. For us and for our entire troop, it was a huge relief.

For the next couple of weeks, A Troop remained in Salisbury, busy through the day, doing routine classroom training and parade ground foot and arms drill and a fair old amount of Support Unit's variety of physical training. That meant many laps of the running track, a few scrambles over the assault course, some hours doing log-drill as well as the rifle and foot drill. As part of our PT exercises we did, on a few occasions, attempt to build a human pyramid. That was done by forming a circle of eight of our sturdiest and heaviest troop members, standing with arms linked through each other's elbows, then less weighty members standing on their shoulders, again with arms linked and so on, tier by tier upwards, until the inevitable point of collapse was reached. We never did make it beyond a third tier and, perhaps more by good fortune than anything else, nobody suffered any real damage in the collapses. All that physical activity left little doubt in any of our minds that if we did get into any hot-metal punch-ups with insurgents, we would certainly be physically fit enough to hold our own. Fortunately, our new Troop Leader, despite his last couple of years spent driving around on Traffic Section duties in Salisbury, was basically young and fit, so capable of putting in his share of the physical efforts needed, individually or whenever a bit of teamwork was called for as with the log drill.

It was during this period in Salisbury that Terry Rowlandson, a confirmed cigarette smoker, managed, while driving his Rover 90, to drop the lighted cigarette he had between his fingers, which were gripping the steering wheel, into the foot-well in front of his seat. Somewhat forgetting there was traffic ahead and behind him, he took his eyes off the road in order to try to pick up the dropped cigarette. The result of his inattention to the road ahead resulted in him driving his car into the back end of a heavy vehicle which had come to a halt ahead of him. Because of the relatively slow speeds involved, Terry got away without injury. Sadly, his Rover 90 came off less well, requiring a fair amount of restorative panel beating and paint spraying, which put it off the road for several days. Terry was fortunate in picking on a very substantial heavy vehicle to argue with because that item was undamaged, so no charges of careless or negligent driving arose from the incident, much to Terry's relief. To his credit, he took the inevitable ribbing from us who were his colleagues and friends with a smile, a laugh and a shrug. It was, however, a reminder to us all to pay attention when behind any steering wheel and not permit ourselves to be distracted by events inside or outside of the cab.

With our other four troops posted in Bulawayo, Sikombela, Salazar and Makuti, it was a day-by-day subject of discussion about where we might be sent to replace one or other of them. In the event, what did happen, did so with some rapidity over a short period of time. Terry Rowlandson reached the end of his two years in the unit and returned to standard duty uniformed branch work. Just a day later, Willie received a transfer to another troop. As replacements, A Troop received two newcomers as section leaders, Patrol Officers 6264 Robert Flynn and 7601 Dermot Creaner. Bob was a senior patrol officer already, having attested on 9th January 1961, but Dermot, having attested only on 6th June 1966, was fresh out of Training Depot and Driving School. However, he came to us with the background of having served for some years in the Royal Ulster Constabulary in Northern Ireland, so he was not exactly a greenhorn in terms of police service, weapons handling and urban terrorism. Moebe barely had time to have a word or two with our newest members of the troop when he was called in by C/Insp. West and advised that we were to leave in 48 hours by plane for a few weeks of guard duties at Vila Salazar and that we could have the next day off, free of duties, in order to get ready for our forthcoming stay in the lowveld. As the only European member of the troop who had any experience of serving at Vila Salazar, I did my best to outline to the others what a tour of duty at Gonakudzingwa was likely to entail.

On Wednesday, 1st February 1967, A Troop arrived at Boli Airstrip, by Dakota aircraft, to start another few weeks of guard duty at the Gonakudzingwa Restriction Camps, where, on the ground, little or nothing had changed since the last time I was there. Using my knowledge from past duty there, I took Moebe, Paddy and Dermot on something of a whirlwind tour of the camps and Malvernia before we settled into the usual routine of guard duties around the restriction camps. Although Camp 1 was technically just a very much smaller replica of the other camps, containing as it did the dozen or so most senior members of ZAPU, Joshua Nkomo, John Fiendo Mpofu and others, it was not permanently or as tightly guarded as the other camps were. We made irregular visits and took an occasional walk around, more to show the flag as it were than anything else. Several days after our arrival, I undertook one such visit. The weather had been dry and hot for a while, so the occasional dust-devil, an item which behaved like a miniature tornado, was not unusual. Joshua Nkomo was strolling slowly around out in the open, wearing his habitual fur hat, when one such dust-devil zipped its whirl-wind way straight over him. It smothered him in dust, sucked his fur hat from his head and whisked it up, up and away, swirling it around with the other dust, debris, leaves and such, before it collapsed as suddenly as it had arisen, a hundred yards or so from the camp perimeter.

Without thinking much about it, I climbed out of the Land Rover from which I had witnessed the brief event, picked my way through the bush to where I had seen the dust-devil collapse and collected Joshua Nkomo's very dusty fur hat. Returning to Camp 1, I found Joshua Nkomo standing just inside the gate, still dusting himself down and watching my approach with a somewhat surprised expression on his face. I beat a little of the dust from his headgear, said, "I do believe this belongs to you Mr Nkomo," and offered the hat to him. Josh, as everyone called him, nodded, took the hat from me and said, "That was a kindly and thoughtful act Majoni, (White Policeman). We are not used to such an attitude here. Do you have a name?"

"Yes I do," I replied, "I am Arnold Woolley."

Josh stuck out his right hand. "This is all I can offer you by way of thanks."

I had no hesitation in shaking his hand, bidding him goodbye and then going on about my other routine duties for that day. Off duty in the evening, while enjoying a pint in the Gonna Stagga Inn as the police station bar was known, I related the incident to those present. Bob Flynn took a long swallow of his beer, wiped his mouth with the back of his hand and declared, "You're too soft Arn. I'd have left his xxxx hat to the white ants!"

Bob's views concerning the African population of the country were clear and unambiguous. Rather like Pete Wilson, he too regarded the African Police members of the BSAP and the ordinary non-political members of the African population as fellow human beings, but a thousand years junior to Europeans. He treated them decently and generally got on well with them. However, wishing, like most of us to have a full-term career in the BSAP and to continue in those years ahead to live in Rhodesia, he regarded the political Africans, of whichever tribal branch, as threats to that aim and therefore hated their guts.

That viewpoint he displayed in no uncertain terms a few days later, when there was a need to make a day trip by road to Nuanetsi Police Station in order to rotate a couple of the constables attached to Vila Salazar Police Station and to pick up some supplies. Bob left at a not too early hour, in one of our Ford 4x4 vehicles, with Driver Constable Kisimis and the pair of brown boot constables due for rotation. That evening, after darkness had fallen, when I was on shift in the guard tent at No. 3 camp, I heard a vehicle approaching from the direction of Nuanetsi and Triangle. Knowing that Bob had gone off that morning with Const. Kisimis and had not yet returned by the time I went on night duty I took no great notice of it as the headlights and engine noise got nearer. However, as the vehicle reached a few yards before the turn-in to Camp 3, someone in the vehicle let loose with a full magazine of bullets on automatic setting. For various reasons, all of us Europeans who were issued with FN rifles, loaded the magazines with one-in-three, or one-in-five tracer bullets. The full magazine burst of gunfire was over in a couple of seconds and the vehicle just kept going towards Vila Salazar Police Station and our Support Unit Camp; however, the damage was done, because a score or more of the restrictees who were still out and about, due to the oppressive heat of the evening which made early sleeping unpleasant, had heard the gunfire and seen the tracer rounds flying not very high over the tops of the buildings. A few flung themselves flat, others dashed for cover inside the barrack blocks and nearly every single one of them started shouting warnings to their friends inside the barrack blocks that the camp was under attack.

Between those dozens who stayed flat on the ground awaiting any further gunfire, those who stayed within the buildings, shouting to know what was going on and those several score who grabbed axes and sticks and rushed at the gate, demanding to be let out to escape any attack, a fair degree of panic briefly became the order of the evening. Their nervousness and agitation transferred itself to some extent to the African staff on duty with me. Reading the mood of the restrictees and by way of giving the constables something positive to do, I had them take up defensive postures, flat on the ground, with weapons facing away from the camp, as if in readiness to protect it and those inside it, while I tried to get the message across to the concerned inmates that I believed the gunfire was a piece of stupid behaviour by a probably drunken police detail and unlikely to be repeated. The simple, visible act of constables on the ground, ready to defend them, along with my, to them rather startling but honest observation about a drunken police detail, did a bit of good to calm down a situation which could have escalated. When ten minutes or so had passed without any more bullets flying, the aura of panicky tension eased and some degree of normality slowly re-established itself, possibly assisted by my firm assurances to the camp spokesperson that, once normality had returned to Camp 3, I intended to go off to our Vila Salazar camp in order to seek out and deal with whoever had been so stupid as to loose off the rounds over all of our heads from a moving vehicle. About an hour after the bullets had streaked over the camp, I felt confident enough to head for the Land Rover parked by our guard tent and drive the short distance to our base camp, which, as I had rather expected at an hour close to midnight, was totally bedded-down and quiet, apart from the activities of the detail then on night guard duties. I explained to the guard on duty the reason for my appearance at base camp at that hour. From that guard I learned that the only vehicle which had entered the camp around an hour or so earlier had been the Ford 4x4 which had returned from Nuanetse, with PO Flynn and Const. Kisimis in it.

Not wishing to disturb the sleeping camp, I invited the camp guard to accompany me and quietly entered the hut in which we Patrol Officers slept. Bob Flynn was seemingly fast asleep, with his FN rifle propped against the wall close by him. Without disturbing Bob, I lifted his FN rifle and took a good long sniff at the front end of the barrel. My nostrils immediately filled with the unmistakable fumes of recently discharged cordite. Without a word, I invited the camp guard to take a sniff, which he did. "It has been fired, Ishe!" was his whispered comment. I nodded a silent agreement, gestured to him to leave the hut and followed him myself, after carefully replacing the FN to where I had lifted it from.

I did not feel it would serve any purpose to waken our troop commander at that hour. I quietly thanked the guard and advised him that I would be speaking with our troop commander once daylight arrived and might need him to confirm what we had both noted. After that I climbed into my Land Rover and as silently as I could, drove out of base camp and returned, unhurriedly, to Camp 3 to see out the rest of the shift. I parked my vehicle as usual, close to the guard tent, doused its lights, switched off the engine and climbed out, taking my own FN rifle with me. Before I could move away from the vehicle, I heard the noise of another vehicle coming towards the camp from the Vila Salazar direction. Somewhat puzzled, I just stood still beside the bonnet of the Land Rover, holding my FN horizontal to the ground at arms-length below my waist. My puzzlement deepened as a Ford 4x4 drove at some speed towards me, sliding to a hard-braked stop on the far side of the Land Rover, its passenger side nearest to my vehicle. Bob Flynn climbed out from the driver's seat, after switching off the engine, but without turning off its lights. He wobbled, rather than walked, around the front of his vehicle until he was standing near the passenger door of the Ford 4x4, facing me. He was shirtless but wearing uniform shorts.

"You took my f---ing rifle and checked it over without my permission you b-----d! Nobody does that to Bob Flynn and gets away with it, so now I'm going to take yours!" The slurred words and wobbly gait told me he was pie-eyed. "Don't think you can stop me, because if you try to I'll put a bullet in you!" He hauled open the passenger door of the Ford 4x4 and started to pull his FN rifle out from where it had been laying along the passenger seat. Whether on the handbrake or on the gear lever, the rifle or its sling caught, preventing him from drawing the weapon out quickly and smoothly.

That gave me ample time to lift my own FN to my shoulder, click the safety catch off, cock it and lean forward, bracing myself on the spare wheel atop the Land Rover's bonnet. As Bob struggled rather clumsily to free his snagged FN, I lined my own weapon up on him and snapped, "Hold it Bob! If you pull that FN out and level it within fifteen degrees of my body, I'll put a bullet through you." Whether it was the sound of me cocking my FN, or the icy-cold tone in my voice, something got through his inebriated mental haze. He stopped trying to get the rifle out and stood silent for a moment, eyeing my rifle pointing at him. Then his gaze focused on my face. Eventually he said, "You f--- well mean it, don't you?"

"Yes, I do and don't you for one second doubt it," was my icy-toned reply, all the while keeping my FN aimed steadily at his breastbone.

Bob Flynn stood there, silent for a full ten seconds. Then he slammed shut the passenger door of his vehicle, spat a slurred "F--k you!" at me, wobbled his way to the far side of the Ford 4x4, climbed in, started the engine and drove off, with the driver's door still swinging wide open. As he drove away, I let out a long-held breath, made safe my own FN and turned towards the guard tent and the on-duty guard, who had clearly heard and witnessed the entire event. "He was very drunk, Ishe!" was all he said, before turning away and resuming his patrol pattern. I had no reason to disagree with his observation.

With the rest of the night passing by quietly, the shift changeover in the morning was a routine affair. I handed over to Dermot Creaner, collected my section's details from the other camps and headed for base camp at Vila Salazar, wondering just what I was going to encounter when I met up with Bob Flynn. As it turned out, while Bob was fast asleep, Moebe Van Wyk was already up and about. I had hardly got within speaking distance when he asked, "What the heck went on between you and Bob around midnight or so? He came back from Nuanetse somewhat on his ear, crash-dived onto his bed and went out like a light. Next thing I heard was him driving out, engine roaring, gears grating and waking up half the camp, including me. The camp guard told me you had been in, sniffed at his FN rifle and left again, with Bob almost on your tail. Then Bob came back, told me you had threatened to shoot him and flaked out again. He hasn't surfaced yet, so what the heck was it all about?"

As briefly as I could, I brought my troop commander up to date on what had gone on, from bullets flying over Camp 3 to my visit to check Bob's rifle and so on. At the end of my detailed narrative, I suggested that Moebe might have a word with Const. Kisimis about the journey back from Nuanetse. Moebe nodded in agreement and went off to do just that, while I took myself off to our bedroom hut, where Bob was still fast asleep, to catch up on a few hours of sleep myself.

Despite the heat, I had no problem in nodding off and slept, undisturbed for six hours or so, until woken by my batman with a call for lunch. In our mess hut I found Moebe, along with Bob, who took one look at me and asked, very reasonably, "You did threaten to shoot me last night, didn't you?"

"Yes," I replied, "but only after you scared the wits out of the entire Camp 3 bunch and my guard team, then threatened to shoot me for having a sniff at your FN."

Bob took a moment to digest my words, shook his head apologetically and said, "I'm not too clear about some bits of last night. I remember thinking it would be amusing to wake up you and Camp 3 with a few rounds fired over your heads. After that it's all a bit vague. Do you want to run it past me?"

As we three ate our lunch, I related the events of the night, in detail, to Bob and Moebe. When I finished, Bob looked at me for a moment, then said quietly, "There are times when I drink a bit too much." He looked at Moebe and asked, "Is there going to be any come-back over it?"

Moebe shrugged. "Depends on Camp 3 and Arn here."

Bob was a senior Patrol Officer with enough service in to take annual promotion exams. Any official report of the night's events could cost him dearly. With that in mind, I assured him there would be nothing formal coming in from me and that if Camp 3 complained, I would report that I had failed to trace the vehicle from which the shots had come. At that suggestion, Moebe nodded his agreement. Bob stuck his hand out across the table and said, "I owe you one, Arn. A big one!" We shook hands and that was the end of it because Camp 3 never did make any official complaint, which rather surprised us all.

Apart from an interesting encounter with an unfortunate tortoise which appeared to have been trodden on by an elephant, resulting in a cracked carapace, which John Williams repaired by some careful drilling and wiring, the remaining days of our latest stint at Salazar passed uneventfully. When word came though that our date for changeover was set for Wednesday, 15th March 1967, the news was gratefully received all round. Even our African members felt a need for some relief from the drenching rain and oppressive heat of the lowveld, which competed well in the discomfort stakes with our periods in the Zambezi Valley. Fortunately, when we needed it, the rains eased back somewhat. It was sufficient to make the Boli Airstrip safe enough for the usual Dakota to once again land on and take off from. With transport all ready and waiting for us once we had landed in Salisbury, it did not take us long to make the journey to Tomlinson Depot, where we were happy enough to learn we were to be stood down for 96 hours of rest and recuperation, which would put us due back on duty on Monday, 20th March 1967. Only after that, would we then be informed of our next assignment, somewhere! As usual, our brief period of R&R flew by. Our African staff often talked of there being two clocks governing the world. One which ran slowly whenever they were on duty and another, which ran much faster, whenever they were off duty. We Europeans tended to agree with their thinking.

Somewhat to our surprise, when we formally paraded four days after getting back to Salisbury, there was still no decision as to where we were to be posted for our next few weeks away from depot. It took another 24 hours before word came through that we were to return to Makuti, for another month or so of border control and counter-insurgency activities. That came as a bit of a surprise, because, we thought we might be off back to Vila Salazar, or Bulawayo. Moebe's observation that at least Makuti was higher than Salazar, so it might be more comfortable than the heat of the lowveld, brought a prompt and heartfelt riposte from me. "Not once you get down into the valley or across to Kariba!"

Two days later, our lunchtime arrival at Makuti camp on 23rd March 1967, caused some head-scratching, because we were simply not expected. E Troop's personnel, except for a small camp guard detachment, were all engaged in duties down in the Zambezi Valley. Rampart reckoned it would take a day or two to get them gathered up, to enable the necessary formal hand-over to take place. That left us looking like having to kick our heels and twiddle our thumbs for the next day and a half. That situation changed following a conversation over evening meal. Moebe happened to remark that he had never been to Kariba Police Station and had never seen Kariba Dam. When every one of us three section leaders assured him that we too had never been to Kariba Town and Dam Wall, it quickly became clear that a very useful way of spending the following day would be for us to undertake a familiarization patrol to Kariba. With that agreeable decision made, we set off per vehicle for a quiet ale at the motel, before getting our heads down relatively early.

The following morning, after a slightly reluctant okay from Rampart, we drove out of Makuti to start the journey to Kariba. We fully expected Kariba to be spectacular but found ourselves applying that word very shortly after we left the Great North Road, at the turn-off close to the Makuti Motel. The set of sweeping hairpin bends as the road descended sharply, over a scant few miles, to almost the level of the Zambezi Valley itself, literally took our breath away. Mile after verdant mile of green treetops, in every shade of that colour that the eye could record and the mind catalogue, demanded our full attention, which nearly became our undoing as Moebe, who was driving, forgot to pay enough attention to the winding road ahead, with the result that we ended up coming to a halt several yards off of the tarmac surface and within a couple of feet of a notably nasty drop.

An hour or so later we arrived at Kariba Dam's wall, parked the Land Rover and walked as far onto the wall as we were allowed. For any visitor, the first sight of the great fresh-water lake on the one side, the massive double-curvature concrete arch dam wall and the grandeur of the river gorge on the other side is bound to have a truly memorable impact. We four uniformed police officers were silent, for several minutes as we simply stood gazing at and taking in the awesome immensity of the largest man-made reservoir anywhere in the world. Created as an economic development project, by the government of the Federation of the Rhodesias and Nyasaland, now Zambia, Zimbabwe and Malawi, work on the dam was commenced in 1956 and completed three years later. At a height of 128m, with a wall crest length of 617m, the dam has a capacity of 181 billion cubic metres of water. When full, the lake created by the dam extends back some kilometres.

The dam was officially opened in 1960, with the intention that it would secure the region's energy supplies and potential development needs for many years ahead. The dam wall houses two underground hydroelectric power stations, fed by water from the reservoir. Between them, the two stations have a total capacity of 1830MW generating more than 10,035 GWh of electricity annually. The North Bank station, when opened had an installed production capacity of 1,080 Megawatts, while the South Bank had slightly less, at 750 Megawatts. Both generating stations were built with thoughts of increased capacity in years ahead. The only event the designers did not foresee was the dissolution of the Federation in 1963. Despite that, a friendly conversation with the Zambian customs and police officers resulted in us being allowed to cross the dam wall and drive to a vantage point on the Zambian side, from which I was able to get a photograph of the dam wall and the mass of water pouring out of the open gates. With that rather unexpected generosity from the Zambian officials, my collection of photographs, for I had carted my camera along for the trip, contains shots from above, below and both sides of the dam.

The building of the dam was not without some controversy, because the flooding of a great length of the Zambezi River Valley meant the displacement of thousands of Batonga tribespeople, who lived on both sides of the river. The Batonga had lived all along the river, mainly upstream from the Kariba Gorge for centuries. In their culture they venerated a creature they called Nyaminyami, who, along with his wife, lived in the river. Not that Nyaminyami was human. Far from it. The Batonga have always claimed that for as long as they have tribal memory, Nyaminyami has occasionally actually been seen by numerous members of the tribe. They claim that the description of Nyaminyami has never altered, but always appeared as a massive snake, with the head of a great fish, akin to the tiger fish which inhabit the river. Nobody among the native population has ever been able to provide any exact size of their river god, because no one through the years has ever claimed to have seen the deity fully out of the water. When I talked the subject over with Batonga elders, nobody could explain how the existence of a wife became known, for while many of the tribe have claimed sight of Nyaminyami, nobody has ever claimed to have seen his reported spouse.

When the word first spread of the intention to build the dam and flood a great swathe of the Zambezi River Valley, the Batonga warned that Nyaminyami would never allow the river to be blocked and controlled. According to them, Nyaminyami and his wife lived in deep pools, or caves, close to the mouth of the Kariba Gorge. Disturbing the natural flow of the river there would incense the river god, who would wreak havoc and destroy those who dared to tamper with his river. The European population of the then Federation and of course those engaged in the construction of the dam, over three years, scoffed at such dire warnings from the Batonga. The detailed history of the Kariba dam wall's construction and the unusually high floods of 1957 and 1958 are well documented.

As I discovered in conversations in later weeks with members of the relocated Batonga tribe, they firmly believed that the "once in a thousand years" level of the floods of 1957 and again in 1958, which really did threaten the survival of the then embryonic dam wall, were caused by Nyaminyami himself, for two reasons. The first being that "his" river and existence were being threatened by the construction work on the dam wall. The second being that the wall had created a barrier between himself and his wife, who had gone downstream to visit relatives and was unable to get back to be with him.

Tribal elders of the Batonga claim that it was only their intervention in 1959, to placate and appease Nyaminyami, which prevented another, greater, flood, which would potentially have destroyed the then incomplete dam wall. Whatever the stories of river spirits and appeasements, it was a fact that as the waters of the dam built up, the weight of the water created geological strains, resulting in numerous, thankfully minor and localised, earthquakes, year on year.

In the first few years of the growing body of water, Operation NOAH was mounted, to rescue all kinds and any number of animals, reptiles, rodents and even the creepy-crawlies that found themselves cut off and stranded on small knolls by the ever-rising level of Lake Kariba. Moebe, Terry, Willie and I were visitors at that time of year when the rains were near their end and the lake's water-level at its highest, resulting in the dam's water-level control gates being fully opened.

Returning from the Zambian side, we stopped on the wall, to take a closer look at the outflow. Watching the massive waterfall effect as the tumbling, foaming water dropped vertically away below us was strangely hypnotic. Tearing ourselves away from it, we stopped long enough to admire the statue of Nyaminyami, before heading towards Kariba Police Station to make our familiarisation visit known to Member-in-Charge and his staff. In carrying out that formal act, we allowed our route to wander somewhat. That permitted us to take in the sights of the burgeoning urban areas, both for European style housing and for the growing number of indigenous people who were finding work suddenly available as the entire community grew steadily year by year. The commercial and recreational fishing, which grew from the creation of the great lake was bolstered by the already well-established Annual Tiger Fishing Contest, which drew anglers from all over the world. Opportunities for water-skiing and all the many other recreational and commercial pursuits opened up by the existence of such a massive body of water gradually attracted more people to the area.

As one would expect, with the gorge and naturally hilly terrain, some of the views from the high points were quite spectacular, so one or two more photographs got added to my collection. Perhaps one of the most treasured is a photograph of the original "Jam Jar Inn", a simple rondavel under thatched roof, created by a handful of European police officers, early in the life of the new police station as an off-duty bar. It was somewhere they could relax and refresh themselves at the end of the working day. Naturally, we four stopped there long enough to sample the wares, but to a strictly limited extent, which guaranteed no impairment of anyone's driving abilities, given the decidedly "interesting" nature of the roads in and around Kariba, with their ups, downs and often very sharp bends. After our single refreshing pint at the Jam Jar Inn, we headed back to Makuti, where we found that radio messages had flown backwards and forward and all was arranged for a formal changeover during the course of the next day.

The following morning, with the formalities of changeover all done and dusted, A Troops received an update briefing from Special Branch, which really told us only that there were lots of trained terrorists sitting in holding camps in Zambia, waiting for instructions and opportunities to cross into Rhodesia. The briefing also instructed us to base ourselves in certain locations along the Zambezi River, to carry out daylight mobile and foot patrols to reassure the local and foreign hunters who were occupying the safari camps A to H which were, at that stage of the insurgency, still routinely functioning. We were also to check all game trails leading from the river, southwards towards the escarpment and carry out night ambushes on any likely to be used by the insurgents. Before dark, I and my section were down in the valley once again, camped around our Land Rover, positioned a couple of hundred yards from the Zambezi itself and not far from hunting camp D. The following day at a mid-morning hour I left two details to guard our base camp and with the rest of the section, drove the short distance to the hunting camp, to pay our respects to whoever was there and to let them know that we were operating in the area.

As it turned out, the camp was occupied by a group of Afrikaans trophy hunters from South Africa. They were destined to leave the following day, having had, from the impressive assortment of game animal heads and horns which they displayed to us, a most successful few days in the valley. Along with their trophy animal heads, they had collected a very impressive number of haunches of venison of assorted kinds, which they had hanging from branches, safely drying in the shade. Since their collection of antelope which they had shot during their stay in the valley was impressive and heavy they feared that the vehicle they had arrived in might not be able to carry everything they wished to take with them to RSA. Our arrival provided them with a solution other than just dumping good meat for the vultures to feast on or pitching it into the Zambezi for the crocodiles. The result was that when we drove away from D camp and the friendly Afrikaans trophy hunters, we had with us an entire carcass of a kudu, less its head and horns, which they had shot the previous day.

Rather than have that bouncing around in the back of our vehicle, for the next few hours, we returned to our base-camp. There we handed over our unexpected meat supplies to the two guards, with orders to get the carcass hung up in the shade. With that done, we set off again, to carry out some more hours of daylight patrolling. In that time, the discussion in the vehicle revolved around just what to do with several hundred pounds weight of venison, far more than we could eat in the entire week we were due to be in the valley, even if we ate nothing but venison at every meal. There was also the small problem of decently butchering the carcass of a kudu. Aside from service bayonets, useless for carving up a carcass, I had a Bowie-type knife with a six-inch blade at my belt. That had a decent edge to it, but, lacking any large blade, or an axe, we had a problem, or so I thought.

Having checked out a dozen or so game trails and found nothing by way of suspicious boot spoor, we returned to base camp at mid-afternoon, looking to have a hearty meal, before setting off to carry out a night ambush activity on a game trail about a mile from our base camp. To my utter astonishment, I discovered that, in the few hours we had been away, our two camp guards had neatly and efficiently butchered and de-boned the carcass. A good deal of it was hanging from branches of nearby trees, while more was laid out on an improvised drying frame over our fireplace, which had expanded to about four times the size I had last seen it at. As I stood there, staring in amazement, Const. Mapfumo came up to me, rifle slung across his shoulders and a broad grin on his face, holding out a leaf-wrapped bundle. "We have saved some fillet steak for you, Ishe. It is fresh and very good nyama" (meat). As I accepted the generous lump of about 8 or 10 pounds' weight of meat, I asked him, "How on earth did you manage to butcher it so fast and so neatly?" Mapfumo took a couple of paces to where his 44 webbing and pack were. Delving into it, he produced one of the biggest and most fearsome flick-knives I had ever seen, with a blade some seven inches or more in length and obviously as sharp as a razor. "I keep it in my pack, Ishe. It is very useful." With the veritable proof of that all around, I simply nodded, said, "Well done, Mapfumo," and walked across to where my own webbing and sleeping bag were. There I unwrapped the great chunk of prime kudu fillet steak which Mapfumo had handed me, carved off a few generously thick slices and not long afterwards enjoyed one of the best "meat only" meals I had ever tasted.

The following day, not having the bush-wise skill to have hung my chunk of meat, but stored it in my pack, when I did come to try to use some more of it, there was a certain sliminess to the surface and a tainted smell which told me I had best not eat it. Seeing that we were going to be with a vehicle for the week and close to the river, I had put a fishing rod and tackle behind the back of the front seats to our Land Rover. I decided to use bits of the inedible chunk of meat as bait and try my luck at catching a fish or two. I found a safe spot at the riverside, with a few rocks directly in front of me, large and uneven enough to stop any crocodile from making an easy and direct dash at me. Behind me, against which I could safely lean back, with my FN rifle beside me, there was about three feet of vertical river-bank, which put the sandy ground behind me as I fished, about level with the back of my head. I cut off enough meat to make a tasty morsel of bait and started to float-fish out over the rocks in front of me. Not only did the fishing prove worthwhile, but I also found myself being fascinated by the antics of an obviously young fish-eagle, whose inept attempts to catch a fish caused a great deal of splash without any successful result. Clearly irritated, the peeved bird flew into a tree not far away and proceeded to tell the world around just what it thought in a series of raucous screeches as it slowly dried out before having another try, this time successfully. Inside of a half-hour I had caught a couple of large barble (catfish), a melana plura (bream) weighing a couple of pounds and a tiger fish weighing four or five pounds. That one took a wee bit of landing. After each of my first three catches, I re-baited my hook from the chunk of meat on the bank behind my head and then concentrated on watching the float out on the calm waters of the river. When I had finished landing the tiger fish, I stood up and turned around, wanting once again to re-bait my hook. To my surprise, my chunk of several pounds' weight of meat was no longer there. However, what was there, in the slightly damp sandy soil, crystal clear and very plain to see, were the pug marks of an adult leopard.

Over the years, I have occasionally wondered just what might have happened, had not several pounds' weight of slightly off venison been between the back of my head and the jaws of an adult leopard. As it was, I simply shook my head in wonderment and relief, gathered up firearm, fishing-rod and catch and took myself back to our base camp, where I presented the assortment of fish to my section, as a change of taste to the mass of venison we had been gifted.

For the remainder of that week in the valley, we patrolled in our vehicle and on foot, checked game-trails, uneventfully, for alien boot spoor and carried out night-time ambushes, without any positive result. My brief spells of fishing each day were very successful, which kept our crude drying rack well-used, put a smile on the faces of the members of my section and meant that at the end of the week, their packs were stuffed full of both well-smoked and dried venison and fish when we headed back to Makuti. At that location, every scrap of smoked and dried venison and fish vanished rapidly into kitbags, to be safeguarded until it could be got back to numerous home villages as good relish, to make the maize-meal dinners just a little bit more palatable. When I related the incident of the bait-thieving leopard to Moebe and the others, they all reckoned that I was one very lucky individual. With that opinion, I could only agree!

Moebe decided that it would be a sensible idea if he rotated duties with us three section leaders, so that he could get some idea of how well each section operated. The result was that we three Patrol Officers spent more days within Makuti Camp, sorting out administrative matters, lending a hand with moving assorted personnel here there and everywhere and assisting with a few hours, whenever needed, manning the movable road-block which operated 24 hours a day on the Chirundu to Salisbury Road. Some days into our tour of duty, Moebe opted to lead Willie's section for a session of day patrols and night ambushes in the valley, where both Bob Flynn and I were already operating to the same pattern, based on Special Branch information that a number of small groups of ZAPU, along with elements of the SAANC, had actually crossed the Zambezi River some days previously.

On his second night out, Moebe and the section sprang their ambush for real, opening fire by starlight alone, just after midnight, when seven ZAPU terrorists entered the killing zone. The proof that the section had paid attention to their hours of training was rapidly demonstrated in what Moebe called, in later recounting the event to us who had not been there, "A short and noisy exchange of gunfire." Short it may have been and certainly noisy, no doubt, but it was also effective, because it resulted in three dead and one wounded terrorist being accounted for then and there and the three remaining members of the group being killed by elements of the RLI during a follow-up operation later in the day. Fortunately, that total success came at no cost or injury to members of the RLI unit or our Support Unit personnel either. Interestingly, but perhaps not surprisingly, that initial success lifted the morale of the entire troop. The many fruitless hours of foot-slogging and mobile patrolling during the day and laying in ambush at night over many months, suddenly became worthwhile.

It was as if the entire troop had been there, not just the one section. That success also had another beneficial effect. The RLI troopers at Makuti began to accept us as equals in the common fight against the insurgents. Previous comments such as, "You lot won't find a riot out here!" and "He's one of the blue-backside boys," suddenly ceased.

Two days after that successful ambush, when I went on radio to make a scheduled routine morning report to Makuti, I was somewhat taken aback to be informed that a helicopter would arrive shortly, with SO Van Wyk on board. He was to take over my section and duties and I was to be airlifted back to Makuti. Since it was not proper to start questioning or arguing over orders from Makuti, I simply acknowledged what I had heard with a standard, "Wilco. Over and out!" As I rolled my sleeping bag, gathered my webbing and prepared to wait for the chopper to arrive in whichever nearby clearing the pilot decided was safe to use, I explained my impending departure to my section and made it clear that I was just as puzzled as they were over whatever might be the cause of the unexpected and sudden change of arrangements.

When the chopper did arrive, there was no time for any conversation between Moebe and myself. The pilot put the aircraft down, but kept the rotor blades whirling while Moebe nipped smartly out and I nipped equally smartly in. Without wasting time, I snapped the seat belt in place and gave a thumbs-up to the pilot, who very rapidly lifted us up and away. A short while later, in the command caravan, Supt Holt answered my obvious question about what was going on, with a somewhat apologetic, "Don't ask me, Woolley. All I know is that I'm ordered to get you back to Salisbury and delivered direct to Camp Hospital just as soon as that can be arranged. Beyond that, your guess is as good as mine. Leave your webbing and pack with the rest of your gear in your tent. Just take what you are standing up in and your FN and head for Salisbury and Camp Hospital. They may be able to tell you what this is all about. Sorry I can't do better than that, but good luck with it whatever it is. Now just get yourself into the Land Rover that's waiting in the car park while I get on to Mash. Prov. HQ to confirm that you are on your way."

Shortly after lunchtime that day I arrived at Camp Hospital to find that they certainly were expecting me. It was clear also that they had been warned that I would be arriving without even the usual pyjamas, dressing gown and toothbrush, all of which they had ready to hand for me. My FN rifle was safely sent off to the Armoury and I was ordered into bed and told to stay there until the doctor arrived to see me. When I asked what the cause was of my being whipped suddenly out of the valley and being put to bed in Camp Hospital all I got back was that they had been warned to expect me and that was that. I was not worried, because I felt perfectly fit and well, but it certainly was puzzling and irritating in that I could get no answer to what I believed were my perfectly reasonable questions.

Once my uniform was safely stowed in the bedside locker and I, in my borrowed pyjamas was in bed as directed, one of the nurses had the kindly thought to ask me if I had had any lunch that day. At my reply in the negative, a tray of tea and biscuits appeared, for which I was most grateful. Another member of the staff brought me that day's edition of the *Rhodesia Herald*. I was still reading that when the doctor arrived, bade me a cheery "Good afternoon, young man," and added, "I gather I have got to give you a thorough physical examination!" At my inevitable question of, "What for Doctor?" he shrugged and replied, "I know not. All that I have had is an instruction to give you a thorough medical and report the result to OC Province." While the doctor got on and put me through a very thorough physical medical examination, I tried my best and failed miserably to think of any reason why my health was suddenly of interest to Duty Uniformed Branch's provincial headquarters rather than to Support Unit.

When that full and thorough medical examination was completed, the doctor said, "Hop back into bed and relax young man. You've just passed that examination with flying colours, which is exactly what I shall pass on upwards." With that certainly re-assuring observation he packed his stethoscope, thermometer and other bits and pieces of equipment into his medical bag and left, leaving me no wiser about exactly what was going on. Having been formally declared to be perfectly well and feeling just that way within myself, I could see no cause for me worry about why I was where I was, so I just relaxed, ate the very appetising meal which was presented to me that evening and settled down to enjoy a very comfortable and undisturbed night's sleep.

That mental tranquillity vanished after breakfast the following day, when an ambulance arrived and I was transferred, temporarily so I was advised, to a bed in Salisbury European Hospital, where they promptly started to take samples of just about everything that could be sampled, blood, urine, stool, nasal mucus and saliva from my mouth. Yet again, my request to be advised why all these samples were being taken, got me nowhere. None of the medical staff was able to tell me. They had merely been instructed to obtain the samples and send them off for laboratory processing. Once I had been able to provide each of the samples they required, I was carted off, back to Camp Hospital, where I promptly requested some communication with Support Unit HQ. I backed that with the comment that if I were not allowed some telephonic communication with C/Insp. West, I would get back into my riot blues and walk down to Morris Depot to see him. The result was that I had a telephone conversation with C/Insp. West, who seemed totally amazed and was actually apologetic, when I complained that I had not been told why I had been whipped out of the valley and dumped into Camp Hospital.

What he told me was just a wee bit worrying, but it certainly killed off any further mutters from me about what I had been subjected to over the past couple of days. C/Insp. West asked me if I recalled helping to take soil samples for the government geological survey teams during their activities in seeking oil deposits in the lowveld along the border fence with Mocambique. At my affirmative reply, he went on to tell me that the laboratory results of the soil sample analysis had, somewhat belatedly, been passed down to BSAP HQ and then on to Support Unit, with the advice to have any police officers who had helped with the digging and sample-taking very rapidly and thoroughly checked over because, although no signs of oil had been found, what had appeared in the soil sample were viable spores, bacteria or whatever, for Anthrax, Botulism, Tetanus and Tuberculosis.

C/Insp. West made it clear to me that, for my own good, I was to remain at Camp Hospital, nominally under observation, until the results of the several samples recently taken from me, were known. Those results were expected to take about a week to come through. For the next six days I was kept in bed at Camp Hospital, being checked over each morning and evening to make sure that each of my vital signs were steady and normal. On the afternoon of the sixth day, Thursday 13th April 1967, C/Insp. West called in at Camp Hospital to advise me personally that the results of the last of the tests had come through and that they were all negative for any of the possible nasties I might have breathed in or allowed entry into my body through any cut or graze on my hands all those several weeks back.

Having delivered that most welcome news, C/Insp. West went on to advise me that a Land Rover would pick me up from Camp Hospital next morning at 09:00hrs and return me to Makuti, where I was to re-join A Troop and resume normal duties. The next morning, I was up at first light, glad to get out of pyjamas and into my Support Unit uniform once again. After an early breakfast I made sure that I thanked all the staff present for their kindness and help over the past week or more, before I headed across to the Armoury to recover my FN rifle and then wait for my transport, which appeared right on time.

On my arrival at Makuti I reported to Supt Holt and explained to him just why I had been somewhat unceremoniously extracted from the valley some 10 days before. At my setting out of the list of nasties waiting in ambush some two-foot underground in the lowveld, Rampart commented, "Good Grief! I wonder what's down there in the valley if we start digging!" He assured me he would get a message through to my troop commander about my return to duty and then sent me off to re-join the few members of A Troop who were in Makuti and to await SO Van Wyk's eventual return from the valley floor. During that deployment, there was only one other piece of excitement that came my way. Bob Flynn and his section were based close by Rekometje Research Station, as visible support to Glyn Vale and Andy Divine, the Tsetse Fly researchers who were determined to keep the station operational, despite the terrorist threat all around them. Bob had applied for a few days of local leave which had been granted. Dermot was tasked to replace him for the few days he would be away and I was directed to do the driving to and from the research station in order to affect the changeover. By then we had adopted the tactic of removing the side doors from our long wheel-based Land Rovers, to facilitate rapid entry and exit in times of urgency. It was also a quiet period in the valley, so the journey out became a matter of Dermot sitting in the front passenger seat, FN rifle to hand and me driving. That outward journey was entirely routine. Lots of game of all kinds, large and small, visible all the while and even a small family of giraffe daintily picking succulent leaves from the various treetops using their impressively long and agile tongues.

With Dermot dropped off and Bob picked up, I began the return drive to Makuti. Just as I also did, Bob had the habit of carting a camera with him whenever out on patrol. Being sat in the passenger seat, with game galore evident literally every yard of the journey, Bob slotted his FN rifle into the front carrying rack and concentrated on getting a few good shots of the plentiful wildlife we passed. A dozen or so miles from Rekometje and well ahead of us on a straight stretch of the dirt road, a herd of what proved to be a score or more of elephants began to cross from right to left in front of us. They were in single file, with several of them, as was quite often seen, with their trunks holding on to the tail of the one directly in front of them. I halted our Land Rover a good fifty yards from their crossing point and prepared to wait until the last of the herd was well clear of the road before driving on. As we were halted, Bob stepped out and, with an eye to the camera's viewfinder, took a couple of shots of the elephants. Obviously not happy with the distance between our vehicle and the elephants, Bob asked if I could get a little closer to allow him to get some better pictures. Warily and keeping the engine noise to a minimum, I eased our vehicle forward until we were no more than the length of a cricket pitch from the unhurriedly moving elephants. The herd ahead comprised a mixed bunch, with a mature matriarch leading the way, followed by others of assorted sizes, until the final one stepped out into view. That one was not only a massive bull, but he was carrying a pair of enormous tusks, among the largest I had seen in the valley. The big fellow took a quick sideways glance at us, dismissed us as no threat and carried unhurriedly on across the road to disappear up the trail the others had taken. Bob was clearly not satisfied with the one "side-on" shot he had taken of the big bull. "I want a head-on shot of that big bugger," he declared and trotted off to where the elephant trail crossed the road. As Bob lined up his camera on the disappearing elephant, I eased the Land Rover forward until I could see over his shoulder. The big bull was some thirty yards or so from the road, moving away from Bob. I took one look and offered, "I don't think he's going to turn around for you Bob." At that, Bob lowered his camera, picked up a sizeable rock from the roadside and set off after the big bull elephant, which, at that point was taking no notice at all of

Bob or our vehicle. Trotting up to within a dozen paces of the retreating grey form, Bob let fly with his rock. I must admit that I did not see exactly where the hurled rock struck the elephant, but it must have been somewhere delicate, because there was an almighty elephantine bellow. After that, the big bull spun around rapidly, ears flapping and head down. Bob, brim full of courage, or stupidity, stood his ground and raised his camera as his photographic target pinned its ears back, put its trunk down, bellowed and charged at him. Bob, eye to his camera's viewfinder, realised dangerously late that he was the target of that elephant's anger. As he turned from the elephant and began to run for his life, I inched our vehicle into position so that the central passenger seats were lined up with the elephant trail along which Bob was fleeing. In a series of fast, almost instinctive moves, I released the Land Rover's handbrake, shoved the gearbox into four-wheel drive and second gear, raised the engine revs to a scream and held down the clutch, all the while with my eyes on Bob and the elephant so close behind him that it was reaching out its trunk towards him. My mind calculated the rapidly dwindling distances, between Bob and the elephant and him and the Land Rover and the relative speeds of each. I judged that it was going to be, as a certain general once said of a famous battle, "a damned close-run thing!" Bob, camera in hand, literally dived headlong through the air and into the vehicle through the open space where a door had once been. I judged and he later agreed that I lifted my foot from the clutch while he was still in mid-air and before he hit the seats. Our vehicle literally leaped forward as I braced my grip on the steering-wheel, waiting for the impact I expected as elephant and vehicle met. Somehow, that never occurred. The angry, bellowing form of the elephant charged across the road, a few bare inches from the back of the Land Rover. I cared not to hang around to see more of it, only stopping to check that Bob was okay some couple of hundred yards further down the road. Apart from a sore hip, Bob and his camera were both okay, but it had been an extremely close call. After he had climbed round into the front passenger seat and I had set the vehicle moving once again, under a more usual gear-box arrangement, Bob turned to me, with a big broad grin on his face and commented, "That's another big one I owe you, Arn, but I got the shot I wanted!" As it turned out days later, he had indeed!

A week or so after that incident, it was my section's turn to be stationed at Rekometje Tsetse Fly Research Station. We made a section camp on a bluff overlooking the Rekometje River, within a hundred yards or so of the research station's buildings. With the valley all green and lush and the river running quite strongly, the first thing I did after we had established our camp, was to take a few photographic shots of the river and terrain around. Our briefing for that week was to keep half the section at our base camp each day, while the other half undertook daylight-hour road patrols in our Land Rover, limited in distance to the Chewore River to the east and the Zambezi River to the north. We were briefed to check all game trails we encountered, greater or lesser and to make sure that there was no sign of them being used by insurgents.

Looking back, it is clear, that those first few months of 1967 were the lull before the insurgent storm. The handful of decidedly amateurish incursions which did take place, both east and west of Lake Kariba were promptly detected and easily dealt with. Apart from my own section's modest encounter and Moebe's successful night ambush, A Troop was not directly involved in any of the small actions which did take place. That is not to say that our days in the Zambezi Valley were uninteresting. Far from it, as our turn at Rekometje demonstrated. By that time, our long wheel-based Land Rovers had been fitted with SSB HF Radios positioned by the left-hand side of the driver and to the right-hand side of the front seat passenger. The aerials which had to be fitted were carried on the outside of each of our Land Rovers just below the roof-rack. Depending upon whichever radio channel was to be used, so the aerial had to be changed to suit that channel. The aerials were six feet in length, half an inch in diameter and could only be safely screwed into their base socket on the side of the vehicle once the vehicle was stationary. My section's first usage for real of that radio arrangement was to contact Makuti Base Camp to report that the changeover of sections at Rekometje had been completed and that I and my section were about to bed down for the night and would be up and about at dawn. I was instructed, as a test for transmission and reception, to change channels in order to attempt to communicate directly with Chirundu Police Station. That meant a change of aerials, which was eventually achieved and, somewhat to our surprise, Chirundu picked up our signals at Strength 3, which made them entirely readable, while their transmission to us came booming in loud and clear at Strength 5. As we closed down our radio for the night, there were smiles and nods of approval among all of us. For the first time in our escapades in the valley, we had the confidence of knowing that we could reliably communicate, if needed, with the police force radio network outside of that geographic feature, without the previously erratic communication and often the need for an overfly by aircraft as had been needed with our VHF radio sets, with their very limited horizontal range. Despite the nuisance of having to change aerials with channels, the fitment of those SSB sets into our Land Rovers was a big step forward.

Next morning, bright and early, after a hot breakfast which would, if necessary, see us needing nothing more until the evening meal, I divided my section into two halves. One half to take with me on the mobile patrol and the other half to remain in camp. With the chosen half-dozen details safely seated in the vehicle, I handed the keys to Dvr/Const. Kisimis and settled myself in to the front passenger seat, my FN rifle, already cocked and loaded, but with safety-catch on, laid across my knees. At my instruction, the others in the vehicle carefully cocked, loaded and made safe their .303 rifles. Kisimis stowed his rifle into the clips which would hold it in place as he drove, but ready to hand should he need it. With everyone settled and ready, I motioned for Kisimis to get us under way, which he promptly did.

It then being in April, towards the end of the rainy season, the weather had been dry, although humid, for the past couple of days, so the dirt road conditions were not too bad. The road eastward from Rekometje Research Station very quickly brought us to the river itself, at a point where it split into two channels to go around a low island of scrubby vegetation, which disappeared under water when the level of the river rose three or four feet as it frequently did at this time of year, whenever it rained further up-river, along the escarpment or the farmlands beyond. On this day, most of the island was above water and neither of the two channels was flowing more than two or three feet deep, which, for our Land Rover was not any real problem. Const. Kisimis drove us slowly and carefully into the water, which was deep enough to flow into the cab at our feet by an inch or two. He drove our vehicle safely across the dozen or more yards of the nearest channel and up on to the island, which was about a hundred yards long and a third of that in width.

It was only when our vehicle reached the low ridge which ran down the spine of the island that Const. Kisimis and I saw, at the same moment, that we were not alone. Turning around, clearly to take a good look at us, from no more than a score of yards away, was a very large bull rhinoceros, its jaws clearly working hard on a great clump of greenery the ends of which were hanging down on either side of its lower jaw. Without taking my eyes from the rhino, I muttered to our driver to keep us moving, which he did. I had hoped that as we were moving on, our large animal companion on the island would simply keep chewing and leave us alone. In that fond hope I was very wrong. He just put down his head and charged at our vehicle, complete with his overflowing mouthful of greenery.

A mature bull rhino can weigh in at between 3,000 and 5,000kg and this fellow was on the larger end of that scale. Despite that, he was good and nimble on his feet and had a fair pace on by the time he did actually hit us. My one worry as he got within a couple of yards of the near side of the Land Rover, was that he would shove his head in through either the front door space or the one behind it. I had no wish to have my left hip or thigh take the impact, so I shifted rather smartly out of my seat, to my right and ended up sitting on top of the radio. Behind me I sensed similar movement among the constables in the centre section of the Land Rover. As it was, our belligerent rhino bull's very impressive horn hit us just where the door frame upright of the bodywork between front and middle door spaces met the floor-level bodywork. The impact knocked our vehicle a couple of feet sideways and rocked it rather alarmingly, causing some concerned yells from the constables behind me. It also caused our driver to bring us to a halt. Not satisfied with having given us an impressive display of rhino-power and still with his mouthful of greenery dangling, our assailant backed off a yard or so, dipped his head, stuck his horn under the skirting board of the Land Rover and began to lift it.

I cared not to wait to see if the powerful animal might have had the ability to turn us onto our side. So, having kept a good firm grip on my FN and not wanting to injure the fellow, I flicked the safety catch off, lined my rifle close by the brute's flickering left ear, but pointing at the ground and pulled the trigger. The crack of the bullet being fired that close to its ear had the effect I intended, because the brute uttered an awful bellow, stopped trying to lift or turn us over and fled, still with greenery dangling from its mouth.

Collectively, we took a few moments to sort ourselves out and recover from the somewhat too-close-for-comfort encounter and marvel at the very visible dent in the vehicle's panel-work. As Const. Kisimis rightly commented, "Ishe, that one was too big, too strong and too close!" That said it for all of us.

The rest of that day's patrol work fortunately proved very routine and unexciting, although my scheduled evening radio report went on a little longer than usual. It was around midnight, with a bright, full moon shining, when I was comfortably asleep in my sleeping bag, laying on my left side, that I was wakened by some gentle nudging in the area of my left shin. The nudging gradually worked its way up, little by little, from knee level to my hip and then my waist. At that point I detected a little simultaneous pressure against my left knee. That length of pressure points apart suggested just one thing, which was a snake, routinely going about its night hunting by trying to see if there might be any tasty little mouse or such hiding away between my sleeping bag and the ground. The immediate problem that I foresaw was that if I remained still, whatever kind of snake it was, it might well be tempted to join me inside my sleeping bag. Since almost all of the assorted snakes of Central Africa are venomous and given my past history, the one thing I did not care to risk was a bite from a venomous snake. Rolling away from it would leave me with the need to then struggle out of the sleeping bag, which would make me vulnerable, should the reptile feel aggressive. There was only one safe way to deal with the problem. I waited, unmoving, until the prodding told me the snake's head was about level with my sternum, then rolled over onto my stomach, trapping the snake's body underneath me and holding its head gripped under both hands, so that it could not wriggle forward. Once I was certain that I had my unwelcome visitor firmly pinned and immobilized beneath me, I called for the guard on duty and explained the situation to him. My terse explanation to Const. Peter that I was laying on and holding down a "nyoka" woke up everyone else. There was some discussion about what was best to do next, into which Const. Phineas said, rather casually, "As long as you have a good hold on its head, Ishe, and can hold that still, I will reach to get a hold on its tail. When I have hold of that we will roll you on to your back and then I can take the snake away from you safely". After I confirmed that, with the material of my sleeping bag between my hands and the snake's head, my grip was very tight indeed, Const. Phineas reached under the bottom end of my sleeping bag until he had hold of the snake's tail. Once he was happy with his grip, he instructed others to roll me on to my back and then step well clear, which is exactly what they did. Once they were backed off, Const. Phineas said, "Let go, Ishe. It will be alright!" Reassured by his confidence I duly let go of the hold I had on the snake's head, whereupon, in the clear bright moonlight, I watched as Const. Phineas dealt with the snake as if he were holding, and vigorously flicking, a whip to get the sound of a crack out of it. There was no sound of any cracking noise, but the effect was dramatic and for the snake, crippling, because Const. Phineas's rapid arm movement broke its back, whereupon Const. Phineas just let go of its tail and, because we all kept our issue boots on at night, simply stamped hard on its helpless head. A close look at the snake showed it to be an Egyptian Cobra almost six feet in length; definitely not something to be sharing a sleeping bag with.

After the body of the dead snake had been hurled away into the nearby bushes, for nature to take care of, I thanked my entire section and particularly Const. Phineas for helping me out of an awkward situation. In doing so I asked him the obvious question of where he had learned that very brave and effective way of dealing with a venomous snake. "My father taught me, Ishe." He explained, "We lived in Rusape. Plenty nyoka there!"

While the rest of the section gradually settled down to sleep away the remaining hours of darkness, I found it difficult to follow suit. When it became my turn for an hour on guard duty I was grateful for the call and just as grateful at the end of my shift that dawn was starting to break, which meant our usual precautionary stand-to, rather than going back to sleep or at least trying to.

The Rekometje River, when in spate, over-spilled here and there into an assortment of flood plains of modest size, which provided perfect nesting areas for all sorts of small birds. Among those, the weaver birds were prolific. Those birds had earned their common name from their habit of building intricately woven nests which hung in sociable profusion from reliably sturdy reeds, or, where reeds were not abundant or were of dubious sturdiness, from some trees. The male birds spent a great deal of time tearing off the long-stranded reed leaves and shredding them into workable widths and lengths. Watching the nest-weaving process going on was quite an education, as the birds possessed nothing more than their beaks and claws as tools. The male birds built the nests and showed them off to the female birds in the spring mating season. If the selected female was interested in any potential mate, she would try out the nest for size and for sturdiness. It was not uncommon for such an inspection to result in the total destruction of the woven nest, with the female tearing it apart strand by strand, before flying off to try out the nest built nearby by another male of her fancy. For obvious reasons, the younger male birds were less adept at nest-building, so it was usually with the more mature birds that the females eventually paired. On one occasion, quietly sitting watching, I saw one female bird energetically destroy the nests built by three males, before becoming satisfied with that of a fourth male bird and settling in with him.

Towards the end of April, we were routinely rotated back to depot, where we spent the next few weeks, apart from one field training session of five days, right at the very beginning of May, which we spent in the Deta Valley, a steep-sided wilderness through which runs the Mukweshe River. As a training location, the Deta Valley had one useful advantage in that there were peaks all around which could be used to do bearings and back-bearings and generally familiarise us and our sergeants in the troop with combined map and compass work. The disadvantage was that the reed grass, brush and scrub was so dense that it was almost impenetrable. In places, the only two ways to make progress were either to hack a way through with a machete or, lacking that weapon, to literally hurl yourself bodily at the reed grass ahead and let the weight of your body and equipment force the grass over and down. Then it was possible to pick yourself up, take a pace or two forward and repeat the process. Working in sections of ten, everyone took brief turns at being lead detail and performing the body-hurling activity when needed. Having been dropped off by heavy vehicle, we were purely afoot for the few days. Towards the middle of the afternoon of the first day, Moebe inquired of me, "How the heck can we make a sensible night-camp in this thickness of bush and grass?" I pointed towards the valley rim, "The vegetation will thin out if we head uphill, away from the valley floor. That's what we have had to do sometimes in other places." Moebe saw the sense in that and promptly changed the direction of our slow progress, to lead us towards the valley wall. It took us another hour of slow slogging before there was anywhere near some thinning of the vegetation which was enough to allow us to find a suitable place for our base camp for those few very worthwhile days of training. Not that our time in the Deta Valley was totally one of sweat and dust. With the Mukweshe River conveniently to hand we found time in the middle of our activities there to enjoy a leisurely bath and a bit of a swim, which I was able to capture on film.

While A Troop was engaged in those few precious training days, more problems cropped up with the dreaded Mars boots. Fortunately, when the Troop paraded at Tomlinson Depot on the morning of Saturday, 6th May, C/Insp. West advised us that replacement boots, of a better and more suitable quality, were waiting for all members of the Troop at the Ordnance Stores. As far as those replacement boots went, they were a vast improvement on the Mars item, but, as we sat having a natter that evening in the bar at Fife Hostel, Moebe, Bob, Dermot and I all agreed that they were not high enough at the ankle to stop us all getting our feet wet in even a couple of inches of water when out in the bush. It was not that any of us were worried about our feet getting wet as such. The problem was that damp feet, socks and boots rapidly created perfect conditions for the appearance of Athlete's Foot and worse. That conversation resulted in all of us making a visit to Ratanje's, a cobbler's shop of good repute in the middle of Salisbury. Mr Ratanje himself listened attentively to the sad story of our issue Mars boots, the nature of the work we were engaged in and our battles with fungal foot infections, caused by continually damp feet. At the end of it, he declared that he was certain he could produce pairs of boots, individually measured for each of us, in black leather, with sides high enough to keep us dry-shod and with soles of military-quality combat pattern, at a reasonable price. When we next visited his shop, some two weeks later, our personalised boots were all ready and waiting. Mr Ratanje was at pains to point out that the NATO quality combat soles had a three-year guarantee. We were all pleasantly surprised at just how comfortable our slightly unofficial style of new black boots felt. We duly thanked Mr Ratanje and gladly paid over the very reasonable price he asked. On the way back to depot we agreed that we would keep the use of our new boots strictly for when we were well away from depot.

Some ten days later, on Friday 19th May 1967, A Troop was flown down to the airfield at Boli, on route to Vila Salazar, with the advice that we would be there until the end of June. As I discovered, little or nothing had changed regarding the situation, layout and operational requirements at the individual camps. Inspector Ron Pilborough was still in charge at the police station, with SO Felix Kutner as his second-in-command. Of the opportunities for rest and relaxation, the police station's bar, called "The Gonna Stagga Inn" was, in the evenings, just as busy as it had been when last I was there, although there was perhaps somewhat less use being made of the swimming pool due to the cold season time of the year. Relations with the Portuguese Customs Officers were still totally cordial, which allowed Bob Flynn and I to swiftly introduce Moebe and Dermot to the welcome offerings available at the motel and station bar and restaurant across the border in Malvernia.

It soon became obvious that a firm friendship was developing between Insp. Pilborough and our new troop leader. From the moment they were introduced it was clear they were going to get along well together. So much so that a couple of months later they went off together on a month-long round the world cruise. I was not surprised to learn that when Moebe inquired carefully about relationships between Insp. Pilborough and myself, Insp. Pilborough had apparently advised my troop leader to keep a close eye on me as I was "Nothing but trouble!" I took a few moments to give Moebe an outline of the events at Camp 3 and the moving of the fence, the shot fired and my accidental listening-in to Insp. Pilborough at Nuanetsi. In view of the friendliness I saw blossoming between Moebe and Ron Pilborough, I did not mention my own full report of the incident getting into Propol's hands somewhat discreetly and outside usual channels. Moebe listened to my story and, commented that he hoped nothing like that would happen this time around. There we left it.

Moebe's wish for a quiet few weeks of guard duties at the restriction camps was, in the main, achieved. However, there were a few incidents worth recording. The first of those was what can only be described as a drunken brawl at No. 2 Camp, which occurred three days after our arrival at Villa Salazar. Dermot went off from our camp at 17:30hrs to carry out a routine shift changeover, which was achieved without anything unusual being noted. However, when he arrived in his vehicle a couple of hours later to check on the guards at Camp 2, he was informed by the constables on duty there that there had been a lot of noise and shouting from one of the barrack blocks.

As Dermot was receiving that verbal report, the door at the end of the block involved burst open and a score or more of the restrictees poured out, all shouting, squabbling and fighting. Dermot, sensible individual that he was, promptly climbed back into the vehicle, got on radio to us and the police station and then flashed lights and blew the horn at those involved.

That apparently had the effect of making some of the brawlers quit the fight and head back inside, but left a lot outside, still fighting. Dermot reported that it would need additional manpower before it was safe for police officers to try to enter the camp in order to restore order and find out the cause of the near riot.

On receiving the report, Insp. Pilborough ordered SO Van Wyk to take a dozen or so Support Unit constables and find out what was going on at Camp 2. Much to our surprise, when Moebe, myself and Bob, with a dozen of our constables, reached Camp 2, about 15 minutes later, the noise and fighting was still going on, with pairs, trios and groups of half a dozen or more all having noisy tussles and struggles. With three vehicles lined up at the gate, each with horn blaring and headlight flashing, the presence of police officers in some strength finally seemed to be noticed. Over the course of the next few minutes those nearest to the gateway and our vehicles quieted down and stopped brawling.

Eventually, we were able to stop the honking of vehicle horns and flashing of headlights and cautiously move into the camp itself. As we did so, those inmates who were nearest to us started to back away, leaving a couple of them apparently out cold, laying on the ground. Moebe, quite properly, requested those inmates nearest to us to call the camp spokesperson so that we could have a conversation with him, to try to find out what had been the cause of the rumpus and whether anyone had been seriously hurt.

While we were waiting for the spokesman to appear, Moebe and I moved forward far enough to allow us to take a closer look at the nearest inmate still laying unmoving on the ground. As we bent to check him over, I detected an unmistakable smell. The fellow reeked of Mlala Palm Wine. Apart from that reeking smell and a small amount of blood around nose and mouth, the fellow did not appear to be seriously hurt in any way. Before I could say very much to Moebe about Mlala Palm Wine, which he had never before encountered, the camp spokesperson appeared and instantly demanded the removal outside of "his camp" of all of us carrying weapons. Moebe patiently advised him that would only happen if we received a sensible explanation about what had gone on to cause the brawling, a firm assurance that it would not start again when we left and whether or not any of the inmates needed medical attention for injuries.

The camp spokesman pushed at the inert figure at our feet with his foot, saying as he did so, "He is not hurt. Just drunk!" At Moebe's question of, "On what?"

The answer was as I expected. "He has been drinking Mlala Palm Wine." Then, somewhat to my surprise, the spokesman continued, "A visitor brought some for us. It was quite a lot, but not enough for everyone." He paused long enough to gesture to one of the nearby dormitory huts. "Then the comrades in that hut tried to keep it for themselves. That is when the trouble started." He looked around at the inmates standing and laying about within sight, but now quiet and with their eyes on us grouped near the gate. Apparently satisfied at what he saw, he went on, "It is over now. Our First Aid people will see if anyone needs medical attention in the morning. If they do, I will tell you." He turned to those still standing around watching us and shouted a few dozen words in SiNdebele, at which those inmates laying on the ground were gathered up and carted off into nearby huts, followed by the remainder of the recently noisy but now quiet bunch of brawlers.

When it was clear that the orders of the camp spokesman were being carried out, without argument or delay, Moebe uttered a polite "Thank you," and gestured for all of us policemen to take ourselves outside of the camp gate. Once we were all on the outside of the gate, Moebe turned to me and asked, "What's all this about visitors taking Mlala Palm Wine into the camp. What were our guards doing for that to happen?" While we stood by our vehicles long enough to see the camp return quite rapidly to its usual situation for any late evening time, I explained that the "visitors" mentioned were more likely to have been a small number of the inmates who had sneaked under the perimeter wire and out of Camp 3 during night-time and gone off on a walkabout of their own for a day or two. Leaving Dermot to resume his standard night-shift routines, the rest of us drove back to our base camp close to the police station. Moebe made a detailed verbal report to Ron Pilborough and that was that.

The great Mlala Palm Wine War at Camp 3 was over. The following day, when Dermot came off shift, he wanted to know what was the Mlala Palm Wine spoken of last evening. Moebe, with his somewhat urban background, had heard of it, but knew little of the how and what of it as an alcoholic drink, apart from the rumoured stories that those Europeans who did drink it, usually swallowed it fast and in one whole gulp, while firmly holding their noses closed, because its smell was so foul. I explained to both of them that the mlala tree was a common item in the lowveld from Nuanetse down as far as Beitbridge, basically in the area of Chief Maseru and his people who were Venda by tribe and spoke Tshivenda as their home language. That was because they owed as much, or more of their heritage to their fellow tribespeople across the river in South Africa as they did to the Shona/Kalanga Group they were usually associated with in Rhodesia.

The traditional Bavenda people used the freshly collected sap of the mlala tree as a health drink. When fresh, it is sweet and pleasant on the tongue and just a little alcoholic in effect. However, whether by accident or design, over the years they had found that if it were left to ferment for a day or two, its potency level ramped up to the stage where very little was sufficient to almost instantly bring on a high degree of intoxication, an urge to vocalise loudly and a serious case of the staggers, which they actually revelled in. It was that fermentation period which also brought with it the foul reek.

At my quite detailed outline of the origins, background and effect of Mlala Palm Wine, my two colleagues promptly wanted to know how come I, as a very moderate drinker, knew so much about it and whether I had ever actually tasted it, fresh or otherwise.

I was happy to explain that the drink had been offered to us months ago, in the Railway Bar in Malvernia, in its fermented state. The foul reek from it had thoroughly put off both Terry Rowlandson and I from even tasting it. However, Reg Crahart, who had actually downed a teaspoonful of the drink, while tightly pinching his nose as he did so, had promptly gone pop-eyed, gasped, "Hell, that's got a kick like a mule," and declined any more. Given Reg's somewhat unfortunate addiction for alcoholic drinks of any and all kinds and his usual capacity for them, that spoke volumes.

That experience had been broadened after 14840 Const. Mutandwa kindly apologised, a day or so later, for appearing drunk on parade last September. He blamed it upon forgetting how potent Mlala Palm Wine was and mixing it with locally brewed beer across the border. When I informed him that I knew very little about it, he related that he had been brought up in the Beitbridge area and volunteered to me all the information I was subsequently able to put before Dermot and Moebe.

A couple of days later, the overnight train, moving fast, managed to run into a herd of elephant. One big bull collected most of the impact, resulting in it being knocked onto its side, with front and back legs on either side of the cowcatcher on the front of the engine. With the speed and weight of the train, the unfortunate animal was pushed along almost a half mile of track, its right side being steadily ground down by the sleepers and ballast between them. By the time the train finally come to a halt and the half carcass of the unfortunate elephant had been cleared away, dawn had arrived. Once the train had gone, every one of nature's scavengers, avian and earthbound, within scenting distance, arrived to join in the unexpected feast. In rapid time, vultures, eagles, kites, buzzards, kestrels, hyena and wild dogs were all briefly contesting for space and the chance to gobble up their share of the unexpected bonanza. Very sensibly, the Game Department's staff just told us to leave the wildlife to clean up the mess, which they did, very efficiently.

It was during that spell at Vila Salazar that I gave a bit of thought to the fact that it was getting on for three years since I had last been back to the UK to see my mother and brother and perhaps it was time I put that right. My bank account was quite healthy thanks to the umpteen days of Travel and Subsistence Allowance which had gone into it on top of my monthly pay. There was also the thought that I would rather not wait until I had completed my full three years in the BSAP because that delay would put me into the UK in winter. With those thoughts in mind and after a conversation about my intentions with SO Van Wyk, I duly submitted the necessary application for long leave, over the months of July and August, which application was quickly approved.

Left to right: Constables Mapuranga, Million, Petros, Itayi

More Time in Support Unit

On the 30th August 1967, I arrived back in Rhodesia, from my spell of long leave in the UK. Returning to my quarters in Fife Avenue Hostel, I found that my batman Shorty had properly remembered my planned date of return. My room was spotless, everything was neat and tidy. My uniforms were all ironed, starched smartly and parade ready, right up to and including my hat, soft, blue.

Guessing, as it proved accurately, that it would not be long before I was off on operations once again, I made sure that my 44 webbing set was all in order. Shorty had clearly paid some attention to my patrol kit because my mess-tins were in very good order and even my spare ammunition belt was noticeably stiff with starch. Perhaps more importantly, both my water bottles were clean inside and out and ready for use when needed. It was with a slight sense of furtiveness that I carefully added to my patrol kit, the set of ex-British Army camouflage jacket and trousers which I had purchased while in the UK. Akin to our strictly unauthorised high-boots from Ratanje's, they were destined for wear only once I was out and about on operations and well away from the eyes of senior police officers, many of whom had openly and loudly expressed their objection to duty uniform branch police officers being converted into soldiers. My greatest concern was that our Support Unit sergeants and constables were still being required to undertake operational duties wearing blue and grey riot gear instead of the camouflage uniforms already being issued to Police Anti-Terrorist Units (PATU) which, under steerage from WWII veterans such as Bill Bailey and Reg Seekings, were slowly but surely beginning to finalise their training and commence combat operations. As it was, in late 1967, Support Unit personnel, aside from us stick leaders with our FN rifles, were still being expected to enter into firefights with terrorists while still equipped with and using WWII .303 rifles against the insurgents' AK47s, SKSs and RPGs.

By the time I reported for duty at Support Unit HQ in Morris Depot on the morning of Friday 1st September 1967, I had already learned of the major terrorist incursion which had taken place just east of the Victoria Falls in Matabeleland, during August. On that occasion the group was much larger than any before. It numbered some 90 terrorists in all, made up roughly of half ZAPU, or perhaps more correctly ZIPRA (Zimbabwe Independent Peoples' Revolutionary Army) and half SAANC (South African African National Congress) members. According to the intelligence gathered by the end of the operation, their intention was to move into the Tjolotjo Tribal Trust Land (TTL) and there establish bases for the recruiting and training of terrorists within Rhodesia. Their idea appeared to be only to move the SAANC element onward once the ZIPRA element was well established on Rhodesian soil. The intended route of the SAANC element was from Rhodesia into Botswana and then into South Africa and on to Soweto Township. However, the presence of that large, combined group was soon detected. That resulted in what was the first major combat operation of the insurgent war. The tail end of that operation was still ongoing as I returned to operational duty. Forty-seven of that group were killed within the first three weeks. A score or so of them were captured, wounded or uninjured, while the remainder, some of whom were wounded, managed to make their escape into Botswana. Instead of returning them to Rhodesia, to be dealt with according to the law of the land, as terrorists, which they were, the Botswana Government, no doubt steered by the UK, imprisoned them, only briefly, before handing them back to the Zambian authorities.

What I and most other Rhodesians of that time did not realise was the eventual ramifications of that particular incursion. What was of immediate note was that our Rhodesian Defence Forces suffered the first men killed in Rhodesia since the native uprisings of 1896-7. What we did not register at that time was the fact that it was that incursion by South African terrorists into Rhodesia which provided the then Prime Minister of South Africa, John Vorster, with justification for subsequently sending South African Police Force contingents to assist Rhodesia in the matter of border control, which at that time really meant, patrolling the length of the Zambezi River in order to prevent further incursions by Rhodesian or South African terrorists into Rhodesia.

At Support Unit HQ I quickly discovered that Inspector Phil Kensett had been added to our numbers, that Supt Ted Mallon had taken over at Makuti in the position of Rampart North East, that A Troop had recently started another stint based at Makuti Camp and that I was ordered to join them the following day. I was to travel to Makuti by Land Rover in company with Insp. Kensett and that I was once again able to take my batman with me. Until 08:00hrs the next day I was off duty to enable me to organise myself in preparation for that deployment.

By 09:00hrs the next day, I was once again under way northward in a Land Rover driven by Phil Kensett, with Shorty as a passenger and all the necessary kit for a few weeks of being based at Makuti Camp. With brief stops at both Sinoia and Karoi, it was afternoon by the time we arrived at Makuti Police Post as it was by then better known. Fortunately, SO Van Wyk was in camp when our vehicle arrived. He carted me off to the caravan which was still the operations room, reported my arrival to Supt Ted Mallon and explained to me that the area between Kariba Gorge and the Chewore River was apparently quiet, with no known crossing of the Zambezi by any insurgent group for many weeks. That was ascribed to the fact that those in Zambia who were orchestrating the incursions had been busy for some time preparing the August crossing into Matabeleland. With that operation now completed and literally hundreds of trained terrorists of ZANU, ZAPU and the SAANC all sitting in camps in Zambia, just waiting to cross into Rhodesia anywhere along the northern border, it was time to be extra vigilant and wary within the area of operation covered from Makuti. Bob Flynn and Dermot Creaner were out with their sections, with vehicles, based at H Camp on the Zambezi and at the Rekometje Research Station. Supt Mallon felt that what was needed was a more thorough scouting of the valley floor from the Chirundu Road to the Chewore River, on foot. His suggestion was that the patrol should commence where the main North Road to Chirundu crosses the Nyakasanga River and finish at the isolated hill called Pfumbe on the west bank of the Chewore River. He reckoned that it would be just about right for a week's patrol by a Support Unit section. As I had been on R&R as he put it, for a couple of months it was just the thing to get me back into a fully operational mindset once more.

I got the distinct impression that Supt Ted Mallon was doing his best to be informal, friendly and encouraging in the manner he was setting out his requirement, but as I could see one or two problems, I pointed them out to our new Rampart. My first concern was water. Although the intended patrol route would walk us across the Ruishi, Rekometje, Cheruwe, Chiremba, Sapi and Mbira rivers on our way to Pfumbe Hill, which I knew could be reached by vehicle from either Rekometje Research Station or Mana Pools, there was little or no chance of finding water in any of them at this late stage of the dry season. Then there was the matter of radio communications, just in case we found anything, or somewhat worse, if some insurgent group found us. Our portable VHF sets, even with their improved aerials had proven erratic in performance in the past and would likely be so again. Finally, I pointed out that I had had some experience of the nature of the bush on the valley floor and was well aware that the bush between the Sapi and Mbira Rivers was tightly packed mopani scrub and between the Mbira River and the Chewore it was dense jesse thorn bush. If the patrol had to cut its way through, then progress could be as slow as just one mile an hour, which might mean missing our intended uplift target date at Pfumbe Hill, which made the need for good radio comms even more essential.

Supt Mallon listened patiently to what I had to say. Then he turned to Insp. Kensett and cheerfully said, "See what you can do to address PO Woolley's concerns, but make sure the patrol starts on schedule tomorrow morning and confirm to me that it has been started, please. Now, Gentlemen, kindly excuse me as I have an SB (Special Branch) meeting to attend." With that polite but clear dismissal, we three left the caravan and retreated to our cluster of Support Unit tents where we pored over our 1:50,000 scale maps of the valley floor. As best we could calculate it, the distance between Supt Mallon's indicated start and finish points was about 70 miles. Nominally that was only 10 miles each day, but by the time we allowed for climbing up and down gullies, of which there were many and doing a few hundred yards up and down any game trails we came across, which were likely to have been used by any insurgents crossing the valley, the likely total distance was going to be nearer a dozen miles or more each day. In distance it was no great burden, which was at least something. What did worry us was how our African members were going to manage with feeding themselves individually rather than communally as could be arranged when we had a vehicle with us or were at a base camp and working around it day by day. No matter how the three of us looked at it, the proposed foot patrol was not going to be a picnic.

In the end, all that we could do was to call my section of A Troop together and brief them on what the morrow would bring. For me, two plus points arose from that briefing. The first one was the realisation that the sergeants and constables were clearly pleased to see me back with them. The second was that Troop Sergeant Isaac asked if he could be included in the patrol in exchange for Sgt Servester as he wished to see more of the valley than he had been able to do so far, having mostly been required to stay in Makuti Camp, supervising guard and other routine activities. Moebe was quite happy with that arrangement. We also arranged that with me away for a week or so and with Insp. Kensett not having brought a batman along with him to Makuti, Shorty would act in that capacity for him while I was away.

The following morning, after making sure that every one of those going on the patrol with me had also had a good breakfast meal and that water bottles were topped up, I joined ten members of No. 1 Section of A Troop as we loaded our 44 webbing sets into two Land Rovers, driven by our troop commander and Insp. Kensett and settled into the vehicles, ready to be driven to our drop off point as chosen by Rampart. It was at that point that Moebe spotted that I appeared to have no sleeping bag strapped under my backpack and asked if I had forgotten it. I had to explain to him that while in the UK I had purchased, at no great cost, a used parachute, made of pure silk and had a tailor convert it into four sleeping-bags. All four layers, when tightly rolled, I could fit neatly into one of the ammunition-pouches on my webbing. Depending on warmth or cool of the nights out on patrol, I could slide, fully dressed, inside one or all four of the layers of silk and, if it were raining, my poncho was quite capable of keeping me dry overnight. That explanation must have set Moebe thinking, because within a couple of weeks, he too had adopted the same very useful arrangement.

It was mid-morning when Moebe and Insp. Kensett set us down at the roadside at its crossing of the Nyakasanga River, wished us good luck and started their drive back to Makuti, leaving us on the ground to commence our foot patrol on a roughly north-east compass bearing. Knowing what we were heading into, I had clipped a large and recently sharpened panga, or machete, onto my webbing belt. It was not long before it had to be brought into use. Moving on foot in the Zambezi Valley is fine if that footslogging can be done using roads, tracks and game trails, but cross-graining, through dense grass, scrub and mopani trees or jesse bushes is something else. Every member of the section, without exception, took a thirty-minute turn at wielding my machete in the thick bush. Whoever was up front, for his half-hour, including me, handed his rifle to the man behind him, who stayed closer than standard patrol formation and distancing dictated. In the thickest patches, visibility was little more than five or six yards. When we reached one of the infrequent small clearings which are scattered all around the valley floor, we viewed it with a sense of relief. However, those clearings brought an absence of the welcome shade which the heavier bush provided. For that reason, once we had established that there was nothing in the way of big game, big cats, or other threat visible in them, my machete was returned to its scabbard and we moved across them without delay.

At the two-hour mark, after a quick conversation with Sgt Isaac, I called a halt to our progress, to avoid moving through the worst couple of hours of the Zambezi Valley's special brand of midday heat. It was not a meal-break. We lit no fires and kept our consumption of water down to a minimum as we were all very well aware that the two water bottles at our belts might have to last us all day and overnight too. What we did do though was to try to establish radio communications with Makuti or Chirundu, or for that matter, anyone who could hear our transmissions. Worryingly, we had no success with those efforts. By two o'clock in the afternoon I decided we needed to push on. Fortunately, the afternoon proved easier than the morning and my machete stayed in its scabbard. The few game trails which we did encounter failed to give us much assistance as they were targeted towards the Zambezi or the escarpment, across our line of patrol, rather than going with it. Each of those we duly inspected for insurgent boot-spoor. Although we found nothing of that kind, the dry dusty ground carried the clear sign of wildlife large and small. In a couple of the large open spaces we had sight of herds of impala, zebra and buffalo.

Close to five o'clock we came across a clump of mature mukwa trees which formed a perfect circle ten or fifteen yards across. Within that circle there were bits and pieces of dead trees, but very little scrub and bush, so it was a perfect place for our first night stop. With most of the grass and undergrowth of the valley in a tinder-dry state, we very carefully cleared an area and excavated a shallow fire-pit so that we could each cook a hot meal before full dark, by which time we needed to have our fire done and finished with. With just one hour of guard duty for each of us, we were able to get a few hours of sleep and to recover somewhat from the efforts of the day just gone.

As dawn approached, we stood-to as usual, in case of any sudden threat of attack. When the threat did appear however, it was not from insurgents, but from a herd of elephant about a couple of dozen strong, or perhaps more accurately, from one of the juvenile bulls in the herd. Instead of busily browsing on the foliage aplenty outside and all around our night camp, this one young bull elephant, standing about six feet at the shoulders, decided that the only place it wished to be was inside the circle of trees, where we were. Fortunately for us, the individual trees in the circle of mature trees were that close together that it was unable to just walk in. However, when it failed to push in between the first couple of gaps it tested, it tried for a third time, where the gap was just a little wider. At that, I cocked and readied my FN, in the hope that the noise, plus our human scent might make it back off.

Not put off at all by that noise or by our human scent which it must surely have detected, it just kept pushing to the point where it actually did get its head within the tree ring before its shoulders wedged just a bit. It was at that point that Const. Svotwa, who was something of a gentle giant, picked up a log of wood about six feet in length and six or seven inches across and smacked the unwanted would-be intruder across the forehead with it. I am certain that I saw the little bull elephant's knees buckle for a moment, before it uttered a clearly distressed squeal, backed away and disappeared at a run into the main body of the herd.

My, "Well done Svotwa!" was echoed by several others in our patrol. With a wary eye on the elephant herd, we re-kindled our fire and each made our own individual breakfast. While the cooking was going on, I had a conversation with Sgt Isaac about finding somewhere, before this day was out, whereat we could replenish our nearly exhausted water supplies. We were all aware that before Kariba Dam was constructed and the valley area below Kariba Gorge was turned into a controlled hunting area and Game Reserve, African people had lived in the valley under Chiefs Nyamunga, Mudzimu, Dandawe and Chundu, with small villages scattered all about. Their survival presupposed reliable and adequate sources of water. Our problem was that we did not have the local knowledge that those villagers had until the time they were re-located out of the valley into the Urungwe Tribal Trust Land above the escarpment. Theoretically, there were two options open to us. The first was to make a radio call for a re-supply. The second was to push on north-easterly until we reached the Ruishe River, or, if we were a little off course, that river's tributary called the Mwashoyeni. Neither would be running at this time of the year, but, with a little bit of luck we might find water if we dug deep enough into the sand of the bed of either water course. Despite our best efforts at making radio contact, before we set off, there was no response to our calls to Makuti or Chirundu. That reduced our options to just one. We needed to push on, which is just what we did.

By my reckoning we had covered less than ten miles on our first day, which left us with about a half-dozen more to cover before reached the Ruishe River, with the potential, if not certainty, for a re-supply of precious water. As we prepared to leave our overnight stop, I issued an order that nobody was to use any of their remaining supply of water until instructed to do so. After that, we pushed on, with Sgt Isaac up front at point for the first hour. Fortunately, the nature and limited denseness of the foliage we were pushing through did not create any need for my machete to leave its scabbard. It was shortly after Sgt Isaac was replaced by Const. Ben at Dermotthat we came across a good broad game trail upon which there was ample proof of its use by elephant, from both spoor and droppings. The not yet quite dry condition of the droppings suggested that the elephant which had left it was not far away, even if it was not within sight. Obedient to our patrol instructions, I sent Sgt Isaac and four constables to check for spoor one hundred paces the one way and took the rest of the section with me to cover a hundred paces or so the other way. Both checks showed nothing but assorted spoor of the natural inhabitants of the valley, so we re-grouped and pushed on along our north-easterly route.

Some few minutes after Const. Itayi had taken over Dermotposition from Const. Ben and in an area where the grass was good and dense, Const. Itayi somehow managed not to see in front of him the entry hole of a spring hare burrow. His left leg sank fifteen inches or so into the hole and he fell. His scream of pain as his left leg broke disturbed a myriad of birds and brought me up at the run from my position in the middle of the section. Const. Itayi's face was grey with pain and shock. It was quite clear he needed immediate evacuation to a hospital. Our patrol routine was always to have the radio carried by the tail-end-Charlie as that individual was least likely to be an immediate casualty in the case of an ambush or other contact. I handed my machete to Sgt Isaac, with instructions to cut a couple of saplings or branches which we could use as splints, while I tried once more to get a message through to ZEF 903, which was the call-sign for Chirundu or to ZEF 908, which was the call-sign for Makuti. Once again, while some indistinguishable chatter could be heard as background noise, my calls were clearly not being heard. Looking around, I could see close by a climbable mopani tree, so with a bit of an initial boost up in from Const. Svotwa, I tried again from some 15 or 20 feet up, once again without achieving any radio contact.

Back on the ground I put my thinking to the members of the patrol. We needed to make a stretcher, using three or four of our blue riot jackets, so that we could carry Const. Itayi. If we did a back-track to the elephant trail which seemed to be heading for the escarpment, that should cross the track from Rekometje Mission Research Station to the Main North Road. We could stop the first south-bound vehicle and ask the driver to take Const. Itayi up to Makuti Camp, from where he could be taken to hospital. There were nods of agreement from all around. While Sgt Isaac supervised the creation of an improvised stretcher, I checked on the splinting which had been applied to Const. Itayi's lower left leg. Although each detail carried a wound dressing, none of us had any rolls of bandage, but I always carried a small hank of cord to help make a night bivvy if needed, so we cut three lengths of that to keep the crude splints in place.

Carting an injured member through the thick bush of the Zambezi Valley on an improvised stretcher was not the easiest of things to accomplish, so it was with a great sense of relief that we got back to the elephant trail. Once there we were able to head south on it and step more smartly along. In under an hour, we reached the track to Rekometje Research Station. By my reckoning we had at least ten miles of walking to get to the Great North Road as it was often referred to. To try to avoid that, I made another effort to make radio contact with Chirundu. That failed. That meant between three and four hours of steady, relentless carting of our injured man. It was no time to rest up through the heat of the midday hours, so we just kept at it. At least we were able to set rotating teams of four to share the burden, so we were able to step steadily along.

After a couple of hours I called a brief stop, to allow us all to rest just a little and to swallow what little was left of our water supplies. In giving them the okay to swallow whatever water each man had still left, I pointed out that once we reached the main road, we would only be an hour's walk from Marongora Dam. There we would be able to drink as much as we needed, camp overnight and set off in the morning with our water bottles full. That outline of intent was met with approval all around, so it was in slightly better spirits that the members of the section, including me, swallowed the last of the water we had set off on patrol with some 30 hours before, picked up Const. Itayi on the crude but fortunately functional stretcher and pushed on.

It was late in the afternoon when we reached the main road, which proved not to be very busy at all, to the extent that it was a full half-hour before a vehicle came into sight, heading southwards. As it approached, I stepped out into the roadway and signalled for it to stop, which it did. It was a Rover 90 saloon car, containing only Assistant Commissioner Gubby Allen, Officer Commanding Mashonaland Province, who must have been on a visit or inspection at Chirundu. As I approached the driver's door and delivered a respectful salute, he lowered the window and took a good hard look at me, before uttering, somewhat sharply, "Good Grief Woolley. You haven't shaved!"

Ignoring that, I informed OC Province of why I had stopped him and the background to how the injury had occurred. Mr Allen climbed out of the staff car, took a good look at Const. Itayi who was still laying on our improvised stretcher in the shade and commented, somewhat dryly but not unkindly, "You really did put your foot into it this time, didn't you constable?!" Then he turned to me and said, "Put him in with his legs along the back seat of the car. He can rest his back against the door until we get to Makuti."

As other members of the section carefully loaded Const. Itayi into the car as instructed, I asked OC Province if he would please pass on the message to the Control Room at Makuti that the patrol would be overnighting at Marongora Dam and setting off to get on with our instructed task as of next morning. That he agreed to do, before getting behind the wheel of the car once again and setting off southwards.

A little over an hour later, having moved along somewhat smartly on well-used trails and tracks and with dusk starting to settle in, we reached Marongora Dam, where we were all, two by two for safety, able to get to the water's edge, slake our thirsts and refill our water bottles. Feeling a whole lot better, we chose a suitable place for a night camp and settled in to the usual overnight routines, except for one. Normally, it would have been unthinkable to set fires and start cooking at that late time of day in an operational area, but, given what the day had held and on the briefing that the area was presently quiet and without any known presence of insurgents, I broke that rule and allowed the fire to be kept going until everyone had eaten an ample meal and swallowed at least a couple of pints of tea.

It took us until noon the next day to get back to the elephant trail which had proved so helpful the previous day. It was only then that I realised, looking at where that trail crossed the Rekometje road and continued southwards towards the escarpment, that it was the very same place where Bob Flynn had nearly come to grief in trying to get his photograph of the bull elephant with the huge pair of tusks.

Towards the end of the day, we were just a few miles beyond where Const. Itayi had come to grief when the level of the land began to take on a decided slope downwards, suggesting a gulley or even a watercourse ahead. Shortly after that, Const. Tirivaviri, on point, made three silent signals in quick order. First was a hand which he held up vertically, to signal a stop, which we all obeyed. Next was a horizontal wavy line with his hand, indicating water or a watercourse ahead. The third was a tap of two fingers of his right hand to his left shoulder, which was the signal for stick leader to appear alongside. What I found myself looking at was a stretch of somewhere in the order of fifty or sixty yards of clear grassland sloping down to a watercourse, the bed of which appeared to be mostly sand, with an occasional smooth rock sticking up. Bringing the rest of the section up to the edge of the grassland from where they could cover our movements, Tirivaviri and I, spaced apart for safety, went to take a closer look at the feature ahead. A quick look at my map and a bit of work with my compass made me feel sure we had reached the Ruishe River, something like 22 or 25 miles along our line of patrol towards Pfumbe Hill. I hauled my machete out of its scabbard and began to use it as a shovel at a likely spot in the sand. Some ten or twelve inches down there was moisture, so I switched my machete for my large mess-tin and dug deeper. At about eighteen inches down I was able to scoop up a palm-full of crystal-clear water, which I displayed to Const. Tirivaviri, who nodded and commented, "We shall be alright for water tonight, Ishe," which we were.

Before we made night camp just inside the bush at the edge of the grassy vlei, I bothered to take our VHF set out into the middle of the open area in an effort to once again make contact with one police station or another. To my pleasant surprise, I received an almost immediate response from Chirundu Police Station, which was some thirty miles distant. I was able to pass our approximate position to Chirundu for relay to Makuti and eventually got back word that Const. Itayi was safe in Sinoia Hospital, which made us all feel a lot better now we knew that our emergency rescue activity had been successful.

A couple of hours of patrolling the next morning brought us to the Rekometje River, some twelve or fifteen miles north of Rekometje Research Station. Knowing what that river was like from our encounters with it close to the research station, we were not surprised to find water just a foot or two down under the surface of the sand. At that point we took the opportunity to top up our water bottles, swallow as much as each of us felt comfortable with and then push on. Walking across the floor of the Zambezi Valley away from tracks, game trails and the like, was always a matter of working with whatever nature decided to throw at you by way of options and challenges. Bush and scrub tree areas, especially when it included, or was exclusively made up of jesse, hook-thorn and the like, meant very little shade and very slow going. Areas of heavy forest were always very welcome, because there was plenty of shade from the scorching heat of the sun, very little undergrowth at floor level to impede progress and very little by way of big game as there was little or nothing for them to browse or graze upon. Then we had the large open areas of low grass, very often clumpy in nature, in which the grazing animals spent a lot of time. Traversing those safely was a matter of sending across men of the section in twos, covered by those who were still in the bushy area. Moving across just two by two avoided the risk of all of us being caught out there by lion, elephant, rhino or buffalo, which could be very risky to say the least.

Fortunately for us on that fourth day out, there were several large vleis, or open areas, teeming with antelope of all kinds and sizes. There was only one which we had to work our way around, because of the presence of elephant and a herd of over fifty adult buffalo, with several young ones among them. The result was that our patrol made better progress than I thought we might until the middle of the day when two things combined to slow our progress. The first was that by my reckoning, we should have by then reached and crossed the upper portion of the Cheruwi River. Admittedly that showed up on my maps as one of the shorter streams running towards the Zambezi as it appeared to start in the valley floor rather than as most did, up on the rim of the southerly escarpment. While I was working on map and compass, trying to fix a position, I noticed a very noisy little bird, about the size of a common sparrow, which was making quite a racket close by us. It kept on chirping loudly, flying a short distance away, each time in the same direction and then returning closer to us. I took no great notice of it, presuming that it was upset by our human presence, which it took as a threat. How wrong I proved to be! It was Const. Bushu who held a short conversation with Sgt Isaac before the pair of them came over to have a word with me. Const. Bushu was certain that the noisy little bird was a honeybird, often known as a honeyguide. According to Const. Bushu, if we followed it, it would lead us to a beehive, which would provide us with some welcome honey to eat.

With all of the section agreeing that they would welcome some fresh honey and me quite intrigued by the story outlined by Const. Bushu, when the little bird took off and flew a dozen yards before settling on a branch and chirruping loudly from there, I moved towards it, with Const. Bushu behind me and others of the stick falling in behind him. This time, on taking note of our movement, the drab little bird flew another dozen or more yards in the same direction before settling and chirruping some more. Eventually, after a half-hour of playing follow-my-leader, avian style, our feathered guide's song changed tone and it started to fly to and fro across our direction of travel. At the same time Const. Bushu, whose eyes were perhaps sharper than mine, or whose bush-sense was better, warned me to go carefully as there were quite a few bees around. I needed no second warning before stopping and starting to look very carefully around me, because even I had heard of the dangers posed by the African bee. It was the sharp eyes of Sgt Isaac who first spotted what we were looking for. Ten or twelve feet up in the trunk of a nearby large marante tree, there was a small hole, with countless bees swarming in and out.

For me and I guessed most of the others there, the next half-hour was highly educational, if somewhat unorthodox in operational area behaviour terms. We quickly and very carefully set a smudge fire, the thick smoke from which covered the tree with the beehive in it. The effect was that the bees started to behave as if sedated. Then Const. Bushu borrowed my machete and cut down a small tree which had branches he could use as a ladder. That he propped firmly against the tree trunk under the beehive. Standing on that and taking no notice of the smoke or the seemingly drowsy bees, which made no effort to attack him, Const. Bushu chipped away at the small hole until it was big enough for him to thrust a bundle of smouldering grass in. Once that was safely within the tree, he did a lot more whacking and chopping until he could reach in and start to bring out chunks of honeycomb which he dropped down to us. Sgt Isaac took the first large chunk, carted it a dozen yards away downwind of our smudge fire and set it on the ground, whereupon our little feathered guide got stuck into it very energetically, pecking open the individual cells and eating the grubs inside, as well as taking in some of the honey itself.

For me, two things arose from that experience. The first was the indelible memory of the encounter with that honeyguide bird. Something few Europeans have ever encountered, so I understand. The second was that when I, who could not recall ever bothering to taste or eat honey before, tasted the honey from that beehive, I found it so tasty and refreshing that whenever it has been available, I have regularly eaten honey on a daily basis ever since, in preference to jams and marmalades.

Once everyone in the section had had enough honey, we set a further chunk down for the honeyguide, carefully put out our smudge fire and returned to working towards our real purpose for being there on the valley floor. While following the little bird, I had taken a glance or two at my compass, which indicated that we were moving in a line not far off from our steady north-east requirement, which was at least some small compensation for the time we had lost in obtaining our unexpected but very welcome feast of honey. It also took us a little closer to what I hoped would be out next source of water, because the heat was unrelenting. At that point, having topped up our water bottles and drunk our fill when we crossed the Rekometje River earlier in the day, we were not too badly off for water. However, if we had to make a dry camp overnight, that adequate water situation would change rapidly. With that in mind we needed to locate the Mbera River which was the next one running across our line of march and hope that we could find water there. With two or three hours of daylight still left, we pushed steadily onward, only stopping briefly to check out two small game trails which crossed our path. While there was no sign of insurgent boot spoor, what did give me some cause for concern was the very fresh spoor of a pride of lion, overlaying all of the other spoor on the second of the two tracks. I did not have to say a word to Sgt Isaac and the others about keeping a sharp eye open. What they all saw on the ground did that job for me.

A short while after finding the lion spoor, it was my turn to take up the Dermotposition for the patrol. Some ten minutes later, we came across another vlei which was something in the order of a quarter mile across. I signalled for the patrol to halt and, without breaking cover, took a good long look up, down and across the open area. No more than thirty yards to my right and a dozen yards or so out in the open, there was a pride of lion, busy eating at the carcass of a buffalo which they had obviously not long ago killed. Silently signalling for the patrol to close up on me, I made them all, in a whispered briefing, fully aware of what I had seen. When I made it clear that I intended to do a left turn, stay just within the cover of the bush and circle around the vlei instead of carrying out our usual method of a two-by-two crossing of it, Sgt Isaac nodded his head in agreement, but then whispered, "Ishe, I have never seen lions. Can I have a look, please, before we move on."

To my amazement, there was a whispered chorus of, "Me too Ishe," which suggested that none of them had actually seen a lion in the wild. Very carefully, making sure that our presence was not detected by the lions, I allowed each member of the patrol a couple of minutes of peering at the contentedly feeding big cats, before leading them away, keeping just inside the bushes bordering the vlei.

An hour or so later, just after I stood down from Dermotposition, we arrived at the Mbera River. At first glance it barely merited being called a river, because it was more like a modest stream, running in a narrow and totally dry gulley and lacking any stretch of sand into which we might dig in the hope of finding water. With my mental fingers crossed, I directed the patrol downstream in anticipation of finding a pool of water or at least some sand into which we might dig. It took us the best part of a mile of scouting before we found a stretch of the river which had a sandy bed. Once more my machete and a couple of mess-tins used as scoops eventually revealed water a couple of feet down below the surface of the sand in the river's bed.

With the welcome confirmation that we were not going to have a dry camp overnight, we crossed the Mbera, found a suitable spot and set about making camp in the thick bush less than a hundred yards from the river itself. As ever, our overnight camp layout was a circular one, with our 44 webbing packs used as pillows by most of us. With no rainfall to bother us most of us set our ponchos as groundsheets, put sleeping bags or bedrolls down on top with our rifles close to hand. With the overnight warmth of the valley in September, I used only one layer of my improvised silk sleeping-bag. Given the thickness of the bush cover at that location, several of us had found bushes to set our packs against. The fact that the foliage of those bushes leaned out and over us was no bother. We soon created a modest fire-pit in the middle of our defensive circle and, in two and threes, used our mess-tins to cook our meal. Before full dark our fire was out, our rifles had been cleaned and the usual quiet murmur of conversation began to die away as individuals, other than the guard, dozed off to sleep, fully clothed and with face-veils in place. For those with sleeping bags, it was a case of keeping bare hands inside them so as to prevent being attacked by mosquitoes, tsetse fly or any other of the dozen and one blood-sucking or egg-laying insects that swarmed at night. Our night-guard arrangement was simple. The thickness of the bush all around meant that there was no visibility, so all that was required was an hour in turn about, simply sitting up, being awake and listening for any potentially threatening noise. Working clockwise and starting at a different point each night, the night guard on duty, upon completion of his hour, quietly awoke the man next to him, waited until that individual was fully awake and attentive and then went off to sleep himself. On that particular night I was positioned between Const. Tirivaviri and Sgt Isaac, who completed his hour on guard and duly woke me close to one-thirty a.m. He waited until I was sitting up and fully awake, with rifle across my lap and then he settled back to sleep. On looking around, the first thing that struck me was the glorious brightness of the full moon above. The second thing was, perhaps due to the effect of the moon, the myriad of insects of all shapes and sizes flittering about and the diving, twisting and sheer acrobatic flying of the bats enjoying their meal among them.

About half-way into my hour of guard duty I began to feel a bit stiff, so worked my way out of my silk sleeping bag, onto all fours and moved to kneel a couple of feet from Const. Tirivaviri's feet, in position to wake him when my hour on guard was completed. A few minutes later, I began to detect something of a rustling in the bushes not far away. As I listened carefully, there came the unmistakable crack of a dry branch breaking as something heavy trod on it. Then, thanks to the bright moonlight, I picked up the unmistakable shape of an adult rhino literally ten or twelve feet distant, but sideways on to our camp circle and apparently oblivious to the fact that we were close by. It was moving slowly, nibbling and chewing at odd clumps of leaves on the bushes. My initial judgement was that its line of movement would take it safely past us, so I remained still and quietly watched its every move. Just when I thought all was going to be okay, it decided to do a ninety-degree left turn and take a mouthful of leaves from the bush which Tirivaviri had his pack and head against.

Obviously liking the taste, it pushed deeper into that bush to the point where its head was vertically over Tirivaviri's head and a bare four feet from me. How the sizeable animal failed to smell our presence I know not. Fearing that its next step would see it tread on the sleeping constable, I reached out and grabbed hold of Tirivaviri's feet, intending to pull him away from the possibility of being trodden on by a rhino. The constable was laying on top of his sleeping bag, on his back, blissfully unaware that by then the rhino's head was a bare eighteen inches above his own. My touch on his boots caused him to immediately sit up, with the result that he really did head-butt the rhino's lower jaw. I added a parade-ground roar of "SCRAM!" at the brute, which, up until that moment, clearly and quite incredibly, obviously had no idea at all about our presence. More than somewhat startled, the rhino uttered a loud snort, stepped back, spun around and galloped noisily off into the night. The combined disturbance of my parade-ground bellow and the rhino's noisy flight immediately had the entire patrol awake, reaching for weaponry and wanting to know what was going on. It took just a little while for me to explain events of the past few minutes and reassure them that all was now well and that they could go back to sleep again.

With the camp quieted down again I formally handed over the guard duty to Const. Tirivaviri who asked, as I settled back into my own sleeping position, "Ishe, did I really hit that rhino with my head?" Upon my assurance that, give or take the wearing of his hat soft blue, he really had done just that, he shook his head in wonderment and said, "Thank you Ishe. I have a good story to tell my family."

During our dawn stand-to the next morning, Sgt Isaac confided to me that he and the constables, who had been literally living on maize meal porridge and sadza, with very little relish to flavour it, for the past four days, would be grateful if they could have some fresh meat for relish. He went on that he had never had the chance to shoot an antelope, so please would I let him shoot something small for their evening meal. To me, that was not an unreasonable request. My affirmative answer to his question put a broad smile on his face and the understanding that they would have fresh meat to eat later in the day put a smile on the faces of the entire section.

After another fruitless effort to make radio communication with Makuti or Chirundu and with an adequate meal inside us, our water bottles full and in good spirits, we set out once again on our north-easterly line of march. By my dead reckoning we had between 22 and 25 miles still to cover. On the map, we still had the Chitemba and Sapi Rivers running across our line of march. Since both of those were more significant watercourses than the Mbera, we felt we might stand a good chance of finding water in one or maybe both. Dealing with the tactical side of Sgt Isaac's request to do a little bit of poaching, carting fresh meat all day long was not a good idea. That we all knew, so we ignored all the plentiful game we came across as we pushed along. Our progress was slowed somewhat by us dutifully checking out, for a hundred yards each way, every one of the half dozen game trails which we encountered, all, perhaps fortunately without any trace of insurgent boot spoor. By late morning we reached the Chitemba River, which proved to be a total disappointment as far as the presence of water was concerned. In the half-mile or so in which we walked along it, its bed was pure rock, without a single trace of water or any area of sand into which we might dig. Rather than waste more precious time and with the Sapi still ahead of us, we moved on, until mid-afternoon, when a good poaching opportunity arose as we came to the end of a stretch of thickly populated jesse and mopani trees. We found ourselves looking out over another vlei in which were grazing at least a couple of hundred assorted antelope. As if to order, there was a young kudu bull no more than twenty yards away. From the cover of the bushes, Sgt Isaac took careful aim. Not wanting to risk a body shot which might only wound and cause the flight of his victim, he aimed for its head and gently squeezed the trigger of his .303 rifle. At the crack of the shot, a neat hole appeared in each of the ears of the kudu, which took off as fast as it could and vanished into the bush some distance away. Sgt Isaac was distraught. "I aimed for the middle of its head, Ishe. I do not know why the bullet went so high." Taking his rifle from him I checked it over. Instead of using the close-range V-sight, he had opted to use the aperture sight, which was designed for accurate shooting anywhere between 100 and 1,000 yards, depending upon how the shooter set it. I had to point out to him that his aperture sight was set on 1,000 yards, probably as a result of some diligent cleaning of his personal firearm, one or more evenings back.

However, I was also able to point out to him that although his intended victim had fled, the single shot, fired from good cover, had only caused all of the other animals in sight to simply pause their grazing for a moment and look around. Finding no visible cause for alarm, they simply got on with their grazing once again. With an impala buck no more than fifty yards away, I suggested that he should use the open V-sight on his rifle and aim for his target's shoulder. This time, at the crack of the shot, the animal dropped where it stood. It was only when I led Sgt Isaac and three other details of the section out to collect the fallen buck that there was any general shift among the animals in view to move away from us intruders. It was clear to all of us that these animals were unaware of humans and what firearms were. That just emphasised we really were in a truly wilderness area.

Sgt Isaac's bullet had hit the impala just wide of its shoulder, but fortunately straight through its heart. As we approached the fallen animal an oxpecker flew off from its body. Oxpeckers and impala have a symbiotic relationship in nature. Oxpeckers live on the ticks, lice and other biting and blood-sucking parasites that make life a misery for the impala by getting into ears, nasal cavities and anywhere that an impala cannot get at to bite, gnaw or scratch at them. In shooting its host, we had deprived that oxpecker of its regular food supply. I had no doubt that it would soon find another impala as its source of bugs to eat. An adult impala buck can weigh anything between 40 to 70kg. This one was middle of the range in age and size, so somewhere about 50kg. Stopping to butcher the animal then and there was not advisable, so it became a question of how best to carry it until we stopped to make night camp in another hour or so. My suggestion of cutting a pole to hang it from so that two constables could carry it between them brought the negative but probably correct reply that it would be too cumbersome to carry it far that way in view of the thickness of the bush we were fighting our way through between the occasional open vleis we were finding. Our dilemma was solved by Const. Svotwa, who tested the weight of the impala before turning to me and saying, "Ishe, if someone else carries my rifle, I can carry this for a while. It is not too heavy."

That was how, as we moved on for the remainder of that afternoon, Const. Svotwa took a permanent position in the middle of the section, with the carcass of the impala draped over his shoulders. My additional burden of his .303 rifle seemed a flyweight one compared to what he was carrying. With about an hour of daylight left, we reached the Sapi River, somewhat suddenly. That was because the thick bush we were hacking our way through at the time grew right up to the top of the bank of the river which was a vertical one at that location. The bank we were standing on top of was some twelve or fifteen feet in height. The riverbed at that point was made up of dry sand with some rock sticking up, while the bank on the far side was just as steep and as high as the side we were on. It seemed logical that we should turn upstream and keep moving until we discovered a safe crossing point. At that moment, my greatest concern was for Const. Svotwa who had set down his load while Sgt Isaac and I briefly discussed our best option for making progress to a night camp. Considering that he had been carting the best part of a hundredweight of dead impala for well over an hour, he appeared unaffected by the effort involved. My question as to his welfare brought a huge grin and an assurance that he was fine and happy to carry on.

The thick bush, a mixture of mopani and jesse thorn, fortunately thinned and to some extent retreated a little from the bank of the Sapi as we moved south along it. That gave us better visibility for a start, which was fortunate as we came across, in quick succession, a family of giraffe and then a rhino, all of them busily engaged in ingesting the umpteen kilos of grass and foliage which they needed each day if they were to survive. Once more the wild and remote nature of that area came to our rescue in that those animals had no cause to be concerned about us. They had most likely never seen human beings before and most certainly had not been shot at. We were a curiosity for just a moment or two, after which they rightly decided that we were no threat to them, so they just returned to their essential task of eating, while we passed them by. Shortly after leaving those animals behind we had sight of a troop of genuine African wild dogs. They were ahead of us and travelling in much the same direction as we were. Not long after we lost sight of those, we came across a small tributary of the Sapi which had a modest game trail angling down into it. That allowed us to get down to the level of the riverbed itself, which was no more than twenty or twenty-five yards across at that point. More helpfully for us, the bank on the far side was low and easily ascendable. Perhaps even more encouragingly, there were signs of animals having been busy digging in the sandy bed, suggesting there was water down below, which there proved to be. Setting two details atop the bank on either side of the river as guards, the remainder of us set about refilling ourselves and also our by then depleted water bottles. When that was done it was a case of changing over the four guards so that they too could load up with water.

With guards out to prevent us being surprised by anything threatening, whether human, or animal, it was time to find a campsite for the night. I was certain in my mind that we were not going to butcher and divide that impala anywhere close to our night camp. That stupidity would guarantee visits from any scavenger or predator in the area that happened to get a whiff of the butchery, starting with that pack of wild dogs. The impala needed butchering down by the river, so our camp needed to be nearby. With just Const. Bushu to accompany me I did a quick scout around beyond the Sapi's east bank. As luck would have it, there was a small stand of trees, perhaps a hundred yards distant, which would suit our purposes. Without waste of time and by leaving two details to protect the impala carcass, on the riverbed, we prepared an overnight camp. With that done and a fire slowly building, it was time to attend to the butchering of our fresh meat ration for the evening meal. Const. Mapfumo's flick-knife and my machete were rapidly put to good use down by the river and in remarkably quick time the carcass was skinned, the viscera were cut out, sorted into usable and unusable parts and the meat carved from the bones. Each man was allowed, in turn, to help himself to as much meat or mutumbu (intestines) as he felt he could comfortably eat that evening. My choice was a good helping of fillet steak, but nowhere near in weight what Sgt Isaac and the rest of the section helped themselves to. When every man was well supplied, we left the remainder of the butchered impala for the scavengers and concentrated on getting our eating done before full dark.

In view of where we were, the knowledge of the wild dogs in the area and the amount of game we had encountered during the day, I set two guards to be on duty, each with a 180-degree arc of responsibility. Hardly had I done that when one of them, Const. Phineas, called me to his side and pointed.

Making their way towards the river, whether drawn by the scent of the impala carcass or a need to dig for water, were half-a-dozen hyena.

Our usual evening cooking arrangements were well established, our fire was kept to a modest size, big enough to allow three mess-tins to be on it at the same time, starting with the three details who had the senior numbers. When one of them took his cooked meal away to eat it, he was replaced by the next most senior numbered detail. I covered the guard as needed and made sure that I was among the last to get to the fire. On this occasion, it grew just a little disorderly and lengthy as some of the section wished to roast their meat, some wished to stew it and others tried a form of frying. What did amaze me was the sheer quantity of meat that my African companions managed to pack away at that one meal, along with quite a lot of sadza, all individually cooked. If I let the rules stretch a little that evening, it was because I felt that with a full five days of hard, sweaty, thirsty patrol work behind them, existing solely on maize meal as porridge or sadza, they deserved a more tasty evening meal as a bit of a morale booster, which that particular evening meal proved to be. In the first hour or so after sundown we were made very much aware of the fact that the remains of the impala which we had left at the river were certainly being competed for and fought over. The assortment of snarls, growls, yelps and whines told its own story. It was only as I prepared to bed down to get some sleep that I realised that I had not even tried to make any radio communication with anyone that evening. My two turns on guard duty came and went without incident. On either side and between them I slept soundly.

After our dawn stand-to, which passed without incident, we ate and drank well, knowing that we would, in threes and a four, top up our water bottles at the river before setting off towards Pfumbe hill, which I reckoned was about 15 miles distant. Just in case there was any scavenger hanging around, I led the first water trip down to the river, with three constables behind me. Where I had expected to see at least the skull, horns and maybe some bones still there, there was absolutely no trace of anything, other than some staining on the surface of the sand. Even the skull and horns were gone. It was a reminder of the reputed power of a hyena's teeth and jaws, which, as I had heard tell, were capable of crunching and swallowing chunks of bone as well as flesh.

The broad game trail following the river on its eastern bank was full of the spoor of animals of all kinds and sizes, from spring hare to elephant. It was a warning for us to keep our eyes and ears open and our wits about us as we set off that morning. It was not long before the Chewore Wilderness Area began to live up to its name. I was taking a turn at point, moving across a small area of long grass when I detected movement ahead of me. Signalling silently for the patrol to halt, I thumbed the safety catch on my FN rifle to the off position and moved slowly and cautiously forward. The cause of the movement in the grass proved to be a sizeable python, at least fourteen or fifteen foot in length. As soon as I saw what it was, I simply froze until it had slithered safely away and out of sight. Signalling for the rest of the section to move forward, I passed word back of why I had stopped them and then moved on.

On the ground around us during the course of that day we saw almost every one of the entire list of antelope and big game of Central Africa from duiker through to a magnificent eland bull. We encountered several herds of elephant and, in one large vlei, a herd of several hundred buffalo. If we had stopped to check out in both directions, each of the many game trails we crossed, our progress would have been minimal, so I used my judgement and tackled only the few which I considered any insurgents might find useful. What we found was much in the way of hoof-prints, but not a boot print anywhere. When I called a halt for a noon-day break, Sgt Isaac produced his official issue notebook and tried to list each of the species of animal we had seen by then. He needed one or two reminders from other members of the section before he felt the list was anywhere near complete. As he said, it was the only way he would be able to tell his family what he had seen.

Shortly after we moved on, we found ourselves in a more forested rather than bushy area. Within that we came across a good broad animal trail which carried, among other animal traces, quite a lot of recent elephant droppings, some of them with dung beetles already busy taking advantage of them. Since it appeared to be heading about north-easterly and would make our progress much easier, I decided that we should make use of it. We were still following it a half-hour or so later when it led us to a place where there was a sheer-sided gulley perhaps a dozen or fifteen feet in depth and some thirty yards across. Sgt Isaac, at Dermotat that time, signalled for the Section to halt and for me to move up to him, which I did. The broad elephant trail we were following went down into the gulley at an angle of about forty-five degrees, maybe a bit more. It crossed the gulley and clearly went up the other bank, which looked to be even steeper than the one where we were standing. However, it was not the gulley or track itself that was the reason for the signal for me to come to the front. It was the herd of elephant visible through the trees, at about a hundred yards distant, which were slowly coming towards us. It was immediately clear to me, as it had been to Sgt Isaac, that we needed to move well clear of where the elephant trail crossed the gulley in front of us, until the herd was well past us. Only then could we cross it safely ourselves. Acting swiftly on that decision, I tested the slight breeze and led the section about thirty yards downwind where we got down flat and stayed still, to give the herd a chance to go past without seeing or smelling our presence. I noticed that most of the section, like Sgt Isaac and myself, settled down close to the edge of the gulley from which point we could monitor the herd as it made the crossing of the gulley.

There were fifteen of them in that herd, led as usual by their matriarch, a very mature female. Somewhat to the surprise of all of us onlookers, when she reached the rim of the bank, instead of simply treading down the trail literally head-first and in the normal elephant walking mode, she stopped, took a good long look all around and then carefully positioned herself in a way that I can only describe as sitting on her tail, right on the edge of the bank, with her hind legs positioned on either side of her front legs, which were actually placed on the sloping part of the down gradient. She then inched forward very gingerly, making small movements, hardly steps, of her front legs. In that odd, ungainly and very careful way she slid slowly downwards until she reached the level ground at the floor of the gulley. Once there, she leaned forward, took the weight from her tail end and stood up on all fours. Once she was upright, she gave a short trumpet call, which appeared to be a signal for the large bull elephant which was next in line, to begin to make his way down the slope, using exactly the same strange technique for the descent. Behind him, each of the other members of the herd waited until they could, in turn, follow those ahead of them. The matriarch waited until five of the herd were on the gulley floor and then, unhurriedly made the climb up the bank on the side of the gulley where we were, all of us, simply staring in silent fascination at what we were witnessing.

As each one more of the herd arrived on the side of the gulley where she was, the matriarch took a few more steps along the trail to allow room for it.

Nine of the herd made the down and up crossing of the gulley routinely in the manner described. However, number ten, a three-quarter grown bull, clearly got it wrong. He managed to start the descent correctly, but, for whatever reason got his backside too far forward and his head and shoulders too far backwards to maintain the controlled sort of slide the others before him had managed. Shrilling either in fear or anger, he fell backwards, with all four feet waving in the air and slid upon his spine down the slope until his backside met the gulley floor, rather suddenly and obviously painfully. Continuing to trumpet his displeasure, the bull elephant rolled himself on to all fours. Once fully upright, with ears flapping and trunk waving he headed for a small mopani tree which had seven or eight feet of trunk with a width of five or six inches. He gave it a good solid nudge with his head, which half uprooted it, then wrapped his trunk firmly around the base of the tree and completed the job. After briefly waving the uprooted tree in the air as if to say, "Look what I can do!" He then set about beating, flailing or flogging the upper end of the tree against every other tree and rock he could find within close range. It was only when most of the branches were shredded and gone that the angry little fellow tossed his impromptu club aside and climbed the trail on our side of the gulley. There he was met by the matriarch of the herd, who, upon hearing the evidently angry shrilling and bellowing from down in the gulley, had clearly felt a need to come back to investigate what was going on. As we watched, there was a brief wrap-around contact of their trunks and a short moment of trumpeting between them. Clearly reassured that that young member of her herd was okay, the matriarch returned to the head of the column. From there she waited until the remaining four of the group had, without any further incident, joined their fellows, whereupon she led them away along the trail down which we had come and out of our sight.

As we all got to our feet once the herd of elephant were safely gone, there was an inevitable buzz of conversation. I looked at Sgt Isaac and asked with a smile, "How are you going to write that one up in your notebook? My Sgt shook his head and tapped a few fingers on his forehead. "No need to write it, Ishe. That one is deep in here. I shall never forget it!" That just about said it for all of us. If ever there was proof that an elephant can throw a temper tantrum, that was it. My only regret was that due to sanctions at that time, my camera was without film and not with me.

Another hour or so of steady progress, made easy along that broad elephant trail, brought us into very much more broken and hilly country. If anything, the thickness of the bush increased, making us even more grateful for the existence of the elephant trail we had been able to follow for some hours. Unfortunately for us, a mile or two into that broken county, the elephant trail, took a clear change of direction to the south, which meant that once again, we had to start pushing and often cutting our way forward. Worse still, there was no way we could maintain a straight north-easterly line of march. We had to go around the hills rather than up, over and down. What bothered me was that if I steered the section too far south, we would encounter the Chewore River south of the Mari-Ya-Tsoro Gorge, very bad country indeed so I had heard tell. My map and some dead reckoning suggested that by turning more directly northwards we could be clear of the hilly country in about five miles. We should then be only five or six miles from the Chewore River where there was bound to be water, with the Pfumbe Hill hopefully within sight. However, that meant that we would be unlikely to find water before we made camp. A quick check with everyone confirmed that each of the section had at least the best part of one full water bottle at his belt. For my part, I had a little more than that, plus the safeguard of a couple of tins of grapefruit in the bottom of my pack, which I regarded as my emergency liquid supply if needed.

Some two hours or so later we were still fighting our way through the thick broken and hilly country when it became time to make our overnight camp, prepare our evening meal and bed down for the night. With the bush around us so thick that visibility was hardly more than a dozen yards, the requirement for each night guard was simply twofold; to stay awake and listen more than look.

The following morning I dispensed with the routine dawn stand-to and any thoughts of an early meal. I set the section moving once there was light enough to see our way. Fortunately, it proved to be the right thing to do. After a couple of hours of hard work, weaving, pushing and when necessary, hacking our way forward, around the hills, at least in the cooler part of the day, we broke out into flatter, if not more open, ground. Once well clear of the hills, I ordered a halt, so that we could light a fire to make our individual and, given the limited amount of water among us, somewhat frugal breakfast meal.

During that break, I once more tried for some radio contact with one or other of the police stations around and about. Ten minutes of effort brought no joy, so I turned the radio off and started to double-check that everyone was okay and ready for the push we needed to make, almost due eastwards according to my dead reckoning, to get to the Chewore River and the Pfumbe Hill. A half hour into that effort, we reached the top of a modest ridge which had an invitingly climbable mukwa tree at its crest. Leaving my rifle and backpack at ground level, I did a little bit of careful climbing until I could get a better view of the countryside around from above the level of the top of most of the surrounding trees. Orientating my map with my compass, I was immensely relieved to see, some five or six miles distant and not too far off of the bearing where I expected it to be, an isolated small hill, which I took to be our destination.

I was about to start a careful descent of the tree when the sound of an aircraft made itself heard and into my view came a low-winged monoplane which made a circle over what I believed to be the Pfumbe Hill and then began to head in our direction.

Map and compass went inside my shirt in a hurry and my climb down the mukwa tree got to be more of a risky scramble until I had both feet on the ground. I need not have worried, for the ever-shrewd Sgt Isaac had recognised that it might be a Police Reserve Airwing aircraft. In my absence up the tree, he had promptly turned on our VHF radio set and established communication with it. It seemed that Insp. Kensett and SO Van Wyk who were both concerned over our radio silence, had persuaded Rampart of the need for an overfly, to which he had agreed. From the very welcome ensuing conversation I learned that we were close to the Mushangwe Stream, which we could follow down to its confluence with the Chewore River just south of Pfumbe Hill. Our RV with transport for our uplift would be on the track just west of the hill. The vehicles would arrive about noon and would wait there for us.

All of that was welcome news to us, but with maybe six more miles to go as any crow would have flown, but likely a quarter again of that to allow for our inevitable ups, downs and diversions, we needed to step along as smartly as we safely could, so it became a case of thanking the PRAW pilot and pushing on, steered by the compass bearing I had taken when up in the tree and the need to stay clear of the heavy hill country to the south of us. A half-hour later, we started to pick up the noise of an animal conflict going on. The mixture of gruff grunts, barking, squealing and yelping told its own story even before we reached the edge of the small open area in which the combat was going on. In the middle of the clearing, less than thirty yards from us, was a half-grown female white rhino, trying to fight off the murderous intentions of better than a dozen hyena. It was clear to us all that even though the rhino was making a valiant effort to fight off her attackers, if it was left to go on, there was going to be only one outcome. Shooting accurately under those circumstances, at targets that were wheeling, darting and bobbing as they sought to hamstring and then get at the throat of their intended prey, was not going to be easy, but I did hold a current Marksman's rating on my record of service and reckoned that even if I missed, the shot would likely stop the attack on the rhino. With that much thinking done, it was time to act, so I picked on the largest of the hyena and managed to put a bullet through its head. Until that moment, the combatants had been unaware of our presence, but the crack of the shot and the sudden dropping of one of the hyena changed all that.

I had fired from the cover of the bushes edging the clearing, so was not easily visible, but the eyes of every one of those animals in the clearing swung in the direction of the sound of the shot. I knew enough about hyena to be aware that packs would attack, kill and eat a human being on their own even if that person were armed. So I snapped an urgent order of "Show yourselves!" and stepped forward into the open, rifle at the ready with Sgt Isaac right beside me. If there was any thought among that pack of hyena to have a go at the two of us, it vanished as the remainder of the section broke out of the screen of bushes and, like Sgt Isaac and myself, promptly aimed their rifles at them. Faced with our full number, the pack of hyena decided we were too much trouble to tangle with. They left the clearing at a run, although one or two of them were bleeding and limping somewhat. Behind them they left the body of the one I had shot. The rhino cow, with her clearly bloodied front horn a testimony to the fight she had put up and herself bleeding a little from the hopefully superficial wounds she had received from her assailants, took herself off in the opposite direction, more likely than not, to find other rhino to keep company with for greater safety in future until she was more fully grown.

With little time to spare ourselves, we too pushed on, but even as we began to move off, Const. Bushu called out "Ishe!" and pointed upwards, to where two vultures were already circling. No doubt, once we were out of sight, they wasted no time in getting down to their waiting meal.

It was shortly after that incident that we came across the Mushangwe Stream. Although it was totally dry, it helped us greatly as there was a narrow, but clear game trail running parallel to it on the northern bank. Grateful for that, but just a little warily in case any insurgents might have heard my single shot, we pushed on until we reached the Chewore River, just a couple of miles south of Pfumbe Hill. It did not take us much scouting, under the watchful eyes of guards, before we found a usable source of water in among the rocks in the riverbed. With a few dry hours behind us, moving as we had through the heat of the day, it was a relief to once more, in careful two and threes, fill ourselves and our water bottles and retreat into the shade of bushes along the western bank of the river, for a brief rest and to try for some radio contact, hopefully with our transport from Makuti. Somewhat to my surprise, but probably because of the short distance between us, that effort succeeded. With that reassurance to bolster our spirits and only a short distance to go, we set off to cover the last couple of miles to our rendezvous with the transport from Makuti. By my wristwatch, it was just on 14:00hrs when we sighted the two Land Rovers which were waiting to uplift us. SO Moebe Van Wyk, our troop commander was driving one and Insp. Phil Kensett the other, each with one constable with them in their vehicle.

It was with a decided sense of relief that I issued the order to make rifles safe, then divided our number into halves and saw to the securing of each of our 44 webbing backpacks on the roof-racks of the vehicles and gave the order to embus. Out of courtesy, I climbed into the front passenger seat of the Land Rover being driven by Insp. Kensett for the journey back to Makuti and set Sgt Isaac in with our troop commander. Insp. Kensett was eager to hear an outline of what we had come across during our seven days out on what had been, until then, in distance, the longest patrol undertaken by Support Unit details operating in the Zambezi Valley. One thing I did discover on that journey of over three hours, was that Insp. Kensett was very worried about us operating in blue and grey riot gear in what he fairly described as a combat zone. Another was that he was one of those drivers who felt unable to hold a conversation without looking at the passenger he was talking to. That trait, common in many drivers, caused a couple of brief and fortunately undamaging excursions off road. He also clearly understood the problem our African members had with the need for individual rations rather than the section or troop arrangements common in the unit until very recently.

Once back at our Makuti Camp, Insp. Kensett hauled me straight off to the control room to provide a debrief for Supt Mallon, whose first question caused me, if not Insp. Kensett, just a little concern, because it was, "Ah, now tell me, where have you been?"

"Exactly where you sent us last week, Sir," I responded very politely, carefully keeping any expression from my face or voice. "From here, Sir, to here." I tapped the two locations for him on the map of the valley which covered one wall, at which he responded with one finger raised and the words "Ah, I remember now. Anything interesting to report?"

Seven incident-packed days flashed through my mind in an instant. "Nothing of any operational importance, Sir," I replied, quite truthfully. "No signs of insurgent spoor or camps or anything of that nature." Supt Mallon looked from the map to me and then to Insp. Kensett, before concluding the debriefing with, "Right then, no need to waste time and paper over a negative report, so shall we just make an entry in the log to cover what you've just told me and leave it at that? Insp. Kensett and I both replied, "Very good, Sir!" and that was that.

On the way back to our Support Unit tents I sought and received confirmation from Insp. Kensett that Rampart had been informed of Const. Itayi's broken leg and hospitalisation and had authorised the PRAW overfly of that morning. Back at our Support Unit tents, I quite literally climbed out of everything I was wearing, wrapped a towel around me and headed for the ablutions block to wash off the sweat and dust of seven sweltering days down in the valley and shave off that many days growth of beard and moustache. When I returned, I discovered that the entire troop was now in camp, waiting for instructions about further deployments. Around the table at our evening meal, I was able to brief the others, including Insp. Kensett, in more detail about how the patrol had gone and what lessons there were to be learned from it. Judging that Insp. Kensett would not be too much of a stickler for rules and regulations when we were away from formality and urban surrounds, I set out matters of Itayi's mishap, Svotwa's unorthodox but effective method driving away of the inquisitive elephant, the encounter with the honeyguide, the neat holes in a kudu's ears, the young elephant's temper tantrum and my shooting of the hyena to save the rhino cow. I made it clear that two water bottles were insufficient under very hot, dry conditions when re-supply of water was uncertain and emphasised the need for better radios and a better rationing system for our African members. The one positive point I was able to make was that the replacement for the dreadful Mars boots had proved fit for purpose. When I was done, Insp. Kensett decided that he would, next morning, compile a brief outline of matters which needed to be known by OC Support Unit and get me to go over it before he sent it off. After six nights of sleeping on hard ground, my Hounsfield bed was a pleasure to settle down upon and with no share of guard duties to do, I enjoyed a sound night's sleep.

On the morning of Sunday 10th September 1967, I found myself pleasantly impressed by the factuality and forthrightness of the debrief report compiled by Insp. Kensett, which I fully approved before it was sent south in the first police vehicle heading to Salisbury. With the valley quiet as far as insurgent activities were concerned and RLI patrols covering that area anyway, A Troop had little to do for the best part of a week, other than to provide guards around the camp both day and night and to provide men and guards for the permanent roadblock on the main north-south road.

I was helping out by putting in a shift on the roadblock, checking vehicles both large and small which were traveling north or south, when a saloon car heading south duly stopped as requested. It carried a European family of two adults and two children of primary school age. At my request for bonnet and boot to be opened so that the required search could be carried out, the male driver promptly inquired as he climbed out of the car, "What part of London do you come from?" At my somewhat raised eyebrows and response of "I was born in Tottenham," he stuck his hand out and said, "I'm from Hackney." As we shook hands he went on, "You Rhodesian guys have been handed a bum deal. I hope it works out for you." The search done, with a negative result, he got back into the car. Before he drove on, he remarked, "You lot should have been given Independence when the Federation was disbanded four years back. Good luck."

As I watched that car disappear on its way, I could only agree with him and think we certainly were going to need all the luck we could get. The Federation, more formally known as the "Federation of the Rhodesias and Nyasaland" was established on 1st August 1953. It lasted until 31st

December 1963 and was disbanded because of the granting of Independence to Nyasaland and Northern Rhodesia, each under black majority rule, in 1964. Rhodesia was refused Independence at that time because it did not have black majority rule. With the USA demanding that the UK got "out of Empire" and with pressure for black majority rule from both the United Nations and the Organisation of African Unity, Britain was far too frightened of world opinion to grant Rhodesia Independence other than under black majority rule, even though there were already 25 black members of the Rhodesian Parliament at that time, with a clear roadmap towards black majority rule in 25 years by way of increasing that number of seats by five at each General Election round.

Nothing of any great moment occurred until the evening of Saturday 16th September, when Insp. Kensett told me that as leader of the Standby Section at that time, I was wanted by Rampart in the Control Room. With the sun having disappeared a while back and full dark not far off, I wondered what the reason for the call might be. What I was instructed to undertake alarmed me no end. Supt Mallon advised me that Special Branch had received information that a small group of insurgents had crossed the Zambezi the day before and were believed to be using a series of game trails which would take them to Nyakasanga Township, which had been a modest retail centre before the valley's population had been moved out but was now simply a small number of deserted and decaying buildings. Rampart instructed me to take my section and set up an overnight ambush on the northern edge of the ruined and deserted township. We were to head out immediately in two Land Rovers, to be dropped off on the main north road a mile or more from the township. We were to be collected from the same location at 08:00hrs the next morning.

My observation to Rampart that there was no moonlight tonight and moving in the dark could be risky, brought the flippant riposte of, "Well, if there's no moon, Woolley, there's no chance of you and your men being seen on the way in, is there? So get going and get on with it. The sooner you're in position the better!"

While Insp. Kensett helpfully went to call the men of my section, I took a quick look at the map. Nyakasanga Township lay about a mile or more almost due west of our starting point for the patrol to Pfumbe Hill. Just north of that starting point for our Pfumbe patrol there appeared to be a track leading from the main road to the township. In total darkness there was no way we could safely footslog through the mile or more of bush which would have been the shortest way from the road to the edge of the township. I decided that we had to use that track, whatever condition it might now be in. Moebe was away in Salisbury for a couple of days, so not present to speak to but both Bob and Dermot were horrified at the tasking I had been given, as was, I might add, Insp. Kensett, who chose to drive one of the two Land Rovers which carried us out of Makuti Camp just before 8:00 p.m. that night. Once we had picked up the small bridge where the Nyakasanga River flowed under the main road, we slowed to a crawl, seeking the turnoff to the track to the township. Once we identified that, my section climbed out of the vehicles and formed up, ready to head off as tasked by Rampart. I had briefed my section on our task for the night once I had got them together at Makuti Camp, so they were fully aware of what was being asked of us. I might add that the comments of Sgt Servester and others were about in accordance with my own thoughts, but orders were orders, so we had to get on with it.

The track, which had once been the main access route into the now deserted township, had rapidly deteriorated and been reclaimed by nature. By starlight alone, and at the end of the dry season, without any rain for around five months, everything was brittle and crackly. Because of an oddity in my eyes, by which my pupils were permanently more wide-open than the average person's, I had excellent night vision, but suffered a bit in bright daylight. Because of that I chose to lead the patrol myself, with Const. Phineas behind me and with Sgt Servester at the rear. With my night eyesight working well, I was able to move forward relatively quietly, with rifle at the ready, to step around dry bushes and clumps of grass and to avoid broken branches and twigs on the ground. Not so Const. Phineas, who manged to crunch into dry bushes, stumble over every wrinkle in the ground and step on every dry branch his boots could find. As the bush on either side opened out and the first of the abandoned buildings came into view, he managed to step on a thickish dry branch, which cracked loudly under his weight and sent him sprawling. Quite naturally irritated by his noisy clumsiness, I helped him to his feet and then hissed at him, "For crying out loud man, what are you trying to do? Get us all killed with your noise?"

I could not have been more wrong! Out of the darkness came a voice.

"Arnie, Arnie Woolley!" It was a voice I knew well. "Tom! Tom Crawford." That brought, "What the heck are you doing moving at this hour of night. You were within five paces of all of you being killed!"

To the utter astonishment of everyone, it turned out that Supt Mallon had, two days previously, briefed an RLI (Rhodesian Light Infantry) patrol, to which he had attached Patrol Officer Tom Crawford, for liaison purposes, to base itself near the deserted township, to carry out day patrols of the area and night ambushes on the township itself. In the darkness, all they had seen was shadowy armed figures coming into the township from the north as they had been briefed to expect. The lieutenant in charge of the patrol had marked out a killing ground, in which we had been. I had reached within five yards or so of where he intended to order his men to open fire on us when Const. Phineas had caused my outburst, which had saved our lives and prevented him from initiating a disaster that would have haunted him and his men for the rest of their lives. His comments upon the operational competence of a certain Police Superintendent were unprintable. They paralleled my own thoughts on the matter.

The result of it was that I and my men bedded down a few yards to the rear of where the RLI ambush was and left that unit to get on with staying operational for the remaining hours of darkness while my unit simply slept the hours away. As dawn broke, the RLI Lieutenant agreed with me that declaring the debacle over the radio, for all too many people to learn about, would be unwise, so we agreed that I would deal with it when my unit reached Makuti Camp later in the morning. By 08:00hrs my section and I were at the allotted rendezvous, but out of sight as far as normal traffic was concerned. Having left from Makuti Camp in something of a hurry, fortunately after evening mealtime, we were all keen to get back there so that we could get a meal inside us, if nothing more. Just a few minutes after 08:00hrs our transport appeared and shortly we were under way towards the escarpment and Makuti Camp. On the way, I provided a full debrief of what had gone on overnight to Inspector Kensett who was driving the lead vehicle. To give that officer his due, he was both astounded and horrified in equal measure at just how close all of us in No. 1 Section of A Troop had come to being killed in an ambush set by Supt Mallon himself. When I expressed my intention to have a few words with our current Rampart, Insp. Kensett cautioned me to be just a little careful in what I might say.

When we arrived at Makuti Camp and climbed out of our vehicles, I sent my African details off duty, lodged my FN in my tent and went to find Supt Mallon, with Insp. Kensett a half-dozen steps behind me. I found Rampart standing outside the caravan which acted as our control room. He was in conversation with a couple of District Uniform details who were part of the team nominally covering the roadblock. To avoid any allegations of misbehaviour or disrespect to a ranking commissioned officer, I marched smartly up, came to an almost parade-ground halt, delivered a very formal salute and said, "Excuse me for butting into your conversation Sir, but I feel that I do have to ask if your right hand really does know what your left hand is doing. You need to know that you came within a whisker of getting me and my entire section all killed last night because you had already established a night ambush on Nyakasanga Township and that I and my section walked smack into the middle of their planned killing ground. Only a noisy constable and a freak of good luck saved our lives." Having delivered that admonishment and before Supt Mallon could recover from his clear sheer surprise at what I had delivered, I took one step back, saluted, about turned very properly and marched away to our Support Unit tents.

It was a couple of hours later, after I had eaten a late breakfast and recounted the overnight debacle to Bob and Dermot, that Insp. Kensett came along and informed me that he had orders to march me in to the control room caravan, as a defaulter, without belt or headgear, as Supt Mallon wished to give me a severe dressing-down and maybe put me on a formal disciplinary charge. A few minutes later, with me dressed as required. Insp. Kensett set about presenting me before Supt Mallon as ordered. Once he had ascertained that Rampart was ready to deal with me, Insp. Kensett did his very best to march me formally in, but the three steps up from ground to caravan floor and my stamped, booted footfall, in time to Insp. Kensett's "Left, Right, Left, Right," proved too much for the second wooden rung, which broke under my right foot. Fortunately, that breakage caused me no great damage, mainly because I was wearing Mr Ratanje's high boots instead of standard issue boots. It did, however, detract somewhat from the full precision of my eventual presentation before Supt Mallon, as a formal defaulter. With Insp. Kensett standing at ease behind me and me at attention, Supt Mallon firstly tore strips off me for what he saw as my rudeness and disrespect in butting, uninvited, into his conversation earlier in the day and alleging that he did not know what he was doing in his role as Border Control Officer, north-east. In his personal opinion, my insubordination merited a formal disciplinary charge, but, in view of the stresses and strains which we were all operating under, on this occasion, he would overlook my misbehaviour, which I must in future be careful not to repeat.

At that point, I expected to be summarily dismissed, but Rampart went on to explain that every single one of us was, as he put it, "Fumbling and stumbling our way forward in attempting to learn how to deal effectively with an insurgency conflict instead of a riot or beerhall brawl." He pointed out that mistakes were being made by all three of our defence forces, Army, Airforce and Police, but hopefully, we would all learn from them, including how to maintain self-discipline when under stress. At that point he finished his remarks and ordered Insp. Kensett to march me out.

Once we had both negotiated the broken step and were some few yards from the Control Room caravan, Insp. Kensett commented, "I have never before heard a bollocking that sounded so much more like an apology without that word being used." I firmly agreed with him. Later that day, Moebe Van Wyk returned to Makuti Camp. When I briefed him on the activities and exchanges of the past 24 hours, he shook his head in sheer disbelief, then remarked, "I think we are all going to need a lucky rabbit's foot before this is finally finished and done with."

With the RLI patrolling the valley, whether it was at their request or a decision from Rampart, A Troop spent a relatively quiet and undemanding week at Makuti Camp. It was on the 23rd September 1967 that Insp. Kensett passed word down that Supt Mallon was somewhat concerned about the accuracy or inaccuracy of the maps we were then using and also about where water was available and was not available along the length of the escarpment east of Makuti. He required one patrol to leave Makuti on foot, heading east along the top of the escarpment, going as far as the Chewore River, checking our current 1:50,000 Ordnance Survey maps against the terrain on the ground and plotting where water existed. He required a second patrol to commence a similar exercise starting at the Tsetse Fly Research Station by the Rekometje River, heading east along the bottom of the escarpment until it reached the Chewore River and then turning north to follow that river to its junction with the Zambezi near Rasenwa Hill. Both patrols were, on the map about a distance of some 50 miles. According to Insp. Kensett, Supt

Mallon had at first believed that the work would only take a few days. It apparently took Insp. Kensett's intervention to point out that cross-graining at the top of the escarpment was going to be a matter of ascending and descending every valley and gulley and that there were plenty of those along the way, while the patrol at the foot of the escarpment would have to contend with some of the heaviest bushlands in the valley. Apparently reluctantly, Supt Mallon eventually agreed to both patrols being aimed at a duration of one week.

Having had the one example of our current Rampart's ability to seriously bungle operational activities, I sought an assurance from Insp. Kensett that before I left Makuti I would be advised of where the RLI patrols were operating and that they would be advised of where I and my section were going to be and roughly when. Fortunately, Insp. Kensett agreed that that would be a very wise move and took himself off to see to it.

That left us with the decision of who was to do which of the two patrols and who was to stay in the relative ease and comfort of Makuti Camp. In the end, Moebe cut three pieces of dry grass and let luck make the decision for us. That resulted in Dermot getting the short straw and the top of the escarpment patrol, me getting the valley floor patrol and Bob getting the cushy number of remaining in Makuti. With that decision made, our troop leader called the troop together and provided a briefing of what each section was going to be doing over the next week. At the end of that briefing, I asked Sgt Isaac if he was thinking of coming out as my Section Sgt again this time. To that he shook his head. "No Ishe. It is better that Sgt Servester should have a chance to see what is down there. It is too wonderful."

By the time we had sorted that out, Insp. Kensett was back with an assurance that the RLI Patrols were stationed at Marongora Dam and the Tsetse Research Station by the Rekometje River or based along the Zambezi River to do shoreline patrols, between Chirundu and the Chewore Mouth, checking for traces of any crossings. Additional to that information, he had phoned the Game Department HQ at Marongora Gate, to let their rangers, who were still carrying out routine work on the valley floor, know of our likely movements. That had resulted in a request that if I and my section did traverse the Mari-Ya-Tsoro Gorge, would I be so kind as to report to their HQ to record the details and sign the book which was kept there for the purpose of registering everyone who traversed the gorge. Insp. Kensett related that it seemed that I would be only the 22nd European to make that interesting journey.

It was agreed that in order to at least start off with full stomachs, Dermot and I, with our respective sections, would leave Makuti next day after an early breakfast. Being very wary of just how dry the area my section was set to patrol through might prove to be, I also scrounged a third water bottle from Bob Flynn. It meant just a bit more weight around my waist, but it was worth it in reassurance alone. By mid-morning the next day, I and my section had checked in with the RLI unit at Rekometje, shown them my line of patrol on a map and, under a blazing sun scorching down from clear blue skies, got under way to follow the outline of the base of the escarpment east of the research station. With just a little bit of a guilty feeling because my companions were stuck with their Greys and Blues, once we were east of the Rekometje River, I changed my blue jacket and blue bush hat for the camouflage items I had brought back with me from my long leave in the UK. The comments from my companions were both envious and approving.

The going on that first day was made easier when we reached the Chikati tributary of the Rekometje River. Unlike many of the small rivers which start at the bottom of the escarpment and eventually flow into the Zambezi, the Chitaki starts way up on the high ground at the head of the escarpment. During the time when the valley was occupied by African villagers, several of the villages of that time, in the area under Chief Dandawa were dotted along the Chitaki, which had clearly been a reliable source of water. It also ran for some eight or ten miles parallel to the base of the escarpment and had a well-used game trail, which perhaps had once been a formal track, running alongside it on the escarpment side. At about the time when I was considering calling a halt to our day's progress and making a night camp, after our six hours or so of walking in relatively thin bush with hardly an animal to be seen, we came across the remains of what was obviously a pair of grain storage huts. The roofs were long gone and so was much of the mud walling, but what they had once been was evident, even to me as a European. The location was as good as any for our first night camp, but before making that decision, I took two constables and walked the short distance to the Chitaki stream, to do a little experimental digging in its sandy bed.

As I expected, a couple of feet down, there was good fresh water to be found. In the reassuring knowledge that we could start the next day's walking with full stomachs and full water bottles, we made our overnight camp not far from the old grain stores. With our defensive circle set, a guard rota established and hot meal inside us, there was the usual chit-chat about the events, or lack of events of the day. Sgt Servester, having had long conversations with Sgt Isaac at Makuti Camp, was decidedly disappointed that, so far, we had seen very little by way of small antelope and certainly nothing of any big game animals, but all too many tsetse fly and mosquitoes. I pointed out to him that as the dry season established itself each year and waterholes grew to be fewer and further between, it was well known that a great deal of the game in the valley, large and small, tended to drift towards the Mana Pools area where there were permanent water supplies some several miles south of the Zambezi River itself. I assured him I felt certain that before the patrol was completed, he would have seen just as much game or maybe more than Sgt Isaac had. The conversations also puzzled over the possible lifestyle of the villagers of years gone by. For the Shona people, cattle are a prized possession and a serious status symbol, yet, with respect to the now vanished villagers, who had clearly survived happily in the valley prior to their being cleared out, we all agreed that those villagers could never have kept cattle, because, what with the lion, leopard, hyena and wild dog packs, not to mention the tsetse fly, their cattle would not have survived for long. There was also wonderment over just how they managed to protect their crops of maize, mhunga and rapoko from the destructive raids of the myriad of wild animals small and large, from duiker to elephant. We were all still puzzling over that when it became time for some sleep, when I noticed that I was not the only one who chose, because of the heat, to simply lie on top of their personal sleeping bag instead of getting into it.

After an uneventful night and our usual dawn stand-to, we all made short work of a substantial breakfast. After that, I did at least make a real effort to get radio contact with Chirundu or elsewhere. Unsurprisingly, those efforts were in vain. With that done and noted, we each topped up our water bottles and set off east once more, doing our best to follow the wandering line where foothills of the escarpment met the flat lands of the valley floor. As the day progressed, the heat grew intense, but, without rain yet, at least the humidity level was low. In terms of direct distance on a map, we made not a lot of progress, but the distance we covered on the ground was far greater, through patches of thick bush, occasional stands of forest and one or two open areas just for variety.

One of the oddities noted by all of us who had operated already in the valley was that tsetse fly always head for the areas of sweat on our grey shirts. What I immediately noticed, wearing my illicit camouflage jacket and bush hat, was that the little pests harassing me were all trying to aim for the darker areas of the mottled colouring. In the hotter part of the day, like others of my section, I simply took off my grey shirt in the hope that the looser jacket would allow some air to circulate between my sweating skin and the jacket's cloth material. What we all found was that the tsetse fly, if not brushed off the moment they settled, could bite quite effectively through any clothing item, be it grey shirt, or blue or camouflage jacket. The heat was literally strength-sapping, so it was maybe a little earlier than usual in the afternoon that I began to think about an evening meal and overnight camp. Hoping that if we took ourselves just a little way up the slope of the escarpment, we might find the air a degree or two cooler than on the floor of the valley, I directed our Dermotdetail to head up slope. A half-hour of quite gentle climbing brought us to a location where there was a modest shelf of flat ground. Just as I was about to give the order for night camp, Sgt Servester, who was tail-end-Charlie at the time, called out, "Smoke, Ishe!" and pointed. A couple of miles away, out on the valley floor, there was a column of smoke, rising vertically in the still air. Given that I had had clear assurances from Rampart, via Insp. Kensett, that there were no Crusader Units operating anywhere in the area my patrol was covering and that the RLI unit at Rekometje Research Station had given me the same message, the sight of that column of smoke concerned me. Hoping that our elevated location would provide some radio contact, I tried calling Chirundu, Makuti and Mt Darwin. Height or no height, our VHF radio set remained stubbornly silent.

If that smoke was a sign of hostile elements, they like us, would be moving in the morning, which raised the risk of an encounter outside of my control. If it was a friendly unit, I needed to know how come I had not been informed and they needed to know we were around. It was no time for indecision. I was wearing camouflage jacket and hat and less likely to be seen by whoever was out there on the valley floor than anyone else of my section members in their blues and greys. For that reason, I put myself at Dermotand led off along the compass bearing I had taken, sighted on that column of smoke. Moving steadily downhill most of the way and through relatively thin bush, we covered the couple of miles or so in quick time. As we got close to where I believed the smoke column was located, I slowed the pace and began to inch warily forward, cautious step by cautious step, rifle butt to my shoulder and ready to fire first if needed. The first indication of a hominid presence nearby was when I noticed scrunched-up used toilet paper on top of a pile of clearly human excreta. Terrorists were not known for carrying toilet paper. The right kind of leaf or a handful of grass sufficed. Looking back, I gave a thumbs-up sign to Const. Peter, pointed downwards, made a backside-wiping gesture and then momentarily held my nose. A clear nod and a grin told me that my improvised silent signals had been understood. A few dozen cautious paces further on brought me to where I could clearly hear European style popular music being played. Through the intervening screen of bushes, my eyes picked up movement of camouflaged figures. I made a silent signal for Const. Peter and the rest of my section to hold their positions. Once I was sure that he and those behind him had acted on it, I inched forward on all fours until I was in position to be sure that it was a Rhodesian Army Unit of some kind whose camp I was warily closing in on. What I saw both astounded and horrified me. The sleeping places of the dozen or more men making up whatever unit it was were randomly scattered around. There was no clear circle or perimeter to the camp. Their generous fire, still smoking away, had a pair of camp kettles hanging over it, with a couple of details attending to them. They carried no weaponry that I could see. They were paying full attention to whatever was in the camp kettles. I could see no sign of any guard on duty and worst of all, aside from the two cooks, every one of those I could see had their personal rifle stripped and were busy cleaning them all at the same time. Determined to make them wake their ideas up for their own safety in future, I inched silently and undetected between two of the sitting details. Taking off my camouflaged bush hat, I then stood up and declared loudly in best parade-ground roar, "Good evening Gentlemen. If I were a terrorist, you would all be dead! Who's in command?"

My bellow and sudden appearance, armed and camouflaged, right there among them, caused a momentary mixture of alarm, confusion and pandemonium. Several of them attempted to rapidly assemble their rifles as they scrambled to their feet. The alarm and confusion rapidly diminished as each of them realised that I was one of their own side. One of them, with a sergeant's cloth insignia on his camouflaged jacket took a couple of steps towards me and demanded, "Who the hell are you and what the f*** are you doing in the valley on your own?!"

My reply was, "Police Support Unit and I am not alone." Before he could say anything more, I turned and bellowed, "Constable Peter, pass the word for Sergeant Servester and the rest of the section to join me, please!" The rapid appearance of almost a dozen armed figures silenced any other comments the sergeant might have intended.

In the short while as full darkness descended, I set Sgt Servester to organise an orderly night camp for us right next to the casually located army unit, which proved to be made up of National Servicemen who had never been on patrol in the valley before. Worse still, when I explained my patrol's tasking, operating out of Makuti, under Rampart and the assurances I had had from Crusader liaison at that location about no other army units operating east of the Rekometje River, the sergeant advised me that his instructions had come from the Crusader commander located at Chirundu, not Makuti. My delicate inquiry about no guard brought the response that their advice had been that guards were only needed during the hours of darkness. My polite advice to the sergeant about having just one roll of four-by-two available and circulating that for weapon-cleaning purposes, so that only one rifle was unavailable at any one time, brought the comment that they didn't teach that during training back in Salisbury. I also pointed out that they really did need to sort out clean, dry wood for their fire, so that there was no repeat of the column of smoke which had first attracted our attention. Noting that there was no indication of water being available in the area of their chosen camp, I did ask about that. The sergeant admitted that he was getting a little worried about that because they had been set down by chopper, with two flights carrying personnel and a third all their packs, rations and water supplies, which they were now getting down to the last of. On that score, I was able to show him the Chitaki stream and mark his map for where we had found good water in it.

The one positive aspect of our encounter was that their army radio kept them in regular contact with Chirundu, so we were able to inform that location that we had met without incident and would be going our separate ways in the morning and ask that that be relayed to Makuti, which was done.

After our routine stand-to at dawn, which had the army unit a little puzzled, I and my section ate our usual hearty breakfast, made sure our own fire was out, wished the army unit well and set off to attend to our own tasking. I was certain that in skirting the base of the escarpment we would be too far south to even see any sign of the Chiruwe River, but hoped that the headwater of the Mbera River, which, according to my map, appeared to start a short way up the escarpment, would be visible and, more importantly, might provide us with a refill of our water supplies. We found the upper reaches of the Mbera River, but, even though we tracked down it for a mile or more and did a bit of digging where there was sand, our efforts proved fruitless. A quick check with Sgt Servester and among the constables revealed that they were all down to about their last half-pint of water. My own situation, having the third water bottle at my belt and tins of grapefruit in reserve, was much better, but with thirty-six hours of activity behind us and a dry night camp ahead of us, finding water next day and preferably early in the day, became something of importance.

Following my philosophy that every member of the section needed to be fully in the picture, I held a section conversation. Thanks to our depot training sessions and mapwork lectures, each of the section had a good grasp of map information and the essentials of relating that to what was physically on the ground around us. We were heading into an area which was known to be largely waterless in the latter part of the dry season or when the rains failed. I was quite confident that we were about five miles from the upper reaches of the Chitemba River and about a dozen miles from the headwaters of the Sapi River. Both had some potential for us finding water in them, but there was no guarantee of that. What we were all beginning to realise was that at this time of the year, there was no water to be found anywhere east of Rekometje River along the line where valley floor met the base of the escarpment. My decision that we should camp overnight without a fire or any cooking and head off eastwards at the crack of dawn, again without cooking, to benefit from the cooler hours of the morning, met with approval. With a touch of luck, we would find water early and be able to make a late breakfast meal mid-morning. After another fruitless effort to achieve some radio contact, I drifted off to sleep that night, on top of my parachute silk sleeping bag, with the words of the Country and Western song, "Cool Water" running through my mind.

After my hour of guard duty I found it difficult to get back to sleep, so was quite relieved when the first light of dawn heralded the beginning of the new day. After dispensing with our usual dawn stand-to and making sure that everyone had swallowed a few mouthfuls of water to start the day, some of it from the third water bottle at my own belt, we set off, with me directly behind Const. Mapfumo at Dermotand with Sgt Servester as last man. We had been moving for about a half-hour, through thin bushland and quite a lot of open vleis with the occasional clump of assorted larger trees, when Const. Mapfumo signalled for the patrol to stop and indicated for me to get alongside him. Once alongside I saw immediately what he had seen. Thirty yards distant there was a fine specimen of the sausage tree, towering fifty feet or more in height. Up in its branches and scrabbling around beneath it, seeking the last of its bright red flowers, which were clearly food for them, was a sizeable troop of baboon at least a couple of dozen strong.

As I learned later, the flowers of the sausage tree are an important source of food during the hot and dry season, when they attract baboon, impala, bush pigs and duiker. The fruits are massive, a foot or more in length and often over ten pounds in weight. Since they drop randomly when the time of the year is right, the sausage tree is not one to camp under. In this case, Const. Mapfumo was right to be cautious because a strong troop of baboon, under an aggressive leader, have been known to attack an individual person, armed or not armed. However, there was no real reason why we had to stick so rigidly to our line of march that we would compete for space with the baboon troop in their foraging, so we diverted sufficiently to skirt around them at a respectful distance. As we did so, a series of raucous bellows from the baboons informed us that they had noted our presence.

Another hour or more of pushing along quite smartly but warily, still faithfully following the outline of the foothills of the escarpment, brought us to a dry gulley just about where I believed we should be meeting the start of the Chitemba River. The gully was dry as a bone, with no trace of sand or any rock pools in which water might be found all year round. Thinking back to our previous patrol to the Pfumbe Hill and remembering that the Chitemba River, at a point much nearer to the Zambezi had proved waterless then, there was little purposes in turning north to follow the gulley. We needed to push on, which is what we did. One of the indicators which worried me somewhat was that as we had been moving eastwards, our encounters with antelope small and large had become less frequent, suggesting that, at this time of the year at least, they did not favour this area of the valley, probably due to the lack of water available.

At that moment, good fortune came to our rescue to a certain degree, because we came across a good, broad game trail going the way we were headed. Life teaches sensible people that when you are handed an Ace, you do not wisely discard it. Following that philosophy, we used that well-beaten trail to shift along, more at a tarmac surface marching rate rather than cautious operational wilderness area patrol pace. That the game trail was well-used by elephant was evident from the frequent droppings we found. The first hour led us into an area of what I can best describe as shallow ditches, which fitted in with the watercourse blue lines on my map, suggesting that we were pushing through the headwaters area of the Sapi River. It was clear that the game trail we were following ignored them and pushed on east, meandering just a little here and there to avoid rocky outcrops. Giving a thought to the fact that if there had been water available somewhere nearby down one or other of those watercourses, the game trail would have diverted towards it, I let myself be guided by the wisdom of the natural inhabitants of the valley, who knew much more about their environment than I did, so we pressed on. Another hour passed, with the heat building. When I called a brief stop to our progress, I discovered that a couple of the constables had reached the point where they had stopped sweating, which was not a good sign. A couple of mouthfuls of water from my third water bottle gave them some small relief, but then we had to push on. We had covered perhaps another couple of miles, through terrain which was interspersed with little rocky outcrops, when Const. Bushu, up at point, maybe under the pressure of our circumstances, forgot all about silent signals and called back to me, "Ishe, there is water ahead!" A while later, when I had time to take some bearings, it was clear that the game trail made by our blessed wild inhabitants of the valley had led us to the very beginning of the Chewore River, at its most westerly point. More immediately, there was water visible in rocky pools over a stretch of the river perhaps fifteen or twenty yards in length. All around were signs that game animals of all kinds regularly frequented the place. If there was ever a sight for dry mouths, then that was it. Having had a little more water over the past hours than my companions and knowing that we would be resting here for a while, I took off my 44 webbing pack and posted myself as guard, while Sgt Servester and the constables divested themselves of their backpacks and made their way down to the waiting water. Over the next little while they each drank their fill from the clearest and cleanest of the pools, topped up their empty water bottles, climbed out of the stream bed and found comfortable spots in which to sit down and relax bare to the waist in the heat.

Right then, nobody even suggested a fire and a meal, despite the fact that it had been more than 24 hours since we had last eaten a cooked meal. With everyone else well-watered and relaxed, I had Sgt Servester replace me as our guard while I drank what was left in my third water bottle, then did exactly what my companions had done. I made my way down to the cleanest little pool, drank some more water and refilled all three of my water bottles. After that, I followed the example of my companions. I stripped off my camouflage jacket, sat down with my FN ready to hand and leaned comfortably back against a granite boulder, bare to the waist and with my left arm out along the top of it, to enjoy a good sweat.

As the first little globules of sweat started to form on my left arm, a bee took an interest, probably because of the salt content, rather than just the water, of which there was plenty nearby. I had been in Africa long enough to know that it is unwise to upset an African bee. Flapping at it, trying to shoo it away, or attempting to crush it, were not wise moves, so I just let it settle on me and shove its proboscis into one of the sweaty globules on my forearm. I knew that if I left it alone it would sup its fill and then take off about its usual business. However, that single bee was quite quickly joined by another and then some more.

As more and more bees started swarming in towards me, Const. Peter called out to me, "Careful Ishe, do not move, they will go away when you are dry." Soon, my arm and shoulder were just one black mass of bees, all busy taking in just as much of my salty sweat as they could. With every one of my companions, including Sgt Servester on guard duty, looking on in a mixture of expressions of concern and fascination, I concentrated on staying absolutely still. I slowly shut my mouth, brought my breathing through my nose down as shallow as I could and with my head already turned to the left, made no move to change that position. In truth, it was not until a couple of them started to investigate my left armpit, while others took an interest in my ears and my nostrils, that it became really difficult to stay totally motionless.

However, my mental order to the physical me of, "If you move a whisker now, we are both dead!" seemed to do the trick. After a few minutes, which felt like a lifetime, the last of the bees flew off. That allowed me to utter probably the most profound sigh of relief I have ever uttered in my life and simply sag limply for a moment or two against the granite rock.

As I did so, Const. Peter exclaimed, "Well done, Ishe. They would have killed you if you had crushed just one of them!"

Our somewhat frequently changed guards, even if they were bare to the waist, stayed alert, armed and ready to provide early warning of any approach of people or animals. The latter being the most likely, because the tell-tale droppings of everything from elephant to duiker were all around. Antelope were highly unlikely to challenge our presence at their waterhole, but an argument with buffalo, rhino, elephant, or perhaps a pride of lion was something to be avoided. During that period of perhaps a half-hour of soaking up the late morning sunshine and, little by little as much water as we each felt comfortable with, I found myself quite fascinated by the efforts of a score or so of dung beetles, busy squabbling among themselves over what must have appealed to them as the juiciest portions of one set of elephant dung. One by one, each having harvested a large marble-sized ball of dung, they started on their journey to wherever they were going, to hide away the fruits of their labours, bury their eggs in it and guard it until their infant offspring, the next generation of dung beetles appeared and were able to feed off of the material until they learned to scavenge for themselves. The little fellows did not push their ball of dung forward in the direction they wished to go. Instead, they almost stood upon their head while rolling the ball of dung, larger than themselves, by pushing at it with their back legs.

With all of us much refreshed, it was time to take ourselves up and away from the stream bed and find a spot where we had some cover and shade, where we could light a smokeless fire and eat a decent meal. Meanwhile, as we were in open ground although close to the escarpment, I tried once more for contact with one or other of our surrounding police stations. Somewhat to my surprise, it was ZEF 209, Mount Darwin who came up, Strength 5, loud and clear. Grateful for that contact, I relayed our position as a map reference and requested they should kindly relay that to Makuti Base Camp, with the message that we were okay and proceeding as tasked.

Finding a suitable spot for a meal break, some few hundred yards from the water hole and well clear of game trails did not take long. After some thirty hours or so without anything other than dry nibbles, just enough to keep away any hunger pains, appetites among all of us were sharp, resulting in somewhat greater quantities of food than normal eventually being consumed. With everyone well fed, well supplied with water and decently shaded from the worst of the sun, I let a couple of hours pass by before deciding to move on. In that length of time, I discussed with Sgt Servester our position on the map and our likely route and distances to be covered. As he and I had our heads together, poring over my map of the area, our guard on duty called quietly to inform us that there was a rhino going towards the watering point we had recently used and that there was a leopard following it. That oddity brought everyone to their feet to take a discreet look. Our peeking confirmed that our guard, Const. Bushu at that time, had nothing wrong with his eyesight. On the game trail which had led us to the water, there was indeed a large male rhino, unhurriedly heading towards the watering point. Some thirty yards behind the rhino was a leopard, also quite clearly not in any hurry and certainly not eyeing the rhino as an item of prey. Both eventually disappeared out of sight down into the bed of the stream, without any indication of competition or strife between the two.

As the crow flies, we were some 16 to 18 miles from the start of the Mariya-Tsoro Gorge. If we followed the winding and twisting of the river as it broadened, it would be more like 20 or 22 miles. What we had to be wary of was entering the four or maybe five-mile length of the gorge too late in the day to reach the far end before dark. We needed to try to at least halve the distance before making overnight camp. That would put us in a good position from which to set off early next day to first reach and then cross the Chewore River itself in order to get to the game trail which ran down the eastern side of the river and led to and through the gorge and by following that, to tackle the gorge itself. With that in mind, we set off, through what was mainly bushland and vlei country, made up of acacia and jesse bushes, both nastily thorny, interspersed with some clusters of really impressive mopani trees.

Possibly because of the water available here and there in the Chewore River which was relatively close by, the abundance of wildlife around us was remarkable. In the next few hours of patrolling, we saw lots of impala, bushbuck, duiker, a magnificent eland bull, several kudu and two whole herds of waterbuck, each one with their distinctive white ring on their buttocks. More distantly there was just a single zebra. Of the larger game, we passed a family group of giraffe, with young and old all busy nibbling daintily at the foliage of a sizeable acacia bush and just one female rhino with her young offspring close by.

We also discovered that there were lots of game trails, both broad and narrow, criss-crossing the area. Where it suited our patrol's general direction, we were only too pleased to take advantage of them, a fact which led to an extraordinary experience. As I have related, I am wary of snakes and wherever possible, give them a wide berth. However, when we were following a stretch of game trail which, from both spoor and droppings, was much favoured and frequented by elephant, with Const. Bushu up front in Point position with me behind him, he signalled a halt and tapped his shoulder for me to join him. As I did so, he pointed at the ground just ahead and said, "Nyoka, Ishe. A piccanin." Laying quite still, right at the edge of the game trail, was a small snake, mottled brown, black and purple. In length it was no more than a yard long and quite stocky in form, with a shortish tail. Its head was broad and triangular, suggesting a viper of some kind, rather than a cobra. Somewhat puzzled by the fact that it was just staying there motionless, I stepped a few feet closer, which made me aware of two things. Firstly, it was more multi-coloured than any other snake I had ever seen and, secondly, sticking out of its mouth was about three inches of the tail of some unfortunate snake or reptile which it had just made a meal of.

Having a detail in the section who clearly knew a whole lot more about snakes than I did, I passed word for Const. Phineas to come forward, which he promptly did. He took one look and in answer to my question of what type of snake it might be, he had no hesitation in naming it as a young Gaboon Viper and offered to kill it then and there, which offer I declined. As for why it was immobile and making no effort to flee from us, his guess was that it had ambushed and swallowed some lizard or another young snake which was much too big for it and was laying there waiting to be able to move once it had more fully digested its over ambitious meal. As what we were looking at was rather unusual, I let each member of the section come up and have a quick look. We could have killed it or left it there to perhaps be trodden on by a passing rhino, elephant of buffalo, but it seemed to me that the little fellow, which Phineas assured me would be double its present size once full-grown, needed a little help. Guided by Const. Phineas, I cut a forked stick from a nearby bush and used it to pin down the snake's head. Then I was able to get a good grip with one hand directly behind its head, take hold of its tail with my other hand and lift the colourful little fellow, which, to my surprise, made no effort to wriggle or object to what was going on. I carted the snake a dozen yards clear of the game trail, set it down and stepped back smartly, but it just stayed still. Const. Phineas gathered some dead leaves and scattered them over it, assuring me that that would help it to be safe and there we left it.

I never counted or checked the time those actions with helping the young snake delayed us, but just re-formed the section into patrol order and set off again. Barely fifty yards further down that game trail, it led out from bushland into a very large area of grassland, which ran a mile or more to our right and was at least a half-mile across. About one hundred yards out, there was one solitary huge baobab tree. The game trail we were following led straight out, passed close by the baobab tree and appeared to lead straight on to the other side of the open area. Given that we needed to move on smartly to make up for the delay with the snake, I indicated for Const. Bushu to lead us on and across the open area, something I would not have done if I had thought that the area was operationally active.

With the numbers of our patrol spread out for tactical safety, Const. Bushu and I were about a hundred yards past the baobab tree, while Sgt Servester as last man, was about level with it when, from way off to our right there came a heavy dull drumming noise. Thundering down towards us, clearly in stampede mode, was a broad front of at least a couple of hundred galloping buffalo, with hundreds more behind them. My bellowed order of, "Back to the tree!" may or may not have been heard above the noise of the stampeding buffalo which were bearing down on us all too rapidly, but it was obeyed with alacrity driven by survival instincts. Those closest to the baobab tree had time to scramble up into its branches, but for those three or four of us furthest out, as a certain General once said of a well-known battle, it really was another close-run thing. No time to get packs off or climb. We made it just in time to huddle tight up against the lee side of the broad trunk of the tree as, so I later discovered, some two thousand panicking buffalo, the Chewore Herd, stampeded past. Some were so close that they stumbled and fell around us, brought down by the above-ground parts of the roots of the baobab tree. Somehow each one got to its feet again and galloped on. Among the last to pass us were two which clearly had blood streaming down their flanks. "Lion, Ishe," was Const. Bushu's observation, which thinking matched my own. As if to prove both of us right, Sgt Servester, from his vantage point well above us in the tree, shouted that there were lions killing a buffalo up at the far end of the open area. That certainly explained the cause of the stampede. When we were all on the ground again, I remarked to Sgt Servester that if the tree had not been there, or if we had been further out, we would all likely have been trampled flat. "We were very lucky indeed Sgt," I observed, to which he shook his head. "No Ishe, not luck. It was the nyoka saying thank you!"

Between the snake rescue and our close call with the Chewore Herd of buffalo, we were somewhat under our targeted distance for the day when it became time to seek a decent location for our night camp. Fortunately, just after I made that decision, we came across a knoll in the mostly level bush country we were traversing. What game trails there were close to it clearly diverted around it and there was sufficient scrub and tree cover on it for us not to be too readily seen. The only problem was that in setting each detail down in a circle, head outwards, it meant laying head downwards on the slope, which was not a comfortable way of trying to sleep, so our defensive circle was formed with our feet outwards and downwards, which was much more comfortable. It did not take long to establish the guard roster, with me first up, gather some good clean dry wood which we could burn without it creating any smoke and for everyone in turn to eat as much as he felt he needed, given our meal-break of not too long before during the day. Another positive point for that location was that our VHF radio liked it. At the first call, Chirundu Police Station came in loud and clear. I advised that we were intending to undertake the traverse of the Mari-ya-Tsoro Gorge the next day and asked for the latest information on any insurgent activity in the area we were heading for. The response from Chirundu was that there had not been any indication of any crossings of the Zambezi or signs of insurgent activity in the entire valley area for several weeks. That much reassurance was welcomed by every one of us and perhaps contributed to what appeared to be a sound night's sleep for everyone, discounting the share of guard duty.

The following morning, given the sitrep we had received from Chirundu I dispensed once again with the usual dawn stand-to and set everyone busy with a very early morning meal. Given the slight elevation we were on and a modest-sized mopani tree in a convenient position, I indulged in a little climbing, so that I could get a better view of the countryside around. Almost due east, at a distance of perhaps four miles, there was a small cluster of hills running north-south. To the north of that feature, there was then a mile or two of apparent flat land and then, clearly visible, the east-west line of the greater hill range through which the Chewore River made its way via the gorge we needed to traverse.

It seemed to me that it would be wiser for us to make our crossing of the Chewore to the south of the small range of hills, where there was likely to be less water, rather than nearer to the gorge where more water would be bound to exist. Accordingly, after our early breakfast and another short radio conversation with Chirundu, we set off, with Sgt Servester at Dermotwith me behind him. We had hardly started when we heard the roar of a lion seemingly dead ahead and not far distant. That put all of us on high alert as none of us wanted any unexpected encounter with a lion, or worse still, an entire pride of lions.

One of the extraordinary experiences of walking that Chewore Wilderness area was that we again appeared to be an oddity, a curiosity or an interest for assorted antelope, large and small. Apparently never having been shot at and probably never having seen any human form before, they reacted completely differently from their counterparts at the Kariba or Marongora Controlled Hunting areas, where antelope of all kinds fled instantly at the sound, smell or sight of human beings. Not long into our morning progress, just after Const. Mapfumo had replaced Sgt Servester at point, we reached an open area which was literally filled, from one side to the other with impala, all with heads down and cropping what little grass they could find. Const. Mapfumo simply kept to our intended line of progress. Once our presence was noted, a few impala heads came up, their ears flicked and their heads went down again. When we got to within touching distance of the animals, there was a little shuffling and nudging among the herd and a gap began to appear which allowed us to simply maintain our steady, if unhurried progress. One or two of the more curious animals gave us a long look and a good sniff. Having no individual or herd memory of us being any kind of threat, they then ignored us and got on with their grazing.

The short line of small hills was entirely visible to us, so my compass stayed in my pocket as we zeroed in on the southern-most tip of that geographical feature. When we reached it, we found ourselves looking down a long gentle grassy slope to what was clearly the line of the Chewore River. Some hundred yards away to the right of our direct line to the river there was a rhino. It appeared to be just laying down, resting, or asleep. Knowing the unpredictable nature of rhino and our individual and collective vulnerability once out in the open, I eased the safety catch of my FN rifle into the "Off" position, instructed the entire section to do the same and added that if the rhino should decide to charge at us on our way to the river, once I fired a first shot at it, they were to fire at it also, as much and as fast as they could reload, until the animal went down. With that possibility in mind, I chose to position myself in the middle of the section and kept a close eye on the rhino as we each in turn moved in open order down towards the river. We were all out in the open before the rhino seemed to notice we were anywhere nearby. Even then, all it did was to turn its head, flick its ears and look at us. I was still eyeing the rhino when a quiet call of "Ishe!" brought my attention back to the front of the section, where Const. Malembo had dropped to his knees and was silently signalling for me to join him, which I did, but deliberately at a steady walking pace in case any rush or hurry raised concern in the rhino's mind.

Sensibly, Const. Malembo had somewhat cautiously approached the point from which he could see up and down the river. Directly in front of us, the riverbank sloped down gently to meet the riverbed, which was about twenty yards wide at that point and just a level bed of sand. However, an assortment or rocks started about a hundred yards downstream.

While we could not directly see any of the water which was obviously there among those rocks, what we could see was the pride of lions which seemed to be drinking there. In taking a long hard look at that group of big cats, it looked to me like a half-dozen or more youngish females only. Fortunately, while my attention was on the lions, or lionesses, others among us had kept an eye on our nearby resting rhino, which resulted in a quiet but urgent call of, "Ishe! The rhino is moving!" By the time I looked round at it, the rhino was halfway to its feet. It got to its feet without any sign of haste or concern, shook itself in a rather dog-like way and started to amble in our direction.

It was no time to dither, with a bunch of lionesses to our left and an apparently inquisitive rhino to our right, so I ordered a two-by-two crossing of the river, at a smart walk, but without running and told Const. Malembo to head at 90 degrees to the river once he reached the far bank and to continue in that line for at least a couple of hundred yards then stop. Two by two, the constables set out to make a steady crossing of the river, with Sgt Servester and myself taking up position as the last pair. As we stepped down the minimal drop from riverbank to sandy riverbed, which was dry and firm, the rhino was barely twenty yards distant and seemingly determined to investigate further these strange two-legged creatures, the like of which it had quite clearly never seen before.

As Sgt Servester and I made the short climb up the far bank, I took a long, hard look at the lions downstream. Fortunately, they seemed to be paying no interest to us at all, which was quite a relief. Whether it was just the water, or that they had made a kill of something at that watering point and were attentive to that, I never knew. Having made sure we were of no immediate interest to the lions, I looked back across the Chewore. Our inquisitive rhino was in the act of stepping down into the riverbed. Once there, he started to follow our footsteps in the sand. Quickly, I instructed Sgt Servester to get to the front of the section, then to turn us left, to parallel the river, while I stayed at the back of the section, to keep an eye on whatever our inquisitive rhino might decide to get up to. The rate at which Sgt Servester took off across the short grassland to where Const. Malembo had halted, probably had more to do with the rhino's presence than any wish to be seen to be obedient to my latest orders.

Safely out of sight of the lions, but with the rhino ambling steadily along after us at about twenty yards distance, we covered the next three miles without any problem. On four occasions Sgt Servester quite rightly signalled a halt to our progress to allow first another rhino and then three small herds of buffalo to clear out of our way. At each of those stops, as I ceased moving forward, while keeping a very close eye on the rhino behind me, that great animal simply stopped as well. On the last of those occasions, I decided that if that rhino had wished to give us any grief, it would have made some aggressive move by now, so I headed of up front and set Sgt Servester to bring up the rear. To the left of us, across the Chewore, the low ridge of hills which had guided us to the river was coming to an end. Another three miles or so distant we could see the hills which contained the Mari-ya-Tsoro

Gorge, through which the river ran on its northward way to join the Zambezi, some 15 to 18 miles beyond the hills.

I decided that it was time to move closer to the river itself, to see if we could pick up the allegedly broad and very well used game trail that would lead us to and through the gorge. Just as on the other occasions, when we moved on, the rhino moved on with us, with Sgt Servester appearing to do as much walking backwards as he did facing forward. With another mile or so of progress under our feet and the midday heat building fast we needed to make a short break from our patrolling, but just what the rhino would do at that was a puzzle. Fortunately, we reached the river again and, more importantly for us, right alongside it, was a broad game trail, which we were only too pleased to start following. Barely a couple of hundred yards on, there was a branch off from the trail we were following, which led down to the bed of the river. Against the far bank, which rose twenty or thirty feet vertically at that point, there were two rhino, both busily licking at the rock face. Looking back, I watched as the rhino which had peaceably followed us for some miles and some hours, ambled down to the riverbed and joined its two companions in having a good lick at the rocks not far from the other two. With our tail-end escort now gone, much to the relief of Sgt Servester, we simply took a break and rested, all of us discreetly watching the three rhinos busy at what was obviously a well-used salt lick. The two rhinos which were down in the river as we arrived both paused briefly to look at us as we passed by, but, perhaps with one of their own kind close to us and showing no concern at all, they quickly returned their attention to the essential business of getting some salt into themselves. They also took no notice as they were joined by our erstwhile rhino companion. It was a strange sight to see three adult rhino within ten feet of each other, without any sign of upset, competition or aggression.

During that refreshing rest period, with ample water to drink and the certainty of refill somewhere not too distant along the Chewore, I discussed our options with Sgt Servester and the rest of the section. We could attempt to push on, helped by that fact that the game trail we were following was wide enough to drive a modern quadmobile along and possibly a Land Rover too, in the hope that we met nothing to delay us. That could give us the opportunity, if not the certainty, that we could get through the Mari-ya-Tsoro Gorge before nightfall. The alternative was to simply move more warily along, aiming to get to within a mile or less of the start of the gorge, make camp overnight there and make an early entry into the gorge the following day. I reminded them that although we had been informed by Chirundu Police Station, via our last radio contact, that the area was operationally quiet, we needed to be operationally alert, for our own safety either way around because walking carelessly in on a pride of lions, or a rhino or elephant with a bad temper, could get us damaged, just as much as a firefight with insurgents. I also reminded them that we were still only five days into our patrol task and that we had, if needed, another five to get to the mouth of the Chewore River to RV with our transport back to Makuti. With the full picture explained, there was total agreement that attempting to get through the gorge today was not wise, so we would push on, carefully, make night camp a little early perhaps and tackle the gorge on the morrow.

With everyone fully in the picture of what our plans were for the rest of the day, all rested, refreshed and alert, we moved on, with Const. Ben up front and me in my usual position as second in line in the patrol formation. We had been moving steadily along for about a half-hour, with the well-trodden game trail making our progress much easier than fighting tussock grass and thorny branches, when we came to the end of a stretch of mopani trees and scrub bushes. That allowed better long-range vision, at which Const. Ben silently signalled a stop and for me to join him. When I did so, he pointed ahead, not at ground level, but up in the sky where, perhaps a mile or more away, there was a column of several vultures soaring and circling.

"Something is dead or dying, Ishe," Const. Ben rightly commented. I gave him a verbal pat on the back for being observant and told him to drop in behind me as I led the patrol cautiously forward, keeping a careful eye on the vultures, to see whether they remained hovering, or if they decided to alight. If the vultures settled, that would warn us that perhaps lion, or hyena, or wild dogs, or whatever had made a kill, had moved off from it. If they kept hovering, either what had attracted them was still alive, or whatever had created that which was attracting them, was still present and smack in our path. My replacing Const. Ben at Dermot was not because I did not trust him, but, because I was the only one wearing a camouflage bush hat and jacket and therefore much less likely to be seen than any of the others in their blues and greys. We had talked it over within the section and they fully understood why I occasionally replaced our Dermotman when we were faced with uncertainties. With the vultures providing us with a very convenient sky marker and no breeze at all to carry our scent ahead of us, I was able to see, before we were seen or scented, which was just as well, because the attraction for the vultures was the half-eaten carcass of a buffalo, still being squabbled over by a pride of lions, consisting of one magnificent male, a few females and a half-dozen yearling cubs. Their kill was lying within a couple of feet of the game trail we wished to proceed along. It became evident that we needed to discreetly backtrack a hundred yards or so and then make a wide detour around the feeding lions and the circling vultures. Fortunately, lions with full bellies are not normally aggressive, but even so, on this occasion, giving them a very wide birth was the only sensible thing to do.

I motioned for Const. Ben to join me so that he could see what I was looking at, then told him to resume Dermotposition to lead us on the detour. He promptly whispered that he thought Sgt Servester would like a look at the lions, which ended up with each member of the section, one by one and vary carefully, coming up to where I was, to take a peek. It was another case of more stories for the families in Salisbury or in their home villages. It did not take us long to work our way through the nearby bush, which, conveniently, was thick enough to hide us from the feeding lions and to work our way back to the game trail by the river. From there it was a case of watching the distant hills grow gradually nearer, keeping an eye open for a decent place to refill our water bottles and keeping an eye open also for a safe place, somewhat away from the riverside game trail, where we could settle for the night. By mid-afternoon we found just what we needed on all three counts. It was a patch of very thick scrub a hundred yards or so to our right. A quick investigation of the sandy bed of the Chewore confirmed that there was good, clean water a couple of feet down. That evening, in our discreet little overnight camp in the bushes by the Chewore River, the conversation was all about what we had experienced during the day and just what the next day might throw up to keep us all on our toes. I did have a small advantage in that during my three years in Nyasaland, much of it spent as an active member of the Police Mobile Force (PMF), I had encountered most of the wild life of Africa, whereas those I was with were raised and had grown to adulthood and, in the case of most of them, had married, within a Tribal Trust Land or an urban township, far away from any wilderness and the big game and assorted antelope roaming freely in the area we were now patrolling through. As several of them commented, they already had many stories to relate to their friends and family. Their hope was that we would not run into any insurgents but would see much more of the animals of the area before the patrol was completed. All I could do was to offer upwards a silent "Amen to that."

With a good meal and plenty of water both inside and beside each of us, all that I needed to do was to supervise the nightly cleaning of rifles, strictly one by one, set up the guard roster and then get my head down for a few hours of sleep. Sgt Servester volunteered to take on the first hour, so my own hour on guard duty began just before dawn started to break. As usual, the dawn chorus of animals and birds as each claimed ownership of its territory was a delight to hear, from the roar of lion to the bellowing of elephant and, somewhere in the hills ahead, the noisy gruff barking of baboon. The dawn chorus was also the signal for the disappearance of the several varieties of bats and birds which had been active all night long. My one beef about the night bats and birds was that they never seemed to reduce in numbers the absolute myriad of mosquitoes, whose whining was incessant.

After a brief stand-to, a decent breakfast meal and a cautious visit to the bed of the nearby river, to top up water bottles, we headed north once again, with Const. Phineas in the lead, me in second position and Sgt Servester bringing up the rear. With ten paces or so between us, the patrol extended around a hundred yards in length from front to rear. Silent signals were all fine and dandy when someone ahead made one, but when it was a matter of passing word from the back end to the front of the patrol, it was often a case of an urgent but muted hiss of "Ishe!" which came to me. That was what happened barely a half-hour after we began to follow the broad game trail northward. A pack of a dozen or more hyena had either picked up our scent or seen us and were showing a distinct interest in Sgt Servester, who had wisely closed up on Const. Ben just ahead of him. With the river beside us running straight at that time, once I had turned and seen what was going on, I called for everyone to close in on me and be ready to do some shooting if needed. Our bunching up together seemed to perplex the hyena, but not scare them off. They kept prowling, approaching us and retreating, as if trying to judge our strength or vulnerability. Being delayed by a probably hungry and potentially dangerous pack of hyena was not on my agenda for the day. I instructed everyone to load and be ready to aim at the ground close to any of the hyena which took their fancy and all fire together when I gave the order. I emphasised they were not to aim at the hyena because all we wished to do was to frighten them off, not kill any of them. The next time the pack approached, I issued the order of "Ready. Aim. Fire!" and to the slightly ragged volley which resulted, added a couple of shots from my own FN. Earth and twigs flew into the faces, legs and torsos of the hyena, at no more than a dozen paces distant. None appeared to have been directly hit but faced with stings from flying bits and pieces of soil and twig, plus the quite loud noise of the single volley, the hyena turned and fled. That allowed us to make safe our firearms, after which we resumed our slightly delayed progress northward.

Thankfully, that was the only untoward encounter we suffered over the now short distance to where the hills rose and the river headed for what was clearly its route through the hills. From the flatlands on one side of the range of hills to the flatlands on the other side was, according to my map, about two and a half miles in a straight line. Given the fact that the river twisted and curved its way through in anything but a straight line, my guess was that we had about four miles to cover. Since it was by then still only mid-morning, clearing the gorge before dusk looked like an easy thing to achieve. Taking up the Dermotposition myself and with the others in close order behind me, we set off to follow the broad and clearly well-used game trail which ran parallel to the course of the river. For the first half-mile the slope of the hills on either side of the river was at about a forty-five degree angle, but then the severity of the slopes grew rapidly until we were walking along what was in essence a four to six feet wide ledge along a vertical cliff. Three things entered my mind as I led the section onward, deeper and deeper into the gorge. The first was a hope that we did not meet anything large and aggressive coming towards us, particularly where vision ahead was limited. The second was that during any decently wet season when the river came down in flood, this game trail would become impassable for greater or lesser periods of time. The third point was that any of the larger adult specimens of animals, such as elephant, rhino or even giraffe would find turning around on the game trail almost impossible along stretches where the pathway was at its narrowest. The game trail, ledge or whatever, faithfully followed each curve and twist of the river, at a nearly level height above the water surface.

It dipped and rose, quite gently, from a dozen feet, to around twenty feet. The horseshoe bends of the river provided either a very limited view ahead on the sharper right hand turns, or a decently long view as the river followed the gorge leftwards. Above us there was perhaps three or four hundred feet of sheer cliff face and much the same on the other side, only some thirty yards distant from us at most. The bed of the river alternated between clusters of rocks and sandy stretches. Some of the pools of water were quite lengthy and extended from side to side of the gorge. Mostly the water was clear enough to see to the bottom of the pools, but not where the water was clearly deepest. As we progressed into the steeper part of the gorge, the direct sunlight died away and a shadowy gloom took control, although we could see the sun shining directly on to the upper level of the cliff face on the western side of the gorge.

We were halfway through the gorge before we reached the point where we could finally see for ourselves just why the gorge was called "Mari-ya-Tsoro". The upper couple of hundred feet of the cliff face on the western side, over a length of a half-mile or so was perforated with hundreds of nesting-holes of birds. It really did look like a giant Tsoro Board stood on edge. Tsoro is a game common across central and southern Africa. Originally it was played with seeds or stones in rows of palm-sized scoops in the ground. Four rows of seven to ten scooped dips with two players. It is a mathematically calculative game, the details of which I never could understand. I likened it to a game of drafts.

The birds living in the nests appeared to be about the size of a European dove, but brightly and multi-coloured in reds, purples and orange shades. Perhaps members of the African roller family of birds. I did not try to count them, but there must have been a thousand or more holes in the face of the gorge, with birds flying in and out all of the time. What struck me was the unerring accuracy which each incoming bird displayed in flying to the right hole out of the many hundred that were there. At a good vantage point, I halted the section for just a few minutes, so that we could watch the avian activity going on above us on the other side of the gorge. During that stop I once again deeply regretted the ongoing sanctions which deprived me of film for my camera. It was while we were standing looking at that Tsoro Board effect in the cliff face that a couple of small rocks came tumbling down from above us on our side of the gorge. When I looked up to see why they had fallen, I found myself looking at a stocky little brown antelope, with two straight, small horns no more than six inches long, which was perched as if on tiptoe on a tiny ledge about thirty feet above us. It was studying us with mild curiosity. Thanks to my days in Nyasaland and more recently in the granite hills of Chibi, I was able to recognise it as a klipspringer, one of the smallest of the antelope in eastern and southern Africa and only to be found in isolated pockets of hilly, rocky country, where its ability to nimbly scale rock faces and leap from crag to crag allowed it to evade its predators. This fellow was still watching us as we decided we had seen enough of the far side of the gorge and its holes in the cliff face and moved on. The fact that we had paused for those few minutes to look at the reason why the gorge had its name, was fortuitous, for wildlife and for us. We had about a quarter of a mile or maybe a little more to go to the end of the vertical cliffs, along a stretch where the game trail was no more than ten or twelve feet vertically above a stretch of water some two to three feet deep and from where I could see most of that quarter mile or so distance ahead of us, when a large herd of elephant, moving rapidly as if something was chasing them or had frightened them, came into view, heading towards us.

The sheer luck of us being at that precise point when those elephant came into view gave me time to order the two constables nearest to me to put down their rifles, take off their packs and then lower themselves over the edge of the game trail and drop down to the river bed. Since every member of the section could clearly see the elephants coming at us at a run and knowing that we could not outrun them even if we did turn tail and flee, there was no hesitation in obeying my order, even if it did mean wet feet and knees.

Once they were both safely down there, I dropped their rifles and packs down to them. It did not need any more orders from me to set the rest of the section following suit, while I kept a wary eye on the lead elephant, which was a female with a pair of ivories most bull elephants would have been grateful for. Because I had the greatest firepower by way of my FN rifle, I chose to go last, although the last thing I wished to do was to have to kill the lead elephant to protect any one of us. Thankfully, there was still a safe although short distance between us, with the lead elephant bellowing warnings and flapping her ears at me, when I was able to follow the others down to the safety of the riverbed. From there I counted as 17 elephant, male, female, young and old, trundled past at a fair old pace, just a few feet above us. When the last of them had gone, Sgt Servester said quietly, "We are lucky, Ishe. The bees, the buffalo and now this. Mwari is with us!" To that my response was, "Let's hope he sticks with us all the way Sgt because we might need him again before this patrol is finished."

With the elephant heading away from us it was time to take stock and consider our next move. All of us were standing in water up to our knees and those few who had stumbled on landing were even wetter. On the plus side, no pack or rifle had ended up in the water. That meant our remaining rations, our bedrolls and our weaponry were all okay. A quick study of the cliff face down which we had dropped to safety showed that it was something of an overhang rather than just a vertical rock face. A quick attempt to see if we could get back up to the game trail, by letting Const. Mapfumo, our best athlete, stand on my shoulders for a start, proved abortive. There were neither handholds nor footholds and the overhand effect made it too difficult anyway. That left us with just one option, which was to get wading and keep our fingers crossed that the water ahead of us remained shallow enough to comfortably wade through. The final quarter mile or more within the confines of the gorge took us quite a while to cover. I led the way, with my pack as high on my back as the webbing straps would allow and my rifle held ready but carefully high above the water. It was a case of testing every forward step before swinging weight on to it and bringing the other foot forward. Thankfully, the deepest part of that lengthy stretch of water soaked us no more than up to our waists as we waded slowly along almost leaning on the rock wall to our right hand side. Eventually, the sheer face of the gorge gave way to more open ground and a more normal riverbank and bed. That lengthy stretch of water ended where a sandbank started. Towards that the water shallowed gently until I was able to step completely clear of it and then lead the section up the eastern bank and on to properly dry ground. For a moment or two all of us stood there, looking back over the water and into the part that we could see of the gorge through which we had so recently made our way. As we each let our eyes rove to and from the narrows of the gorge to the sandbank at our feet that, it was Const. Ben who flung his arm out and pointed at the far side of the sandbank, "Ah! Ishe, Ma croc! A quick glance at what he was pointing at from the advantage of height which we had not had when down at water level, clearly showed the unmistakable slide-marks of where one or more crocodile had slithered in and out of the water at that point. In getting us out of the somewhat sticky position we had been in with the elephant coming at us, I had never even thought for one moment of the possibility of there being one or more crocodiles in that stretch of water. I doubted that any of my companions had thought of it either. Sgt Servester looked long and hard at the clear slide-marks less than a score of yards distant and said, "It is Mwari again Ishe. He is still with us."

By that time the heat of the midday was really making itself felt, to the point where we were beginning to steam dry. Close by we found a suitable clump of mopani trees under the shade of which we stopped for a short while, to pour the water out of our boots and step out of our soaking clothes and socks, in order to let them dry in the sun while we just relaxed, albeit with a guard out who was appropriately alert, if not quite appropriately dressed. More in hope than expectation I made another attempt at radio communication. Very pleasingly, Chirundu, ZEF 903 came in at strength 5, loud and clear at my first call. That allowed an exchange of situation reports in which I provided them with our location, which was about four miles south of Pfumbe Hill and they confirmed that the valley in our area was free of insurgency activity as far as they were aware. It was that phrase, "As far as we are aware," which kept us all alert and watchful as we eventually moved on into the afternoon, with the peak of Pfumbe Hill on the western side of the river growing closer and closer as we progressed steadily along on the well-trodden game trail beside the river.

That stretch of eighteen or maybe twenty miles from the gorge to the Chewore River mouth contained both open vleis and lengthy stretches of thick bush, with the greatest assortment of thorny varieties that I had ever encountered in Rhodesia. There were acacia bushes and trees, camel thorn, knob thorn, buffalo thorn and lots and lots of bush willow, some of it demonstrating its ability to adopt a vine-like style of growth as it wove its way into more mature trees. The fact that we were able to avoid most of their assorted spikes by sticking with the game trail following the river was greatly appreciated by us all. It was when we were pretty close to Pfumbe Hill, in a patch of thick bush, when I was beginning to feel it was time to seek a suitable place for our next night camp, that Const. Mapfumo, ahead of me at point, suddenly signalled a stop and tapped his shoulder. When I got alongside of him, he just pointed. We were at the edge of a small patch of open grassland leading away from the riverside. About a hundred yards from the river there was a single large tree. Leaning and I do mean leaning, against that large tree, was one adult bull elephant. It had its front legs crossed and was swinging its trunk slowly and gently from side to side, as if it were a pendulum. "Mapfura Ishe?" Const. Mapfumo suggested quietly, to which I nodded. The marula tree, or mapfura tree, one of the largest to be found in Zimbabwe, produces a plum-like fruit, which, when properly fermented was used by the locals all over southern Africa to produce a thick, creamy liqueur which rivalled Mlala Palm Wine in potency. The kernel inside the nutty shell under the flesh of the fruit has been a source of nutritious food for the locals for literally thousands of years as evidenced by archaeological digs in the Pomongwe Caves. I have eaten it myself on several occasions and found it similar to a cashew nut in taste and texture. It was not unknown for elephant to consume a hearty meal of the fallen and partly fermented/rotting fruit and become somewhat drunk as a result. The elephant we were looking at was a perfect example of the stories many people had heard of, but never seen for themselves. After a moment or two of studying the obviously contentedly inebriated elephant, Const. Mapfumo quite rightly suggested that it would be okay to go on as there was no way that elephant was going anywhere. He would eventually either lay down or fall down and sleep off his boozy binge. Provided we made no effort to go anywhere near him and his marula fruits, he would not trouble us, which is exactly how it worked out.

Not long after our safely distanced encounter with the drunken elephant, we found a suitable place to camp for the night. It was a little earlier than usual, but after the eventful day we had just had, an early night seemed appropriate. The first task after establishing a safe perimeter and the usual guard roster, was another effort to contact one of other of the surrounding police stations by our VHF radio set. That effort failed. As we cooked and ate our individual meals and afterwards relaxed, there was quite a lot of discussion about cliffs that looked like tsoro boards, elephants, crocodile and Mwari and a general puzzling as to whether or not elephants suffered hangovers just like human beings.

The following morning, after an untroubled night and a precautionary dawn stand-to, followed by an unhurried morning meal, we set off northward once again, with two immediate tasks in mind. The first was to find a safe location along the Chewore where we could refill our water bottles. That meant a rocky pool or stretch of dry sand into which we could dig for clean water, safely away from the longer and deeper stretches of water we were beginning to encounter, which might just hide a crocodile lurking in its depths. Fortunately, we found a decent stretch of sand which, although dry at surface level, had plenty of good clean water eighteen inches down. The second was to find a location which might allow me to pass a morning situation report to one of the surrounding stations. That took three efforts before I could make contact with Chirundu, who were able to pass on our location to Makuti and confirm for us that there was still no information of any insurgent activity in the area of our patrol.

The thickness of the jesse bush all around us made me wonder whether the broad game trail which we were cautiously progressing along was perhaps the only north-south game trail east of the Chewore for some distance. With that in mind and our instructions to scout round the area, just following a well-trodden game trail seemed not really to be doing a full job. Acting upon that thought, when we encountered the next clear game trail running east-west, which was half the width of the one we were progressing northward on, I turned the section on to it so that we could explore it for a mile or two. In just over an hour of steady progress, covering perhaps three miles on the ground, the only game trails that we found which were running north-south, were tiny, clearly used by the many small animals and probably a rodent or two and not much else. That is not to say that there was not a proliferation of antelope and other game in the area, for we had close encounters with eland, kudu and a family of giraffe, most of which just stood and watched us pass by. What was clear also was that the bush and grasslands were parched dry and badly in need of some early rain. After a little over an hour of following that east-west game trail, I called a brief rest period, after which we back-tracked on our own spoor until we were once again on the major game trail on the east side of the Chewore River, from where we set off again on our northward route. With a break to let the heat of the midday sun pass by, we continued on, without any incident of note, until I called a halt to our day's progress at a point where we were no more than five or so miles from the 4-500ft high peak of Rusemwa Hill which stands on the west side of the Chewore River. Rusemwa Hill has its peak at its southerly end. From that peak is slopes steadily downward for about two miles to meet the flatlands barely a couple of hundred yards from where the Chewore River flows into the Zambezi River itself.

I had been carefully studying the river as we moved northwards alongside it, watching carefully as it gradually grew in width, because our transport would be on the track to the west of Rusemwa Hill, which meant that we needed to find a suitable point where we could cross the river to be on the western side of it. I also had in mind that we needed to find a location which might provide good VHF radio communications with Chirundu or some other police station, because I needed to plan for our uplift on the following day. Probably as much by luck as good judgement, my chosen overnight camp location satisfied both of those requirements. There was good water to be had in the bed of the Chewore, where crossing it in the morning would be easy and Chirundu came in loud and clear after only a couple of calls. With Chirundu kindly acting as our relay, arrangements for our uplift, timed for midday next day, at a convenient point just west of Rusemwa Hill were made firm. That gave us about five miles of ground to cover the following morning, which meant about a three-hour effort at most. Provided we met no cause for delay on route, that distance we could cover before the midday heat really kicked in. With my section fully briefed for the morrow, a decent meal inside me and the usual overnight routines all established, with me on the first hour of guard duty, I was content to fix my face-veil into place to hopefully keep the worst of the mosquitoes at bay and then settle down to our usual night-time routine.

The following morning, with dawn stand-to done and a good meal inside us, we made our way to the river, refilled water bottles and then completed the crossing to the western bank, where we found that there was a very useful, if not quite as broad, game trail which seemed to parallel the river in its meanderings. The grasslands and the bushes close to the river on the western side showed just as much sign of having been grazed and probably over-grazed, as those on the other side. That was to be expected really, as water became scarce all over the valley floor as the dry season developed, apart from locations such as the Chewore or the Mana Pools, where water at least could be found.

What was an operational patrol seemed more like a game-viewing safari as we made steady progress towards our designated uplift point. It reached the point where Const. Mapfumo, with a great smile on his face, volunteered the opinion that they had all come along to say goodbye to us because they knew we were about to leave them. There were murmurs of agreement to that from others. With nothing to stop our steady but careful progress, we made it to our designated RV in good time. There, as the temperature rapidly started to reach somewhere between 35 and 40 degrees Celcius, we were all quite content to seek some shade and wait for uplift, in the middle of our ninth day of that most interesting and memorable patrol. On the way back to Makuti, we stopped off at the Game Department's Offices at Marongora Gate. There, of course, I related our encounter with the elephant and our dropping down into the water of the gorge to avoid them. The senior Ranger there looked at me with a rather odd expression on his face, which made me ask if something was wrong. "Nothing wrong at all, really," he offered, "but didn't anyone warn you that there is a twenty-foot croc that lives in that gorge?"

When I returned to the two vehicles waiting for me and imparted that piece of information to the men in my section, there were some sharp intakes of breath, gasps and comments. The ever traditional but pragmatic Sgt Servester thought about it for a moment and then observed, "It was Mwari again, Ishe. He made us all lucky and you specially, because you were in front." I could hardly argue with that. After making a full verbal report to Supt Mallon, who, somewhat to my relief, did not require a full, written report, I headed to my tent, stripped off everything I had been wearing for the past ten days and headed to the ablutions block to get properly cleaned up. As I stepped clear of the tent, the ever-efficient Shorty, gathered up my discarded clothing, took one long sniff and commented, "Ah, Ishe, too much smell!" That about summed it up! Round our meal table that evening, in the company of Insp. Kensett and SO Van Wyk, Dermot and I compared what we each had encountered on our respective patrols. Dermot's patrol across the top of the escarpment had revealed that there was plenty of water at that level, that the bush was a lot lighter in density than on the valley floor and that his patrol had been physically taxing, with a great number of ridge crests to scale and then carefully descend from, during each of the seven days he had been out. My recounting of what I and my section had encountered, especially the matter of our journey through the Mari-ya-Tsoro gorge, with its resident 20ft croc, was cause of much comment. That night laying on the relative comfort of a Hounsfield camp bed and with a real pillow under my head, I drifted off to sleep fast. Helped perhaps by the fact that I did not have my boots on, rifle by my side or thoughts in my mind of a share of guard duty to do.

Water in the Rocks & Four Gold Bars

For the next four days, we were left in relative peace, with just routine camp activities to attend to and an hour or two of assisting with the manning and moving of the permanent roadblock on the main road. Coming off from roadblock duty on the fifth day, Insp. Kensett sought me out, with the interesting news that Rampart wanted me and my section to undertake a sweep through the valley from a point a dozen miles south of Chirundu to Pfumbe Hill on the Chewore River. It was to be a compass-bearing line of patrol with a total distance of about 65 miles, which he wanted covered in the next six days. The only good piece of news was that Rampart had accepted that water in that area was hard to find, so he had arranged for an African Game Ranger, one who knew the valley well, to accompany us, to help us in finding water.

Obedient to those latest orders, on Monday, 9th October 1967, after a decent breakfast, I and my section climbed into two Land Rovers and headed out of Makuti Camp once more, as fully equipped as we could be for another week in the Zambezi Valley. By borrowing a few water bottles from details who would be remaining in Makuti for the next while, I ensured that each of us had three full water bottles at our belts or in our packs, whichever way each individual preferred to carry them. Stopping off briefly at Game Department's HQ, as arranged, we picked up our guide, who cheerfully introduced himself simply as Chundu. In appearance, he reminded me more of a Kalahari Bushman than a typical member of the Shona tribe. It was impossible to tell how old he was, but from the fact that he had reached beyond the grey-beard stage, with his hair colour heading more towards white, he was certainly no youngster.

When I helped stow his Bergen-style pack on the roof of the Land Rover, I commented about the fact that he appeared not to have any firearm with him. At that he gestured to our vehicles and replied, in very passable English, "You are my firearms, Ishe!"

Some half-hour later our transport dropped us off a few miles beyond the bridge over the Nyakasanga River, 10 or 12 miles south of Chirundu Police Station. I had already set my compass to a marching line of 60 degrees, which by my calculations would steer us, in a few days, at least within visible distance of Pfumbe Hill, if not spot on at it. When Chundu took an interest in what I was trying to do, I explained the matter of the compass bearing to him and my trying to see if I could find a hillcrest on the Zambian Escarpment which I might use as an aiming point. He listened politely and then said, "No need, Ishe. There are many pathways that the Mudzimu, Dandawa and Chundu villagers used before we were moved out of the valley. I know them, they will take us to Pfumbe." He gestured at the thick wall of the mopane bush a few yards from the roadway. Not good," he commented, "Better we go back a short way to a pathway we can walk on."

That seemed eminently sensible to me. After all, he was our guide for this patrol, so it was only good common sense to accept his advice. There was no need to explain to the other section members because they had all been listening in on the exchange between Chundu and myself. As it turned out, Chundu's "short way" was nearer a couple of miles, but when he eventually pointed and said, "We go there Ishe," it was clear that our couple of miles of walking back along the main road had been worthwhile, because what he had gestured at was a gap in the mopane scrub some six to eight feet wide, which was a clearly well-trodden pathway and game trail.

With Chundu directly behind me and Sgt Servester bringing up the rear, I gave the order to load and make safe our rifles and then set off along the trail our guide had steered us to. At the half-hour mark I called a brief halt to let me drop back from Point, to be replaced by Const. Ben, with Chundu directly behind him. I asked Chundu if we would be able to find water when we stopped for our overnight camp. "It will be alright, Ishe," was his quiet assurance before we pushed on, carefully and warily just in case we encountered insurgents or any of the larger and more aggressive of the valley's many animal species.

Without rain or a cloud in the sky, the sun beat scorchingly down and rapidly raised the temperature as noon approached, so I called a halt and steered for a clump of trees which offered at least some shade. While we rested and consumed some of our water to replace what we had sweated out, I asked Chundu about how people had been able to live for many years in the valley and grow crops to live on with all the wild animals around, without losing their crops to those animals. Chundu's face lit up with a smile from chin to hairline as he explained they had maize as their main crop, but also grew millet, sorghum and rapoko. Because the soil in the valley was so very rich, they did not need to grow the large areas of crops which villagers outside of the valley had to grow. The smaller fields were guarded by deposits of lion droppings, which kept most of the valley antelopes away and fences woven from the acacia bushes, with their quite fearsome thorn spikes, which also helped to keep most animals out. To those fences they added sharpened wooden spikes and as the time neared to reap the crops, if they were worried, they lit carefully controlled fires at the corners of the fields. He explained that it was the task of the young boys and girls to keep the fires burning but controlled through the nights when they were needed. If a fire went out because its attendant had fallen asleep, a sound beating would result. He explained also that if there was ever any shortage of grown crops, the valley abounded with edible plants and there were all sorts of fruits too. On top of that, there were fish in the rivers and of course plenty of animals to hunt for meat, so that in those years of poor harvest nobody ever went hungry.

When I asked about the availability of water all year long, Chundu explained that there were places where water always existed in the bed of the several streams like the Nyakasanga, Rekometje, Cheruwe and Chewore, which was why most of the old villages were established close to those places. He also explained that there were certain places away from the rivers where water was, as he put it, hidden underground. He also assured us, as a unit, that we could drink as much water as we wished at this rest period, because we would meet the Nyakasanga River in another hour or so at a place where Gandarera village had once been. With that assurance, we all perhaps drank a little more of our precious water supplies than we might otherwise have done.

With the worst of the heat of the day gone, it was time to push on, along well-beaten pathways, now just game trails, as they wound their way through the thick mopane bush country which covered the valley floor in this area. Using the old pathways was something of a trade-off, because they wandered considerably, adding a fair few miles to the distance as measured in a straight line. At least the going was much easier than pushing and even hacking our way in a straight line along a compass bearing. When we left our transport, I explained to Chundu that one of our tasks was to check carefully any game trails which insurgents might use from the river to the southern escarpment and asked that he should point out to us any of those which he knew of. We were about an hour into our afternoon stretch when Chundu closed up behind me to quietly inform me that one such track was a little way ahead. With that warning provided, I moved up to lead the section a little more slowly forward with Chundu directly behind me, until we reached a small open area, at which point Chundu assured me that there was a crossing of the paths in the middle of it. On that assurance and not wanting the entire section out in the open all at once, I caused the rest of the section to fade into cover and moved forward with Chundu in order to check the pathway he had warned us of.

The pathway was there, as expected. Less expected, but there in plain sight, was the boot spoor which was clearly to be seen upon it. Among the variety of tread patterns there were some of the very easily identifiable "Figure of Eight" tread pattern commonly worn by insurgents. Not only was the spoor clear, heading for the distant southerly escarpment, but there was quite a lot of it and it was very fresh too, without any sign of animal spoor on top. My guess was that that we had come close to bumping into an insurgent group numbering about twenty, which number Chundu agreed with. As for how old that spoor was, our best estimate was maybe 30 or 60 minutes at most.

It was the work of a few moments to put my section into ambush positions looking out over the open area in case there was any other group following along behind the one whose spoor we had seen. Then I had to do some quick map and compass bearing work in order to get a rough, if not precise map reference for our present position. Then I got on to our VHF radio set and crossed my fingers that I was going to be able to make contact rapidly with one or other of our surrounding stations.

Just as luck had played its part in I and my section not coming into direct contact with the group of insurgents which had crossed our path, luck came into it again, as ZEF 908, Makuti, came in strength 5 at first call. Rampart, to give him his due, grasped the situation at once. Within fifteen minutes of my call Copper 19 was visible and in radio communication with us. I was quickly able to steer him to overfly our location which enabled him to get a precise map reference of our position. That allowed me to put him on a course in the direction the insurgent group were moving. Some three miles south of our position tracer fire was directed at the aircraft, which wisely gained height rapidly but kept circling. Shortly after that, Fire Force's helicopters appeared, heading for where the tracer rounds had gone up at the PRAW aircraft and a noisy contact ensued, the sounds of which we could easily hear.

It was about fifteen or twenty minutes after my warning words to my section to stay alert and aim low if any fleeing insurgents came our way that two armed insurgents appeared, running hard away from the contact area, where the helicopters of Fire Force were still circling. My admonition to my companions to aim low in the hope of taking wounded insurgents as prisoners worked reasonably well. At our gunfire both insurgents fell, dropping their weapons as they did so. My bellowed order of, "Cease fire!" brought a comparative silence apart from the screeching of numerous alarmed birds.

On the assumption that any of their fellow insurgents coming along behind them would have heard our gunfire and headed away from us, I tapped Const. Phineas on the shoulder and motioned for him to come with me to examine the two groaning insurgents while the rest of the section covered us. Both had been hit more than once. One had leg and shoulder wounds, while the other had gunshot wounds to both legs. Rapidly securing their weapons, which consisted of one SKS and one AK47, we then did what we could to stem the most obvious flows of blood before we returned to our ambush site, from where I was able to make radio contact with Copper 19 and explain to him our sprung ambush and the result of it. Once I had finished my conversation with Copper 19, Sgt Servester asked if it was possible for each of the section to have a souvenir of the contact. Something to take home to show family and friends and to act as a good luck charm for the future. The two wounded terrorists had not been carrying packs and even if they had been, the contents would have had to be left for Special Branch details to go through. That left just one thing which they both had with them in plenty. That was ammunition for their weapons. The problem was that if any of my section were later to be found in possession of a live 7.62mm round, it might prove awkward. After a moment's thought I checked the AK47 and found its magazine to be full. Warning my section of what I was about to do, I aimed the rifle at the base of a bush close by and loosed off a burst of a dozen or more rounds. As I cleared and made safe the rifle, I gestured to the ejected cartridges scattered close by. My instruction to Sgt Servester to gather up the doppies and share them out was swiftly obeyed. I noted that even Chundu gladly accepted the one offered to him and that Sgt Servester pocketed a couple more than just one.

About a half-hour later, an Alouette helicopter made radio contact with us and brought in a Special Branch detail, supported by four RLI troopers. To them we handed the recovered weapons, showed them the two wounded insurgents and then went on our way, leaving them to clear up the aftermath of our latest contact with the enemy. Before we moved on, I did not need to caution my companions about staying alert, but what I did do was congratulate them all over how well they had handled themselves in that brief engagement. However, I deliberately chose not to mention the fact that one of them had failed to heed my call for them to aim low. One thing was evident. Modest though it may have been, that successful contact clearly lifted the morale of us all. Countless hours of lectures and training and fieldwork exercises suddenly became worthwhile.

Just as Chundu had said, another hour of patrolling brought us to the Nyakasanga River, where we found ample water a couple of feet down in the sand and a decent location for an overnight camp not far from the river. Given the events of the day, I was at pains to ensure that, one by one, we each carefully cleaned our rifles. As a safety precaution, I posted double guards prior to allowing the section to settle into the routine of establishing a smokeless fire and cooking and eating an evening meal before darkness descended. Before daylight faded completely, I studied my map of the valley and did my best to work out, as accurately as I could, just how far we had walked since being dropped off and just where we were. Forgetting the couple of miles that we had walked along the main road, it looked as though we had covered something like eight miles along the generally eastward line towards Rupimbi Hill. It was not a great start, but, given that the unexpected ambush and aftermath had delayed us somewhat and that we had another five days of patrolling still left, with about 50 miles to do, it was not any great cause for concern. Remembering Chundu's words earlier in the day about Gandarera village having been near where we now were, I asked him about it. As a result, he promised to show me that location before we moved on in the morning.

With a double guard system and the almost stifling heat, there was not a lot of sleep for any of us, so it was a case of up and about early for everyone, after a thankfully normal Zambezi Valley night. Once our cooked breakfasts were eaten and our cooking fire safely and thoroughly doused, Chundu led us a very short distance towards what appeared to be just another thicket of mopane bushes. However, on closer examination of what Chundu indicated, it was clear that there were the remains of several pole, dagga and thatch huts, now almost obliterated by some ten years of the natural plant-life growth of the valley. As we all stood there, staring at what was left of probably many and perhaps hundreds of years of occupation, questions started to come in from my companions. I sensed that if Chundu started answering them then and there, we might have been there for quite a while, so I told him to hold the answers until our lunch or evening break and set my section off once again in a generally eastward direction, following pathways of greater and lesser width and usage as indicated by Chundu.

With Chundu's quite amazing knowledge of the trails, many of which, as he explained, had been used equally by villagers and animals in the times when the valley was populated, our progress, although wary, was steady. That allowed for longer than usual breaks and with his certainty of plenty of water at the Rekometje River, we were all able to keep well hydrated, which compensated somewhat for the blistering heat of an October month in a year when the annual rains seemed determined to arrive late.

That lateness of the rains probably accounted for the relative absence of antelope and larger game compared with our earlier patrols in the year. The Mana Pools area which lay some 15 or more miles to the north of our line of march was always a reliable source of water, which, as the rest of the valley away from the Zambezi River dried out, naturally attracted both antelope and their predators, leaving the rest of the valley less populated by animals, as we were finding. Despite that, there were sufficient rustlings and similar noises to keep us alert, as small game and large rodents became aware of our presence and chose to move away from us.

The dryness of the valley was brought home to us when we reached the Rekometje River, which, for the length of the stretch which we could see, was just a bed of dry sand. At my question of whether we needed to go up or down river or to dig in the sand for water, Chundu assured me that we would find surface water just a few hundred yards downstream where there were reliable rock pools. When those turned out to be dry, Chundu guided us back upstream to where the bed of the river was sand from bank to back. "There will be water here, but we must dig for it," he assured us. In that he proved right. With guards posted up and downstream on both banks, it took the remainder of us quite a while and a good deal of effort to use our mess-tins to dig down some four feet or more into the sand to where there eventually was a plentiful supply of good clean water.

In the quiet conversation of our overnight camp a short distance from the river, Chundu expressed his surprise and concern over how far down we had had to dig. He feared that the smaller rivers ahead of us, the Chiruwe and the Mbera would be totally dry. If that happened, we would, he declared, need to walk a little to the south to where there was a place where there was always water inside the rocks. He asked if I had any string with me. When I assured him there was a length of quarter-inch rope in the bottom of my pack, he nodded approvingly. "That is good, Ishe. It will save us having to make some." With that intriguing picture in my mind, I settled down for another hot, sweaty night of fitful sleep between my turns on guard duty.

Our routine pre-dawn stand-to passed uneventfully, after which I decided that it would be wise to use the relative cool of the early daylight hours to cover a few miles before we settled down to morning meal. My thinking was simple. If Chundu's worry over there probably being no water in either the Chiruwe or the Mbera River proved right, we would need some daylight time to reach the place where there was water in the rocks as he had put it. Thankfully that third day passed uneventfully. We reached the Chiruwe River nearly half-way through the afternoon, only to find that Chundu's worry had been justified. Where he had expected to find water, there was none. That raised the question as to what the water situation might be in the Mbera River, some several miles ahead. Our guide's concern was clearly written on his face, so I asked him what his thoughts were. There was no immediate concern, for all of us had better than one full water bottle available, but, even so, while Chundu thought through our problem, I issued the order that there was to be no drinking until we made night camp. After a moment or two Chundu said, quietly but firmly, "Better we go now to where I know we will find water. That way we will have plenty water for tonight and more for the morning." From me and from the members of the section who heard his words, there were nods of agreement.

Without more ado, we moved into patrol formation and set off, this time firmly south at ninety degrees to our target line of patrol. After some two hours of steady walking, with the mopane bush gradually thickening and with fewer pathways to use, Chundu led us to a cluster of huge granite boulders piled one atop the other to a hundred feet or more in height. Two of the biggest boulders at the bottom of the jumble were leaning against each other so that they created a cave, which our guide gestured towards. "There is good water there, Ishe, but there can be snakes and bees and scorpions too. It is better we go carefully. You must bring your string."

Setting Sgt Servester to organise the constables into a semi-circular defensive screen around the cave entrance, I set down my pack and delved into it until I was able to lift out the length of nylon rope I always carried, kept tidy by a couple of spare bootlaces wrapped around it. I tucked the bundle into my belt, cocked my FN, took off the safety catch and nodded to our guide that I was ready to follow him. On seeing I was ready, Chundu picked up a fist-sized rock and threw it into the cave. Apart from the clatter of it landing and rolling, there was no other noise resulting from his action. When that negative result was evident, he stepped warily, pace by pace and with his axe at the ready, out from the afternoon sunlight into the gloom of the cave, with me close behind.

The cave proved to be about 20 yards in length, about 12 feet across but only just sufficient in height for me to remain standing upright in. As my eyes became accustomed to the gloom, I noticed a few knee-high boulders scattered about, each of which Chundu carefully examined all around, before moving past. Finally, we arrived within a few feet of the vertical end wall of the cave. It was only when Chundu pointed that I realised that there was a gap of a couple of feet between the end of the granite floor of the cave and the vertical granite end wall. "That is where the water is, Ishe." He picked up a small stone, held it out over the gap, said "Listen!" and let it fall into the narrow void. After a second or two there was the distinctive noise of a stone hitting water, which made totally clear our guide's earlier somewhat puzzling references to water being in the rocks and needing string to get at it.

The one worry I did have was whether the thirty or forty feet of nylon rope which I had to hand was going to be long enough. I tied a fist-sized rock to the end of my nylon line and lowered it until it was clear that it had hit water. Measuring the length of rope needed against my outstretched arm-span of better than six feet indicated that the surface of the water was close to 24 feet down, fortunately several feet short of the full length of my nylon rope. How to bring the water up I solved by taking the cup from the bottom of one of my water bottles. By tying it through its handles to the nylon rope, using one of my spare bootlaces and jiggling the cup up and down when it hit the water's surface, I was able to detect when it had filled with water. Some cautious hauling up of the nylon rope produced a nearly full water bottle cup of what tasted as clear sweet water, which brought a sigh of relief from me. A couple of further up and downs proved that it needed three lifts to fill one of our water bottles, which suggested that getting everyone fully refilled with water was going to be a somewhat slow and lengthy process.

Returning to the rest of my section, I found that dusk was already falling. Given the fact that we were well away from any beaten track and that our morning meal-break had been several hours ago, I told everyone to drink their fill of the water they were carrying as there was now plenty available. The next thing was to direct the collection of sufficient dry wood to make a cooking fire inside the cave where it would not be seen and, after a meal, then to bed down in their semi-circular positions around the cave mouth. While the constables, bar one who was on guard, were at those tasks, I took Sgt Servester into the rapidly darkening cave and showed him the hole in the granite floor, below which the water was and explained how it could be raised for us to use, even if only slowly. Sgt Servester looked, listened and shook his head in wonderment, then said, "We shall have another story to tell our people when we get home, Ishe."

The larger than usual cooking fire inside the cave mouth served two purposes. It provided sufficient light to allow the slow process of lifting water to go on, while two or three of the section cooked their meal in turn about. Even with that larger fire and a rota system for bringing their water bottles up for refill each in turn, it was much later in the evening than usual before we were able to settle into our normal night routine of sleeping, interrupted by just one or two hours of guard duty before dawn. It was only when I was awoken for my hour on guard duty that I suddenly realised that I had forgotten to try to make radio contact at all with Chirundu or Makuti the previous day.

Next morning saw us up with first light. While others were soon busy cooking and eating, I tackled the matter of trying for radio contact with Chirundu or any other ZEF station which might hear me. Strangely, it was

ZEF 4, Darwendale, which responded promptly and came in loud and clear. That station passed my message of our location and my situation report as all okay on to Makuti. With that done I got on with preparing for the day ahead. Once each of us had finished eating and had drunk our fill of water, I supervised sufficient lifting of water activity to ensure that everyone's water bottles were full and to thoroughly douse the remains of our fire. Then it was time to move out and head north for several miles to get back onto our designated direct line of patrol from drop-off point to Rupimbe.

Day four of our patrol passed relatively routinely. As we had feared, the Mbera River was dry as a bone. Chundu expressed a worry that the Chitemwa River, some six or seven miles to the east, might be dry also. That would mean no likely refill of water until we reached the Sape River, another half-dozen miles or so beyond the Chitemwa. With water discipline established as a precaution, we pushed on, warily but steadily, stopping only briefly and drinking little. When we reached the Chitemwa, close to 14:00hrs, it too proved waterless. With a dozen or more miles of patrolling behind us already that day, under a cloudless blue sky and searing heat, my worry was that should we encounter any insurgents, the top-level combat efficiency needed to deal with a contact and firefight might not be there. That made me decide to call it a day and make early camp just east of the Chiruwe River.

Given the lack of water in the area, I asked Chundu how the locals managed when the valley was populated. What he explained, both to me and Sgt Servester made sense. There was no water even in good years between the Mbera and Chewore Rivers, from the Zambezi right back to the bottom of escarpment, where wells could be dug. There were also too many elephants, rhinos and buffaloes and too many lion, leopard, hyena and wild dog packs. For all of those reasons there never were any villages established in that wild and dry area.

I also explained to them both where I thought our present position was, about twelve to fifteen miles from the north end of the Mari-ya-Tsoro Gorge. That re-assured me that even if we found, in the morning, that the Sape River was as dry as the Chitemwa had been, we would not be without water for long. My thinking met with their approval and that of the rest of the section as my intentions were passed around. It also brought from Chundu the question of how I knew of the certainty of water in the Chewore and of the Mari-ya-Tsoro Gorge. I doubt he would have believed me when I told him of our patrol down the Chewore and of meeting elephant and dropping down into the water if Sgt Servester had not verified every word of the story I related. In return, Chundu explained that even in the days when there were villages in parts of the valley, there were crocodile living in the gorge, mainly at the northern end.

Before last light I was able to make radio contact with Chirundu and pass our location to that station for relay to Makuti. Once that was done, we settled into our normal night routine, much of which, between turns at guard duty, was spent laying on top of our sleeping bags rather than in them and just twisting and turning in the unforgiving overnight heat and humidity until exhaustion kicked in and sleep took over. That night there was no moon, so the stars were extra bright. Despite the absence of any moonlight, the busy nightlife of the valley buzzed, chittered, rattled and chirruped all around as each of the many nocturnal creatures went about its business, whether flying, climbing, walking or crawling according to its nature. In past nights in the valley, we had been investigated by porcupines, pangolins, hyena and even elephant. On this occasion, when I was sitting up during an hour on guard just after midnight, a small movement less than a dozen yards away drew my attention. With no moon to help me identify it at first, all that I could detect was that it was about the size of a hyena, but more streamlined in shape. Without fuss or noise, I brought my FN to bear on it as it came slowly a yard or so nearer, with its head raised, clearly testing the unfamiliar human scents it was picking up. Finally, I registered that I was looking at a honeybadger, which, despite its name, does not closely resemble any other badger species, but is more like a very large weasel. They are carnivorous, with few natural predators. Honeybadgers also have the reputation of being no danger to anything which they do not consider to be their natural prey, but they also have a reputation as being ferociously capable of defending themselves if attacked. That identification put me in a dilemma. If it got too close and ended up frightened by a sudden movement, its sharp claws and teeth could inflict considerable damage, but the last thing I wanted to do was to fire any warning shot in order to scare it away.

I decided that a quiet conversation was needed, which went along the lines of, "Good morning, Mr Honeybadger. How nice of you to visit us. We are not good eating for you and wish you no harm, so how about leaving us alone and going away to find something that you can eat?" My few words, although quietly spoken clearly reached the honeybadger, whose ears flickered. They also caused Chundu, some few feet from me, to sit up and ask, "Ishe?" as he clearly wondered why I appeared to be talking to myself in the middle of the night. I pointed in the direction of our unwanted visitor and replied, "I'm having a polite conversation with a honeybadger which seems inquisitive and intent on joining us. I don't wish to have to shoot it." Chundu's response was not quite what I expected. "Better we all slowly stand up, Ishe. We are something strange to it. It will be trying to decide whether we are something to attack and eat or to move away from." By now the rest of the section were all wide awake, so up we all stood, while my conversation with the honeybadger continued along the lines of, "There you are, my friend, we are much too big for you to eat, but we mean you no harm, so why don't you just leave us in peace, please and go off to hunt your usual prey?" Whether it was my words, or the sight of a dozen upright humans, or at least the several he could probably see, our unwanted visitor took itself off and vanished into the darkness of the night-time bush, leaving all of us to get back to our normal and, after that, uneventful night routine.

Next morning, we all cooked and ate a meal adequate to see us through the day if need be. That left all of us with little more than a cupful of water to drink as the day wore on. For once, my radio call was answered directly by Makuti, to which station I explained our location, situation and options for the day. A couple of hours of steady patrolling brought us, by mid-morning, to the Sape River. Despite some digging where Chundu indicated and repeating that activity a quarter mile up and down stream, we failed to find water.

We were at least twenty miles from the Chewore River at Rupimbe Hill, where water would most certainly be available as that was close to the Zambezi itself. It was too far to try to reach in the remainder of the day, so heading for water at less distance became an imperative. That meant certainly aiming for the Chewore at the north end of the Mari-ya-Tsoro Gorge, only some ten miles or so from our present position.

Five more hours of cautious but steady progress, with just one short stop, at which we all consumed the last of our available water and after a surprising number of sightings of giraffe, elephant, rhino, buffalo and a pride of lions, which latter item caused us to make a wary detour, we arrived at our intended position on the Chewore River. There, to the immense relief of all of us, there was ample water visible in the rock pools. Cautiously and in pairs, we slaked our immediate thirsts and refilled our water bottles. With that priority need dealt with, the second thing needed was some radio contact, to make our location known to the control room at Makuti and to let them know that we had twelve to fourteen miles in distance to cover next day to make our designated pick-up point. That made it likely that it would be after midday or maybe early afternoon before we arrived at the map reference provided, just west of Rupimbe Hill. To my relief, Chirundu came in loud and clear. With that station acting as relay for us once again, the necessary information was passed on and acknowledged by Makuti. Our transport would be in position by midday and would simply wait for us to appear. In the quiet of our chosen night camp, I commented to Chundu over my puzzlement at the amount of game we had seen during the day compared with the lack of it over the previous two days. Chundu's face took on the expression of a parent when asked an idiotic question by a child. Gesturing in the direction of the river, he said, "Ishe, they know the water is here for them. They can move more quickly than us to it and away from it. That is why this year, until the rains come, the animals will be close to the Chewore and to Mana Pools." With that blindingly obvious answer, which I had managed not to think of for myself ringing in my ears, I decided it was time to get my head down until my turn at guard duty came around.

After an uneventful night and a relatively brief dawn stand-to I urged the section's members to get a swift but ample meal into themselves as it was unlikely that we would be able to stop for any meal-break before we were uplifted and back at Makuti towards evening. So it was that we set off with full stomachs and full water bottles, to tackle the dozen or more miles to our RV point.

Under Chundu's guidance we followed a game trail on the west side of the Chewore River. The initial ease of progress was welcome but, what was not so welcome were time-consuming encounters with a herd of elephant and a rhino, both coming towards us on the game trail, within ten minutes of each other. The time it took for us to get safely away and out of sight of them in order to avoid the possibility of any need for more drastic defensive action made me decide that it might be better to get off of the well-trodden game trail and make progress through the mopane bush and occasional trees a little more distanced from the river. When I put that thought to Chundu he was agreeable, so we left the game trail and pushed steadily on through the virgin bush. There was little need for me to consult my compass, because, over the first four or five miles we had sufficient glimpses of the hill called Pfumbe which rises just west of the river, to keep us on track. Despite the area being mostly mopane bush country, there were areas of open grassland. Our standard procedure for safe crossing of such areas was to bring the entire section up just inside the bush-line, to provide cover for two or three of us to make the crossing to cover on the far side and then for the section to cross safely in twos or threes. Applying that pattern, towards late morning, gave us all a truly memorable experience. Sgt Servester, at point, had stopped just inside the bush-line before one open area and signalled for us to all close on him, which we did. Before we could consider making our crossing of the open area in our usual wary fashion, we were presented with the sight of a herd of impala fleeing frantically from a cheetah, which literally erupted out of the bush a hundred yards or so to our right and caught and killed a young doe. Silencing the awes, aahs and gasps from section members, I joined with them in silently watching the cheetah, clearly a female, start to drag her kill towards the spot from which she had erupted so unexpectedly.

"She has cubs somewhere over there, Ishe," Chundu voiced quietly. As if to prove him correct, when the cheetah was close to the bush-line, one half-grown cub appeared to meet her and then another. Rapidly, Cheetah, cubs and kill vanished into the bush. Chundu pointed leftwards to our line of march. "Better we move more that way so that we do not disturb them, Ishe," he advised. It was advice we were all very happy to take. Before Sgt Servester set off, I commented to him, "Another story to relate to your family, Sergeant?" His answer was a huge grin and several emphatic nods of his head.

The remainder of that morning and early afternoon passed uneventfully. Apart from two brief stops for a bit of rest, we pushed steadily on. If we were all beginning to feel a little weary after midday, we had two incentives to spur us on. The first was the sight of Rupimbe Hill, initially as a small rise on the horizon, which grew in size as we got nearer and nearer. The second was that at our last brief rest stop, we made radio contact with our waiting transport, which we were then able to rendezvous with as planned. Once again Insp. Kensett had set himself as one of our uplifting drivers, so I was able to brief him on what we had encountered over the past six most interesting days.

The only stop we made on the way back to Makuti was to drop off Chundu from where we had collected him, at Game Department HQ, after thanking him profusely for guiding and educating us over the past week. Back at Makuti as dusk was settling in, I took time to thank Sgt Servester and the constables for their efforts over the past six days before sending them off to get a decent meal and an uninterrupted night's sleep. When I put my head into the control caravan, I found that Rampart was not there to provide any immediate de-brief to. After a welcome shower, a total change of clothing and a decent meal placed in front of me by Shorty, I was only too ready to put myself down onto the welcome relative comfort of a Hounsfield camp bed, instead of the hard ground of the Zambezi valley and rapidly fall asleep, aided by the thought once again that nobody was going to wake me in the night to take a turn at guard duty.

Next morning, 15th October 1967, when I reported to provide a debrief to Supt Mallon, he decided that all that he required was a short written report for record purposes. His guidance on the nature of that report was, "Keep it brief and factual, please. I don't want a game-viewing diary. Just what's essential for operational purposes." To give him his due, when I handed in three foolscap sheets of my handwritten report at lunchtime, he carefully read through them, before commenting, "That's fine, Woolley. Just as well that you didn't bump head-on into that bunch whose tracks you reported. They could have given you some serious grief." As it was, it all turned out well and SB picked up some useful intelligence from one or two of the wounded Terrs and the contents of their packs.

Two days later, the first rains arrived. Initially a few towering thunderheads which flickered, flashed and rumbled for a while, before letting loose with one almighty crack, accompanied by a vivid lightning strike which hit a tree only a dozen yards outside the perimeter of our camp. That was the signal for a downpour which lasted some hours. Over the next few days, the hardest-working item of our equipment was our individual poncho cape. Makuti camp went, within a few hours, from bone dry underfoot to sodden.

After a brief lull, the pouring rain resumed and continued until next day. We had to erect a canvas covering over the cooking fire so that Shorty and the other batmen could produce hot food for us. Our shifts on the permanent roadblock were endured rather than enjoyed. The water steadily pouring from the flysheets of our tents soon created pools where the ground was flat and little streams where it sloped. The temperature did drop a degree or two, but the humidity steadily rose until almost any movement created sweat which stuck clothing to skin in a most uncomfortable way.

On Wednesday, the 25th October 1967, A Troop was rotated back to Tomlinson Depot and stood down for a welcome week of R&R, which we all reckoned that we had genuinely earned. I sent my batman off for the week, with strict orders to be back in seven days. After that, the most pressing item was once more to sit down to compile and then submit my Travel & Subsistence Claim form for the 17 shillings and 6 pence per day which was payable when out and about from normal allocated quarters. My number two priority, as ever, was to write a fairly long letter to my poor worrying mother back in the UK, who never really did get used to the fact that I could only reply at any real length to her letters when I was in Salisbury rather than when I was out and about on other duties.

On Thursday 2nd November 1967, A Troop paraded once more as a unit, at Tomlinson Depot, which promptly produced some clear evidence that right across the troop, our last stint at Makuti and into the valley, had made itself felt by way of wear and tear on uniforms and equipment. In strict rule and regulation terms, each item of uniform had a set lifetime of usage before any routine exchange for new could take place. Very fortunately, from our OC, Bert Fremantle, to C/Insp. West and the staff at our Ordnance Stores, there was a pragmatic recognition that uniforms designed to be worn to deal with occasional riots in urban areas were not intended to deal with the rigours of weeks of Zambezi Valley foot patrols. Even so, it took two whole days before each troop member, black and white, had individually handed in those items which had suffered damage to the extent whereby they needed to be replaced and drawn appropriate replacements.

That exercise had barely been completed, on November 5th, when Moebe was called in to see C/Insp. West, who advised him that A Troop would be taking another turn at Restriction Camp guard duties at Villa Salazar in two days' time. That was how it was that once again, early on the morning of 7th November 1967, A Troop flew out in a Dakota from New Sarum to Boli Airstrip and settled in for a stay of a month or more of guarding the four camps containing the political restrictees from Joshua Nkomo downwards.

That tour of duty at Vila Salazar proved to be a very routine and unexciting few weeks. Periodic heavy rain competed with scorching sun while the four sets of inmates of the camps behaved in their usual way, by trying to make our shifts on duty as uncomfortable as they could.

One event which I recorded on camera was that I painted an A Troop emblem on the mud wall of the large hut which, before the ZAPU restrictees were placed into the four camps and all unauthorised visitors to them were prohibited, had been Joshua Nkomo's meeting room. On it I recorded our stays at Vila Salazar throughout the year and the names of section leaders and troop commander. My photograph of us all by that badge, with Moebe wearing only a skin loincloth brings a smile to my face whenever I view it. Mention there of our troop commander, who was ever thoughtful for us all, reminds me that as he was aware of my date of attestation, he carefully arranged for me to be off duty for the 8th of December, on which date I completed three years of service. That meant that I was no longer a Junior Patrol Officer, but automatically, without examinations or such, moved up to the status of a Senior Patrol Officer. That change of status, formally and properly, required the carrying of a second gold bar on my shirt's epaulets and on my slip-ons. As it was, there was no way of sorting that out down at Vila Salazar, so I just carried on displaying the Junior Patrol Officer badges of rank. I celebrated my elevation by buying a round of beer for everyone at the Gona Stagga Inn that evening. As it turned out, that 8th December date was good for us all, in that we received information that we were to be rotated back to Salisbury a week later. When that was passed down to our sergeants and constables and to our batmen, there were smiles all round, for it meant the probability of having Christmas and the New Year in Salisbury. It also had us all wishing, hoping and praying for a spell of dry weather so that the landing strip at Boli would be usable on the appointed day. Fortunately, the weather was kind and by the middle of the afternoon of 15th December 1967, we were back at Tomlinson Depot, where we were stood down overnight, with orders to be back on parade for 09:00hrs next day. The following morning, before I could raise the matter, the ever-efficient C/Insp. West called me in to his office and handed me a requisition for my additional insignia bars and the necessary tailoring work and sent me off to present it at Ordnance Stores, along with the necessary shirts, tunics, jackets riot blue and slip-on tabs which I was not immediately wearing. By the end of that day, my uniforms and slip-on tabs were back with me, all properly sorted out to show my Senior Patrol Officer status, which I duly showed up wearing the following morning. However, that situation changed very rapidly, because at tea-break, C/Insp. West called me in to his office again to advise me that, somewhat to my pleasant surprise, I had been made up to the rank of Lance Section Officer in the Force Orders published that day. With something of a smile on his face he handed me another set of requisition forms and instructed me to get over to Ordnance Stores once more to get my uniforms adjusted to carry the three gold bars indicative of Section Officer rank.

The result of that little exercise was that the following day I duly appeared wearing the three gold bars of my new rank. Apart from the congratulations offered by my troop commander and other comrades, Bob Flynn took a long thoughtful stare at my shoulder tabs and then said, "You've gone up one bar each day since we got back. I bet you a pint you won't dare to come in tomorrow with four bars showing." Not being one to back off from a bit of a prank and a dare, I stuck my hand out and said, "You're on!" A handshake sealed the bet. With a little smiling connivance from my troop commander and a visit to Ordnance Stores, where, fortunately, the staff were only too willing to go along with the planned prank, the following morning I duly paraded with four gold bars at each shoulder tab. Bob duly acknowledged that he owed me a pint in the Fife Hostel bar in the evening and I just carried on in and out of the offices, lecture room and on the parade square until tea-break when I felt sure that C/Insp. West would probably have something to say about the oddity on my shoulders. Even though I felt sure he had noticed it, nothing was said until our afternoon tea-break, at the end of which C/Insp. West requested me to follow him to his office. Once seated behind his desk he gestured at my four bars and inquired, "Presumably a bet Mr Woolley?" At my nod and confirmatory "Yes, Sir," he simply said, "I hope you've won it, whatever it was, but be a good fellow and be sure to appear in proper regulation order tomorrow will you?"

My assurance that I would do so brought a polite dismissal and that was that. My free beer from Bob and the circulation of the story behind it was a five-minute amusement that evening in the Fife Hostel bar. As promised to C/Insp. West I appeared on parade the following morning wearing the correct insignia for my newly acquired LSO rank. However, that little escapade gave rise to a conversation with my troop commander, SO Moebe Van Wyk, in which he reminded me that having now served for a full three years, I would be eligible to sit for promotion when the annual examination dates for 1968 were set, which was usually late April or early May. He pointed out that while my Lance Rank carried the pay level of a confirmed Section Officer, to maintain it I would need to pass the annual examinations and the sooner the better. Moebe was of course quite right, because having entered the force at the top of the Patrol Officer pay scale, the only way of increasing my income was to gain additional rank. In any UK Police Force, an entrant who was happy to remain as a constable could do so for a full thirty years, with a pay rise each year through to retirement. That was not how the pay scales for the BSAP were structured. There the pay scales were designed to encourage, members to get on in rank in order to also get on in income earned. The Section Officers' exams were threefold. Common Law, Statute Law and Administration, which really meant Standing Orders. If one succeeded in gaining a pass-mark in each, then one attended a Promotion Interview before a Selection Board consisting of three officers. If you passed that scrutiny, then there was a two-week Promotion Training Course to get through, during which it was not uncommon for a number of members to be Returned to Unit, for one or other reason, at the decision of whoever was the Senior Officer in Charge. If any applicant made it through those various hurdles, eventually a promotion list appeared in Force Orders, pay scales changed and, quite likely, a transfer followed.

A Troop as a unit was fortunate in that we were able to remain in depot across Christmas 1967 and over the New Year into 1968, engaging in each of the assorted routines of depot activity, from training in and out of classrooms to covering the essential guard duties. What did happen was that the rainy season set in with more and more vigour as the weeks went on, which had us all discussing just how bad conditions might be back in the Zambezi Valley or down in the lowveld at Vila Salazar, whichever one came our way as our next tasking.

What also happened was that word filtered down to us of the start of Operation Cauldron going on in the Zambezi Valley. What first reached us was that there had been a major incursion between Mana Pools and the Chewore River and that elements of both RLI and RAR had been deployed to engage them and that there had been casualties on both sides.

During that period in depot, I did mention to C/Insp. West that I was thinking of taking Section Officer promotion exams in 1968 and asked him if there were any past examination papers which might be obtainable so that I could study the type of questions likely to crop up. I also asked him how I could guarantee that I would not be stuck somewhere on duty in the valley or lowveld when I needed to be sitting down to take the exams. On the matter of not being out in the wilds when the examination days arrived, he gave me an assurance that if needed I would be replaced by AN Other as he put it, so that I could take the exams. On the matter of previous question papers, he promised to see what he could do. A few days later he called me into his office and handed me a file of papers with the comments that I might find the papers useful and not to be worried if they were not from the immediate past couple of years as the habit seemed to be not to repeat recent questions but to reach back a few years and repeat those. He also made it clear that if any others in the unit decided that they too wished to sit the exams, I would be required to see that they too received copies, which seemed completely fair to me. I thanked him for his help and put the file aside to be looked at back at Fife Hostel. They turned out to be copies of all the examination subject papers for the years from 1963 to 1965.

In the second week of January 1968 A Troop was once more sent off to Makuti Camp for another tour of duty. We were aware of the ongoing Operation Cauldron as units of the RLI and RAR tracked down and killed or captured the ZIPRA and SAANC insurgents. Because of the ongoing activities associated with that operation and the fact that Makuti Camp had grown to form a combined Operations HQ, our duties were mainly limited to providing camp guards, supporting the floating checkpoint on the main road, at which all southbound traffic was routinely stopped, checked out and searched through the 24 hours of each day and carrying out some patrols of the valley floor, as directed by Rampart, based on intelligence supplied by Special Branch, or as we all regarded it, guesswork. Up at Makuti Camp level, it was possible to keep routines rolling, despite the rains. I also found time to put in a few hours of study towards the promotion exams later in the year. Down on the valley floor, it was another matter. The dirt roads were hardly passable and patrolling on foot was nigh on impossible, between inches of mud underfoot, soaking wet grass and bushes and trees and every stream and river inches or feet deep in water.

Our Capes, Poncho were our sole waterproof item. Trying to set up an overnight bivvy in a teeming downpour and stay dry at the same time, was an interesting exercise. That was because of the need for that useful piece of equipment to be converted into our personal overnight bivvy tent. Each morning that we encountered heavy rain when we needed to be up and about, we all had to try to stow everything by way of sleeping bags and blankets into our packs and webbing pouches while sitting in our individual bivvy. We each then had to undo the strings and pull up whatever pegs we had used to set up our bivvies and then literally stand up from inside the then shapeless bivvy, thrusting our heads through the aperture for our heads, where the hood was. That was the only way by which we could start the day in a reasonably dry state.

Whatever the reason, A Troop was relieved and returned to depot right on four weeks to the day, for which we were all grateful. However, a certain amount of that gratitude disappeared when we were notified that our time off was to be limited to a short 72 hours, after which we were to relocate to Bulawayo Police Camp, for a three-month tour of duty. There we were to come under the command of Propol Matabeleland. The one cheery note was that both European and African members of the Troop would be housed in standard accommodation within Bulawayo Camp itself and not under canvas for the entire tour of duty. Another piece of good news was that Patrol Officers and above could drive to Bulawayo in their own cars, so that we might have that useful item available when off duty during the three months posting.

Bulawayo & Matabeleland

The day after we arrived in Bulawayo Camp, we were all pleasantly surprised when Senior Assistant Commissioner Paddy Ward arrived to have a conversation with our troop commander and us stick leaders concerning what the Troop might be called upon to undertake during the next three months. His main briefing to us was that we should keep up a steady foot and mobile patrol presence in the African townships, which covered quite an area and be ready to respond to any calls that might arise for us to create a presence in the tribal areas north and south of Bulawayo, or to undertake patrols along the border with Botswana, running down to the Limpopo River and the border with South Africa. His briefing was pretty much what we had been expecting, but we all appreciated the fact that he had taken the time and trouble to make us welcome and to introduce himself to us. It was more than most senior officers ever did.

Bulawayo proved to be a most interesting posting. Apart from being a major railway centre, it also had Mpilo Hospital, the second largest in the country and for our off-duty days, the Matopos Hills, with Rhodes' Grave, were worth several visits.

As for the townships, there were several. The original one, which grew as the European heart of the city grew, was Makokoba. That was located a little distance from the main centre. In 1931, the Southern Rhodesian Government under Sir Godfrey Huggins, built the more formally laid out Luveve Township. Following on after the end of WWII, Mzilikazi Township was brought into being. As the growth of the city progressed in those post-war years, more townships appeared, Barbourfields, named after a mayor, Nguboyenja, named after one of Lobengula's sons and others. As the railways developed, townships such as Matshobuna, Sizinda and two which were for single men, Iminyola and Mabutweni were developed. The last two kept the authorities busy carrying out frequent raids to remove the wives, girlfriends and prostitutes who sneaked in alongside the menfolk, to benefit from their regular earnings working within the railway system.

Somewhat to our surprise and relief, we found that our patrol presence in the assorted townships was well tolerated. In many locations, it was welcomed. Whereas our encounters with the Zimbabwe African Peoples' activists held in the camps at Vila Salazar had been mostly unpleasant, that was not at all the case in the African townships of Bulawayo, apart from a natural resentment when it came to the removal of females from the supposedly bachelor townships, which rather reminded me of my experiences when operating in the Mashaba Mine compounds.

For me, there was also the added benefit of being based in decent quarters wherein I could spend my spare time studying for the looming promotion examinations. With a whole lot of understanding from my fellow stick leaders and from my troop commander, who all made sure that I had as much study time as possible, when it came to time to sit the exams, I at least felt that I had done all that I could to stand a fair chance of passing. I found no problem with the Common Law question paper or that for Statute Law. However, on completing the last exam, which was the Administration item, largely based on Force Standing Orders, I left the room feeling just a wee bit concerned about whether or not I had done enough to earn a pass mark. Walking away from the exam room I encountered OC Province. Being his usual thoughtful self, Mr Ward asked me how I had got on, to which I replied quite honestly that I was not certain I had done well enough to earn a pass-mark in that last exam. His response was an encouraging one. He tapped the officer's leather cane that he was carrying on my shoulder where the three gold bars of my Lance Rank were. "Cheer up, Mr Woolley," he said, "just remember that those are worth a few points to you anyway." It was a very welcome word of encouragement.

With the promotion exams behind me, one thing I did not wish to do was lurk around Bulawayo Camp wondering and worrying until the results of the exams were made known a couple of weeks hence. I asked Moebe if the next bush patrol could be allocated to me and my section. Two days later I and my full section headed out on foot from Plumtree Police Station at the start of a nominally fourteen-day long border patrol all the way down to Mphoengs and on to Beitbridge. That meant firstly following the Ramaquebane River to its junction with the Shashi River, then along that river until it met the Shashani River. Then following the Shashani, past Fort Tuli and on until that river fed into the Limpopo River about where it was joined by the

Umzingwane River and then continuing further along the Limpopo River to Beitbridge.

At first sight, it was a monumental distance of some 250 miles, which was just a little shorter than the drive by road, which is on record as 261 miles. However, rather than the wilderness of the Zambezi Valley, the entire stretch was through inhabited Tribal Trust Land. As the Special Branch details who briefed us advised, ours was to be a flag-flying and possibly intelligence-gathering patrol. Since the sizeable incursion of August 1967, east of Victoria Falls, there had been no further indication of any incursion into Matabeleland. However, we would still need to be on the look-out for any signs of terrorist presence, recruiting activities by local political activists and so on. In land altitude terms, we would be dropping from 900 metres above sea level at Plumtree to 600 metres at Beitbridge. The rainy season, which had not been heavy in the border areas had by now almost totally ended, so the temperature and humidity ranges would be far more comfortable than down in the Zambezi Valley.

With fourteen days of time nominally available, with more if needed and certainly eight hours a day available for walking, with a two-hour break across the hottest part of the day, I did not feel we were being asked to do too much. A brief bit of calculating set it out that if we kept to our eight full hours of patrolling each day, we would need to move steadily along at around 2.25 miles per hour, which at least seemed doable. For me, having acquired a Bergen rucksack along with my camouflage jacket and bush hat during my recent leave in the UK, starting off carrying 14 days of consumables was no problem in bulk terms, particularly as I had obtained a fair supply of dehydrated vegetables to keep the weight down. However, what did concern me was the matter of rations for my African companions. 44 webbing was never designed to carry the bulk of two weeks' rat-pack consumables which they would need. In the end, it was agreed that there would be an air-drop re-supply on day eight of the patrol. The news of that arrangement, imparted to my companions the day before we set off, was greeted with approval and clearly a degree of relief.

Matabeleland South is the least populated of the several regions in Zimbabwe. It has an area of 54,172 square kilometres (20,916 sq. mi), equal to 13.86% of the total area of Zimbabwe. However, it may have been on record as about one-seventh of the total area of Rhodesia, but it certainly did not contain one-seventh of the population. That became very clear as we progressed generally south and slightly east, following the course of the Ramaquabane River, which there formed the boundary between Rhodesia and Botswana. The villages were well scattered and there seemed to be ample farmland, a good deal of grazing land and good stretches of virgin forest.

It soon became clear to us all that while we seemed to be something of a novelty to the local tribespeople, they were perfectly polite and friendly as we moved among them. Typical of the Tribal Trust Lands everywhere, there was everyday work going on, with fields being worked, cattle being herded and water and firewood being collected. Much of that workload being undertaken by the womenfolk and youngsters.

We were able to make our scheduled morning and evening radio situation reports directly to Bulawayo without difficulty. We also managed radio contact with Plumtree, Gwanda and Beitbridge. Another small bonus was that in having a section at full strength and with little or no indication of terrorist activity, just one single guard on duty at a time was quite adequate, so none of us lacked sleep. We also benefitted from the fact that with the rainy season barely ended the Ramaquabane River, although a modest one in size, still had an ample number of pools scattered along its length, so water was plentiful.

Somewhat to my surprise, and probably because the pressure of human habitation was lighter here than other TTL areas I had patrolled in the past, we still encountered a broad assortment of game animals large and small. The tally on our second day out included a solitary rhino, a family of giraffe and an assortment of small antelope. As Sgt Servester commented during our conversation over evening meal on the second day out, "This is a good patrol, Ishe, we are among people who are welcoming us and that makes us all feel happy."

On our third day out, the Ramaquebane River ran into the Shashe and the waterway assumed that name. On the morning of our fourth day out, when we came across a cluster of village huts some few hundred yards back from the river, we stopped to pay our respects to the village headman. We explained that we were just passing through as it were and inquired if all was well with them. Although the headman declared that all was well, it was clear that both Sgt Servester, who was interpreting for me, and I read something different in his body language and facial expression, so Sgt Servester pressed him a little further and assured him that we were there to help if there was anything troubling the villagers. The headman hesitated for a moment or two, then poured out his tale of woe. He related that whereas the Shashe River near the kraal had been free of crocodile for several years, a big one had appeared with the peak of the recent rains and seemed intent upon staying. It had already taken a young child, one of his grandsons and they were afraid it would take others or even some of their precious cattle. If we could shoot and kill it, it would be a wonderful thing for their village.

Whatever I might have expected we would encounter during the patrol, a request to eliminate a child-eating crocodile was not one of them. However, it was clear that the presence of this predatory crocodile was a major worry for the villagers. It would have been wrong to ignore the clear plea for help that the kraalhead presented to us. At my invitation to show us the reptile if it was anywhere to be seen, the kraalhead, along with a few other villagers led us down to the bank of the Shashe, which was about 75-80 yards across at that point. With the sun shining steadily down from a cloudless sky, it was no surprise to any of us to find the crocodile was out of the water, just resting on the far bank, soaking up the sunshine, with its back toward us and its tail just a foot or two from the water. As best I could judge from where we were, it was certainly a large fellow, probably 16-18 feet in length.

It did not take me long to decide. In theory, we had no permit, licence or authority to eliminate the crocodile. However, since the border between Rhodesia and Botswana ran down the middle of the Shashe and not on one side or the other, the reptile was not, technically in Rhodesia, so shooting it would not be any offence committed on our territory. A quick question or two to our guides confirmed that there were no kraals in Botswana within a couple of miles of this location and that nobody on that side would hear any shots we might fire. Finally, at the distance involved, although I was classified as a marksman, there was no guarantee that I would get my bullet into a killing point. If I wounded it, or missed completely, the reptile would be into the water and out of sight very rapidly. With nearly a dozen rifles at my disposal, I turned to Sgt Servester and explained my thoughts to him that a dozen bullets into the brute would be better than just one and perhaps he and the constables might enjoy doing a bit of target practice on the reptile across the river. My proposal clearly met with his approval. "We can do it, Ishe," He declared with a broad grin. "It will make all of us very happy."

When we explained to the kraalhead and the villagers what we were about to do, the smiles on their faces were as big as my sergeant's had been.

In quick time everyone was briefed and set down into a comfortable firing position from which we were each able to get a good sighting on our target. After a double-check that everyone had their aperture sights set for 100 yards distance, my orders of "Load" and "Safety Catches Off" brought the appropriate rattles and clicks. I made sure that I had a good steady sight on the reptile before uttering a clear, steady "Ready, Aim, Fire," and squeezing the trigger of my FN as I uttered the last part.

The volley that cracked out upon my order was a very respectable one in terms of togetherness. Through the aperture sight of my FN rifle, I saw a few spurts of sand kick up alongside the crocodile. However, not everyone had missed the target which had clearly taken several hits because it reared up, tail lashing and then flopped down, commencing a slow but clear intention to get into the water. My orders of reload, ready, aim and fire again brought a second very satisfactory volley. Clearly there were again a few misses, but not many, because the impact of that second volley caused the crocodile's tail to give a few feeble twitches before the reptile became totally motionless.

As I knelt up and gave the orders to unload and make weapons safe, the kraalhead, literally jumping up and down on the spot, yelled, "Yafa, Ishe, Yafa!" (It's dead, Sir. It is dead!) He clapped his hands in approval of our action in clearly eliminating the threat from the now obviously dead reptile across the river. As my section members rose to their feet there was some light-hearted bantering between them as to who might have hit the mark and who might have missed. What was abundantly clear was that everyone was in high spirits at a job well done.

As something of a final postscript to our action in support of the villagers, as we moved on southwards and the village dropped out of sight, Const. Mapfumo called out and pointed skywards behind us, to where two vultures were circling. By nightfall most of the remains of that crocodile would have disappeared into the bellies of the assortment of scavengers, winged and hoofed, which nature provided to keep the land tidy.

That evening, the roll of four-by-two which passed from detail to detail for rifle-cleaning purposes was accompanied by my personal ramrod which unscrewed into 10" long sections, so that the dirtied rifle barrels were all cleaned up and shiny before darkness descended on a genuinely happy bunch of police officers.

Three days later, with something like 120 miles of steady, but mostly undemanding foot-slogging behind us, we made radio contact with Bulawayo for the purpose of setting up the necessary re-supply of rations for my African companions on the patrol. We chose a good broad patch of grassland better than a quarter of a mile across, provided a reasonably accurate map-reference for our position and waited for the aircraft to make radio contact with us. Pretty well on time, in mid-morning, a Rhodaf Dakota made contact. Just to provide an aiming mark for the Dakota crew, we had laid out four ponchos in the middle of the vlei and then retreated to the edges of the clearing to be well away from any of the packages that were about to be dropped. With a full section of ten men, each needing seven rat-packs, i.e., one per day for food for the remainder of our patrol, there were 70 packs to be delivered.

Where I had fondly thought the whole lot might have been packaged together, well-padded in order to survive a parachute drop from low level, I discovered that each rat-pack had been individually wrapped in straw to create something like an over-sized football and then encased in typical fishing net material to hold it all together. To give the Rhodaf boys their due, the pilot did get down low. He came in as slowly as he could, but it took three passes before all the necessary packages had been pushed out of the aircraft and had bounced and trundled their way all over the vlei.

As the Dakota gained height and vanished towards Bulawayo, I sent a VHF radio message thanking the crew for their efforts and then an HF radio message to Bulawayo to confirm that the re-supply had been completed. After that, I joined my companions, less two on guard duty, as we started to gather up and strip down the re-supply of rations to enable them to be squeezed into packs and pouches until they could be gradually consumed over the remainder of our patrol. Such was the pressure on space available that my rucksack, which had had seven days of foodstuffs taken out of it, ended up taking on board 10 of the 8oz tins of corned beef. The scattered straw and discarded cardboard I was not bothered about leaving there because nature would guarantee its eventual degradation, but the netting material was another matter. Leaving 70 chunks of clearly nylon-based netting scattered about was unthinkable, so that we carted with us until evening when we were able to safely dispose of it all in our several small cooking fires. Eventually, with our dropping zone safely cleared and somewhat late in the morning, we were able to resume our steady movement southwards, paralleling the course of the Shashe River. In an attempt to make up for some of our lost patrol time, I kept our steady movement going perhaps an hour or so longer than I might otherwise have done. Then I called a halt to progress and we settled into an all-round defended night camp, a few hundred yards distant from the river so that we might get just a little relief from the myriad of flying insects that swarmed close to the water.

I had one of the early shifts on guard duty that night. That hour passed quite quickly and without incident. I was soon settled down again and fast asleep, but not for very long. Just after midnight the guard on duty woke me. There was clearly something large making its unhurried, but certainly noisy way, not necessarily towards us, but at least fairly close by. It was a moonless night, but the stars were bright, which had caused us to keep our five small fires burning a little longer than just to cook our evening meal. A couple of them were still smouldering and I would have expected any wild animal to have detected the tang of smoke and stayed away from it. Not so our clearly heavyweight nocturnal companion, which, from the sounds we were hearing, was unhurriedly browsing its way towards us, fires or no fires. As I somewhat had expected, what eventually got close enough to be clearly identified in the starlight was a hippo. By now, every member of the section was awake, so I quietly instructed them to just stay still, but for Sgt Servester to stir up the fire nearest to him to get some flames going. My words caused the hippo to pause its browsing. Its head lifted and its ears did some rapid twitching, while it also did some clear scenting, looking and listening. At a distance of no more than ten paces, I started a conversation which went along the lines of, "Good evening, Mister Hippo, please mind where you are stepping, because you are a bit large and heavy, but if you really want to have a better look at us, I am sure that Sgt Sevester can put a few more sticks on one of our fires so there are some flames for you to see us by. I really don't want to hurt you, but my FN rifle is set on automatic, with the safety catch now off and it is pointing straight at you, so please don't be aggressive towards us. You go about your browsing and let us go about our sleeping and we shall all be good friends."

As I was talking to the hippo, Sgt Servester was already busy adding some small dry sticks to the fire nearest to him and puffing and blowing to get some flames going. As he did that, I continued my one-sided conversation with the hippo which appeared to be quite curious about us. To me, that curiosity was entirely understandable because while it would have been quite used to humans in the form of local villagers being out and about by daylight and visible to it as it spent the daylight hours in one of the pools in the nearby river, it had probably never encountered humans out and about at night in the middle of its usual browsing area. Fortunately, Sgt Servester's efforts with the fire quickly brought some flames into life, at which the hippo snorted a couple of times, then turned away and wandered unhurriedly off out of sight and hearing.

Taking a bit of a liberty, on the reasoning that we were not exactly in a known operational area, I issued instructions for those on guard duty for the rest of the night to keep the one fire burning and then for everyone else to get back to sleep. Fortunately, the rest of the night passed by without further incident.

The following day's patrolling was routine and uneventful. Our overnight camp was undisturbed. After a decent breakfast we set out on day 10, with the map telling me that before midday we should be approaching the convergence of the Shashe and Shashane Rivers. I noted from the contour pattern on my map that the Shashane flowed into the Shashe between two hills, one greater than the other, which was exactly what we encountered when we reached the junction of the two rivers. However, what the map failed to tell us to expect was that both hills clearly showed evidence of stone walling at various locations upon them. Since our arrival there was only just a little before the time when I would have called a noon-time break, I called a halt to our progress and organised a temporary camp to allow everyone to make tea if they wished and have a bite to eat if they felt like it, while I took myself off to scout around some of the walled areas of both hills.

What I found were clear indications of walling similar to the Zimbabwe style of walling I had become familiar with and also signs of huts. I bothered to collect a few of the shards of broken pot, concentrating on those with rims and/or decorations on them, with thoughts of taking them to the Bulawayo Museum when our patrol work was over. Little did I know then just what collecting those few pieces of pottery would lead to and how much they would change my life.

When I got back to re-join my section, I showed them the bits and pieces I had collected. That promptly brought about a request from several of them to also be allowed to go to gather a few bits and pieces to take back to show their relatives in Harare and in their home villages. The request seemed fair to me, so we re-located to a better position for an overnight camp, after which I allowed time for each member of the section to take a look at the walling and signs of huts on the hills. That resulted in Const. Phineas bringing back a few pieces of pottery which were far better specimens than I had gathered. I was very grateful that he presented a couple of them to me, to add to my collection.

That evening, there was much discussion about who had occupied the two hills and when, although there was general agreement that they must have been related to, or part of the people who had built Great Zimbabwe many hundreds of years ago.

The next two days were again uneventful as far as the patrolling went, but when I made radio contact for our afternoon situation report on the second day, there was a message for my personal attention, which was to advise me that I had been successful in passing all the written promotion exams for Section Officer and would be going on the promotion course in a few weeks' time. While that news really did make my day, what made it even more gratifying was the fact that the members of my section were all clearly as pleased as I was and full of congratulations.

Two days later, we completed our lengthy foot-patrol, were uplifted as arranged and returned to Bulawayo. There, after a detailed debrief, during which I did not mention the small matter of shooting a crocodile, I and my section were given a couple of days off. That provided me with some time to visit the Bulawayo Museum in order to have a conversation with Graham Guy, the curator. To him I related what I had come across at the Shashe/Shashane river junction and handed over to him the collection of pot shards I had gathered there. Graham Guy listened to my story, looked at the assorted bits of broken pottery and promptly declared, "You have clearly visited Mapila and Little Mapila. Those are the names of those two hills." He went on to explain that they were an offshoot of the Mapungubwe culture, whose people first occupied and then expanded from a hill of that name, a few miles south of the Limpopo River in what is now South Africa. He kindly invited me to return the following day when he would allow me to read the book on the Mapungubwe culture which had been compiled after excavations from 1923. It was an invitation I was only too pleased to accept.

What I learned the following day, in conversation with Graham Guy and via my perusal of the Mapungubwe book, a collection of the archaeological reports and photographs of the many sessions of digging over the years on the Mapungubwe Hill, was certainly an eye-opener for me. Until then I had firmly believed, like many others, that Great Zimbabwe was the centre of a culture generally thought to date from 1,000 AD through to 1,500 AD which spread out from that location to cover most of Rhodesia. I had read the book *The Arab Builders of Zimbabwe* and was aware of the contending theory which pointed to a culture called Leopard's Rock, named after a location in Northern Rhodesia, which dated to about 800 AD, which some believed had developed into the Zimbabwe culture. However, until my encounter with Mapila and Little Mapila and my conversations with Graham Guy, I was totally unaware of the existence of the Kingdom of Mapungubwe, or Maphungubwe which dated from about 1,075 through to 1,220 AD and which, some scholars believed was the predecessor of the Zimbabwe culture centred upon Great Zimbabwe near Fort Victoria.

From my hours at the Bulawayo Museum, I learned that the name Mapungubwe is derived from either the TjiKalanga or Tshivenda languages. The name might mean "Hill of Jackals". According to what I read the kingdom was the first stage in a development that would culminate in the creation of the Kingdom of Zimbabwe in the 13th century. There was, from the excavations carried out, clear linkage between Mapungubwe and a recorded trade centre called Rhapta, on the south-east coast of Africa. The records indicated a strong likelihood of there also having been trade connections with the Sultanate of Kilwa Kisiwani. That latter kingdom was centred on a small island just off the coast of present-day Tanzania. It was occupied between the 9th and 19th centuries AD, controlled by the Omani Sultans and much used by Persian merchants seeking mainly gold and ivory. One of the strangest pictures in my mind as I read through the Mapungubwe records, was the apparent peaceful co-existence and co-operation between the Kalanga, Nambya and the BaVenda peoples, who all appeared to be closely involved within the Mapungubwe Culture.

Having discovered my interest in archaeology and prehistory, Graham Guy drew my attention to the Ranch House College in Salisbury, which he described as a multi-cultural education centre, which held an annual two-week course in archaeology, with one week of lectures and one week of practical work on a site of interest. Graham Guy advised me that the annual courses were usually over-subscribed and urged me to make an inquiry about the September course without delay, which is exactly what I did. Fortunately, I discovered there were a few places left on the Ranch House archaeological course for that year, so I booked to attend it.

Aside from our routine patrolling of the townships and some of the district areas in Matabeleland, one other most interesting issue arose when one or two items of our troop weaponry required attention. As the provincial headquarters, Bulawayo possessed a substantial armoury, sited in Bulawayo Camp. The armourer, Peter South, kindly showed us one of his favourite items in the armoury, which was one of the two Maxim machine guns which had seen action at the Battle of Bembezi, fought on 1st November 1893. It came about when the Matabele people, under their king, Lobengula, rebelled against the growing presence of the Europeans in the country who had put a stop to the annual raids by the Ndebele into the Shona/Kalanga areas of Mashonaland. In 1893, the Ndebele, without warning, launched a series of murderous attacks on Europeans around Bulawayo. A relief column of a score of waggons and 700 men was despatched from Salisbury to relieve the Ndebele siege of Bulawayo. Nearing Bulawayo, at a place called Bembezi, the column made an overnight stop and moved into a protective circle. A small party of troopers went for water supplies to a stream a half-mile from the waggons. That water party was ambushed by some Ndebele Impis intent on wiping out the relief column. All but one of the water party were caught by the Ndebele and killed. The sole survivor was Trooper White, who, being a noted athlete, was able to outrun the ambushers and make it safely back to the laager. In later years that area became known as "White's Run Farm". Initiating the ambush on the water party was the signal for an all-out attack by the Ndebele warriors, whose massed impis totalled some 5,000 men, including King Lobengula who had gone along himself to oversee the wiping out of the relief column.

What the Ndebele warriors, with their traditional shields, spears and knobkerries were unaware of was that the relief column's troopers not only had their usual Martini-Henry rifles and some side-arms for defence, but also two Maxim machine guns available. As the impis moved into their standard "buffalo horn" formation with the intention of surrounding and overwhelming the circle of waggons and its defenders, the two machine guns, spewing out bullets at close to 1,200 rounds per minute, literally decimated their ranks. With at least one quarter of their number dead and dying, King Lobengula called off the attack and left the battlefield. That battle, at which the Ndebele Impis, brave as they were, suffered casualties of a nature they had never before encountered, presaged the end of the first Matabele Rebellion.

With Pete South's story of the battle and after sitting on the firing position of his favourite gun, there was only one thing to do, which was to visit the location of the battle. That I was able to do a few days later, to read the wording of the memorial which had been erected some years after the event and to try to understand and to an extent empathise with the feelings of those tribal warriors who had been willing to fight and die in defence of their traditional way of life, some three-quarters of a century before.

Once I and my section were back on duty after our lengthy border patrol, we returned to a few more days of routine township patrols and the ongoing drill and lectures which were intended to keep us all up to date with changes in laws and procedures. Those lectures included both theory and practice in matters of first aid, to equip us to offer at least some practical assistance for injuries likely to arise from beer hall brawls or traffic accidents and even contacts with insurgents.

After a week or so of purely routine activities there was a call from Provincial HQ for one section to undertake what was described as a routine patrol from the main road between Bulawayo to the Victoria Falls, just south of Wankie, now Hwange, in a direct westerly line to the Botswana border. Despite the patrol being called a routine one, Special Branch required it to commence the following day. Moebe decided that the only fair way to deal with it was for us three section leaders to draw straws. Somehow, I managed to draw the short straw, so by mid-morning the next day, I and my section were dropped off at the side of the main road some ten miles south of Wankie Police Station, which was home to Joint Operations Command (JOC) North-West's control room. That put us about half-way along the main road from Bulawayo to Victoria Falls, a total distance of about 275 miles.

After a definite rush-around the previous afternoon, I and my section were all rationed and ready to spend the next seven days covering a distance of some 70 miles, much of it through the Wankie National Park. For radio communications we carried both an HF and a VHF radio set, with orders to report in, morning, noon and evening and in particular to promptly report anything interesting or unusual which we might come across.

The Special Branch detail who met us at the roadside was also at pains to make sure that our ability to communicate was sound. He insisted that we test both HF and VHF sets before starting our patrol. Once we had successfully done that, he urged us to carry out the patrol carefully and thoroughly, so that we missed nothing of interest as he put it. I was able to assure him that with only about 10 miles a day to cover, ours would be a thorough look-see, but my question as to whether there was anything specific which we should be on the look-out for, brought only, "No, but go carefully and just keep your eyes wide open, that's all." The only useful comment that he made was to warn us that the rainy season had been a poor one all over Matabeleland and particularly so in the northern part of the province. Water was scarce all over the area, which could be a problem. Fortunately, A Troop had been in Bulawayo long enough to have learned that fact, so I had ensured all members of the section were once again carrying three full water bottles, just as we had done on certain patrols in the Zambezi Valley. At the bottom of my rucksack there was, as usual, also a large tin of Mazoe Valley Crushed Grapefruit, there just in case of any urgent need for its liquid content rather than the fruit itself.

As I led my section away from the main road, on a compass bearing due west, I wondered how the area would compare for game with the Zambezi Valley. I was aware the area had been declared a Game Reserve as far back as 1928 and subsequently declared a National Park in 1961. In area it covered about 5,600 square miles. Much of the western boundary abutted the border with Botswana, edging onto the Kalahari Desert. Although the insurgency had diminished the flow of tourist safaris all intent on game-viewing, such activities were still occurring, based upon the main camps scattered throughout the park. According to the 1:50,000 Ordnance Map of the area, which I was carrying with me, none of those lay directly on our intended line of patrol. Our line of march was to be across the lower third of the national park, traversing the north of the Dzivanini Wilderness Area and the centre of the Shakwanki Wilderness Area.

Whatever we might come across, it was a clear hope that we would probably be seeing just as much and maybe more in the way of wild animals and birds than we had seen in our recent Zambezi Valley patrols. Some newspaper reports of the time had carried articles on the apparent over-population of elephant in the Wankie National Park and the need for a carefully managed culling exercise. Whatever lay ahead as we set off, the one pleasant difference between the Zambezi Valley and our present task in Matabeleland was that as it was now in the dry, cool season, the temperature was way down and very comfortable for some long-distance walking at an unhurried pace. Having said that, I had barely covered a few hundred yards before I found it necessary to draw my panga from its scabbard at my belt and start hacking a path through the dense and head-high grass which barred our way. Fortunately, after a quarter of a mile or so, that dense grass gave way to more open grassland which allowed me to put my panga back into its scabbard. As I moved into the shorter grass, my presence clearly disturbed a bird the size of a turkey, which ran away instead of flying. It was jet black in colour with a decidedly red wattle and long, curved beak. Days later I was able to identify it as a southern ground hornbill, one of the rarer birds of the area. Over the next hour or so we only found three modest game trails, all running north-south. We took time to patrol up and down each for a couple of hundred yards. All three bore plenty of spoor of assorted antelope and one displayed some fairly fresh spoor of a big cat, probably a cheetah as it was a solitary track.

With no great worry over distance to cover and time to do it in, I called a lunchbreak for an hour, to rest up a while and make radio contact with Wankie Police Station, rather than for cooking and eating purposes as every one of us had started the day with a good morning meal which would see us through until we made our first overnight camp. We tested both our HF and VHF radios, with good contact being achieved via both. The main topic of conversation was a question of where all the game was hiding? We had certainly seen little or nothing of anything yet, whereas in the Zambezi Valley we had got used to seeing, except towards the end of the dry season, antelope and other wild creatures almost every few yards. The general thinking was that the dry conditions and lack of ground water had created a movement towards the north, where the several natural pans were kept from drying up by having water pumped into them from boreholes which also provided the water for the chalets and viewing cabins built to encourage tourists.

As we pushed steadily and warily onward after our rest, we began to encounter a little more by way of small and large antelope and had a distant view of a pack of wild dogs. Their very presence suggested there was probably more in the way of antelope to be found in the area than we were seeing. In the afternoon we found another half-dozen game trails criss-crossing our line of patrol and dealt with each in our set manner, without finding anything other than the spoor, both new and old, of a broad assortment of wild animals, including elephant.

Late in the afternoon we came across a modest stand of teak trees which I decided would make a decent place for our first night stop, particularly as I thought that we had probably covered our ten miles for the day. What concerned me though was that we had seen nothing by way of any stream or pan at which we could refill our water-bottles. Fortunately, with the cooler weather none of us had drunk much during the past several hours. My cautionary words to my section not to use too much water was met with nods of approval and agreement. Without any visible mountains or other high ground to do back-bearings from, it was difficult to pin-point our exact position. In accordance with our orders to maintain regular radio contact and provide plenty of feed-back, I did some dead-reckoning and worked out a probable map reference for our overnight camp, before getting onto our HF radio and making contact with Wankie Police Station.

After an uneventful night, a pre-dawn stand-to and an early radio conversation with Wankie Police Station, we made and ate our individual breakfasts at an unhurried pace, before setting off due west once again. After about an hour Const. Mutandwa who was at point, stopped the patrol and pointed to where several vultures were circling about a half-mile away and somewhat north of our intended line of patrol. Quite obviously, we needed to find out what, on the ground, was the cause of the vultures taking an interest.

Approaching very warily, through the grass and scrubby trees, we reached a point where we were looking out onto a more open area, which was only a hundred yards or so across, which had a large anthill just about in the middle. It was directly over that anthill that the vultures were circling, although, from where we were, we could see no reason why. As we watched, one of the vultures descended to ground level on the far side of the anthill and out of line of sight to us. Something snarled or growled, somewhat feebly. There was a screech from the vulture which took to the air once more and resumed circling along with its fellows. As quietly and as warily as we could go, I led my section around the edge of the open area, staying as much under cover as we could, until we were able to see what was attracting the attention of the vultures. What we were eventually able to see was a natural, but still pitiful sight. It was an adult male spotted hyena, backed into a defensive position between two wings of the anthill. The poor brute looked as though it had lost out in a fight with one or other of the big cats of the area. It had lost one eye and its left hind leg was clearly broken. Its left flank was torn and bloodied. As we watched from our viewpoint, another of the circling vultures decided to try to have a go at the clearly injured and probably dying hyena, only be rebuffed by a snarl and gaping jaws.

Watching the scene before us, I was torn between two disciplines. The one being never to interfere when nature was taking its habitual course. The other, my training as a tracker under Game Rangers, who had instilled in me their policy of never leaving a wounded animal to suffer. Track it, find it and finish it! As if he could read my thoughts, Sgt Servester whispered, "It is suffering, Ishe!" Those few words helped me. With a steady rest on the branch of a growing tree, I put a bullet from my FN through the dying hyena's skull and put it out of its misery. As we moved on to resume our line of patrol, the vultures were already descending.

By the end of that second day, we had checked out so many criss-crossing game-trails that we were probably behind in the distance we should have travelled. What we had found upon each was plenty of animal spoor, but nothing to indicate human usage. We had also not come across any potential or actual source of water. After we had made our individual evening meals, I checked with each member of the patrol to find out what water supplies they still had available. No one had much more that would be needed to make a decent breakfast, washed down with a mug of tea. That section conversation brought an agreement that with a decent meal to start the following day we would be alright until noontime. If we had not found water by then it would be necessary to call for an overfly to steer us towards the nearest pan or other source of water. My evening sitrep to Wankie carried that message.

About an hour after resuming our line of patrol the next morning, we came across the course of a modest stream. Nominally, at first sight it was dry, but a bit of digging with my panga suggested there was water below. Just how far and how much there might be, were unknowns. I set a four-man screen of guards around us, while the rest of us prepared to dig. With my panga acting as a rudimentary spade and some energetic use of a mess-tin, we set to in our attempt to find the answers to those two questions. With our crude tools and a somewhat sandy stream bed, it was not possible to just dig a narrow hole, because the walls kept collapsing. After an hour of energetic activity, we ended up with a gradually narrowing pit about four feet across at the top and three feet deep in the centre. At that point I was able to scoop up a palm-full of clear, drinkable water. A little more digging allowed me to put the smaller portion of my mess-tin into the bottom of our makeshift well and watch it slowly fill with water. With the slow seepage, rather than any flow from of our newly won water supply, it was midday before thirty water bottles were all refilled and we had each slaked our own personal thirsts. That fortuitous re-supply of water I duly commented upon when I made our required radio-call on our VHF set to Wankie Police Station.

The remainder of that third day passed as a carbon-copy of our second. Game animals were around, but not in the numbers we had become used to in our Zambezi Valley patrols and there was nothing on any of the several trails which we checked, apart from old and new animal spoor. My evening sitrep to Wankie relayed just that, along with the observation that due to our essential digging for water, we had covered not a great deal of mileage as the crow flies.

After another uneventful night and a routine sitrep to Wankie Police Station, we set off a little early the next morning, with the intention of covering more mileage than we had done the previous day. The first few game trails we inspected turned up just what all the others had in previous days, which was nothing of interest, but then we came across an oddity. Sgt Servester was at that time our Dermotman. He made a silent signal for the patrol to halt and then tapped a hand on his shoulder, the usual quiet request for me to join him, which I did. What he and I were looking at was what appeared to be a newly created game trail through the grassland we were traversing. It was flattened grass, some four or five feet wide, running in a straight line, north-south, at ninety degrees to our line of patrol. The knee-high grass we were patrolling through appeared to have been trampled down by something, but there was no grassless surface from which we could, at that point pick up a sign of what had created the trampling.

A careful look at a few ends of trampled and broken grass showed that they were dry, suggesting the trampling was not very recent. It was obvious that we needed, if possible, to ascertain what had caused this odd pathway, so we turned due south and began carefully to follow the trail of trampled grass. As luck would have it, we did not have far to go before we came across what was certainly an overnight camp for literally scores of people. There had obviously been a clear perimeter and several areas where fires had been set. Around the fireplaces where the grass had been scraped away to prevent the cooking fires from spreading, there was clear spoor of human footwear, some of it the figure-of-eight pattern we had often seen in our Zambezi Valley patrols. Having prowled around the extensive camp with me, Sgt Servester summed it up by shaking his head and saying, "Too many Gandanga, Ishe!" With that observation I could only agree. In our skirting around the overnight camp, we had picked up where the occupants had headed southwards. We also noted there were some bird and small game tracks over the boot spoor which was of interest to us. That suggested the camp had been empty for a couple of days at least.

Clearly what we had located required to be reported to Wankie Police Station, so I got on to our VHF set in order to do just that. What happened next was utterly bizarre. I had not quite finished delivering my report to Wankie over the airwaves when Fire-Force, headed by a K-car, came flying in from over the horizon, heading on a flight path a few miles north of us. As I broke off my transmission to Wankie, that station came back with a directive for me to link in by radio with Fire-Force and guide them to our location, which I promptly did. With Fire-Force on the ground and its troopers roaming all around us, looking at what we had found, I asked their commander how the heck they had appeared so fast. His laconic reply of, "We've been shadowing you and your section, day by day, ever since you set off, just in case you got yourselves into any trouble you couldn't handle!" left me momentarily speechless.

I pointed out to him the boot spoor which had convinced me this was an insurgents' overnight camp and showed him their clear trail heading to the south. At that he made radio contact with Wankie Police Station and requested that the Joint Operational Command (North-East) Officer (JOC for short) should speak with him as there was clearly a need for some skilled trackers to take a look at what we had found, in order to sort out how fresh or old the overnight camp site was and get a better idea of how many it had held.

That conversation resulted in the arrival about a half-hour later of a helicopter carrying two European and one African Game Department Rangers. Those three spent a good half hour or more looking around and following the track south for a few hundred yards before reporting back to the Fire-Force Commander that the camp had held around 90 people and that it was two days, or maybe three days old.

All that information was duly passed on by radio to JOC at Wankie. The report brought back a, "Roger. Stand-by!" That period of standing by lasted only a few minutes before orders came for Fire-Force and the Game Department staff to return to Wankie and for I and my ten men to continue our patrol to the Botswana border. It took but a few minutes for all six helicopters which were on the ground close by to embark their human cargo and lift off, heading back east, towards Wankie. However, before he left, the Fire-Force commander took a moment to tell me and my ten men that we had done a good job in finding the insurgents' camp. When I asked him if they would be shadowing us for the rest of our patrol, he shook his head and said, "No. You're on your own from here on, but we don't think you're likely to find another crossing of that size and you guys are quite capable of dealing with any strays or stragglers you may bump into." We shook hands and that was that. It was only then that I looked at my wristwatch and discovered it was already early afternoon.

When we settled into our overnight camp that evening, after another uneventful few hours of progress westwards, the general topic of conversation was how lucky we were that the terrorists' camp had been old and empty, because if it had been occupied by nearly a hundred terrorists, we would not have stood a chance, even with Fire-Force close by. I pointed out that the only reason I had felt it safe to follow the odd trail of trodden down grass that Sgt Servester had noted was the total dryness of the ends of the broken grass, which told me the trail was not very fresh. Had it appeared fresh I would have been on the radio to Wankie very fast indeed. What I did promise my companions was that when we got back to Bulawayo I would try to find out why we had been sent out on patrol as we had been when it was clear that JOC knew more than they had bothered to tell us via our roadside briefing.

Several days later, I was able to do just that. The story was that there had been some unconfirmed reports of a major incursion of 92 terrorists, some ZAPU and some SAANC (South African African National Congress) north of Victoria Falls. The actual date of the crossing was uncertain, but, according to the information, it was "recently." Thoughts of searching for the insurgents by air were discarded because it was reckoned they would simply scatter into tiny groups which would be difficult to deal with. However, a contact with a small patrol of our forces would keep them all together for long enough to permit the shadowing Fire-Force enough time to engage them as one large target. When I was eventually able to relate that story to my section, there was much shaking of heads in sheer disbelief. Const. Phineas was the first to comment and he was dead right, "They could have got us all killed, Ishe!" The final piece of information I was able to pick up was that the trail we had seen leading south from the overnight camp was followed by an entire RLI platoon and Game Department trackers, without making any contact because the entire group of insurgents crossed over the border into Botswana before contact could be made.

The morning after our discovery of the insurgents' deserted camp we set off west once more. In the first half of the morning, we began to encounter much more in the way of game, large and small, than we had been seeing over the previous four days. We had sight of a large herd of elephant, a decent number of impala, a magnificent eland bull and a pack of wild dogs. The general view among all of us was that there must be a water supply somewhere in the area, perhaps a small pan. When we came across a well-used game trail, with a great deal of animal spoor on it, most going one way, I decided to follow it for a while to see if it might lead us to water, which it did, an hour or more later. It was a small stream with shallow, gently sloping banks and stands of trees, mostly mopani, along its length. Strewn along its course it had surface water visible in pools. It was clearly the reason why we had seen more game that morning. With our water supplies somewhat deplete since our last refill, we were all grateful to top up our water bottles, although I had to issue an order that there was to be no drinking of the water until it had been boiled for tea or become part of the cooking for a meal.

That was because of the ample sign that the local wildlife was not too careful about where it deposited its droppings and likely its urine too.

By my admittedly crude dead reckoning we were at that point a little more than twenty miles from the end of our patrol, so I decided to have an hour's break before we pushed on. With one detail on guard duty the rest of us settled down in the shade of the trees amid some inevitably thick bush. After about ten minutes, Const. Malembo, who was nearest to me, uttered a fairly muted "Ishe" and pointed upward to a branch of a tree a dozen or more yards away. There almost invisible in the dappled shadows, was a civet cat. It was laying along the branch, with front and back legs just hanging down on either side of the branch, obviously very comfortable and relaxed. It was clearly awake and watching us, but seemingly totally unworried by us, so much so that when we started to rise to resume our patrol, it just watched us go without any attempt to shift from where it was.

The next forty-eight hours of our patrol were uneventful. We checked an assortment of game trails without finding anything interesting, apart from some dung beetles working busily away on some elephant droppings. Our regular situation reports to JOC at Wankie were all along the lines of, "Nothing to report." What the JOC did do, given that we had no way of knowing our precise position on the ground, was to arrange an overfly by a Police Reserve aircraft on the afternoon of our sixth day out, for the purpose of getting a fix on where we would likely meet the border track and fence the next morning. When I advised the pilot that while we were not totally out of water yet, it would be useful if we could find a re-supply by morning of the seventh day, the pilot gave me map references for where we were at that time and for a place called Kukulawani Pan, right alongside the border track, where there appeared to be some water. That location would also make a reliable fixed point to rendezvous with our transport for the journey back to Bulawayo.

With that most useful assistance I was able to adjust our direction of patrol just a little to the north of strict east/west, so as to aim for the pan indicated. When we finally reached it, 11:00hrs on our seventh day out, we had to back off to a safe distance because a herd of elephant, all the members of which, were stomping around in what little, very muddy, water still showed in the centre of the pan.

Shortly after we had backed off a little from the pan, and were resting at the track side, we heard the noise of a motor vehicle approaching. Looking discreetly down the track, I saw an airdrop jeep approaching from the north. It contained four people. They were all stripped to the waist, with one of them actually sitting on the bonnet, clearly sunning himself as the vehicle drove unhurriedly along. I waited until the vehicle was thirty yards away and then stepped out in front of it. The sight of my camouflage clothing and FN Rifle caused a bit of bother. The driver stood sharply on the brakes. The unfortunate fellow doing the sunbathing on the bonnet was pitched off his perch and landed in a heap on the dirt track, fortunately being unhurt by his tumble. It turned out they were part of the South African Police unit working out of Victoria Falls. As I gently pointed out to them, with my section on their feet behind me, if we had been insurgents, they would have been in real trouble, because not one of them had a weapon in their hands. They were also not carrying any water at all with them and worse still, no ammunition other than what was in the magazines of their rifles.

I was still politely telling them some of the facts of operational life, including finding the camp for 90 or so insurgents, when more vehicle noise made itself heard, this time coming from the south. It was two police Land Rovers with just a constable driver and one escort in each of them. After friendly handshakes with the four somewhat chastened but better-informed members of the South African Police, I followed the rest of my section into our uplifting transport. After that, it was a matter of siting back and relaxing during the three-hour drive to Bulawayo. There I delivered a quick debrief to my troop leader and fellow section leaders, all of whom agreed that my section and I had been very lucky not to have actually bumped into that insurgent group, Fire-Force or no Fire-Force. That conversation brought up the fact that while I had been away on leave in the UK, in August 1967, there had been a similar sizeable crossing east of Victoria Falls. That group, again made up of SAANC and ZAPU had penetrated as far as the Tjolotjo Tribal Trust Land, where they were eventually located. In the firefight which followed, 47 of the group were killed and a score captured. The survivors fled into Botswana. It seemed that having learned of the fate of their predecessor group this latest bunch had decided to simply get through Rhodesia and into Botswana as fast as they could. In that they had succeeded.

After another couple of uneventful weeks in Bulawayo, I was required to return to Salisbury to attend an interview with the Promotion Board. If I passed that, I would be allocated a place on the two-week-long Promotion Training Course in depot. When I marched in before the three senior officers comprising that year's board and stamped to a parade-ground halt at attention, there were a few quizzical glances and comments. It seemed I was the first person to appear before them wearing black leather, rather than brown. At the board's request, I did a few about-turns, marched up and down the length of the room and then returned to a position of attention in front of them, for which I was duly thanked and stood at ease. The first question was whether I had decided what to do if successful with promotion this year. My reply that I understood that a tour of duty with Support Unit was a two-year posting, that I was already beyond that and had recently submitted a request to return to Duty Branch brought what I took to be sympathetic and understanding nods from all three officers on the board. After that there were a few questions about my previous police experience in the UK and Nyasaland/Malawi, after which I was thanked once more for appearing and duly dismissed.

Ten days later, I received confirmation that I was to attend the Promotion Training Course in depot. My pleasure at that news was somewhat dampened upon discovering that the Officer-in-Charge of that course would be Supt Ted Mallon. With the history between us, I felt that I would need to be spot-on with parade inspection, drill performance and lecture attentiveness, because any course attendee could be sent packing and back to station if he incurred the displeasure of the Officer-in-Charge of each year's course.

As it turned out, I was right to be wary. At the start of our first parade, Supt Mallon made it clear that he would be warning any of us just once concerning any defaults or lapse in expected standard of turnout, but a second time would result in an immediate dismissal from the promotion course and an order to return to station. After that, Supt Mallon, spent far longer checking my turnout than he did any of the other two-dozen members of the squad. When that same pattern repeated itself the next day, I clearly noticed a frown appear on the face of Insp. MacIntosh, the depot Instructor assisting with the running of the promotion course. It was also noted by some of my companions on the course, who later bothered to ask me why Supt Mallon did not seem to like me very much. When I explained our past encounter, there were a few raised eyebrows and rolled eyes. Over the first three morning parades four members of the squad were ticked off by Supt Mallon. The alleged defects were carefully written down in a notebook by Insp. MacIntosh. On the Thursday, Supt Mallon gave me his usual detailed scrutiny. Glancing down at my boots, he declared, loudly, "You've not polished the laces of your left boot Woolley. I've warned you before, so if you cannot take notice of a fair warning, you can fall out right now, pack your kit and return to station."

Before I could protest that no such warning had been given, Insp. MacIntosh spoke up, gesturing with his right hand at the notebook in his left hand. "Beg pardon, Sir," he said, "but I've no such warning written down in my notebook and I don't believe I would have missed it." Supt Mallon's lips tightened.

"Very well," he snapped. "Get it into your notebook now!" and moved on.

At morning tea-break Insp. MacIntosh found a moment to step alongside of me and mutter quietly, "Watch it Woolley. Supt Mallon's clearly after you. Try not to give him the chance!" before moving on. For the remaining days of that promotion course, I made sure that the laces on both boots were polished and shiny for each day's inspection parade. Supt Mallon maintained his habit of spending more time examining my turnout each morning than any other member of the promotion course, but, despite his best efforts to find some fault, he was unable to do so.

Unfortunately, three other members of the course were not so lucky, or perhaps not so diligent, for they were ordered to leave the course and return to station after repeating turnout defects for which they had been previously warned and which had gone down in Insp. McIntosh's notebook.

It was only when the inspection parade on our final day was over and we were dismissed to attend the day's lectures that I felt able to relax somewhat and breathe a little easier, knowing I could no longer become a victim of Supt Mallon's resentful attitude towards me for having dared to inform him somewhat bluntly of his operational incompetence which had damned nearly got my section and I wiped out by our own side.

By the time I was finished with matters of potential promotion to full Section Officer rank instead of the Lance (Acting) rank of that time, A Troop had been recalled from Bulawayo and redeployed to Makuti to assist in the mopping-up operations which were ongoing in the aftermath of Operation Cauldron which had started in March.

It seemed that the SAANC and ZIPRA command elements in Zambia had learned nothing from the virtual wiping out of their sizeable incursion east of Victoria Falls in August 1967, even if their more recent incursion into Matabeleland, which my section and I had nearly bumped into, had made it safely over into Botswana. That odd complacency had led them to launch a major, combined, crossing of the Zambezi River, close by the mouth of the Chiwore River, in March 1968. Some 123 terrorists had crossed over. They created a major supply base within a half-mile of the Zambezi River. Working from there they built a chain of re-supply camps, between the Zambezi River and the top of the Southern Escarpment, with the intention of recruiting Africans from within the European farming area. The main base was well dug-in and defensible. The fact that the terrorists had been able to work undetected for some time was put down to the fact that while some parts of Rhodesia such as Matabeleland North, had had very little or even no rain at all, the Zambezi Valley had had more than its fair share, resulting in very little actual foot-patrolling having been carried out for some months. What happened eventually was that a Game Ranger undertaking a routine patrol came across the unmissable trail created by the toing and froing of many terrorists over several weeks. That resulted in a sizeable operation led by elements of the Rhodesia Light Infantry, supported by the Rhodesian Airforce, with Police Support Unit taking on a more backed off role. Within several weeks, 70 or so of the terrorists had been killed, a score or more had been captured and the remainder had fled back to Zambia.

Operation Cauldron had effects all round. The South African Prime Minister, Mr Vorster, saw fit to bolster the until then decidedly lightweight presence of the South African Police in Rhodesia, while the ZIPRA and SAANC commanders decided that large-scale incursions were inadvisable, so began to infiltrate smaller groups more frequently as the year wore on. A Troop arrived in Makuti in the last week in July 1968, just in time to become involved in the tail-end of the operation which dealt with a crossing of some 30 terrorists, just below the Kariba Gorge. One member of that group, who was a decidedly unwilling terrorist trainee, having been literally dragged away from where he had been happily working in Lusaka, took the opportunity to desert during the night. He then ran the considerable distance to Chirundu Police Station to report the incursion. That distinctly useful piece of very current information led to an immediate counter-insurgency operation which was so successful that within a couple of days, 25 of the insurgents had been killed and the remainder captured.

In the second week of August 1968 I was back down in the Zambezi Valley, leading my section on day patrols and night ambushes, much as we had been doing some eight or nine months before. Making a routine radio call one morning, I was advised that I had indeed been successful in my bid for promotion to full Section Officer Rank. While that news was very welcome, it briefly crossed my mind to wonder what had become of my written request for a return to Duty Branch policing. However, with plenty of work to keep A Troop and every member in it fully occupied on a day-by-day basis, that thought simply became shelved.

By then, the additional personnel supplied by the South African Police had allowed a chain of surreptitious Observation Posts to be established along the length of the Zambezi River. With a great deal of Defence Force activity going on, we were advised to keep our VHF radio open. That resulted in my section and I listening in to an RLI patrol's conversation with one of the SAP Observation Posts based near H Camp. They had come across the spoor of what was clearly a single insurgent, heading north towards the Zambezi River, just a mile or two away. They reckoned he had probably hidden after Op. Cauldron and was now intent on trying to get back to Zambia rather than surrender to Defence Forces, which he could have done. The RLI unit reckoned that the individual would reach the river not far from the SAP position. Their prediction proved right, because the OP reported a short while later that they had sight of a single African male, in civilian clothing but armed with an AK and carrying a pack on his back. A few moments later they reported that the individual had set down his pack, put his rifle down by it, taken off his boots and entered the water, clearly intending to swim to the other side which was at least a hundred yards or more distant. The next transmission from the RLI patrol asked if the SAP unit could get a shot at the individual to prevent him from escaping. That brought the laconic reply. "No need. That guy has just been grazed by a flatdog!" (flatdog being common slang for a crocodile.)

On 2nd September 1968, A Troop was rotated back to Salisbury where we were stood down for four days, which, as usual, saw us all taking our separate ways of making best use of our time off. On the morning of the second day of time off, i/c Fife Hostel advised me that he had received a telephone call from C/Insp. West, asking me to call in to see him about my promotion. Wondering what it was all about, I duly drove the short distance to Tomlinson Depot and went in to see C/Insp. West, who did not beat about the bush. "Sorry for the short notice, Woolley, but your request for transfer back to Duty Branch has been approved. You've been posted to Bindura District. Return your black leather items to Ordnance Stores this afternoon. Draw whatever you may be short of after your time with us and get yourself off to Bindura tomorrow, because it seems you are a little bit overdue." He handed me a set of Route Instructions and blank Requisition Forms, wished me well and that was that.

Back at Fife Hostel I read through my Route Instructions, which seemed to emphasise that until very recently I had been on operational duties in the Zambezi Valley. The rest of that day passed in something of a blur as I did just as C/Insp. West had instructed. In addition, I advised i/c Hostel that I would be vacating my room the next day, provided Shorty with the wherewithal to get to Bindura by bus within the next day or two and packed everything except the uniform items I needed for the morrow. The one thing which rankled somewhat was that with all the rush and hurry, I had no opportunity to say a proper farewell to my European and African comrades in A Troop.

Shortly after breakfast the following day, properly dressed in Duty Branch colours, I loaded my car, handed the key to my room to i/c Hostel and drove off, headed for the Mazoe Valley and Bindura which was where District HQ was located. Little more than an hour later I parked my car in the car park at Bindura Police Station and made my presence known to the detail behind the reception desk. That individual pointed out the offices of District HQ close by and advised me to report to Supt Ron Dick. He kindly pointed me towards a further car park nearby where a uniformed figure had his head and shoulders deep into the engine compartment of a Peugeot 405 Station Waggon. Clutching my Route Instruction document, I marched over to within a yard or so of my new OC District, stamped to a parade-ground halt and said simply, "Section Officer Woolley, Sir!"

Without ceasing his mechanical activities or lifting his gaze from the engine Supt Dick responded with, "You won't find him here. The bastard's AWOL!"

My reply of, "I am he, Sir and I am not AWOL," caused Supt Dick to jerk his head and shoulders up so fast that he collided with the prop holding up the bonnet of the Peugeot Estate Car and knocked it aside. That brought the metal bonnet down on top of him. Between the combined efforts of both of us we got the bonnet propped back up, which allowed Supt Dick to stand upright, glare angrily at me and demand, "Where the hell have you been for the past month? You were supposed to have been here at the beginning of August."

I offered him my Route Instructions document, with the words, "This may help to sort it out, Sir. I've been at Makuti and down in the Zambezi Valley and only learned of my transfer out of Support Unit two days ago."

Supt Dick read carefully through what was written on my Route Instructions before handing the document back to me. "Hand that over to District Clerk. You are posted to Bindura Police Station, so get yourself over there and get settled in at the mess where there's a room for you. You'll find that Bindura is an interesting station with lots to keep you busy."

In saying that, he was absolutely right!

Op Cauldron fresh fish

⑤×3. In 1968 120 Terrorists entered Rhodesia from Zambia. Most were aged 14 to 20. Some women. I was involved in Operation Cauldron for some months until all of them were accounted for. In quiet moments I caught fish for my stick of men. Ration Packs are grim! Note the uniforms and doorless landrover, with anti-landmine reinforcement. The photo with vehicle is us trying to dry out after a storm.

Op Cauldron 1968 drying out after a storm

Cauldron 1968 Fresh fish for dinner
Consts. Mapfumo, Mapuranga and Bushu

Printed in Great Britain
by Amazon